D1252023

Morning Star, Midnight Sun

Morning Star, Midnight Sun

The Early Guadalcanal-Solomons Campaign of World War II August–October 1942

Jeffrey R. Cox

Osprey Publishing
c/o Bloomsbury Publishing Plc
PO Box 883, Oxford, OX1 9PL, UK
Or
c/o Bloomsbury Publishing Inc.
1385 Broadway, 5th Floor, New York, NY 10018, USA
E-mail: info@ospreypublishing.com

www.ospreypublishing.com

OSPREY is a trademark of Osprey Publishing Ltd, a division of Bloomsbury Publishing Plc.

First published in Great Britain in 2018

A CIP catalog record for this book is available from the British Library.

ISBN: HB: 978 1 4728 2638 1
ePub: 978 1 4728 2639 8
ePDF: 978 1 4728 2640 4
XML 978 1 4728 2641 1

18 19 20 21 22 10 9 8 7 6 5 4 3 2 1

Index by Zoe Ross
Typeset in Trajan & Adobe Garamond
Cartography by bounford.com
Originated by PDQ Digital Media Solutions, Bungay, UK
Printed in China through World Print Ltd.

Osprey Publishing supports the Woodland Trust, the UK's leading woodland conservation charity. Between 2014 and 2018 our donations are being spent on their Centenary Woods project in the UK.

To find out more about our authors and books visit **www.ospreypublishing.com**. Here you will find extracts, author interviews, details of forthcoming events and the option to sign up for our newsletter.

CONTENTS

PROLOGUE: VISITORS

As light started taking over the eastern sky on the morning of August 7, 1942, the officers and men of the Imperial Japanese Navy's 13th Construction Unit began to rouse themselves. Their commander, Captain Monzen Kanae, knew it was going to be a hot day, as days here on the island the Japanese called Gadarukanaru always were.[1] And a busy day. He was expecting visitors.

A month earlier, Captain Monzen's 13th Construction Unit, joined by the 11th Construction Unit under Lieutenant Commander Okamura Tokunaga, had been sent down to this island in the southernmost corner of the Empire of Japan – or, more accurately, the "Greater East Asia Co-Prosperity Sphere." That was what the Japanese called their empire, though this island was neither in Asia nor blessed with prosperity.

Captain Monzen was in a land as alien to him as Tokyo Bay was to Commodore Matthew Perry when he barged in, literally, in 1853 and started the dominos falling, the first of which was the so-called "Meiji Restoration" and with it the creation of the Japanese Empire. The foundation of the Meiji Restoration was Japan's desire to establish itself as a great power so that nothing like the humiliation of the Commodore Perry visit could ever happen again.

And in establishing itself as a great power, Japan put itself on a collision course with other great powers. It was most fortunate for Japan that its first European rival for control of Asia was the most inept of the great powers – Tsarist Russia. The Combined Fleet of the Imperial Japanese Navy destroyed the Russian Far East Fleet off Port Arthur. The tsar sent his Baltic Fleet halfway around the world to relieve Port Arthur. The Japanese destroyed that fleet, too, at the decisive Battle of Tsushima in 1905. It became part of the Japanese national psyche, the "decisive battle" that stopped the European imperialists.

After World War I, Tsarist Russia was replaced as a rival by Great Britain and t United States, who became the focus of Japanese military preparations. As rela between Japan and the West deteriorated, Japan moved to modernize its navy a out how it would fight the next war at sea. The Imperial Japanese Navy refused t its long-held idea of the "decisive battle" like it had enjoyed at Tsushima in 1905 during the Russo-Japanese War. However, the Washington Naval Treaty, a noble attempt by the victorious Allies to prevent another arms race through the limitation of naval construction, ostensibly forced Japan into a set disadvantage against its likely rivals. As a result, Japanese naval strategists looked for creative ways to gain a decisive edge. And achieved several breakthroughs.

Seeing that, at least in the days before radar, darkness could hide their inferior numbers, the Combined Fleet, the main ocean-going combat component of the Imperial Japanese Navy, trained relentlessly in night combat.[2] They perfected high-quality optics for night spotting and developed illumination rounds, flares, and floatlights that were more reliable and burned more brightly than their American counterparts. The Imperial Japanese Navy's Naval Air Force, known as the "Sea Eagles," became the world leader in naval aviation, both in its pursuit of carrier aviation and in its development of seaplanes and seaplane tactics.

It was during this period that the Imperial Japanese Navy developed what was arguably the crown jewel and definitely the most dangerous weapon of its surface fleet – the Type 93 torpedo. By far the finest torpedo of its time, the Type 93 was 24 inches in diameter and, at 29 feet 6 inches, unusually long. It carried an explosive charge of 1080lb, the largest of its kind. But what made the Type 93 so special was its range. At its high-speed setting of 48 knots, it had a range of 20,000m – more than 10 miles. At its slowest speed of 36 knots, it could go an incredible 40,000m – more than 20 miles. By comparison, the US Navy's Mark 15 torpedo, used by destroyers, had a maximum range of just 5,500m at its high-speed setting of 45 knots and a range of 13,700m at 26 knots – a speed so slow that it could be outrun by Japanese warships. On top of that, the Mark 15 was powered by steam, which left a trail of bubbles that was easily spotted, and seemed overly prone to duds. In contrast, the Type 93 was powered by oxygen, which left no bubbles and little visible wake. The Japanese went to great lengths to conceal the Type 93; its devastating power would be a rude shock to the US and Royal navies in the Pacific. Much later, the torpedo's extreme effectiveness and unusual length earned from noted historian Samuel
iot Morison the title by which the Type 93 would become famous – "Long Lance."

he Washington Naval Treaty of 1922 was arguably Japan's last attempt at outwardly
ing its expansionist ambitions in the name of "peace." As the Treaty was concluded,
Taisho, whose lack of interest in politics had helped Japan agree to the
Treaty, was forced from power by health issues. His son Crown Prince
dily gained more power until December 25, 1925, when Taisho died and
ce became Emperor of Japan. The new era of Showa ("enlightened peace")
Hirohito would use this period of enlightened peace to start two wars.[3]
val ingenuity, her first aggressive act was in fact on land with the
arting in earnest in 1937. It was never called a war, at least not in
as always called an "incident" – one that was supposed to last a
"incident" that the behavior of the Imperial Japanese Army

exhibited some of the most barbaric conduct of the 20th century, including the literal "Rape of Nanking". Some 20,000 women were raped, most repeatedly, many in front of husbands, fathers, or children who were murdered when they attempted to intervene.[4] In Nanking alone some 260,000 civilians were killed, more than a third of the city was left in ruins, and everything of value was shipped to Japan.[5]

Ultimately, Japan conquered everything worth conquering in China – its ports, its industrial areas, the majority of its arable land, most of its navigable rivers. Yet it meant nothing. In 1940, the Sea Eagles received a new toy: the Mitsubishi A6M Type 00 (*Reisen*) Carrier Fighter, Model 11, which would become famous as the "Zero."[6] It literally chased what little air power China had from the skies. It still meant nothing. The Chinese would not surrender, could not be made to surrender.

As a result, the "China Incident" kept consuming more and more resources – $5 million a day, a staggering sum for that time – while the continuing Japanese atrocities were alienating the very countries on whom Japan depended for import of those resources, such as the United States.[7] Only 10 percent of the oil Japan used was produced in the home islands. Another 10 percent came from the Netherlands East Indies. The remainder, 80 percent, came from the United States. And that flow of oil was in danger of being cut off if relations between Japan and the West continued to deteriorate.

And continue to deteriorate they did, as World War II in Europe began. In June 1940, a month after President Roosevelt had moved the Pacific Fleet from San Diego to Pearl Harbor, the US Congress authorized the Two-Ocean Navy Act, providing for a massive expansion of the US Navy. In a few years, the US Navy would achieve quantitative superiority to the Imperial Japanese Navy in the Pacific, and any chance of the Japanese assembling the East Asian hegemony that was now the clear goal of Emperor Hirohito would be gone unless immediate action was taken.[8] Tokyo did its calculations. Based on the Two-Ocean Navy Act and Japan's own continued naval expansion, Japan's naval strength relative to the US would peak in late 1941.[9]

Meanwhile, the army's continued brutality increased international sympathy for the Chinese, who received a trickle of military support. The Japanese seized northern Indochina to cut the last remaining routes for that support to get to China. The U Britain, and the Dutch government-in-exile rationalized that Japan was simply tryin cut the Chinese supply line through Indochina and did not suspect that a fu invasion of their Far East interests was in the offing. However, in July 1941, the moved into southern Indochina, seizing a major air complex in and around S

The strategic ramifications of this action were obvious. The Japanese n surrounded the Philippines, with Saigon to the west, Japanese-held Formo and the Japanese-held Marshall Islands to the east. Saigon was in range and all-important Singapore, as well as northwest Borneo, which co into the East Indies. Their intention was clear. The response from W – and, on August 1, 1941, Japanese assets were frozen and a total imposed. The British and the Dutch quickly followed suit.

Japan and the United States were now at an impasse. Washington would not lift the trade embargo until Japan had withdrawn from both Indochina and China. Japan would not withdraw as to do so would mean a loss of "face" – that vague but important Asian concept that remains imperfectly understood in the West – and Japan's inevitable reduction to a second-rate power.

So the long-held Japanese ambition to seize the resources of Malaya and the oil-rich Netherlands East Indies was now a national imperative. Becoming self-sufficient through the seizure of Southeast Asia was now more than philosophical; it was essential for national survival. Imperial General Headquarters, the rather informal organization roughly equivalent to the American Joint Chiefs of Staff that grew in wartime to coordinate (in theory) the activities of the Imperial Army's and Navy's general staffs on behalf of the respective services, needed options.

The Naval General Staff had been planning an operation to seize Malaya, Borneo, and the Netherlands East Indies for a long time. However, Admiral Yamamoto Isoroku, head of the Combined Fleet, knew what going to war with the US would mean – a likely catastrophic defeat for Japan. As Yamamoto famously said, "In the first six to twelve months of war with the United States and Great Britain I will run wild and win victory upon victory. But then, if the war continues after that, I have no expectation of success."[10] Nevertheless, he fine-tuned those plans for war.

While the Japanese would have the advantage in the short term, they knew they could not match America's industrial and military might in the long term. What they were hoping for was a continuing manifestation of the American political weakness and isolationism that had kept it out of the war so far. Admiral Yamamoto's projection of six months was key. The Japanese hoped they could build up their East Asian empire during that timeframe – adding the Philippines, Malaya, the East Indies, Siam (already an ally),
d Burma, and building up a defensive web of islands including Guam and the Marianas,
olines, the Marshalls, the Gilberts, Wake, and New Britain. By the time the United
mobilized, Japan hoped its new defensive network would make the American
whether retaking far-away East Asia was worth the cost in lives and in
door to a political settlement that could allow Japan to keep its
strategy relied on doing nothing to so outrage the
fuse to listen to any settlement short of Japan's

moto and the Japanese had developed were put
Nagumo Chuichi were assembled. Six aircraft
ose names would become infamous – *Akagi*,
Hiei and *Kirishima*, two fast battleships that
Tone and *Chikuma*, two bizarre-looking
nally the 1st Destroyer Flotilla of eight
aze, *Kagero*, *Shiranuhi*, *Arare*, and *Kasumi*
as the "Japanese Carrier Striking Force"

in US Navy circles, it was and is more commonly known by the informal name of *Kido Butai* – “Striking Force.”

They headed to Pearl Harbor and a date with history on December 7, 1941.

But even before *Kido Butai* struck Pearl Harbor – an act that indeed so outraged the American people that they refused to listen to any settlement short of Japan’s unconditional surrender – the Japanese began what US military theorists would later call “the Centrifugal Offensive,” the conquest of Malaya and the Netherlands East Indies being the prime objectives, but also including the Philippines; Guam and the Marianas; and an outer defense web with the Carolines, the Marshalls, the Gilberts, Wake, and New Britain. The Japanese conquered almost all of them. And they did so even more quickly and at a much cheaper cost in men and materiel than their plans had predicted.

Japan’s drive to seize the Philippines, Malaya, and the Netherlands East Indies was later called the Java Sea Campaign. The key combat engagements included destroying most of the US Far East Air Force on the ground at Clark Field in the Philippines, effectively ceding control of the air to the Japanese for the entire campaign. There was the sinking of the Royal Navy battleship *Prince of Wales* and battlecruiser *Repulse* off Malaya by the Japanese Naval Air Force, destroying the most powerful Allied surface ships in the first days of the war. And then there was the Battle of the Java Sea, in which a motley, multinational collection of Allied warships slapped together at the last minute was decisively defeated by the Imperial Japanese Navy.[11]

The key component to Japan’s victories during this time was air superiority, whether by land-based air or *Kido Butai*, which topped off this first round of conquests with a rampage through the Indian Ocean, viciously lashing at British bases and ships almost unopposed. Admiral Yamamoto had indeed run wild.

But those early victories had come with a heavy, albeit intangible, price. Almost inevitably the Japanese suffered from a bout of what they called “Victory Disease” – t
Naval General Staff and the Combined Fleet thought they simply could not lose. R
Frank defined the symptoms of Victory Disease as “overextension and dis
forces.”[12] This was true on a strategic level, but it also manifested itse
overconfidence, and sloppiness all the way down to unit level.

The arrogance, sloppiness, and overconfidence showed u
Java Sea Campaign. Just before the Battle of the Jav
surface forces escorting a very large convoy of ar
admiral was so contemptuous of Allied oppositi
his charges, barely reaching them before the
transports started landing troops in northw
opposition that they positioned their forc
invasion transports. The Allied cruisers USS
trying to escape, got in between the helple
in a melee in which the Japanese sank bo
own transports, including the flagship of

nowhere to be found. They had vanished during the night, a development that was reported to Rabaul.

Meanwhile, in late July, Lieutenant Commander Ito Haruki of Japanese radio intelligence, known as the Owada Communications Group, had detected two new Allied unit call signs in the southwest Pacific. Both were on the commander-in-chief circuit series, and both communicated directly with Pearl Harbor. On August 1, radio direction-finding equipment located one of the call signs in Nouméa, French New Caledonia, and the other near Melbourne, Australia. Ito guessed Nouméa was for a new South Pacific command and Melbourne for an Australian or British force. Deducing the Allies were about to start a new offensive in the Solomons or New Guinea, he sent word to Truk, where Admiral Yamamoto was on the battleship *Yamato*, and to Rabaul as well. His messages were ignored and not passed on to Gadarukanaru or Tulagi.[24]

At least not directly. On the morning of August 1, the 4th Fleet radioed, "According to information received the enemy's condition is as follows: enemy is gathering power along the east coast of Australia … You should keep close watch." On the evening of August 6, the 84th Guard Unit received a bizarre message from the 8th Base Force in Rabaul, stating that the remnants of the 81st Guard Unit, most of which had already been withdrawn from the area and were headed back to Rabaul, should be withdrawn as soon as possible, although, because "conditions" were increasing the "probability of danger," the withdrawal should be postponed.[25]

Even so, there was a slowly developing sense of urgency at Lunga. Lieutenant Commander Okamura of the 11th Construction Unit had been urging for weeks the deployment of aircraft to Gadarukanaru despite its lack of a finished runway.[26] On August 5, the 84th Guard Force joined him in that request. But the request was rejected, as it was believed that the US Navy could not mount a counteroffensive until 1943.

Nevertheless, aircraft would be here soon. Three officers of the Yokohama Air Group had visited the airfield on August 5 to inspect the progress. Satisfied that the work was on schedule, they told Captain Monzen that elements of the 25th Air Flotilla would stage into the Lunga field on August 8.[27] That was the reason for the visitors on this day. Two staff officers of the unit were coming from Rabaul to inspect the airfield and figure out where to put the aircraft. Maybe they wouldn't notice the big hole.

The completion of the airfield had been a cause for celebration for the Japanese. They had been drinking *sake* and singing in celebration until midnight.[28] Now, the men of the 11th got to sleep it off while the men of the 13th, nursing hangovers no doubt, had to cross the Lunga to make the airfield truly operational.[29] Before heading out, the men of the 13th, such as Captain Monzen, performed their morning religious rituals and settled down to breakfast and crushing headaches …

There was an explosion. A big one. It came from the kitchen building at Lunga or, more accurately, what had been the kitchen building, which was now just a pile of rubble.

What happened? Another bombing raid? There was no time to consider the question. In quick succession came more blasts. And aircraft making strafing runs on the Lunga base.

The Americans were here. Well, he had been expecting visitors.

There was panic among the Japanese and the Korean labor force. After carefully considering the question of whether they wanted to die for their Japanese masters, the Koreans decided "Not my emperor" and fled. The crack Special Naval Landing Force troops, with a well-earned reputation for never surrendering, turned their tails and fled. Captain Monzen reported his men "had gotten out of hand."[30] Some fortunate ones fled to a coconut grove, from which Monzen would try to figure out a way to defend Gadarukanaru – the island known in the West as "Guadalcanal."

The time was 6:14 am. It was, as Petty Officer 2nd Class Kaneda Sankichi of the 3rd Kure Special Naval Landing Force called it, "the beginning of Hell."[31]

CHAPTER 1

FIGHTING THE PROBLEM

At 5:19 am, more than two hours after battle stations had sounded, a new command post came to life on the transport USS *McCawley*. The "Wacky Mac," as the *McCawley* was known, was the flagship of Rear Admiral Richmond Kelly Turner, commanding the ships of an amphibious invasion force, the first such force for the US in World War II. Indeed, the first amphibious invasion since 1898.

The US Navy would not have done this – because too many senior officers believed it simply could not be done – but for the iron will of the commander-in-chief of the US Fleet, Admiral Ernest J. King. After Pearl Harbor, President Roosevelt believed he needed new people in place to deal with the new reality of war, people who were fighters, not politicians. King was certainly no politician. The man described by official US Navy historian Samuel Eliot Morison as "a hard man with little sense of humor" had made few friends ascending the ranks, but had done enough to be noticed by the right people.[1]

Pearl Harbor had convinced President Roosevelt to replace Husband Kimmel with Chester Nimitz as commander-in-chief of the Pacific Fleet, whose acronym CINCPAC was usually verbalized as "sink pack." Admiral Thomas C. Hart was already commander-in-chief of the Asiatic Fleet (CINCAF, verbalized as "sink aff") and, indeed, most of what had been the Asiatic Fleet was now sunk.[2] King himself had been commander-in-chief of the Atlantic Fleet (CINCLANT, verbalized as "sink lant") before he was named commander-in-chief of the US Fleet (CINCUS, verbalized as "sink us"). King quickly decided he would rather not have all the officers and sailors fighting the war at sea under his naval command saying "sink us." The new acronym for the same title would be COMINCH.

The 63-year-old admiral would become a somewhat controversial figure. A trained aviator, King was brilliant, determined – and arrogant. Historian William Tuohy would say King "believed he could do any job in the US Navy better than anyone else," and would run the Navy "with an iron fist and no velvet glove."[3]

The eminent Guadalcanal historian Richard B. Frank describes him this way:

> Besides intelligence and dedication, one other pillar supported King's professional reputation: his toughness. He regarded exceptional performance of duty as the norm and evinced insensitivity or even callousness to his subordinates, upon whom he also frequently exercised his ferocious temper. But if King proved harsh with subordinates, he was no toady to superiors. Those who fell short of King's standards found he could be hostile, tactless, arrogant, and sometimes disrespectful or even insubordinate.[4]

According to Morison, Admiral King knew he was "respected rather than liked by the Navy." He was hated by such a distinguished cast of characters as Secretary of War Henry Stimson; British Prime Minister Winston Churchill; Chief of the Imperial General Staff Field Marshal Sir Alan Brooke; and Royal Navy Admiral Sir Andrew Cunningham.[5] None came close to the opinion of General Dwight Eisenhower. The man who could make friends with pretty much everyone once said, "One thing that might help win this is to get someone to shoot King. He's the antithesis of cooperation, a deliberately rude person, which means he's a mental bully." Why? Because King wanted to press the Pacific War against the Japanese, not drain it to support the fight against Germany.

Nevertheless, Admiral King was appointed to the renamed COMINCH on December 30, 1941. Why? Although he may have been dark and humorless, King had a can-do philosophy. He approached the Pacific War with the idea of "Make the best of what you have":

> There must be no tendency to excuse incomplete readiness for war on the premise of future acquisition of trained personnel or modernized material … personnel shall be trained and rendered competent … existing material shall be maintained and utilized at its maximum effectiveness at all times.[6]

With the thin reed of resources available in the Pacific at this time, it was an essential philosophy.

The man with whom Admiral King would be working in the Pacific would be Admiral Nimitz, the new commander-in-chief of the Pacific Fleet. Nimitz was almost King's alter ego. Every bit as brilliant as King, Nimitz was in some ways a contradiction, a soft-spoken Texan almost without ego. "[Q]uiet, thorough, and thoughtful – a natural diplomat," was how Tuohy would later describe him.[7] Nimitz was loyal to his subordinates and was good at avoiding the poisonous personal relations that seemed to follow King. Morison described him as having:

> … the prudence to wait through a lean period; to do nothing rash for the sake of doing something. He had the capacity to both organize a fleet and a vast war theater, the tact to

> deal with sister services and Allied commands, the leadership to weld his own subordinates into a great fighting team, the courage to take necessary risks, and the wisdom to select, from a variety of intelligence and opinions, the correct strategy to defeat Japan.[8]

That was with the benefit of hindsight. Things looked different in those last days of 1941 and early days of 1942. The demands of the war and the politics involved exhausted even Nimitz. He wrote to his wife, "I'll be lucky to last six months."[9]

Together, King and Nimitz would have to wrestle with the big philosophical issue dominating these hard early days of the Pacific War: identify the fine line between "mak[ing] the best of what you have" and "[doing something] rash for the sake of doing something." Indeed, early on Admiral King did not trust Nimitz and tried to steamroll him. But soft-spoken did not mean weak and Nimitz stood up to him. King backed down and the two ultimately worked well together, especially at finding that line.

As Japan swept across Southeast Asia and the Pacific, President Roosevelt and Prime Minister Churchill were having their first secret conference, codenamed "Arcadia." It was at Arcadia that the "Europe First" policy was firmly established by the US and Britain. Nevertheless, the Pacific was not to be neglected, and the Allies were not to remain passive in defense of this theater. It was at Arcadia where the ill-fated organization known as ABDACOM (American-British-Dutch-Australian Command) was formed to pool Allied resources in the defense of Malaya and the Netherlands East Indies in what has been called the Java Sea Campaign.

It was from Arcadia that, on December 31, 1941, Admiral King issued his first substantive orders to Admiral Nimitz. The Pacific Fleet was, first, to hold the line at Hawaii-Midway and protect the lines of communication with the West Coast. Second, and "only in small degree less important," the fleet was to protect the lines of communication with Australia.[10]

Even though the agreement out of Arcadia was very clearly "Europe First" for resources and efforts, Admiral King got in a few helpful lines about the war against Japan. The carefully worded and intentionally vague declaration said efforts in the Pacific would involve "maintaining only such positions in the [Pacific] theatre as will safeguard vital interests and deny to Japan access to raw materials vital to her continuous war effort while we are concentrating on the defeat of Germany." "Vital interests" was conspicuously left undefined, though the term was used a second time as a title for a tiny section:

> The Safeguarding of Vital Interests in the Eastern Theatre
>
> 18. The security of Australia, New Zealand, and India must be maintained and Chinese resistance supported. Secondly, points of vantage from which an offensive against Japan can eventually be developed must be secured.[11]

This authorization to seize "points of vantage from which an offensive against Japan can eventually be developed" was added at Admiral King's insistence.[12]

The declaration also identified "main sea routes which must be secured," including "the Pacific routes from United States and the Panama Canal to Alaska, Hawaii, Australia and the Far East." Securing those routes required holding and capturing "essential sea bases," which included Hawaii and Samoa. There were also "main air routes which must be secured," which included "the U.S. to Australia via Hawaii, Christmas Island, Canton, Palmyra, Samoa, Fiji, [and] New Caledonia." This required securing "essential air bases," including Hawaii, Christmas Island, Palmyra, Canton, Samoa, Fiji, New Caledonia, and Townsville.[13]

Allied action in the Pacific seemed to be severely limited by this document. But Admiral King had a lawyer's eye. For instance, Australia was some 7,000 miles from San Francisco. As Vice Admiral George Dyer pointed out in discussing King's seemingly limited options:

> A straight line on a mercator chart from San Francisco in California to Townsville [...] passes just south of the island of Hawaii and just south of Guadalcanal Island in the Solomons. In Admiral King's belief, the Japanese should not be permitted to impinge on this line, if the line of communications from Hawaii to Australia through Samoa, Fiji, and the New Hebrides was to be secure.[14]

Did that mean in order to "secure" the air and sea lane to Australia, under the Arcadia declaration, Guadalcanal "must be secured"? The New Hebrides? One could make the argument that it did. That is how all these locations would come up again and again as King looked for ways to wedge his allowances under the Arcadia declaration ever wider to position US forces in the Pacific for not just defense but offensive operations as well.

Under pre-existing defense plans, Admiral King was able to send small garrisons to Palmyra, almost 1,000 miles south of Pearl Harbor, and to American Samoa, another 1,300 miles toward New Zealand. South of Palmyra on the route to Samoa were Canton and Christmas islands, which the Army under Arcadia garrisoned with 1,500 and 2,000 troops respectively.

Things started to get strained when the issue of French New Caledonia came up. New Caledonia was Free French, with strategically important nickel and chrome deposits. With France under Nazi occupation and a Vichy government, it was almost defenseless. Australia had agreed to garrison it, but was stretched too thin to do so beyond a company of commandos. Aside from these 300 Australians, there was a local force of native troops of dubious effectiveness. New Caledonia could not withstand a major Japanese effort.

With New Caledonia specifically listed on the Arcadia declaration, Admiral King forced the Army to scrape up something to defend it. They gathered loose units totaling some 17,000 troops, including the Army Air Force's 67th Pursuit Squadron, and threw them in a secret, heavily guarded convoy from New York to Nouméa, where they arrived in March. The Army also scraped together a 4,000-man garrison for Bora Bora, where King established a fueling base.

While trying to secure these supply lines, King prodded Nimitz to carry on a sort of naval guerilla warfare against exposed Japanese positions. On February 12, he told Nimitz, "a strong and comprehensive offensive [is] to be launched soon against exposed enemy naval forces and the positions he is now establishing in the Bismarcks and Solomons." Three days later came a reminder: "Current operations of the Pacific Fleet, because of existing threat, should be directed toward preventing further advance of enemy land airplane base development in the direction of Suva and Nouméa…" Then, on February 26 came yet another reminder: "[O]ur current tasks are not merely protective, but also offensive where practicable…"[15] In other words, make the best of what he had.

It was this nudging that resulted in an attempted raid by the carrier *Lexington* on Rabaul on February 20 that was aborted when Japanese flying boats from the Yokohama Air Group spotted the carrier, spooking it enough to withdraw, but not before having to fight off an attack by twin-engine "Mitsubishi G4M Type 1 Land Attack Planes" – the Allies called this aircraft the "Betty" – of the 4th Air Group. Fighter pilot Lieutenant Edward H. "Butch" O'Hare was credited with shooting down five bombers in six minutes. This made him the Army Air Force's first Flying Ace and earned him the Medal of Honor and his name on an airport in Chicago. Admiral King's pestering also brought the successful attack on the Japanese invasion force off Lae and Salamaua on March 10.

The leadership of the US Army, in the form of General George C. Marshall and Army Air Force General Henry H. "Hap" Arnold, was committed to the Europe First policy. Taking much of their cue from General Eisenhower, Marshall and Arnold were determined to quash any offensive actions in the Pacific and not send any reinforcements there:

> To set a limit to future movements of Army forces into the Pacific and find a basis for increasing the rate at which Army forces would be moved across the Atlantic became, during February and March, the chief concern of General Marshall and his advisors on the War Department staff, and the focus of their discussion of future plans with the Army Air Forces and the Navy.[16]

Nevertheless, the continuing Japanese advance that imperiled Australia obliged President Roosevelt to send Army troops there, which meant a supply line for those troops had to be maintained and protected. And an American public still enraged over Pearl Harbor and filled with "unbridled fear, hatred, and distrust" toward Japan meant that a passive posture in the Pacific was politically unacceptable to Roosevelt.[17]

In Admiral King's estimation, that advance meant the Japanese would soon conquer positions to threaten the lanes through Samoa, Fiji, and New Caledonia with air attacks. On February 18, King suggested Tongatabu in the Tonga Islands would be the ideal location for "the principal operating naval base in the South Pacific," while aircraft there would provide mutual support for those on Fiji and Samoa. King also suggested taking Efate, in the New Hebrides, which would "deny a stepping stone to the Japanese if they moved South [sic] from Rabaul" and provide a strong point "from which a step-by-step general advance could be made through the New Hebrides, Solomons and Bismarcks."[18]

General Marshall did not like that. Six days later he wrote back: "It is my desire to do anything reasonable which will make offensive action by the Fleet practicable."

But:

> a. What is the general scheme or concept of operations that the occupation of these additional islands is designed to advance? Are the measures taken purely for protection of a line of communications – or is a step-by-step general advance contemplated?
> b. What islands will be involved?
> c. What Army troops, particularly Air, will your proposal eventually involve? [...]
> d. Your proposal contemplates the employment of Army forces as occupational troops. Has the question of the availability of the Marines been fully explored? [...]

Marshall went on to state that American operations in the South Pacific must "for several reasons be limited to the strategic defensive" so far as air and ground forces were concerned. He concluded:

> I, therefore, feel that if a change in basic strategy, as already approved by the Combined Chiefs of Staff, is involved, the entire situation must be reconsidered before we become involved more seriously in the build-up of Army ground and air garrisons in the Pacific islands.[19]

It was a flat refusal to provide any help, behind a thin passive-aggressive veil. But Admiral King was deft. He answered each of Marshall's questions with his "frankly more offensively minded concepts of our future Pacific endeavor."[20]

At a March 2 meeting of the newly formed Joint Chiefs of Staff, Admiral King handed out a memorandum detailing his proposal. King summarized his proposal with nine words: "Hold Hawaii; Support Australasia; Drive northwestward from New Hebrides."[21] "The general scheme or concept of operations is not only to protect the lines of communication with Australia," he wrote, "but in so doing to set up 'strong points' from which a step-by-step general advance can be made through the New Hebrides, Solomons, and Bismarck Archipelago."[22] For this proposal, King said he needed two, maybe three, Army divisions and maybe eight groups of aircraft.

By this time, Singapore had fallen only a few weeks earlier; defeat in the Battle of the Java Sea had spelled the end of the Allies in the Netherlands East Indies. President Roosevelt needed something, anything, on which to hang some hope. Admiral King's proposal did just that. King was the man with a plan, which was more than anyone else had at that time. Roosevelt gave his tacit approval.[23]

However, by now the Joint Chiefs could not even agree if keeping the lines of communication open to Australia was necessary, as had been contemplated in the Arcadia declaration. On February 28, 1942, General Eisenhower told General Marshall:

> The United States interest in maintaining contact with Australia and in preventing further Japanese expansion to the Southeastward is apparent … but … they are not immediately vital to the successful outcome of the war. The problem is one of determining what we can spare for the effort in that region, without seriously impairing performance of our mandatory tasks.[24]

As a result, Roosevelt now prohibited further reinforcements for the Pacific. The Army had convinced him to give everything to Europe and nothing to the Pacific.[25] Touring the Pacific, General Arnold later said, "it was impossible not to get the impression that the Navy was determined to carry on the campaign in that theater, and determined to do it with as little help from the Army as possible."[26]

The Army's refusal to provide additional units to the Pacific or to agree to offensive action softened when General Douglas MacArthur was rescued from the fall of the Philippines in March 1942. When the Japanese first attacked the Philippines on December 8, 1941, MacArthur, already a national hero, "demonstrated his unique leadership style: when he was good, he was very, very good[;] when he was bad, he was horrid."[27] After long predicting the Japanese could not attack until spring of 1942, MacArthur had refused to consider evidence that a Japanese attack was, in fact, imminent. Then, after being informed of the Pearl Harbor attack, MacArthur disappeared for the next several hours, the first hours of the war, apparently shell-shocked that his predictions were actually wrong. Most of his aircraft were destroyed on the ground at the Clark Field base complex, due largely to MacArthur's willful violation of orders. The result was an inability to contest Japanese control of the air over the Philippines, and, later, the Netherlands East Indies. MacArthur refused to position supplies on the Bataan Peninsula for a protracted campaign because the idea of withdrawing there was "defeatist," so that when he ultimately did withdraw there, his troops had neither the ammunition nor the food for prolonged resistance. After the situation in the Philippines went south, Roosevelt ordered MacArthur to go south, too, all the way to Australia, leaving the troops he had so poorly served behind.

But MacArthur was still a national hero, with a formidable public relations machine that covered up much of his horrid performance – and made him a domestic political threat to Roosevelt. Keeping him on the sidelines was out of the question. Now the Army was interested in reinforcing the Pacific – for an offensive led by Douglas MacArthur. Like a protagonist in his own movie, MacArthur needed something interesting to do.

Which brought up the question of whether the Pacific needed to be like Europe under General Eisenhower and have one theater commander. Douglas MacArthur was the obvious choice. To the Army, at any rate. To the Navy, MacArthur was the one who had constantly berated the Asiatic Fleet and its commander Admiral Hart as not being worthy of the name; allowed the Japanese to completely destroy their base at Cavite; then, to top it off, blamed the fleet for the collapsing situation in the Philippines. Finding MacArthur's performance more "horrid" than "very, very good" and rightly believing MacArthur knew nothing about sea power, Admiral King, with the full backing of the Navy leadership, vowed that MacArthur would never have operational command of the Pacific Fleet.[28] The Army believed MacArthur bore no responsibility for the disaster in the Philippines – that public relations machine at work – and would not agree to command by a Navy admiral.

To break the impasse, on March 9, the Joint Chiefs created two command areas of the Pacific theater. One, a "Southwest Pacific Command," encompassed the Philippines, the Netherlands East Indies, Australia, the Solomon Islands, and adjoining ocean areas. Most of these were not currently under Allied control. It would be up to its commander, General MacArthur, to retake them. As part of the command, MacArthur even got his own little navy to abuse just as he had Admiral Hart and the Asiatic Fleet. And he did. At his new headquarters in Melbourne, MacArthur told a reporter, "[T]he best navy in the world is the Japanese navy. A first-class navy. Then comes the British navy. The US Navy is a fourth-class navy, not even as good as the Italian navy."[29]

Nimitz got the rest as part of a "Pacific Ocean Area," and, like General MacArthur, he reported to his respective service chief on the Joint Chiefs of Staff, who would be conducting this Pacific War by committee. Nimitz's Pacific Ocean Area was further divided into three regions: North, Central, and South, with boundaries at 40 degrees north latitude and the equator. Admiral Nimitz could directly command the first two, but the new South Pacific Command for the area south of the equator would have to be handed off to a subordinate, with Vice Admiral Robert L. Ghormley, who had just finished his term as special naval observer in London, eventually selected.[30]

On April 18, while Lieutenant Colonel Doolittle conducted an operation initiated by Admiral King in leading 16 B-25 Mitchell medium bombers from the deck of the aircraft carrier *Hornet* in a bombing attack on Japan that left little damage but humiliated the Japanese military establishment, King issued orders to Admiral Ghormley that, as Ghormley later recalled them, read like a summons to jury duty:

> You have been selected to command the South Pacific Force and South Pacific area. You will have a large area under your command and a most difficult task. I do not have the tools to give you to carry out the task as it should be. You will establish your headquarters in Auckland, New Zealand, with an advanced base at Tongatabu. In time, possibly this fall, we hope to start an offensive in the South Pacific. You will then probably find it necessary to shift the advanced base as the situation demands and move your own headquarters to meet special situations. I would like for you to leave Washington in one week if possible.[31]

Admiral Ghormley, 59, had served in destroyers and battleships followed by multiple staff assignments, culminating in a stint as chief of the War Plans Division in 1938–39 in which he earned a reputation as "a brilliant strategist."[32] Considered by King to be "a very able man," Ghormley was highly respected for his intelligence and well-liked by his subordinates. Even so, many shared the opinion of Marine Lieutenant Colonel Samuel Griffith, who later wrote, "It is not entirely clear what prompted King to this appointment."[33] While one cannot rise to flag rank without some sense of politics, and, indeed, there has been some suggestion that Roosevelt, a fan of Ghormley's, may have interceded on his behalf, Ghormley seems to have been shy and introverted, especially among peers.[34] An outgoing personality is not needed to be an outstanding commander or a capable administrator, but Ghormley's previous positions never required the proactivity he would need now.

They had required diplomacy, however, and so would this new assignment. And Admiral Ghormley did have considerable diplomatic skills. He arrived in Nouméa, New Caledonia, on May 17 to find Admiral George Thierry d'Argenlieu, who had taken the island for the Free French, unhappy that he and his commander-in-chief, George de Gaulle, had not been consulted on Pacific strategy. But Ghormley managed to smooth things over and then flew to New Zealand.

Of his first impressions of the area, Ghormley wrote:

> The vast distances, the shortage of aircraft, the ease with which the Japanese could slip between defended points, the large size of many islands, the high mountains on most of them, the primitive state of the natives, the total lack of harbor or base facilities, the lack of cable facilities, the lack of ships.[35]

Grim first impressions did not count for much in Admiral King's planning. On April 16, King's assistant chief of staff for planning, Rear Admiral Richmond Kelly Turner, presented a four-phase "Pacific Ocean Campaign Plan." Phase One was the buildup of forces and bases in the South Pacific to secure the area and position for an offensive against the Japanese. Phase Two was an offensive up through the Solomons and New Guinea to seize the Bismarck and Admiralty Islands. Phase Three would extend that offensive to the central Pacific, such as the Marshall and especially the Caroline Islands. Phase Four would involve a drive into the Philippines or the Netherlands East Indies, "whichever offers the more promising and enduring results." This document would become the basic plan for the US Navy in the Pacific.[36]

To make this plan work, earlier Admiral Turner had also recommended the [illegible]lishment of an amphibious assault force in the South Pacific. King agreed and [illegible]d Admiral Nimitz to create it. When Nimitz arrived back in Hawaii after his [illegible]24 conference with Admiral King in San Francisco, he was carrying the specific [illegible] Admiral Ghormley to "prepare to launch a major amphibious offensive [illegible]ons held by the Japanese." The Pacific Fleet staff conducted studies that [illegible]anta Cruz and lower Solomon Islands. King made Turner commander of [illegible]us force. Turner, very uncharacteristically, admitted that he knew little [illegible] responded, "Kelly, you will learn."[37] It was a new war, with new [illegible]and new ways of thinking. How this all interacted, no one knew. [illegible]rn on the fly, something that American officers would later call

Like King and Nimitz, Admiral Turner, who went by "Kelly," would leave his sizable and controversial imprint on the Pacific War. Thin, 57 years old, he looked like a college professor, with the intellect, the vision, and the patronizing manner to match. A trained aviator, Turner would be described by eminent naval aviation historian John Lundstrom as "a tough, bright, even brilliant officer, 'Terrible Turner' was also arrogant, abrasive, irascible, and domineering, grasping for power where he had no business. Only strong-willed commanders kept him in check."[39] Nimitz remarked that Turner was like King in that he was "brilliant, caustic, arrogant, and tactless – just the man for the job."[40]

Then-Lieutenant Colonel Merrill B. Twining, operations officer of the 1st Marine Division, later worked extensively with Turner and remembered him as having "a colossal ego that sometimes led to decisions that ignored the dictates of ordinary common sense." Twining meant it with all due respect, as he did the following description of Turner:

> A loud, strident, arrogant person who enjoyed settling all matters by simply raising his voice and roaring like a bull captain in the old navy. His peers understood this and accepted it with amused resignation because they valued him for what he was: a good and determined leader with a fine mind – when he chose to use it.[41]

While Admiral Turner got to work building the "South Pacific Amphibious Force" from scratch, Marine Major General Alexander Archer Vandegrift was busy training the 1st Marine Division in New Zealand. In March, Vandegrift had been ordered to prepare a regiment to be sent to Samoa. Suspecting the regiment would see combat, Vandegrift cannibalized the rest of the 1st Marine Division to pack the 7th Marine Regiment with as many of the most experienced officers and noncommissioned officers as possible, and the 7th was shipped off.[42] The general's suspicions would have been correct if Midway had resulted in defeat, but it didn't.

On April 15, General Vandegrift was ordered to move the 1st Marine Division – without the 7th Marine Regiment – to New Zealand to form the new Landing Force of the South Pacific Amphibious Force, which was expected to be seeing combat soon. So, right after he assembled his most combat-ready men to send to a place where they would see no combat, the general was now to get the rest of his division – the 1st, 5th, and 11th Marine regiments, all green – ready for combat. Vandegrift got to work trying to very quickly mold these green recruits into a fighting force.

The Japanese were pushing ahead with their next offensive, the capture of Tulagi in the Solomons and Port Moresby, the only remaining position of value in Allied hands in New Guinea. Always keeping his eye out for opportunities to attack, Nimitz believed the Tulagi position was exposed and proposed raiding it using the 1st Marine Raider Battalion. This started another tug of war between General MacArthur, who, though he would shortly field slightly more than three divisions, admitted he did not have the forces to take Tulagi, and Admiral King, who thought Tulagi was too small and wanted something more.[43]

And there things sat while carrier battles took place in the Coral Sea, in which the Japanese invasion force directed at Port Moresby was turned back, and near Midway, in which four Japanese carriers were sunk. Despite the losses of the carriers *Lexington* and *Yorktown*, destroyers *Sims* and *Hammann*, and oiler *Neosho*, the positive effects of both actions, especially Midway, on sagging American morale cannot be overstated. But the American victory at Midway would not have been possible without "Magic."

"Magic" was a subset of what is more commonly and famously known as "Ultra," the term adopted by the Allies to reference signals intelligence (in military acronym SIGINT) obtained by breaking encrypted enemy radio and wireless telegraph communications. While Ultra covered all such intelligence, the US adopted the term *Magic* for its decrypts specifically from Japanese sources. In the case of Coral Sea and Midway, a breakthrough had come in the Japanese naval high-level command and control communications code the Allies called "JN-25."[44] The Allied breakthrough had been the result of painstaking intelligence work. With the Japanese unaware of the breach, *Magic* and signals intelligence would be the gift that kept on giving.

As it was, Midway was its own gift, of which some could not wait to take advantage. The *Yorktown* was perhaps still on her way to the bottom of the Pacific when on June 8 General MacArthur told Washington he could overrun New Britain and New Ireland in a few weeks, "that important area, forcing the enemy back 700 miles to his base at Truk," thus obtaining "manifold strategic advantages both defensive and offensive."[45] All he would need to do this were only the three infantry divisions he already had – which earlier had not been enough to seize Tulagi – plus "one division trained and completely equipped for amphibious operations and a task force including two carriers."

That sounded fine to General Marshall, who believed this potential operation needed to be run as quickly as possible. He was in the process of requesting the necessary forces from Admiral King when King preempted MacArthur's proposal with one of his own. The Navy was already preparing operations against the objectives MacArthur mentioned, operations that would be more gradual. Capture of intermediate air bases was necessary to help neutralize the air power based at Rabaul. Such a campaign would be "primarily of a naval and amphibious character supported and followed by forces operating from Australia."[46] In short, the Navy would do it, with MacArthur's help.

Admiral King was continuing to lay the groundwork for offensive operations in the Solomons. On June 11, King asked Admiral Ghormley when he could go on the attack. Ghormley replied that he planned to occupy the New Hebrides, Santa Cruz, and Ellice islands, which were unoccupied, "as soon as the prospect of reinforcement is favorable." This did not answer the question. It was a sign of things to come.

But General MacArthur did try to answer the questions posed to him. Or at least obfuscate them. In a June 24 message, MacArthur addressed the criticism of his plan by claiming his original proposal was only an outline. Quite obviously, he said, a "gradual" approach with seizure of intermediate bases in the Solomons and New Guinea would be required to capture Rabaul. What MacArthur meant by "gradual" he did not say, but plans at his headquarters indicated his version of gradual was 14–18 days. He would not need any more time. He spent the rest of the message explaining why only he, Douglas MacArthur, should be in command of this offensive.[47]

Correctly figuring MacArthur was "blackmailing the US Navy into greater reinforcements in the South Pacific," Admiral King was having none of it. He tried to explain to MacArthur that Tulagi had to be taken before Rabaul or else the air power based there posed too great a risk to his ships.[48] That same day King ordered Nimitz to prepare a plan to capture "Tulagi and adjacent islands." The next day, King told General Marshall they needed to strike now before this "golden opportunity" arising out of Midway passed. The admiral recommended a single unified command to perform the seizure of the Santa Cruz Islands as the start of an offensive to begin around August 1 that would culminate in the capture of New Guinea and Rabaul.

The day after that came General Marshall's response. He continued to push for General MacArthur's command, mainly on the grounds that the operation lay "almost entirely in the Southwest Pacific area" and that it was "designed to add to the security of that area," though he did acknowledge that the boundaries were not necessarily controlling. He went on to make the case, such as it was, for General MacArthur to lead this offensive through the Solomon Islands and New Guinea to Rabaul and New Britain.[49]

By now well aware that he was in a political pissing contest, Admiral King responded in writing the same day. "[General Marshall's] basic trouble," he later said, "was that like all Army officers he knew nothing about sea power and very little about air power."[50] So, King later explained, he had "to 'educate' the Army people." King told Marshall that he had agreed to have an Army general in command of the European theater – "unity of command" – because it would be fought primarily by the Army. The Pacific was being fought primarily by the Navy and Marine Corps; hence it made more sense to have a Navy admiral in charge. The offensive "must be conducted under the direction of CINCPAC and cannot be conducted in any other way." He finally said he was going to start an offensive "even if no support of Army forces in the Southwest Pacific is available." King gave Admiral Nimitz orders to this effect on June 27.[51]

General Marshall was furious. Without approval from President Roosevelt or the Joint Chiefs, Admiral King had ordered preparation for a major offensive into General MacArthur's Southwest Pacific Area. He also seemed to be defying Roosevelt's order not to reinforce the Pacific; once Admiral Nimitz started his attack, reinforcements would be forthcoming. But King could point to Roosevelt's approval of his March 2 memorandum for limited actions in the Solomons. And he had only ordered Nimitz to prepare for an offensive.

MacArthur was beyond furious. He had not even seen Admiral King's letter to Marshall; he had just picked up King's orders to Admiral Nimitz and Nimitz's response in which he listed some units under MacArthur's command for the attack. In "one of his more remarkable tantrums of the war," in the words of the historian Richard B. Frank, MacArthur on June 28 radioed General Marshall:

> It is quite evident in reviewing the whole situation that the Navy contemplates assuming general command control of all operations in the Pacific theater, the role of the Army being subsidiary and consisting largely of placing its forces at the disposal and under the command of Navy or Marine officers ... I shall take no steps or action with reference to any components of my Command except under your direct orders.[52]

Evidently MacArthur thought it was patently ridiculous that an invasion of Pacific islands across thousands of miles of ocean be commanded by someone from the Navy. Especially when it could be commanded by Douglas MacArthur.

But it was about more than that, the general alleged. It was all part of a master plan for "the complete absorption of the national defense function by the Navy." A plan he had "accidentally" uncovered when he was Chief of Staff of the Army.

> ... By using Army troops to garrison the islands of the Pacific under Navy command, the Navy retains Marine forces always available, giving them inherently an army of their own and serving as the real bases of their plans by virtue of having the most readily available units for offensive action.[53]

General Marshall, of course, backed his Army colleague. But even he admitted that General MacArthur was "supersensitive about everything" and "thought everybody had ulterior motives about everything." MacArthur's "hypersensitivity" was something of a joke in defense circles. His "paranoia, lust for personal publicity, political ambition, structured and comfortable lifestyle, and hypochondria were well-known in the army… His emotional balance was precarious. These personal foibles […] made George Patton look n[illegible]l."[54]

It [illegible] General Marshall, after he had sufficiently calmed down himself, to initi[illegible]he impasse. During the last two days of June, Marshall and Admiral King [illegible] the "Joint Directive for Offensive Operations in the Southwest Paci[illegible]n by the United States Chiefs of Staff" that consisted of three phases. Pha[illegible] given its own code name of "Watchtower," would involve the seizure of Tu[illegible] Santa Cruz Islands. This task would be completed by the Pacific Fleet. MacA[illegible]outhwest Pacific Command boundary would be moved up the Solomons, so this [illegible] would lie entirely within the South Pacific Command. MacArthur himself would [illegible]erdict "enemy air and naval activities westward of operating area," meaning Rabaul and New Guinea.[55] Phase Two would be the capture of Lae, Salamaua, the rest of the northeast coast of New Guinea, and the central Solomons. Phase Three would involve the reduction and capture of Rabaul. Phases Two and Three would be under the command of General MacArthur. This three-part plan was given the cheerful name of "Pestilence."

Admiral King and General Marshall – curiously not General Arnold – formally adopted *Pestilence* on July 2. Phase One – *Watchtower*, involving the capture of the Santa Cruz Islands, Tulagi, and adjacent positions – was scheduled to begin August 1.

King scheduled a meeting with Admiral Nimitz for July 3 in San Francisco to brief him on these developments. In the interim, Nimitz had been working on *Watchtower* as he understood it. On June 27, he expanded the planned attack on Tulagi to include the capture of an unspecified airfield site, if not a finished airfield.[56]

On July 2, Admiral Turner briefed Nimitz on how *Watchtower* was developing. In what he called a "Limited Amphibious Offensive in South and Southwest Pacific," Turner planned to capture various islands to create a web of mutually supporting airfields. His first target would be Ndeni in the Santa Cruz Islands, some 250 miles north of Espiritu Santo in the New Hebrides, where Admiral Nimitz had already authorized development of a base, and 350 miles southeast of Tulagi. Turner thought Ndeni would make a great air base to guard the eastern flank of the Solomons, largely because he had never been there and knew nothing about it.[57] But as Admiral King had said earlier, he would learn.

Next would be the Tulagi and Florida islands. The problem was that there was no place on either island to build an airfield. So Admiral Turner suggested a coastal plain on Guadalcanal, 18 miles to the south, where an airfield could be built. Neither he nor Admiral Nimitz had any idea as yet that more than a few parties were suddenly interested in Guadalcanal.

Among those parties was, like *Magic*, a uniquely useful form of Allied intelligence gathering in the South Pacific: an organization called "Ferdinand." Named after the children's story *Ferdinand the Bull*, whose title character preferred smelling flowers to fighting, *Ferdinand* was the brainchild of Australian naval reservist Lieutenant Commander Eric A. Feldt, a veteran of the British Grand Fleet in World War I. Feldt had been local affairs administrator on New Guinea, where he became familiar with the talented, temperamental, and fiercely independent Melanesian natives. When Feldt was recalled to service, he came up with the idea of enrolling plantation managers, government administrators, missionaries, and anyone who wanted to serve, but not to fight, not to be noticed, not to cause any trouble for the Japanese, except to watch and warn of Japanese movements, actions, and other developments. By December 1939, *Ferdinand* had 800 members, located everywhere in New Guinea, the Bismarcks, and the Solomons, including chief observers trained to communicate by radio.[58] They would become known as "coastwatchers."

Upon the arrival of the Japanese, the coastwatchers became dependent on the goodwill of the local Melanesians. Whether due to the respect and humanity with which the Australian local colonial officials had treated them, the general brutality with which the Japanese treated everybody including them, or both, the vast majority of Melanesians remained loyal to the Allied cause. They became essential to the Allies by gathering information, carrying equipment and supplies, providing cover, and infiltrating Japanese construction details.

As the Japanese advanced and began consolidating their hold on the Solomons, the coastwatchers, directed from Townsville, Australia, became eyes and ears – but not hands – for the Allies. Six in particular became critical to the South Pacific war effort. In a hilltop hideout in Pora Pora, northern Bougainville, near the Buka Passage, where the local Melanesians had, unlike the others, switched sides to the Japanese, was Lieutenant W. J. "Jack" Read. At the other end of Bougainville, overlooking the Shortland Islands, was Paul Mason, a short, bespectacled radio hobbyist and former plantation manager with 25 years' experience in the islands. At a plantation on Segi Point on New Georgia was Donald Kennedy, a middle-aged former district officer who, according to Feldt, projected "a natural aura of command."[59]

Guadalcanal had three coastwatching posts. On Gold Ridge, 15 miles from the coast, was naval reservist Donald MacFarlan, working with Kenneth D. Hay, a sizable plantation manager with sizable intelligence. On western Guadalcanal was F. Ashton "Snowy" Rhoades, working with an older former Norwegian trader, Leif Schroeder. Filling the role of chief coastwatcher on Guadalcanal was former district officer Martin Clemens, positioned east of Lunga at Aola Bay.[60]

It was Martin Clemens who first noticed Japanese activity in the Lunga area. By radio and by native runner, he, MacFarlan, Hay, and Rhoades compared notes to determine what the Japanese were doing. When the convoy carrying the 11th and 13th Construction Units arrived, they deduced the Japanese were building an airfield. Construction on the base progressed under the watchful and thoroughly enraged eyes of Martin Clemens.

As a result of the work of Clemens and friends, *Ferdinand* reported work at the Lunga site on July 1. *Ferdinand* was joined the next day by *Magic*, who concluded the Japanese had landed construction troops on Guadalcanal.[61] Admiral Nimitz had wanted to seize an airfield site. Now he had one. King and Nimitz agreed to replace Ndeni in Phase One with Guadalcanal for the time being. But that airfield construction was an hourglass, and as it got closer to completion, the sand was running out.

In the midst of all this politicking, Admiral Ghormley was dealing with a South Pacific Command that was little more than a paper and a cabin on the command ship *Argonne* – given the happy nickname "Agony Maru" – in Auckland. On June 25, he had been ordered to arrange the capture of "Tulagi and adjacent positions."[62] Ghormley was "flabbergasted." His "immediate mental estimate of the situation was that [they] were far from ready to start any offensive."[63] And they weren't. At the moment all Ghormley had was a tiny staff that was largely scavenged from the Asiatic Fleet, with Rear Admiral Daniel J. Callaghan, former skipper of the cruiser *San Francisco* and formerly President Roosevelt's naval aide, as its chief.[64] Ghormley had little information, no major units under his command, and no bases anywhere close to the target.

Nimitz was trying to help with that by directing the seizure of Espiritu Santo, 125 miles north of Efate in the New Hebrides, where an airfield was to be constructed. But, in a pattern that would reveal itself more and more over the coming months, Ghormley actually complicated his own reinforcement when he refused to shift troops from rear bases to Espiritu Santo, without which Nimitz would not authorize the airfield. Ultimately, just to get moving, on July 3 Nimitz ordered construction of the air strip, on the next day specifying that it be made ready for B-17s by July 28.[65]

The arrival of the new orders from Admiral King for the seizure of Guadalcanal and Tulagi, before the issuance of the Joint Chiefs' directive, had done nothing to improve Admiral Ghormley's sinking mood. General Vandegrift had come from his own headquarters in Wellington to pay his new superior an official call in Auckland on June 26 when he was summoned to meet the admiral. Vandegrift had met Ghormley in Washington and was surprised at his "harassed, almost brusque manner" now.

They had barely shaken hands when Admiral Ghormley declared, "Vandegrift, I have some very disconcerting news."

"I'm sorry to hear that, Admiral."

"You will be more sorry when you read this," Ghormley said as he handed the Marine general a piece of paper. Vandegrift pulled a chair up to the admiral's desk to read it.

It was a set of top secret orders. General Vandegrift's 1st Marine Division was to seize Guadalcanal and Tulagi as part of an amphibious operation. Vandegrift had to read it again to be sure of the shocking words they contained. The most shocking was the date: August 1.

General Vandegrift folded the orders and silently pushed them across the desk to Admiral Ghormley. Then the general leaned back in his chair. He had to think.

The admiral tapped the orders with his index finger for a moment, then looked at Vandegrift. "Well?"

General Vandegrift went over his issues. He had been given command of the 1st Marine Division, but it came with the disclaimer "Some assembly required." The 7th Marine Regiment was garrisoning Samoa. The divisional command and the 5th Marine Regiment were in Wellington, New Zealand; the 1st and the 11th Marine regiments, the latter less two of its battalions, were en route.[66]

To compound matters, they had to break in new equipment and their supply situation had to be determined. Most importantly, they needed information on Guadalcanal; Vandegrift didn't even know where Guadalcanal was. The general concluded, "I don't see how we can land anywhere by August first."

"I don't see how we can land at all, and I am going to take it up with MacArthur," Ghormley responded. "Meanwhile, we'll have to go ahead as best we can."[67]

And with that inspiring declaration, the meeting was concluded. A rather subtle but important distinction had been exposed. General Vandegrift thought *Watchtower* could not be started by August 1; Admiral Ghormley thought it could not be started at all. Admiral King, with his belief in making the best of what you have, was conscious of the difference.

General Vandegrift had to redouble his work. He tried to arrange to assemble his division as quickly as possible, at sea if necessary. His staff informed him that to replace the 7th Marine Regiment, which was staying in Samoa for the time being, they were getting the 2nd Marine Regiment from the 2nd Marine Division; the catch was that the 2nd was sailing in from San Diego. They were getting the 1st Raider Battalion back from the 7th Marine Regiment, but it was still in Samoa. They were also getting the 3rd Defense Battalion, sailing in from Hawaii.

But the general had to assemble more than just his division. Admiral Turner would be commander of the amphibious force, but he would not arrive until mid-July, so Vandegrift had to draw up the plan for the landing and the amphibious force himself. He had to assemble his supplies for the cargo ships and transports. "Combat loading," it was called. Upon landing, the most essential supplies, such as ammunition, food, water, fuel, and medical supplies, would be positioned to be unloaded first. Less essential supplies, such as accordions, shoe polish, and hats, would be at the back of the supply queue. With the dock workers at Wellington trying to heist the government for more money, the 5th Marine Regiment had to take up the loading arrangements itself – in the midst of heavy rains that lasted for some three weeks.[68]

With the two most important elements in any combat operation being communications and information, General Vandegrift gave Lieutenant Colonel Frank B. Goettge, 1st Marine Division's intelligence officer and former football star at Ohio State, the task of redressing the distressing lack of the latter. Goettge and his section interviewed former Solomons residents, civil servants, and merchant ships' officers in New Zealand. On July 1 Goettge even flew to Melbourne, where he spent a week scouring General MacArthur's headquarters for everything he could get on Guadalcanal. He found out about the *Ferdinand* organization and was able to establish contact. Goettge then spent a few days in Sydney, continuing to dredge up and interview former residents of the Solomons. Soon, Guadalcanal got its code name, a name that would become famous: "Cactus." Other locations got code names as well. Tulagi was "Ringbolt," Espiritu Santo "Button," New Zealand "Spooner," and Efate "Roses."[69]

The orders for *Pestilence* included a directive that Admiral Ghormley meet with General MacArthur to coordinate planning. The South Pacific commander went to Melbourne on July 8, but he wasn't happy about it. He informed MacArthur's command: "On account of early commencement of [Phase] One and the great detail of planning necessary, [I] will be accompanied by minimum officers and my stay must be as short as possible." For his part, MacArthur was still brooding over not being given the entire command over the first offensive in the Pacific. Like most meetings involving Ghormley, this was not going to be a happy meeting.

The two announced their lack of confidence in the planning, preparation, and execution of *Watchtower*, now only three weeks away:

> The two commanders are of the opinion, arrived at independently, and confirmed after discussion, that the initiation of the operation at this time without a reasonable assurance of adequate air coverage would be attended with the gravest risk… surprise is now improbable… successful accomplishment is open to the gravest doubts. It is recommended that this operation be deferred.[70]

The issue, as they saw it, was airpower; more precisely, lack of the same. The landing force would need carrier support from 36 to 96 hours, "where they will be outside the range of any supporting air and exposed to continual hostile surface and submarine attacks." General MacArthur did not have the air power to sufficiently suppress that of Rabaul. "The carriers will be themselves exposed to attack by land-based air while unprotected by our land-based aviation." Consequently, it was "extremely doubtful that they will be able to furnish fighter escort to the transport area, especially should hostile naval forces approach." Surprise was "improbable" due to "the depth of the existing hostile reconnaissance."[71]

Moreover, with their nearby bases the Japanese were better positioned to rush reinforcements to the Solomons that could destroy the invasion and covering forces. "The initiation of this operation at this time without a reasonable assurance of adequate air coverage during each phase would be attendant with the gravest risk."[72] General MacArthur and Admiral Ghormley recommended *Watchtower* be "deferred" pending the further development of force to enable all three phases [of *Pestilence*] to take place, "in one continuous movement."[73] Which sounded suspiciously like MacArthur's proposals from early June.

Admiral King saw exactly what was happening: Douglas MacArthur was sulking over not being given complete command over *Pestilence*. Likely speaking for the naval leadership, King told General Marshall, "Three weeks ago, MacArthur stated that if he could be furnished amphibious forces and two carriers, he could push right through to Rabaul. He now feels that he not only cannot undertake this operation but not even the Tulagi operation."[74]

With the Japanese already on Guadalcanal, the sand in that hourglass was running out. *Watchtower* now needed speed, not delay. Admiral King contemptuously responded to their statement with a one-word order: "Execute."[75]

Perhaps appropriately, the MacArthur-Ghormley memo of hopeless optimism crossed one in which Admiral Nimitz told Ghormley, "I have full confidence in your ability to carry this operation to a successful conclusion."[76] More appropriately, the missive got the attention of General Marshall, who tried to bolster the operation by sending the 11th Bombardment Group to the South Pacific. The first of its B-17s arrived at the newly completed airfield at Espiritu Santo on July 30. The completion of the airfield in such a short time, especially given how the "Sea Bees" (men of the construction battalions) were fighting heat and malaria, was, said the commander of land-based air Rear Admiral John S. "Slew" McCain, "a truly remarkable achievement."[77]

On the opposite end of the remarkable spectrum was the situation in Wellington. The 1st Marine Division and its supplies were still straggling in. Organizing the supplies in the driving rain was still a headache, with a lack of dock space in Wellington being the major culprit, becoming a drag on the operation. To try to speed things along, General Vandegrift ordered that "all units ... reduce their equipment and supplies to those items that are actually required to live and fight," helping earn Operation *Watchtower* the nickname "Operation Shoestring."[78] The supply difficulties caused Vandegrift to ask for a slight delay in *Watchtower*. On July 16, the date was officially reset for August 7, but the Japanese were so close to completing the airfield that the date could not be pushed back further.

That same day, Vice Admiral Ghormley published and distributed a 174-page operational plan for *Watchtower*. Given the catchy title of "Op-Plan 1-42," it was not a particularly complicated plan from an organizational standpoint. Under his South Pacific Command were two task forces. One, Task Force 63 under Rear Admiral McCain, consisted of all the land- and water-based aircraft. Everything else he placed in what he called Task Force 61, "The Expeditionary Force."[79]

The Expeditionary Force was under the command of the newly promoted Vice Admiral Frank Jack Fletcher, the most experienced carrier admiral in the Navy, veteran and victor of both the Coral Sea, where he had lost one aircraft carrier, and Midway, where he had lost another aircraft carrier. And who was currently sailing from Pearl Harbor under radio silence. Identified under his direct command were six task forces. Three of them were carrier groups, each consisting of one aircraft carrier plus an escorting screen. Task Force 11, under Fletcher's direct command, was centered on his flagship carrier *Saratoga*, escorted by heavy cruisers *Minneapolis* and *New Orleans*, and destroyers *Phelps*, *Farragut*, *Worden*, *MacDonough*, and *Dale*.

Task Force 16 was commanded by Rear Admiral Thomas C. Kinkaid on the carrier *Enterprise*, with the new battleship *North Carolina*, heavy cruiser *Portland*, light cruiser *Atlanta*, and destroyers *Balch*, *Maury*, *Gwin*, *Benham*, and *Grayson*. The *Atlanta* was a new class of light cruiser, featuring 16 rapid-fire 5-inch guns in eight dual mounts. The weapons layout would be good in air defense, and she was classified as an antiaircraft cruiser.

Task Force 18 was under Rear Admiral Leigh Noyes, the only trained aviator of the three carrier admirals. His flag was on the aircraft carrier *Wasp*, which was the only one of the three carriers whose air group was trained in night operations. She was screened by heavy cruisers *San Francisco* and *Salt Lake City*, and destroyers *Lang*, *Sterett*, *Aaron Ward*, *Stack*, *Laffey*, and *Farenholt*. Providing fuel to the carrier task forces were five oilers: *Platte*, *Cimarron*, *Kaskaskia*, *Sabine*, and *Kanawha*.

As a general rule, each of the American fleet carriers had an air group that consisted of four squadrons. Each squadron was assigned a particular role – fighting, bombing, scouting, or torpedo. Originally, the squadrons were designated according to their role and the hull number of their carrier. So, for instance, the hull number of the carrier *Enterprise* was 6. The fighter squadron on the *Enterprise* was officially designated "VF-6" but was informally known as "Fighting 6." Normally, carrier fighter squadrons like Fighting 6 would have 27 Grumman F4F Wildcats, the US Navy's primary fighter. The rather stubby-looking Wildcat would be the primary opponent for the famous Japanese Zero. It had a slightly lower top speed and inferior rates of climb, acceleration, and maneuverability compared to the Zero. But, unlike their Japanese counterparts, pilot protection was a major priority for American combat aircraft procurement, and the Wildcat was no exception. The Wildcat was rugged, with an armored cockpit and self-sealing fuel tanks combining to provide excellent protection for the pilots. The F4F was considered obsolete, but when flown with even moderate skill it could more than hold its own against the Zero.

The typical torpedo squadron, to use the *Enterprise*'s original squadron as an example, had the official designation of "VT-6" and was called "Torpedo 6." Normally, it would have 18 of the Grumman TBF Avenger. The Avenger was a brand-new torpedo plane, rushed into service because its predecessor the Douglas TBD Devastator was not only obsolete but had become a deathtrap. At Midway every single one of the Devastators from the carrier *Hornet*'s Torpedo 8 had been shot down by Zeros and antiaircraft fire. The Avenger was fast for a torpedo plane, with long range and even an enclosed bomb bay. Like its fellow Grumman Wildcat, the Avenger was a very rugged plane with good protection for the pilot. The TBF was easily recognizable by its .50cal dorsal tail gun. It also carrier a ventral .30cal tail gun and a .30cal "peashooter" for the pilot.[80] Its enclosed bomb bay could carry two 1,000lb bombs, four 500lb bombs, or one torpedo. The big drawback here was that the torpedo was the Mark 13, which, like the American Mark 14 and Mark 15 torpedoes, seemed to be less than effective.

To continue with the *Enterprise* as an example, each carrier had two squadrons of dive bombers, each with 18 Douglas SBD Dauntlesses. One squadron was dedicated to dive bombing, carrying the official designation of "VB-6" or "Bombing 6." The Dauntless was also used to conduct long-range reconnaissance, which was an additional focus for, originally, "VS-6" or "Scouting 6." The Dauntless did not look like much and its aerial ratings were not all that impressive, either. But the Dauntless was the hero of Midway and beloved by its pilots.

As the war went on, the numerical designations for carrier squadrons would get mixed up as carriers were lost or sidelined for repair, or carrier squadrons were rotated. For instance, the *Enterprise*'s scout bombing squadron was now actually "VS-5" – "Scouting 5" – moved over from the sunken *Yorktown*, as was the *Enterprise*'s torpedo squadron, "VT-3" – "Torpedo 3."[81]

Admiral Turner's force, called Task Force 62, was subdivided nine ways. The group of transports headed for Lunga was officially called Task Group 62.1 but codenamed "Transport Group X-Ray." It was commanded by Captain Lawrence F. Reifsnider with transports *Fuller*, *American Legion*, *McCawley*, *Barnett*, *George F. Elliott*, *Hunter Liggett*, *Alchiba*, *Crescent City*, *President Hayes*, and *President Adams*; and cargo ships *Alhena*, *Betelgeuse*, *Bellatrix*, *Libra*, and *Fomalhaut*. This transport group was further divided into two groups of three transports and one cargo ship each; one group of two transports and two cargo ships; and one group of two transports and one cargo ship.

The distinction between "transports" and "cargo ships" might seem academic, and indeed in most reports they are both lumped together as "transports."[82] But, in fact, there was considerable difference. Each transport was assigned to carry one combat team, three "units of fire" – roughly the amount of ammunition consumed in a day of heavy combat – 30 days' rations, and quartermaster, ordnance, engineer, chemical, signal, and medical supplies. Each cargo ship was to carry supporting troops, heavy equipment, seven more units of fire, 30 days' rations and other supplies, and clothing stocks were assigned to each cargo ship.[83] Indeed, some very important people would demonstrate they were quite conscious of the difference.

Providing artillery support to the landing at Lunga was Task Group 62.3, with heavy cruisers *Quincy*, *Vincennes*, and *Astoria*, each cruiser with two spotter planes, and destroyers *Hull*, *Dewey*, *Ellet*, and *Wilson*, commanded by the *Vincennes*' skipper Captain Frederick L. Riefkohl.

The landing at Tulagi centered on, officially, Task Group 62.2, coded "Transport Group Yoke" under Captain George B. Ashe. Not surprisingly given its target, it was much smaller than its Guadalcanal counterpart, consisting of transports *Neville*, *Zeilin*, *Heywood*, and *President Jackson*, and four old destroyers converted into fast – by transport standards – transports: *Colhoun*, *Little*, *McKean*, and *Gregory*.

The Tulagi landing would get fire support from the official Task Group 62.4 under Rear Admiral Norman Scott, flying his flag in the light cruiser *San Juan*, a designated antiaircraft cruiser like her sister *Atlanta*. In addition to the *San Juan*, the fire support would come from the destroyers *Monssen* and *Buchanan*.

Task Group 62.5 was a group of minesweepers, creatively dubbed the "Minesweeper Group," under Commander William H. Hartt, Jr. Its job was to sweep for mines around both Tulagi, Guadalcanal, and Savo Sound in general with minesweepers *Hopkins*, *Trever*, *Zane*, *Southard*, and *Hovey*.

Given the task of providing protection from surface forces was "MacArthur's Navy," the Allied ships supporting General MacArthur's Southwest Pacific Command. They were normally designated Task Force 44, but for *Watchtower* they were called Task Group 62.6, the "Screening Group." It consisted of Royal Australian Navy heavy cruisers *Australia* and *Canberra*; US Navy heavy cruiser *Chicago*, Australian light cruiser *Hobart*, and American destroyers *Selfridge*, *Patterson*, *Ralph Talbot*, *Mugford*, *Jarvis*, *Blue*, *Helm*, *Henley*, and *Bagley*. This squadron was commanded by Rear Admiral Victor Alexander Charles Crutchley, a British admiral on loan to the Royal Australian Navy, which was such a new organization that it lacked experienced flag officers of its own.

Generally, Americans did not and do not like serving under foreign officers, especially after what they considered the subpar performance of the Dutch Admiral Karel Doorman during the Java Sea Campaign. Victor Crutchley seems to have been an exception. He was a distinguished Royal Navy veteran known for his physical courage, having fought in the Battle of Jutland, been awarded the Distinguished Service Cross for one attempt to block the German U-boat fleets in harbor, been awarded the Victoria Cross (Britain's highest award for bravery) for gallantry and seamanship during another, and on top of all that the French *Croix de Guerre* – all during World War I.[84] He commanded the battleship *Warspite* to an impressive victory against the German *Kriegsmarine* off Narvik early in World War II. "His intelligence, careful demeanor and meticulous approach to planning and operations deeply impressed his American colleagues."[85]

Because almost everything needs a numeric designation, the carrier planes supporting the landing were officially called Task Group 62.7, the "Air Support Group." This would be the air support provided by the carriers *Saratoga*, *Enterprise*, and *Wasp* in the form of fighter cover and bombing attacks. Fighter director officers were placed on the flagship *McCawley* and the transport *Neville* to direct air support for Guadalcanal and Tulagi respectively. Another fighter director officer would be placed on the cruiser *Chicago* to direct the intercept of the expected Japanese air attacks on transports.[86] The direct air support for General Vandegrift's Marines was called Task Group 62.8, with floatplanes from the *Astoria* and *Quincy* spotting for the Guadalcanal landing, while those from the *Vincennes* would support the landing on Tulagi under Brigadier General William H. Rupertus. The Marines set to land on Santa Cruz were not given a numeric designation for some reason, though they appeared in Admiral Turner's table of organization.

The transport *McCawley* would serve as Admiral Turner's flagship, a far more grandiose term than this ship actually deserved. Like many transports, the *McCawley* was a hurried "conversion" from a cruise liner, in this case the *Santa Barbara*, who for some 12 years had carried passengers, most recently for Grace Lines. Whether she carried them in luxury is open to question. Even by Navy standards she was cramped, with staff officers crammed together three in a room, and the more junior ship and communication officers stacked up in bunk rooms.[87]

Moreover, by the time the US Navy got the *McCawley*, she was "a dirty ship."[88] Not that this was unusual for the transports on this mission, as many of the Marines noticed. The *American Legion* was so "filthy" that the men on board were said to resemble "wild gypsies," many choosing to sleep out on deck – so many that individual squads would protect areas on deck they had settled.[89]

It was even worse on the transport *John Ericsson*, transporting Marines from San Francisco to Wellington, New Zealand.[90] Navy officers had to step in to prevent the *John Ericsson* from loading rancid butter and rotten eggs – but not the spoiled beef and chicken and fouled cooking grease that later sickened most of the men on board. Marine Corporal Grady Gallant called the food "genuine slop" and declared "none of it was fit to eat." Marine Robert Leckie said there was not an ounce of fresh food on the ship.[91] Even the Marine history, though not mentioning the *John Ericsson* by name, admitted, "The standard of health [for Marines arriving in New Zealand] remained fairly high, except for troops on board one transport of the second echelon. Among those marines rotten food on the voyage to New Zealand had caused a loss of weight varying from sixteen to twenty pounds per man, as well as a diarrhea epidemic."[92] Leckie would say the *John Ericsson* was "little better than an African slaver" that "stank like a floating head." The only ones left healthy were the ones who had refused to eat the horrid food, subsisting only on peanuts and Pepsi Cola.[93]

The 13,000-ton *McCawley* was rated for 17 knots, which by transport standards is practically light speed. But she also had "an intermittently flaming stack, visible for miles around as we charged along for all the world like a horse-drawn steam fire engine."[94] The fire-breathing smoke stack, which was dangerous inasmuch as it could act as a beacon at night for interested and not necessarily friendly parties, had been troublesome for the last 18 months, but no one had gotten around to fixing it yet.

This was largely because the *McCawley* had a completely dysfunctional command staff. Her skipper was Captain Charles P. McFeaters, whom Lieutenant Commander Twining of the 1st Marine Division described as "a superannuated hypochondriac" who "was in no physical condition to command a ship."[95] The deficiencies of a skipper can be addressed by a good executive officer, but the *McCawley*'s was Lieutenant Commander George K. G. Reilly, "a Marine-hating mustang, a sadist determined to haze Marines," who worked to abuse them 24 hours a day. A bit more gentle than Twining, Admiral Turner's biographer said of them, "These two officers struggled constantly to meet the demanding requirements of a stern taskmaster and an eager beaver staff, but never quite made the grade."[96]

The problems did not end there. The two most critical elements in any military operation are information and communications. And in communications the *McCawley* was sorely deficient, lacking even a voice radio. A radio suite was brought in, including 16 field radios, but the range of the radio was not much more than 5 miles and still could not regularly monitor the frequency used by Admiral Fletcher.[97] It was a common problem on the *McCawley*. Of Admiral Turner's staff, only the meteorologist filed a "satisfactory" report on the particular flagship facilities needed for his efficient functioning.[98]

In the judgment of Lieutenant Colonel Twining, the *McCawley* was a "Hell Ship" that was "definitely not battle worthy."[99] Twining's opinion was prevalent among the Marines. General Vandegrift was so disgusted by conditions on board the *McCawley* that he requested "a vessel better suited in communications and accommodations," but had been denied.[100] Only the exigent circumstances can explain why the *McCawley* was chosen as the flagship for the first US offensive of the Pacific War and the first US amphibious invasion since 1898.

Admiral McCain deployed his Task Force 63 for primarily reconnaissance and antisubmarine patrols. He had at his command the Army Air Force's 11th Bombardment Group, consisting of the 26th, 42nd, 98th, and 431st Bombardment Squadrons, newly formed in July as a sort of mobile fire-fighting force under the direct command of the Joint Chiefs. The brand-new airstrip at Espiritu Santo had five Boeing B-17 Flying Fortresses of the 98th, five of the 26th were at Efate, ten of the 42nd were split between two airfields on New Caledonia, and the 12 of the 431st were used as a kind of reserve and based at Nandi in the Fijis.[101]

Also on hand were 28 Consolidated PBY-5 Catalina flying boats. Of these Catalinas, 12 were based on shore – six at Nandi in the Fijis, four at Efate, and two in New Caledonia. The remainder were on seaplane tenders to be positioned for the flying boats to conduct air searches. The seaplane tenders *Curtiss* and *McFarland* were moved up to Segond Channel, just off Espiritu Santo, from where the *Curtiss* would deploy her ten PBY Catalina flying boats to search south and southeast of the Solomons. The *McFarland* would continue on to the Santa Cruz Islands so its six PBYs could search north and northeast of Guadalcanal. The seaplane tender *Mackinac* would be positioned in the Maramasike Estuary on the east coast of Malaita to serve as a base for nine Catalinas, whose primary job was to search to the northeast.[102]

Task Force 63 could also call on 79 Bell P-39 Airacobras of the Army Air Force's 67th, 68th, and 70th Fighter Squadrons, and 22 Martin B-26 Marauders of the Army Air Force's 69th and 70th Bombardment Squadrons. The B-26 was the closest American equivalent to the Japanese Naval Air Force's Mitsubishi G3M Type 96 Land Attack Plane – the Allies would call it the "Nell" – and G4M "Betty" bombers, inasmuch as it could carry torpedoes. There were also 50 Grumman F4F Wildcats of Marine Fighting 111 and 212, and Observation 251, 12 Hudsons of the Royal New Zealand Air Force, 25 Navy Vought OS2U Kingfisher floatplanes, and 17 Curtiss SBC Helldivers of Marine Observation 151.[103] Given the area Task Force 63 had to cover and the bases it had to protect, this was a woefully inadequate force in both numbers and types of aircraft. It was just the best that could be done. Even so, the most forward base, the new airfield at Espiritu Santo, had exactly three fighters in addition to its five B-17s, one of which crashed at sea on August 6 and had to be replaced from Efate, and three floatplanes.[104]

With the Bismarcks and the northwestern part of the Solomons still under General MacArthur's jurisdiction, his cooperation was required for *Watchtower* to succeed. MacArthur was indeed a good soldier and amenable to working with Admiral McCain to coordinate search efforts within the Southwest Pacific Command area. The most important aspects of the agreement included the arrangement, from five days before the invasion to four days afterwards, of four daily reconnaissance flights from Port Moresby covering an area including Madang, Kavieng, Ontong Java, Santa Ysabel, and the central Solomons. Naval targets discovered in this area within a 550-mile range of Port Moresby would be attacked in separate airstrikes. On the day of the invasion and for four days thereafter MacArthur's air force was to suppress Japanese air operations in and around Rabaul and Kavieng.[105]

In the meantime, 1st Marine Division intelligence officer Colonel Goettge was still trying to dredge up anything he could on Guadalcanal and Tulagi. And not having much success. The Marines had no maps of the area and their charts were inaccurate, so they decided to make a map from aerial photographs. Demonstrating a commendable degree of foresight, Admiral Ghormley, who had been instrumental in setting up a US Navy aerial photography unit, was able to take one with him when he was sent to the South Pacific.[106] Ghormley had an aerial photograph collage made of the Lunga area, but the weather during the mission had been cloudy so there were blank spaces in the picture. General MacArthur's intelligence people promised aerial photography of the objectives. They put together a good set of photographs of the Lunga area, then sent it to the wrong address; General Vandegrift never received it.

Lieutenant Colonel Twining was familiar with the criteria for a good landing beach, so he volunteered to personally perform an aerial photographic reconnaissance of the beaches. He went to Auckland to talk to Admiral Ghormley, who told him he needed to take a plane from Nouméa. So the Marine went to Nouméa, where Admiral McCain told him his aircraft could not scout the Solomons due to a lack of range. The Army Air Force's could, McCain said, but wouldn't, as the local Army Air Force commander would not allow it. But McCain had a friend commanding the Army Air Force in Port Moresby who would arrange it. Twining would have to go there. As the Marine headed out, he was stopped in his tracks. "What do you know about aerial reconnaissance anyway?" the admiral was asking. Before Twining could reply, McCain said, "Well, you got to go anyway. Even if they burn you up. Good luck."[107]

With that last bit of encouragement, Lieutenant Colonel Twining and his crew made their way to Port Moresby, where Admiral McCain's friend had indeed arranged for a specially modified B-17 to take him over Guadalcanal and Tulagi to scout the area. Their Fortress took off on the morning of July 17 headed for Guadalcanal, their only map a reprint of a prewar *National Geographic* with a map showing the Solomon Islands, which was just as good because the navigator was too engrossed in a comic book to pay much attention to it.

They arrived in the Guadalcanal area around 2:00 pm. The Fortress headed toward Tulagi first, due to reports of enemy aircraft. Flying low to take photographs, they found Tulagi ringed with coral. Landings could only be accomplished with light craft. They also found floatplanes – the "Nakajima A6M2-N Navy Type 2 Interceptor/Fighter-Bomber," which did not exactly roll off the tongue, so, as they did with all other Japanese aircraft, the Allies identified it with a common given name: "Rufe." The Rufe was literally a Japanese Zero with floats. And the Rufes were taking off.

Twining's Flying Fortress made a quick run over Lunga on Guadalcanal. The beaches looked good; there was indeed a runway there, or, more accurately, most of one, with a big gap in the center that would not be there much longer. Before the Fortress could make another pass, the float Zeros were onto it, holing the Boeing with 20mm gunfire and forcing it into evasive maneuvers before it escaped into a cloud. The B-17 managed to get away, but the exchange had caused it to use most of its fuel and it still had to get back to Port Moresby. On top of that, they were lost. They managed to grope their way in the dark toward Papua, where bursts of antiaircraft fire and searchlights in Port Moresby led them back to base. On fumes. But Lieutenant Colonel Twining got what he needed.

On July 21, Admiral Fletcher ordered all units to rendezvous southeast of the Fiji Islands at 2:00 pm on July 26. The 12 transports and cargo ships of the amphibious force, carrying the 1st and 5th Regiments of the 1st Marine Division, and their 14 escorts under Admiral Turner, sailed from Wellington on July 22. The 2nd Marine Regiment, coming from San Diego, was being escorted by the *Wasp* task force. The 1st Marine Raider Battalion was to be carried by the destroyer transports *Colhoun*, *Little*, *McKean*, and *Gregory* that were currently with the *Saratoga* task force. All in all, 72 of the 76 US Navy ships arrived on time. Once assembled, they all headed for the Fijis to perform a dress rehearsal of the landing.

With the rendezvous completed, on July 26, Admiral Fletcher called the various commanders involved in *Watchtower* to his flagship *Saratoga* for a conference. It was to be a large conference – Admiral Turner's flagship *McCawley* alone sent 17 officers – and one that would become infamous and somewhat bizarre.

The bizarre nature of the conference stemmed from the absence of the man who should have been its dominant participant, Vice Admiral Ghormley. This was the first major operation in his new area of command, and he was not going to attend the final meeting to iron out details and disputes? Ghormley would later explain, "I was desirous of attending this conference, but found it impossible to give the time necessary for travel with possible attendant delays."[108] Though his headquarters was in the process of moving from Auckland to Nouméa, Ghormley never gave an adequate explanation for his absence. In fact, though he had ordered the conference held, he had never planned to attend and apparently only sent his chief of staff, Admiral Callaghan, along with his communications officer, at the insistence of Admiral Fletcher.[109] The absence of the admiral from the conference had a definite effect.

The destroyer *Hull* arrived at the *Saratoga* carrying the aforementioned Admiral Callaghan, the head of land-based air Admiral McCain, and members of their attendant staff. En route, the destroyer had also picked up Admiral Turner and General Vandegrift and their staffs.[110] When they arrived, they all got into a cutter, but the carrier rolled, and McCain ended up "waist deep in the ocean." Protocol required the senior officer to board first, in this case McCain. He stepped on the ladder, known as a Jacob's ladder, to climb aboard the flagship. As he was climbing, someone opened a garbage chute along the side and inadvertently dumped a torrent of sour milk on the admiral. McCain was, in the words of Vandegrift, "one mad little admiral."[111] *Watchtower* was off to a great start.

While the junior staff officers attended subsidiary conferences of intelligence, communications, and other topics, the senior officers held a private meeting in the wardroom that lasted nearly four hours. It would become a conference to remember, and nearly all of its participants would remember it differently.

With Ghormley absent and having delegated tactical command to Admiral Fletcher, the carrier commander effectively dominated the meeting and the conversation. Years later, General Vandegrift would write that Fletcher, whom he had never met before, was "a distinguished-looking man but seemed nervous and tired," graciously allowing that the recent combat at Coral Sea and Midway could do that. The Marine general first detected something amiss when he sensed Fletcher "lack[ed] knowledge of or interest in the forthcoming operation." Vandegrift soon found out why, when Fletcher "quickly let us know he did not think it would succeed."[112]

It wasn't exactly Henry V's St Crispin's Day speech.

Admiral Fletcher seemed to direct particular ire toward Admiral Turner. According to Turner's chief of staff, Captain Thomas G. Peyton, "the conference was one long bitter argument between Vice Admiral Fletcher and [Turner]. Fletcher questioned the whole upcoming operation. Since he kept implying that it was largely Turner's brainchild, and mentioning that those who planned it had no real fighting experience, he seemed to be doubting the competence of its parent."[113]

"Fletcher's main point of view was the operation was too hurriedly and therefore not thoroughly planned, the Task Force not trained together; and the logistic support inadequate."

Admiral Turner kept responding with, "[T]he decision has been made. It's up to us to make it a success."

"To [Admiral Fletcher's] arbitrary objections, expressed forcefully," wrote General Vandegrift, "we replied as best we could but obviously failed to make much impression."[114]

Admiral Fletcher himself remembered saying, "'Now Kelly, you are making plans to take that island from the Japs and the Japs may turn on you and wallop the hell out of you. What are you going to do then?" Admiral Turner answered, "I am just going to stay there and take my licking."[115]

At one point, Admiral Fletcher interrupted Admiral Turner to ask how long it would take to land the troops on Guadalcanal. Turner answered five days.[116]

The veteran carrier admiral then announced, "Gentlemen, in view of the risks of exposure to land-based air, I cannot keep the carriers in the area for more than 48 hours after the [initial] landing."[117]

One can imagine that the immediate reaction in the wardroom to Admiral Fletcher's dissonant declaration was a moment of stunned silence. Admiral Callaghan was apparently shocked. Admiral Turner was outraged. General Vandegrift felt betrayed. "My Dutch blood was beginning to boil," he later wrote, "but I forced myself to remain calm while explaining to Fletcher that the days 'of landing a small force and leaving' were over.'"

> This operation was supposed to take and hold Guadalcanal and Tulagi. To accomplish this I commanded a heavily reinforced division which I was to land on enemy-held territory, which meant a fight. I could hardly expect to land this massive force without air cover – even the five days mentioned by Turner involved tremendous risk.[118]

Admiral Turner "heatedly backed" Vandegrift. Admiral Fletcher "curtly announced" he would stay until the third day, then dismissed everyone.

The difference of opinion on Admiral Fletcher's withdrawal of the carriers did not end there. Afterwards, Admiral Turner reportedly confronted Fletcher, snarling, "You son of a bitch. If you do that you are yellow."[119]

It was vintage Admiral Turner, though whether he actually did it is uncertain.[120] Admiral Callaghan reported back to Ghormley with the notation, "Task Force must withdraw to South from objective area (i.e. general advanced position) within two days after D day!"[121] It would seem that Callaghan did not agree with this early withdrawal of the carriers. Not that he did anything about it. As representative of Fletcher's superior Admiral Ghormley at the conference, Callaghan did nothing to overrule Fletcher or hold the withdrawal decision in abeyance until Ghormley as senior officer could settle the dispute. For that matter, during this "acrimonious conference, Callaghan reportedly "sat in silence" and "never said a word."[122]

Admiral Turner did not even bother appealing the decision, as to do so would be going outside the chain of command. When, two decades later, he was asked why not, he explained, "Whom to, and who was I to do so? Fletcher was my old boss, and at that moment the most battle experienced commander in our Navy. It was his judgement, and it was my job to live with it."[123]

The conference on the *Saratoga* would be remembered differently by different people for different reasons. Captain Peyton was not surprised by Admiral Fletcher's position nearly as much as he was by how the admirals spoke to each other. "I was amazed and disturbed by the way these two admirals talked to each other," he recalled. "I had never heard anything like it." One witness went so far as to describe the conference on the *Saratoga* as "stormy."

Admiral Kinkaid disagreed, calling the mood of the conference "animated rather than stormy," adding, "Turner asked for a lot of things, much of which he didn't get, because they were not in the realm of the possible."

Vice Admiral Fletcher later described the conference, as was his wont, in more gracious terms, saying, "[T]here was no bitterness in the discussion. Plenty of opinions vigorously expressed as to what or could be done."

Nevertheless, Captain Peyton seems to have been accurate when he later said of the conference, "In my opinion too much of the conference was devoted to 'fighting the problem,' as we used to say at the [Naval] War College, and too little time to trying to solve the problem."[124]

Admiral Turner's jaundiced comment notwithstanding, fairness to Admiral Fletcher, at that time the US Navy's most battle-experienced carrier flag officer – although significantly not an aviator – requires some digression to discuss what seems to have been his logic in providing such a tight and hard limit to the presence of his three carriers in covering the initial landing on Guadalcanal.

Indeed, there was a certain military logic to it. The landing needed air support. The closest Allied base was Espiritu Santo, 580 miles away from Savo Sound. The major Japanese base at Rabaul was 540 miles away. The Japanese-held airfields at Buka (392 miles) and Kieta, Bougainville (340 miles) were even closer. Thus the Japanese bases were closer than the Allied bases. Worse, the range of the Grumman F4F Wildcat was too short to fly from Espiritu Santo to Guadalcanal and provide air cover. But the range of the Japanese Zero and the simply incredible range of the G4M Betty meant that Guadalcanal was within range of Rabaul, let alone Buka and Kieta.[125] So, while providing air support for the invasion, Fletcher's carriers would be in range of Japanese land-based air power. That's even before the question of the location of the Japanese carriers was addressed.

Admiral Fletcher may have had his decision on the timing of the carriers' withdrawal come down to a question of cargo ships. On July 25, Admiral Turner gave Fletcher word that if the landings proceeded well, he envisioned sending back all of the transports and "about all of the

Pacific Fleet combatant ships" by the evening of August 8, basically a day-and-a-half after landing. What would remain were the five cargo ships – the *Alhena, Betelgeuse, Bellatrix, Libra*, and *Fomalhaut*. "The greatest difficulty," Turner said, "would be with the five cargo vessels." He couldn't predict when the cargo ships would be unloaded, estimating three to six days. "We will need air protection for the entire period," Turner concluded.

The carrier admiral might have been taken aback by that one. Fletcher had to have wondered, "Seriously? You want me to risk three aircraft carriers – three fourths of the remaining US Navy carriers in the Pacific – for *cargo ships*?" Did it matter that the entire Allied offensive in the Pacific depended on those cargo ships, more specifically the supplies they carried for the Marines ashore?

In order to provide air cover, the carriers had to be within about 60 miles of Tulagi, and toward the south. Those requirements put the flattops in a very tight box in which they could move. The Japanese would find them eventually. Before the Battle of Midway, Admiral Nimitz had issued the following directive to Admiral Fletcher:

> You will be governed by the principle of calculated risk, which you shall interpret to mean the avoidance of exposure of your force to attack by superior force without good prospect of inflicting, as a result of such exposure, greater damage to the enemy. This applies to a landing phase as well during a preliminary air attack.

This order was general in nature but still in effect. The key phrase was "calculated risk." Admiral Fletcher likely had the question of whether exposure of his force to attack by the superior Japanese forces at Rabaul and elsewhere to protect *cargo ships* came with good prospect of inflicting greater damage on the enemy. His performance at the conference shows that his answer to that question was quite obviously "no." But was that the right question? Was Fletcher interpreting his orders properly? Would providing the air cover for the cargo ships, arguably, inflict greater damage on the enemy by allowing creation of an air base in enemy territory?

Even General Vandegrift's operations officer Lieutenant Colonel Twining of the 1st Marine Division agreed that Admiral Fletcher had a point. "[…] Fletcher's view on a strategic level […] in a way […] was correct." Then there is the inevitable, "But his somewhat brutal conduct of the *Saratoga* conference was totally incorrect from every point of view."[126]

This is where Captain Peyton's statement that "too much of the conference was devoted to 'fighting the problem,' […] and too little time to trying to solve the problem" must be considered. It says something that Fletcher reportedly opened the meeting by saying he thought *Watchtower* would fail because it was too hurriedly and therefore not thoroughly planned, the Task Force not trained together; and the logistic support inadequate. That was all true. It was also irrelevant. As Turner would respond, "[T]he decision has been made. It's up to us to make it a success." Maybe Fletcher was just venting. But it's hard to see what he hoped to accomplish by starting the conference not so much critiquing the plan as completely dismissing it.

The question of how long the carriers would stay might have been made moot if land-based aircraft had been provided to the Lunga airfield immediately once it became operational. But that was not the case. Admiral King's order of June 24 directed the Pacific Fleet to provide two squadrons of fighters and two of scout bombers in addition to the observation squadron already in the South Pacific. In fact, two squadrons of Marine fighters and two of dive bombers had been formed as part of the newly organized 23rd Marine Air Group at Pearl Harbor. But none could immediately be sent to Guadalcanal. Half of the new air group would be sent on the escort carrier *Long Island*, which would take two weeks to get to the South Pacific after leaving Pearl Harbor on August 1. Of the fighter squadrons currently in the South Pacific, none of the Wildcats had the range to make it to Guadalcanal without belly tanks with extra fuel. And no belly tanks were available. It was likely a result of the necessarily hurried preparation, but the lack of available land-based aircraft for the Lunga field was a major failure in planning *Watchtower*.

Lieutenant Colonel Twining described General Vandegrift's demeanor after the conference as "deeply disturbed and in no mood to talk." But the general had no time to dwell on it. He had to get ready for the rehearsal for the landing, scheduled for July 28–31. If the first amphibious assault by US Marines since 1898 was to be successful, they would need to practice first.

On the first day of the dry run, Admiral Fletcher released his table of organization. Of the three carrier admirals Fletcher, Kinkaid, and Noyes, only Noyes was a trained aviator, so Fletcher delegated tactical command of Task Group 61.1 – which consisted of all three of the carrier task forces – to him. Admiral Turner's force was called Task Force 62 under Admiral Ghormley's chart but Task Group 61.2 under Admiral Fletcher's chart; the Japanese by no means had a monopoly on duplicative and confusing unit names.

By this time, Admiral Turner, General Vandegrift, and their respective staffs were completely immersed in the practice run. With units coming from San Diego, Hawaii, New Zealand, and Australia, the Fijis seemed like a convenient meeting point. The Fijis were also 1,100 miles from Guadalcanal, far enough into the rear so Japanese scout planes would not find this massing of Allied ships. For the rehearsal, the island of Koro, in the coral reef-locked Koro Sea, was used as a stand-in for Guadalcanal. But not a very good stand-in. In hindsight, maybe they should have checked Koro for coral before practicing for an amphibious invasion there.

As a result, the practice landing, in the words of Vandegrift, "did not work out well."[127] Two complete landing exercises had been planned, but coral reefs made landing on the beaches almost impossible. Lieutenant Colonel Twining called it "a complete fiasco."[128] Much later, Vandegrift tried to recognize the value in the practice, saying, "At the very least, it got the boats off the transports, and the men down the nets and away. It uncovered deficiencies such as defective boat engines in time to have them repaired and gave both Turner and me a chance to take important corrective measures in other spheres."[129]

For now, though, General Vandegrift thought the rehearsal was "a complete bust." One Marine officer remembered that the only time he saw Vandegrift dejected during the

Guadalcanal campaign was after the rehearsal at Koro.[130] For his part, Admiral Turner was unhappy about the selection of the Koro beaches and thought the partial rehearsal "unsatisfactory," but thought it far from being "a complete bust." Vandegrift hoped for truth in the old show business axiom: "A poor rehearsal traditionally meant a good show."[131]

And with that, the American armada left the Fijis on July 31, heading for *Cactus* and *Ringbolt*. Trying to avoid or at least mislead Japanese reconnaissance efforts, the amphibious force first headed southwest, away from the Solomons. Under the protective watch of Admiral McCain's air force and – for now – Admiral Fletcher's carriers, Admiral Turner's ships trudged along in three concentric circles, with the transports in the center, the cruisers in the circle around the transports, and the destroyers in the outer circle. When the invasion fleet reached a point some 400 miles south of Rennell Island, the fleet was to turn north and make a beeline for Savo Island.

Admiral Turner took this time to handle some organizational matters. First, he told Royal Navy Admiral Crutchley that he would be designated as second-in-command. Crutchley demurred, believing that since this was primarily an American operation it should be an American flag officer, perhaps Admiral Scott, as second-in-command. Turner was unmoved; in selecting his commanders, Turner would display a pattern showing he regarded seniority above all else. Crutchley it was.[132]

Turner was also putting the finishing touches on the landing plan with General Vandegrift. The practice landing had indeed revealed shortcomings which they were correcting, but there was also a substantive dispute: Turner wanted to use the incoming 2nd Marine Regiment to take Ndeni after Tulagi and Guadalcanal were secured. Vandegrift wanted to use the 2nd Marines as a reserve in case the attacks on Guadalcanal or Tulagi needed reinforcements. Ndeni was a "malaria-infested fever hole" in the eyes of Vandegrift's staff, who never understood why it was so important in the first place. Supposedly, Admiral King had said it did no good to possess Ndeni and could not be held if Guadalcanal was lost.[133] The 2nd would be the rope in a tug-of-war between Turner and Vandegrift.

There was also mounting concern regarding the whereabouts of the 3rd Defense Battalion. It had been loaded on the transports *Zeilin* and *Betelgeuse*. Traveling as part of Convoy 4120 from Pearl Harbor, they would arrive too late for the rehearsal, it was known. But they had missed the rendezvous in the Fijis altogether. And no one knew where they were.

Admiral Turner had the cruiser *Chicago* launch a floatplane to head back to the Fijis and ascertain the whereabouts of the two ships. He also dropped off destroyers *Dewey* and *Mugford* to wait for them in Suva to escort them back to the fleet. As it turned out, Convoy 4120 had been hamstrung by one ship, the *Nira Luckenback*, that had "engine trouble" and was unable to keep speed. Under strict radio silence, the heavy cruiser *San Francisco*, escorting the convoy, dashed ahead to look for the invasion fleet but could not find it. They all arrived in Suva, finding the *Dewey* and *Mugford* waiting for the *Zeilin* and *Betelgeuse*. Together the four ships left to chase down the invasion armada, but pushing the speed envelope caused a fire in the engine room of the *Betelgeuse*. The cargo ship had to stop to make repairs and was left behind with the destroyer *Dewey* while the *Mugford* and *Zeilin* went ahead. On August 4, all four made the fleet and took their respective positions.[134]

As the invasion convoy began its northward run to Guadalcanal and destiny, it received the tragic news of the sinking of the American destroyer *Tucker*. The *Tucker* had been sailing through the western entrance to Segond Channel in Espiritu Santo when she struck a mine that broke her keel. Not a Japanese mine but an American mine laid as part of the defenses for the new base, in a new minefield about which no one had told the destroyer's skipper. It was at least the second time in this Pacific War that an Allied ship had been sunk by an Allied mine. The chartered transport *President Coolidge* also hit a mine in the same field.

But the next two days brought better luck, as a weather front moved in with cloud cover and sporadic squalls. Air operations were limited. The Expeditionary Force was now hidden by a protective blanket that got thicker as they approached Guadalcanal.

The tension got thicker as well. Appreciating the gravity of what they were about to attempt, the night before the assault landing, Admiral Turner sent out to the amphibious force a message he had personally written:

> PUBLISH TO ALL HANDS:
>
> On August seventh, this Force will recapture Tulagi and Guadalcanal Islands, which are now in the hands of the enemy.
>
> In this first step forward toward clearing the Japanese out of conquered territory, we have strong support from the Pacific Fleet, and from the air, surface and submarine forces in the South Pacific and Australia.
>
> It is significant of victory that we see here shoulder to shoulder, the U.S. Navy, Marines and Army, and the Australian and New Zealand Air, Naval and Army Services.
>
> I have confidence that all elements of this armada will, in skill and courage, show themselves fit comrades of those brave men who already have dealt the enemy mighty blows for our great cause.
>
> God bless you all.
>
> R. K. Turner, Rear Admiral, U.S. Navy, Commanding.[135]

Admiral Ghormley sent out words of encouragement as well: "We look to you to electrify the world with news of a real offensive. Allied ships, planes and fighting men carry on from Midway. Sock 'em in the Solomons." Apparently Ghormley did not personally write this message.

Late in the afternoon of August 6, the three carrier groups that had been protecting the invasion convoy broke off contact and headed to the south to position themselves to cover the invasion. The transports were shifted into a column of squadrons of transports so as to narrow the front profile of the formation headed into restricted waters. During the approach Admiral Fletcher had continued to monitor the latest intelligence reports. There was some difficulty for Allied intelligence because *Magic* was temporarily blinded as the Japanese had switched to a newer version of the JN-25 code. The latest estimates had 5,275 Japanese troops at Lunga – these numbers were why the Marines were landing at a beach east of the airfield and not at the airfield itself – and 1,850 defending Tulagi. General MacArthur believed 139 Japanese aircraft (56 fighters, 38 bombers, 24 flying boats, and 21 floatplanes) were operating from Rabaul. Radio intelligence had placed four heavy cruisers of the 6th Cruiser Division, two light cruisers of the 18th Cruiser Division, one light cruiser and 12 destroyers of the 6th Destroyer Flotilla, eight submarines, and two seaplane tenders in and around Rabaul. Radio intelligence placed the still-fearsome Japanese carriers in the waters of the Japanese home islands. The latest development was the most curious – a new Japanese fleet, the 8th, had been formed, and its commander was now in Rabaul with his flagship, probably the cruiser *Chokai*.[136] It was, indeed, suggestive of a new Japanese offensive.

All the more reason to get the Allies' own offensive underway, rushed though it may have been. "Seldom has an operation been begun under more disadvantageous circumstances," General Vandegrift would later say. Lieutenant Colonel Twining feared, "The stage was rapidly being set with all the props needed for a first class disaster."[137]

General Vandegrift and the Marines, admirals Ghormley, Fletcher, and Turner, and the sailors had all this on their minds that morning of August 7 as the sun started rising to the east. The invasion moved forward all the same. With the invasion forces at battle stations, Admiral Turner asked General Vandegrift to set H-Hour for landing.

The Marine general chose 9:10 am to start the first Allied offensive since Pearl Harbor.

CHAPTER 2
MAKEE LEARNEE

"I felt like the Greeks going to Troy or something."[1]

Those were the thoughts of Marine Captain Paul Moore. Not a thousand ships, to be sure, but at 82 ships and 19,000 Marines, it was the largest armada yet assembled by the US Navy in the Pacific. It included three aircraft carriers, one brand-new battleship, and two brand-new light cruisers intended for antiaircraft work. The impressive picture was misleading as to just how desperate the circumstances in the Pacific remained for the Allies, but it was a start.

And it was why, like the invasion of Troy, *Watchtower* was more than a military operation. Not a cultural phenomenon and the end of a historical epoch like Troy was, but the changing of a mindset from desperate hunted to opportunistic hunter and, for the enemy, vice versa. It was a mindset Admiral King had been trying to install in his men since he took command.

But it was complicated. Admiral King saw a Japanese airfield under construction, the completion of which would complicate Allied efforts in the Pacific. Others, like Admiral Fletcher and Admiral Ghormley, saw obstacles, regarding the forces under their command as outnumbered, outgunned, and outsupplied: not ready to take the offensive.

Maybe they were right. Historians and military analysts would comment, not always favorably, on "the sheer audacity of taking the strategic offensive" here.

> King catapulted 'Watchtower' off at a velocity that mocked all conventions and under conditions that affronted a fair portion of the principles of war. The theater commander and his principal subordinates were confused about the objective of the enterprise […] Unity of command had been forfeited by the division of the Pacific into two theaters […] The selected instruments for conducting the landings consisted of approximately 19,000 marines – such was the rush that a certifiable count was never made – of a hybrid, half-trained division and a hastily fabricated Amphibious Force led by an admiral who arrived at the eleventh hour before sailing.[2]

In the words of the historian John Prados:

> This resulted from one of the most gigantic improvisations imaginable – makee learnee on a grand scale […] Rather the 'Canal – or "Operation Watchtower," to give it its proper code name – became the first major American amphibious landing of the war, an application of doctrines hitherto extant only on paper, practiced in small-scale exercises with rudimentary techniques and novel, unproven equipment. The landing boats, cross-shipping, and fire-support arrangements […] were mostly experimental at Guadalcanal. Moreover, Watchtower would be carried out by an untried area command, viewed with some suspicion by another theater boss quite zealous in protecting his own prerogatives. All of this amounted to something far less than a formula for success.[3]

Maybe. But so far it seemed to be going better than the Greek expedition to Troy. They had not been compelled to appease an angry Greek goddess by sacrificing the general's daughter. Nor had they attacked the wrong place, as the Greeks did.

The invasion force approached Savo Sound and then split up, as planned. Transport Group Yoke headed north around Savo Island and later turned east toward Tulagi. The remainder, Transport Group X-Ray, headed for Lunga. Destroyers dropped out of formation to guard the entrances to the channels behind them.

As the light improved and the ships got closer to the invasion beaches, almost everyone got their first views of Guadalcanal. One Marine war correspondent recorded his first impressions:

> … Guadalcanal is an island of striking beauty. Blue-green mountains, towering into a brilliant tropical sky or crowned with cloud masses, dominate the island. The dark green of jungle growth blends into the softer greens and browns of coconut groves and grassy plains and ridges.[4]

Admiral Turner described Guadalcanal as a "truly beautiful sight that morning."[5] The men about to land who would have to live there had other ideas. Maybe they had a collective premonition. Morison described the feeling:

> There is something sinister and depressing about that Sound […] between Guadalcanal and Florida Islands. Men who rounded Cape Esperance in the darkness before dawn on August 7 remember that "it gave you the creeps." Even the land smell failed to cheer sailors who had been long at sea; Guadalcanal gave out a rank, heavy stench of mud, slime, and jungle. And the serrated cone of Savo Island looked as sinister as the crest of a giant dinosaur emerging from the ocean depths.[6]

The heavy cruiser *Chicago* led Transport Group X-Ray in steaming along the shore of Guadalcanal. The 15 transports were arranged in two columns of seven and eight ships, arranged in the same order in which they would lie for the initial landing. There was no sign of the Japanese. Indeed, not much sign of anything. There were no guns, no planes, no men. The land was peaceful. Quiet. Too quiet for Lieutenant Colonel Twining, who remembered, "We almost felt disappointed by our unbelievable good luck. No one likes to be ignored."[7]

Too quiet for the young Marines anticipating with little relish their first contested landing. It can't be this quiet. Was it a trap? "I can't believe it," one lieutenant told Richard Tregaskis. "I wonder if the Japanese can be that dumb. Either they're very dumb or it's a trick."[8]

The fire-support ships had received instructions not to fire on wharves, pontoons, jetties, bridges, or lighters which were offering no threat; they would be needed later. The warships were ordered to use starshells against flammable (and inflammable) targets such as fuel dumps.

At the direction of Admiral Crutchley, the heavy cruiser *Quincy* moved from the rear of the fleet to the front. The time was 6:13.

The quiet was abruptly broken by the roar of the 8-inch guns of the *Quincy*, the prime fire support for the invasion, targeting the western part of the landing beach closest to the airfield. She was soon joined by the heavy cruisers *Australia*, *Astoria*, and *Vincennes*, and the destroyer *Ellet* targeting other parts of the landing area.[9] That the cannonade had more than just a military meaning was not lost on Lieutenant Colonel Twining:

> Every gun in the covering force that could be brought to bear joined in a deadly salute to the emperor. Ours was a salute that would bring him into the twentieth century and his prime minister to the gallows. We were announcing that the way back had begun. It was an unforgettable moment in history.[10]

General Vandegrift was not mesmerized by the show of gunfire. He was noticing that maybe the intelligence information brought to him by Colonel Goettge was not totally accurate. There was supposedly a "grassy knoll" 4 miles south of the airfield. The 1st Regiment had been ordered to take it. As more and more of Guadalcanal drifted into view, the grassy knoll turned out to be 1,514-foot Mount Austen. Called *Mambula* by the locals – "rotting body" – for reasons that would soon become apparent, it was too far away and far too big to be taken by a regiment on that day. The 1st was ordered to stop at the airfield.

Flares were seen shooting into the sky, from whom is unknown. The crack of the gunfire had rolled across from Guadalcanal to Tulagi and its satellite islands Gavutu and Tanambogo, where the Yokohama Air Group was based. Three of the big four-engine "Kawanishi H6K Type 97 Large Flying Boat[s]" – yet another mouthful, which was why the Allies eventually called this seaplane the "Mavis" – were moored off Tulagi's east coast. Four others were lounging off Tanambogo's north shore. Also at Tanambogo were two of the Nakajima Rufes or float Zeros. Another six were sitting off Halavo, a village on Florida Island 1 mile east of Tanambogo. Lieutenant Commander Courtney Shands of the *Wasp* led 11 Grumman F4F Wildcats toward Tulagi. Two Wildcats got guard duty while the remaining nine roared in directly at the veteran Yokohama.[11]

The flying boats were supposed to take off at dawn. Apparently seeing the danger, one tried to get under way but was quickly destroyed by Shands' pilots flying only 50 feet off the water. The other two were torched, as were four boats trying to service them. Shands and his wingman Ensign Samuel W. Forrer continued toward Halavo, where they saw Japanese pilots frantically running across the beach toward the Rufes. All six float Zeros were set afire in succession. Meanwhile, Lieutenant S. Downs Wright and wingman Ensign Roland H. Kenton went to Tanambogo and destroyed the remaining four Kawanishis. It had taken mere minutes to utterly destroy the Yokohama Air Group.[12]

Lieutenant Commander Shands had his Wildcats head back for the *Wasp* around 7:00 am. The *Wasp* was the southernmost of the three carriers, now in an arrowhead about 30 miles off the west coast of Guadalcanal. Flagship *Saratoga* was the point of the arrowhead, with *Wasp* 5 miles off her starboard quarter and *Enterprise* 5 miles off her port quarter. Two of the carriers were in plain view of a Japanese lookout post on the southwest coast of Guadalcanal, but by then the Lunga headquarters had been abandoned and there was no one to take his sighting report.[13]

"Land the landing force!"

The call went out over loudspeakers and bullhorns. The Marines went over the sides to crawl down netting to their boats and started making their way ashore. The first landing target was actually in the Tulagi sector: Haleta, on Florida Island, which was taken without opposition. The village controlled the western flank of Tulagi.

The landing point on Tulagi itself was "Beach Blue" on the island's west side. It was blocked off from the sea by coral and so was considered the least likely beach for a landing. Which is precisely why the Americans struck there with a few companies of the 1st Marine Raider Battalion, brought in on the fast destroyer transports. As an incentive the Raiders' commander, Lieutenant Colonel Merritt A. Edson, spread word to his men that during the night of August 6, Tokyo Rose had taunted, "Where are the United States Marines hiding? The Marines are supposed to be the finest soldiers in the world, but no one has seen them yet."[14]

Edson's Raiders landed with gunfire support from the light antiaircraft cruiser *San Juan*, and the destroyers *Monssen* and *Buchanan*. The Japanese, including members of the 3rd Kure Special Naval Landing Force, retreated to the southern end of the island into some caves and prepared positions. Digging them out would prove to be a nasty affair.

The landing point on Guadalcanal was called "Red Beach," some 3 miles east of the airfield. As the Marines sailed toward the shore in their landing craft, there was a second bombardment by the cruisers *Quincy* and *Astoria*, and the destroyers *Dewey*, *Hull*, *Ellet* and *Wilson*, with cruiser floatplanes spotting fire and doing some scouting ashore.

One of those floatplanes, a Walrus from the *Australia*, puttered along over the *McCawley* at masthead height, staying low to avoid misidentification. An irritated Admiral Turner ordered, "Shoot down that plane." Instead of passing on the order, his talker said,

"Admiral, that's the Walrus plane from the *Australia* … sir." Turner just looked at him silently.[15]

At around 9:10 am, right on schedule, the bombardment ceased and the Marines came ashore to find … nothing. There was no enemy anywhere. The Marines had been pumped full of adrenaline to take out on the Japanese and were puzzled to find no opposition.

Opposition was on its way, however. At around 11:30 am warnings came in of Japanese countermeasures. Two came from Pearl Harbor, arising from messages deciphered by *Magic*. One was a set of instructions sending 18 bombers and 17 fighters to attack the mass of ships off Guadalcanal; the second ordered submarines to head toward Tulagi. Then came a message from coastwatcher Paul Mason on Bougainville: "24 bombers headed yours."[16]

But the American carriers were more than 60 miles from Turner's ships, for whom they had to provide fighter cover and air support. The carriers also needed fighter cover for themselves. And all of these aircraft would return when they were low on fuel; they had to be replaced. It would prove to be a difficult juggling act for Admiral Noyes.

By 1:15 pm, Noyes had succeeded in putting 24 fighters over the carriers and 18 over the screen.[17] That was the good news. The bad news was that ten of those 18 fighters for the screen were only on the way there. The screen would have had six more Wildcats of Fighting 6 under Lieutenant Louis H. Bauer. The fighter director on the *Chicago*, Lieutenant Robert M. Bruning, Jr., vectored them toward the approaching bombers, but the fighter director on the *Enterprise*, Lieutenant Henry A. Rowe, overruled him and sent them back toward the carriers to try to catch the bombers with four fighters under Lieutenant Theodore S. Gay. However, Rowe's plan depended on the bombers heading for the carriers. The bombers simply continued heading toward Guadalcanal, and Rowe had just moved Bauer's Wildcats out of position.

The mistake left only eight Wildcats from the *Saratoga* – four under Lieutenant James J. "Pug" Southerland II and four under Lieutenant Herbert S. Brown – to face the incoming airstrike. The Japanese were coming with Lieutenant Egawa Renpei leading 27 G4M Bettys escorted by Lieutenant Commander Nakajima Tadashi's 18 Mitsubishi A6M2 Type 0 carrier fighters, given the reporting name of "Zeke" but immortalized simply as "Zero."

Among Lieutenant Commander Nakajima's Zeros of the Tainan Air Group was Petty Officer 1st Class Sakai Saburo, then Japan's top fighter ace with some 48 aerial victories. With most of those victories over inferior aircraft like the P-40 and inferior pilots, the veteran Sakai was intrigued about fighting US Navy carrier pilots for the first time.

Sakai's day had not gotten off to a good start, however. He knew the flight from Rabaul to Guadalcanal would be the longest ever for a Zero, so he had arranged for his own in-flight food and beverage service. After he started to head southeast, Sakai reached down to grab a soda out of his lunch box. When he started to open the bottle, it exploded all over the cockpit and, critically, his flight goggles. Sakai had forgotten the altitude and its accompanying low air pressure. He spent 40 minutes looking like he was flying while intoxicated as he struggled to clean the soda from his goggles and his instruments, causing his Zero to weave all through the formation. Sakai "had never felt more ridiculous."[18]

Over Vella Lavella, the Japanese airstrike moved to higher altitude. About 50 miles from Guadalcanal they got their first look at the American invasion fleet. Sakai was stunned at the sheer size of the operation. He estimated at least 70 ships below, with more on the horizon. Sakai called it "almost unbelievable."[19]

The G4Ms descended from 16,000 feet to just beneath the cloud cover at 13,000 feet. The eight Wildcats under lieutenants Southerland and Brown moved to intercept, but they were kept at bay by five Zeros under Lieutenant Kawai Shiro. The covering Wildcats were so out of position that the Bettys just strolled in and dropped their bombs; 156 bombs were dropped, all at once. And, as Sakai watched, they all missed. Badly. He was furious. "It was obviously stupid to try to hit moving ships from four miles up!… Our entire mission had been wasted, thrown away in a few seconds of miserable bombing inaccuracy."[20]

As the Bettys turned away to return home, the Wildcats continued to lash away at them, and the Zeros struck at the Wildcats. Lieutenant Brown was wounded and his Grumman shot up, apparently by Japanese ace Petty Officer 1st Class Nishizawa Hiroyoshi, who pulled up alongside Brown, smiled, and waved.[21]

Lieutenant Southerland had gotten close enough to take some shots at the Bettys. From long range he raked the fuselage of Petty Officer 2nd Class Sato Tamotsu, causing the G4M to burst into flames and plunge into the sea, the first aerial kill of the Guadalcanal campaign. Southerland emptied his magazines into a second, but could not bring it down as Japanese gunners took a few bites out of his Grumman. Southerland turned away to try to make it back.

He immediately got attention from a Zero who zoomed in behind. The Zero was joined by two friends. Now three Zeros chased Lieutenant Southerland's damaged Wildcat, which had no ammunition left. He would have to improvise.

And improvise he did. Southerland kept getting the faster Japanese fighters to overshoot him. At one point he got all three to overshoot him, leaving him behind them for a change. Sakai Saburo saw what looked like one Wildcat chasing three Zeros, two of whom where his wingmen, and decided to take over. Then began another dogfight, one that would become epic, as Japanese ace Sakai Saburo struggled to get the better of "Pug" Southerland. Sakai, who "had never seen such flying before," was amazed by his flying skill. "There was a terrific man behind that stick," Sakai later wrote.[22]

With a damaged plane and no ammunition, the issue was never in doubt. Sakai perforated Southerland's Wildcat with 7.7mm fire. And then Sakai received another shock. "I could not believe what I saw; the Wildcat continued flying almost as if nothing had happened. A Zero which had taken that many bullets into its vital cockpit would be a ball of fire right now. I could not understand it."[23]

Southerland's maneuvering got Sakai to overshoot him, but with the Wildcat's guns dry, the *Saratoga* pilot could do nothing. Sakai opened his cockpit canopy to look at the pilot and plane that had given him such a battle. The Grumman F4F Wildcat "was a shambles. Bullet holes had cut the fuselage and wings up from one end to the other. The skin of the rudder was gone, and the metal ribs stuck out like a skeleton. […] It was incredible that his plane was still in the air."[24] Their eyes locked. And for the first time in his many victories, Sakai could see the human being at the opposite end of his guns.

Southerland was wounded, Sakai could see. Now he understood why Southerland had stopped maneuvering his fighter. "This was no way to kill a man! Not with him flying helplessly, wounded, his plane a wreck."[25] Sakai shook his fist in frustration at Southerland:

> I had never felt so strange before. I had killed many Americans in the air, but this was the first time a man had weakened in such a fashion directly before my eyes, and from wounds I had inflicted upon him. I honestly didn't know whether or not I should try and finish him off. Such thoughts were stupid, of course. Wounded or not, he was an enemy, and he had almost taken three of my own men a few minutes before.[26]

It's one of those horrible moments in war, when one realizes that in the target reticle, underneath the bomb, at the opposite end of the gun, is a human being. Killing the enemy is easy. Killing a fellow human is hard. Quite simply, it is why propaganda campaigns often seek to dehumanize an enemy. Because that realization causes hesitation. And that hesitation can mean death for you and for your comrades. That a moment of humanity in that most inhuman of enterprises can cost you your life is part of the horror of war.

Sakai decided he "wanted the airplane, not the man," and finished off the Wildcat with 20mm cannon fire.[27] Southerland, who had been looking for a place to bail out anyway, escaped his now burning plane and parachuted to safety on Guadalcanal.[28]

Sakai Saburo would go on hunting Americans. He and his wingmates found a flight of … what were they? More Wildcats? That's what they looked like. Eight of them in two flights. He came up behind as the Americans tightened formation. That meant they had not seen him. Sakai kept closing the range on their tails. For him and his wingmates, this would be easy. And then Sakai realized they were not Wildcats …[29]

Too late. While Sakai later thought his targets were actually Grumman TBF Avengers, historian John Lundstrom determined they were eight Douglas SBD Dauntless dive bombers from Bombing 6 and Scouting 5.[30] Their rear .50cal guns caught Sakai in a brutal crossfire. One round shattered Sakai's windshield and pierced the top of his skull above his right eye. Sakai was temporarily blinded by the blood and severe pain. Regaining some of his sight, he turned his battered Zero to make the long, long flight back to Rabaul – if he could.

The first air battle over Guadalcanal was over. It was the first US Navy battle versus Japanese land-based Zeros. On this day it was the Tainan Air Group, widely respected as perhaps the best land-based unit in the Japanese Naval Air Force. They sent up 17 Zeros to battle 34 US Navy aircraft, of which 18 were Wildcats and 16 were Dauntlesses. The results were not pretty. Nine Wildcats and one Dauntless were shot down, against the Japanese loss of two Zeros. Four of the G4M bombers were shot down, one had to ditch off Buka, and one crashed back at Rabaul.[31] For the US, it amounted to a loss rate of 50 percent of Wildcats deployed, a figure noticed by Admiral Fletcher.

Something else was noticed by Admiral Fletcher: Japanese dive bombers. At 2:00 pm, Admiral Turner warned of attacking dive bombers. Shortly thereafter, the *Saratoga* picked up a garbled message: "25 planes about 8,000 feet disappearing bearing 100 degrees," its origin a mystery.[32] The reports of dive bombers, which normally operate from aircraft carriers, set off alarm bells on the flag bridges of the *Saratoga*, *Enterprise*, and *Wasp*. There had to be a Japanese aircraft carrier out there. There was no way Japanese dive bombers had the range to make it to Guadalcanal from Rabaul.

They didn't. But all the same, nine of them attacked at approximately 2:45. They were nine "Aichi Type 99 Carrier Bombers," – code-named "Val" by the Allies – of the 2nd Air Group, commanded by Lieutenant Inoue Fumito. Each Type 99 was carrying two 132lb bombs. With the ships off Tulagi hidden by cloud cover, Inoue directed three Aichis under Warrant Officer Ota Gengo to attack the warships on the western edge while he attacked the transports anchored off Lunga with the remaining six.

On board the destroyer *Mugford*, the westernmost of the destroyers providing antisubmarine protection for the transports, one of the lookouts – who was lying on his back – saw two aircraft emerge from the low clouds. "Planes!" he shouted to the bridge. "They've got wheels!" Fixed landing gear was a distinctive feature of the Vals. Two more planes popped out of the clouds. Four were now diving on to the destroyer, three of them Vals.

And one Wildcat, piloted by the *Enterprise*'s Lieutenant Albert O. "Scoop" Vorse, Jr., had latched onto the third Type 99 of Ota's section, the one of Petty Officer 2nd Class Iwaoka Minoru, and was hacking away at it.

The *Mugford*'s skipper, Lieutenant Commander Edward W. Young, ordered right full rudder. Diving from off the destroyer's starboard quarter, Ota and his wingman Petty Officer 2nd Class Takahashi Koji released their bombs. One struck the *Mugford* just forward and to starboard of Number 3 5-inch mount. The blast demolished the aft deck house, disabled the Number 3 and 4 5-inch mounts, and blew 14 men overboard. They were never seen again. Seven were killed on board. The two mounts, however, would be repaired within a few hours.[33]

Ota and Takahashi were able to speed off and escape. Iwaoka's dive bomber, left smoking by Lieutenant Vorse, dove straight into the water.

Lieutenant Inoue led his six Type 99s in a string, but rapidly attracted attention from six *Saratoga* Wildcats under Lieutenant Richard Gray, who tried to claw their way to altitude to engage the Vals. Two more *Saratoga* Wildcats to the north also saw the Vals and moved to intercept.

With enemy fighters closing in from multiple directions and no fighter escort, Lieutenant Inoue decided he'd never reach the transports and instead moved to attack a light cruiser – actually the destroyer *Dewey* – on the western edge of the antisubmarine screen like the *Mugford*. The Aichis all reached their pushover points, but one was flamed during the dive. The Vals managed to get one near miss on the *Dewey*. As they headed away, four Wildcats from the *Enterprise* joined the fracas. Three more Vals were splashed, for a total of five of the nine Vals shot down.

The attack by the carrier dive bombers was almost completely ineffective but had a major psychological effect. From where had they come? A carrier? Admiral Fletcher thought they needed to scout the area thoroughly the next morning. Admiral Kinkaid on the *Enterprise* thought it important to scout immediately. Admiral Noyes on the *Wasp* thought it wise to scout the next morning, but believed the dive bombers were "probably land based from Rabaul via Buka or Kieta."[34] The presence of the Vals would continue to nag at Fletcher.

And at Admiral Turner. By then, it seemed that whatever General MacArthur's efforts at suppressing the Rabaul airfields had been, they had failed. He also wondered about the efficacy of the searches by both General MacArthur and Admiral McCain. Turner wanted the routes from Rabaul to Guadalcanal to be covered. The most obvious route was the channel, called New Georgia Sound – for now – between the double lines of islands that are the Solomons. It appeared that the searches by the Navy Catalina flying boats would cover only part of that route, only up to the southern tip of Choiseul Island. Beyond that would be the responsibility of General MacArthur. Did he really want a search of that important sector dependent on Douglas MacArthur?

To ask the question was to answer it. At 5:42 pm, Admiral Turner asked Admiral McCain to launch a supplemental search by a Catalina flying boat from the tender *Mackinac* anchored off Malaita to cover this sector. "Southwest Pacific is responsible for this sector," Turner said, "but I consider a morning search by you is necessary for adequate coverage."[35]

The coverage was necessary, for the objectives on neither Tulagi nor Guadalcanal had been secured. On Tulagi, the 3rd Kure Special Naval Landing Force had holed up in caves at the southern end of the island, and also on the islets of Gavutu and Tanambogo. On Guadalcanal, the Marines continued to move inland slowly and cautiously, the heat and humidity doing far more to slow down them down than the Japanese, who were still nowhere to be found.

Corporal Gallant and his buddies had landed with the second wave of Marines. They waited by the beach and "watched more boats arrive and got a kick out of the expressions of Marines as they jumped out and charged across the beach. They didn't know what to expect – no more than we had – and they always had an expression of surprise when they found everything quiet."[36]

Well, not everything was quiet. The troops from the first wave were still nearby. From the heavy brush just ahead, Gallant heard shouting and gunfire. And squealing.

A pig burst out from the tall grass and ran off.

A nearby Marine quipped, "They're giving them pigs hell." It was true. The first wave of Marines to land on Guadalcanal was now in a firefight with wild pigs.

The nearby Marine offered his suggestion for improving future amphibious operations. "They ought to [have] told them guys they was to fight Japs, not pigs."[37] It was another bit of the fine tuning that was lost in the rush to launch *Watchtower*.

The pigfight ended and things on Guadalcanal got quiet again.

"It was quite peaceful," said journalist Richard Tregaskis, "despite the rifle shots [...]"[38]

August 7, 1942, had been the busiest day in the history of American carrier operations, with 703 takeoffs and 687 landings. Losses to enemy action were nine Wildcats and one Dauntless; operational losses were five Wildcats and one more Dauntless.[39] The morning of August 8 was not promising to be any less busy.

Admiral Noyes had issued orders for the *Wasp* to search to the northwest toward Rabaul to find those elusive Japanese carriers, if there were any. The carrier dutifully launched 12 Dauntlesses to perform the search. The entire air group from the *Saratoga* was to be kept in reserve in case of emergency, while the *Enterprise* and *Wasp* provided air cover for the carriers and the transports. Once again, Noyes had a lot of balls to keep in the air.

In fact, even more than Noyes had anticipated, because during the night Admiral Turner had been busy. First, he had been digesting sighting reports. At midnight, Southwest Pacific Command reported that at 12:13pm on August 7, a B-17 had sighted one heavy cruiser, three light cruisers and one destroyer headed west some 25 miles north of Rabaul. That afternoon another B-17 reported six unidentified ships in St George's Channel between New Britain and New Ireland headed southeast.[40] At 7:38 on the morning of August 8, Southwest Pacific forwarded from submarine *S-38* a sighting report from 8:00 the previous night of "two destroyers and three larger ships of unknown type, heading 140 degrees True [southeast], at high speed, 8 miles west of Cape St George."[41] But there were more immediate concerns.

The unloading of the transports on Guadalcanal had reached chaos proportions, with supplies being delivered faster than they could be moved off the beach. At one point some 100 boats lay "gunwale to gunwale" on the beach, while another 50 or so waited, some as many as six hours, for a chance to land. At 2:00 am, Turner had suspended the unloading because "the beaches were so congested." Unloading did not resume until 7:00 am.[42]

The stubborn Japanese resistance on Tulagi, Gavutu, and Tanambogo was continuing to be a problem. It compelled Admiral Turner to finally relent to General Vandegrift concerning the 2nd Marine Regiment, originally slated to take Ndeni, and release it to General Rupertus to try to finish off the Tulagi area. It was apparently in reference to this move that Turner signaled Admiral Fletcher, "Owing to reinforcements [to] Florida area[,] will not commence retirement as planned."[43]

Admiral Turner had requested dawn airstrikes on the stubborn Japanese resistance at Tanambogo. Because of radio silence, Captain Dewitt C. Ramsey of the *Saratoga* had been unable to forward that request to Admiral Noyes. So, Ramsey decided to launch the airstrikes – 19 Dauntlesses and eight Avengers – himself, against orders. For all the good that did. Turner had decided to centralize the airstrike direction to the *McCawley*, from which he could not even see Tanambogo. The Dauntlesses ended up returning without launching any attacks.

Captain Ramsey also reminded Admiral Fletcher that they had lost five Fighting 5 pilots the previous day, with one possibly spotted on a beach on the northwest coast of Guadalcanal. And just to help things along, he launched four Wildcats in a special, unscheduled combat air patrol that happened to cover the area where the pilots had gone down.

By 8:00 am, 16 Wildcats were operating over the carriers and 16 were over the transports. But the fighters had to be constantly rotated because of the Wildcats' limited fuel. Admiral Kinkaid requested adding eight F4Fs from the *Saratoga* to the 8:30 and 10:30 combat air patrols. Admiral Noyes answered, "[N]ot approved. *Saratoga* must be ready to launch for or in case of attack."[44] A little more than an hour later, Noyes found out *Saratoga* aircraft were in the air.

Noyes promptly gave Captain Ramsey a gentle reminder that his orders to hold the *Saratoga* in reserve were not suggestions, not even guidelines, but orders. "*Saratoga* does not appear to be complying with my orders for today's operations which require her until noon to maintain fighters and attack group ready for launching at all times in case of bombing attack or locating of enemy [carrier]. Please refer conflicting request [for air support] to me."[45]

Captain Ramsey relayed a second request from Admiral Kinkaid for eight additional fighters from the *Saratoga* for air cover. Apparently not aware of the previous conversation between Kinkaid and Admiral Noyes, and assuming the request would be approved, he launched eight Wildcats at 9:52, against orders – again – before the *Wasp* had replied. In the meantime, the *Saratoga* had to re-spot her flight deck – that is, reposition the aircraft currently on her flight deck – to recover the Dauntlesses and Avengers she had launched earlier.[46] Against orders.

Admiral Noyes found out about that, too. By this time, Noyes apparently suspected the problem might not be Captain Ramsey but Admiral Fletcher, who was on the *Saratoga* and was commander of the fleet for this operation and thus superior to Noyes, but subordinate to Noyes in the operations of the carrier task forces. It was so confusing.

Noyes was incensed, no mean feat for this laid-back officer, and sent about as polite a message as one could to someone who was his superior but also his subordinate: "Your [request] negative. Invite your attention to present situation if enemy [carrier] should be located and I ordered your attack group launched. Your fighters should also be ready for launching for actual bombing attack until noon."[47]

Except there was no way the *Saratoga* could do that, because she had re-spotted her flight deck to recover the Dauntlesses and Avengers she had launched without orders that morning, and now had to re-spot to recover the Wildcats she had also launched without orders. Captain Ramsey started getting a new airstrike ready, with an escort of Wildcats fitted with belly tanks for extra fuel. Ramsey later "strongly recommended" the fighter director officer be located on the air task force flagship to eliminate such "confusion" in the future.[48]

For the time being, Captain Ramsey had to simply hope there were no Japanese carriers out there. The *Wasp*'s returning scouts had found none, although, 40 miles north of Santa Ysabel, Lieutenant Commander Ernest Snowden, the commanding officer of Scouting 72, had shot down a Japanese floatplane which he believed had been a float Zero.[49] That was a short-range fighter. Where did it come from?

At 10:38, Admiral Crutchley's flagship *Australia* picked up a report from another coastwatcher, Lieutenant Jack Read, located 400 miles northwest of Lunga in northern Bougainville. Read reported at 9:48 am 40 twin-engine bombers heading northwest to southeast had passed low over him. Admiral Turner immediately had his ships get under way, moving to the center of Savo Sound to gain maneuvering room.

And, like a well-oiled machine, the US Navy fighter control got to work. Fighter director Lieutenant Bruning on the *Chicago* estimated the Japanese airstrike would arrive around 11:15, while Lieutenant Rowe on the *Enterprise* guessed between 11 and noon, which was a rather sizable window. Ten fighters – three from the *Enterprise* and seven from the *Wasp* – were circling the transports, with eight more from the *Wasp* on the way. Eight fighters were circling the carriers. The *Wasp* had nine Wildcats on her flight deck, the *Enterprise* 15, and the *Saratoga* 26. At 11:01, the *Enterprise* immediately launched 13 fighters to protect the carriers, who now had 21 fighters overhead.[50]

Lieutenant Rowe suggested sending up the *Saratoga*'s fighters to protect the transports. But since she was being held in reserve for a possible airstrike, Admiral Noyes had to authorize it. And Admiral Fletcher himself got involved. Commander Harry D. "Don" Felt, the commander of the *Saratoga* air group, went to the carrier's flag bridge to explain why the *Saratoga*'s fighters had to be sent to protect the transports. But Fletcher was grim, responding that the Japanese "won't attack the transports. They're going after us and get us."[51]

Commander Felt pointed out that the transports were between the Japanese and the carriers; theoretically deploying fighters over the transports could protect the carriers as well. "Let's get our fighters off and protect those fellows," Felt said. Fletcher "gave in and said all right."[52] With the search planes reporting no Japanese carriers, Admiral Noyes agreed as well and authorized the launch at 11:05. It took 30 minutes for the order to go from Noyes' flagship *Wasp* to the *Saratoga*.

Getting approval to launch was only half of the equation, and arguably the easier half. *Saratoga* had to actually launch the fighters. She was still trying to get the airstrike spotted on the flight deck with the escorting Wildcats carrying belly tanks. Now she had to launch fighters for air cover over the transports. But the Dauntlesses and Avengers for the airstrike were in the way. And the Wildcats still had their belly tanks, which would inhibit their combat performance. The Wildcats' radios had to be reset from the strike to the combat air patrol frequencies, which was not as easy as pushing a preset button on a car radio. At 11:41, the carrier finally got off eight Wildcats, one of which lost an improperly attached belly tank on takeoff.

Meanwhile, over the transports, Lieutenant Bruning had positioned his 18 fighters at 17,000 feet to have a proper altitude advantage over the incoming attackers. But he had underestimated the airstrike's time of arrival and now those 18 Wildcats were running out of fuel. At 11:30, out of fuel concerns, Admiral Noyes recalled the fighters from the *Wasp* – not just the seven over the transports who were running out of fuel but the eight en route who had plenty of fuel.

Thanks to the finely tuned fighter direction machine, when the Japanese finally arrived at 11:55 am, there were only three fighters, all from the *Enterprise*, defending the all-important transports.

The Japanese came round the mountains of Florida Island, from the east. As on the day before, they were G4M "Betty" bombers – 14 from the 4th Air Group and nine from the Misawa Air Group, all led by Lieutenant Kotani Shigeru of the 4th. Unlike the day before, these were armed with torpedoes and were thus much more dangerous. Escorting the Bettys were 15 Zeros of the Tainan Air Group under Lieutenant Inano Kikuichi.

Lieutenant Kotani had indeed come later than the American fighter directors had predicted. That was intentional. He was trying to hold off his attack in the hope that Japanese air searches would find the elusive American carriers northeast of the Solomons. If they did, he could get the carriers' position from the scouts' radio report and direct his airstrike there. So Kotani looped to the north around Santa Ysabel and Florida islands, the mountains of each screening his aircraft from radar. There was no such report, no such sighting, though one flying boat did pass to within a few miles of the carriers without seeing them. So Kotani came around the mountains of Florida and led his Type 1s down low at altitudes 10 to 150 feet roaring toward the west. He chose as the target of his attackers the ships off Tulagi. He chose poorly.

"[B]oth transports and screening ships at Tulagi opened an intense and effective antiaircraft fire as the planes passed them," understates the narrative of the Office of Naval Intelligence.[53] Among those ships was the light cruiser *San Juan* with her 16 5-inch dual-purpose guns, perfect for antiaircraft defense. She and her Yoke mates unloaded on the Japanese attackers. Eyewitnesses reported, "the fire of all these ships was so extensive and of such volume that the Japanese pilots showed utter confusion and state of mind and reacted accordingly."[54]

Trying to keep his formation together, Lieutenant Kotani switched targets to the transports off Lunga, but it didn't get much better. Admiral Turner led his flock of transports, now arrayed in four columns, in two 30-degree turns so that they steamed away from the attackers. One trio of Bettys skirted the northern edge of the transport formation; another trio skirted the south. The remainder were caught in vicious crossfires of all the ships in Savo Sound, from machine guns to the 8-inch guns of the heavy cruisers. "The [antiaircraft fire] must have been intense," says the Office of Naval Intelligence's Narrative, "with over 50 ships delivering the most concentrated fire of which they were capable for about 10 minutes." The bomber formation broke up, the Bettys maneuvered individually and not always intelligently. Some passed over the transports, some between the columns, some ahead, some astern.

The Mitsubishis were cut to ribbons. No fewer than eight were seen crashing in flames. One burning Betty barely missed the stern of the cruiser *Vincennes*. Another slashed through the rigging of the transport *Barnett* before splashing. At 12:02, a third, that of Reserve Lieutenant (jg) Sasaki Takafumi, crashed on to the boat deck of the transport *George F. Elliott*, the former liner *City of Los Angeles*.[55] This was a particularly nasty crash, rupturing an oil lubrication tank, "driving one [G4M] engine down on deck, spreading parts of plane and parts of bodies of Japanese on deck, exploding and throwing gasoline and lubricating oil all over the topside and down into [chief petty officer] quarters and the engine room and fireroom."[56] Heavily afire, the *Elliott* staggered out of formation.

As far as anyone could tell, only three of the G4Ms made it through the entire formation of ships, and two of these were shot down on the way out. Only a very few aircraft were able to release their Type 91 torpedoes, but one torpedo buried itself in the starboard side of the destroyer *Jarvis*, blowing a 50-foot hole in her forward boiler room and stopping her dead in the water.[57]

As the remaining G4Ms tried to head northwest away from the murderous gunfire of Savo Sound, they were jumped by those three remaining *Enterprise* Wildcats still providing air cover under Machinist Don Runyon and alerted to the Japanese intruders by radio. Runyon himself managed to shoot down one Betty from the 4th Air Group and one Zero from the Tainan Air Group, whose efforts at escort were thwarted by the heavy antiaircraft fire. His wingmates shot down three more Bettys.[58] The Japanese sped away as best as they could, not in anything resembling a combat formation, but in ones and twos.

In ones and twos was how the Japanese returned to Rabaul as well. Their commander Rear Admiral Yamada Sadayoshi of the 5th Air Attack Force – the operational name of the 25th Air Flotilla – watched in shock as exactly five Mitsubishi G4Ms returned, all badly shot up. No fewer than 17 had been shot down; one more crashed on the way back. Two Zeros had been shot down as well.[59]

However, the Japanese pilots returned to Rabaul reporting major successes against the invasion convoy: four large cruisers, three light cruisers, two destroyers, and three transports sunk; a large cruiser, a destroyer, and six transports severely damaged. Even Admiral Yamada didn't believe it. He reduced the tally to one heavy cruiser, one destroyer, and nine transports sunk, with three light cruisers and two unknown types badly damaged.

While not in the same galaxy as the damage reported by the Japanese, the damage was bad enough. The gashed *Jarvis* was towed into shallow water by the *Dewey*. However, the *Jarvis*' engines were intact and her damage control restored power. Fourteen of her crew were missing and seven had to be hospitalized on the *McCawley*.[60]

While the other transports were moving to anchor themselves again for unloading off Lunga, the *George F. Elliott* had lost power and was struggling with the fire caused by the crashing bomber. The destroyer *Hull* had moved alongside and was training five or six fire hoses on the flames. An attempt to tow the transport to Lunga 10 miles away to try to salvage some of the supplies on board failed. The fire continued to gain in strength and intensity. Eventually, the heat caused an internal bulkhead to rupture and leak bunker fuel, which fed the conflagration uncontrollably. The *Elliott* had to be abandoned as a total loss. Three officers and seven enlisted men had been killed.

At 5:30 pm, Admiral Turner ordered the transport sunk so the fire and smoke would not act as a beacon for the Japanese. At close range, the *Dewey* fired three Mark 15 torpedoes at the burning hulk. There was no apparent effect – one of many proud moments for the Mark 15 torpedo. The *George F. Elliott* just drifted into shoal water near Florida Island, where she grounded herself. Now, she could not be sunk and just kept burning, illuminating the area after dark and acting as a beacon for anyone looking for the landing zone.

A second air raid warning compelled the transports to get under way again. The warning turned out to be a false alarm, but the transports took hours to anchor themselves back at Lunga to unload their cargo in chaotic fashion. It also served to remind Admiral Fletcher that his carriers were on borrowed time. Admiral Kinkaid later said, "We could not reasonably hope that Japanese search planes would fail to locate us during the period of our operations south of Guadalcanal – it seemed obvious we were there – but that is just what happened."[61] How long could it continue?

By early afternoon, the Marines had seized the airfield. Now incoming supply boats were vectored to the beach north of the airfield just east of the Lunga River, which they jammed up as well. Marines stripped to their waists to manhandle the supplies off the beaches in the brutal heat and humidity.

Journalist Richard Tregaskis watched as Lieutenant Evard J. Snell, an aide to Colonel Leroy P. Hunt commanding the 5th Marine Regiment, was hauled into the old Japanese headquarters at Kukum, now being used as a Marine command post. Snell was paralyzed, although he could speak. Snell was no casualty of the Japanese. In the suffocating heat and humidity, he had lost consciousness four times that day without telling anyone and was now apparently gripped by heat stroke. Colonel Hunt wanted to cheer up the despondent Snell, so he took an 8-inch by 12-inch American flag that Snell had purchased in Vineland, New Jersey on Memorial Day 1934, and kept in his pocket through tours in China and the Philippines. Colonel Hunt had the tiny flag run to the top of the captured Japanese flagpole. Struggling to smile, Snell's face lit up. He would make a full recovery.[62]

It was the first time in this Pacific War that the American colors were raised over land liberated from the Japanese.

Admiral Turner stared at the message. In disbelief, though he should have expected it. In anger, though that was not all that unusual. It was a message that his communications staff had picked up at 6:07 from Admiral Fletcher to Admiral Ghormley, copied to admirals Turner, McCain, and Noyes:

> Total fighter strength reduced from 99 to 78. In view of large number of enemy torpedo and bomber planes in area recommend immediate withdrawal of carriers. Request you send tankers immediately to rendezvous decided by you as fuel running low.[63]

This changed everything. His ships had survived two days of Japanese air attacks. His transports and cargo ships were still not unloaded, not even close. Especially at Tulagi. How could he continue unloading without protection from more air attacks?

As Admiral Turner undoubtedly tried to calm down, there were several other matters of concern tugging at him. At 6:30, the executive officer of the damaged destroyer *Jarvis*, Lieutenant James H. Ray, reported to him on board the *McCawley*. The commander of Destroyer Squadron 4, Captain Cornelius Flynn, had inspected the damage to the destroyer and suggested that she head to Sydney alone. Turner disagreed; a single torpedo is usually fatal to a destroyer, and the admiral believed the damage was too great.

After discussing the situation with Lieutenant Ray, Admiral Turner told him to pass an order to the *Jarvis*' skipper, Lieutenant Commander William W. Graham, that the destroyer was to head to Efate by the eastern entrance to Savo Sound, escorted by a destroyer-minesweeper after the minesweepers had refueled around 10:00 pm. Furthermore, the *Jarvis* was to sail via sheltered waters and as close to land as possible so she could be beached if necessary. The order would be confirmed by signal later on. Ray headed back to the *Jarvis*.[64]

At about 6:45 pm, Admiral Turner was passed a report that at 10:25 am, a Royal Australian Air Force Lockheed Hudson had sighted off Kieta, Bougainville, "three cruisers, three destroyers, and two seaplane tenders or gunboats" on a course 120 degrees True – southeast – speed 15 knots. Towards him. The report could not have improved his mood. The sighting was eight hours old.

Something more about this report caught his attention – "two seaplane tenders." Hadn't a scout plane from the *Wasp* shot down a Japanese floatplane that morning? The Japanese must be setting up a seaplane base, most likely at Rekata Bay only 130 miles away. So he could expect more air attacks tomorrow just as his air cover was leaving.

Admiral Turner needed to know about the possibility of defending against air attack without the carriers providing fighter protection. And he needed to know the status of the unloading of supplies on Guadalcanal and Tulagi. At 8:45 pm, Turner sent for Admiral Crutchley, who was commanding the surface screening ships and was Admiral Turner's designated second-in-command, and General Vandegrift to meet him on the *McCawley* to discuss the situation.

On board the Australian heavy cruiser *Australia*, Admiral Crutchley received the message: "Please come on board as soon as possible. I will send boat as soon as you approach."[65] He and his staff had been expecting such a call. They, too, had picked up Admiral Fletcher's message. They had also picked up the report from the Australian Hudson about the "three cruisers, three destroyers, and two seaplane tenders." They worked the calculations and determined that this force could reach them that night. But those "seaplane tenders"? They portended an air attack.[66]

By this time, as he had done the previous evening, Crutchley had ordered his ships into nighttime cruising disposition, established in his order "Special Instructions to the Screening Group." Under his command for the nighttime screening were the Australian heavy cruisers *Australia* and *Canberra*, the US heavy cruisers *Chicago*, *Vincennes*, *Quincy*, and *Astoria*, the Australian light cruiser *Hobart*, US light antiaircraft cruiser *San Juan*, flying the flag of Rear Admiral Normal Scott, and American destroyers *Monssen*, *Buchanan*, *Selfridge*, *Patterson*, *Ralph Talbot*, *Mugford*, *Jarvis*, *Blue*, *Helm*, *Henley*, and *Bagley*.

With the defense of the *Watchtower* transports, the veteran Royal Navy admiral had been presented with a difficult tactical problem. There were two separate groups of transports to be protected, one off Tulagi, the other off Guadalcanal. There were two entrances to Savo Sound from which an enemy surface force might attack the transports. One entrance was to the east, with Lengo and Sealark Channels. Here was stationed Admiral Scott's force of cruisers *San Juan* and *Hobart*, and destroyers *Monssen* and *Buchanan*, who had been working together off Tulagi during the days. This entrance was considered unlikely for an enemy attack, but required protection nonetheless.

The real danger was from the western entrance to Savo Sound, the entrance closer to the Japanese bases at Rabaul and Bougainville. To complicate matters, this entrance was divided into two avenues of approach by Savo Island. Believing that handling four cruisers at night was unwieldy, Admiral Crutchley had decided to guard both entrances almost equally with forces centered on three cruisers. The avenue south of Savo, between it and Guadalcanal, was patrolled by a column of the *Australia*, *Canberra*, and *Chicago*, with the destroyers *Patterson* and *Bagley* on either bow of the *Australia*.

Commanded by Admiral Crutchley himself, this was a natural arrangement, as the two Australian cruisers had worked together before, and the *Chicago* had been with them ever since early 1942. This southern group of ships sailed in a general line of 305 degrees True [northwest] to 125 degrees True [southeast]. The group would reverse course approximately every hour, the cruiser column turning around by a column turn and the destroyers reversing course independently so that *Bagley* stayed between the column and Savo and the *Patterson* between the column and Guadalcanal.

Between Savo Island and Florida Island to the north was a northern group of ships. The center was a column of the heavy cruisers *Vincennes*, *Quincy*, and *Astoria*, screened by the destroyers *Helm* and originally *Jarvis*, but with the *Jarvis* badly damaged the destroyer *Wilson* had to step in to replace her. Due to a relative shortage of flag officers, this group was commanded by the *Vincennes*' skipper, Captain Riefkohl. Riefkohl had decided to go with what was called a box patrol, a square concentric with the midway between Savo and Florida islands. They would start on a course of 45 degrees True [northeast] then make a 90-degree turn to starboard approximately every half-hour, traveling at 10 knots.

The remainder of the destroyers were deployed in an antisubmarine screen around the transports, except for the destroyers *Blue* and *Ralph Talbot*. Both destroyers were deployed in New Georgia Sound some 5 miles outside of Savo Island as radar and antisubmarine pickets. Both destroyers would be patrolling courses southwest to northeast, *Ralph Talbot* north of Savo, *Blue* west.

Admiral Crutchley had thus committed the cardinal sin of dividing his forces, though in this case it was probably the best he could do given the geography with which he had to work. He intended for the northern and southern groups to act independently, but still support each other. Crutchley had gotten the approval of his superior Admiral Turner for these dispositions. "I was satisfied with arrangements and hoped the enemy would attack," Turner later wrote. "I believed they would get a warm reception."[67]

Now, however, Turner had added a complicating factor: he had ordered Admiral Crutchley to meet with him, requiring him to leave his guarding force, and to leave his flagship *Australia*.

Admiral Crutchley signaled to Captain Howard D. Bode on the cruiser *Chicago*. "Take charge of patrol. I am closing CTF 62 and may or may not rejoin later."[68] The flagship *Australia* then pulled out to travel the 20 miles and look for Admiral Turner's flagship *McCawley* in the dark. Crutchley's departure meant that Captain Riefkohl in the northern force was technically in command of the entire force, but Crutchley did not tell Riefkohl that he was leaving. As was common practice in the Royal Navy, he simply assumed that Riefkohl had picked up the same signal from Turner ordering Crutchley to meet him that Crutchley did.

As the veteran Royal Navy admiral sailed off, the southern force was left in the hands of the skipper of the *Chicago*, Captain Bode. His nicknames of "King Bode" and "Captain Bligh" suggest a skipper who was none too popular with his crew. He was known for being a "strict disciplinarian," with a manner that was "insulting and intimidating when he was not entirely aloof. He visited the wardroom only for meetings, and his presence always chilled the company."[69]

Bode did not take advice from his subordinates well. "His officers were scared to death of him," said Bode's Marine orderly Raymond Zarker. "The minute I would walk in there they would freeze, like a bunch of frightened rabbits." One officer who knew Bode on another ship described him as "short and stocky." This likely suited the skipper because "he used to stick one of his hands in his blouse in front and he postured a little like Napoleon postured and looked a little like I thought Napoleon was supposed to look."[70]

Naturally, Captain Bode believed himself destined for flag rank. And probably took this chance to command as a taste of things to come. But the situation was tricky. Normally, the commander of a force would place his ship in front. But Bode's *Chicago* was in back. Moving to the front would require maneuvering around the *Canberra* in the dark, in restricted waters between two islands, and then doing it again when – if –

the *Australia* returned that night. After conferring with the *Canberra*'s Captain Frank E. Getting, Bode decided to stay where he was.[71]

As the night went on, the stage formed by Savo Sound had action of some sort going on everywhere. The *McCawley* had tried to visually signal orders to the damaged destroyer *Jarvis*, but the destroyer did not acknowledge. A cutter sent later to deliver the orders by hand could not find the *Jarvis*, nor could the destroyer-minesweeper *Hovey*, sent to escort the holed destroyer to Efate. On the transport's flag bridge Admiral Turner seethed as he waited for his conference. His flagship took in another sighting report of "two heavy cruisers, two light cruisers, and one unknown type" sighted at 3:00 pm. It was now 9:30. The report was more than six hours old.

At Lunga and Tulagi, the Marines were scrambling to unload supplies they would need to hold the islands. Off Florida, the transport *George F. Elliott* continued to burn, mocking the efforts of the destroyer *Hull*, who fired four Mark 15 torpedoes into the blazing hulk without any effect, another proud moment for the Mark 15, the second on this day.

Near Savo Island, the flagship of the screening force made for the *McCawley*, while behind it the two groups of cruisers made their boring patrol rounds, headed by exhausted captains and worn-out crews. Captain Bode was so spent he went to sleep in his emergency cabin off the bridge.

Out in New Georgia Sound, two lonely destroyers went back and forth, on opposite sides of the western entrance to Savo Sound. Both were keeping watch. One was also being watched.

Radioman 2nd Class Douw MacHaffie of the destroyer *Ralph Talbot* had gone to the bridge to report that he had been relieved of duty at the end of his shift when they first heard it – the soft growl of aircraft. One was flying over the destroyer. Skipper Lieutenant Commander Joseph W. Callahan tapped MacHaffie on the shoulder. Better report this, he ordered.

MacHaffie got on the warning net and broadcast it: "Warning Warning plane over Savo headed east."

They didn't get an acknowledgment. Nevertheless, they assumed everyone had heard it.

The short message had left out some details, however. In the rush to get out the warning, they had not included their belief that the aircraft was a cruiser floatplane. It didn't seem important. The plane had to be Allied, they figured.

At the Marine command post on Guadalcanal, Lieutenant Colonel Twining found the major concern for the evening so far was poor communications. Their radios could not penetrate the jungle. They had land lines, which were constantly being accidentally cut by Marines. Communication with the ships offshore, however, was perfect – "a mixed blessing," he admitted.[72]

Lieutenant Colonel Twining was in the command post with Major Kenny Weir, the air officer, learning just how hot and humid a night on Guadalcanal could be. A little after midnight it got even more humid, as a thin mist came in and hung in the air.

About an hour later, there was something else in the air. Like a growl, but not from any animal. Aircraft engines. Major Weir listened, with increasing alarm. "Cruiser floatplanes," he said. "And not ours."

Floatplanes were usually carried on battleships and cruisers to run errands, perform antisubmarine patrols, scout, and spot the fall of gunfire.

The air officer paused for a moment. Listening to the rumble overhead. Letting his words sink in …

"Where there are cruiser planes, there are cruisers."[73]

CHAPTER 3
THE SLEEPING WATCH

The admiral stood on the bridge of his flagship watching the movements of the small dark shadow ahead of him with a mixture of trepidation and no small measure of amazement. The enemy ship was about to cross his path. Almost collide with his ship. Hadn't it seen him?

For Japanese Vice Admiral Mikawa Gunichi, the whirlwind of the last two days, indeed the last two months, had come down to this.

The whirlwind had begun after the debacle at Midway. The Japanese advance across the Pacific was mostly over. Even though the Imperial Navy had canceled the *FS* operation to isolate Australia, Imperial General Headquarters didn't quite accept that the offensive phase of Japan's war had ended and had decided to revert to its own strategy of isolating Australia to prevent it from becoming a staging area and jumping off point for the inevitable Allied counteroffensive. The only question was how to accomplish it.

While the Imperial Japanese Navy had canceled its own operation – for now – to isolate Australia, the Imperial Japanese Army had approached the problem from New Guinea, quite literally. Seeing Papua-New Guinea as a physical shield for Australia, they had invaded the island and succeeded in conquering the northern half of it, with a bastion at Lae. The Australians still held the southern half, centered on the colonial capital of Port Moresby. But the campaign had stalled. To capture Port Moresby by land, the Japanese had to start at Buna on the north coast and cross the 13,000-foot Owen Stanley Mountains that divide the Papua Peninsula roughly down the middle, which was a tall order.

To make matters worse, the Japanese could cross the Owen Stanleys only by using the Kokoda Trail. Even today, the trail is a primitive, single-file footpath that makes Thermopylae look like Texas. Going from tropical lowlands up the Owen Stanleys and back down to tropical lowland, the Kokoda also ranges from hot humid days with torrential rain to frigid nights, all wrapped up with deadly animals, frightening insects, and nasty diseases.

For General Hyakutake Harukichi, commander of the Japanese 17th Army, the best way to advance down the one-man-wide track was obvious: send more men. That meant moving more troops across the ocean to New Guinea. For that, they needed the Imperial Japanese Navy, the same people who had just canceled the *FS* operation out of fears they were overextending themselves. Specifically, the general would need Admiral Inoue Shigeyoshi's 4th Fleet. Never content with a simple numeric designation, the Japanese gave the 4th Fleet the operational designation of "South Seas Force." But the "South Seas Force" had proved less than totally effective in its conduct of combat operations at Coral Sea, in which the seaborne invasion of Port Moresby that would have precluded all this Kokoda Trail foolishness had been turned back.

Which is where and why Admiral Mikawa came in. On July 12, Mikawa, a 1910 graduate of the Japanese naval academy at Etajima, third in his class of 149, was named commander of the newly created 8th Fleet, responsible for the Solomons, the Bismarcks, and New Guinea, to be carved out of the operational area of the 4th Fleet. The Japanese designated the 8th Fleet the "Outer South Seas Force" and the 4th Fleet the "Inner South Seas Force." With this move, the New Guinea operations and the expansion of the Japanese defense line from the Solomons southward to isolate Australia would have a dedicated fleet.

But it was the makeup of the 8th Fleet that showed what the Combined Fleet really thought of these Outer South Seas operations. The fleet would consist of the heavy cruiser *Chokai*, the heavy cruisers of the 6th Cruiser Division, the light cruisers of the 18th Cruiser Division, and whatever destroyers Admiral Mikawa could find lying around.[1] While the 8th Fleet would be based at Rabaul, on the northeastern tip of New Britain, the designated fleet flagship would be the *Chokai*, a member of the *Takao* class of heavy cruisers with a main armament of ten 8-inch guns, a secondary armament of eight 5-inch guns, and eight torpedo tubes to launch the devastating 24-inch Type 93 torpedo. Their superstructures as originally built resembled squashed versions of the famous "pagoda" masts of Japanese battleships, which provided very large, very spacious bridge areas that, by warship standards, were nothing short of luxurious. For that reason, the *Chokai* and her sister ship *Atago* were very popular with flag officers and would spend most of the war serving as fleet flagships, as *Chokai* would be now. Admiral Mikawa's flagship was nothing short of a maritime monster.

Her fleetmates, however, were not in the same league. The balance of the 8th Fleet's heavy cruisers was provided by the warships of the 6th Cruiser Division, under the command of Rear Admiral Goto Aritomo. These were the four heavy cruisers of the almost-identical *Furutaka* and *Aoba* classes. The *Furutaka* and her sister ship *Kako*, and the *Aoba* and her sister ship *Kinugasa* were the navy's oldest heavy cruisers, started in the mid-1920s, back when Japan made a pretense of abiding by the Washington Naval Treaty that limited warship tonnage and armament. After extensive modernization that made the ships almost identical, they had a main armament of six 8-inch guns in three twin turrets. By the start of the Pacific War, this main armament was hopelessly outgunned, especially when compared with later Japanese heavy cruisers like the *Chokai*. But they all still had eight torpedo tubes each, capable of launching the deadly Type 93 Long Lance.

Meanwhile the 18th Cruiser Division, commanded by Rear Admiral Matsuyama Mitsuharu, consisted of ships no one else wanted, so old that Admiral Mikawa derided them as "rabble."[2] The *Tenryu* and her sister *Tatsuta* had been laid down in 1917, during World War I, and seemed more at home in that war than in this one. In their time the *Tenryus* had been somewhat revolutionary. They were the first Japanese cruisers to have triple torpedo tubes, though they could only use 21-inch torpedoes. And they set the standard for light cruisers that would lead Japanese destroyer squadrons throughout the war – they were long, blocky, upright, ugly things, armed with six of those torpedo tubes and a main armament of four 5.5-inch guns.

Not normally with the 18th but also part of the "rabble" was the light cruiser *Yubari*. Completed in 1923, the *Yubari* looked nothing like other Japanese light cruisers such as the *Tenryu*. Instead, she looked like a miniaturized Japanese heavy cruiser – sleek, clipper bow, raked funnel. That was intentional. She was originally an experimental design by the famed Japanese naval architect Baron Hiraga Yuzuru and would form the prototype for the *Furutaka* class and later. Like other Japanese light cruisers, though, *Yubari* had been the flagship of a destroyer squadron, the 6th Destroyer Flotilla. When that organization was deactivated, *Yubari* was sent to the South Seas, where she didn't seem to be doing much. She was a beautiful ship that was woefully underarmed, with six 5.5-inch guns and four torpedo tubes, albeit tubes that could handle the Type 93.

These weren't the best tools overall, but they were pretty much the only tools in the admiral's shed. He also had some submarines and logistics ships. But the Combined Fleet had not seen fit to give Admiral Mikawa any air power; the air elements in the 8th Fleet's operating area, the 25th Air Flotilla, were not under his command, but were instead under the umbrella of the 11th Air Fleet, headquartered in far-off Tinian in the Marianas. And he had to fight to keep even these limited tools, as Combined Fleet wanted to withdraw the 6th Cruiser Division to Truk.

So, on July 20, the admiral's operations officer Captain Ohmae Toshikazu flew down to Rabaul, the main Japanese base in the South Pacific, to start setting things up. Two days later Ohmae flew to the headquarters of the 4th Fleet at Truk in the Caroline Islands to brief the admiral himself on the very unpleasant situation he had found in Rabaul. Admiral Mikawa arrived in the *Chokai* on July 25 for two days of meetings with the 4th Fleet to get their take on the situation in the Solomons and New Guinea before turning that part of their command over to him. Admiral Inoue seemed happy to be rid of the area, but Mikawa was concerned; while the focus of the army and Combined Fleet was on New Guinea, he had noted frequent American reconnaissance missions over Guadalcanal and a buildup of Allied aircraft in the New Hebrides. Although he believed the Allies could not mount a full-scale counteroffensive until 1943, he surmised that the Allies would in some way attack the new Guadalcanal airfield before it could be brought on-line. Those concerns were laughed off by the 4th Fleet, dismissed as "the mere anxiety of a newcomer" who didn't understand the situation.[3]

So Mikawa sailed off in the *Chokai*, arriving in Rabaul on July 30. He found it just as bad as Captain Ohmae had described. The 25th Air Flotilla, one of the Imperial Japanese Navy's land-based air units that had no equivalent in the US Navy, and the 8th Base Force, in charge of the administration and logistics of the Rabaul base, were bickering. The 25th was about to be rotated out and, in anticipation, seemed a little too laid back about the war situation. But one thing on which the 25th and the 8th agreed was that "a new higher command organization in Rabaul would be most unwelcome."[4] When told he wanted his headquarters ashore, the staff of the 25th Air Flotilla responded by saying any surface commander would certainly prefer to keep his headquarters in his flagship. In the alternative, they kindly told him he could have his headquarters ashore – if he could find the space. But Mikawa, a thoughtful commander not known for his ego, made the most of it, and took stock of his new surroundings.

And Rabaul was in many respects an excellent military base. It was strategically located on the northeastern tip of New Britain, so it could serve as a waypoint between the main Japanese Pacific stronghold at Truk and points south like Japanese-held New Guinea and the Solomons. It controlled access to the St George's Channel between New Britain and New Ireland, which was a major route between Truk and the Solomons. For the Navy itself, Rabaul boasted an excellent harbor, 7½ miles long and 5 miles wide.[5] It consisted of a large outer harbor, alliteratively called Blanche Bay, with multiple smaller harbors around its periphery, Keravia Bay, Matupit Harbor, and, closest to Rabaul proper, Simpson Harbor, which would become the main Japanese navy base.[6] It had two airfields: Lakunai (or "Rabaul Lower Airstrip" or "Rabaul East," as the Japanese pilots would call it), 2 miles southeast of Rabaul between Simpson Harbor and Matupit Harbor, and Vunakanau ("Rabaul Upper Airstrip" or "Rabaul West"), 11 miles south-southwest of Rabaul near Keravia Bay.[7] And plenty of room for the Japanese to construct a few more airfields as needed. All in all, Rabaul had a lot of things that would be very helpful to Admiral Mikawa.

And a lot of things that would be less helpful. Rabaul is situated within a circular fault line within the Earth's crust, and so is perhaps the most geologically active place on Earth. It can have hundreds or even thousands of earthquakes a month.[8] Even worse is its annoying habit of getting itself buried in volcanic ash. Rabaul is also located within an eponymous caldera and is literally surrounded by volcanoes. In 1937, a new volcano, called Vulcan, popped out of Simpson Harbor with a bang and combined with Rabaul's reigning resident active volcano, Tavurvur, to destroy Rabaul with volcanic ash. The Australians abandoned the area.

Nevertheless, the Japanese reoccupied Rabaul very enthusiastically, though the vociferous volcanoes did affect operations, especially air operations. Ash from Vulcan ate away at aircraft fuselages at Vunakanau.[9] Persistent ash clouds and gases from Tavurvur ate fabric wings and prevented essential maintenance to the nearby Lakunai airfield, which Sakai Saburo called "the worst airfield [he] had ever seen anywhere."[10] "Rabaul," said Sakai, "was plucked from the very depths of hell itself." But when faced with the question of whether having the finest harbor in the South Seas was worth the very real risk of becoming a Pacific Pompeii, the choice for the Japanese was obvious.

The soft-spoken, highly respected Admiral Mikawa did not let such mundane things as erupting volcanoes or uncooperative base personnel hinder him. Mikawa's staff located a headquarters for him – a "dilapidated wood-frame shack" near the Lakunai airfield and the admiral proudly ran up his flag.[11] He cited his concerns about Allied activities in the lower Solomons in a successful effort to keep the 6th Cruiser Division, which he placed along with the *Chokai* at Kavieng, on the northern tip of New Ireland, out of range of General MacArthur's nosy B-17s from Port Moresby.

With his cruisers protected, Admiral Mikawa threw himself into preparing for the 8th Fleet's support of the 17th Army's operations in New Guinea, especially the advance from Buna over the Kokoda Trail. There was to be a move to capture bases on Milne Bay, on Papua's eastern tip, to support yet another seaborne invasion of Port Moresby that would itself support the advance down the Kokoda Trail. It was not going to be easy. On July 31, MacArthur's bombers attacked a convoy consisting of the minelayer *Tsugaru*, transport *Nankai Maru*, and submarine chaser *CH-28*. No ships were sunk, but the convoy was prevented from entering Buna. Another convoy, consisting of the transports *Nankai Maru*, *Kinai Maru*, and *Kenyo Maru*, the light cruiser *Tatsuta*, the destroyers *Uzuki* and *Yuzuki*, and submarine chasers *CH-23* and *CH-30*, was scheduled to make the run to Buna on August 8. Mikawa figured MacArthur would try to sink this convoy and hoped a large Japanese air attack scheduled for August 7 on Rabi, on Milne Bay, where the Allies were building an airfield, would distract from MacArthur's effort.[12]

But developments in the lower Solomons just kept nagging the admiral. Mikawa was given an intelligence report that a US Navy task force of three aircraft carriers and several escorting cruisers had left Pearl Harbor on August 2. It was in the context of this report that Mikawa read another report that came in from Japanese radio intelligence on August 5. They had picked up increased radio traffic in the 8th Fleet's area and were predicting increasing enemy activity there. Mikawa suspected that this meant Allied air attacks on Japanese supply lines running through Buna. The reconnaissance and air attacks on Tulagi and Guadalcanal were merely diversionary, he presumed. And it would take those US carriers a while to get down to the Coral Sea to bomb the Buna supply line. He had no way of knowing that those carriers had not left Pearl Harbor on August 2, but had instead left Fiji on August 1.[13]

The Tulagi-based Yokohama Air Group had reported the increase in bombing raids against the Lunga airfield. US submarines were sighted moving into the area. On August 5 and 6, a storm front had prevented Japanese reconnaissance in the Solomons and to the south and east from both Tulagi and Rabaul.[14] That same day, August 6, the Japanese garrison on Guadalcanal reported that all the native laborers working on the airfield had fled into the jungle during the night.

The Japanese shrugged it off. The New Guinea operations would proceed as planned. The air attacks on Rabi were scheduled for the morning of August 7. And there would the nut that was Port Moresby start cracking …

"Large force of ships, unknown number or types, entering the sound. What can they be?"[15]

The message came after dawn on the morning of August 7 into the headquarters of the 25th Air Flotilla, where the flotilla's commander Rear Admiral Yamada Sadayoshi immediately suspected the question posted by this cryptic message mostly answered itself. Guessing that this was an enemy raid, he ordered three G4Ms from the 2nd Air Group to check out the Tulagi area.[16] The report that came in to Admiral Mikawa was slightly less cryptic: "0630. Tulagi. Enemy task force sighted."[17]

This was still not a lot to go on, but Mikawa and his staff had suspected for some time that something bigger than a mere raid was afoot in the lower Solomons. Previously scheduled scouting missions involving two long-range Type 97 Large Flying Boats were directed to the Tulagi area and beyond, out to 700 miles.[18] He tried to recall the *Chokai* and the 6th Cruiser Division, both of which had just sailed out of Kavieng, and summoned the senior naval and air officers and staff to his humble "command post" that lacked even a bathroom. As they gathered, at 7:25 am Mikawa received a second report:

"Enemy task force of 20 ships attacking Tulagi. Undergoing severe bombing. Landing preparations underway. Help requested."[19]

Admiral Tsukahara, head of the 11th Air Fleet, operationally designated "Base Air Force," had been informed of the situation and took off for Rabaul to oversee the reaction, in effect replacing Admiral Mikawa as area commander, but not before sending a message to Admiral Yamada urging the 25th Air Flotilla, operationally called the "5th Air Attack Force," to "destroy the enemy invasion forces with all its might."[20] That had just become a lot more difficult after Mikawa received a report from the Yokohama Air Group on Tulagi: "All large flying boats burned as a result of 0630 air attack."[21]

Forced to improvise, Mikawa was formulating a plan for a night raid with his heavy cruisers, of which he was sorely lacking at the moment. The only ships in Simpson Harbor were the "rabble" – the *Tenryu* and *Yubari* of the 18th Cruiser Division – and the destroyer *Yunagi*, none of which he considered suitable for this operation because of their age. The *Chokai* and the 6th Cruiser Division were operating out of Kavieng. *Furutaka* and *Kinugasa* were heading for Rabaul, but the *Chokai* was leading the *Aoba* and the *Kako* to Manus Island in the Admiralties, and thus heading west – away from Rabaul. At 7:49 am the *Yunagi* was dispatched to chase down the *Chokai*, *Aoba*, and *Kako* to bring them back.[22] Fortunately for Mikawa, the cruisers had heard the pleas for help from Tulagi, and Admiral Goto ordered them to rendezvous and make haste for Simpson Harbor. Meanwhile, the senior staff officer of the 18th Cruiser Division had pleaded with Mikawa to allow the old light cruisers to take part in this operation. The admiral was inclined to acquiesce to his request, and the 18th was told to prepare to sortie at 1:00 pm.

While Admiral Mikawa was preparing the 8th Fleet's response to the American attack, Admiral Yamada was preparing the 5th Air Attack Force's response. Yamada called a quick and not-entirely pleasant meeting with his air commanders to order the day's regularly scheduled air raid on Milne Bay redirected to the Tulagi-Guadalcanal area to deal with this new threat.[23]

That posed some serious problems. It was some 560 miles to Guadalcanal. The G4M Type 1 bombers could make it there and back easily, but it was at the far end of the range of their Zero fighter escorts. And these were no mere fighter escorts – these were the pilots of the Tainan Air Group, perhaps Japan's best fighter group and among the best fighter groups in the world. They had not shirked from flying from Formosa beyond the end of their operational range to strike at Clark Field in the Philippines in the first days of the war. But this was different – the range was even longer, and there was no time to experiment with fuel mixtures to achieve the desired range. It would be the longest mission ever flown by Zeros.

The officer who would lead this escort, Lieutenant Commander Nakajima Tadashi, vociferously objected to the prospect of leading his pilots beyond the maximum range of their aircraft, predicting half of them would be lost.

Admiral Yamada was adamant. "Take every Zero that will fly."

Lieutenant Commander Nakajima, just as adamant, offered a compromise. "This is the longest fighter mission in history," he said. "Not all my men are capable of it. Let me take only my best twelve pilots. They would have a chance of making it."

An enraged Admiral Yamada silently shoved a piece of paper into Nakajima's face. It contained the last message received from the Japanese garrison on Tulagi, sent at 8:05 am: "Enemy forces overwhelming. We will defend our posts to the death, praying for eternal victory."[24]

Chastened by the finality of the message, Nakajima agreed to send 18 Zeroes to escort the 27 Bettys. Stragglers low on fuel were to land at an abandoned Australian airfield on Buka, north of Bougainville on the route to Guadalcanal, where they would be picked up later.[25] Nakajima went to brief his pilots, some of whom had been sitting inside their cockpits waiting to start the scheduled attack on Milne Bay.

The pilots, having heard bits and pieces of Nakajima discussing the mission with the staff officers, were bemused. "Where is Guadalcanal, sir?" one of the petty officers asked Sakai Saburo.

"I don't know," Sakai replied. Then he turned to the group of pilots. "Does anybody know where Guadalcanal is?" They shook their heads. The petty officer grumbled, "Nobody knows! Then, it cannot be an important place."[26]

The mood turned more serious, indeed somber, when the pilots were briefed on the situation and the mission. The airfield at Lunga Point on Guadalcanal and the naval air base at Tulagi were the targets of an enemy invasion. The Tainan were to fly there, engage the enemy's covering fighters – US Navy carrier fighters, this would be the Tainan's first battle with US Navy aviators – and return. It was a trip of 560 miles. "Don't waste fuel!" was the theme. They would carry external drop tanks, but contrary to accepted practice were not to drop the tanks before their first engagement with enemy fighters. They needed every drop of fuel.

At 9:50 am Nakajima led 18 Zeros through the volcanic ash from nearby Tavurvur (quiet on this day, Sakai noticed) covering the Lakunai runway into the air. At about 10:05 Nakajima was joined by the 27 G4Ms of the 4th Air Group taking off from Vunakanau, armed with high-explosive antipersonnel bombs intended for land targets in Rabi – there had been no time to rearm them for naval targets. Finally, at about 10:45 came 16 "Aichi D3A Type 99 Carrier Bombers" that the Allies would call the "Val" from the 2nd Air Group. Even staging through the Buka reserve airfield, the Aichi definitely did not have the fuel for the trip. Nevertheless, just after the Japanese Naval Air Force had lost dozens of experienced dive bomber crews in the Midway debacle, Admiral Yamada believed the offensive capabilities of these additional aircraft justified risking more of these precious pilots on a one-way trip. The air crews, he hoped, could be fished out of the water by the seaplane tender *Akitsushima* after they ditched, which he estimated would be southeast of the Japanese seaplane base in the Shortlands area.[27]

Meanwhile, Admiral Mikawa sent four of the five submarines of the 7th Submarine Squadron towards Guadalcanal to hopefully prey on the Allied transports.[28] He requested permission from Tokyo to conduct his surface attack on the Allied ships the following night, August 8. He also tried to get some ground reinforcements for the embattled garrisons on Tulagi and Guadalcanal. But Mikawa's suspicions that this was more than a mere raid were not shared by all. Admiral Mikawa went to General Hyakatuke, who had no idea the Navy had even been building an airfield on Guadalcanal. When informed of the Marine invasion, Hyakutake, "a man of optimism and a supreme confidence bordering on arrogance," had first asked, "What is a Marine?"[29] When Mikawa asked about infantry reinforcements, the general demurred, saying he could not provide any of his infantry, already committed to the New Guinea operation, without the approval of Imperial General Headquarters. The general firmly believed that the developments in the lower Solomons were merely a diversion intended to draw Japanese attention and resources from the pending operations in New Guinea.

General Hyakutake's belief may have been genuine, but it was also convenient from a bureaucratic standpoint. The early advance in Southeast Asia requiring cooperation between the Imperial Army and Navy had been extraordinary inasmuch as the Army and the Navy traditionally were bitter rivals in Japanese politics, each only dimly aware of the operations of the other. The Navy had not even told the Army the extent of the disaster at Midway, out of fear of losing "face" in front of their rivals. The Army was fully committed to the New Guinea plan and had never been sold on this lunacy in the lower Solomons. The airfield on Guadalcanal was a Navy operation, the enemy attack a Navy mess. Rebuffed, Mikawa proceeded to scrape together 310 members of the 5th Sasebo Special Naval Landing Force, and 100 sailors of the 81st Guard Unit, who had recently returned from Guadalcanal, gave them a few machine guns and not quite enough rifles, stuck them on board the transport *Meiyo Maru* and the supply ship *Soya*, and, with the minelayer *Tsugaru* and a few small combatants serving as escorts, in the loosest sense of the word, ordered them toward Guadalcanal.

It was at 12:03 pm that the *Yunagi* finally stumbled across the *Chokai* and the 6th Cruiser Division headed for Rabaul. Accompanied by the destroyer, the *Chokai* would speed on ahead to Simpson Harbor. Admiral Goto's ships would wait outside the harbor, launching their floatplanes to conduct antisubmarine patrols. Admiral Mikawa knew that submarines could be an issue on this mission. Aircraft were good at spotting submarines, even submerged ones, and could attack them for a limited time, but for sinking submarines or simply holding them down so they wouldn't interfere with operations, nothing could beat a destroyer. And Mikawa had only one destroyer available to him, the ancient *Yunagi*, already being overworked on this hectic August 7.

Yet submarines were far from the only danger around Rabaul. Still some 25 miles north of Rabaul in St George's Channel, the old cruisers watched 13 Army Air Force B-17s flying out of Port Moresby approach Rabaul. The cruisers prepared for air defense, but though the Flying Fortresses had seen the cruisers and would send in a woefully inadequate contact report, they focused on the Vunakanau airfield. The Zeros of the 2nd Air Group and those left behind by the Tainan Air Group – 21 in all – rose to meet the threat. It was a common confrontation early in the Pacific War, unescorted B-17s versus Japanese Zeros. Eight Zeros were damaged, but as the Fortresses left the area, the Zeros swarmed the one trailing B-17 after it had lost an engine. They set its auxiliary fuel tank afire and left it staggering to crash in the jungle some 40 miles south of Rabaul. The damage to Vunakanau was only superficial, and the airfield was operational in time for the bombers of the 4th Air Group, returning from their attack on the Allied ships near Guadalcanal and Tulagi, to land safely. Nevertheless, Douglas MacArthur's air force considered this limited attack a rousing success.[31]

Admiral Mikawa and his staff walked outside to watch part of the air attack with mild interest; they had never seen one. But they had too much on their plate in preparing for this operation to worry about an unrelated air raid and went back inside.[32] The admiral had decided, "depending on the results of the reconnaissance and the counterattacks of our air force to the south, to strike the anchored enemy convoys at night and destroy them."[33] He knew the results of neither the reconnaissance – which would hopefully locate the enemy carriers from where the air attacks had come – nor the counterattack, but he knew he would receive these eventually. There were more immediate concerns.

This striking force was the best Admiral Mikawa could do, no doubt, but nevertheless, except for the ships of the 6th Cruiser Division, none of these ships had ever worked together or even trained together. While the skipper of each ship was a veteran and very skilled in the methods of the Imperial Japanese Navy, a night operation with maneuvering and targeting was a potentially dangerous proposition. Nor was that all.

There was also the question of the waters in which Admiral Mikawa's ships would be sailing. The Japanese charts of the area were old and incomplete. Soundings of the depth of the waters were few. The admiral was concerned that one of his ships would run aground on an uncharted reef. The commander of the 8th Base Force advised that the New Georgia Sound, the central channel of the Solomons that Americans would call "the

Slot," was almost deep enough for battleships. It was also the most direct, most obvious route to Guadalcanal. Mikawa agreed.

The admiral wired his plan to Tokyo for approval. Admiral Nagano Osami, the chief of the naval general staff, was furious. He thought the plan was "dangerous and reckless" – the *Chokai* and six cruisers no one else wanted would be badly outnumbered and outgunned as they tried to break through to the Allied transports – and initially ordered that it be stopped immediately.[34] To him, the plan seemed like suicide. However, at the urging of his staff officers, Nagano reported the plan to Admiral Yamamoto himself. Yamamoto was an inveterate gambler. Admiral Mikawa was not, he knew, but the soft-spoken Mikawa was aggressive in his own way. Yamamoto radioed Mikawa directly: "Wish your fleet success."[35]

At 1:30 pm the *Yunagi* led the *Chokai* into Simpson Harbor to await orders from Mikawa. About a half-hour later the 6th Cruiser Division arrived outside Simpson Harbor in St George's Channel and waited. During this time the aircraft of the 5th Air Attack Force started returning from their attack on the Allied ships off Guadalcanal and Tulagi. If the men of the 6th Cruiser Division looked up, they might have seen fighter ace Petty Officer 1st Class Sakai Saburo of the Tainan Air Group staggering back to Lakunai. His duel with the Dauntlesses had left him gravely injured, the severe head injury leaving him blind in his right eye and paralyzed over the left side of his body. In severe pain, Sakai had considered a proto-kamikaze run on an Allied ship, but he somehow kept himself awake and flew for four hours and 47 minutes over 640 miles, flying over the speeding *Aoba* and *Kinugasa* to get back to Lakunai, where he landed with his fuel gauge on empty. So was he. As Sakai reported to his superiors, he collapsed from his injuries. But Sakai would survive to tell his epic story.[36]

If Admiral Mikawa's ships saw the wounded ace, they could only give him passing attention. One issue remained: who was to command this force? Mikawa had multiple flag officers from which to choose, including Rear Admiral Goto of the 6th Cruiser Division and Rear Admiral Matsuyama of the 18th Cruiser Division, both of whom would be involved in this operation. Nevertheless, Admiral Mikawa decided that the best person to command this operation was Admiral Mikawa himself. He had been admonished by Tokyo to command this operation from ashore in Rabaul, but there seemed little point to that in his mind. He could not effectively command the 8th Fleet while at sea, but Vice Admiral Tsukahara was on his way to take command of everything, including specifically relieving Mikawa as commander of the 8th Fleet, pursuant to contingency plans in the event of an Allied offensive in this region. Mikawa was the senior and most experienced flag officer present. And he had the most familiarity with the battle plan, since he himself had created it. It made sense.

At 3:30 pm, Admiral Mikawa got the intelligence information he had been seeking, a summary compiled from the reports of the 5th Air Attack Force's bombers, the scout planes launched that morning, and a later scout plane also launched to check the area to see what damage the air attacks had caused:

a. Enemy making landings on Guadalcanal air base; three fires on the airfield.
b. One fire in the area of the Tulagi seaplane base.
c. Three heavy cruisers, several destroyers, and about thirteen transports off Tulagi.
d. Several destroyers and twenty-seven transports off Guadalcanal air base.
e. From 1320 to 1440 there were sixty to seventy enemy planes over the anchored transports.
f. At about 15:30 no enemy planes were sighted over the anchorage.[37]

The 5th Air Attack Force would report that of these ships its attacks had sunk two cruisers, a destroyer, and six transports, and heavily damaged three cruisers and two destroyers.[38] The summary likely gave the admiral the cold comfort of vindication. This was no diversion, this was no raid. This was a full-scale invasion. Except where were the enemy carriers? Sixty enemy planes suggested multiple aircraft carriers. Where were they? The question – and the possibility of air attack on his ships as they made their way to and from Guadalcanal – weighed heavily on Admiral Mikawa's mind.

But those would have to be what are called "known unknowns." At 4:28 pm, the *Chokai*, now flying Admiral Mikawa's flag, steamed out of Simpson Harbor, with the *Tenryu*, *Yubari*, and *Yunagi*.[39] "It was a fine clear day, the sea like a mirror," Captain Ohmae would later write. "Our confidence of success in the coming night battle was manifest in the cheerful atmosphere on the bridge."[40] Shortly after 6:00 pm, the *Chokai* and her consorts made their rendezvous with the 6th Cruiser Division, whom Mikawa had fall in column behind the flagship. The *Yubari* moved to the starboard bow of *Chokai*, and the *Tenryu*, followed by the *Yunagi*, moved to the port bow to screen against submarines.

Not that they were especially effective. At 7:42 pm, when the Japanese formation was some 8 miles west of Cape St George, it literally ran over the old US submarine *S-38*. Having detected the Japanese ships at around 7:25, the submerged submarine tried to move into an attack position, but she ended up square in their path. Apparently without realizing it, the *Yubari* and *Tenryu* bracketed the *S-38* in between the two Japanese cruisers, *Tenryu* ahead and *Yubari* astern. Three minutes later came the heavy cruisers passing overhead, one so close that its wash caused the *S-38* to roll seven degrees. The nice fat Japanese targets were too close for torpedoes to arm. As soon as the ships had finished passing, the *S-38* turned to try to follow them, but they were moving at a "very high speed" – too fast for a submarine, and she lost track of them at around 8:10 pm.[41] She radioed a contact report to MacArthur's headquarters. Missing out on these large, valuable men-of-war was a disappointment to the *S-38*, but she would keep trying.

During the night, Mikawa had his force loop around the northern coast of Bougainville, the northern "plug" to "The Slot." He had to maintain a very careful balance. He needed more information on the makeup on the enemy force, so he wanted to be close enough at daybreak to be able to launch his floatplanes to reconnoiter the enemy dispositions off Guadalcanal and hopefully find those missing aircraft carriers, but not so close that his ships would attract the attention of said carriers or divulge his ultimate objective.

Accordingly, at about 6:25 am, the *Chokai*, *Aoba*, *Kako*, and *Kinugasa* each launched a floatplane; the *Furutaka* would have joined them but its plane developed engine trouble at the last minute.[42] The *Aoba*'s was to search the Guadalcanal area; the others headed east to try to find the elusive enemy carriers.

With the scout planes launched, Admiral Mikawa had his ships disperse and change course periodically in order to launch the remaining floatplanes on antisubmarine patrols and deceive Allied scout planes as to his intentions.

At 10:20 am a Royal Australian Air Force Lockheed Hudson bomber was sighted circling high overhead. In an attempt to throw the Hudson off his intentions, Mikawa had his ships change course toward Rabaul. The Hudson remained over the cruisers for 16 minutes before heading back to its base at Milne Bay. The *Chokai* intercepted the contact report from the Hudson: "Three cruisers, three destroyers, and two seaplane tenders or gunboats, course 120 degrees True, speed 15."[43] During this time, the *Kako* was informed, apparently by the *Aoba*'s floatplane, that another Hudson was inbound.[44] Mikawa was now convinced he was being tailed. The *Chokai* and *Kinugasa* recovered their floatplanes, which had found nothing, by 11:00 am, when that second Hudson finally appeared. Mikawa thought this was the same Hudson that had circled them earlier, while Admiral Matsuyama thought it was actually a B-25 Mitchell. All the same the Hudson came in low from the northwest trying to get a close look at the mysterious ships, but a few shots from the *Chokai*'s forward main battery were impressive enough to drive it away. Mikawa was certain his position had been reported and the enemy now knew where he was. He was half right.

Though the *Kako*'s floatplane, an Aichi E13A1, had been shot down by Lieutenant Commander Snowden, at around noon the *Aoba*'s floatplane returned and reported "one battleship, one auxiliary carrier, four cruisers, seven destroyers and 15 transports" off Lunga Point, Guadalcanal, and two heavy cruisers, 12 destroyers, and three transports off Tulagi.[45] This was a troubling report for Admiral Mikawa. The biggest threat to his ships were the enemy carriers, and they were still nowhere to be found. Moreover, there were more enemy ships than the 5th Air Attack Force's report of damage inflicted during the previous day's air attacks had led him to believe there would be.[46] But the 5th's damage assessment could not have been wrong. Could it?

Nevertheless, the report from the *Aoba*'s scout did give Admiral Mikawa some encouragement. The Allied naval power in the Guadalcanal area exceeded his own, true, and could overwhelm him if massed against him. However, it was divided between Guadalcanal and Tulagi. And Mikawa could overwhelm each group before the other could come to its aid. The admiral discussed the latest information, such as it was, with his staff over lunch. Though the enemy carriers still had not been found, if they were not within 100 miles or so of Guadalcanal, he would not have to worry about air attack until the next morning – that is, unless he got too close to the island in the afternoon and thus exposed his force to air attack from the carriers. He expected the 5th Air Attack Force to attack the enemy around Guadalcanal and inflict serious losses – again – of which he would be informed in the late afternoon. So at 1:00 pm the admiral made the final decision to go forward with the mission. Mikawa re-formed his scattered ships, ordered speed set at 24 knots, and headed for the Bougainville Strait and the New Georgia Sound. It wasn't exactly crossing the Rubicon, but the admiral felt no hesitation.

"The sea was dead calm, and visibility was, if anything, too good," Captain Ohmae would later say.[47] Perfect weather, one might say, for bombing, which the Japanese feared was coming when, about 45 minutes after lunch, the lookouts in the Japanese force sighted aircraft approaching from the southeast. There were sighs of relief when they turned out to be Japanese bombers of the 5th Air Attack Force returning to Vunakanau. But the Mitsubishi G4Ms were hardly an impressive sight, straggling in twos and threes. They must have been in a hell of a fight over Guadalcanal, chewed up, presumably, by US carrier fighters. Admiral Mikawa went to the surprising length of breaking radio silence to ask the 5th Air Attack Force if they had any information on those carriers; he never received their negative reply.[48]

The admiral probably never appreciated the irony of their situation, indeed of his situation. Not even six months earlier, it was the Allies who were slapping together a force of warships who had never worked together to desperately strike at enemy transports in the Java Sea. Now it was the Japanese. Then it had been the Allies sailing into waters they occupied but did not fully understand. Now it was the Japanese. Then it was the Allies who had left their base that was suffering from repeated air attacks – Soerabaja – to go into a battle in which they never had a clear idea what they were facing. Now it was the Japanese. It had been the Allies who were in constant fear of daylight, and feared the sight of even one enemy plane and what it could and almost always did portend. Now it was the Japanese. Admiral Mikawa was not one of the arrogant admirals whose insidious influence had largely caused the Japanese defeat at Midway, but he was still paying the price. How times had changed. How Midway had changed everything.

At around 4:00 pm, the scratch Japanese force passed through the Bougainville Strait, separating Bougainville Island from Choiseul to the southeast, and entered the New Georgia Sound – "The Slot." Battlefield commanders are always desperate for information, and Mikawa was no different. Still having heard nothing from the 5th Air Attack Force in Rabaul as to the results of their attacks, Admiral Mikawa ordered the *Aoba* to again launch her floatplane to scout the Tulagi-Guadalcanal area once more, passing between Choiseul and Vella Lavella first. He wanted information in his hands in time for the plane to return to the *Aoba* before sunset. If the aircraft could not return to the *Aoba* before sunset, it was to head to Shortland.[49]

Preparations for the coming attack began in earnest at 4:40 pm, when Admiral Mikawa signaled his orders for the conduct of the battle. Except for the four heavy cruisers of the 6th Cruiser Division, none of these ships had worked together or maneuvered together before. The battle plan had to be kept simple. The force would operate in a column – that is, single file: *Chokai*, followed by the 6th Cruiser Division, which in practice would be the *Aoba*, *Kako*, *Kinugasa*, and *Furutaka*; then the *Tenryu*, *Yubari*, and

Yunagi – arranged with the strongest ships in front and the weakest in back. "We will penetrate south of Savo Island and torpedo the enemy main force at Guadalcanal. Then we will move toward the forward area at Tulagi and strike with torpedoes and gunfire, after which we will withdraw to the north of Savo Island."[50] So, it would be a counterclockwise sweep around Savo Island. Speed would be 24 knots. So the Japanese ships could recognize each other, long white sleeves were to be flown from the signal yards on each side of each ship's bridge.[51] Mikawa's operations officer Captain Ohmae would later write, "While drafting this order, I had the firm conviction we would be successful."[52] Admiral Goto was of the opinion that "(Mikawa's) decision to attack at night and his direction of the operation offered an opportunity of great success."[53]

The confidence continued to build when at 4:54 pm the force turned to the southeast to make the dash to Guadalcanal through The Slot, starting between Santa Isabel and New Georgia Islands, course 120 degrees True, speed 24 knots.[54] Yet while the confidence built, the tension built as well, as about 20 minutes later they sighted a mast off the starboard bow. An unexpected enemy ship? No, the mast turned out to belong to the seaplane tender *Akitsushima*, now on her way to set up a seaplane base at nearby Gizo Island after her errand of mercy trying to fish out the downed Val pilots the previous day.[55] There were sighs of relief; they had not expected enemy ships. Not out here, not yet. But they had expected enemy aircraft – more scout planes, carrier-based dive bombers and torpedo planes. According to Captain Ohmae, "The very existence of the enemy flattops in the area was a major concern to Admiral Mikawa, and this dominated our later tactical concepts."[57] And the Japanese radio operators had been picking up radio chatter from the American carrier planes, referring to their carriers with code names like "Green Base" and "Red Base." Yet since those two Australian Hudsons that morning the Japanese had seen no enemy planes. All afternoon, not one, not even a scout plane. Strange.

Mikawa was not complaining, though, and as the sun dipped lower and lower in the sky, setting at 6:16, the possibility of an attack from the American carriers diminished and the spirits and confidence of the officers and sailors continued to rise. That confidence would be further energized by Mikawa's inspirational speech – drafted by Captain Ohmae – to his men. The *Chokai*'s Aldis lamp flashed his message at 6:40 pm to each of the ships: "In the finest tradition of the Imperial Navy we shall engage the enemy in night battle. Every man is expected to do his best."[58]

With that, pursuant to Admiral Mikawa's order, each ship disposed of everything it had above the waterline that was flammable. It may seem like a little thing, but Mikawa was taking no chances. Fire has been the biggest dread of sailors since the beginning of sail; the replacement of flammable wood by steel in most ships had merely changed the dimension of that dread. Steel would not burn or melt easily, but it does not breathe, either, and a fire below decks could turn a ship's interior into a relative smoke-filled pressure cooker that would hamper firefighting efforts. Moreover, a fire could give away the ship's position to the enemy – a cloud of smoke visible over the horizon by day, a glowing beacon by night. So anything and everything that could burn – light oil, loose wood, paint, depth charges, munitions for the floatplanes, anything – was either stowed below decks or jettisoned over the side. The floatplanes themselves were fire risks, as well, but the admiral had special plans for them.

At 9:00 pm, while Admiral Mikawa and his staff were gathered in the flag plot preparing for battle, they finally received the report from the 5th Air Attack Force as to the damage caused by its attacks on the Allied ships off Guadalcanal. The flotilla claimed it had sunk two heavy cruisers, one "large" cruiser, two destroyers, and nine transports, and left two heavy cruisers and one transport burning.[59] The report buoyed Mikawa's spirits and gave him more confidence in the coming clash; these Japanese airmen had just made his job easier by damaging the enemy so badly.

The report was wrong, of course. Badly wrong.[60] It was around this time – one can argue that it was this very battle – that saw the start of the distinctively Japanese habit of reporting combat damage inflicted on the enemy that was inversely proportional to the damage actually inflicted. The Naval War College would later say the Japanese had "a tendency, which became more pronounced throughout the war, to make exaggerated claims concerning enemy damage without first making every effort to verify the truth."[61] "Japanese claims seem almost to have been almost deliberately inversely related to reality," says naval historian H. P. Willmott. "What seems truly extraordinary about the Japanese situation … is what seems to be the usually uncritical acceptance of the most preposterous of claims on the part of higher authority."[62] Though Mikawa and his staff seem to have been on the verge of discounting the 5th Air Attack Force's battle damage assessments of the previous day, that apparently did not lead them to question the 5th's assessments on this day. Not that it would matter.

For the admiral was once again leaving as little as he could to chance and continuing what might be called battlespace preparation. Between 11:00 and 11:13, the *Chokai*, *Aoba*, and *Kako* each launched a floatplane. The Imperial Japanese Navy had a peculiar preoccupation with seaplanes, both floatplanes and flying boats. The navy was extremely aggressive with seaplanes, far more so than its American counterpart, and seemed to be of the opinion that there was no problem that could not be solved by adding more seaplanes.

For now, however, in launching their floatplanes for a night battle the Japanese were using a unique tactic that the Allies would never counter, let alone match. And on this night, it would be especially dangerous. The ships could not stop to lower the floatplanes into the sea for a water takeoff, so the aircraft had to be shot off the catapult. Not like a catapult on today's aircraft carriers, which act somewhat like a slingshot. A cruiser catapult was more like a cannon, with an explosive charge used to basically shoot the floatplane off the rail – of a moving ship – into the air. At night. The aircrews – nine men, led by First Lieutenant Kiyose Fumio – had never done this at night before, but remarkably they were able to do so without incident.

Yet the dangers did not end there. The mission of these three floatplanes on this night was threefold. First, they were to drop navigational markers, in the form of floatlights or flares that burned on the water, to help guide the Japanese ships into the battle area.

Second, they were to scout and report on the dispositions of the Allied ships. Third, they were to drop flares to illuminate and preferably backlight the enemy ships when the Japanese force was some 20 miles from the enemy. The problem here was that once the mission was complete, the floatplanes could not be recovered; Admiral Mikawa's cruisers would be speeding as fast as possible to get as far away from the as-yet-unsighted American aircraft carriers as they could, so they could not stop to pick up the floatplanes. They would have to somehow make their way back to the Japanese base in the Shortlands off Bougainville in the dark. In other words, for these nine men this was quite possibly a one-way mission to drop flares.[63]

What had been a sunny day had, the closer one got to Guadalcanal, devolved into a moonless, completely overcast night. It was hot, humid, sticky, and oppressive. Between the lack of a moon, the clouds now blanketing the area blocking all starlight, and the absence of light from the Solomons, underdeveloped as they were, the darkness was beyond the extreme version often found at sea. It would swallow anything that sailed into it. Or at least seem to do so to the untrained eye. But the Japanese eyes on duty at night were not untrained. Quite the opposite, in fact.

Part of the strategic emphasis of the Imperial Japanese Navy was on night fighting, in order to, in their minds, even the odds against a United States that had its naval superiority written into law ever since the Washington Naval Treaty. Part of that night-fighting ability was detecting the enemy before the enemy detected the Japanese. The Japanese had no radar at this time, so they depended on the eyes of the lookouts stationed on their ships. The lookouts were specifically chosen for their excellent eyesight. They were thoroughly trained in ship recognition in low-light conditions. And they had the excellent Japanese optics in the form of oversize binoculars with strong magnification and even polarized lenses to filter out haze. In practice, at least at this point in the Pacific War, Japanese nighttime eyes often outperformed American radar.

As excellent and unparalleled as these lookouts were, Admiral Mikawa did not want to depend exclusively on them. Which is why he had sent up his floatplanes to drop flares, to make the lookouts' job easier.

And the lookouts in the scratch Japanese force started spotting those flares. At 11:35 pm, the *Tenryu* sighted a floatlight dropped by one of the floatplanes. This flare was dropped to burn on the water as a navigational aid, to mark 30 miles from Cape Esperance on Guadalcanal on a bearing of 140 degrees True. It was hoped this floatlight would be far enough out to escape Allied detection.[64] At midnight, the crews went to battle stations. The ships moved from their cruising formation into the battle formation as Admiral Mikawa had ordered – a single column, led by the flagship *Chokai*, followed by the *Aoba*, *Kako*, *Kinugasa*, *Furutaka*, *Tenryu*, *Yubari*, and *Yunagi*, in that order. Increasing speed to 28 knots, they would go in by the south entrance to the sound, that is, south of Savo Island.

However, the closer they got to this tiny, volcanic island, the visibility had, if anything, gotten worse, with squalls now popping up. Squalls had a habit of appearing around Savo

Island, especially to its south and east, late at night. As the squalls drifted to the southeast, they would usually break up. But not tonight.

Admiral Mikawa had the *Chokai* flash two last messages to his ships at 12:25 am. The first was relaying a report from one of his floatplanes: "Three heavy cruisers south of Savo Island, course 290 degrees true, speed 18 knots."[65] Now they had some idea of what to expect in this imminent battle south of Savo Island. Mikawa indeed had the local superiority he had wanted. He also signaled, "Prepare to fire torpedoes." Launching torpedoes was the preferred Japanese method for launching a nighttime attack. Torpedoes don't reveal positions in the dark, and have a much longer range than guns. At least the Japanese Type 93 torpedo did.

At 12:30, the floatplanes reported about 20 transports in the anchorage and three or four cruisers at the eastern end of the channel. The odd and encouraging part of the report was that the transports were using their lights to illuminate the offloading of cargo.[66] They would not be using their lights if they were expecting combat. Somehow, Admiral Mikawa's surprise had been preserved.

Soon the lookouts were seeing a different kind of flares in the dark – actual fires – in the direction of Tulagi. And they saw a reflection of fire in the clouds overhead, one that didn't quite fit the fires they were seeing.[67] Tiny, volcanic, Savo Island finally came into view at 12:40 am. The tension went up yet another notch …

"Ship approaching, thirty degrees starboard!"[68]

The loud call came from a lookout on the *Chokai* at 12:43 am. The *Aoba*, directly astern of the flagship, spotted the unknown vessel a minute later. The ship was on a bearing of 162 degrees True, 10,900 yards away.[69] In other words, the Japanese lookouts had spotted a ship over 5 miles away on an overcast night with intermittent squalls and no moon. The training of the lookouts was paying off; their work here was nothing short of incredible.

"On the flagship bridge all breathing seemed to stop while we waited identification of this sighting," Captain Ohmae would later write.[70] They were in territory where no Japanese ships were known to be operating, but where enemy ships were known to be present in large numbers. It was really only a question of what type of ship it was.

It was, as the Naval War College put it, "a ship resembling a destroyer."[71] And it was on a northeasterly course to cross the path of Admiral Mikawa's ships. Almost a collision course, even. The admiral was caught somewhat off guard. His scouts had not indicated an enemy destroyer this far out.

But here it was. After all this, this whirlwind of events, it all came down to this one destroyer. Admiral Mikawa stood on the bridge watching the destroyer's movements with a mixture of trepidation and no small measure of amazement. The enemy ship was about to cross his path. Almost collide with his ship. Hadn't it seen him?

"Stand by for action," radioed the *Chokai*. The action would come from the Japanese only on the admiral's order to open fire. Every gun was trained on the lone destroyer; the *Tenryu* had even started pulling out of the column to head toward her. Would he give the order?

The admiral was decisive. "Left rudder. Slow to 22 knots." Blow the surprise? For a mere *destroyer*? Admiral Mikawa thought not. He turned away from the destroyer, course 100 degrees True, signaled "Enter by the north entrance" and slowed down, hoping to reduce the wakes of his ships. For not only were they kicking up a lot of water, as ships tend to do, the wakes they were leaving were almost glowing, a luminescence caused by disturbing the *noctiluca scintillans*, a microorganism indigenous to South Pacific waters. The bioluminescence earned the species the nickname "Sea Sparkle." The admiral did not want anything sparkling about his ships this night.

If the destroyer gave any indication of seeing them, the guns of the Japanese cruisers, now trained on her, would open fire. So many guns firing at one little destroyer at a range that kept decreasing would not end well for the destroyer. There was complete silence on the *Chokai*'s bridge. The lone destroyer got closer and closer. The range was now down to less than a mile; the Japanese could look down on her, even see crewmen walking around on her deck.

Captain Ohmae, like most of the Japanese watching, was fascinated by the encounter:

> From her deliberate, unconcerned progress, it was plain that she was unaware of us – or of being watched – and of the fact that every gun in our force was trained directly on her. Seconds strained while we waited for the inevitable moment when she must sight us – and then the enemy destroyer reversed course![72]

She reversed course and sailed away.

"With no change in speed she made a starboard turn and proceeded in the direction from which she had come, totally unaware of our approach," according to Captain Ohmae.

The Japanese lookouts were shocked. Admiral Mikawa was incredulous. *How could the enemy miss us?*

But miss them she did. The destroyer, the USS *Blue*, went back to her assigned patrol course, heading back toward the southwest, "blind as a sleepwalker," according to one historian.[73]

"Ship sighted, twenty degrees port!" came the call from the *Chokai*'s lookouts, almost simultaneous with the *Blue*'s turnabout. It was … another destroyer? That's what the Japanese believed. It was the *Ralph Talbot*. The ship was steaming away from them too.[74]

"Right rudder. Steer course 150 degrees," said Admiral Mikawa.[75] The *Chokai* signaled "Enter from south passage."[76] The *Blue* and *Ralph Talbot* had not coordinated their patrol routes, so both were heading away from The Slot, the main and most obvious avenue for a Japanese approach from Rabaul to Guadalcanal, at the same time. There was a gap some 9 miles wide.[77] Not very wide, by naval standards, but enough.

At 26 knots, the deadly Japanese squadron steamed coolly, quietly, and confidently between the two destroyers whose job was to warn of approaching enemy ships. These destroyers were not the ships they were looking for; there was far bigger game ahead.

Just how and why the *Ralph Talbot* and, especially, the *Blue* missed the approach of the Japanese has never been conclusively determined. The two destroyers employed two methods for detection of enemy ships – radar and lookouts. On this night, both failed.

Radar was still a relatively new invention at this time. When people think of radar today, they think of what they see on television when a storm is coming: the meteorologist refers to a map showing the storms, with a line originating at the center of the map that rotates – the line representing the sweep of the radar, and the origination point the radar antenna. The sweep of the line refreshes the echo of the storms, so as a storm moves the radar can track that movement. This type of display is called a plan position indicator (PPI), and is the most common type of radar display in use today. While the electronics and physical principles involved can be complicated, the display is relatively easy to understand.

That is not what the *Blue* or *Ralph Talbot* had. The type of radar the destroyers had was called SC radar. It was a search radar used for detection of ships and aircraft, but it was in detecting the latter that it was far more effective. The display for this SC radar is called an A-scope, which looks less like the PPI with its top down view than an EKG. The scope shows a line across the screen, usually with tiny lines emanating from it caused by the interference of the receiver itself, and by their appearance earned the nickname "grass." Radar returns were represented by vertical lines emanating from this line. Without going into detail, the vertical line on an SC radar display would indicate that *something* was out there and how far out there that something was, but only that. That vertical line could represent a plane or a ship – or an island. With so many islands in the Solomons, it would be easy for inexperienced radar operators to mistake the line actually representing a ship as being from an island. Or, the line from the ship could be lost in the bigger line from a nearby island. It was for this reason that the SC radar was better at detecting incoming aircraft than it was incoming ships. Indeed, the *Blue*'s radar had earlier that night detected the unknown aircraft reported by the *Ralph Talbot*. But on this night when surface ships were about, as the Naval War College put it, "Suffice it to say that the *Blue*'s radar was highly ineffective."[78]

More troubling in many respects is the failure of the *Blue*'s lookouts. Naval historian Samuel Eliot Morison said the main problem with the lookouts was that they were looking in every direction but astern, a common enough issue.[79] It appears, however, that the lookouts on the *Blue* were not looking in every direction but astern; rather, they were all focused on Cape Esperance on Guadalcanal, trying to make sure the navigation was correct so the *Blue* could maintain the course that gave her the best chance of spotting incoming attackers.[80] How all the lookouts watching Cape Esperance and none looking at the single most obvious avenue of Japanese approach – The Slot – gave the *Blue* the best chance of spotting incoming attackers has never been explained.

Naval historians Bruce Loxton, who served on the *Canberra*, and Chris Coulthard-Clark, in their extensive analysis of the engagement, probably put it best:

> … [N]o one on watch in *Blue* saw, at a range of about a mile, a column of eight ships, five of which were about 10,000 tons, moving across the line of sight at high speed, and this on a night when *Chokai*'s lookouts could see a single destroyer, proceeding at 12 knots, at eight miles… *Blue*'s failure to see the Japanese is inexplicable and inexcusable.[81]

"Inexplicable" is also the description used by Australian Rear Admiral Galfrey George Ormond Gatacre, then a commander serving as Admiral Crutchley's operations officer, who acidly added:

> The Japanese had sighted our destroyers at long range, but to pass a few hundred yards from one of them without being seen, can not be credited to Japanese night battle practice and night lookout training; they needed to collide with *Blue*, that night, to make their presence known![82]

In fairness to the lookouts on the *Blue*, one must call attention to the words of Captain Stephen Roskill, naval historian and skipper of the Royal New Zealand Navy's light cruiser *Leander* (which would have its own odd role of sorts in the events of this night) which would take part in the fighting in the Solomons in 1943:

> The reader who feels strongly about the unreadiness of the ships, the failure of communications and the poor lookout maintained, should himself experience the strain of trying to remain alert for several consecutive nights after long and anxious days in the deadening and exhausting heat of the Solomon Islands' climate.[83]

It is a fair point and one that should always be kept in mind here. But war is not fair and cares little for intentions. The Japanese had a history of not being fair in war – especially the current one – and Admiral Mikawa, honorable officer though he may have been, had no intention of being so tonight.

So as they passed through the 9-mile gap, Admiral Mikawa, not quite believing what was happening, turned to the *Chokai*'s skipper, Captain Hayakawa Mikio, and shrugged, "The Americans must be asleep."[84]

In ancient Rome, when a legion set up camp for the night, a small group of soldiers would have the duty of providing a night watch for the camp. Tired after a hard day of martial duties, these unfortunate legionaries still had to stay awake and keep their eyes open for the approach of an enemy army or spy. The punishment for falling asleep on night watch duty was death.

The Allies were about to find out why.

Imagine driving a semi-tractor trailer rig to meet a friend in a darkened parking lot full of semi-tractor trailer rigs with their lights off. This was Admiral Crutchley in the *Australia* trying to find Admiral Turner in the *McCawley*. He had been maneuvering for almost two hours hoping to find the *McCawley* without running into any of the thin-skinned transports in the dark. As a result Crutchley did not arrive on the *McCawley* until about 10:30 pm.

Because General Vandegrift had not yet arrived, Turner and Crutchley discussed the very delayed report from the Hudson that morning of three cruisers, three destroyers and two "seaplane tenders or gunboats." Delayed by, as it turned out, simple lethargy among Allied communications personnel still getting used to the concept of messages being time-sensitive.[85] Both agreed that the force could arrive off Guadalcanal that night, but those "seaplane tenders" also suggested that the Japanese would set up a seaplane base, probably near Rekata Bay, and attack with seaplanes the next morning. The idea that the report may have been wrong in identifying the ship types doesn't seem to have occurred to anyone. Besides, there had been no report from the search Turner had ordered to cover the Slot that morning. It must not have found anything, Turner thought, or, more accurately, assumed. Turner had no way of knowing the supplemental search had, for reasons that have never been fully established, never been carried out.

General Vandegrift finally arrived around 11:15 pm. As exhausted as he was by his duties on Guadalcanal, he thought the admirals "looked ready to pass out."[86] But Admiral Turner made sure everyone had ample supplies of coffee and the meeting got under way.

Turner showed General Vandegrift Admiral Fletcher's message about withdrawing the carriers. The Marine general snarled that Fletcher was "running away twelve hours earlier than he had already threatened."[87] He was preaching to the choir, but Turner felt his hands were tied. It was known that Japanese air reinforcements were headed into the Rabaul air complex. The report of those "seaplane tenders" suggested an air attack coming in the morning. And now their air cover was being pulled. The only option was to withdraw the transports.

Unfortunately, Admiral Turner had badly underestimated the time it would take to unload the transports. Everyone had. Turner asked Vandegrift about maximizing the little time they had left to unload the most badly needed supplies on Guadalcanal. The general noted that the 1st Marine Division would face shortages of food, ammunition and other essentials. Nevertheless, he said, "We are in fair shape on Guadalcanal."[88]

On Tulagi, however, the combat had delayed offloading, and Vandegrift wanted to check its status. Professorially peering over his glasses, Turner replied, "I thought you would want that. I have a minesweeper standing by to take you over there."

Admiral Crutchley offered to have his launch drop the general off at the minesweeper on his way back to the *Australia*. Vandegrift declined, but Crutchley insisted, "Your mission is much more important than mine."[89]

They boarded Admiral Crutchley's launch at around midnight, then struggled through a torrential downpour until they could find the minesweeper. As the general departed, the admiral shook his hand. Frustrated with the entire situation, caught in the middle, the veteran Crutchley empathized with the plight of the Marines and how much they needed the Navy right now, but closed with a word of understanding for his superior: "I don't know that I can blame Turner for what he's doing."[90]

It was 1:30 am when Crutchley returned to the *Australia*. By his calculations, any Japanese surface attack would have to take place by 2:00 am in order to get back within the range of air cover from Rabaul before US carrier planes could strike. It was only theoretical inasmuch as Admiral Fletcher was having the US carriers bravely run away, but the Japanese did not know that.

It would be nearly 3:00 am before the *Australia* could rejoin the *Chicago* and the *Canberra* in the southern group. The flagship would have to maneuver to take the head of the column – in restricted waters, without radar or voice radio, with visibility reduced by the night's rainstorms and the lack of a moon.[91]

Or he could avoid all those risks and keep the *Australia* with the transports protected by the antisubmarine screen until dawn, when he could rejoin the southern force. The admiral chose the latter option.

After all, that 2:00 am was only a half-hour away. And there was no indication the Japanese were coming tonight.

In a silent, ghostly procession, the *Chokai* led a gaggle of warships into the swallowing darkness west of Savo Island – unseen, unexpected.

Starting at 1:12 am, Admiral Mikawa had the Japanese column loop to the south of Savo, coming within some 1,200 yards of the shore.[92] He continued the loop until 1:24 am, when the *Chokai* extended the loop further to the southeast to avoid a large mass of clouds and rain that covered the southern part of the island and extended several miles to the south. If Mikawa had been hoping the island and the clouds would help camouflage his ships, he was to be rewarded far more than he had any reason to expect.

At around this time, the Japanese finally saw the cause of the mysterious orange glow reflected off the clouds – the American transport *George F. Elliott*, still burning, helping the Japanese by acting as a beacon to the anchorage, illuminating the Allied ships, and fouling the night vision of the already-tired Allied lookouts.

The floatplane pilots were now chomping at the bit to begin dropping their flares but Mikawa, not quite ready, told them to hold off.[93] At 1:26 the admiral signaled to his ships, "Proceed independently."[94] In theory, this meant that the *Chokai*, the 6th Cruiser Division, the 18th Cruiser Division, and the *Yunagi* would each determine its own targets. Six minutes later, Mikawa had the column turn to port to course 95 degrees True for the dash into the Allied anchorage off Guadalcanal. He signaled, "All ships attack."[95]

"Cruiser, seven degrees to port!"[96]

As close as Mikawa had gotten to Savo Island, somehow this ship had managed to get even closer, in between the island and the Japanese. Some 3,000 yards away from *Chokai*, it was moving very slowly to the west. The lookouts thought it was an *Achilles*-class light cruiser – the HMNZS *Leander*, maybe? Captain Ohmae thought it too small for a cruiser, so it must be a destroyer.[97]

Which it in fact was – the USS *Jarvis*, crawling across this battlefield-to-be, the exact reason for her presence a mystery to everyone, including her, that will never be solved. She wasn't supposed to be there; with her radio suite out, Admiral Turner had given an order for her executive officer to carry to her skipper, Lieutenant Commander Graham, to head for Efate via the eastern channel, but to wait for the destroyer minesweeper *Hovey* to escort her before doing so. The order was also flashed to her by an Aldis lamp. But she never acknowledged the order; she may have never received it, exactly why a mystery. She also did not follow standard protocol in requesting permission to leave.

So it seems that, without telling anyone, around midnight the *Jarvis* started toward Sydney, Australia, where the destroyer tender *Dobbin* could help with her repairs, by creeping through the western channel, taking the same route she had taken to get to Guadalcanal in the first place – and blundering into the Japanese intruders.

To Mikawa, the *Jarvis* appeared to be in a good position to launch torpedoes, but with a combination of incredible nerve and even more incredible luck, he held fire as the destroyer moved like some black phantom in the opposite direction along the entire 5-mile-long Japanese column, at one point coming within 1,100 yards of the *Tenryu*.[98] The *Jarvis* gave no indication of having seen them, and had no crew visible on her deck. Both whether she saw them and what she could have done if she had are open to question: she was suffering severe structural issues with a large torpedo hole in her side that limited her speed to 7 knots or so; her radio was out; and she had jettisoned her torpedoes and other top-side nonessentials to save on weight and thus improve her battered buoyancy, which left many of her weapons offline. And she was alongside an enemy column of seven cruisers and a destroyer.

"Three cruisers, nine degrees to starboard, moving to the right!"[99]

The call came from the *Chokai*'s lookouts at 1:36 am, the range about 12,500 yards on a bearing of 120 degrees True.[100] They were the *Canberra* and *Chicago*, with the destroyers *Patterson* and *Bagley* screening, almost at the western end of their patrol line. Admiral Mikawa ordered a course change toward them. A minute later, another group of cruisers was sighted to the north, bearing 300 degrees, range 18,000 yards.

So the Allies were indeed divided into two groups. And Admiral Mikawa had superiority over each of them; he needed to eliminate each quickly before they could combine. And he had the element of surprise. Just as he had hoped.

The *Canberra* and *Chicago* were headed almost directly toward the Japanese ships, presenting a narrow bow profile that would be difficult for torpedoes to hit. Unless the Allied cruisers changed course.

Captain Hayakawa boomed the order: "Torpedoes fire to starboard – fire!" It would take the torpedoes six minutes to reach their targets.

Overhead, Lieutenant Kiyose was finally given permission to begin dropping the flares.[101]

On a night when every American and Australian around Guadalcanal and Tulagi desperately wanted even a little rest and relaxation, the skipper of the US destroyer *Patterson*, Commander Frank Walker, allowed no such thing. He had seen the Hudson's sighting report of "three cruisers, three destroyers, and two seaplane tenders or gunboats" and had calculated that whatever Japanese force this described could arrive off Savo tonight. What if the Hudson's description of the ships was wrong? What if those ships were all cruisers? Walker stayed on the bridge and kept his torpedo tubes loaded and ready for firing.

Supposedly, Commander Walker was not the only one expecting a battle that night. According to Jack Coombe:

> Everyone had been expecting an attack that night because of reports of heavy Japanese ship movements at Rabaul, but no one knew the direction from which it would come. Most concluded it would come from the north, which offered the best approach with possible reinforcements from Truk.[102]

But expecting and prepared are not the same. Commander Walker and his crew were prepared.

On the *Patterson*'s starboard quarter, Captain Getting of the *Canberra*, like Commander Walker, had concluded with his staff that the Japanese ships reported by the Hudson could reach Savo that night. Unlike Walker, however, Getting had taken the report at face value and assumed it was correct.[103] Those two seaplane tenders meant he could expect another air attack in the morning. He had better get some long overdue sleep, which he was getting in a chair in his sea cabin when he was summoned to the bridge, one deck above. At 1:43 am, the senior officer on watch, Lieutenant Commander E. J. Wight, had detected an explosion off the starboard bow, almost due north. Almost immediately thereafter, the port lookout had reported a ship dead ahead. But against the dark amorphous mass of the squall south of Savo, no one else could see it.[104]

Except for a lookout on the *Patterson*. He saw a strange black shape almost dead ahead, distance about 5,000 yards. Commander Walker immediately ordered battle stations and, speeding up to 20 knots, ordered a hard port turn to unmask the starboard torpedo tubes for a launch at the unidentified shape, actually the *Furutaka*, fifth in the Japanese column. Critically, he ordered a message to be broadcast by radio and by Aldis lamp: "Warning! Warning! Strange ships entering harbor!"[105]

As the *Patterson* swung to port, her guns opened up on the *Furutaka* and she quickly reached a favorable torpedo launch position. But the torpedo officer apparently could not hear Commander Walker's order to launch torpedoes over the roar of the guns, and the destroyer's torpedoes never left their tubes.[106] Not so the *Furutaka*. She launched one torpedo from her four starboard tubes at the *Patterson*. The destroyer did not even see the torpedo until it had sped by harmlessly. Curiously, the *Patterson* could not see her companion destroyer *Bagley*, but she did see two more Japanese cruisers, *Tenryu* and *Yubari*, enter the fray. She broadcast a second warning by voice radio: "All ships. Warning! Warning! Three enemy ships inside Savo Island."[107]

Now, over the defenseless, anchored transports near Lunga Point Lieutenant Kiyose's flares started to appear, five of them, attached to tiny parachutes, about a mile between each. Intense light providing brilliant illumination – and perfectly backlighting the *Canberra* and *Chicago*.[108] On the former, while Captain Getting was on his way to the bridge, Lieutenant Commander Wight spotted wakes from three ships off the starboard bow, then saw the *Patterson* flash her warning message. The cruiser went to battle stations.[109] Wight shouted, "Alarm starboard; load, load, load!" for the 8-inch guns, and ordered a port turn to unmask the rear turrets and thus allow all the guns to fire at the intruders.[110] But the skipper had other ideas.

Captain Getting arrived to see torpedoes passing down each side of the ship; they were from the *Chokai*, the premature explosion of the fourth had been seen from the bridge. With her target now nicely silhouetted, the *Chokai* opened fire with her 8-inch main armament, the other Japanese cruisers following the lead of the flagship. Getting ordered, "Hard to starboard" and "Full ahead!" He was more concerned about keeping a blocking position between the Japanese and the transports he was supposed to be protecting. The *Canberra* began picking up speed in her turn to starboard, toward her own screening destroyer *Bagley*. In theory, anyway; curiously, no one could see the *Bagley*.

While switching to a combat footing was happening smoothly if not totally effectively on the *Patterson* and *Canberra*, it seems that *something* was happening on the *Bagley*, but precisely what was never recorded. What is known for certain is that upon sighting the Japanese, the *Bagley* increased speed to 25 knots and made a sharp turn to port, toward the *Canberra*, apparently passing her to starboard. The turn was ostensibly to unmask the starboard torpedo tubes for firing at the approaching enemy, but the starboard tubes were not fired at this time, for reasons that remain disputed. The *Bagley*'s skipper, Lieutenant Commander George A. Sinclair, said there was no time to insert the firing primers that ignited the explosive charges that launched the torpedoes.[111] But Torpedoman 3rd Class Eugene McClarty would later say the primers were always in place whenever the destroyer was at sea; rather, he said that the *Bagley* was turning too fast to be able to aim the tubes properly.[112]

Mistakes in handling a ship at the beginning of combat are hardly unusual – the *Canberra* already had made one this night – but the curiosities do not end there. Lieutenant Commander Sinclair, "apparently a highly nervous man," was an engineer by training, inexperienced at ship-handling and was at best uncomfortable doing so.[113] In a command arrangement that might most politely be described as unusual, it was "normal" on the *Bagley* for Sinclair to hand over control of the destroyer to his executive officer Lieutenant Commander Thomas E. Chambers in "awkward" situations. Presumably, combat would qualify as just that.

Afterwards there was talk on the *Bagley* that Sinclair had panicked and thrown the destroyer into the hard port turn away from the Japanese column. At some point, Lieutenant Commander Chambers took command, possibly forcibly, from Sinclair.[114]

The *Bagley*'s sharp port turn was steadied on a northeasterly course, and the port torpedo tubes were brought to bear on the Japanese. The situation was critical as the *Bagley*'s lookouts could see the Japanese salvoes starting to find the range on the *Canberra*. At 1:49, the Number 2 torpedo mount launched four torpedoes toward the northwest at what she identified as two *Tenryu*-class light cruisers and two *Ashigara*-class heavy cruisers. But while the torpedoes were launching, the Japanese ships seemed to disappear.[115] The black background of Savo Island and the ephemeral murk of the squall were posing difficulties for the Allied lookouts. The sound gear reported an explosion at the time their torpedoes should have hit their targets. The *Bagley* couldn't see what her torpedoes had hit, but the explosion was "in [the] enemy area," as Lieutenant Commander Sinclair put it, so it had to be something Japanese.[116] Right?

Like a well-oiled machine, the *Canberra* was swinging into action both figuratively and literally. Captain Getting ordered a report of the sighting of the three cruisers to be signaled to *Chicago*. Her four turrets were manned, loaded, and ready, as were her torpedo tubes. She continued her starboard turn, essential for blocking the route to the transports, but also throwing off the firing solutions for her own guns and torpedo tubes. She was still silhouetted by the flares and the burning *George F. Elliott* and the Japanese guns were starting to find the range, but now the Japanese cruisers were themselves coming into the light provided by those flares.

And their column was beginning to fray. The *Chokai*, still firing at the *Canberra*, had begun to turn to the northeast, which would take her toward the transports in the Tulagi area and also allow all five of her turrets to bear on the Allied ships. The *Furutaka* had pulled out of the column to starboard for some reason, possibly to unmask her four port torpedo tubes, possibly because of steering issues that cropped up at about this time. She was now off the starboard quarter of the 6th Cruiser Division. She thus had a clear view of the *Canberra* about 9,000 yards away, so she immediately followed the *Chokai*'s 8-inch salvoes with several of her own, as well as four torpedoes, which missed.[117]

The *Aoba*, second in the Japanese column, was now leading two cruisers of the 6th Cruiser Division right at the *Canberra*, and opened gunfire at a range of 4,200 yards. The Australian lookouts spotted the *Aoba*'s torpedoes approaching from the port side; they, too, missed. The *Kako*, third in the Japanese column, unloaded on the Australian cruiser at a range of 4,000 yards with 8-inch and 4.7-inch gunfire and four torpedoes.[118] The Japanese salvoes were creeping up to the Australian cruiser, but a few more seconds and her gun director would have a firing solution on the Japanese and those 8-inch guns could train to port and fire.

At about 1:48, the *Canberra* was rocked by two explosions, as Japanese 8-inch shells finally found their mark. Both hit the area of the port side of the bridge; one wrecked the plotting room, killed the gunnery officer, and mortally wounded Captain Getting. Fires started spreading amidships. Some crew members saw and felt a sickening thud just before a third explosion that sent a large column of water over the ship – oddly, from the starboard side, the side away from the Japanese. The *Canberra* immediately lost all power – no engines, no guns, no torpedoes, no pumps – took a 5-degree list to starboard, and had a midships fire that made a fine point of aim in the darkness. She could not move, she could not fight. She was utterly helpless. Her 8-inch guns had fired exactly one shell; her 4-inch guns no more than a few. A sailor had run to the radio room to send out the warning message only to find the transmitter was smashed.[119]

In the next few minutes, the *Canberra* was hit no less than 24 times, including hits on "A" and "X" turrets, the 4-inch gun deck, the torpedo space, the after gun director, and both engine rooms. Fred Tuccitto of the *Chicago* was watching the carnage. "I can still see them shooting at the *Canberra*," he lamented. "One event I can't get rid of is seeing the *Canberra* taking hit after hit. How could anyone live through such an ordeal?"[120]

While the *Canberra* was taking a pounding, Captain Bode's earlier decision to lead from behind was coming home to roost. Bode had been in a deep sleep in his emergency cabin near the bridge when things started happening. The lookouts reported two small flashes low on the water in the direction of Savo Island. Then flares started appearing astern, flares that were immediately identified as the type used by cruiser floatplanes for illumination purposes. The senior officer on watch, Lieutenant Commander George Holley, then watched the *Canberra* ahead of him make an unplanned turn to starboard, revealing two rather vague, dark objects between the Australian cruiser and the *Patterson* to port and a third to the right.[121] They were the *Kako*, *Kinugasa*, and *Aoba* respectively.[122] At this point Holley ordered battle stations.

The clanging sounds of general quarters brought "King Bode," the officer in tactical command of the southern force, out of his slumber and back to the bridge, where he, in the words of Samuel Eliot Morison, "acted as if dazed." [123] Bode ordered both banks of 5-inch secondary guns to fire starshells, but before they could do so the lookouts started reporting torpedoes approaching from a dizzying number of angles. First, the starboard bridge lookout reported a torpedo wake (from the *Chokai*) to starboard. The bridge crew could not see it, but nevertheless Bode ordered right full rudder to try to parallel the wake. The words were hardly out of his mouth when the main battery control officer reported two torpedo wakes coming from slightly to port, so Bode ordered left full rudder to "comb the wakes" (or "comb the torpedoes"); that is, go to a course parallel to that of the torpedoes, presenting either a bow or stern profile that is narrow and thus minimize the chances of a torpedo hit. Both torpedoes crossed in front of the bow, one 70 yards away, the other a mere 20 yards.[124]

At about 1:47 am, Main Battery Control reported yet another torpedo approaching the port bow. There was a thunderous explosion near the bow, shaking the entire ship, and sending up a column of water as high as the foremast to ultimately drench the forward half of the ship. "It was like a kitchen full of pots and pans," said Ken Maysenhalder, manning one of the *Chicago*'s starboard 5-inch guns.[125]

This tin fish had bitten off a chunk of the *Chicago*'s bow below the waterline. "I knew we were hit," said Art King, manning one of the searchlights, "and I knew that we were going too fast. When word got up here that the bow had been blown off, I figured somebody's got to get word to the captain to slow down otherwise those forward bulkheads were going to collapse one by one."[126] Someone did. The *Chicago* slowed to 12 knots.

Not unreasonably, Captain Bode thought the explosion came courtesy of the torpedo seen off the port bow. In fact, it came from the starboard side, launched by the *Kako* as part of a spread targeting "what appeared to be a battleship"; the *Chicago* resembled a modernized *Pennsylvania*- or *Nevada*-class battleship, in miniature, anyway.[127] A second torpedo of that spread struck near the engineering spaces. It did not detonate, common for US torpedoes but rare for the Type 93, though it did leave an unsightly dent.

With the cruiser's port turn having accomplished its objective, to a degree, Captain Bode kept the *Chicago* turning to port because the bridge crew and the lookouts could see heading for them, some 4,000 yards away, "what was then believed to be a destroyer in a position to discharge torpedoes."[128] The "destroyer" was actually the *Furutaka*, who had already launched the torpedoes that had missed the *Chicago* to port, but Bode never quite figured that out.

It was hardly unusual this night. "King" Bode's strict disciplinarianism was reaping its fruits in what was now revealed to be his tenuous control of the *Chicago*. "There was mass confusion on the bridge as nobody had any idea what was happening," came a rather damning indictment from Doc Wallace, a member of the bridge crew. Wallace was manning one of the phone circuits, and overheard Bode arguing with his gunnery officer over who was to control the radar.[129]

According to Bode's report, at about this time, 1:47 am, the *Chicago*'s lookouts saw gunfire ahead, both off the starboard bow and some 40 degrees off the port bow. The Naval War College found it "singular" that this was the first gunfire reported by the *Chicago*, when the *Canberra*, only 600 yards away, had been taking a pummeling from the Japanese for at least the preceding three minutes.[130] Perhaps he missed it when he was arguing with his gunnery officer about the radar. No matter. Soldiers have been trained to head to the sound of the gunfire when they do not know what is going on and have no overriding orders. Bode was not a soldier and he could see, not hear, the gunfire, but the difference was immaterial. He headed toward this newly detected gunfire. Away from the transports he was supposed to be protecting but toward the gunfire.

The gunfire off the *Chicago*'s starboard bow was from what were thought to be "two destroyers." They were actually Japanese light cruisers *Tenryu* and *Yubari*, who were exchanging fire with the US destroyer *Patterson*, the source of the gunfire off the *Chicago*'s port bow. As tactical officer in command of the southern force, Captain Bode also had authority over the *Patterson*. But he issued no orders to the destroyer, gave her no guidance, indeed, did not contact her at all. This was why the force clearly needed a flag officer to command it and not a skipper.

So the *Chicago* groped her way along, as if dazed, heading west. The bridge crew had seen the *Furutaka* in an attack position, yet somehow the main battery director could not get a fix on a target for her 8-inch guns to start shooting, and the *Furutaka* had subsequently sped off out of range. The bridge crew could see the battle between the *Patterson* and the 18th Cruiser Division, yet somehow the main battery director still could not get a fix on a target for her 8-inch guns. Captain Bode was responsible for the destroyer *Patterson*, yet he watched the destroyer take on two larger warships by herself. The *Patterson* was outnumbered, outgunned, and now pinned by the searchlights of the *Tenryu* and *Yubari*, but she was snarling and snapping at the two larger Japanese ships like a rabid dog.

Now the 5-inch secondary batteries finally got their chance to fire the starshells. Two 4-gun salvoes fired from the port side to illuminate the area beyond the *Patterson* and hopefully backlight her tormentors so the *Chicago*'s gun director could get a fix on them. But none of the shells ignited; they just plopped into the sea. Two 4-gun salvoes from the starboard side intended to reveal a target behind the *Canberra* – the *Aoba* – also failed to burst. A frustrated Captain Bode would later report, "All star shells fired on the first two spreads failed to ignite, apparently because of the failure of the candles to ignite." The Naval War College thought it more likely that the fuses for the starshells had not been set properly.[131]

Unfortunately for the *Chicago* and her crew, the fuses on the Japanese shells were set properly. One such shell, its source unknown, struck the starboard leg of the *Chicago*'s tripod mast and detonated over the forward stack, spreading shrapnel topside, killing two, and bending the topmast so it interfered with the fire-control radar for the main battery director.[132]

Unlike the main battery director, the secondary battery director of the *Chicago* was able to get a fix on a target, and thus made itself felt, somewhat, in the battle between the *Patterson* and the Japanese 18th Cruiser Division as it reached a rather anticlimactic apex. Unlike the *Chicago*, the *Patterson* had gotten her starshells to ignite, silhouetting the *Yubari*. The destroyer was trading shots using her 5-inch guns at a range of about 5,600 yards. But despite her small size and evasive zigzag maneuvers, she took a hit on the Number 4 5-inch mount, which ignited the ready ammunition, killing ten, setting the after part of the ship on fire, and knocking the Number 3 and 4 5-inch mounts offline. The *Patterson* turned eastward to parallel the two Japanese cruisers while trying to contain the fire enough to bring the guns back online, but was only successful as to the Number 4 gun. Nevertheless, the *Patterson* managed to get a hit – a 5-inch dud – on the *Yubari*, who reported "some scratches (during the night action) from the light fire of an enemy destroyer."[133] Now the *Chicago* entered the fray, to a degree, with one of her 5-inch secondary mounts on the port side, firing 25 rounds and scoring maybe one hit on the *Tenryu*. The director then lost track of the cruiser; the main battery director still could not find a target. Captain Bode, frustrated with the inability to find something at which to shoot, took the dangerous but defensible step of ordering the cruiser's searchlights turned on. At 1:51 am, two searchlights snapped on and scanned the waters off the port side for a moment, but found nothing.

Captain Bode was given a report from damage control. The damage to the bow meant the *Chicago* could not go more than 25 knots without risking the forward bulkheads collapsing like dominoes. But she just kept heading west, slowly, although for no known reason. Gunfire was sighted some 14,000 yards to the west at 2:00 am, apparently two ships fighting, but the cruiser could not close before the flashes petered out and the ships involved could not be identified.

So, Howard Bode had effectively abandoned the defenseless transports he was supposed to be protecting. It was a dilemma, a judgment call – head for the gunfire or guard the transports. And Bode was not in the best shape to make that call. Bode, like all the other officers and men in the Allied force, was exhausted mentally and physically. He had been asleep in his emergency cabin when the engagement brought him to the bridge and forced him to immediately assess the situation. Perhaps not knowing where exactly Admiral Crutchley was, Bode may not have even understood he was still in command. The conditions were far from ideal.

But war rarely happens under ideal conditions, for either side. It is up to the battlefield commander to make the most of whatever hand he is dealt in order to protect and effectively lead his men. On this night, in the midst of battle, Howard Bode got into an argument with his gunnery officer over who should control the radar. He had imposed an overly strict regimen of discipline on the *Chicago*, which could have and seems to have left many of those under his command so fearful of making a mistake, so tightly wound that they struggled to function in battle: they did not set the fuses on the starshells properly; they could not find the Japanese at all; they missed a good portion of the battle raging around them; they could not advise Captain Bode for fear of his wrath.

Bode was not fighting off the Japanese, had not fought off the Japanese. Neither was he protecting the transports. He had given no orders to the *Canberra*, *Patterson*, or *Bagley*. He had not checked on their status. He had basically left them to fend for themselves. For reasons known only to him, he had directed the *Chicago* to slowly move into a kind of no-man's-land, where she could not protect the transports, could not engage the Japanese, could not be any kind of asset in this situation.

Most astonishingly, he had told no one outside the *Chicago*, warned no one – not Captain Riefkohl, not the northern group, not his superior Admiral Crutchley, not Admiral Turner – that the Imperial Japanese Navy was finally here.

"Proceed independently." That was what Admiral Mikawa had told the various factions of his cruiser force. It could have easily applied to the Allied southern force, given the lack of direction from Captain Bode. The Allied ships were like cows milling in a field. The *Canberra* was disabled, burning, and adrift. The *Chicago* was simply wandering to the west. The *Bagley* was loitering between Savo and Guadalcanal. Hit by the *Yubari*, the *Patterson* was snarling like a kicked puppy, fruitlessly looking for someone on which she could exact her revenge.

Taking the admiral's "proceed independently" order to perhaps a bit of an extreme was the destroyer *Yunagi*. At the tail end of the main column, the *Yunagi* had literally been forgotten. Admiral Mikawa had actually seen the *Yunagi* break off from the column, and wondered aloud at the identity of the destroyer. But the *Yunagi* had a good reason to turn away, because she had seen a nice, fat, juicy target – a light cruiser of the *Achilles* class, moving slowly, presumably because of the big hole visible near her starboard bow. Maybe, just maybe, the Japanese destroyer could finish her off.

But that was no cruiser. That was the destroyer *Jarvis*, still creeping across the battlefield, apparently only dimly aware of what was going on around her. The *Yunagi* overtook the damaged American destroyer on her starboard quarter and at 1:55 am brought her guns to bear. Though wounded, the *Jarvis* still had some bite to her, however, and replied with gunfire of her own. This short exchange was witnessed by the *Chicago*, who doesn't seem to have done anything about it. The *Yunagi* was not hit or damaged, but claimed to have hit the *Jarvis*. Whether she did or not will never be known. Perhaps surprised at the amount of return fire from and maybe a bit intimidated by this "cruiser," at about 2:00 am the *Yunagi* broke off the gun duel and headed north to rejoin her comrades when they completed their trek around Savo and passed north of the island on their way out.[134]

So the *Jarvis* was left to continue what was never intended to be her own lonely trek, hugging the coast of Guadalcanal. She simply wanted to be left alone, but 50 minutes later, after she had rounded Cape Esperance and began heading south, another ship began tailing her. The *Jarvis* sped up as much as she dared, but the mysterious ship closed to about 500 yards and issued a visual challenge – it was the US destroyer *Blue*. The Naval War College would later say that on this night, the *Blue* was "not vigilant, at least on certain bearings."[135] True enough, though she had seen flares and flashes of gunfire around Savo Island, the same alleged watchdog destroyer that had completely missed seven Japanese cruisers and one Japanese destroyer pass within a mile of her, the *Blue* had similarly completely missed the approach of the *Jarvis*, only seeing the crippled destroyer after she had passed and actually crossed the *Blue*'s line of sight to that all-important Cape Esperance. The *Jarvis* was ominously leaving a large oil slick, quite visible to the *Blue* even on this darkest of nights.[136] Using her Aldis lamp, the *Blue* told the *Jarvis* she was trailing oil; the *Jarvis* replied that she was aware of it. The *Blue* signaled, "Are you all right?" And, lying, the *Jarvis* answered, "Affirmative."[137] The *Blue* went on to resume her watch, if one could call it that. The *Jarvis* slowly crawled away to the south, one lonely destroyer, the smallest of all men-of-war, crippled and barely clinging to life, proceeding independently, proceeding alone, in the dark out to sea.

The dark has a way of pulling apart even the best-led, the best-trained combatants, and Admiral Mikawa's force was no exception. After his attack on the southern force, Mikawa had the column turn northeast, initially heading for the transports at Tulagi. But he had seen the northern group of cruisers and knew he could not go after the transports with three US Navy heavy cruisers in his rear, blocking his exit. He had to take care of them first. So the flagship *Chokai* had led the 6th Cruiser Division in a turn to the north to continue rounding Savo Island counterclockwise.

The Battle of Savo Island

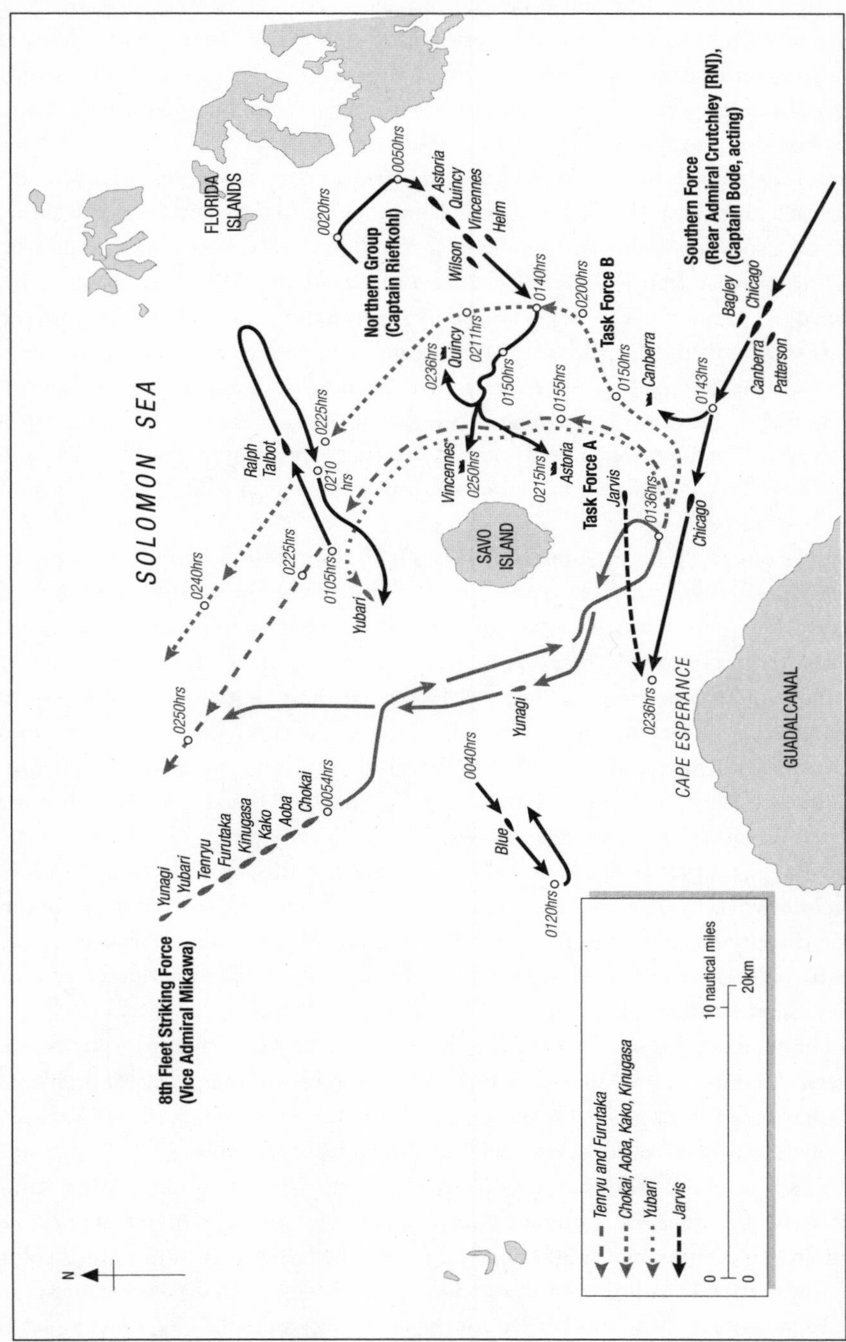

The *Furutaka*, the last ship in the 6th Cruiser Division's column, was not with them. Her steering difficulties had pulled her out of the column well to starboard. She tried to turn back to rejoin her sister ships, but the disabled *Canberra* drifted in the way. Apparently steering with her engines, the *Furutaka* turned to port – due north – to avoid a collision, then gave the helpless Australian ship a blasting with her main and secondary armament. Still, she couldn't rejoin the main Japanese column.

Enter the "rabble" of the 18th Cruiser Division. The *Tenryu* and *Yubari* had just finished their duel with the *Patterson*, believing they had sunk her, when the *Furutaka* came up on a collision course with the *Yubari*. Admiral Matsuyama ordered an immediate line turn to port, and both *Tenryu* and *Yubari* turned at roughly the same time. *Tenryu* had turned her gunfire on the *Bagley* and thought she had heavily damaged the destroyer; the *Bagley* was not hit and had never even realized someone was shooting at her. The *Yubari* would have joined in this effort to get the *Bagley*'s attention but her range was fouled by the *Furutaka*, who now fell in behind the *Tenryu*. They were now completely separated from the main Japanese column. How they could rejoin was not clear; if they tried to do so, they risked running into the northern group of Allied cruisers or fouling the eastern group's line of fire.[138]

This was not exactly how Admiral Mikawa had planned it. The once-simple column of Japanese cruisers was now two groups, an eastern one with the *Chokai*, *Aoba*, *Kako*, and *Kinugasa* all in column, and a western one with the *Tenryu* leading the *Furutaka* and the *Yubari* slightly to port. Both were east of Savo Island heading north on parallel courses.

It was on the *Chokai*, leading the more eastern of those brackets, where one of those sharp-eyed Japanese lookouts had, in the dark, made a startling discovery. Her executive officer Kato Kenkichi would later explain, "When the *Chokai* approached the enemy, the main battery of the first ship we saw, which I think was the last ship in the column, was not trained on either of our groups of ships."[139]

The 8-inch gun turrets of all the US cruisers, not just the *Astoria*, which was the ship Kato mentioned, but also the *Quincy* and *Vincennes*, were trained in – the forward turrets all facing directly forward, the aft turrets all facing directly aft. As if they were in port.

Clearly oblivious to the Japanese presence – again – the US Navy cruisers were about to be bracketed by enemies.

The aircraft flares that had backlit the southern group for the Japanese were in the wrong direction for illuminating the northern force. But that in itself was not a major problem; the Japanese had very good searchlights and were very good at using them. Captain Kato would say the crews went into battle "very easy mindedly, without any worries."[140]

At 1:48 am, the *Chokai* launched four torpedoes.[141] Two minutes later, Admiral Mikawa gave the order for the main guns to open fire. The searchlight of the *Chokai* snapped on. An intense, blinding beam that caught the last cruiser in the Allied column.

No, it was not how Admiral Mikawa had planned it, but it would work better than he could have imagined. Two arms headed for the northern group of Allied cruisers, ready to give them the embrace of death.

At midnight, Lieutenant Commander William Truesdell had come on duty as the gunnery officer for the US cruiser *Astoria*. A figure who was either loved or hated aboard the cruiser, Truesdell was nevertheless well-respected and something of a stickler for being prepared.[142] He took his post in the forward main battery control station and noticed the forward fire-control radar seemed to be malfunctioning. Specifically, the display was about half its horizontal size. Otherwise it was functioning normally. The technicians had decided they could not identify and fix the problem at night with the ship blacked out, so they would wait until morning. Truesdell insisted it be fixed immediately. At 1:45 am, the technicians began work on the radar and had it fixed within a few minutes.[143] Truesdell tested it on the other ships in the group to satisfy himself that it was indeed fixed.[144]

Radar was proving to be a continuous problem on the *Astoria*. The after fire-control radar was already out because of a shorted transformer, and no replacement parts for it were available at sea. According to skipper Captain William Garrett Greenman, the search radar was not of much use either. "What we got only lent to confusion," he later said. "The officer on watch in radar frequently reported to me early in the evening that he was picking up strange objects in the area where these ships were supposed to be." Greenman decided that those strange objects were indeed ships – his comrades in the screening force.[145]

Up on the *Astoria*'s bridge, Lieutenant Commander James Topper, the senior officer on watch, had just overseen the cruiser's course change at 1:44 am to a northwesterly course, following the *Quincy* and *Vincennes* on this leg of the box patrol. Except Topper thought he had just felt a slight tremor. Probably a destroyer dropping depth charges some distance away, he presumed. Maybe a submarine had managed to sneak into the harbor and was going after the transports. But he could find nothing amiss among either the transport groups or other ships. Topper told everyone to be alert.

Then the lookouts reported they could hear a plane overhead, but they could not see it. Lieutenant Commander Topper went to the starboard side of the bridge to hear for himself, but his investigation was interrupted by the voice radio, which carried an order from the *Vincennes*. The cruisers were having navigational issues in the dark and had strayed from their intended course on the box patrol. If there were indeed submarines inside the perimeter, maintaining their proper course and station in the formation was important to preserve the antisubmarine protection of the destroyers. To help get back on course, Captain Riefkohl was delaying the next turn in the box patrol for ten minutes – from 1:50 am to 2:00 am. In acknowledging this order, the *Astoria* missed the second warning issued by the *Patterson*.

Someone on the port side of the bridge reported seeing starshells off the port quarter. Lieutenant Commander Topper saw that they were not starshells but aircraft flares, about 5,000 yards away. He sent for the captain and prepared for general quarters.

And was shocked by a tremendous BOOM! and an accompanying concussive shock. Without warning, the *Astoria*'s main guns had fired a salvo. "This gave me quite a surprise," Topper later wrote, "as I had not given an order about opening fire, nor could I make out any ships in the vicinity of the flares."[146] General quarters sounded as the 5-inch secondary battery fired a salvo of its own.[147]

Lieutenant Commander Topper could not see any ships, but Lieutenant Commander Truesdell could. He had seen the aircraft flares and knew exactly what they meant. Truesdell had run back to his station just in time to see the shell splashes off the port bow from the first Japanese salvo, fired by the flagship *Chokai* at a range of 7,000 yards. It had missed, but was only 500 yards to port and 200 yards ahead. The time was 1:50 am.

"All stations alert!" came the order to the gun crews from Lieutenant Commander Truesdell. Reacting quickly and completely in line with his training – a rare feat on this night – Truesdell put his men at battle stations and trained the *Astoria*'s gun director to port, along with all three main turrets.[148] The lookouts reported three cruisers of the *Nachi* class. Truesdell thought he saw four on the radar screen. He requested general quarters and permission to open fire. There was no reply.

At 1:51 am there were more shell splashes, 500 yards to port but ahead by only 100 yards. A second salvo from the *Chokai*. She was zeroing in on the *Astoria*.

Lieutenant Commander Truesdell was mystified as to why general quarters was not sounding when very clearly enemy ships were shooting at them. He made a second request. But again no reply.

He could wait no longer. "Commence firing!" At least eight of the *Astoria*'s nine 8-inch guns fired, followed by all of the port 5-inch guns.

More shell splashes, dead on but still 500 yards to port. The *Chokai*'s salvos were getting closer to the mark.

"What are you firing at? Cease firing!" came the order from the bridge.[149]

Still groggy from his aborted nap, Captain Greenman had arrived at the bridge and was puzzled as to why his ship was at general quarters firing its guns. "Who sounded the general alarm? Who gave the order to commence firing?" Topper replied that he had done neither.

Seeing the flares and maybe two searchlights, Captain Greenman arrived at the conclusion that the Allied ships had sighted a surfaced Japanese submarine and were shooting at it. He couldn't see any submarine, but that didn't mean anything. There couldn't be enemy ships inside the harbor. Which meant the *Astoria* was shooting at Allied ships.

"Topper, I think we are firing on our own ships," said Captain Greenman. "Let's not get too excited and act too hastily. Cease firing." Lieutenant Commander Topper agreed with his assessment.

Except it just wasn't adding up to that. Captain Greenman had shell splashes 500 yards to port – the third salvo from the *Chokai*. He saw shell splashes straddle the *Vincennes*. A member of the bridge crew, on the internal phone with the gunnery officer, declared, "Mr Truesdell said for God's sake give the word to commence firing."

Captain Greenman could now see fire from at least five ships. There were more shell splashes, this time only 200 yards to port, close enough that an 8-inch shell struck the *Astoria* well forward, passing through the paint locker without causing a fire. The *Chokai*'s fourth salvo. She was getting ever closer.

After a single minute that felt like an hour, Captain Greenman finally got the hint. He remarked, "Our ships or not, we will have to stop them." Lieutenant Commander Topper would later explain, "I believe this remark was caused by the splashes that had just landed ahead and to port of the *Astoria*."[150] As far as battlefield speeches go, it left room for improvement, but Greenman next shouted, "Sound general quarters! Commence firing!"[151]

Lieutenant Commander Truesdell immediately complied by firing all six guns of the two forward turrets at the *Chokai*, the *Astoria*'s third salvo. The 8-inch shells fell only about 100 yards short. He was close.

But the *Chokai* had the element of surprise and Captain Greenman's indecision, giving her a head start on getting her shells on their target. And that head start paid off at 1:55 am, when the *Chokai*'s fifth salvo landed at least four 8-inch shells amidships on the *Astoria*. The direct recipients of the Japanese flagship's largess were the *Astoria*'s boat deck and the hangar – where she kept her SOC Seagull floatplanes.

Now the wisdom of Admiral Mikawa's decision to jettison all flammable (and inflammable) materials topside was shown. By contrast, the *Astoria*'s floatplanes were supposed to be drained of their fuel every night, but the crews grumbled about this duty and the aircraft were scheduled for an early morning mission anyway, so each carried 175 gallons of volatile aviation fuel.

The hangar and catapult area was a fire marshal's nightmare. Not only did each Seagull carry that aviation fuel it should not have had, but the planes themselves were wood and fabric. Their fuel and ammunition were also stored in the hangar. A kerosene tank was nearby. It all meant that when the *Chokai*'s shells hit, midships on the *Astoria* became an inferno.

No longer could the *Astoria* try to hide herself in the darkness, no longer could she even hope that any evasive maneuvers would be effective, because she now unwillingly carried a giant torch. The *Chokai* now shut off her searchlights, eliminating her own bright points of aim in the night. The *Astoria*'s midships fire was now a giant glowing target for the Japanese gunners.

Captain Greenman received an order from the *Vincennes* to increase speed to 15 knots. Fifteen knots? In a battle? He ordered speed increased to 20 knots and a turn to port.

With the Japanese column speeding at 26 knots about to pass some 4 miles astern of the US column – between the northern force and the transports they were supposed to protect – the two forward turrets were reaching the limit of their train, their ability to rotate to port. Lieutenant Commander Truesdell had begged the bridge to turn to port to keep the Japanese within their firing arcs. Turret 3, the aft turret, the turret that was most able to fire on the Japanese, lost power as a result of the fire. But it could have been worse.

And it quickly was. At 1:56 am, three 8-inch shells, believed to have come from the *Chokai*, hit the forward Number 1 turret. One penetrated the faceplate and detonated in the gunroom, killing everyone there and destroying the interior of the turret. The other two penetrated the barbette, killing all but two in the upper powder room and the shell deck. Turret Number 1 was now permanently disabled, and another fire was burning on the *Astoria*.

In response came the *Astoria*'s fourth salvo – only two shells from the only functioning turret, Number 2. They missed. Now that she had the range, the *Chokai* apparently went to rapid fire with her 8-inch guns. The *Kinugasa* joined in the carnage. And for the *Astoria*, now the real agony began.

The *Astoria* was in the curious position of being the last ship in the northern force to go to general quarters but the first to fire at the Japanese. The *Quincy*, just ahead of her, had been the first to go to battle stations. She had been having communications problems all night; they certainly did not get better now. She had received the second warning from the *Patterson*, but it was never passed to the main battery control. At 1:46 am, lookouts had spotted three dark silhouettes to the southwest, one with three turrets forward. Since no American cruiser had three turrets forward, they decided that these ships were probably Japanese. But apparently this information also never reached main battery control, or, for that matter, the bridge.

Nevertheless, when she received that second warning from the *Patterson* at 1:47 am, the supervisor of the watch, Lieutenant Commander Edward E. Billings, had the *Quincy* go to general quarters, and skipper Captain Samuel Nobre Moore was called to the bridge.[152] He arrived just as the cruiser was pinned in Japanese searchlights, those of the *Aoba*, operating just behind the *Chokai* in the Japanese eastern column.

But these could be friendly ships seeking that curiously unseen Japanese submarine that everyone thought had penetrated the harbor. So Captain Moore ordered the recognition lights – colored lights up either side of the bridge that identified the ship as American – turned on. This was a bad idea.

Next, Captain Moore asked his officer of the deck, Lieutenant Charles P. Clarke, Jr., which way he should turn. Clark answered, "To the right." This was to try to clear the supposedly friendly ships illuminating them. Moore asked again, and Clarke gave the same reply.[153]Another bad idea, of which, on this night, the Allies had no shortage.

The shells were now starting to fall. The lookouts could see shell splashes near the *Astoria*, the *Chokai*'s first salvo having fallen short, and near the *Vincennes*, the first salvo from the *Kako* also having fallen short. Captain Moore was saved from acting on his own misunderstanding by orders which came in from the *Vincennes* over the voice radio: "Steam at standard speed, 15 knots!" and "Fire on the searchlights!" So, the skipper appropriately directed his gunners to "Fire on the searchlights!"[154] A good idea, at long last.

The gunnery crews had been completely in the dark about the situation and the sounding of battle stations until the *Aoba* literally shone the light on them at 1:50 am.

Nevertheless, a minute later fire-control quickly got a fix on the *Aoba*'s searchlight – 8,400 yards – for the *Quincy*'s 8-inch guns to open fire. And ... nothing. No earth-shattering kaboom, no concussion, no flash from the *Quincy*'s 8-inch guns.

The *Quincy* was now bracketed by shell splashes. The first 8-inch salvo from the *Aoba* had landed off the port bow, the second some 200 yards off the starboard side. And still nothing from the *Quincy*'s 8-inch guns.

At 1:52 am, the *Aoba* finally got a hit with her third salvo, well aft on the *Quincy* and starting a fire on the fantail, which was quickly contained. Still no response from *Quincy*'s 8-inch guns.

A minute later came the *Aoba*'s fourth salvo of 8-inch shells, which hit the bridge, "accomplish[ing] more damage to personnel than to material, and wounded several persons," in the words of the Naval War College.[155] Still nothing from the *Quincy*'s 8-inch guns.

Though the *Quincy*'s main armament was having obvious issues, the cruiser's secondary armament was trying to get in the game. In an attempt to illuminate the cruiser's tormentor, starshells were loaded into the four port-side 5-inch guns. But no order to fire them was received – those communications issues again – and the guns simply sat there, loaded. Just long enough for the *Aoba*'s next salvo at 1:54 to hit the guns, setting off the starshells "like Roman candles" as well as the nearby ready ammunition. The guns were wrecked and most of the personnel killed.[156]

The Japanese eastern column was moving astern of the northern force. If the US cruisers wanted to keep the Japanese cruisers within the firing arcs of their forward guns, they would have to turn. Seeing the *Vincennes* about 600 yards ahead make a sharp turn to port, Captain Moore immediately had the *Quincy* turn to port as well. Thus, the Japanese remained within the firing arcs of all nine 8-inch guns. Now, if only those guns would fire.

Less than a minute later, the *Aoba*'s sixth salvo hit the *Quincy*'s well deck, where it set one of the cruiser's Seagull floatplanes afire. Burning gasoline was sprayed all over the well deck, boat deck, and the floatplane on the port catapult.

"Shoot it off!" screamed Captain Moore.[157] He wanted the explosive charges normally used to catapult the plane into the air detonated, to instead blow off its flaming carcass into the sea. But the order was never carried out and the fire soon spread to the starboard catapult, the floatplane located there, and everywhere amidships. Enemy gunfire had set a floatplane on fire yet again just like the *Astoria*.

But unlike those of the *Astoria*, the *Quincy*'s guns had yet to fire a shot, a full eight minutes after she had gone to battle stations, some five minutes after she had first been under enemy fire. Captain Moore fumed. The *Aoba* shut off her searchlight.[158] And for the *Quincy* now the real agony began.

It was remarkable that on this night, when the Allies were plagued by assumptions and errors, inference and incompetence, Captain Riefkohl of the *Vincennes*, the officer in tactical command of the northern group, had received the report of the Japanese cruisers and "seaplane tenders or gunboats" and had actually calculated that if those ships had wanted to reach Guadalcanal, they could do so that night. Equally remarkable was that

Riefkohl did next to nothing about it, only making an order to a few on the *Vincennes* to keep a lookout for approaching enemy ships between midnight and 2:00 am and to make an all-around sweep with the search radar. He said nothing more to the crew of the *Vincennes* and nothing at all to the other ships of the northern group. Then he went to bed after nearly 21 hours on the bridge for some inarguably badly needed sleep.[159]

Captain Riefkohl was awakened 45 minutes later.[160] The lookouts had noticed some curious things. Flares had appeared over the area of the transports. Gunfire had been spotted, and some ships were silhouetted by "a great display of light" southeast of Savo Island. Arriving on the bridge, Riefkohl took a look for himself.

The skipper could see the flares, and a battle going on to the south between two ships who were shooting starshells to try to illuminate each other, later determined to be the *Patterson* exchanging fire with the *Yubari*. Seeing no other ships or heavy gunfire and having received no communications from either Admiral Crutchley or the southern force – the *Patterson*'s warning had reached the *Vincennes*' radio room but not the bridge, for reasons known only to the communications personnel – he surmised that the southern group had intercepted a Japanese destroyer trying to penetrate the harbor. The destroyer must be a diversion – to lure his ships to the south and leave the north channel unguarded for the main force of Japanese ships to plow through and attack the transports. But Captain Riefkohl would not be fooled so easily. His ships would stay right where they were and continue their box patrol.[161] Surely, the southern group could handle a single destroyer?

Nonetheless, Captain Riefkohl ordered the *Vincennes*, but not the rest of the northern force, to battle stations at 1:48 am.[162] With no information aside from what his lookouts reported and no direction from Admiral Crutchley, he was plagued by indecision. Riefkohl considered shooting up starshells, but those would reveal his position and might illuminate the southern force. He wanted to position his ships to best oppose an enemy charge through the north channel, which meant he should turn to starboard. But turning to starboard took him further away from the southern force, which may need his help. He chose to increase speed to 15 knots but keep his current course to await developments, or, better yet, orders.

And so the northern force was still cruising northwest when at 1:50 Captain Riefkohl saw off his port quarter a pair of searchlights snap on, shining on the *Astoria*. Twenty seconds later came another pair, shining on the *Quincy*. Twenty seconds more and there was a third pair, shining on the *Vincennes*.

Captain Riefkohl presumed it was the southern force. Chasing that destroyer, which was doing quite the opposite of clearing out the north channel. Politely, the *Vincennes* radioed these unexpected visitors: "Turn those searchlights off of us. We are friendly."[163]Not quite as politely, the unexpected visitors responded with an avalanche of 8-inch shells – the *Chokai* firing at the *Astoria*, the *Aoba* firing at the *Quincy*, and, now, the *Kako* firing her first salvo at the *Vincennes*, landing some 500 yards off the port beam.

Captain Riefkohl looked to port and saw a long line of gunfire, seemingly aimed at him. He was starting to reach the conclusion that these ships were not the southern force, not even friendly, though not convinced enough to stop the *Vincennes*' radio room from continuously broadcasting, "We are friendly."[164] He ordered starshells to be fired to attempt to illuminate their tormentors. Gunnery officer Lieutenant Commander Robert Lee Adams responded with a salvo from the 5-inch guns. At the same time, the *Kako*'s second salvo landed only about 100 yards short.

"Open fire on targets of opportunity," Captain Riefkohl ordered his gunners.

But for the Japanese, the *Vincennes* was already the target of opportunity. At 1:52 am the *Kako* fired her next salvo from both her main and secondary armament. The *Vincennes* took a 5-inch shell on the bridge that killed the communications officer and several others. She also took several hits amidships, in the carpenter shop and in the hangar. The floatplanes had been drained of fuel, but the planes themselves were still wood and fabric and they caught fire, which gave the *Vincennes* her own illuminating flaming torch. The *Kako* shut off her searchlights.[165] And for the *Vincennes* now the real agony began.

All three heavy cruisers of the northern force had thus been branded not with a scarlet letter, but with a glowing target, courtesy of their own floatplanes. They could no longer hide from the Japanese. Conversely, the fires helped hide the Japanese. The flames and smoke ruined night vision and fouled sighting and range finding on the American ships, while the Japanese, having no more need of their searchlights, had turned them off and thus robbed the Americans of any point of aim for their guns.

Indeed the American guns were struggling to make their presence felt. At 1:53 the *Vincennes* finally got her first salvo off – nine 8-inch shells directed at the *Kako*. It was 500 yards short, largely because she had gotten her firing solution off the *Chokai*'s searchlight. Her gunners recalculated. The *Kako*'s did not, and the *Vincennes* took several hits in her antenna trunk, knocking out her searchlights, communications, and, temporarily, power to the gun control equipment.

Captain Riefkohl, the officer in tactical command of the northern force, presented his gunnery officer, Lieutenant Commander Adams, with the question of "What do you suggest now?"

Lieutenant Commander Adams replied, "Let's get out of here until we can see what we are doing. I'm not sure of my targets." Captain Riefkohl told his gun crews, "Cease firing. I am going to swing around. When we come back in we'll give them hell!"[166]

The *Vincennes* increased speed to 20 knots, or tried to, anyway, and turned 40 degrees to port, in an effort to keep the Japanese now rapidly passing astern within the firing arcs of her forward turrets – but also surrendering to them a position between her and the transports she was supposed to be protecting. By the time power had been restored to her fire-control, another target had appeared: the *Kinugasa*. As the fourth and last cruiser in the Japanese eastern column, she did not have an opposite number among the northern force cruisers and was trying to decide on a target. Despite the fact that her most likely targets were all illuminated by fires, the *Kinugasa* continued to use her searchlights. A nine-gun salvo from the *Vincennes*, her second, detonated in her port steering room. Her steering control temporarily disabled, the *Kinugasa* stumbled out of the column to port.

Having learned the error of her ways, the *Kinugasa* shut off her searchlights and the *Vincennes* lost her target.[167]

Captain Riefkohl tried to shift his target back to the *Kako*, but he found the *Vincennes*' port turn had not been enough to keep the *Kako* within the forward turrets' firing arcs. So he turned back to starboard to try to parallel the Japanese. While in this turn, at 1:55 the *Vincennes* suffered an underwater explosion on the port side underneath sick bay. Riefkohl thought she had been hit by a torpedo from a submarine. He was half right; the cruiser's starboard turn took her close to her original course from when the battle started – and into the path of the torpedoes the *Chokai* had launched before opening gunfire on the northern group.[168] One of those torpedoes had hit.

Things went downhill even more quickly. The shell hits kept coming. The *Vincennes* lost power to her main guns; two were able to run off backup generators, but Turret 2 had to be operated by hand. Steering had to be moved aft after the bridge lost steering control. At least three shells struck aft near the backup command center known as "Battle II" that was manned during battle and commanded by the executive officer. The salvo ended up killing most of the personnel there, smashing the station, and actually blowing the aft 5-inch director overboard.[169]

Damage to the firerooms was costing the *Vincennes* more and more engine power, and with most internal communications destroyed, Captain Riefkohl was unable to give steering instructions from the bridge to the after steering engine room.

The *Vincennes* finally lost sight of the eastern column of Japanese cruisers at 2:00, only to have the battle cross from injurious to insulting by taking fire from the *Furutaka* and the *Yubari* of the western section of Japanese cruisers to port. Illuminating by searchlight, the *Furutaka* used her 8-inch main guns and 4.7-inch secondary guns to pummel the *Vincennes* further, knocking out the remaining fire-control position and forcing the guns to go to local control, meaning the individual turrets and mounts had to sight their own targets, determine the range and deflection, and fire on their own. The *Yubari* sent a "low order detonation" torpedo into the *Vincennes*' port side, destroying the Number 1 fireroom and killing everyone in it. The *Vincennes*' forward engine room took a shell hit that ruptured the main steam line. With the loss of the last of the steam pressure, the engine rooms were abandoned and the *Vincennes* lost all propulsive power. Desperate for help from any quarter, Riefkohl watched as his two screening destroyers *Helm* and *Wilson*, whom he had earlier ordered to carry out a torpedo attack, nearly collided with each other. The *Helm* did try to carry out the attack, charging all by herself at an unidentified ship in the gloom southwest of Savo Island. As she prepared to launch torpedoes, a lightning flash illuminated her target; it was the *Bagley*, who had never sighted the *Helm*.[170]

The eastern group cruisers continued to fire on the *Vincennes* from starboard, disabling both forward turrets and knocking down the American flag with shell hits. Finding this gunfire "rather irritating," Captain Riefkohl tried to use the *Vincennes*' remaining momentum to turn to port, where the *Furutaka* and the *Yubari* were still pounding him. Incredibly, the captain ordered another American flag run up from the starboard yardarm and illuminated;

he still thought the ships shooting at him from starboard were friendly. The Naval War College found this "difficult to understand." In fairness, though, when the flag went up, the *Furutaka* and *Yubari* quit shooting, turned off their searchlights, and sailed off.[171]

But it was too late for the *Vincennes*. Powerless, afire, adrift, and listing badly to port from the torpedo hits, the cruiser was doomed. Curiously, the *Chokai* shone her searchlight on the disabled cruiser and fired on her for a few minutes, but it was superfluous. At 2:16 am, Captain Riefkohl gave the order to prepare to abandon ship. As the cruiser continued to heel over to port, the order to abandon ship was given at 2:30 am. 20 minutes later the *Vincennes* slid into the deep, her foremast striking the water just a few feet from where Captain Riefkohl was swimming desperately to get away.[172]

The *Chokai*'s actions here are part of her own little mystery. She had broken away from the main Japanese eastern column around 2:00 am and wandered off northeast toward Tulagi. The *Aoba*, *Kako*, and *Kinugasa* had not followed, but had continued heading north, engaging the northern group but also placing themselves between the northern group and the *Chokai*, who later had to chase after the 6th Cruiser Division like a puppy chasing after its owner. Why the *Chokai* did this is unknown. Admiral Mikawa later indicated it was planned, but the course information for the *Chokai* during this period was curiously absent from her after-action report, suggesting a cover-up. The Naval War College thought she may have been having steering troubles, and that her use of her searchlight may have been to try to establish her bearings and find her cohorts. It may sound like a small matter, but it would have outsized consequences.

Thanks to the *Quincy*. Captain Moore's ship could no longer see the eastern group of Japanese cruisers, who had killed their searchlights. As if that did not blind her to her tormentors enough, the midships fire on the cruiser had fouled her fire-control stations and forced the evacuation of the after stations. The smoke from the blazing *Vincennes* ahead of her made it worse still. But at 1:56 am she was finally able to see through the smoke a light – a searchlight, to be precise, had snapped on from the southwest. Her exasperated skipper and gunnery officer were elated, and for the first time in this battle the *Quincy* got off a nine-gun salvo from her main armament. It missed, but her 8-inch guns had finally fired, after a sickening eight-minute interlude since the ship had gone to battle stations.

The absurd length of time it took for the *Quincy*'s main guns to fire was the subject of considerable comment in the Naval War College's post-mortem of the battle. The issue for the *Quincy* was not poor performance by her skipper, her officers, and men, or any problem with her equipment. Rather, it was organizational.

The *Quincy* had just transferred to the Pacific from the Atlantic, where there were standing orders to keep the secondary guns manned at night in case they came across a surfaced German U-boat. It made sense for operations in the Atlantic, flooded as it was by German U-boats that were employed strategically, but not in the Pacific, where the Japanese operated their submarines quite differently. No one had thought to change it when she came to the Pacific. For purposes of this engagement, this difference might not have mattered, except when the *Quincy* went to battle stations, those crewmen manning the guns had to move to their battle stations elsewhere, while others had to come in to man the guns. There was a similar issue with communications personnel. The result was that when the *Quincy* went to battle stations a lot of men were running from one station to the other. When the watertight doors and hatches were closed and dogged down, their movement was slowed to a crawl. So her battle stations were not fully manned for a period of time that was utterly ridiculous, and, since they were under fire from the Japanese, deadly.

Which more than adequately described the *Quincy*'s predicament. The searchlight they had just seen was not the ship that had been firing on them all along, the *Aoba*, but a different one, from a group to the southwest. It belonged to the cruiser *Furutaka*. The *Quincy*'s lookouts then spotted gunfire from a ship with three stacks ahead of the *Furutaka* – the *Tenryu*.

Admiral Mikawa's unintentional embrace of death had clutched the *Quincy* close to its bosom, and Captain Moore realized he was caught in a crossfire between two groups of Japanese cruisers. Seeing the *Vincennes* make a wobbly turn to starboard, Moore turned to starboard as well. He snarled at his gunnery officer, "We are going through the middle! Give them hell!"[173]

His plan was that the *Quincy*'s aft turret would deal with the *Furutaka* while the forward turrets could fire on the eastern group. In this he would be disappointed. An 8-inch shell from the *Furutaka* hit the aft turret's faceplate and jammed it in train.

It seemed nothing could go right on this night for the Allies. Once the *Quincy* in her turn had cleared the flaming *Astoria*, Captain Moore had the starboard 5-inch guns fire a salvo of starshells. The forward turrets were to fire on anything the starshells revealed. But the salvo burst short of any targets and above the clouds, so they provided no illumination. Two subsequent ones also burst above the clouds.[174] Moore tried to aim the searchlights, but communications broke down and his orders never got through.

Fortunately, if one could call finding targets shooting at one fortunate, three sets of searchlights had been spotted to the south – the *Aoba* leading the *Kako* and *Kinugasa*. The *Aoba* had switched from pounding the *Quincy* to pounding the *Astoria*. But in her turn to starboard the flaming, struggling *Quincy* looked to the *Aoba* like she was making a kamikaze run at them. "She was a brave ship, manned by brave men," Captain Ohmae would later say.[175]

A suicide run was always guaranteed to get the Japanese attention, so the *Aoba* switched her guns back. The American cruiser took another vicious salvo that knocked out a fireroom, her forward antiaircraft director, and most of her starboard guns. The *Quincy* responded with her second 8-inch salvo; the *Aoba* shut off her searchlight before the shells landed, over in range.

Behind the now-surrounded ship, the ancient, ugly *Tenryu* off the western group, was starting to get her licks in, and devastating licks they were, too. She launched a volley of torpedoes that ran for about two minutes before at least two of them buried themselves into the *Quincy*'s port side, destroying two firerooms and slowing her further. A salvo from the light cruiser knocked out the "Battle II" secondary command center.[176]

The *Quincy* was now a staggering inferno, sinking, surrounded, taking shots from all directions, yet unable to see who was doing the shooting. She was desperate for a target to dish out just a little of what had been so brutally served to her.

And a target appeared – a new set of searchlights off her starboard quarter farther to the southeast. Her six remaining functional 8-inch guns let loose for only their third salvo – their final salvo, their final defiance – at these mysterious lights.[177]

A lookout saw the target burst into flames, backlighting another cruiser, apparently the *Kako*, crossing in front of her and badly separated from the other Japanese cruisers, for some reason. The lookout didn't realize they had just hit Admiral Mikawa's flagship *Chokai*.

One 8-inch shell hit near the aviation crane. But Admiral Mikawa had had the foresight to dump all flammable objects and had launched his planes, or the *Chokai* would have had a burning scout plane like the *Vincennes*, *Quincy*, and *Astoria* did. As a result, the hit was not serious. The other two 8-inch shells hit just aft of the bridge in the flag operations room, about 15 feet from Mikawa himself. The explosion left the admiral, Captain Ohmae, and the rest of the staff "shocked and disconcerted momentarily," but it was not a serious hit.[178] Nevertheless, inasmuch as it burned up all the navigational charts, it was a very annoying one.[179]

The *Quincy* could only wish the response was limited to annoying. At 2:06 am, a devastating blast from the *Aoba* smashed the starboard side of the bridge and "cleared the pilot house," killing or mortally wounding everyone there. Lieutenant Commander Billings, who had brought the ship to battle stations, staggered to the starboard wing of the bridge, half of his face gone, and collapsed in the arms of Lieutenant Clarke, reassuring "I'm all right, I'm all right. Keep calm. Everything will be all right. The ship will go down fighting."[180]

The junior officer of the deck Lieutenant (j.g.) J. H. Mee, Jr. and Lieutenant (j.g.) Douglas C. Skaife ran onto the bridge and found Captain Moore slumped to the right of wheel. "Transfer control to Batt II," the skipper groaned. A signalman came in and took over the wheel. Mee ran around trying to get in touch with Battle II, not knowing it had already been destroyed.[181]

The list of things destroyed on the *Quincy* was rapidly lengthening. At about the same time the bridge was hit, a shell running on an almost flat trajectory passed through, appropriately enough, the shell deck, and hit the barbette of Turret 1, damaging the turret so badly it could not fire. Turret 1 took two more hits in quick succession and had to be abandoned. Turret 2 took a hit near the top of the barbette, setting the ammunition on fire and leaving the turret ablaze, to explode a few minutes later with such ferocity that the executive officer on the *Astoria* thought the *Quincy* herself had exploded.

With both the guns and the fire-control stations now disabled, assistant gunnery officer Lieutenant Commander John D. Andrew went to the bridge to ask for instructions. He found the pilothouse a slaughterhouse – bodies and pieces of bodies strewn about in often grotesque positions, windows smashed, blood everywhere. The only sign of life was the signalman still at the wheel, now spinning it in a futile effort to turn the ship left. He turned to Andrew.

"The Captain is dead," he said. "He told me to beach the ship but I can't steer." As he finished, Captain Moore half rose from the deck and, moaning, collapsed for the final time.[182]

His ship had only a few moments more – blazing like a furnace, badly listing, communications so bad no one knew who was in command, helplessly meandering to starboard, no longer aware of what was going on around her. The equally blazing *Astoria* heading in the opposite direction was barely able to avoid a collision. A late torpedo hit at 2:16 to starboard from the *Aoba* flooded a fireroom and cost the *Quincy* what little power she had left, but was otherwise redundant. Her bow awash, the *Quincy* completed her roll to port and sank at 2:38.[183]

The *Astoria* was blazing in more ways than one. In the unfortunate position of being the last cruiser in a column whose "T" was being crossed astern by the Japanese, she had taken the brunt of the gunfire from the Japanese eastern cruisers and could only respond with Turret 3. At 2:01 the cruiser *Kako* had launched four torpedoes, which missed; the *Astoria* could not respond in kind because of the unbelievably stupid decision by the US Navy to remove the torpedoes from their cruisers. Captain Greenman had turned to starboard to bring Turret 2 to bear on eastern cruisers – she was apparently unaware of the western group – and to clear the line of fire of the *Quincy*. But the *Quincy* unexpectedly turned right as well, so Greenman had to turn the *Astoria* more than he had wanted or expected to try to clear the *Quincy*'s line of fire. It meant that the *Astoria* continued to take the bulk of the gunfire.

Of that gunfire, she had taken only two worrying shell hits to her hull, both 8-inch hits that had punched holes in the hull in the second deck above the waterline. So the *Astoria* was structurally sound, more or less, and would remain so, if the damage did not get any worse from combat or the fires blazing on and inside her.

Though she was blazing from her foremast to her hangar, her remaining 8-inch guns were blazing, too, in a different sense, thanks in large part to the energy and coolness of Lieutenant Commander Truesdell. But it was sound and fury signifying nothing; her range setting was far short of the actual ranges on the Japanese, largely because the Japanese had turned off their searchlights and her fire-control equipment was fouled by her smoke and fire. Thus her first 11 8-inch salvos missed, mostly falling short. But the Japanese did not, and, as they passed aft, the *Kako* and *Kinugasa* continued to give her a vicious lashing.

At 2:02, the *Kako*'s 25mm guns raked the *Astoria*'s bridge, killing her helmsman and crippling her communications. A minute later an 8-inch shell from the *Kinugasa* exploded on the well deck – again – and detonated a kerosene tank. Midships now became a firestorm, and dense smoke entered the after engine room, forcing its abandonment. The ship slowed down. Captain Greenman realized they couldn't take much more of this pounding and at 2:04 am ordered a turn to port away from the Japanese.[184] It was a fortuitous order, for at 2:05 the *Kako* launched another two torpedoes, which missed – again.

But Japanese torpedoes were not the only things the *Astoria* had to avoid. As the cruiser had turned to port, she saw the *Quincy*, out of control and burning furiously, still turning to starboard and about to cross in front of her in the opposite direction. Only a left full rudder averted a collision.[185]

A collision averted was small comfort as the shells continued raining on the *Astoria*. Fire-control was now a memory. Steering was lost from the bridge and had to be moved to the main damage control station. She settled on a wobbly course to the south, for all the good it would do; the forward engine room lost all power and was shut down.[186] And the *Astoria* staggered to a halt.

Then the gunfire stopped. Lieutenant Commander Truesdell was flabbergasted. "Why the enemy did not completely destroy the *Astoria* that night is a mystery to me as we had ceased firing; but for some reason they withdrew and did not come in for the kill."[187]

They certainly thought about it. The *Kinugasa* turned her searchlight on the *Astoria*, evidently to assess her damage. Defiantly, the *Astoria* got off one last salvo – three 8-inch shells from Turret 2, fired by local control.

Naturally, they missed, instead flying over the intended target *Kinugasa* into the darkness beyond. One landed on the left side of the forward 8-inch turret on the *Chokai*, knocking it out of commission.

Perhaps chastened, a little, the *Kinugasa* shut off her searchlight, and the Japanese disappeared into the night.

With them two Allied cruisers were about to disappear. Two more were helpless: dead in the water. Burning.

And alone.

While the Americans and Australians had been going through hell, the Japanese were virtually celebrating. By any standard Admiral Mikawa's operation here had gone ludicrously well, due to an incredible streak of good luck combined with an incompetence bordering on criminal on the part of the enemy. So well that Mikawa was not so much a military commander as a symphony maestro. The searchlight on the *Chokai* was his baton. Captain Ohmae would later explain:

> The *Chokai*'s searchlights were used for the double purpose of spotting targets and also informing our own ships of the flagship's location. They were effective in both roles, fairly screaming to her colleagues, "Here is the *Chokai*! Fire on *that* target!… Now *that* target… This is the *Chokai*! Hit *that* target![188]

Most symphonies don't have the audience shooting back at you, and for the most part this one did not as well. "For incredible minutes the turrets of enemy ships remained in their trained-in, secured positions, and we stood amazed, yet thankful while they did not bear on us."[189]

Except Mozart never had to deal with his musicians running off in the middle of a performance. Admiral Mikawa did. His scratch force was now badly divided. Destroyer *Yunagi* was somewhere west of Savo Island. *Tenryu*, *Yubari*, and *Furutaka* were close to the northeastern coast of Savo, heading northwest. The other cruisers of the 6th Cruiser Division were further northeast, headed northwest as well. Mikawa's own flagship *Chokai* had wandered off further still to the east. This tends to happen at night.

To make them an effective combat formation again, he had to get them back together. That would take time. Admiral Mikawa predicted that a half-hour to slow down and assemble, a half-hour to regain formation, a half-hour to get back up to battle speed, and another hour to get to the transport anchorage would suffice. And all that time, the clock was ticking, getting closer to dawn, when his cruisers would be as vulnerable to US carrier planes as the hapless *Mikuma* and *Mogami* were during the retreat from Midway. He needed to get away fast, and hopefully draw the US carriers into the range of the G4M bombers at Rabaul.[190]

Admiral Mikawa still did not know where those carriers were located, and he was apparently beginning to think his intelligence information was inaccurate. He had not been told about the two picket destroyers west of Savo Island. He was surprised by the appearance of the northern group of US cruisers. It seemed the Allies had warships "everywhere" and he did not know where they were, did not even know where the transports were, for that matter.[191] Had the reports of damage inflicted on the Allied ships by the 5th Air Attack Force been … wrong?

Finally, there was likely an emotional consideration. Admiral Mikawa was well aware of how far he had pressed his luck. He had been "greatly impressed … by the actions of the northern group of US cruisers… Had they had even a few minutes' warning of our approach, the results of the action would have been quite different."[192] They could have been different anyway, as that 8-inch shell from the *Quincy* came very close to killing the admiral. As it was, the *Chokai* had taken more of a beating than her consorts, with her forward 8-inch turret now disabled.

Admiral Mikawa looked around him at the flaming ships and debris around Savo Island. It reminded him of the water lantern festival at Lake Hakone.[193] He was also reminded of the words of Admiral Nagano, who had opposed the Savo operation, before Mikawa had left Japan: "The Japanese Navy is different from the American Navy. If you lose one ship it will take years to replace."[194] He was unwilling to press his luck further. The 17th Army had said the Americans could be easily pushed off Guadalcanal. Why risk his precious ships to sink noncombatant transports and supply ships? It was just not the Japanese way.

"All forces withdraw," Admiral Mikawa ordered at 2:23 am. The *Chokai* signaled, "Force in line ahead course 320 degrees speed 30 knots."[195]

There was considerable grumbling, especially from the *Chokai*'s skipper, Captain Hayakawa.[196] Perhaps in protest, Captain Sawa Masao had the *Kinugasa* empty her starboard torpedo tubes at the transports off Tulagi 13 miles away. The torpedoes missed, but no one would have been surprised if these Long Lances had hit. Nevertheless, the *Aoba*, *Kako*, and the *Kinugasa* complied, the *Chokai* trying to overtake them, but not trying too hard; the *Aoba* still had her charts easily accessible.

Off to port, they could see the western group – the *Tenryu*, *Yubari*, and *Furutaka*. These three ships were not quite ready to go home yet; they had come across the picket destroyer *Ralph Talbot*.

When the *Ralph Talbot*'s lookouts had seen Lieutenant Kiyose's flares to the east, the destroyer had gone to battle stations and had increased speed to 30 knots. Then ... nothing. No orders were issued to her, so she simply stayed on her patrol line as she watched gunfire to the east. She still did not suspect Japanese ships were in the area until about 2:12 am, when a single searchlight stabbed out of the darkness on the *Ralph Talbot*'s port bow and pinned the destroyer for about 10 seconds before swinging away.[197] Her skipper, Lieutenant Commander Joseph W. Callahan, had no idea what that was about – the Japanese usually used two searchlights, the Americans used one – but it seemed ominous.

It was even more ominous when, at 2:14 am, as she continued her patrol heading southwest, another single searchlight off the port beam snapped on, found the *Ralph Talbot*, and kept her pinned. More ominous yet were the colored shell splashes that started sprouting around her. Only Americans used colored dyes to mark the fall of their shots. Between that and the single searchlight, it must be friendly ships firing at her. Lieutenant Commander Callahan ordered the destroyer to go to top speed and start zigzagging. The *Ralph Talbot* turned on her identification lights and frantically broadcasted on the voice radio that she was being fired on by friendly forces. She took one hit on the starboard torpedo mount, killing two and knocking out one tube. Then, after seven salvos, all but two of which were short, the shooting stopped, though the searchlight did not. Maybe her messages had gotten through.[198]

Or not. At 2:18, Lieutenant Commander Callahan saw a Japanese light cruiser, the *Yubari*, crossing astern headed northwest. The *Ralph Talbot* turned to starboard to engage, only to be pinned by the *Yubari*'s searchlight – approximately 1,000 yards to port of the searchlight already on her, from the *Tenryu*. Those had not been friendly ships that had been firing on her earlier, but the *Tenryu* and the *Furutaka*. Now the *Furutaka* unloaded with her secondary guns, while the *Yubari* unloaded with her main guns.

In rapid succession, the *Ralph Talbot* took five hits, all from the *Yubari*. The first hit the charthouse under the bridge and knocked out the port torpedo director and the searchlights. The second destroyed the radars and some of the fire-control equipment, the third hit the wardroom, the fourth the starboard side near the torpedo tubes, causing the destroyer to ship water, and the fifth hit the Number 4 gun mount. Twelve men were killed.[199]

The *Ralph Talbot* struggled to respond, her radars knocked out by the early hit, and her lookouts blinded by the Japanese searchlights and unable to get effective firing solutions. Lieutenant Commander Callahan launched three torpedoes from the functioning starboard tubes; they all missed. He swung back to port and tried to launch torpedoes, but was only able to get off one that missed. The *Ralph Talbot* thought she had gotten one hit on the *Yubari*, with which she had knocked out the cruiser's searchlight. It had not. The *Yubari* had merely shut it off.

Lieutenant Commander Callahan no longer had a target, but he had no time to worry about that. The *Ralph Talbot* was a picket destroyer northwest of Savo Island, widely separated from her Allied consorts. She was rapidly taking in water and quickly developed a 20-degree list to starboard. At around 2:30 she lost all power, so she couldn't move. Her radios were smashed.[200] She was sinking, powerless, alone – and with no way to call for help.

The *Yubari* could have finished her off, but having received Admiral Mikawa's order to withdraw, she joined the *Tenryu*, *Yunagi*, *Chokai*, and the 6th Cruiser Division in their headlong flight to get away from the US aircraft carriers, the same US aircraft carriers who were in a headlong flight to get away from the Japanese.

Admiral Mikawa knew he would have to request air cover from Rabaul later in the morning. But for now, he, Captain Ohmae, and the flag staff had the skippers submit their battle reports so they could assess the damage they had inflicted on the enemy. Their conclusion: five enemy cruisers and four destroyers sunk.[201]

For once, it was not that much of an exaggeration.

The first warning Admiral Crutchley on the *Australia* had that something was amiss was when Lieutenant Kiyose's flares appeared over the transports. Like the able, experienced veteran officer he was and unlike most of the other Allied commanders on this night, Crutchley immediately realized that the flares presaged a Japanese attack. Like those other Allied commanders, though, he misinterpreted what he was seeing, in his case still clinging to the bizarre notion that the flares were meant to aid a Japanese submarine attack on the transports.[202] Why submarines, who rely on stealth and surprise, who hide until the right moment to make a devastating strike without warning, would want bright objects illuminating the area around them just before they strike was never fully explained.

The admiral came to his senses once he saw gunfire south of Savo Island, gunfire that intensified as it moved north and east. "The gunfire was very heavy, and I thought it must have been the *Vincennes* group coming into action against an enemy being engaged by the *Australia* group."[203] Which was correct, technically. Crutchley was puzzled as to why he had not received any reports about this engagement, but felt the lack of communications confirmed what he and Admiral Turner firmly believed: that the forces they had deployed were more than adequate to deal with the situation. Still, in an example of the "better safe than sorry" philosophy that had been sorely lacking in the Allies over the past 24 hours, he tried to form a battle line by moving the *Australia* to a blocking position some 7 miles west of the transports off Guadalcanal and ordering all destroyers not currently engaged with the enemy to form up on his flagship. A sensible action that, like most everything else the Allies did this night, went awry. Because of a communications error, most of the destroyers interpreted his order in the context of an earlier order Crutchley had issued, and instead went northwest of Savo Island, where they were completely useless for combat but, critically, were able to help in rescue operations.

Still having heard exactly nothing from his subordinates on the battle that had clearly taken place but whose specifics were not clear, at 2:26 am Admiral Crutchley sent out a message asking the commanders of the three screening groups, "Are your groups in action?" Admiral Scott on the *San Juan*, far to the east guarding the eastern channel, answered, "This force not in action. Appears to be surface force between Florida Island and Savo." There was only an ominous silence from the *Vincennes*. Captain Bode on the *Chicago* responded, "Were but not now."[204]

Historians may debate how Admiral Crutchley could have found fault with a battle report as complete, informative, and insightful as Captain Bode's, but apparently find fault with it he did. After seeing three burning ships between Savo and Florida islands, at 2:42 Crutchley sent a second, much more terse, message to the *Chicago*: "Report situation!" Three minutes later Bode responded, "We are standing toward Lengo on course 100."[205] Crutchley's original message had apparently caused Bode to order the *Chicago* to reverse course and head back to the east. Another three minutes went by before Bode started sketching the picture for his admiral: "*Chicago* south of Savo Island. Hit by torpedo. Slightly down by bow. Enemy ships firing to seaward. *Canberra* burning on bearing 125 degrees True five miles from Savo. Two destroyers standing by *Canberra*."[206] It was useful information, except the *Canberra* was about 9 miles east of where Bode said she was, and she had no destroyers standing by her.[207] Bode actually had no idea where they were and seems to have been just making things up as he went along. At 3:10 am a frustrated Crutchley could only report to Admiral Turner, who had seen the gun flashes and was aware that something that happened, of a "Surface action near Savo. Situation as yet undetermined."[208]

In a missive that in the world of military reports and their dry language counts as nothing short of brutal, the Naval War College speculated that after an hour of "acting as if dazed," to use Morison's words, the demands of his immediate superior for an update had finally awakened Captain Bode to his own inglorious role in the events of this night, about which he was "deeply concerned".[209] *Canberra* survivor Bruce Loxton agreed, suggesting Bode was trying to cover up his conduct.[210] That may very well be, but in fairness, one must recall the words of Captain Roskill in "surviving the strain of trying to remain alert for several consecutive nights after long and anxious days in the deadening and exhausting heat of the Solomon Islands' climate."[211] There is also the small matter of Bode, exhausted as he was, probably not knowing if he was in charge of the southern force or not. Even so, he did, in what could be described as the finest military tradition, head for the sound or at least the sight of the gunfire, as even the War College admitted.

Against that must be balanced that the two most important commodities in military actions are information and communications. Captain Bode had vital information that the Japanese were attacking, yet he did not communicate it to anyone at a time when it might have had value. He would later give multiple explanations as to why, saying he tried to and the message never got through, or – a truly bizarre defense considering the Japanese had just hit his ship with a torpedo – he did not want to give away his position to the Japanese. While he could not be bothered to communicate this vital information to anyone, Captain Bode did, in the middle of battle, find time to argue over who should be controlling the radar, which Bode had turned off to again avoid giving away his position to the Japanese. When Captain Bode lacked information, specifically as to who was in charge, he did not communicate that, either. While it is almost an absolute that every commander makes mistakes in every battle, and that allowances must be made for such mistakes, it is hard to find any judgmental justification for the silence from the bridge of the *Chicago*.

Heading east, toward the transports, as he probably should have been doing all along, Captain Bode stumbled across the *Patterson*, who, apparently without orders, took position on the *Chicago*'s starboard bow as an antisubmarine screen. At 3:35, the lookouts sighted the *Canberra* – 2 miles astern. The *Patterson* was dropped off to assist her.[212]

The disabled and burning Australian cruiser was desperate for any and all the help she could get, but as the *Patterson* approached, the *Canberra*'s ready 4-inch ammunition began to explode. "You had better wait," she flashed the destroyer.[213] A little after 4:00 am, the situation had cleared up enough for the *Patterson* to come along side and help fight the fires and take off the wounded. Things seemed to be turning around. And then Admiral Turner sent a message.

Admiral Turner was in an impossible position, but one that would nevertheless provide the mercurial but brilliant admiral one of his frequent vague moments. He knew something had happened off Savo Island, and as information came in in bits and pieces he was realizing what a disaster it was. He was furious but not surprised when he was informed that Admiral Ghormley, almost in a perfunctory manner, had approved the withdrawal of Admiral Fletcher's carriers. He tried to talk Fletcher out of it, at 3:45 signaling, "Surface attack on the screen coordinated with use of aircraft flares. *Chicago* hit by torpedo. *Canberra* on fire."[214] For all the good that would do. Captain Sherman of the *Wasp*, with its pilots trained in night operations, asked Admiral Noyes three times to request permission from Fletcher to quickly head north to launch a strike at the fleeing Japanese ships. Three times Noyes refused to even forward the request.[215] He knew what the answer would be. Fletcher had never wanted to fight over Guadalcanal, and sure enough he wasn't going to fight.

Which left Admiral Turner desperate to get out his unarmed and unarmored transports. At about 5:00 am the *Patterson* intercepted his message directed at Admiral Crutchley. "It is urgent for this force to depart this area at 0630," and, "If *Canberra* cannot join retirement in time she should be destroyed before departure."[216]

Samuel Eliot Morison would later call this the "death warrant" for the *Canberra*.[217] Her crew was outraged. She was burning, she was listing 10 degrees to starboard, but she wasn't actually sinking. Now what? The *Canberra*'s executive officer, Commander J. A. Walsh, acting as captain in place of the mortally wounded Captain Getting, kept salvage efforts going until 5:15 am, but as it was obvious she could not get under way in time for the 6:30 departure, he ordered the cruiser abandoned.[218] The *Patterson*'s Commander Walker called in the destroyer *Blue* to assist.

Before the *Blue* arrived, a lookout on the *Patterson* reported, "Strange ship on the port quarter."[219] The *Patterson* challenged the ship, but received no reply. Signaling the *Canberra* "Out all lights!" the destroyer cast off – to the cheers of the Australian crew. "There were no outcries or entreaties," Commander Walker would later write, "rather a cheery 'Carry on, Patterson – Good luck' – and prompt and efficient casting off of lines, brows, etc. Not a man stepped out of line." Walker concluded by saying everyone in the *Patterson* felt "privileged to have served so gallant a crew."[220]

The *Patterson* approached the unknown ship, challenging her two more times. Still no reply. The destroyer snapped on her searchlight. The ship responded by opening fire. Commander Walker ordered his guns to return fire, and a snap firefight was under way. In the glare of his searchlight, Walker thought he recognized the other ship. After three 5-inch salvoes, he thought he better make the emergency recognition signal. The other ship, the *Chicago*, stopped shooting. Her jittery gunners had started shooting without orders from Captain Bode, who, now being a stickler for procedure, noted that the *Patterson* had used the wrong emergency identification signal.[221]

In the meantime, the destroyer *Blue* had managed to find the *Canberra*, and tied up to the cruiser's port side. Now the *Patterson* returned, tied up to starboard, and together they removed the *Canberra*'s survivors. *Patterson* would take off 398, of whom 46 were seriously wounded. Among them was Captain Getting; emergency surgery could not stabilize him before he could be transferred to a medical transport. The *Blue* took 343, of whom 18 were seriously wounded.[222] It was the *Blue*'s only positive contribution to this Battle of Savo Island, or as the Japanese called it, the First Battle of the Solomon Sea. Her battle report summed up her performance as, "This vessel took no offensive measures, inflicted no damage to enemy and sustained no loss or damage." Or, as one historian put it, "No runs, no hits, one error."[223]

While all this was happening, at around 5:15 some good news came around: the *Ralph Talbot* had managed to get up some steam power and crawled close to Savo, where she jury-rigged her radio to send out a distress call.

Meanwhile, things had gotten more complicated. Admiral Crutchley had asked the *Patterson* for an update on the *Canberra*'s condition. Commander Walker responded: "Disabled on fire in position 7 miles southeast of Savo."[224] The message said it all, except for what ship was disabled and on fire: the *Canberra* or the *Patterson*.

Having heard nothing more about it, Admiral Crutchley ordered the destroyer *Selfridge* to check up on both the *Canberra* and the *Patterson*, and to sink both if they could not join the retirement.[225]

Meanwhile, General Vandegrift reported to Admiral Turner that only three days of rations and 36 hours of ammunition had been landed at Tulagi. He pleaded with Turner to allow six more hours for the transports to unload critical supplies. Turner agreed, and at 6:21 am canceled his original order for withdrawal.[226]

The *Selfridge* was continuing toward the *Canberra* when she stumbled across the *Astoria* – disabled, burning, if anything in even worse shape than the *Canberra.* At 6:44 the destroyer reported the cruiser's position and that four destroyers were trying to pick up survivors. This was the first news that Admiral Crutchley or Admiral Turner had on the northern group. Turner would add that he had no information on the *Vincennes*, the *Quincy* and *Ralph Talbot* were believed sunk, and the *Astoria* was burning, but the crew was trying to save the ship.

Having passed the *Astoria*, the *Selfridge* finally arrived at the *Canberra*, finding the Australian cruiser deserted. Her skipper asked Admiral Turner if she should continue with scuttling the *Canberra*. Even though he had delayed the evacuation of the transports – the very reason why the *Canberra* had to be sunk – Turner quickly said she should. So at 7:10 the *Selfridge* opened fire with her 5-inch guns on the derelict.

But nothing came easy on this day. The destroyer *Ellet* came along and saw the *Selfridge* shooting at a cruiser. She assumed it must be a Japanese cruiser, so the *Ellet* opened fire as well. She had fired 106 5-inch rounds and seen several hits before the *Selfridge* could break the bad news that she was shooting at a friendly ship. Even so, the *Canberra* still wouldn't sink. The *Selfridge* fired 263 5-inch rounds. She launched four torpedoes, only one of which exploded, another fine performance for US torpedoes. At 7:47, the frustrated destroyer called on the *Ellet* to finish the job. At close range, the *Ellet* fired one torpedo, which really did explode against the Canberra's starboard side, and the cruiser sank at 8:00 am.[227]

Which left the *Astoria*. The cruiser was for all practical purposes divided in two, with the bow and stern not burning but everything in between an inferno so intense that no ship could come alongside. The destroyer *Bagley*, with Lieutenant Commander Chambers conning in this awkward situation, put her starboard bow alongside the *Astoria*'s starboard bow. By 4:45 am, she had taken off all wounded from the forecastle. Then she saw a light flashing from the stern. Survivors were there, too, so she headed there, in the process picking up survivors, some of whom were from the *Vincennes*, in rafts and in the water.

At about 5:45, the *Bagley* returned and Lieutenant Commander Chambers brought the ship to the *Astoria*'s starboard quarter. Captain Greenman believed that even though she had a 3-degree list to port, the cruiser could still be saved. He went back aboard with 325 men. They set up a bucket brigade to try to douse the intense fires. Lieutenant Commander Topper took a damage control team to try poking around the lower decks.

At around 7:00 am, the old four-piper destroyer *Hopkins*, now a minesweeper, came up to help. Captain Greenman asked the *Hopkins* to tow her to the shallow water off Guadalcanal so they could effect more repairs and hopefully keep those gaping holes in the port side from submerging. The burning, water-logged heavy cruiser was really too much for the old destroyer to manage, but after a fashion they made a tow line, and got the *Astoria* pointed southeast. Morale soared as they slowly built up speed, soon moving at 3 knots.[228]

And they needed to get moving; at around 8:50 am word spread that a coastwatcher on Bougainville had heard a large formation of aircraft headed southeast. The Japanese were on the way.

Captain Greenman reported to Admiral Turner that there was a chance of saving the *Astoria* if she could get power and water to fight the fires. At the order of Turner, the destroyer *Wilson*, in her one known useful act in this action, came alongside the cruiser shortly thereafter to pump water into the fire. Between the *Wilson* and the bucket brigade, they were slowly whittling down the fire – except for a very intense one below decks near the wardroom.

Nevertheless, things were slowly turning for the worse. The list had increased to 10 degrees. Lieutenant Commander Topper could not ascertain whether the sprinkler system and flooding valves had been able to flood the forward 5-inch magazine; Captain Greenman believed they had not, but because of fires and damage no one could get there to check. The answer to their question came at 11:00 am, more felt than heard. A big shudder came from the ship, followed by the grind of collapsing bulkheads. All in the vicinity of the Number 2 turret. Yellow gas bled out of the shell holes. Topper tried to get down a hatch to the forward 5-inch handling room, but the hatch was too hot. Another rumble, more crashes from collapsing bulkheads. The magazines were exploding. It was over.[229]

At 11:19, Admiral Turner ordered the *Hopkins* and *Wilson* away to begin escorting the transports leaving Guadalcanal, but he was sending the *Buchanan* to help fight the fires and the transport *Alchiba* to tow the ship. Yet all they could do was pick up survivors. The port list was enough so the shell holes started shipping water. The explosions below decks were venting out the ship.

At five minutes past noon, Captain Greenman bowed to the inevitable and ordered the *Astoria* abandoned. She rolled over to port and sank by the bow at 12:15, joining the *Canberra*, *Quincy*, and *Vincennes* on the bottom of what would thereafter be known as "Ironbottom Sound."

Except for an intermission preparing for the Japanese air attack that, strangely, never came, Admiral Turner kept the transports unloading for those additional six hours; for, as much room as they could free up by unloading food, ammunition, and other supplies for the Marines on Guadalcanal, was as much room as they had for the wounded. Why he placed so much effort on saving the American *Astoria* but not the similarly situated Australian *Canberra* is a question Turner never answered, but the discrepancy, perceived or otherwise, would be a source of friction between the American and Australian governments.

Nevertheless, in acceding to General Vandegrift's wishes, Admiral Turner had been exceedingly courageous in exposing himself and his men to Japanese air attacks for which they had little defense, but they could not stay exposed. Beginning at 4:00 pm and ending at dusk, the Allied ships left in three convoys.

It was the start of the first Allied offensive of the Pacific War, but it felt like a retreat from Moscow, no mean feat in the south Pacific. Four first-line cruisers sunk, 1,077 American and Australian sailors dead in the worst defeat in US Navy history.[230] The mood was glum. "It was a big mess," said Fred Tuccitto of the *Chicago*. "We had no idea that the Japanese were so good."[231]

Admiral King would call it "the blackest day of the whole war."[232]

About an hour after dawn on August 9, an SBD Dauntless from the carrier *Saratoga* was out scouring the Coral Sea southwest of Guadalcanal for any sign of the Japanese. Not to attack them, of course, but to make sure they were not following. The crew did not find any Japanese, but did find something curious all the same.

The bright blue Coral Sea was marred by a long rainbow coming from a small ship. The Dauntless approached. The ship was friendly, a US destroyer, but she appeared to be in dreadful shape. She was inching along at about 7 knots, down by the bow, and trailing that rainbow – a large oil slick.

The air crew radioed in the contact and the grim picture it presented, not even knowing the half of it. The ship was the destroyer *Jarvis*, who in the previous day's air attack had suffered a torpedo hit that left a 50-foot hole in her starboard bow. The attack had knocked out her radios. Most of her guns were disabled. All her lifeboats, torpedoes, and floatables had been jettisoned.

The SBD resumed her mission and left the *Jarvis*. The destroyer was barely clinging to life all alone in the middle of the broad expanse of water between Guadalcanal and Australia. No way to contact anyone, but at least the Americans now knew where she was.

And so did the Japanese.

While escaping the US carrier planes that had no intention of attacking him, Admiral Mikawa had reviewed the battle reports from his skippers. He found the action report of the destroyer *Yunagi* intriguing: she had damaged "one "*Achilles*-class" cruiser trying to "escape in the outer bay."[233] When Mikawa radioed Admiral Yamada of the 5th Air Attack Force in Rabaul requesting air cover, he also told him about the cruiser.

Admiral Yamada was already taking action. He had launched his own reconnaissance planes around dawn to see what they could of the Allies around Tulagi and Guadalcanal and to find those elusive American aircraft carriers. One Betty bomber of the 4th Air Group reported at 9:35 am that it had spotted "a large enemy destroyer" some 100 miles southwest of Tulagi. At 11:00 am, a second Betty of the 4th Air Group reported sighting a damaged "*Achilles*-class cruiser" slowly retiring from the battle area.[234]

Now here was a nice target. A cruiser. Undoubtedly the same ship reported as the "large enemy destroyer" earlier. Hurt and limping away. Shortly before 8:00 am, Admiral Yamada had already launched 16 bombers of the Misawa Air Group and 15 Zeros of the Tainan Air Group and sent them toward Guadalcanal, likely to attack the transports, who, unbeknown to him, were now without fighter protection; or better yet, to find those American carriers. Yamada decided to go for the quick, almost-certain kill. At about 11:16, he ordered the Betty from the 4th Air Group to maintain its station over the cruiser and redirected the 31 aircraft already in the air to that position, with the "Primary Assignment: To attack enemy cruiser."[235] At 1:00 pm, they found their badly wounded prey – not an *Achilles*-class light cruiser, but the destroyer *Jarvis*.

As one historian put it, "Her crew had no boats, no life rafts, and no chance."[236] The knowledge of imminent death often has a way of focusing the mind, and in the case of the *Jarvis* the eyes of her gunners. Like a wounded animal caught in a trap, the destroyer growled and snapped at her tormentors. Despite the Zeros strafing her decks to try to keep her gunners down, her antiaircraft fire seems to have been unusually effective, as she shot down two Bettys and damaged four more, one so badly it had to make an emergency landing.[237] But with 16 torpedoes aimed at a destroyer that could barely move, the issue was never in doubt. Admiral Yamada would later dryly record: "Results: Attacked and sank one *Achilles*-type ship."[238]

No way to call for help. No lifeboats. No one friendly anywhere near her. All alone. Any survivors of the *Jarvis*' 264 officers and men were doomed to drown in the Coral Sea. Trying to swim in the midst of a nauseating oil slick until they could swim no more, then sinking into the cold depths forever. As far as the US Navy knew, she had just vanished. Even by the impossibly dark standards of war, the fate of the *Jarvis* and her crew was a unique twist on absolute hell.

But an absolute hell that saved the lives of perhaps thousands of American and Australian servicemen on Guadalcanal by diverting from them an air attack against which they themselves were largely unprotected.

Pleasantly surprised that he had not encountered an air attack on his return trip, Admiral Mikawa entered Simpson Harbor in the *Chokai* with the 18th Cruiser Division and the *Yunagi* at 5:39 am on August 10.[239] His flag was struck from the luxurious flagship and raised back above the dump of a building next to the Lakunai airfield. The admiral who had been unwanted in Rabaul was now greeted with cheers, with which the soft-spoken Mikawa could not have been entirely comfortable.[240]

Yet the cheers were well-earned. This operation had been assembled on the fly, with ships that had never worked together, with only the barest amount of information concerning the enemy, and no air cover. Yet through the planning and skill of Admiral Mikawa and his crews, and through pushing their luck to its absolute limit and maybe even past it, they had inflicted on the US Navy the worst defeat in its history. With barely a scratch in return, relatively speaking.

The only thing that went wrong the previous night was the reinforcement convoy Mikawa had slapped together. Some 14 miles west of Cape St George, the *Meiyo Maru* took two torpedoes into her port side aft, compliments of Lieutenant Commander Munson and the US submarine *S-38*, eager to make up for being unable to attack Mikawa's cruisers. The transport went down just after 8:00 pm, taking down with her 342 of the Special Naval Landing Force troops and 31 of her crew. Escorts *Tsugaru* and minesweeper *W-21* counterattacked but Munson's boat made good her escape.[241] Yet compared with Mikawa's tactical success of that same night, it was merely an inconvenience.

When Mikawa stepped ashore he even found a message from Admiral Yamamoto waiting for him. It read: "Appreciate the courageous and hard fighting of every man of your organization. I expect you to expand your exploits and you will make every effort to support the land forces of the Imperial Army which are now engaged in a desperate struggle."

A nice message on the surface. But the reference to the "land forces" of the Imperial Army's "desperate struggle," in that oblique way that is so Japanese, recalled the transports of the US "land forces" that Admiral Mikawa had not attacked. Privately, Yamamoto was furious with Mikawa.

For now, though, there was cause for celebration, a celebration badly needed after the catastrophe of Midway. The *Chokai* was being repaired by the 8th Base Force. Mikawa hoped his men could get some rest and relaxation in Rabaul. And he hoped for celebration, rest, and relaxation for the men of the 6th Cruiser Division, whom he had ordered up to Kavieng with no destroyer escort the previous morning.

Most of them would get that rest and relaxation.

Admiral Goto and the men of the 6th Cruiser Division were indeed in a celebratory mood. Having escaped air attack off Guadalcanal, they had just escaped submarine attack in the natural choke point of the St George's Channel between New Britain and New Ireland. Yesterday, they thought they had spotted a periscope in the channel – wrongly, as it turned out – and had to endure a night of evasive maneuvers. But they had left the channel with its submarine threat behind them and dawn had produced a bright, sunny day. With dawn, Goto had ordered the zigzagging stopped, and now the *Aoba* led her consorts in a column at 16 knots. With the beautiful weather present and combat unlikely, the skippers were allowed to open the portholes of their ships to vent out the stifling heat below decks.[242] They were some 16 miles off Simbari Island. Kavieng was less than 100 miles away.

At 9:10 am, there was an underwater explosion and a huge geyser of water erupted abreast the Number 1 forward turret on the starboard side of the last cruiser in the column, the *Kako*.[243] Within seconds there were two more explosions and aquatic eruptions on her starboard side, further aft, in the vicinity of the forward magazines and boiler rooms 1 and 2.[244] Maybe they had stopped those evasive maneuvers a little too soon.

For the explosions were from three torpedoes, out of a spread of four launched by the 17-year-old US submarine *S-44*, stewing off New Ireland under the command of Lieutenant Commander John R. "Dinty" Moore. The range had been a ludicrously close

700 yards; "We were close enough to see the Japs on the bridge using their glasses," Moore later said.[245]

Within three minutes, the *Kako* groaned as her bow dipped from the first hit and twisted, letting water ship in through those open portholes, another great idea implemented just a tad too soon. The dying cruiser continued rolling over onto her starboard side, her holes big and small sucking in more and more water, her forward stack belching steam.

Having dived to 130 feet, the 850-ton *S-44* could only listen to what followed as the cold sea water reached the *Kako*'s boilers. "Evidently all her boilers blew up," Moore recalled. "You could hear hideous noises like steam hissing through water. These noises were more terrifying to the crew than the actual depth charges that followed. It sounded as if giant chains were being dragged across our hull, as if our own water and air lines were bursting."[246]

Just some seven minutes after the first torpedo had hit, just short of the safety of Kavieng, the *Kako* sank bow first; 8,800 tons gone, just like that. Their luck from Savo Island had definitely run out. Admiral Goto and the other ships of the 6th Cruiser Division tried to find the undersea predator in their midst. The *Aoba* cryptically recorded, "Carried out embarrassing depth charge barrage."[247] The *S-44* escaped rather easily, having bagged the largest ship sunk by US submarines so far in the Pacific War.

Perhaps now a little more conscious of the threat from submarines, the remnants of the 6th Cruiser Division spent most of the rest of the day picking up survivors; the destroyer *Uzuki* came up from Rabaul to rescue a few more the next day. Ultimately, the vast majority of the *Kako*'s crew, including her skipper, Captain Takahashi Yuji, were rescued, but 34 crewmen were lost. The arrival of the *Aoba*, *Furutaka*, and *Kinugasa* in Kavieng at 5:11 that afternoon was not nearly the happy one they had expected.

The *Kako* was a Parthian shot from a foe who had already been defeated – defeated in battle, but not the war. This was no longer the Philippines, the Java Sea, the Indian Ocean, when the Imperial Japanese Navy could steamroll its enemies, usually without taking losses, often before the enemies could even organize to fight.

No more. Now, their enemies fought hard. Now, even a victory for the Imperial Japanese Navy came with a price. A price they could not afford to pay.

How times had changed.

How Midway had changed everything.

CHAPTER 4
PANDAEMONIUM

Marooned.

That was the feeling running through the 1st Marine Division. Having all of their transports and cargo ships up anchor and leave, carrying most of their supplies, with no definite timeframe as to when they would be back, can leave one with that feeling. The Marines were shocked, a feeling intensified by news of the disaster at Savo Island.

Marooned. On a jungle island. Holding only a tiny part of a jungle island. Shared with the enemy.

Almost all of the Marines' heavy equipment had been on the cargo ships at whose defense Admiral Fletcher had balked. The Marines had enough food for maybe 37 days. Enough ammunition for just four days of combat.

General Vandegrift called his senior officers for a briefing on the situation:

> I told them of Fletcher's carriers precipitately retiring, which meant that the transports were leaving. [... L]ess than half of our supply was on the beach; all of our heavy equipment remained aboard the transports; God only knew when we could expect aircraft protection much less surface craft; with the transports gone the enemy would shift his attacks against us and we could expect surface attacks as well.
>
> Then I ordered them to relate these unsavory facts to their junior officers, NCOs and men. But they must also pound home that we anticipated no Bataan, no Wake Island. Since 1775 Marines have found themselves in tough spots. They had survived and we would survive – but only if every officer and man on Guadalcanal gave his all to the cause.[1]

Lieutenant Colonel Twining described their predicament:

> We were left without exterior communications or support of any kind and with no assurance that help would be forthcoming. We had no source of information or observation except what we could derive from a twenty-four foot observation tower constructed of

> palm logs inherited from the emperor. We were on half rations, had little ammunition and no construction equipment or defensive materials whatsoever, and no one would talk to us when we improvised a long-distance transmitter from captured Japanese radio equipment. Outside of that we were in great shape.[2]

The Marines got to work: finishing the airfield, establishing a defense perimeter around it, and lugging the dropped-off supplies to hidden caches. It was now that the Marines really got to know Guadalcanal.

It might be hard to imagine Guadalcanal. People hear "South Pacific" and they think sun and lots of it, palm trees, beaches, and the like. Guadalcanal sounds like a virtual paradise, except with people shooting at you.

Many English speakers not versed in history find it shocking that Guadalcanal does not have an actual canal. The very name suggests a fundamental dishonesty about the island. The island, as many a writer has opined, looks like paradise but is more like Paradise Lost.

The Marines quickly picked up on the dishonesty, that Guadalcanal was a lie. William Manchester called it "a vision of beauty, but of evil beauty."[3] Remembering how Guadalcanal looked from the deck of a transport on D-Day, one Marine said, "From our vantage point we couldn't see what a putrefying shithole it really was."[4]

Before the American invasion, information on the Solomons was sorely lacking. The Europeans first discovered the Solomons in 1568, and various European powers made efforts to colonize the Solomons, along with New Britain and New Georgia, which is how the island names seemed like little pieces of European imperialism tossed into a pot and shaken, not stirred. But with no riches, hostile natives, and an unpleasant climate, no one particularly wanted to go there, so the islands were largely forgotten. The Australians preferred to pretend the Solomons weren't there. Those few who had been there usually refused to talk about them. The very few who did talk about them, who had visited Guadalcanal, called it a "bloody, stinking hole."[5]

Mostly volcanic in origin if not current behavior, the Solomons are largely a double column of islands running from northwest to southeast. To the northwest the large island of Bougainville, itself bracketed by Buka to the northwest and Shortland, the name of an island and its associated island group, to the southeast, acts as a block on the big channel between the double line of islands, technically called New Georgia Sound but known in American parlance for obvious reasons as "The Slot." The major islands on the north-northeast side of The Slot are, from northwest to southeast, Choiseul, Santa Ysabel, and Malaita. On the south-southwest side of the Slot are New Georgia and associated islands around it, the Russell Islands, Guadalcanal, and San Cristobal.

The centerpiece of the campaign, Guadalcanal is some 90 miles in length and about 25 miles wide. On the other side of the newly and unhappily named Ironbottom Sound, between Guadalcanal and Malaita, was the island of Florida. And snuggled into an elbow of Florida Island in Ironbottom Sound was Tulagi, home of the best natural harbor in the lower Solomons. Also between Guadalcanal and Florida, off the northwest corner of Guadalcanal, was Savo Island, tiny and conical, albeit not sharply so. The Indispensable Strait – named after a British warship – separates Florida from neighboring Malaita. The strait between Florida and Guadalcanal to the south, part of Ironbottom Sound, is known generally as Sealark Channel.

The Marines had no idea what they had gotten themselves into. As official US Navy historian Samuel Eliot Morison explained, "The Marines, usually prepared to land anywhere at any time, possessed information on almost every group of Pacific islands except the Solomons."[6] This should probably have been a tipoff that the decisive Pacific campaign would be fought there.

There was information out there, however, if one knew where to look and whom to ask. Coastwatcher Martin Clemens described Guadalcanal:

> On the inside she was a poisonous morass. Crocodiles hid in her creeks or patrolled her turgid backwaters. Her jungles were alive with slithering, crawling, scuttling things; with giant lizards that barked like dogs, with huge red furry spiders, with centipedes and leeches and scorpions, with rats and bats and fiddler crabs and one big species of landcrab which moved through the bush with all the stealth of a steamroller.[7]

The first thing one notices about Guadalcanal is the heat. And it's not a dry heat; the air is completely saturated. The public affairs officer Major Frank O. Hough described it, saying, "No air stirs here and the hot humidity is beyond the imagination of anyone who has not lived in it."[8]

The Solomons have two seasons, "wet" and "dry," though to the Marines the seasons were more like "wet" and "really wet." The *New York Times*' F. Tillman Durdin wrote, "It rains almost every night – weepy tropical rain that soaks into the bed rolls and seeps through the tarpaulin. The nights are passed in wet chill and discomfort and the days in mud and filth."[9] Marine Captain Joe Foss said the foxholes where most of each night was spent "never dried out" and "smelled like an owl's nest," a description to which probably everyone can relate.[10]

The rain has more of a negative effect than just wetness, mud, and general discomfort. It feeds the primordial jungle and keeps it primordial. The jungle canopy combines with the dense undergrowth to keep much of the jungle floor in darkness for years, decades, centuries. Anything that dies, plant or animal, in that damp darkness, rots. In ghastly, horrifying, nauseating fashion.

"Rot lies everywhere just under the exotic lushness," explained Major Hough. "The ground is porous with decaying vegetation, emitting a sour unpleasant odor. [...] Freshly killed flesh begins to decompose in a matter of a few hours."[11]

William Manchester listed a few of the enemies American forces had to face:

> [S]erpents, crocodiles, centipedes which could crawl across the flesh leaving a trail of swollen skin, land crabs which would scuttle in the night making noises indistinguishable

> from those of an infiltrating Jap, scorpions, lizards, tree leeches, cockatoos that screamed like the leader of a banzai charge, wasps as long as your finger and spiders as large as your fist. And mosquitoes, mosquitoes, mosquitoes, all carriers of malaria.[12]

But it wasn't just the mosquitos and the malaria. The standing water also bred mold and other unfriendly microbes that permeated the air and got into every wound, every scratch, and turned them into "malignant ulcers." Private Leckie called them "Guadalcanal rot," an exceedingly painful type of tropical ulcer or jungle rot.[13] The travel writer Jack London described them in *The Cruise of the Snark* as "excessively active ulcers. A mosquito bite, a cut or the slightest abrasion, serves for the lodgment of the poison with which the air seems to be filled." One Marine described the ulcers as "flesh encrusted with oozing pus by the canteen-cup."[14] And those ulcers easily turned septic. One could lose a limb from jungle rot.

The constant rain also played havoc with equipment. Vehicles got stuck in deep mud. Anything metal rusted. Electrical circuits and batteries were disrupted. And it was impossible to keep oneself clean through all this with no clean place to shower or shave or wash clothes with any regularity. Especially since most of the personal care items had been on those cargo ships Admiral Fletcher would not protect; indeed, with most of the toilet paper stashed aboard those cargo ships, Marines who had to use the toilet cleaned themselves with pages from the *New York Times*.[15] Between the mud, the mold, and the men unable to bathe or wash, the smell was nauseating.

Even the plants were unfriendly, particularly the notorious kunai grass – also called blood grass because the tips can be the color of blood, and can draw blood. Kunai can grow to a height of 7 feet or so. It is stiff, serrated, and sharp. Manchester said kunai "could lay a man's hand open as quickly as a scalpel..."[16] But kunai was just the vanguard of botany's assault on humanity. Most of the island that was not kunai was what historian William J. Owens called "pestilential rain forest." Massive trees, sometimes 40 feet across at their base, were often dead and rotten, liable to topple at the merest disturbance. There were at least 11 kinds of thorn bushes, and vines with "large razor-sharp thorns like hooks that ripped through uniforms and human flesh." Bamboo, which according to Private Richard William Harding seemed to grow even as it was hacked down.

The rain. The rot. The mosquitos. The malaria. The kunai. Then there were the animals. Poisonous snakes. Bats that can foul any exposed food. Salt-water crocodiles. It was this South Pacific paradise in which the 1st Maroon Division, as Lieutenant Colonel Twining cheekily renamed the unit, got to work.[17]

The supplies were hauled off the beach and dispersed among small caches hidden in the jungle and inside the perimeter. Within four days most of it was completed. Engineers improved the old coastal road to Lunga and bridged various waterways inside the perimeter to speed movement.

There was one piece of good news for General Vandegrift and his men. Some of the Japanese had left in a panic; others thought the Americans were just going to raid the island and so decided to hide out until the Americans left. In both cases, the Japanese had left everything behind, including hot meals sitting on tables. Most of what the US could not supply for the time being, due to pulling out the transports too soon, the Japanese did, including huge quantities of rice, plums, tinned crabmeat, and other foods. Also, beer and *sake*, useful since you couldn't drink the local water. A complete radio suite, which since there had not been time to get the radios off the transports was a godsend that, with some tinkering, allowed them to communicate. Thirty-four operational trucks, numerous bicycles, a 1940 Plymouth, and a headquarters building shaped like a pagoda, which became the US headquarters and was nicknamed, unsurprisingly, "the Pagoda." Even rifles, machine guns, ammunition, basic earth-moving equipment, and two functional radar sets were all salvaged.

The Marines set up their defense perimeter, some 9,600 yards in length. In the east, the line was the waterway east of the airfield, which the Marines had dubbed "Alligator Creek." Even though it did not have alligators and was not a creek. It was actually the Ilu River. Even though it was not a river but a tidal lagoon. The Marines kept confusing it with the Tenaru River further east, on the other side of thick jungle. This part of the line was held by the 1st Marine Regiment, as was the beach all the way around Lunga Point. On the west side the perimeter looped around the village of Kukum across the flat land between the beach and the hills, and was held by the 5th Marine Regiment, except for one battalion.

The perimeter was thin. Most of the combat forces were held inland as a reserve to counter any penetration of the line. The line to the south of the airfield, facing the interior jungle, was especially thin, and mainly outposted, since it was believed this was the least likely direction from which an attack would come.

The Marines were able to sprinkle the perimeter with artillery. The 1st Special Weapons Battalion placed its 75mm half-tracks inland from the beach, but could move them on to the beach if necessary. The 11th Marine Regiment deployed its 75mm pack howitzers and 100mm howitzers around the airfield. But they had not been able to unload their 155mm howitzers. The 3rd Defense Battalion placed their 90mm antiaircraft guns within the perimeter, but they had not been able to unload their 5-inch coastal defense guns. The absence of both the 155s and the coastal defense guns would prove painful in the days ahead.

Outside of this perimeter, infantry patrolled the jungles and started tangling with Japanese defenders almost immediately. Captain Monzen had originally planned to launch a suicide attack against the Marine invaders, but with the pitiful number of men he had been able to scrounge up, he figured such a venture would be all suicide and no attack, so he melted back into the jungle.[18] He then started forming the core of Japanese resistance between the Matanikau River, some 4 miles west of the Lunga, and Kokumbona, a native village some 4 miles west of that.

Most importantly, while this was going on, the 1st Engineer Battalion completed the airstrip. This was no mean feat, since the cargo ship *Fomalhaut*, which had been carrying most of the earth-moving equipment, had left after offloading only about 15 percent of her cargo. The cargo that made it ashore included no power shovels or dump trucks, and only one bulldozer.[19] That's where the earth-moving equipment left behind by the Japanese, primitive as it was, came in most helpful, especially the two small trains with hoppers that were able to cart off some 7,000 cubic feet of earth. General Vandegrift reported that the new airfield could handle 38 fighters and nine dive bombers.[20]

It was on August 10 or so when General Vandegrift had a small but quite meaningful ceremony. Major Weir had taken a small American flag from a disabled landing boat. Then the resourceful air officer scrounged up a Japanese flagpole, asking the general to come to the Pagoda for the first flag raising over the new airfield.

But a new airfield, a new base, needs a name. Major Weir didn't want it named "after some potbellied old SOB behind a desk in the Pentagon." He thought of one Marine named Major Lofton R. Henderson.

"Joe" Henderson, as he was sometimes called, had been the commanding officer of Marine Scout Bombing Squadron 241, which had been stationed at Midway during the pivotal battle. He bravely led 16 SBD Dauntlesses flown by inexperienced Marine pilots without fighter escort in a dangerous glide-bombing attack on the Japanese carrier *Hiryu*. Zeros and antiaircraft fire cut them to ribbons. Flying in the lead to calm his green air crews, Henderson was the first shot down, his left wing set afire, he himself badly wounded over the *Hiryu*. He was never seen again. Henderson was the first Marine aviator killed in an attack on the enemy.

In his honor, Major Weir, endorsed by General Vandegrift, christened the new runway "Henderson Field."[21]

The head of the Japanese naval general staff, Admiral Nagano Osami, stood in his dress whites before his emperor. Answering questions about the American attacks on Guadalcanal and Tulagi, Nagano was firm: "It is nothing worthy of Your Majesty's attention."

That answer did not itself seem worthy of His Majesty. Not when the man giving the answer, Admiral Nagano, had traveled all the way to the emperor's summer villa in Nikko to brief him on the Guadalcanal situation, in order to short-circuit the emperor's own plans to return to Tokyo upon hearing about the attack.[22]

Admiral Nagano went on to explain. It was only a raid, nothing more. Their information was that only 2,000 American troops were on Guadalcanal, there only to destroy the airfield and leave. The Japanese military attaché in Moscow had received this information directly from the Russians. Exactly how the Russians would have known is rather vague and apparently not an issue the Japanese considered. It was what the Japanese wanted to hear.

"Don't worry, Your Majesty," Admiral Nagano concluded. "The landing is a reconnaissance. We can push them off with just our naval landing force. There would be danger if we let them consolidate, so we will move quickly to mount an operation against them. Please set your mind at rest and stay there."[23]

The emperor's mind was not at rest, however. Nor were some of the minds at Imperial General Headquarters and elsewhere. The Army operations section was questioning the interpretation that this was a mere raid, based on reports of a large convoy having left San Francisco in mid-July that correlated with the large number of transports sighted off Lunga. Those transports suggested to Admiral Mikawa's 8th Fleet that the Americans had landed a full division. Nevertheless, General Hyakutake's 17th Army resisted the interpretation that the landings on Guadalcanal and Tulagi represented a new Allied offense, unwilling to be distracted from his desire to take Port Moresby.[24]

In fairness, however, the Imperial Army's belief that the invasion was likely a raid and could not be more than a few thousand troops was based largely on the assessment that the Pacific Fleet could not mount an offensive before 1943. That assessment was based on the Naval General Staff's report of US losses at Midway. It was an assessment which deliberately overstated those losses, to put it mildly. In effect, the Naval General Staff had lied to the Imperial Army about the extent of the disaster at Midway.[25]

In the meantime, the Japanese were taking some action. Admiral Tsukahara, as previously arranged, headed to Rabaul to take over naval operations in the South Pacific as "Southeast Area Commander." Under his command was Admiral Mikawa's 8th Fleet and his own 11th Air Fleet, the latter now operationally titled "Base Air Force."

Under Base Air Force was the 5th Air Attack Force (25th Air Flotilla), which was supposed to be rotated out and replaced with the 6th Air Attack Force (26th Air Flotilla). Now, because of the developments on Guadalcanal and Tulagi, the 6th would instead be reinforcing the 5th. The 6th consisted of two groups of medium bombers – the Misawa and Kisarazu air groups – and one group of fighters from the 6th Air Group. The 5th still had the star-studded veteran Tainan Air Group of fighters, plus the 4th Air Group of medium bombers, depleted by their disastrous attack on Guadalcanal on August 8; the seaplanes of the Yokohama and 14th air groups, and the fighters and carrier bombers of the 2nd Air Group. All told, Base Air Force had about 114 aircraft on hand.[26]

It was Base Air Force's aerial reconnaissance that showed little activity at the Lunga airfield and no aircraft. It was Admiral Mikawa's 8th Fleet whose destroyers ran sweeps of Savo Sound, where they found no evidence of American activity. These efforts buttressed the idea that the landings were small scale, which is exactly what everyone wanted to believe.[27]

Admiral Nagano and General Sugiyama Hajime, his chief of staff counterpart for the Army, reached an agreement on August 10 concerning operations in New Guinea and the Solomons. Port Moresby, New Guinea was still to be the ultimate objective in the South Pacific, but now General Hyakutake's 17th Army would first retake Guadalcanal and Tulagi.

It was an annoyance to General Hyakutake. He considered Guadalcanal and Tulagi to be "insignificant." He neither needed nor wanted them to suck resources off his main goal of taking Port Moresby.

As it was, his command of the 17th Army came with the caveat "some assembly required," since reinforcements intended for his command were strewn across the Pacific and Southeast Asia. The 2nd "Sendai" Division was divided between Java and the Philippines. The 38th "Nagoya" Division was in the East Indies. The 35th Brigade under General Kawaguchi Kiyotake was in the Palau Islands. The 28th Regiment from the 7th Division under Colonel Ichiki Kiyonao was on Guam. Various antitank units were scattered hither and yon, some even in Manchuria.

Where General Hyakutake saw a burden, Admiral Yamamoto saw an opportunity. An opportunity to avenge Midway and bring about the "decisive battle" with the Americans that he had always wanted. Yamamoto assembled a fleet of five aircraft carriers, four battleships, 16 cruisers, one seaplane tender, and 30 destroyers. Once again, he could have just assembled an armada and advanced. But that was just not the Imperial Japanese Navy way. No, the Imperial Japanese Navy way was, once again, to divide the fleet into bite-sized pieces for purposes of deception. It had not worked at Coral Sea. It had not worked, most famously, at Midway. But Yamamoto was certain it would work eventually.

So on August 11, Admiral Yamamoto started moving the pieces into place as the 2nd Fleet under Vice Admiral Kondo Nobutake, designated the "Advance Force," went to sea. It consisted of the 4th Cruiser Division, with the heavy cruisers *Atago*, also serving as Kondo's flagship, her sister ship *Takao*, and her other sister ship *Maya*. The fleet also had the 5th Cruiser Division under Vice Admiral Takagi Takeo, the victor of the Battle of the Java Sea, with the heavy cruisers *Myoko* and *Haguro*. All were screened by the 4th Destroyer Flotilla under Rear Admiral Takama Tamotsu, with the light cruiser *Yura* as his flagship, and destroyers *Kuroshio*, *Oyashio*, *Hayashio*, *Minegumo*, *Natsugumo*, and *Asagumo*. Air cover would be provided by the seaplane tender *Chitose*.

It was part of a new three-pronged operational strategy being tried out in the aftermath of Midway. In addition to the Advance Force there was also the "Vanguard Force," which would screen the reconstituted, slimmer *Kido Butai* until the former was ordered to move ahead of the carriers. The Vanguard Force was under Rear Admiral Abe Hiroaki, with *Kido Butai*'s traditional escort battleships *Hiei*, serving as Abe's flagship, and *Kirishima*, as well as the hybrid heavy cruiser/seaplane carrier *Chikuma* from the 8th Cruiser Division, and two ships of the 7th Cruiser Division, *Kumano* and *Suzuya*, under Rear Admiral Nishimura Shoji. These ships would be screened by the 10th Destroyer Flotilla under Rear Admiral Kimura Susumu in the light cruiser *Nagara* with destroyers *Nowaki*, *Maikaze*, and *Tanikaze*.

Kido Butai itself, technically the 3rd Fleet, would have a core of two large carriers *Shokaku* and *Zuikaku*, the light carrier *Ryujo*, the heavy cruiser/seaplane carrier *Tone* from the 8th Cruiser Division, and destroyers *Kazegumo*, *Yugumo*, *Kamigumo*, *Akigumo*, *Hatsukaze*, *Akizuki*, *Amatsukaze* and *Tokitsukaze*.

In support of both Admiral Kondo's and Admiral Nagumo's ships was the appropriately named "Support Force," with the battleship *Mutsu*, whose skipper, Captain Yamazumi Teijiro, commanded this force, and destroyers *Harusame*, *Samidare*, and *Murasame*. Also in support was Admiral Yamamoto himself in the battleship *Yamato*, with destroyers *Akebono* and *Ushio*, and the escort carrier *Taiyo* providing some air support. As usual, however, Yamamoto's Support Force, including the most powerful battleship in the world, would be hundreds of miles behind the action, in no position to provide actual support.

Also hundreds of miles behind the action would be a "Standby Force" consisting of the aircraft carrier *Junyo*. The *Junyo* was a strange ship. Converted from the passenger liner *Kashiwara Maru*, she was not quite big enough or fast enough to be a fleet carrier, but was too large to be a light carrier. The lack of speed would cause her problems in launching the heavy Type 97 carrier attack planes – the Allies called the B5N the "Kate" – in the absence of a headwind, though that in itself was not a problem because her air group had been cannibalized to bring the air groups of the *Shokaku* and *Zuikaku* up to full strength.[28]

All these ships were to act in support of the work of Admiral Mikawa's 8th Fleet, with his victors of Savo Island – his heavy cruiser flagship *Chokai* and Admiral Goto's 6th Cruiser Division with the old heavy cruisers *Aoba*, *Kinugasa*, and *Furutaka*. For this operation, Rear Admiral Tanaka Raizo and his 2nd Destroyer Flotilla would be dropping off some 900 men of Colonel Ichiki's 28th Regiment on Guadalcanal and then speeding off. From his traditional flagship light cruiser *Jintsu*, Tanaka would lead destroyers *Suzukaze*, *Kawakaze*, *Umikaze*, *Kagero*, *Isokaze*, *Yayoi*, *Mutsuki*, and *Uzuki* with Patrol Boats *1*, *2*, *34*, and *35* thrown in. *Jintsu* and Patrol Boats *34* and *35* would escort the transports *Boston Maru* and *Daifuku Maru*, carrying the balance of the 28th Regiment. Patrol Boats *1* and *2* would escort the big transport *Kinryu Maru*, carrying some 800 troops of the 5th Yokosuka Naval Landing Force. They would all join to form a big convoy to Guadalcanal.[29]

This battle plan, such as it was, would be called Operation *Ka*, after the first syllable of Guadalcanal – Gadarukanaru, as pronounced in Japanese. The mission Admiral Yamamoto gave to this conglomerate of ships in support of the reinforcement of Guadalcanal had a simple breakdown: carrier aircraft were to keep the waters around Guadalcanal clear of American ships; Base Air Force was to attack the airfield by day; 8th Fleet's ships were to attack the airfield by night.

In the words of Private Leckie, "All of this was in support of 2,400 troops: it was a whale backing up a weasel."[30]

In theory. In reality, Admiral Yamamoto was more interested in his "decisive battle" with the Pacific Fleet than protecting the reinforcements. How exactly he planned to bring the Pacific Fleet out to battle in response to this reinforcement convoy to Guadalcanal is actually rather vague.

The first issue was getting reinforcements to Guadalcanal as quickly as possible, which was a big reason why the closest unit, the 28th Regiment, was selected. The 28th was famous in Imperial Army circles. Shock troops, in 1939 they had fought the Soviets in an underpublicized war on the border between Japanese-controlled Manchuria and Soviet-controlled Mongolia. The war culminated in the Battle of Nomonhan, giving that tiny village its one claim to fame.[31] That the Japanese lost the battle and lost the war – badly – did not seem to affect the elite reputation of the 28th.

Colonel Ichiki Kiyonao, commander of the 28th, had twice been an instructor at the Army's infantry school and was considered an expert in infantry tactics.[32] Especially in what the Japanese called "bamboo spear" infantry tactics. Bamboo spear tactics were what was known in the West as the "banzai charge" because they involved making frontal attacks with bayonets and swords, usually at night, and always yelling "Totsugeki!" – "Charge!" – or "Banzai!" The banzai charge would, Ichiki and many, many others in the Imperial Army firmly believed, take advantage of the superior "spiritual power" of the Japanese soldier that would overcome any numerical or technological advantage on the part of the enemy. So firmly had this idea taken hold that pretty much every Japanese land attack culminated in at least one banzai charge. In a way, it was their trademark. It had worked well in China, abeit with heavy losses. Now Ichiki would get a chance to try it against the hated Westerners.

Ichiki had been promoted to colonel at the outbreak of the Pacific War and given command of the 28th Regiment, ostensibly of the 7th Division, but it usually operated independently and was called *Ichiki Butai* – usually translated as "Ichiki Detachment." It was the Ichiki Detachment that had been given the honor of occupying Midway, but the colonel had been denied his moment of glory.

He would get another chance. Colonel Ichiki was ordered to go to Truk to meet the 17th Army's Colonel Matsumoto Hiroshi, who was coming from Rabaul to give him new orders and brief him on the Guadalcanal situation.

The Ichiki Detachment was to travel to Guadalcanal in two echelons. The first, of about 900 troops, was to be transported to Guadalcanal on fast Navy destroyers, and land on the night of August 18–19 at Taivu Point, some 20 miles east of Lunga. The second echelon, about 1,100 troops, was to be ferried on two transports with naval escort.

Because of the uncertainty about American strength on Guadalcanal and Tulagi, the orders issued to Colonel Ichiki were necessarily vague and flexible:

> The strength of the enemy which landed in the Solomons area is still unknown, but there is no enemy activity as we had expected. Even to this day, August 13, it is certain they are not utilizing the airfield there.
>
> The Army will cooperate with the Navy and quickly attack and destroy the enemy in the Solomons while the enemy is trying to complete the occupation. It will recapture and maintain these vital places.
>
> The Ichiki Detachment will cooperate with the Navy and quickly recapture and maintain the airfield on Guadalcanal.
>
> If this is not possible, the Detachment will occupy a part of Guadalcanal and await the arrival of troops in its rear. For this purpose, a spearhead unit of approximately 900 troops will be organized and loaded on six destroyers that are near at hand and will advance toward Guadalcanal by a direct route.[33]

Colonel Matsumoto went on to give additional details to Colonel Ichiki. Matsumoto said the Marines' activity had not been "vigorous" since landing and that they might be "withdrawing to Tulagi." On the other hand, Japanese intelligence indicated the Americans on Guadalcanal might be at divisional strength – about 10,000 troops. If that was the case, Ichiki was to wait for reinforcements.[34]

But Colonel Ichiki was arrogant, overconfident, and racist. There would be no need for reinforcements, he firmly believed. Without any advance scouting or any further information on the terrain or weather, Ichiki decided to have his 900 men launch a surprise attack on the Marine positions on the second night. His men would each carry only seven days' rations and 250 rounds of ammunition.[35]

So, on August 16, Colonel Ichiki took 916 men and boarded six destroyers – the *Kagero*, *Hagikaze*, *Arashi*, *Tanikaze*, *Hamakaze*, and *Urakaze*, forming the "Transport Unit" under Captain Sato Torajiro. Sato, in turn, was answerable to the newly designated "Commander Reinforcement Group" – Rear Admiral Tanaka Raizo. They left Truk at 7:00 am.[36]

The commander of the 2nd Destroyer Flotilla, Admiral Tanaka was a Combined Fleet veteran. He had made a name for himself at the Battle of the Java Sea and was considered a transport and amphibious expert. He was also very opinionated and outspoken. Tanaka read his orders from the 8th Fleet with shock and extreme consternation. He would later write of the orders:

> With no regard for my opinion, as commander of the reinforcement force, this order called for the most difficult operation in war – landing in the face of the enemy – to be carried out by mixed units that had no opportunity for rehearsal or even preliminary study. It must be clear to anyone with knowledge of military operations that such an undertaking could never succeed. In military strategy expedience sometimes takes precedence over prudence, but this order was utterly unreasonable.[37]

Nor did he care for Colonel Ichiki's bamboo spear tactics. Admiral Tanaka had great respect for Ichiki himself, whom he had met on the Midway operation, and of whose "magnificent leadership and indomitable fighting spirit" he was well aware.[38] Before the transport force had sailed, Tanaka had stepped aboard the destroyer *Arashi* to meet with Ichiki, who described his plan for Guadalcanal.[39] The admiral was again dismayed. He had dealt with these Americans in the Java Sea and knew them to be dangerous, far more dangerous than the Chinese Ichiki had previously fought. Tanaka felt bamboo spear tactics had "no chance against an enemy equipped with modern heavy arms," and was more like "a housefly attacking a giant tortoise."[40]

He was not alone in this estimation. General Kawaguchi Kiyotake, who was leading the 35th Brigade slated to reinforce Colonel Ichiki, told a reporter on August 13, "This is our new destination – Gadarukanaru. I know you think this might be small scale warfare. It's true there will be nothing heroic in it, but I'd say it will be extremely serious business." He predicted the island would be the focal point in the struggle for the Pacific. He told his men they were embarking on "a very important mission." And many would die.[41]

So General Kawaguchi's troops boarded their own transports to head to the battle area, leaving on August 15.[42] Cramped on board, the Japanese Army troops amused themselves with exercises and singing, and comforted themselves with what the Japanese battle studies had told them about the Americans and the Europeans:

> Westerners – being very superior people, very effeminate, and very cowardly – have an intense dislike for fighting in the rain or the mist, or at night. Night, in particular (though it is excellent for dancing), they cannot conceive to be a proper time for war. In this, if we seize on it, lies our great opportunity.[43]

They had already seen it themselves, to an extent, in the East Indies. Some reminisced about the easy conquest of Borneo. "After we got through firing there wasn't one blade of grass," said one soldier. "I'm not going to let any grass grow on Dakarunaru."

A sergeant growled, "It isn't Dakarunaru. It's Gadarukanaru. Remember the name, will you?"[44]

The old adage holds that victory has a hundred fathers but defeat is an orphan. An exception to the rule was the Royal Navy Admiral Crutchley, who understood that he himself shared responsibility for the disaster of the night of August 8–9 off Savo Island. "The fact must be faced that we had an adequate force placed with the very purpose of repelling surface attack," he said, "and when that surface attack was made, it destroyed our force."[45]

In the case of that disaster, multiple investigations by the US Navy, including an "informal" board of inquiry known as the Hepburn Investigation, and independent inquiries and analyses over the years established that in this case defeat did indeed have a hundred fathers – a hundred fathers who could all share at least some portion of the blame, but almost all of whom had some factor mitigating their involvement in the defeat.

Beginning in December 1942, Admiral Hepburn's crew interviewed most of the major Allied officers involved over several months. Once his investigation was completed, he issued his findings and recommendations. Admiral Hepburn's main conclusion was fairly obvious: "The primary cause of this defeat must be ascribed generally to the complete surprise achieved by the enemy." As to how this surprise was achieved, he listed five reasons:

> 1. Inadequate condition of readiness on all ships to meet sudden night attack.
> 2. Failure to recognize the implications of the enemy planes in the vicinity prior to the attack.
> 3. Misplaced confidence in the capabilities of radar in the picket destroyers *Blue* and *Ralph Talbot*.

> 4. Failure in communications which resulted in the lack of timely receipt of vital enemy contact information.
> 5. Failure in communications to give timely information of the fact that there had been practically no effective reconnaissance covering the enemy approach during the day of August 8.

Though not listed with the causes of the surprise, Admiral Hepburn did add:

> As a contributory cause … must be placed the withdrawal of the carrier groups on the evening before the battle. This was responsible for Admiral Turner's conference, which in turn was responsible for the absence of the *Australia* from the action. It was furthermore responsible for the fact that there was no force available to inflict damage on the withdrawing enemy.[46]

Admiral Hepburn recommended official censure for only one officer, the *Chicago*'s Captain Bode, for his inexplicable failure to warn of the presence of Japanese ships. It was a devastating blow for Howard D. Bode, who in that report saw his dreams of flag rank die. He never recovered. Upon learning of the report's conclusions, on April 19, 1943, Bode shot himself in his quarters at Balboa, Panama Canal Zone. He died the next day.

Admiral Hepburn was critical of some of the actions of admirals Fletcher, Turner, McCain, and Crutchley, and Captain Riefkohl, but he recommended no formal action against any of them. Captain Riefkohl never commanded ships at sea again, and told anyone who would listen that he had driven the Japanese away by putting a shell into the chart room of Admiral Mikawa's flagship *Chokai*; how the survivors of the *Quincy*, who actually sent that shell into the chart room, felt about his claim is not recorded. The careers of Turner, Crutchley, and McCain do not appear to have been affected. Crutchley was even awarded the Legion of Merit in 1944.

For its part, Australia held its own investigative proceedings. The Australian Commonwealth Naval Board set up a "Board of Enquiry" to investigate the loss of the *Canberra*. The Board made a preliminary report dated August 23, 1942, and a final report dated September 30, 1942. The final report found that the *Canberra* was not torpedoed, but was hit by 24 Japanese shells. Admiral Crutchley vehemently disagreed with this finding, as did a number of other survivors from the *Canberra*.[47] It was only years later, thanks largely to the work of Australian Commodore Bruce Loxton and historian Chris Coulthard-Clark, that evidence linking the sinking of the *Canberra* to the frantic launch of torpedoes by the US destroyer *Bagley* came to light and has rapidly gained acceptance in history circles.

Even almost 40 years later, for Admiral Turner, the disaster at Savo Island "stuck in his craw." He would give his theory as to how the Navy could have suffered such a defeat:

> The Navy was still obsessed with a strong feeling of technical and mental superiority over the enemy. In spite of ample evidence as to enemy capabilities, most of our officers and men despised the enemy and felt themselves sure victors in all encounters under any circumstances… The net result of all this was a fatal lethargy of mind which induced a confidence without readiness, and

> a routine acceptance of outworn peacetime standards of conduct. I believe that this psychological factor, as a cause of our defeat, was even more important than the element of surprise.[48]

That was, with the wisdom of hindsight, in the future. In the now, the South Pacific Command had a major problem: it had to supply the 1st Marine Division on Guadalcanal – "Cactus" – and Tulagi – "Ringbolt." And do so having just squandered the initiative back to the Japanese with the inept performance at Savo Island, to which the Marines derisively referred as "The Battle of the Five Sitting Ducks."[49]

On August 11, General Vandegrift radioed Admiral Ghormley his first situation report and requested another Marine regiment.[50] That same day, Ghormley ordered Admiral Fletcher to destroy the Japanese aircraft carriers, but also to:

> a. Cover the Espiritu Santo-Nouméa line of communication.
> b. Support Guadalcanal and Tulagi against enemy ships; and
> c. Cover the movement of friendly ships to Guadalcanal.[51]

The disgusted Marines on Guadalcanal would likely have told Ghormley he was a few days too late. Even so, Admiral Fletcher kept his carriers at sea between Espiritu Santo and Guadalcanal, but out of range of the Japanese search planes in the Shortlands. And by the end of August 12, Fletcher had completed what many said was his favorite pastime – refueling.[52] He was in a very difficult position, however, as explained by his air operations officer, Lieutenant Commander Oscar Pederson:

> The lack of air facilities at Guadalcanal required the carriers to be in position to furnish support; the lack of facilities also by necessity forced the long range searches to the northward to be conducted from Espiritu Santo and Vanikoro [in the Santa Cruz Islands] some 400–600 miles away. This shortened the margin of warning we could receive of any impending attack and forced the carriers to operate closer to Guadalcanal in the more dangerous waters between the Solomons and the Santa Cruz Islands.[53]

As Admiral Fletcher had feared, the area of operation for his carriers was severely restricted. Already, there were rumblings of Japanese countermoves, moves more dangerous than anything seen at Savo Island. Allied intelligence did not know exactly what those countermoves would be, or when they would take place. Admiral Fletcher's carriers kept sending out air searches, out to 200 miles. However, the performance of *Magic* leading to Midway had spoiled the Americans a bit. They expected to know precisely when and where the Japanese would strike.

Yet *Magic* was not perfect. It was periodically reduced in effectiveness when the Japanese changed call signs or went to a new version of their JN-25 code. That was happening at this rather inconvenient time for the US Navy. The Japanese had modified their fleet code and, just before the *Watchtower* landings, changed their call signs. There were also hints that they were about to shift to a new version of JN-25. To top it off, the Japanese were making some efforts at radio deception, having other units assume the call signs of their aircraft carriers. Allied radio intelligence had to resort to traffic analysis to figure out what the Japanese were doing.[54]

On August 13, Allied intelligence determined that *Kido Butai* was headed to the South Pacific. Three days later, some intelligence analysts noted radio silence by the Japanese 3rd Fleet, the new official designation for *Kido Butai*, and deduced the silence meant it had sailed. Not everyone agreed, however, and on August 17 Pacific Fleet intelligence placed the *Shokaku*, *Zuikaku*, and *Ryujo* in the Japanese home islands, though they were expected to head south shortly. But that very night, at midnight, the Japanese changed their call signs again, which usually indicated a major operation was imminent.[55] A major operation meant *Kido Butai*. Where was it? Had it left Japan? If so, when? None of the Allied Pacific commands could agree on the answers to these questions.

Expecting action soon, but not knowing when, and with orders to protect the supply line to Guadalcanal, Admiral Fletcher was forced to keep his carriers in something of a dance between the Solomons, Ndeni, and Espiritu Santo. Normally, he would head towards Guadalcanal during the day and head away at night. In so doing, he would be out of range of the Japanese morning searches. Ideally, the carriers would stay within 12 hours of airstrike range of Guadalcanal.[56]

So the supply line was protected. But what about actually getting the supplies to Guadalcanal? Admiral Ghormley was unwilling to risk – a phrase that would come up more and more often – his few transports and cargo ships to run supplies to Guadalcanal. They resorted to using fast transports, which were old destroyers that had been fitted to carry supplies. Some had already been used in the Tulagi landing. They would become supply workhorses in the days ahead.[57]

In the meantime, they had the airfield on Guadalcanal. An airfield without aircraft is just a field but worse, since a normal field does not attract enemy attacks but an airfield does, even an empty one. And it did seem like something of an oversight in *Watchtower*, trying to capture an airfield without aircraft ready to operate from said airfield.

Certainly Admiral Nimitz was trying to get aircraft to the new Henderson Field. The *Long Island*, a tiny escort aircraft carrier, the first of her kind in the US Navy, arrived at Fiji on August 13 with two squadrons of the 23rd Marine Air Group. But while in Fiji, the carrier's skipper, Commander James D. Barner, informed Admiral McCain that the Marine fighter pilots he carried were not carrier-qualified and probably could not even take off from the *Long Island*. Admiral Ghormley was not pleased: "I need fighter planes on Guadalcanal now."[58]

McCain had a suggestion: if the pilots on the *Long Island* were not qualified, exchange them with the more experienced fighter pilots he had available at Efate. The escort carrier arrived at Efate on August 17 and the exchange was made. Admiral Fletcher arranged to meet the *Long Island* on August 19 and escort her to within range of Guadalcanal to launch her aircraft.[59]

It added up to a well-covered but nevertheless rickety supply line to a 1st Marine Division that already did not have all the supplies it needed. As it was, the primary support base for Guadalcanal, Espiritu Santo, in both its port and airfield, was not much better off:

> At Espiritu [Santo] existed a fair example of South Pacific logistics. On 18 August Colonel [Laverne G.] Saunders [Commander of the 11th Bombardment Group] described its unloading facilities as "one barge, a sandy beach and a prayer." Heavy equipment was slung over the side of cargo vessels into a lighter. Ashore there were no cranes and the small, finger piers made of coconut logs salted down with coral washed out and disappeared after 2 or 3 weeks' use. Since the supply officer seldom was informed of arrival dates, boxes and crates accumulated in the coconut groves. There was no question of living off the country; each item of food, clothing, and housing had to be brought in. The mud was there in abundance. Espiritu Santo [had] a foot-thick covering of soft black dirt, a quagmire after the tropical rains.
>
> [...] Getting the fuel out of the drums and into the tanks of the B-17s was one of those impossible jobs which somehow got done. Gas trucks and trailers did not exist; the steel drums were dumped over the ship's side, floated ashore in nets, hand-rolled up under the trees, and dispersed in dumps of 20 to 30. From these they were loaded on trucks, rolled up on stands, and emptied into the tank wagons which serviced the aircraft.[60]

The Army Air Force commander in the South Pacific, Major General Millard F. Harmon, himself familiar with Espiritu Santo, said to General Marshall in a letter on August 11:

> The thing that impresses me more than anything else in connection with the Solomon action is that we are not prepared to follow up... We have seized a strategic position from which future operations in the Bismarcks can be strongly supported. Can the Marines hold it? There is considerable room for doubt.[61]

It rains in the Solomons. A lot.

Even though August was part of what was ostensibly the "dry" season, in reality it could, and frequently did, rain. Indeed, the Solomons are susceptible to very sudden downpours; the Americans called them "gully washers."[62] A lot of rain would fall in a very short time, quickly filling the gullies and ravines – and trenches and foxholes.

But it was not just storm clouds that were gathering. The Japanese began harassing the marooned Marines, not necessarily causing a significant amount of damage or casualties, but always keeping them on edge, nibbling away at energy and morale. Base Air Force was first on the act. On August 11 around noon six Zeros attacked. The next day it was three Bettys who dropped bombs in the jungle to the west.

Then came the submarines. It wasn't enough for them to be lurking in Ironbottom Sound, watching and waiting to pounce like one of Guadalcanal's crocodiles, terrorizing traffic between the island and Tulagi and watching every move in the Lunga roadstead. Now they began to harass the Marines with their 5.5-inch deck guns, too. Late in the morning of August 12 the submarine *I-123* surfaced some 700 yards from the Marine positions, at which she fired 14 5.5-inch shells. The lack of those 5-inch coastal defense guns left aboard the cargo ships was a problem. The Americans improvised with the 75mm halftracks they had positioned just inland of the beach, to be moved up to provide fire support. A captured Japanese 3-inch gun and a few pack howitzers deployed on the beach joined in to convince the *I-123* to dive.[63]

The next day, it was the *I-122*. She surfaced around 5:30 pm and raised the Japanese battle flag as encouragement to any Japanese hidden ashore who could see it. Whether those Japanese were still encouraged when the aforementioned Marine artillery chased the *I-122* and her Rising Sun back into the depths from whence she came is unknown. [64]

Unable to differentiate between the submarines, the Marines just referred to them as "Oscar." Oscar tended to shell Lunga at 6:00 am and 3:00 pm, but he would also surface at night to shoot illumination rounds that would disturb the Marines' sleep. According to Lieutenant Jack Clark, who managed the remaining landing boats on Guadalcanal, Oscar would make midnight high-speed runs on the surface up and down Ironbottom Sound, creating larger waves that washed Clark's boats higher on the beach, making them harder to refloat.[65] The submarines became a major thorn in the Marines' side.

Patrols started sparring almost daily with the remnants of the Japanese garrison and the laborers. The laborers were a problem. Groups of them wandered the jungle, without food or water, but because they were uniformed they looked somewhat like combat troops but had little combat value. "Termites," they were called.[66] Marine intelligence had to sort the termites from the real combatants, the remnants of the 3rd Kure Special Naval Landing Force, to determine the actual Japanese positions. The area west of the perimeter between the Matanikau River and Kokumbona continued to come into focus as the center of Japanese activity. Probes into the area were met with heavy resistance, with the area between the Matanikau and Point Cruz especially dangerous.

A strong patrol was arranged to go by boat to Point Cruz and explore up the Matanikau, gathering information on the terrain and the enemy, spending the night near the inland high ground then returning to American lines cross country. The plan for the patrol was changed in the aftermath of two developments. First, on August 12, a Japanese warrant officer of the Special Naval Landing Force, "powerfully built and of surly demeanor," was captured. Once a few alcoholic beverages had properly loosened his tongue, the recalcitrant and probably tipsy prisoner admitted his unit was between the Matanikau and Kokumbona.[67] He also admitted that possibly hundreds of laborers and naval infantry were wandering through the jungle without food and might be willing to surrender under certain conditions. That same day, a Marine patrol reported seeing a white flag west of the Matanikau. Both the reported white flag and the admitted position of the Japanese willing to surrender were in the general area where the patrol was supposed to go. As a result, Lieutenant Colonel Goettge, the 1st Marine Division's intelligence officer, decided to lead the patrol himself, taking the prisoner, several intelligence officers, a Japanese linguist, and a surgeon with him. General Vandegrift reluctantly approved, but Goettge was warned to avoid the mouth of the Matanikau.

Without telling headquarters, Lieutenant Colonel Goettge led his 25-man patrol out around 6:00 pm on August 12. Almost 12 hours later, one member of the patrol, Sergeant Charles C. Arndt, returned, sent back to report that the patrol had encountered resistance and needed reinforcements. A few hours after that, two more men, Corporal Joseph Spaulding and Platoon Sergeant Frank L. Few, returned to relate the story of knife-wielding Japanese prowling among American bodies on the beach, of "swords flashing in the sun."[68] The patrol had apparently landed in the dark too close to the mouth of the Matanikau. Goettge had gone ashore, keeping the prisoner literally on a leash, when Japanese bullets cut him down.[69] That's when the slaughter began, lasting until the morning, with the Marines caught in a crossfire of Japanese machine guns. A second patrol sent to help them never made contact with the Japanese and found no sign of Goettge's patrol. Arndt, Spaulding, and Few were the only survivors.

With the death of its intelligence officer and much of its intelligence staff, the demise of Lieutenant Colonel Goettge's patrol was a disaster for the 1st Marine Division. And almost a national catastrophe. The linguist on the patrol, Lieutenant Merle Ralph Cory of the 5th Marine Regiment, had been a cryptanalyst in Washington, privy to *Magic* and the breaking of the Japanese codes. Had the Japanese questioned Cory, he could have been an intelligence gold mine for them, crippling the entire American Pacific War effort. But the Japanese naval troops shot Cory and, after he was down, bayonetted him.[70]

The 1st Marine Division's intelligence section was decimated while, as many Marines believed, on an errand of mercy to save starving Japanese willing to surrender. A humane gesture but a false hope from the beginning. The unwillingness of Japanese to surrender was still an alien concept to the men of the 1st Marine Division, which may help explain the lack of preparation for an ambush. The white flags seen by the scouts were most likely not flags of surrender, but Japanese Rising Sun flags, with the *hinomaru* – the red sun disk – in the center of the white flag hidden by folds of fabric. That one white flag could be mistaken for another white flag is understandable. That the patrol's preparations evidently had not accounted for this possibility is less so.

The incident left the Marines rattled, even more rattled than the small earthquake that had shaken them awake at 2:35 am on August 14.[71] But it also left them angry. "Swords flashing in the sun." That was the phrase that went around camp. There were rumors that one of Goettge's Marines had his tongue cut out, another had his hands cut off.[72]

Swords flashing in the sun. "That was the phrase and the image," said Private Leckie, "that carried Vandegrift's men from a merry to a murderous mood."[73] What had been green troops, just out of training with little actual combat, were now US Marines seething with rage. Young Marines who had been timid and fearful of combat now sought it. Patrols went from cautious to aggressive. Air attacks by Japanese Bettys turned into dark sporting events, as men watched "with gleeful hate" as the heavy antiaircraft guns of Henderson Field traded shots with their tormentors, each bomber shot down bringing cheers. After an attack in which five of their bombers were damaged, Base Air Force reported to Tokyo, "Enemy AA guns are rather accurate."[74] Their G4Ms went from bombing from an altitude of 10,000 feet to 25,000 feet. At that height bombing was not nearly as accurate.

No more cowering within the Lunga defense perimeter. "From now on," Leckie explained, "there would be no quarter."[75] None given, none expected.

Lieutenant Colonel Edmund J. Buckley was tabbed to try to rebuild the division's intelligence section. He got a major boost on August 15, when a double rank of native Melanesian constables, properly shouldering rifles, showed up at one of the outposts of the Lunga perimeter.[76] In their midst was a tall, bearded, white man, shambling in what were actually his last pair of decent shoes shielding badly blistered feet. The Marine guards raised their weapons. The man walked up to one of the guards, Private William J. Carroll, and in a perfect British accent whispered his name: Captain Clemens of the British Solomons Protectorate Defense Force. The head of the *Ferdinand* organization on Guadalcanal, coastwatcher Martin Clemens, had arrived. He asked to be taken to headquarters.[77] Clemens had come down from his lookout post to put himself, his most senior subordinate Sergeant Major Jacob Vouza, a Melanesian, and some 60 of their men in the service of the Americans. They would help fill, albeit along different dimensions, the void left by the loss of Goettge, his trained scouts, and his intelligence men.

It was almost sundown on August 15 when American ships appeared off Lunga for the first time since August 9. Not an impressive fleet, they were just destroyer transports *Colhoun*, *Little*, *Gregory*, and *McKean*. Carrying nothing all that important, simply 400 drums of aviation gasoline, 32 drums of lubricant, 282 bombs – from 100- to 500-pounders – ammunition, tools, and spare parts. Also dropped off was part of a naval construction base unit called "Cub-1." "Cub" was a code name for advanced fleet and fuel bases of medium size. It was commanded by Major Charles H. Hayes, executive officer of Marine Observation Squadron 251. He had experience at running primitive airstrips, and he would need it. This unit was to aid the Marine engineers in work at the field and to serve as ground crews for the aircraft that, Admiral McCain promised in a letter Hayes delivered, would come on August 18 or so.[78]

On August 15, Japanese Naval Air Force bombers out of Rabaul dropped baskets by parachute to the remnants of the Japanese garrison still holed up west of Kukum. Some of the parachutes were carried by the wind inside the Marine perimeter. The Americans examined the containers, whose contents included food, ammunition, medical supplies – and a note. It read "Help is on the way! Banzai!"[79]

Help was indeed on the way. Closer than anyone thought. The next day, the old Japanese destroyer *Oite* dropped supplies and 113 members of the 5th Yokosuka Special Naval Landing Force off near Tassafaronga, where they and their commander, Lieutenant

Takahashi Tatsunosuke, were greeted by Captain Monzen.[80] Their primary mission was to bring in new long-range radio equipment, since the original radio suite had been abandoned when the Japanese fled Lunga.[81]

The foreboding portents continued. On the night of August 18, the outposts guarding the beaches reported larger waves washing ashore from Ironbottom Sound. They were unable to see the waves' source in the dark far out on the water, but they could tell the wash came from ships heading east at high speed. Around 3:00 am, the pickets reported an almost identical wash, this time heading west.[82] It seemed like someone had gone to and come from a position east of the Marine perimeter, most likely dropping something off.

Sunrise on August 19 found the 1st Marine Division with its hands full on three sides of the Lunga perimeter. To the east, they were trying to determine just who or what had been dropped off in the night. To the north, loitering in Ironbottom Sound were three destroyers, *Kagero*, *Hagikaze*, and *Arashi*, who had been among those Japanese ships speeding in the night, now lazily lobbing shells at Tulagi and Lunga. To the west, the Marines were determined to clear the Japanese from the Matanikau area and Kokumbona – mainly the remnants of the 3rd Kure Special Naval Landing Force, plus the newly arrived 5th Yokosuka Special Naval Landing Force, totaling maybe 600 men under Captain Monzen – who had slaughtered the Goettge patrol.[83]

With too few Marines to take any new ground, the Marine attack on the Matanikau was more of a sortie than anything else. A three-pronged attack was planned, one prong in the middle to keep the enemy engaged, while the two prongs on the outside, one inland, the other using landing boats, would cut off the Japanese retreat.

The Marine company traveling by boat to the Matanikau attracted the attention of the Japanese destroyers, who started gunning for them without success. Marine artillerymen on the Lunga beach manhandled the captured Japanese 3-inch gun into position to duel the destroyers. After 20 rounds all fell short, it became apparent that the gun did not have the range. But the destroyers' guns did and chased the Marines from the 3-inch emplacement. The lack of those 5-inch coastal defense guns was becoming a serious problem. There was no way to drive off the obnoxious destroyers.

Enter Army Air Force Major James Edmundson, survivor of Pearl Harbor and Midway, commanding a B-17 of the 11th Bombardment Group flying out of Espiritu Santo. Word had reached Espiritu Santo that Japanese ships were interfering with the Marine sortie on the Matanikau. Edmundson's Flying Fortress was the only one ready to go, so up he went. At around noon he came over Ironbottom Sound and began to harass the harassers. Circling at an unusually low altitude of 5,000 feet, from which Edmundson had been one of the few B-17 pilots to have had success bombing ships in the past, he made multiple bomb-dropping passes. They culminated in a stick of four 500lb bombs, one of which landed on the Number 3 5-inch mount of the *Hagikaze*, the explosion drawing cheers from the hundreds of Marines watching from shore. The bomb hit wrecked the mount, flooded the magazine, and damaged the destroyer's rudder and propeller shafts, reducing her speed to six knots. Edmundson circled the wounded *Hagikaze*, keeping the Japanese on edge and likely delaying repair efforts, until his fuel ran low; he headed back to Espiritu Santo, roaring low over the Marines at Lunga who saluted him with more cheers. With 33 dead and 13 wounded, the *Hagikaze* had to crawl out of Ironbottom Sound, escorted by the *Arashi*, back to Truk for emergency repairs.[84]

Back on the Matanikau, the Special Naval Landing Force fell back to an ancient Japanese army custom: when in doubt, launch a banzai charge. In this case, it was the first daylight banzai charge of the war. And it was against US Marines with automatic weapons. After some 65 killed and an unknown number wounded, Captain Monzen decided to retreat back into the jungle. The Marines returned to Lunga, having lost four killed and 11 wounded.

That left the issues on the eastern flank. For about a week the Marines had received rumors of a Japanese presence east of Henderson Field. Upon his arrival, Captain Clemens had confirmed part of those rumors, including a radio station near Taivu.

With four of Martin Clemens' men as guides, Captain Charles H. Brush led part of a company from the 1st Marine Regiment out at around 7:00 am to investigate these reports. They followed the coastal road heading east toward Koli Point. Just short of Koli Point they stopped to rest and eat some lunch – and watch the bombing of the *Hagikaze*. Second Lieutenant John J. Jachym had been to this area before and remembered an orange grove up ahead. Brush had the patrol saddle up again for another half-hour of marching.

Before they got to the oranges, Captain Brush's patrol ran into a Japanese patrol headed in the opposite direction. In fact, it was a group of five officers and 33 men, not in any military formation, with no guarding in the front or on the flanks, just strolling between the road and the beach.

The encounter caught both the Americans and Japanese by surprise, but the Americans, all of whom were seeing their first combat, recovered much more quickly. Captain Brush ordered Lieutenant Jachym to send one platoon to envelop the Japanese from their left while the remainder of Captain Brush's patrol attacked from the front. An action lasting less than an hour left 32 of the 38 Japanese on the expedition dead, most killed in the first few minutes. Six fled. The Marine patrol suffered three killed and three wounded.[85]

Captain Brush and his men examined the dead Japanese, looking for intelligence information to help them prepare for the days ahead. The first thing they noticed was the headgear. The helmets and hats of the Special Naval Landing Force each had an anchor and chrysanthemum emblem, but the headgear these men were wearing each had a star – the logo of the Imperial Japanese Army.

Lieutenant Jachym noticed a lot of swords, map cases, binoculars, and documents for such a small patrol. Too many officers as well.[86] What were these men doing? Some of the Japanese had been carrying radios, telephone equipment, and spools of wire.[87] Were they laying communications cables in preparation for a larger force landing? They also found a code for ship-to-shore communications used for a landing operation.

Captain Brush's examination of the captured documents left him shocked and horrified:

> With a complete lack of knowledge of Japanese on my part, the maps the Japanese had of our positions were so clear as to startle me. They showed our weak spots all too clearly. For example, the First Battalion, First Marines, had been preparing positions on the right of the Second Battalion, but were not occupying these positions. On the right of the First Battalion there was nothing. This fact was clearly shown on the Japanese map which I inspected on the scene of the patrol action.[88]

The captured documents were translated back at Lunga, confirming Captain Brush's belief that the patrol was an advance party of a much larger force. A force that knew exactly where the Marines' weak points were. General Vandegrift ordered the east flank strengthened, and native scouts also sent out to the east. Most of August 20 was spent in these endeavors.

It was late in the afternoon when that familiar buzzing sound returned. Aircraft engines. "It became a drone," wrote Martin Clemens, "and then the drone became a roar…"[89]Another air raid? The normal warnings from the coastwatchers had not come through. The men scattered and dove for cover, bracing for the bombing and strafing…

"They're *ours*!"

Whoever yelled these words is unknown, but the words themselves were both shocked and shocking. And yet true. The aircraft overhead were marked not with the *hinomaru*, but a blue disk, inside which was a white star.[90]

Two of the American planes made a slow, deliberate circle around Henderson Field and the Marine defense perimeter, so that the beleaguered men on the ground could see they were no longer alone. Tired, filthy, sick, Marines came out of tents, dugouts, and trenches, to stand up cheering, hollering, weapons held high, punches thrown in the air, tossing defiant curses at the enemy they could not see but knew was coming, a joyful noise for the first time inside the Lunga perimeter.

"Our planes had come at last," Marine photographer 2nd Lieutenant Karl Thayer Soule later wrote. "[O]nly thirty-one, but in that joyful moment they seemed to darken the sky."[91] The sight gave Martin Clemens "a tingle right down the spine."[92]

The sight of 31 aircraft – 19 Grumman F4F Wildcat fighters of VMF-223, "Marine Fighting 223" – under Captain John L. Smith and 12 Douglas SBD Dauntless dive bombers of VMSB-232 – "Marine Scout Bombing 232" – under Major Richard C. Mangrum. They had taken off at 1:30 pm from a position southeast of San Cristobal some 200 miles away from the flight deck of the *Long Island*.

How the arrival of these friendly aircraft had lifted much of the stress that these past two weeks had placed on General Vandegrift soon became apparent. The general later said their arrival was "one of the most beautiful sights of my life." As the first Dauntless taxied following a ground-control Jeep to a dispersal area, Vandegrift would recall, "I was close to tears and I was not alone." After the propeller had stopped, Major Mangrum climbed out of the cockpit and jumped to the ground to a hero's welcome. The general commanding the 1st Marine Division rushed up to greet the young aviator. "Thank God you have come."[93]

Now, there was hope. "That night we went to bed early and slept well," Lieutenant Soule later wrote. "The fleet that had sailed away so long ago had not forgotten us after all."[94] The meaning was not lost on Martin Clemens. "[W]e were in a position to hit back for a change."[95]

And with that, the "Cactus Air Force" was born.

Some 20 miles east of Henderson Field, others heard the growl of arriving aircraft headed to the airfield. It brought a very different reaction.

A Japanese interpreter, known ever since – inaccurately – as "Ishimoto" paused for a moment, as if making a mental note of the new visitors.[96] With him Colonel Ichiki undoubtedly noted their appearance as well. Maybe he also deduced what it portended for his mission, or perhaps not.

The Ichiki Detachment had indeed been dropped off by those Japanese destroyers speeding by Lunga at around 1:00 am on August 19 after a trip under "difficult conditions." After meeting no resistance, Ichiki radioed Rabaul, "We have succeeded in invasion."[97]

As Colonel Ichiki had his men move into position, he radioed Rabaul again, "No enemy at all. Like marching through a no man's land."[98] That would change, he hoped. Ichiki had said the Americans would be "dog meat" for his "die-hard soldiers."[99] The colonel even went so far as to write in his diary, "18 Aug. The landing. 20 Aug. The march by night and the battle. 21 Aug. Enjoyment of the fruits of victory."[100] He had written these entries on August 19, post-dating diary entries of his victory just in case he was killed. The contradiction doesn't seem to have occurred to him.

The next order of business was to send a reconnaissance party ahead. Ichiki ordered Captain Shibuya Yoshimi to lead 38 men forward to the Nakagawa area – what the Japanese called Alligator Creek – to inspect the Marine defenses and find a specific point to attack. In the process, they would lay telephone wires to communicate with the regimental headquarters. Captain Shibuya and his lightly armed patrol took off around 9:00 am.

It was around 4:30 in the afternoon when a few members of Captain Shibuya's expedition started staggering back in to camp. They reported the patrol had been wiped out. Colonel Ichiki was shocked and dismayed. He had sent these men forward without adequate weapons; he had sent them forward to their deaths. Worse, Ichiki had lost the element of surprise.

Another expedition was immediately sent forward, this time better armed. They found no Americans and no survivors, but they did find Sergeant Major Vouza, who had been returning to his village to hide his small American flag. They dragged him back to Colonel Ichiki.

With Ishimoto translating Japanese into the pidgin English dialect spoken by most of the Melanesian natives, Colonel Ichiki questioned Sergeant Major Vouza.[101] The big Melanesian answered by silently looking back with undisguised contempt.[102]

The Japanese Army troops tied Vouza to a tree in the hot sun. Vouza still would not answer. The Japanese smashed his face with rifle butts. Vouza still would not answer. They slashed him with a sword. Vouza still would not answer. They made him lie on a hill of red ants. Vouza still would not answer. They hanged him from a tree until he lost consciousness from his wounds and from exposure. After dark, the Japanese took the sergeant major down, and tied his wrists. The men of the Ichiki Detachment had shed their knapsacks and nonessential gear and were moving out to begin their attack. And Vouza would be shoved along with them.

It was after midnight by the time the Ichiki Detachment reached Alligator Creek, having chased off some Marine pickets. The waterway was really a tidal lagoon, separated from Ironbottom Sound by a sandspit. The sandpit was, to Colonel Ichiki, a perfect avenue of attack.

With no more need of Sergeant Major Vouza, the Japanese guards were ordered to kill him. He was bayonetted seven times in the chest and once in the throat. Vouza staggered away, rivers of blood falling from his wounds. The Japanese let him go. Surely he would bleed to death.

It was about 2:00 am when a flare went up over Alligator Creek, bathing the area in eerie green light. Some 100 Japanese infantry crouched low, rifles held like spears, bayonets in front, looking like a twisted re-creation of an ancient Greek phalanx. This was bamboo spear tactical theory at its finest. Shouting "Banzai!" or "Totsugeki!" the Japanese troops charged forward …

… into an American line laced with barbed wire borrowed from a farm and pockmarked with foxholes filled with members of Lieutenant Colonel Edwin A. Pollock's 2nd Battalion of the 1st Marine Regiment armed with .30cal and .50cal machine guns. The 1st Special Weapons Battalion chipped in with two 37mm antitank guns firing canister antipersonnel rounds that turned the guns into giant shotguns, leveling Japanese troops like a tornado through a cornfield.[103] The first attack was almost entirely wiped out.

One of the Ichiki Detachment's company commanders suggested to Colonel Ichiki that they suppress the Marine defenses with artillery to reduce the gunfire the troops would have to face on the charge in. But Ichiki figured you can't make an omelet without breaking some eggs. He ordered yet another banzai charge across the sandspit. Again the Japanese charged in a tight phalanx and again they were cut down. A few made it to the other side of Alligator Creek to engage the "dog meat" Marines in hand-to-hand combat. The combat was fierce and confused, with Japanese soldiers at one point stabbing each other with their bayonets.[104] It was not enough, and once again the Japanese were compelled to retreat after suffering horrendous losses.

By this time, the sandspit was a veritable killing field, covered with Japanese bodies and parts thereof. Colonel Ichiki was running out of eggs for his omelet. As the eastern sky was starting to lighten, Japanese knee-mortars and 70mm guns opened fire on Colonel Pollack's troops, while a flanking group moved out into the surf and took over a disabled landing craft on which they positioned a machine gun to start trying to knock out the 37mm antitank guns. Ichiki moved up to personally take the lead and ordered his men to spread out along a longer front to cross the shallow creek. Then they charged again. They ran completely upright, not even trying to duck the hailstorm of gunfire.[105]

The fighting became thick and heavy, and several Japanese got through to toss grenades into the Marine entrenchments and start slashing with their bayonets and swords. The Marines had preregistered fire with 75mm pack howitzers positioned near Henderson Field itself and opened fire in support of the hard-pressed men of Colonel Pollack. The Japanese attackers were hit, but as the gunners tried to adjust to the Japanese closing in on the line, many of the shells landed inside the Marine positions. A further adjustment brought the barrage across the creek at the deadly Japanese machine guns. As the light improved, the fire of the 75s was replaced by that of 81mm mortars, all from the 11th Marine Regiment, the artillery regiment of the 1st Marine Division.

Around 7:00 am, a badly wounded native Melanesian approached the Lunga perimeter. Bleeding profusely from multiple stab wounds, including a particularly bad one in his throat, he asked the Marine pickets to call Martin Clemens for him. Clemens drove over in a Jeep and found his sergeant major, Jacob Vouza, barely alive. Left for dead, Vouza had instead chewed through his restraints and walked and crawled some 3 miles through the battle area. A gurgling Vouza reported what he had seen of Japanese numbers and armaments, which Clemens telephoned in. After dictating a last letter to his wife and children, Clemens took Vouza back for medical treatment. The doctors operated on Vouza, replaced his lost blood, and to Clemens' amazement, helped him make a full recovery.[106]

At around the same time, the 1st Battalion of the 1st Marine Regiment under Colonel Lenard B. Cresswell moved up the creek and crossed its dry bed in an attempt to envelop the Ichiki Detachment. By now, it was clear the Marine line was going to hold and the Ichiki were confined to a coconut grove. The Marines cut off all escape routes to the south and swung north to encircle the Ichiki.

For the first time, the "Cactus Air Force" took off from Henderson Field, in the form of four Fighting 223 Wildcats under Captain Smith. They began strafing runs on the remaining Japanese to try to herd them back into a killing zone. But a little after noon Smith's flight fell foul of 13 Zeros of the Tainan Air Group under Lieutenant Kawai Shiro, who had been released from escorting an abortive bombing mission to harass Henderson. A one-sided air battle resulted in two Wildcats badly damaged, one crash-landing upon return, for no Japanese losses. Not a good score at first blush, but there was a silver lining. Smith believed the mission "did a great deal of good" because the pilots were impressed that the Grummans could still fly after taking so much damage.[107]

Yet even encircled and attacked from the air, the Japanese troops still would not surrender. General Vandegrift was appalled at their conduct:

> I have never heard or read of this kind of fighting. These people refuse to surrender. The wounded will wait until men come to examine them and blow themselves and the other fellow to pieces with a hand grenade. You can readily see the answer to that…
>
> The answer was war without quarter.[108]

With the action dragging on throughout the day, General Vandegrift ordered a platoon of five M2A4 light tanks from the 1st Tank Battalion to cross the creek and crush the surviving Japanese – literally, if necessary. One tank was immediately disabled by a Japanese soldier damaging its track; the crew recovered, but the remainder, in the only Pacific combat action for the M2A4 tank, took to blasting Japanese with 37mm canister and .30cal machine guns. Those they did not shoot, they ran over and indeed crushed, leaving in their wake large lumps of barely recognizable flesh. Vandegrift recalled, "The rear of the tanks looked like meat grinders."[109]

It was over by sundown, the first major battlefield victory in the Pacific War over the Imperial Japanese Army by formerly green US Marines who had joined since Pearl Harbor, now seeing their first combat. The action cost the 1st Marine Division 34 dead and 75 wounded. They added to the division's lean armory by capturing from the Ichiki Detachment ten heavy and 20 light machine guns, 20 grenade throwers, 700 rifles, 20 pistols, three 70mm guns, an undetermined number of sabers and grenades, large quantities of explosives, and 12 flame throwers.

But this battle was more than the cost in men and materiel, more than the capture and destruction of enemy men and materiel. For all of Colonel Ichiki's belief in "spiritual power," it was the spirits of the Marines that rose:

> In but hours its psychological effect grew out of all proportion to its physical dimensions. Yesterday, the Jap seemed something almost superhuman, a kind of mechanical juggernaut that swept inexorably through the Philippines, through the Dutch East Indies, over the beaches at Guam and Wake Island, through the jungles of New Guinea […]
>
> But today *we* had beaten the Jap. The Jap no longer seemed superhuman. The Jap was a physical thing, a soldier in uniform, carrying a rifle and firing machine guns and mortars and charging stupidly against barbed wire and rifles and machine guns. We stopped this, decimated his ranks […]
>
> Confidence is a vital factor in a unit. It was wondrous to see the infectious wave of confidence that swept over the Marines on Guadalcanal.[110]

Private Leckie would write, "The soft, effete Americans had shown how savage they could be."[111] In contrast, the Japanese at Taivu Point radioed Rabaul, "Ichiki advance force this morning failed to reach the airfield. On verge of annihilation." Of the 916 men of the Ichiki Detachment who landed only 128 were able to assemble at Taivu Point, about 80 of whom had remained there and not taken part in the attack.[112]

The exact fate of Colonel Ichiki Kiyonao himself is uncertain. After he headed to the front to take personal command, there were no confirmed sightings of him. One Japanese soldier later said he saw a man he believed to be Colonel Ichiki shoot himself in the head, which has become the generally accepted version of the end of Ichiki.[113]

Afterwards, Admiral Tanaka would say, "[T]his episode made it abundantly clear that infantry-men armed with rifles and bayonets had no chance against an enemy equipped with modern heavy arms. This tragedy should have taught us the hopelessness of 'bamboo-spear' tactics."[114]

The virtual destruction of the first echelon of the Ichiki Detachment was met with shock and disbelief in Rabaul. The Americans had annihilated a Japanese unit? Can they do that? General Hyakutake, commander of the 17th Army, did not know what to make of it, but he was very concerned, a concern perhaps not entirely evident in his report to General Headquarters which simply said the following:

"The attack of the Ichiki Detachment was not entirely successful."[115]

CHAPTER 5
IS HE LUCKY?

The events on Guadalcanal sent ripples across the Solomons, indeed across the Pacific.

The evening of August 20, while Colonel Ichiki's troops were still inching their way to the Marine perimeter, the Guadalcanal lookout post radioed news of the arrival of the first American aircraft at the Lunga airfield. The news caused extreme consternation on the *Yamato*. At 10:42 pm, Admiral Yamamoto issued new orders: all combat commands were to destroy the airfield, using air attacks and naval artillery bombardments.[1] At the same time, he ordered Admiral Tsukahara to find those American carriers.

Admiral Tsukahara had already found one American carrier. At 11:30 am on August 20, a Type 97 large flying boat from the 14th Air Group commanded by Warrant Officer Taguchi Iwao spotted one carrier, one cruiser, two destroyers, and other ships about 250 miles south of Guadalcanal headed north-northeast at 14 knots. Taguchi started to tag along, but was chased off by a Scouting 71 Dauntless from the *Wasp* flown by Ensign Harlan J. Coit on an antisubmarine patrol.[2]

This first sighting of an American aircraft carrier since June drew a significant reaction. Base Air Force quickly determined the carrier was out of range. Admiral Mikawa figured the carrier was looking for his Guadalcanal reinforcement convoy, as did Admiral Tsukahara and eventually Admiral Yamamoto. Yamamoto ordered Admiral Kondo, who had not even left Truk, to head south to protect the convoy. Tsukahara told Admiral Tanaka to turn the convoy to the north to lure the carrier within the range of Base Air Force's bombers at Rabaul. Then, at 2:57 pm Mikawa ordered Admiral Tanaka to turn the convoy south-southwest towards Rabaul – conflicting orders that sent him in almost opposite directions. An exasperated Tanaka averaged the orders and turned northwest.[3]

But Admiral Tanaka had a question of his own: since he was now taking his transports toward an operating enemy air base, who was going to give him air cover? Tanaka's immediate superior, the 8th Fleet's Admiral Mikawa, asked his own immediate superior, Admiral Tsukahara, who also commanded Base Air Force, to provide air cover. But Tsukahara refused because he "preferred to support the convoy by offensive rather than defensive means," meaning he found it more fun to attack the enemy rather than defend his own ships. He suggested Admiral Nagumo's carriers provide that air cover. But Admiral Yamamoto stepped back in, saying *Kido Butai* was to attack the enemy carriers, not reveal its presence by defending a convoy. If the American carriers had not been found by noon on August 24, then the carriers would protect the convoy.[4]

All of this for one slow, tiny escort carrier, the *Long Island*. In fleeing the Dauntless and some Fighting 71 Wildcats that were vectored to catch her, Taguchi had missed the big news: the *Long Island* had launched 31 aircraft for Henderson Field.[5]

Having received word of Colonel Ichiki's attack, Admiral Fletcher headed for Guadalcanal to be in range to strike any Japanese surface ships positioning themselves to bombard Henderson Field. He sent up air searches and requested Admiral McCain to send up air searches of his own.

It was a pair of scouts from the *Wasp*, Lieutenant (jg) Charles Mester and Ensign Robert Escher, who made an interesting sighting around 8:00 am on August 21 in Ndeni's Graciosa Bay – a seaplane tender and two destroyers, with a few seaplanes aloft. Recognition signals went unanswered, and they certainly looked Japanese, so the scouts both pushed over to make dive-bombing attacks.

It was only then that Lieutenant Mester recognized the seaplanes as Catalina flying boats. Mester pulled away, but Ensign Escher did not recognize the target and dropped his 500lb bomb. It landed just off the starboard beam – of the USS *Mackinac*. Two of its Kingfisher floatplanes wrecked, its fueling system damaged, the angry tender treated the ensign to heavy antiaircraft fire as he sped away. At 8:20, the *Mackinac* signaled that it had been bombed, then quickly issued a "correction."[6]

Japanese aerial searches were getting much closer to finding the American carriers. A large Mavis flying boat commanded by Warrant Officer Tokunaga Yasuichi of the reconstituted rump of the Yokohama Air Group spotted five ships, type unknown, 530 miles southeast of Shortland at 10:45 am. It was promptly set afire by a scouting Dauntless flown by Lieutenant Robert M. Ware of the *Wasp*. This propensity for the *Wasp*'s scouts to shoot down intruders before fighters could be vectored in was starting to bug the fighter pilots. "Wish the damn scouts would tend to their own business," wrote *Saratoga* fighter pilot Ensign Foster "Crud" Blair.[7]

But there was some welcome news on August 21. The dawn search found no enemy ships near Guadalcanal, though just after noon a report from one of Admiral McCain's PBYs revealed four enemy cruisers and one destroyer near Ontong Java Atoll, some 300 miles north of Tulagi.[8] But Admiral Fletcher's carriers received a reinforcement of surface ships, Task Force 44, with the Australian heavy cruiser *Australia*, Australian light cruiser *Hobart*, and three US destroyers under Admiral Crutchley.

An increased surface capability was necessary given the Japanese propensity for running troops into Guadalcanal using destroyers, as evinced by the recently concluded combat with the Ichiki Detachment. Admiral Nimitz had warned of this possibility, ordering "Carrier aircraft must be employed to prevent landing, particularly if attempted prior to arrival [of] enemy carriers." General Vandegrift wholeheartedly agreed, saying, "Strength of enemy force uncertain. If not prevented by surface craft enemy can continue night landings beyond range of action and build up large forces. Request every means available be used to prevent this."[9]

Admiral Fletcher was conscious of surface capabilities, albeit not to protect Guadalcanal but to protect his own carriers as he approached Guadalcanal. Believing that Japanese search planes had already found his carriers, he deployed a "vanguard force" of his own – heavy cruisers *Minneapolis*, *New Orleans*, *San Francisco*, and *Salt Lake City*, and six destroyers under Rear Admiral Carleton H. Wright – to advance 20 miles ahead of his carriers to prevent a night ambush by Japanese surface forces. Admiral Ghormley was happy with the arrangement as it allowed Fletcher to help protect a convoy of those precious cargo ships heading up to Lunga, scheduled to arrive early on August 22.[10]

Indeed, it was into the early hours of August 22 when that tiny, almost timid flotilla chugged into Ironbottom Sound, bearing gifts for the Marines on Guadalcanal.

Entering at 1:40 am were cargo ships *Fomalhaut* and *Alhena*, veterans of the original August 7 landing, bringing badly needed supplies that should have been left at that time, as well as Army Air Force Lieutenant Robert E. Chilson with 30 enlisted men of the ground echelon for the 67th Fighter Squadron.[11] Guarding the freighters from possible Japanese opposition were the destroyers *Blue*, *Henley*, and *Helm*. It promised to be a boring job if the Japanese didn't show.

But in the gloom of a moonless, murky night, four dark shapes were seen heading out. The American crews went to battle stations. Guns and torpedo tubes were trained on the shadows. The *Blue* flashed a challenge. No response. From the bridge of the *Blue*, Commander Robert Hall Smith, in charge of the 7th Destroyer Division, ordered a second challenge flashed. Still no response. Smith was ready to open fire – then someone noticed they were old flush-deck destroyers, American ships now serving as high-speed transports, about the arrival of which no one had told Smith.

With that crisis averted, the *Fomalhaut* and *Alhena* slowly poked their way into Lunga Roads off Kukum, where the *Helm* stood by them as they unloaded. The *Blue* and *Henley*, on orders from Admiral Turner to sweep for Japanese ships that were expected that night, headed out into the middle of Ironbottom Sound. They took to steaming at 10 knots from east to west and back again, the *Blue* leading the *Henley* by some 400 yards.

At 3:24 am, the *Blue*'s radar picked up a fast-moving contact that crossed her bow, closing range from 4,500 to 2,900 yards, showing up only sporadically on the screen before vanishing altogether 11 minutes later. Smith guessed it was a "small, 20-knot surface craft, assumed to be friendly patrol boat."[12] The destroyers went back to their patrol.

But not for long. At 3:55, while she was heading east, the *Blue* picked up a contact on radar off the starboard beam at a range of 5,000 yards, a rather uncomfortably close range for a first contact. Sonar picked up high-speed propeller noises and was able to pin down the speed as between "20 to 50" knots.[13] Both destroyers trained out their guns and torpedo tubes in the direction of the contact, but all the lookouts could see was maybe a wake. The *Blue* informed the *Henley* that, after closing the range to 3,200 yards, the contact had passed astern. It must have been that friendly patrol boat. The two destroyers maintained their course and speed.[14]

"Torpedo!"

The call came from one of the *Blue*'s lookouts as two phosphorescent wakes headed straight for her stern. Skipper Commander Harold N. Williams quickly barked two orders – "Full speed ahead!" and "Right full rudder!" – hoping to swing the stern out of the way.[15] But it was too late.

The *Blue* rocked under the force of an explosion starboard side aft as several feet of her stern was blown off and men and gear were tossed as much as 50 feet in the air. Her steering gear was wrecked and her propellers were disabled. Nine were killed and 21 injured.[16] The *Henley* moved to guard her stricken comrade.

They never knew what had hit them. With only radar and sonar contacts to evaluate – and the guess that the contacts were of a friendly patrol boat – Commander Smith now figured it was an enemy patrol boat. The assailant was actually the destroyer *Kawakaze*. The submarine *I-121* had sighted this American reinforcement convoy on August 22.[17] In response, Admiral Tsukahara ordered the destroyer *Yunagi*, who had been escorting the 6th Cruiser Division to the Japanese seaplane base at Rekata Bay, to intercept it. He didn't want her doing that by herself, but he was short of destroyers, so he ordered Admiral Tanaka to send one ahead to meet her. Tanaka chose to send the *Kawakaze*, then guarding the troop convoy. The *Yunagi* was forced to turn back by bad weather, but skipper Lieutenant Commander Wakabayashi Kazuo had the *Kawakaze* press on ahead. Her lookouts had spotted the American destroyers on an opposite course, and Wakabayashi had let loose with six torpedoes from an unfavorable angle before she scooched across the wakes of the American destroyers and headed toward Savo Island and safety without firing her guns once.[18]

The *Blue* was severely damaged and immobilized, but her bulkheads were holding and she was not sinking. At daybreak, the *Henley* ran a towline to her and starting towing her towards Lunga so she would be close to shore. The *Blue*'s stern was so mangled and twisted that it dragged in the water, making the tow extremely slow going and causing the tow line to snap at 7:09 am. While a Marine lighter and some landing craft tried to rig another towline, the *Henley* went to cover the cargo ships unloading in Tulagi. At 11:10 am, Admiral Turner ordered the *Blue* towed to Tulagi.[19] That is, in the opposite direction from which she had been towed earlier.

So the *Henley* went back out to try to drag the recalcitrant destroyer to safety. Again the towline snapped. The former-destroyer-now-fast-transport *Manley* came in to attempt a tow, as did more landing boats from Lunga. The destroyer, the former destroyer, and assorted boats tried to cajole and coerce the *Blue* toward Tulagi while her mangled stern resisted by clawing the water behind her for a full 36 hours almost to Tulagi.

However, they were then informed that a large Japanese surface force was expected to enter Ironbottom Sound the night of August 23. To prevent the Japanese from capturing the *Blue* and towing her away – not that that was easy in her current state – or sinking her with men still on board, Commander Smith recommended to Admiral Turner that the destroyer be scuttled. Turner approved.

And at 9:00 pm on August 23, the crew was taken off, the watertight doors were all opened, and the *Blue* was left to sink. Except she didn't. To make sure she did, the *Henley* fired one Mark 15 torpedo at the abandoned hulk. It missed. Another proud moment for the Mark 15 torpedo.

The *Henley* then opened fire with her 5-inch guns. The *Blue* exploded and gave off a cloud of steam; the shells had struck her boilers. She sank stern first.[20]

This small engagement was the first night combat since the August 9 engagement off Savo Island. It was a stunning lack of situational awareness by multiple US Navy ships, including and especially the *Blue*, which made that disaster possible. The *Blue*'s situational awareness doesn't seem to have improved much since then, despite the presence of the division commander on board. Moreover, as at Savo Island, the Americans were inhibited by an unfounded belief that they were firing on their own ships. In this case, the near accident with the fast transports colored judgments concerning the subsequent contacts. And once again, the *Blue* did not get a visual on a target at close range. The US Navy still had a lot of work to do at night surface combat. For now, the Imperial Japanese Navy still ruled the night.

But its grip on the day was slipping, slowly but surely. After the sun had risen on the disabled *Blue*, a Kawanishi of the 14th Air Group commanded by Petty Officer 1st Class Shakata Shoichi, who had made a pest of himself on previous missions, disappeared. At 10:18, the *Enterprise*'s radar picked up an unidentified aircraft 55 miles to the northwest. Because clouds and intermittent squalls inhibited radio reception, the carrier was unable to raise the eight fighters currently providing air cover, so the carrier launched 12 more fighters. Four under Lieutenant Vorse were vectored toward the contact. Vorse raced ahead of his group to catch the Mavis and sent 100 rounds straight into the fuselage. The burst started a gas fire in the fuselage of the flying boat, which disintegrated at 7,000 feet. Shakata had not gotten off a contact report, and the *Enterprise* remained in the ether.[21]

The Americans tightened their grip on Guadalcanal as Army Air Force Captain Dale Brannon led five P-400 fighters – the export version of the Bell P-39 Airacobra – of the 67th Fighter Squadron into Henderson Field.

Of more immediate concern to the Japanese, as the *Kawakaze* sped back north toward her convoy some 75 miles north of Tulagi, were two SBD Dauntlesses. They made diving runs on the dancing destroyer without success. Then they made a few strafing runs, injuring one sailor before heading for home, the *Saratoga*.[22]

Lieutenant Commander Wakabayashi and the men of the *Kawakaze* had gotten off lucky. They could only hope this attack was not a sign of things to come.

It is said that Napoleon was asked to consider the qualifications of a particular general. Napoleon is said to have responded, "I know he's a good general, but is he lucky?"

At some point, people in high places began to ask a similar question about Vice Admiral Frank Jack Fletcher.

In the days after Pearl Harbor, Admiral Fletcher commanded a task force built around the *Saratoga* in a relief operation for Wake Island. The task force was delayed by refueling, an act which became associated with Fletcher. It was also delayed by indecision on the part of the interim head of the Pacific Fleet, Vice Admiral William Pye. The operation was canceled and Wake fell to the Japanese after heroic resistance.

Admiral Fletcher was the senior naval officer for the Battle of the Coral Sea. The Americans had clearly won a tactical and strategic victory, turning back a Japanese invasion convoy intended for Port Moresby and sinking the light carrier *Shoho* in exchange for the loss of the oiler *Neosho* – issues of fuel, again – and the destroyer *Sims* and damage to the carriers *Lexington* and *Yorktown*. Until a fuel vapor explosion gutted the *Lexington* and forced its scuttling, turning the battle into a tactical draw.

Admiral Fletcher was the senior naval officer for the Battle of Midway. Again, the Americans had clearly won a tactical and strategic victory, sinking four Japanese front-line carriers in exchange for damage to the carrier *Yorktown*. Until a floatplane from the heavy-cruiser-seaplane-carrier-thing *Chikuma* found the damaged *Yorktown* being towed away from battle. The Japanese submarine *I-168* was vectored in, crept inside the American antisubmarine screen, and finished off the *Yorktown* with torpedoes.

For *Watchtower*, Admiral Fletcher was the commander of both the Expeditionary Force and the carrier task forces. His announced withdrawal of the carrier task forces – over the expressed objections of his subordinates in the landing force albeit not those of the carrier task forces themselves – was the first in a series of dominoes that led to the disaster at Savo Island. Concern about fuel was, once again, alleged to have played a part in his decision, a concern that Fletcher disputed.

The question lingered. *Is he lucky?*

At 9:42 am, Admiral Fletcher picked up a report from one of Admiral McCain's Catalina flying boats, this one piloted by Lieutenant Leo B. Reister. He reported eight enemy ships – two heavy cruisers, three destroyers, and four transports – course 190 degrees – south southwest – speed 17 knots.[23] Every American flag officer in the South Pacific knew this was an invasion convoy. This was it. The start of the Japanese counteroffensive.

At that moment, the commander of that invasion convoy, Admiral Tanaka, was finding something else even more offensive. Tanaka personally saw the "Consolidated" flying boat shadowing his convoy and, within 200 miles of the Guadalcanal airfield and without air protection of his own, deduced air attacks were in-coming. After Tanaka reported his plight, 8th Fleet's Admiral Mikawa ordered the convoy to turn to the north and stay out of danger. It made sense to Tanaka, even though it would delay landing until August 25, so he turned the convoy around. Of course, at 4:30, Admiral Tsukahara radioed Tanaka, "The convoy will carry out the landing on the 24th."[24] Contradictory orders from his superiors yet again. The well-oiled machine of the Imperial Japanese Navy continued to hum beautifully.

And hum it did. When told of Admiral Tanaka's turnabout, Admiral Kondo's Advance Force turned around and headed north for 12 hours before heading south again. So did *Kido Butai*. All in order to maintain the delicate timing of this Operation *Ka*.

Admiral Tanaka need not have worried. Just like Admiral Yamamoto, Admiral Fletcher wanted those enemy carriers. Those transports Lieutenant Riester spotted would not threaten Guadalcanal for at least another day, so the American carriers, Admiral McCain's Catalinas, and the Flying Fortresses of both Admiral McCain and General MacArthur kept scouring the seas.

The carriers *Saratoga*, *Enterprise*, and *Wasp* had their hands full anyway, as their own scout planes kept finding surfaced Japanese submarines, apparently forming a search line to find the American flattops. At 7:25 am, Lieutenant Turner F. Caldwell, Jr, head of Scouting 5, spotted a surfaced submarine, the *I-19*, skippered by Lieutenant Commander Kinashi Takakazu. Caldwell bombed the submarine but apparently missed. It was a miss the Americans would come to dearly regret.

Not even a half-hour later, at 7:45, two other Dauntlesses piloted by Lieutenant Stockton B. Strong and Ensign John F. Richey sighted another surfaced submarine north of the Stewart Islands (now Sikaiana), this one the *I-17* under Lieutenant Commander Harada Hakue. The SBDs bombing attack came to nothing when Harada crash-dived. A half-hour later, the *I-17* surfaced – in full view of Strong and Richey, who proceeded to strafe the submarine, forcing it to dive again, now with four new bullet holes in her starboard main ballast tank cover.[25]

In the meantime, Admiral Fletcher had changed his mind about that convoy Lieutenant Riester had found. At 11:40 he received a report that one of General MacArthur's Flying Fortresses had spotted an enemy force – two transports and two destroyers – in the Shortlands. It sounded like it was another convoy bound for Guadalcanal. In reality it was two minesweepers and two destroyers refueling.[26] The possibility of two convoys headed for Guadalcanal sent Admiral Ghormley into a panic and convinced both General Vandegrift and Admiral Fletcher that maybe they should attack at least one of them.

Commander Felt led 31 Dauntlesses armed with 1,000lb bombs and six Avengers armed with torpedoes against the convoy spotted by Lieutenant Riester, with orders to spend the night at Henderson Field. General Vandegrift launched every attack plane he had at the same convoy. However, the weather was rapidly deteriorating. Both strikes were compelled to head to Henderson Field and bed down for the night. Their late-night entertainment would consist of a bombardment of the Marine positions by the Japanese destroyer *Kagero*, which was the entirety of the "large Japanese surface force" that had led to the scuttling of the *Blue*.

Now, the pesky fuel issues that always seemed to trip up Admiral Fletcher appeared again. Confusion continued as to the location of the Japanese carriers. Pacific Fleet intelligence believed a Japanese surface force would reach the Solomons by August 20, but carriers could not arrive before August 25. Yet on August 22 Pacific Fleet intelligence admitted that the Japanese carriers may have departed undetected any time after August 16.[27]

That same August 22, Admiral Ghormley had signaled Fletcher: "Indications point strongly to enemy attack on Cactus area 23–26 August," which he helpfully clarified with "Presence of carriers possible but not confirmed."[28] Pacific Fleet intelligence indicated on August 23 that such a presence would not be confirmed because the *Shokaku* and *Zuikaku* were still en route from Japan to Truk, while the *Ryujo*, *Zuiho*, *Hayataka* – actually the *Junyo* – and the *Hitaka* – actually *Junyo*'s sister carrier *Hiyo* – were still in the home islands.[29]

So, the scout planes had found no carriers, and the best intelligence they had placed the Japanese carriers no further south than Truk. Admiral Ghormley wanted the American carriers refueled before the projected Japanese attack date of August 25. So, at 6:23, Admiral Fletcher ordered Admiral Noyes to take the *Wasp* task force south toward Espiritu Santo and refuel on August 24, returning as soon as possible.

That meant 26 fighters, 26 dive bombers, and 11 torpedo bombers – about a third of the American carrier air strength – would be unavailable. But only for about a day. In Admiral Fletcher's best judgment, they would be back in time for the battle on August 25.

If he was lucky.

As dawn approached on August 24, from the tender *Mackinac* at Ndeni six Consolidated Catalina flying boats fanned out to search northwest in the area north of the Solomons. It was common procedure for a scout or two to sight the enemy and report it in, then for the brass to decide what to do about it. It was a little different this day – while aerial searches launched by the *Enterprise* at around the same time found nothing, all six PBYs sighted the Japanese.

At 9:37, the *Enterprise* picked up a report from a Catalina piloted by Ensign Gale C. Burkey that had spotted one carrier, two cruisers, and four destroyers heading due south at a position northeast of Malaita some 280 miles northeast of the American carriers.[30] Admiral Fletcher had not received the report, but Admiral Kinkaid passed it along to him. Fletcher told Kinkaid to get an airstrike ready for when this target was in range.[31]

In rapid succession, three more Catalinas reported contact with the Japanese. Ensign Theodore S. Thueson, flying the closest to the Solomons of the Patrol 23 scouts, reported running into three Zeros around 9:00 am. At the opposite end of the scouting fan, Lieutenant Leo Riester reported two heavy cruisers and two destroyers, who shot at him. Then he reported being "attacked by aircraft planes fighting type Zero."[32] Lieutenant (jg) Robert E. Slater, scouting the sector to the west of Riester, reported running into enemy aircraft as well.

This was rapidly becoming a pattern. At 11:10, Admiral Fletcher's *Saratoga* received another report of an aircraft carrier, this time with two heavy or light cruisers and one destroyer. It was the same composition as the force reported over an hour earlier, at almost the same position, reported by the same pilot, Ensign Burkey. But Burkey's PBY had been intercepted by two Zeros, who despite an hour-long chase had failed to shoot down his slow, lumbering flying boat.[33]

There was more. Yet another garbled report came in at 11:16 from Ensign James A. Spraggins, although the pilot call sign was misreported, of one heavy or light cruiser and four unidentified ships near Ensign Burkey's carrier. Then at 11:25 came a report from Ensign Thueson of two heavy cruisers and one destroyer northeast of Burkey's carrier headed north-northwest at 20 knots.

It was a plotting officer's dream and an intelligence officer's nightmare, which was something of the point of the unique Japanese take on the old strategy of divide and conquer. But it was also becoming clear that at least one Japanese aircraft carrier was already here. A day early. And Admiral Fletcher had just sent one of his aircraft carriers off to refuel.

By now, the *Enterprise*'s airstrike was ready and Admiral Kinkaid wanted to launch it at the carrier they had sighted. Admiral Fletcher was not so sure. He had done that at Coral Sea back in May, attacking the light carrier *Shoho*, and had shortly after launch found out about two bigger carriers in range, *Shokaku* and *Zuikaku*, who attacked him the next day. He did not want that to happen again, so he ordered Kinkaid to launch more search patrols to look for more carriers.[34]

But Admiral Fletcher's time was running out. At 11:50 am, the *Saratoga* picked up an unidentified aircraft, known in parlance as a "bogey," some 50 miles to the southwest. Fighting 5 flight officer Lieutenant David Richardson, leading four Wildcats, was vectored in to intercept. The bogey turned out to be a Kawanishi flying boat commanded by Warrant Officer Ata Kiyomi of the Yokohama Air Group. But this was a new kind of Kawanishi, not the Type 97 Mavis, a faster, more modern 8HK1 Type 2 Flying Boat that the Allies would christen "Emily." Ensign Foster Blair set the Emily's inboard port engine afire, sending the flying boat careening into the water, where it exploded. It had sent out no contact report.[35]

There would be more chances. At 12:45, the *Saratoga* vectored Lieutenant Richard Gray's four Wildcats toward a contact to the south. Gray saw what "appears to be a B-17" skimming over the water, which is something a B-17 would almost never do. A closer look revealed it to be "a Jap bomber," specifically, a G4M of the Misawa Air Group commanded by Petty Officer 1st Class Takahashi Sachito. The carrier task force's lookouts watched as Gray and his airmates brought the Betty down in flames only 7 miles away. Takahashi, too, had not gotten a contact report out, though Admiral Fletcher presumed he had.[36]

At 12:35, the *Saratoga*'s radar picked up a larger group of unidentified aircraft, bearing 350 degrees True (north-northwest) heading southwest. They were heading away from the American carriers and toward Guadalcanal.[37] OK, Admiral Fletcher thought, maybe there really is a carrier just to the north. And maybe he should take care of it.

Henderson Field did not yet have radar, so for early warning they had to make do with fighters in the air during the most likely time for attack – the period between 11:00 am and 3:00 pm – with more aircraft on alert on the runway. Four Wildcats of Marine Fighting 223 under Captain Marion Carl were over Sealark Channel when they saw incoming Japanese aircraft. Carl sounded the alarm. The Pagoda sounded the air raid siren and signaled "Condition: Red" by hoisting a black flag. Ten more Marine fighters took off, followed by two P-400s of the newly arrived Army Air Force's 67th Pursuit Squadron.[38] Four 90mm antiaircraft guns of the 3rd Defense Battalion trained upwards in preparation for the intruders.

The attack came in two waves. The first consisted of six Type 97 Carrier Attack planes, each armed with six 132lb high-explosive bombs, escorted by six Zeros. Lieutenant Murakami Binichi commanded the former, Warrant Officer Shigemi Katsuma the latter. This group was followed by a second group of nine Zeros under Lieutenant Notomi Kenjiro.[39] Flying at just under 10,000 feet, the first wave ran into a hornet's nest. Shigemi's Zeros were driven away from their charges as the harassed Kates closed in on their target, dropped their 36 bombs to negligible effect, and headed away to the north under intense fire. On their heels came Lieutenant Notomi's Zeros, roaring in low to strafe Henderson Field from three directions – and catching the aircraft of 2nd Lieutenant "Rapid Robert" Read slowly gaining altitude after takeoff, injuring Read and riddling his fighter so badly it had to be ditched near Florida Island. The Cactus Air Force slashed at all three Japanese groups. For the loss of three Wildcats, only one of whose pilots, Read, survived, the Cactus Air Force shot down three Zeros and three Kates, only one of whose pilots, Petty Officer 1st Class Okamura Takeo, was recovered. A fourth Type 97, that of Petty Officer 1st Class Sato Takamori, had to ditch off Ndai Island north of Malaita, where he was recovered by the destroyer *Mochizuki* the next day.[40]

This had been the first combat for most of the Cactus Air Force pilots, who, despite the losses, returned to Henderson Field "hilariously elated."[41] Even so, the Japanese pilots sent a message describing their strike as "successful."[42] The *Ryujo*'s skipper, Captain Kato Tadao, would report his aircraft "delivered a strong attack on the airfield at Guadalcanal, destroying fifteen enemy fighters in the air, bombing antiaircraft and machine gun emplacements, and silencing them." Kato would go on to say, "[H]aving been thoroughly deceived by this maneuver, the enemy believed this small force to be our main strength."[43]

Kato Tadao, apparently not the brightest of stars in the Combined Fleet firmament, was wrong on both counts. But for now, it would not matter.

The message from the Japanese strike planes was intercepted by the destroyer *Amatsukaze*, who along with the heavy-cruiser/seaplane-carrier *Tone*, flying the flag of Rear Admiral Hara Chuichi, and destroyer *Tokitsukaze*, was escorting the source of the strike, the light aircraft carrier *Ryujo*.[44] The *Amatsukaze*'s skipper, Commander Hara Tameichi, wondered how successful such a small strike could be.

Calling the light carrier a "big concern," Commander Hara always got apprehensive even simply looking at the *Ryujo*. About a decade old, her air group had never been part of the Japanese Naval Air Force's "A-Team," inasmuch as she never got the best pilots or the best equipment. Now, after so many air crews lost at Midway, Hara was sure the *Ryujo* was getting the dregs of the pilots available.[45]

The attack on Henderson Field had come from the *Ryujo* in a tactical move that defies simple explanation. The disappearance of the Kawanishi Type 97 of Petty Officer Shakata on August 22 convinced Base Air Force in Rabaul that an American carrier was in Shakata's search sector. Admiral Tsukahara asked Yamamoto to have Admiral Nagumo's carriers suppress the Lunga airfield on August 23 and provide air support over Taivu Point on August 24, when the convoy was supposed to land there. Admiral Tanaka seconded the request. Yamamoto was not willing to risk *Kido Butai* for this request, but he did authorize an air attack if necessary on August 24.[46]

To handle this air attack, at 1:45 am on August 24, Nagumo had detached from *Kido Butai* this small force under Admiral Hara, with the *Ryujo*, the *Tone* from the 8th Cruiser Division, and destroyers *Amatsukaze* and *Tokitsukaze*. This creatively named Detached Force would race ahead of *Kido Butai*. If the American carriers were not located before noon, the *Ryujo* would attack Guadalcanal.[47]

No one knows exactly what Admiral Yamamoto and Admiral Nagumo were thinking in sending this small force ahead of *Kido Butai* into a position exposed to the enemy, and likely neither did they. The traditional belief, exemplified by the *Amatsukaze*'s Commander Hara as well as official US Navy historian Samuel Eliot Morison, has been that the *Ryujo* was a decoy, a diversion meant to draw air attacks from the US carriers, who would both be diverted from attacking the reinforcement convoy and reveal themselves for devastating air attacks from the *Shokaku* and *Zuikaku*.[48] This theory is typical of Imperial Japanese Navy doctrine of division and deception. And, to be sure, the *Ryujo* had already been sighted multiple times by American scout planes, and was causing considerable confusion for the staffs on the *Saratoga* and *Enterprise*.

The problem is that the *Ryujo* was, as Admiral Ugaki put it, "a valuable carrier."[49] The Japanese had just lost four fleet carriers at Midway. The Japanese were so desperate for new carriers that they had started conversion of the hull of what was supposed to be the third *Yamato*-class battleship, the *Shinano*, into an aircraft carrier, or at least a reasonable facsimile of one. They were also planning the conversion of the *Ise* and *Hyuga*, two perfectly good battleships, into hybrid battleship-aircraft carriers that could perform the function of neither effectively. The *Ryujo* was hardly a perfect aircraft carrier, to be sure, even by the standards of light carriers. She had a small, narrow flight deck, small and poorly placed elevators, and poorly designed hangar decks, all of which crippled flight operations.[50] Nevertheless, simply put, the Japanese needed any carrier they could get right now.

The other theory, which has gained more traction in recent years, is that the *Ryujo* force was sent ahead to be an "indirect escort" to the reinforcement group and attack the airfield on Guadalcanal, with no reference to being a decoy or a diversion at all.[51]

The problem with this theory is that the *Ryujo* was simply not powerful enough to do either by herself. After Midway, the Japanese carriers and their air groups were reorganized, with fighters added at the expense of torpedo bombers. This idea was taken to an extreme length in the *Ryujo*. Designated a "fighter carrier," the flattop – literally, since she had no island superstructure on one side of her flight deck – carried 24 Zeros and nine Type 97 carrier attack planes.[52] Nine attack aircraft against an active airbase is nothing short of pitiful. Her 24 fighters could strafe the airfield or protect Admiral Tanaka's convoy, and Tanaka, who from the *Jintsu* saw the carrier and her escorts head south that afternoon, was happy at her presence.[53] However, this concept had been attempted during the Coral Sea action in May, in which the light carrier *Shoho* was to provide air cover to an invasion convoy directed at Port Moresby. The *Shoho* could not even protect herself, as she was simply overwhelmed in an attack from the *Lexington* and *Yorktown*. There was no reason to believe the *Ryujo* would fare any better based on that experience.

And Admiral Hara would remember that experience. At Coral Sea, he had commanded the 5th Carrier Division, with the *Shokaku* and *Zuikaku*. With the loss of the *Shoho*, for which Hara bore little responsibility, the invasion convoy was forced to turn back. Hara was able to sink the *Lexington*, damage the *Yorktown*, and escape with the *Shokaku* and *Zuikaku* still afloat. Hara had thus lost no aircraft carriers under his command. A few weeks after Coral Sea, Admiral Nagumo lost four under his command at Midway. As a result, Hara's carriers were taken away from him, renamed the 1st Carrier Division, and given to Nagumo, while Hara – "one of the Navy's most brilliant leaders," in the words of the unrelated Commander Hara – was stuck with the 8th Cruiser Division.[54] Rank has its privileges.

And it had privileges for Lieutenant Commander Charles M. Jett, commander of Torpedo 3 from the carrier *Enterprise*. At 2:40 pm, Jett and his wingman Ensign Robert J. Bye had spotted the *Ryujo* and made a contact report before heading north to gain altitude in their Grumman Avengers. Two SBD Dauntlesses flown by Lieutenant Stockton B. Strong and his wingman Ensign Gerald S. "Rich" Richey also saw the *Ryujo*, drawing to within 5 miles of her before sending out a contact report. They also saw Jett and Bye moving on up. Having done his good deed for the day by reporting the carrier's location, and with Jett and Bye positioning themselves for an attack, Strong decided to head back without attacking the carrier. It was a decision he immediately regretted. Approaching from the southwest, Ensign John H. Jorgensen, flying an SBD Dauntless dive bomber with Ensign Harold L. Bingaman as a wingman – in a TBF Avenger torpedo bomber – also found the carrier.[55]

On the *Amatsukaze*, Commander Hara had just finished his lunch on the bridge when at 2:55 a lookout shouted, "A plane, looks like the enemy, coming from 30 degrees to port." The skipper turned and looked through his binoculars just in time to see the first plane joined by a second. To Hara, they looked like B-17s; they were actually the TBF Avengers flown by Jett and Bye.[56] Having first allowed the prowling Grummans to loiter for 15 minutes before mistaking the single-engine Avengers for four-engine B-17s suggests that, apropos of Hara's fears for the *Ryujo*, the carrier's escorts had indeed not brought their "A" game.

Then again, neither had the *Ryujo*. Commander Hara directed his antiaircraft guns trained upward into the path of the intruders. Seeing what was going on, the flagship *Tone* and destroyer *Tokitsukaze* quickly joined in. But the *Ryujo* was slow on the uptake. Hara stared at the carrier, his jaw dropping. She was doing nothing. "All was so quiet and serene on board the carrier," the *Amatsukaze*'s skipper recalled, "that I thought the skipper must be asleep."[57]

After what seemed like an eternity to Commander Hara, the *Ryujo* finally turned into the wind to launch one Type 97 for antisubmarine patrol and three Zeros under Petty Officer 1st Class Sugiyama Teruo. At 2:58, the carrier's skipper, Captain Kato, the former executive officer of the *Akagi* and a trained aviator, swung the *Ryujo* into a tight starboard turn just in time for all four 500lb bombs dropped by the two Avengers to miss about 150 meters astern. Jett and Bye rapidly took their leave, not even noticing Sugiyama's vain attempt to catch them. He returned to circle the carrier.[58]

Commander Hara was flabbergasted by the *Ryujo*'s lethargic performance. He angrily ordered a message sent to the carrier, directed specifically to her executive officer Commander Kishi Hisakichi, who was an Etajima naval academy classmate of his. "Fully realizing my impertinence, am forced to advise you my impression. Your flight operations are far short of expectations. What is the matter?" Hara later admitted the message was "probably rude and certainly audacious"; and knew of no other Japanese naval officer who had ever sent such a message during an operation.[59]

Commander Kishi quickly responded, "Deeply appreciate your admonition. We shall do better and count on your cooperation."[60] This seemed to placate the *Amatsukaze*'s commander, though the message could be interpreted with a whiff of indignity at being lectured on air operations by a destroyer skipper with no flight training.

In any event, the *Ryujo* soon launched two Zeros led by Petty Officer 1st Class Miyauchi Yukuo; the launch of a third had to be aborted. They got into the air just in time to catch another pair of *Enterprise* scouts, Lieutenant John N. Myers and Machinist Harry L. Corl, who were trying to get into position to bomb the *Tone*. The *Tone* began evasive maneuvers and opened up on the new intruders.[61] The Zeros harangued the two Avengers, driving off Myers and shooting down Corl, who was killed. Corl's gunner, Radioman 3rd Class Delmer D. Wiley, survived the crash, inflated his rubber boat, and drifted northwest, alone. For 15 days. Then he finally reached Carteret Island, 40 miles northeast of the Japanese base at Buka, where he was taken in by friendly natives. Wiley did not return to Allied-held territory until April 11, 1943, 218 days after being shot down.[62]

The leaking sky that had drip-drip-dripped US Navy planes now caved in as the drips became a torrent. The lookouts on the *Amatsukaze* shouted, "Many enemy planes approaching!"[63] Commander Hara watched in horror as the *Ryujo* sluggishly turned into the wind and scrambled two more Zeros, then ordered her aircraft returning from the strike on Henderson Field to make for Buka. Hara was again mystified as to why the carrier did not recall the fighters from the airstrike.[64]

It was too late. Admiral Fletcher had waited as long as he could for the *Enterprise*'s scouts to locate the additional carriers he knew were out there before concluding he had to deal with the birdhouse in the hand. At 1:40 pm, 30 Dauntlesses and eight Avengers took off from the *Saratoga*, led by the head of her air group, Commander Felt. Because of the distance, Fletcher did not authorize any fighter escort. One dive bomber and one torpedo bomber had to abort because of mechanical issues.[65] Almost a half-hour later, a Catalina piloted by Lieutenant Joseph M. Kellam reported one small carrier, two cruisers, and one destroyer headed southeast, but 60 miles northeast of where Felt was heading.[66] Fletcher tried to inform Felt but could not reach him.

Even so, while on the way, Commander Felt intercepted Lieutenant Commander Jett's sighting report that placed the *Ryujo* some 75 miles further northeast than anticipated. Felt's air group followed him to the site mentioned in Jett's report, but after finding nothing Felt had them turn southwest again. Finally, at 3:36 the *Ryujo* and her three escorts came into view, heading southwest at about 30 knots.[67]

As the *Saratoga* strike approached, the Detached Force opened, with the *Tone*, *Amatsukaze*, and *Tokitsukaze* positioning themselves some 5,000 meters from the *Ryujo*.[68] It was a tactic the Allies had used during the Java Sea Campaign, having the ships scatter to gain "fighting room." Scattering gave the ships room to maneuver, but at the cost of minimizing their antiaircraft defense, which could be fatal if all the attacking aircraft decided to pile in on one ship. The Allies had learned this the hard way in the Java Sea Campaign, and had still not quite digested the best way for ships to position themselves for air defense. The Japanese were still new to Allied air attacks and had yet to learn it. For now, in essence, the *Ryujo* was on her own.

This seemed to work well, at first. Commander Felt had ordered six dive bombers and one torpedo plane to attack the *Tone*, with the remaining planes to concentrate on the *Ryujo*. It was the SBDs of Lieutenant Commander Louis J. Kirn, skipper of Scouting 3, who first reached their pushover points from 14,000 feet at 3:50. As the Dauntlesses screamed downward, Captain Kato threw the *Ryujo* into a tight starboard turn, and all of the 1,000lb bombs from Kirn's group missed. Next came Lieutenant Commander Dewitt W. Shumway, head of Bombing 3, leading down seven of his Dauntlesses. All of the 1,000lb bombs from his group missed as well.

Commander Felt watched the rain of bombs missing the target with growing alarm until he finally ordered all remaining aircraft to attack the *Ryujo*. Felt himself dove and thought he got a hit, though he probably got a near miss. Six Dauntlesses of Bombing 3 led by Lieutenant Harold S. Bottomley followed Felt and finally got … something. Captain Kato admitted no bomb hits, but it seems at least two bombs hit the flight deck very close to the edge. A third planted itself on the flight deck near the stern toward the starboard side.[69]

Meanwhile, Lieutenant Bruce Harwood of Torpedo 8 had his five torpedo bombers attempt the classic anvil attack, with Harwood leading three Avengers from the starboard bow and two more coming from the port bow, coming in at 200 knots and releasing from 200 feet altitude at an average range of 800 to 900 yards.[70] It was a perfectly executed anvil attack – except for the Mark 13 torpedoes themselves. One of the torpedoes passed under the stern of the carrier, three more missed, but one torpedo smacked into the starboard side of the *Ryujo* near the engine room. The engine room itself was flooded, with the starboard aft boiler room possibly flooded as well. The carrier lost helm control and started listing to starboard.[71]

As the American strike headed back to the *Saratoga* while being ineffectually harassed by Zeros, black smoke was billowing from amidships aft of the carrier, with fire visible on the hangar deck.[72] "It was a pathetic sight," moaned Commander Hara. "*Ryujo*, no longer resembling a ship, was a huge stove, full of holes which belched eerie red flames." From the *Jintsu*, Admiral Tanaka had watched the air attack on the eastern horizon, from where he could now see "a gigantic pillar of smoke and flame."[73] There went his air support.

Admiral Hara ordered the Detached Force to head back to the north, but the *Ryujo* could not comply. Then he signaled, "Destroyers, stand by *Ryujo* for rescue operation."[74] Commander Felt stayed behind to amuse himself with the carrier's woes, watching as the *Ryujo* "continued to run in circles to the right pouring forth black smoke which would die down and belch forth in great volume again."[75]

Then the *Ryujo*'s aircraft returned from the attack on Guadacanal, to find their home in flames with a 23-degree list to starboard.[76] Captain Kato had been late – again – this time in sending the order for them to head to Buka. Now they did not have the fuel to get there. Several of these second-string Sea Eagles circled their burning nest, ditching near the destroyers, where the crews were rescued. Others headed off toward Buka to at least get as close as possible to the Japanese base.[77]

The *Ryujo* was dying. She had stopped her circling and was now dead in the water. After recovering some pilots who had ditched for lack of fuel, Commander Hara's *Amatsukaze* tried to come alongside. But when three B-17s under Major Ernest Maniere from the 11th Bombardment Group appeared overhead, the *Amatsukaze*, *Tokitsukaze*, and *Tone* had to get under way to evade the long strings of 300lb bombs. All missed. One of the B-17s was shot up by escorting Zeros, but made it back to Espiritu Santo; a second, undamaged Fortress crashed on landing, killing its crew.[78]

By the time the Japanese escorts could get back to their rescue work it was nearly dark. The *Ryujo*'s list was now 40 degrees and she had lost all power. Her signalmen used flags to signal "We are abandoning ship. Come alongside to rescue crew."[79] The *Amatsukaze*, *Tokitsukaze*, and *Tone* came back to rescue the crew.

Taking a tremendous risk, Commander Hara brought the *Amatsukaze* along the listing starboard side. The carrier's canting hull brushed against the destroyer's bridge, sending streams of cold sweat down a nervous Hara Tameichi's back. Strong crewmen used poles to keep the destroyer away from the *Ryujo*'s canting deck, while others ran planks from the destroyer's port side to the sinking carrier. Wounded were transferred across, then the crew and officers. The *Amatsukaze* alone took some 300 survivors.[80]

The *Ryujo*'s list suddenly increased sharply; the danger of her capsizing on top of the *Amatsukaze* and taking the destroyer with her was very real. Commander Hara shouted, "Evacuation finished?" An officer at the end of a plank answered, "Yes, sir! Please cast off. It's getting dangerous!"[81]

The *Amatsukaze*'s engines roared to life and she sprinted away, barely getting 500 meters before the *Ryujo* finally capsized to starboard, slowing just long enough to reveal the holes in her hull, and slipped stern first beneath the waves.[82] The suction caused by her sinking made the *Amatsukaze* "bob like a cork."[83] Seven officers and 113 petty officers and men went down with the carrier. A distraught, half-drowned Captain Kato visited Commander Hara to express his gratitude and that of his men. But Kato was compelled to inform Hara that Hara's friend Commander Kishi did not make it.[84]

If her mission had indeed been to destroy or at least suppress the Lunga airfield, the carrier had failed miserably, not only by not damaging the airfield but by getting herself sunk in the process. Her failure was her own doing, but not her own fault. An effective attack on the airfield was simply beyond her abilities, so much so that historian John Lundstrom called the attack "a useless gesture."[85]

Nevertheless, Commander Hara, for one, pinned responsibility for her demise on the incompetence of Captain Kato, whom he blamed for what he believed were the *Ryujo*'s sluggish air operations; whether he knew that the carrier's design inhibited efficient flight operations is anyone's guess. To be sure, however, the retired Marine and highly respected Imperial Japanese Navy historian Paul Dull would describe Kato's behavior in this action as "puzzling."[86] But Hara's fury was also directed at Admiral Yamamoto, for ordering Kato to complete this "decoy" mission.[87]

Commander Hara would later admit that the decoy mission "had met a dismal end; and yet it had not been a failure," because the "sacrifice of *Ryujo* had deflected the enemy from the main Japanese force[.]"[88]

If the light carrier's mission had indeed been to divert the American carriers from the main Japanese force to allow *Kido Butai* to get the first licks in on the American carriers, the *Ryujo* had succeeded admirably.

Admiral Hara's flagship, the *Tone*, which even Commander Hara admitted was "weird-looking" because all of her turrets were in the front, commanded the 8th Cruiser Division, whose only other member was her sister ship, the *Chikuma*.[89]

At this moment, the *Chikuma* was not with the *Tone* as she normally was, nor was she with *Kido Butai*, for the support of which both cruisers had been specifically designed. No, the *Chikuma* was currently with Admiral Abe's Vanguard Force, whose job should not be confused with that of Admiral Kondo's Advance Force. The Vanguard Force – battleships *Hiei* and *Kirishima*, heavy cruisers *Kumano*, *Suzuya*, and *Chikuma*, light cruiser *Nagara*, and destroyers *Nowaki*, *Maikaze*, and *Tanikaze* – had screened *Kido Butai* until Abe's ships moved ahead by about 6 miles or so to act as an early warning. And *Kido Butai* would now need that early warning, for now the Japanese Carrier Striking Force was mostly carrier and less force, comprising only *Shokaku* and *Zuikaku*, and destroyers *Kazegumo*, *Yugumo*, *Kamigumo*, *Akigumo*, *Hatsukaze*, and *Akizuki*.

As part of this early warning, the battleships and cruisers sent out scout planes to find the enemy carriers. To make up for the aerial search capacity the aircraft carriers lost when they replaced bombers with fighters, the escorting battleships and cruisers carried more seaplanes – another example of the Japanese belief that there was no problem that could not be solved by adding yet more seaplanes. The *Chikuma* was an old hand at this. And she had a scalp or two to her scouting credit. At Midway, it was one of her scout planes that had found the American carrier *Yorktown*, disabled but making good progress on repairs. It was the contact report of the *Chikuma*'s floatplane that had allowed the Japanese submarine *I-168* to find the *Yorktown* and finish her off with torpedoes. The *Chikuma* hoped to add another scalp when, at 11:00 am, she launched one of her scout planes, a last-minute addition to the Japanese late-morning search.[90]

About two and a half hours later, this scout plane, an Aichi Type 0 reconnaissance seaplane – the Allies called this aircraft the "Jake" – commanded by Special Duty Ensign Fukuyama Kazutoshi, showed up on the radar of the carrier *Enterprise*.[91] A full eight *Enterprise* Wildcats were vectored to swarm the Jake, but the *Chikuma* scout pilots were veterans; the floatplane took advantage of clouds, rolled, and danced in the air. However, Wildcat pilot Gunsmith Charles E. Brewer killed the Jake's gunner, then Machinist Doyle C. Barnes flamed the Type 0 some 28 miles short of the American task force.

But Ensign Fukuyama had gotten off a partial message: "Spotted large enemy force. Being pursued by enemy fighters, 1200 [2:00 pm local time]." The *Chikuma* passed the report on to Admiral Nagumo. Fukuyama had not reported the position of the force, nor its composition, nor its course and speed.

Despite the encounters between the Japanese scouts and the American fighter patrols all day long, Ensign Fukuyama had gotten off the only contact report. So, unlike his US Navy counterparts who had to sort through multiple contact reports, not all of them complete or accurate, Admiral Nagumo and his staff had to deal with only one, albeit a partial one. The timing of the message was plotted against Fukuyama's planned search course, leading to the deduction that the force was 260 miles away on a bearing of 153 degrees True – southeast.[92] East of Malaita. There were no airfields around there, so the fighters who attacked Fukuyama had to be coming from an enemy carrier …

He had them. The *Chikuma* had done it again.

While Admiral Nagumo and his staff had been making their calculations, the flagship *Shokaku* had added to her patrolling air cover by launching three Zeros under the fighter squadron commander Lieutenant Shingo Hideki. After that, the carrier could focus on launching the airstrike under air group skipper Lieutenant Commander Seki Mamoru – 18 Aichi Type 99 carrier bombers, escorted by nine Zeros under Lieutenant Shigematsu Yasuhiro. They started taking off at 2:50 pm. Ten minutes later, the *Zuikaku* started launching her contribution to the airstrike – nine Type 99 carrier bombers under Lieutenant Otsuka Reijiro and six Zeros under Lieutenant Hidaka Saneyasu.[93] All 42 attack aircraft formed to head out and gain altitude …

"Hell divers!" The call came from the *Shokaku*'s lookouts.

It was two scouts from the carrier *Enterprise*: Bombing 6 skipper Lieutenant Ray Davis and his wingman Ensign Robert C. Shaw. They were about to attack Admiral Abe's ships, now some 40 miles ahead of *Kido Butai* and trying to close the range to the US task force, when they saw a big aircraft carrier with what looked like aircraft spotted on her flight deck for launch. The veteran Davis was a savvy pilot and managed to lead Shaw in avoiding the Japanese combat air patrol.

But not the new Type 21 radar installed on top of the *Shokaku*'s island superstructure. The radar, the first and so far only one in the Combined Fleet, had detected them, but the operator could not get a message to the bridge in time. Nor could anyone tell the patrolling Zeros that wolves were in the fold. The outgoing airstrike saw the two Dauntlesses, and five of Lieutenant Shigematsu's planes peeled off to pursue them. But they had not caught them before 3:15, when Davis and Shaw pushed over into their dives from 14,000 feet.

Admiral Nagumo must have groaned as Dauntless dive bombers screamed down on his flagship – again. His protective flight of Zeros was ineffective – again. The howls got louder and louder as the SBDs plunged down. The *Shokaku*'s skipper, Captain Arima Masafumi, threw the carrier into a hard right turn. One 500lb pound bomb hit just 10 meters off the starboard side, killing six; the second splashed another 10 meters beyond the first.[94] Physical damage was negligible.

That was far too close for Admiral Nagumo. His carriers scrambled more Zeros, four from the *Zuikaku* and the last 11 aboard the *Shokaku*. Nagumo also ordered Admiral Abe in the Vanguard Force to close on the American carriers and destroy them in surface action that night.[95]

Lieutenant Davis and Ensign Shaw headed back, making contact and attack reports. Davis was very careful to give his identification, the Japanese carriers' position, course, and speed. Not that it mattered much. Radio reception on this day was not ideal, so much so that on his way back to Ndeni Lieutenant Kellam felt obliged to detour his PBY to the *Enterprise* and flash his earlier contact report, and also a new report of three light cruisers, two destroyers, and three transports 50 miles from his first contact.[96] As for Davis and Shaw's report, the only thing that got through to the *Enterprise* and *Saratoga* was "Two [carriers] with decks full."[97] This wasn't much use unless, like Admiral Nagumo, one had enough information to deduce their position.

A report of "Two carriers with decks full" was disturbing enough, but it was nothing compared to what showed up on the *Enterprise*'s CXAM radar at 4:02: a large contact, bearing 320 degrees True – northwest – distance 88 miles. The *Saratoga*, about 10 miles from the *Enterprise*, picked it up, too, at a range of 103 miles. The contact faded. But no one believed it was a phantom. It was a Japanese airstrike. Admiral Fletcher's worst nightmare had been realized – his carriers were about to be attacked, with no idea of where the Japanese carriers were and with his own airstrike already committed.

Admiral Fletcher had to send up additional fighters, but launching planes off an aircraft carrier is not easy. At that moment, the *Saratoga* was some 140 miles east of Malaita, heading northwest at a speed of 20 knots. The *Enterprise* was about 10 miles off her port quarter. To create enough headwind to generate enough lift for aircraft to take off from their short flight decks, both carriers had to turn into the wind, which was from the southeast, as it almost always was in this area, and speed up. So both forces turned to the southeast and rang up 25 knots, driving the carriers and their escorts into "long heavy swells" with destroyers "bouncing almost out of the water."[98]

The *Enterprise* immediately launched her remaining fighters and vectored ten already aloft northwest toward the contact, hoping to catch them well short of the carriers. At the same time, another Japanese floatplane, this one from the battleship *Hiei*, helpfully provided updated location information on the US carriers to the Japanese. Not as helpfully, the information the floatplane provided had the American flattops 50 miles further south than they actually were, and headed southeast instead of northwest. Lieutenant Commander Seki adjusted his course slightly more toward the south, hoping to chase them down.[99]

Two minutes later, the *Enterprise* CXAM radar detected another, smaller contact. Now she turned those ten Wildcats more toward the west and the new contact. She also vectored another group of four fighters toward the northwest, followed by another group of 16 Fighting 6 fighters that had just launched. Now three groups of fighters were fanning out to the northwest in three different vectors, leaving no fighters over the *Enterprise*.[100]

Fletcher ordered Admiral Kinkaid to close the *Enterprise* force on the *Saratoga* and launch his currently spotted small attack force so the Japanese attack would not catch the *Enterprise* with flammable aircraft on deck.[101] The *Saratoga* cleared her own deck of aircraft – two Dauntlesses, five Avengers, and six Wildcats. Both groups were ordered to join up, head north, and attack anything Japanese they found, preferably that carrier reported by Lieutenant Commander Jett, that is, the *Ryujo*. When Lieutenant Harold H. "Swede" Larsen, head of the reconstituted Torpedo 8, heard they were going to attack something instead of just marking time beyond range of the Japanese attack, he came out and bodily threw a pilot out of an Avenger to take it over himself.[102]

The *Enterprise* fighters aloft managed to isolate that new, small bogey – it was a returning Avenger scout. With that mystery solved, at 4:18, the large inbound contact appeared, now only 44 miles away on a bearing of 320 degrees True – northwest. Its altitude was estimated to be 12,000 feet. Four *Saratoga* fighters had to land to refuel – quickly, hopefully – but Admiral Fletcher still had 11 Wildcats 40 miles to the northwest, with another 16 en route, now ordered to move up to 12,000 feet. Closer to the carriers themselves were 15 more. Seven were to escort the *Enterprise* airstrike and could be redirected. All in all, 53 fighters were waiting for the Japanese attack.[103]

But not necessarily in the right place. The *Enterprise* and her escorts in a "ring formation" came into Lieutenant Commander Seki's view at 4:20. With the carrier still 40 miles away and off to his left, Seki had the attack group turn toward the east in order to attack from the north. As he had his Sea Eagles head east, Seki saw another carrier, the *Saratoga*, beyond the *Enterprise* to the southeast. And as he had his Sea Eagles head east, Seki unintentionally outwitted the *Enterprise*'s fighter director officer Lieutenant Commander Leonard J. "Ham" Dow, who, seeing Seki's earlier turn toward the south, had concluded that the Japanese would attack from the west and so had directed 11 Wildcats in that direction. Seki passed them headed in the opposite direction.

Lieutenant Commander Seki's observer, Special Duty Ensign Nakasada Jiro, sent out the message "Assume attack formation." Lieutenant Shigematsu's four remaining Zeros moved out in front to carry out their mission, which was technically called "air control." How these four Zeros planned to control 53 enemy fighters has never been satisfactorily explained.[104]

But the Japanese air control was made so much easier when 11 of the *Enterprise*'s Wildcats had been sent too far west and missed the inbound Japanese entirely. Worse, the defending Grummans were too low. The Japanese were at 18,000 feet, the defenders at 12,000 to 15,000 feet. Four Wildcats under Lieutenant Vorse tried desperately to climb and hack away at the Vals, but Lieutenant Shigematsu's Zeros ripped through them.[105]

With the Japanese now at 27 miles and closing, the *Enterprise* finally launched her airstrike – 11 Dauntlesses under Lieutenant Caldwell and seven Avengers under Lieutenant Rubin H. Konig, all commanded by air group skipper Lieutenant Commander Maxwell F. Leslie, a hero of the Battle of Midway. They were told to head north, attack anything they could find, and land on Guadalcanal if they had to. The seven Wildcats originally slated to escort them were pulled off the strike, but since they had been part of it, their radios were tuned to the strike frequency and not the fighter director frequency. They were told to orbit the *Enterprise* at 15,000 feet and keep an eye out for incoming Japanese.[106]

As the wheels of Lieutenant Commander Leslie's command TBF Avenger bounced off the *Enterprise*'s flight deck at 4:38, Seki's radio operator Ensign Nakasada sent another message: "All forces attack."[107] Lieutenant Otsuka's nine *Zuikaku* Type 99 carrier bombers made for the *Saratoga*, while the *Shokaku* Type 99s were lined up in a column on the *Enterprise*'s port quarter as the carrier turned away to starboard toward a course 170 degrees True – south-southeast.[108] It was time for the Sea Eagles of *Kido Butai* to avenge Midway.

Only now did the defending US Navy fighters realize that all was not sunny above them. Lieutenant Hidaka's six Zeros from the *Zuikaku* momentarily pulled away from Lieutenant Commander Seki's bombers to ambush a flight of three Wildcats from the *Saratoga* commanded by Fighting 5 flight officer Lieutenant David C. Richardson. The flight was scattered and one Wildcat, piloted by veteran Lieutenant Marion W. Dufilho, vanished. Two more Wildcats from the *Saratoga* tried to intervene and were driven off.

More fighters from the *Saratoga* headed northwest toward the threatened *Enterprise*, but they were all too low. For now.

"The enemy planes are now directly overhead!" reported the *Enterprise*'s radar plot in desperation.[109] But the lookouts could not see the enemy planes in the sun. To make matters worse, the fighter director officer, Lieutenant Commander Dow, was struggling to position the defending fighters because both his communications and communications among the fighters shared the same radio frequency. And many of the younger pilots were talking too much. Dow tried desperately to break in to the fighter frequency.[110]

Starting at 4:41, one by one, the Aichi Type 99s pushed over into their dives on the *Enterprise*, whose fire-control radar just went out.[111] The carrier's gunners struggled looking into the sun to pick out the attackers. It was a puff of smoke from above the port bow that caught the attention of Marine 1st Sergeant Joseph R. Schinka, commanding a 20mm antiaircraft battery on the carrier's port side. With the target still out of range, Schinka opened fire, not to hit the target but to attract attention. For the *Enterprise* was not alone.

The *Enterprise* was in the center of, as Lieutenant Commander Seki had described it, a ring formation, with a radius of 1,800–2,000 yards. The ring included six destroyers – *Balch*, *Maury*, *Ellet*, *Monssen*, *Grayson*, and *Benham* – but off the *Enterprise*'s port bow was the heavy cruiser *Portland*, off the starboard bow was the light antiaircraft cruiser *Atlanta* with 16 5-inch dual-purpose guns in eight twin mounts, and astern was the brand-new post-Pearl Harbor battleship *North Carolina*.

Though aircraft carriers were supplanting battleships as the queens of the seas, battleships were still vital. The *North Carolina* was the first modern US Navy battleship completed since World War I, the first of a new class – indeed, a new generation – of American battleships. With all of the Pacific Fleet's battleships disabled in the humiliating disaster of December 7, the arrival of the new *North Carolina* at Pearl Harbor in July was inspiring for the hard-pressed sailors on hand. Even for Admiral Nimitz himself:

> I well remember the great thrill when she arrived in Pearl Harbor during the early stages of the war – at a time when our strength and fortunes were at low ebb. She was the first of the great new battleships to join the Pacific Fleet, and her mere presence in a task force was enough to keep morale at a peak.[112]

The presence of the *North Carolina* did not go unnoticed on the *Enterprise*. Nor did the presence of the battleship's massive antiaircraft battery of 20 5-inch dual-purpose guns in ten twin mounts and 15 1.1-inch guns.

Lieutenant Commander Seki led his dive bombers down, pushing over at precise intervals of seven seconds, like a long, long train going over the top of the big hill of a roller coaster, gaining speed, plunging, screaming downward. But Seki's dive bombers had gained four planes diving with them, a flight of four Grummans under Lieutenant

Richard E. "Chick" Harmer from the *Saratoga*. Too late to prevent the dives, his angry Wildcats joined the dives instead, snarling and slashing at the Vals as the Sea Eagles tried to stay on target.[113] Harmer and his pilots did not have to shoot the Vals down; they just had to disrupt their attack.

Lieutenant Commander Seki himself was harassed and harangued by Lieutenant Harmer's wingman, Ensign John McDonald, driving the Japanese air group commander to miss with his bomb. Harmer himself drove the second Val, that of Petty Officer 1st Class Imada Tetsu, to distraction and a miss with its bomb. Lieutenant Howard Crews ripped into the third Val, that of Petty Officer 1st Class Sasaki Mitsuo, but had to pull away before he could see what happened to the Japanese. Sasaki's pilot, Seaman 1st Class Akutagawa Takeshi, released his bomb too early, and it splashed some 200 yards off the *Enterprise*'s port quarter. Sasaki's Val caught fire, then spun into the water 600 yards off the carrier's port beam. The fourth member of Harmer's flight, Ensign Benjamin "Mole" Currie, was forced into a twisting dive that prevented him from taking any shots.[114]

Lieutenant Crews had to pull up because the antiaircraft fire from the US Navy ships was becoming too intense for him to risk being a victim of friendly fire. The normally dry narrative from the Office of Naval Intelligence opined, "The volume of our antiaircraft fire was tremendous."[115] The fiercest came from the *North Carolina*. Ensign Fred Mears, heading out in one of the *Enterprise*'s Avengers, was stunned when the *North Carolina* opened up with her antiaircraft battery. "The battleship accompanying our carrier lit up like a Christmas tree."[116] On the *Enterprise*, Admiral Kinkaid could not believe what he was seeing from the *North Carolina* and had the carrier signal her, "Are you afire?"[117]

The next six Vals pushed over into their dives with little in the way of fighter opposition, but seemed to be having difficulty with the unexpectedly heavy antiaircraft fire. The eighth and ninth Vals of Seki's group were those of Petty Officer 1st Class Yasuda Nobuyoshi and Petty Officer 2nd Class Kitamura Kenzo. Diving into a nightmare of shellbursts, Yasuda's Val was torched, forcing his pilot, Petty Officer 2nd Class Shirai Goro, to release his bomb too high. The bomb splashed into the water off the *Enterprise*'s starboard bow, the flaming Aichi following right behind it. Kitamura had antiaircraft gunfire coming from the front and machine gunfire from the *Enterprise* Wildcat of Gunsmith Brewer behind him. Brewer had to pull up because of the friendly flak, but by then the Val was doomed. Fatally damaged and flaming like a comet, the Aichi plummeted downward into the blizzard of burning lead as pilot Petty Officer 2nd Class Miki Isamu released his bomb too high – again – and aimed the burning, barely-under-control dive bomber for the *Enterprise*'s fight deck. His bomb missed to starboard while his Type 99 "screamed past sky control in a fiery blur" and plunged into the water to port.[118]

The first nine Vals of Seki's attack had missed with their bombs. The last nine, led by Lieutenant Arima Keiichi, had an additional handicap of being clawed by four *Enterprise* Wildcats under Machinist Barnes, who had been directed too far west to intercept the Japanese on the inbound and had to chase them from behind to catch them as they pushed over. Barnes shouted, "OK, let's go give them hell!" One Val immediately went down to

Barnes' wingman, Ensign Robert A. M. "Ram" Dibb, but Barnes himself took the full force of a 5-inch antiaircraft burst that blew the wings and tail off his fighter, sending them both to their doom some 2,000 yards off the port quarter of the destroyer *Balch.*[119]

Lieutenant Arima pushed over to lead his Aichis in the dive into a hellstorm of flak far more intense than anything he had ever seen in his years of service in China.[120] Arima watched in horror as the Type 99s of petty officers Yasuda and Kitamura were set alight in front of him. But his pilot Petty Officer 1st Class Furata Kiyoto grimly held their dive and released their 551lb bomb. Furata pulled out very low, and Arima watched the bomb burrow through the flight deck's Number 3 elevator to explode at 4:44 in the chief's quarters on the third deck.

About half a minute after and 20 feet away from Lieutenant Arima's bomb hit came another bomb, this from the Type 99 of Petty Officer 1st Class Koitabashi Hiroshi, flown by Petty Officer 1st Class Akimoto Tamotsu. This bomb detonated in the Number 3 5-inch gun gallery, disabling both guns, setting off ready powder, threatening the 5-inch magazines, and killing all 38 men operating the guns.

Following Petty Officer Koitabashi was Petty Officer 2nd Class Iida Yoshihiro. His own bomb was set afire by 20mm rounds from the *Enterprise*'s guns. While the whole idea of a bomb involves setting it on fire to quickly explode, it is considered preferable that it do so after it has hit the target, or at least after it has left the plane. Iida's Val "disintegrated in a tremendous burst [in] mid air and nothing but small pieces came fluttering down, just like confetti on Wall Street."[121]

Three more Type 99s, those of Lieutenant (jg) Motoyama Hiroyuki, Petty Officer 2nd Class Tsuchiya Ryoroku, and Petty Officer 2nd Class Horie Kazumi, pushed over to attack the *Enterprise.* Motoyama and Tsuchiya between them managed only a near miss to starboard. Horie's Aichi, pounded by gunfire, began to break apart during his dive, but he released his bomb at an altitude of about 1,500 feet to hit the *Enterprise*'s flight deck just aft of the Number 2 (center) elevator, disabling the elevator and leaving only the forward elevator operable, blasting a 10-foot hole in the flight deck, and damaging some of the arresting gear.

But these were the last attacks on the *Enterprise.* The last three Aichis under Warrant Officer Argane Masaki, for reasons known only to him, did not attack the *Enterprise* but instead went astern of the carrier to attack the *North Carolina.* All three were shot down after dropping their bombs, their sacrifices netting only three near misses.

That left Lieutenant Otsuka's nine *Zuikaku* Type 99 carrier bombers to fight their way to the *Saratoga.* And fight they would have to, because the American fighters were now swarming. The first to challenge Otsuka and his Vals were three *Saratoga* Grummans under Lieutenant Hayden Jensen. Otsuka was trying to form his Type 99s into a column for the dive on the *Saratoga*, but that just left Jensen and his pilots to stalk them from astern. Jensen was quickly joined by four *Enterprise* Wildcats under Machinist Don Runyon. More Wildcats appeared ahead. Otsuka decided he would not make it to the *Saratoga* and opted to turn back toward the *Enterprise.*

He turned just in time for his close air cover, four Zeros from the *Zuikaku*, to join in what became a wild air melee. It was also just in time for Lieutenant Otsuka to be shot down, by whom is unknown. Leaderless, the remaining seven Vals scattered to different targets. Four bombed the *North Carolina*, netting four misses, with all four shot down. Three ganged up on *Enterprise*, losing one of their own without a hit.

Even so, some on the *Enterprise* were highly impressed with the work of Lieutenant Commander Seki's men. Captain Arthur C. Davis described the dives as "steep, estimated at 70 degrees, well executed, and absolutely determined."[122] Senior Landing Signal Officer Lieutenant Robin Lindsey was more effusive:

> These Jap planes launched about the most beautiful awe-inspiring attack I have ever seen. It was almost suicidal, in fact, they came so low. They used a roll-over approach, a rather shallow dive … about 60 to 55 degrees … came down and released about a thousand feet and were pulling out at 200 feet.[123]

But beauty is indeed in the eye of the beholder. The gunnery officer of the cruiser *Portland*, Lieutenant Commander Elliott Shanklin, who had seen five other Japanese dive-bombing attacks, was less impressed. He found their technique wanting, as pushing over in a line one at a time left each one's view of the target obscured by the plane ahead.[124] Moreover, Shanklin saw some of the Vals "veer from their dive rather than continue." Many "released early at high altitudes," others "appeared deflected to a considerable extent from the course of their dives" by the heavy antiaircraft fire, which left them with "both the physical and the psychological handicap imposed by the barrage."[125] In short, while the attacks were good, Shanklin had seen better.[126] It is for very good reasons that eye witness testimony is the least reliable form of evidence.

But there were other attackers about, who might be better. At 4:51 pm, the *Enterprise*'s radar showed a large contact 50 miles away, bearing 265 degrees True – almost due west – heading southwest. This was Admiral Nagumo's follow-up strike, launched a little before 4:00 pm and led by Lieutenant Takahashi Sadamu, head of the *Zuikaku*'s air group. It consisted of 18 Type 99s from the *Zuikaku* and nine from the *Shokaku* under Lieutenant Yamada Shohei, escorted by six Zeros from the *Zuikaku* and three from the *Shokaku* under Lieutenant Shirane Ayao, who headed the *Zuikaku*'s fighter group.[127]

On board the *Enterprise*, anxious eyes watched the radar. The carrier was still burning, still could not handle aircraft. Everyone had to go to the *Saratoga* for the moment. Though her damage was not serious, the *Enterprise* herself was currently helpless.

But Lieutenant Takahashi's strike was going the wrong way. Another search plane from the *Chikuma* had the *Enterprise* in sight, had watched the decimation of Lieutenant Commander Seki's strike, and had radioed the carrier's position. Takahashi didn't pick up that message. That contact report was rebroadcast by *Kido Butai*; Takahashi didn't pick that up either. At 5:30, Lieutenant Commander Seki radioed his report of the results of his strike and the position of the American carriers. Takahashi missed that one, too. Some of his pilots had copied the messages, but no one thought to tell him.[128]

So Lieutenant Takahashi led his strike over empty water more than 80 miles south of the *Enterprise*. Then he turned to search to the west, getting further and further away from his quarry. The damage control on the *Enterprise* was very efficient. At 5:40, Admiral Kinkaid reported to Admiral Fletcher that the carrier had suffered two bomb hits and some underwater damage but said "damage [was] apparently light."[129] Less than ten minutes later, the *Enterprise* was conducting flight operations, landing 33 planes in the next 21 minutes. At 6:10 she stopped for a bit to spot and launch five Wildcats for combat air patrol. The radar guys and fighter director started breathing a little easier as Lieutenant Takahashi's strike moved off. Things were looking up.

But nothing looks up for very long around Guadalcanal. It's as if the island's fundamental dishonesty infects everything around it. Pandaemonium. The first bomb hit on the *Enterprise* blew off a ventilating trunk line, allowing smoke from the fire caused by the second bomb hit into the steering compartment. The seven-man crew in the compartment shut off the ventilation system and covered the vent, but eventually temperatures in the confined compartment reached 170 degrees, requiring the vent to be reopened. Water and foamite as well as smoke and fumes flooded the compartment through the open vent. The steering engine shorted out and before the crew could switch to the reserve engine they were overcome by smoke.

The upshot was that without warning the *Enterprise*'s rudder jammed 20 degrees to starboard. The carrier plowed through her protective screen like the proverbial bull in a china shop chasing its own tail. Her siren sounded to warn the ships around her. Destroyer *Balch* had to scurry out of the way to narrowly avoid being run down, as the *Enterprise*'s Captain Davis frantically rang "all stop." Davis tried to regain control by steering the carrier with her engines, but they could not overcome the torque of the rudder. He brought the carrier to 10 knots, so she would be steaming in smaller circles.

But the *Enterprise* was now helpless, with Lieutenant Takahashi's airstrike still on the hunt for her. Admiral Fletcher signaled that the *Enterprise* might need a tug, though how the torque of the rudder could be overcome with a tow is anybody's guess. Carrier *Saratoga* took over providing air cover for the beleaguered flattop. During this time, she managed to land her strike that had brought the *Ryujo* to grief.

The *Enterprise*'s damage control was working feverishly to restore helm control. Everyone kept calm and let Chief Machinist William A. Smith handle it. He donned breathing gear and went to hack his way into the smoke and fumes of the steering compartment. Twice he was overcome and pulled back by a safety line, but on the third try Smith got in and switched the rudder over to the standby motor. Helm control was restored at 6:58, exactly 38 minutes after the rudder had jammed. In the words of Morison, "That's the kind of thing that wins battles, no less than good shooting and accurate bombing."[130]

There would be no more good shooting or accurate bombing from the Japanese this day. Lieutenant Takahashi's strike was forced to return to *Kido Butai* and land after dark, the carriers turning on their searchlights to guide the Sea Eagles back, meeting only limited success.

The strikes launched in desperation by the *Enterprise* and *Saratoga* met with a bit more success. Not against the Japanese carriers, which they never found, but against Admiral Kondo's Advance Force. Lieutenant Larsen led five Avengers of Torpedo 8 boring in from port against Kondo's cruisers, claiming one hit but in reality getting none. However, on the way back one Grumman, piloted by Lieutenant (jg) Edward "Frenchie" Fayle, was jumped by two Zeros from the *Shokaku*, flown by Petty Officer 1st Class Iwaki Yoshio and Petty Officer 2nd Class Ohara Hiroshi. Together they perforated the Avenger's right wing and fuselage and shattered the plexiglass of the turret. But the Sea Eagles continued to wither away as Iwaki, a Japanese ace who had gunned down members of Torpedo 8 at Midway, was killed by Fayle's gunner, aviation radioman Petty Officer 3rd Class Edward Velazquez. Fayle would have to ditch short of Guadalcanal, but would be recovered August 29.[131]

Two more *Saratoga* aircraft, Dauntlesses flown by Lieutenant (jg) Robert M. Elder and Ensign Robert T. Gordon, got their own shot at Admiral Kondo's Advance Force. They only glimpsed Kondo's surface warships in passing over them to target the seaplane tender *Chitose*, who was stopped recovering her floatplanes after a long day of sparring with Catalina flying boats. Diving from 12,500 feet, Elder and Gordon got at least one near miss with a 1,000lb bomb portside aft. Three floatplanes were set afire. More seriously, hull plates were ruptured, damaging her port engine and ultimately flooding her port machinery spaces, leading to a 30-degree list. She had to be towed clear by the destroyer *Minegumo*.[132]

The Japanese spent the night trying to make Admiral Yamamoto's dream of surface ships finishing off damaged enemy carriers come true. Admiral Abe's Vanguard Force had linked up with Admiral Kondo's Advance Force and together they swept southward in an impressive armada, with the heavy cruisers in a Homeric-like line abreast, deploying floatplanes to scare up the enemy.[133]

But the American carriers were out of reach. The *Enterprise* was heading due south. At half-past midnight the Japanese submarine *I-17* spotted the carrier, followed shortly thereafter by the *I-15*, but neither boat could position itself for an attack and the *Enterprise* would make her way to Pearl Harbor for repairs. The Japanese only found the destroyer *Grayson*, left behind to search for downed pilots. She prudently turned tail and fled. To avoid morning air attacks, so did the major Japanese forces.

Except for one.

Despite the loss of his putative air support, Admiral Tanaka turned around to head toward Guadalcanal. Though he had definitely been sighted, he had not been attacked; in the chaos surrounding the Japanese attack, Lieutenant Kellam's report of Tanaka's convoy had been overlooked on the *Enterprise*. Moreover, the Japanese thought they had at least set two American aircraft carriers on fire and thus had at least driven off the American air power.[134] But there was now a new player in the South Pacific.

Admiral McCain's Catalina flying boats bravely patrolled in the night over the South Pacific. One, piloted by Ensign William C. Corbett, found seven ships, which were later determined to include one aircraft carrier. The report of one carrier, one light cruiser, and five destroyers located 180 miles north of Guadalcanal, course 190 degrees True, speed 17 knots reached Henderson Field at 4:30 am.[135]

During that same night, General Vandegrift's men had endured a shelling by Japanese destroyers *Kagero*, *Isokaze*, *Kawakaze*, *Mutsuki*, and *Yayoi*, a bombardment that was far more annoying than damaging. The general also received a welcome reinforcement in the form of Lieutenant Caldwell's 11 *Enterprise* SBD Dauntlesses, who, having searched in vain for the enemy, were guided in for the night landing by flare pots marking the runway. Despite their unfamiliarity with Guadalcanal, all the Dauntlesses landed without mishap. Vandegrift decided to take a whack at the approaching carrier with his little Cactus Air Force. He assembled a strike of five Marine and three *Enterprise* SBD Dauntlesses under Major Mangrum, escorted by ten Marine Wildcats under Captain Smith, all of whom took off at 6:00 am.

The Wildcats, lacking belly tanks, were forced by fuel issues to turn back, leaving their charges on their own. While heading back, north of Malaita the Marine fighters roughed up the Mavis of Warrant Officer Fujiwara Tomosaburo of the Yokohama Air Group. They thought they shot him down, but Fujiwara was able to get back to the Shortlands and run his badly damaged Kawanishi aground before it sank.[136]

Major Mangrum's unescorted bombers searched for the Japanese aircraft carriers who had pulled back and were nowhere to be found. But the Dauntlesses did stumble across the actual subjects of Ensign Corbett's sighting report: Admiral Tanaka's convoy, now with no air cover. By 8:00 am they were 150 miles from Guadalcanal, planning to land their troops that night. Tanaka was issuing orders for the positioning of his ships for the landing when Mangrum's bombers spilled out of the clouds.[137]

The Japanese had been "caught napping," in Admiral Tanaka's words; there was not even time to train the antiaircraft guns up at the attackers. The Cactus Air Force pilots made shallow dives on the convoy. At 8:05, 1st Lieutenant Lawrence Baldinus planted a 1,000lb bomb between the Number 1 and 2 5.5-inch guns of Admiral Tanaka's trusted flagship *Jintsu*, an Allied nemesis since the beginning of the war. Shrapnel and flaming fragments were strewn everywhere, including the cruiser's bridge, where Tanaka himself was knocked unconscious. The blast killed 24, started a fire that forced the flooding of her forward magazines, and badly damaged the cruiser's bow.[138]

Lieutenant Colonel Mangrum was not done. Two minutes later, Ensign Christian Fink of the *Enterprise* 6 plopped his own 1,000lb bomb amidships on the auxiliary transport *Kinryu Maru*, carrying 800 members of the 5th Yokosuka Special Naval Landing Force. Mangrum himself got a near miss on the *Boston Maru*, carrying more troops of the Ichiki Detachment.[139]

The Marine and Navy SBDs headed back to Henderson after a job well done. The stricken *Kinryu Maru* suffered a massive explosion as the stored ammunition began cooking off; she would not last much longer. Destroyers *Mutsuki* and *Yayoi,* who had hurried back from their largely ineffective bombardment of Henderson Field, and Patrol Boats *1* and *2* pulled alongside to take off the Special Naval Landing Force troops. Their mission of mercy was complicated when a flight of three B-17s under Captain Walter E. Chambers of the 11th Bombardment Group appeared overhead. The *Yayoi* and the patrol boats got under way for evasive maneuvers, but the *Mutsuki* stayed motionless where she was. Her skipper, Lieutenant Commander Hatano Kenji, wasn't all that concerned about B-17s or other American high-level bombers. Noting the B-17s were especially high, Hatano said, "[I]f they should hit us we would be the first ship struck by horizontal bombers in this war."[140]

Commander Hatano was mistaken.[141] In more ways than one. At 10:15, the high-flying B-17s plopped at least one bomb in the *Mutsuki*'s engineering spaces. The blast killed 41, injured 11, and left his command sinking. But Hatano was right in one sense: his *Mutsuki* had the honor of becoming the first Japanese ship sunk by horizontal bombers. Hatano was surprised but unapologetic. "Even the B-17s can make a hit once in a while."[142]

So now the *Yayoi* was left rescuing survivors from both the *Kinryu Maru* and the *Mutsuki*, who while sinking nevertheless managed to perform one last service for her emperor by sending a torpedo into the *Kinryu Maru* and putting the burning derelict under. Admiral Tanaka regained consciousness and, with his flagship too damaged to continue into what was obviously a combat zone, switched his flag to the destroyer *Kagero*.

"My worst fears for this operation had been realized," Admiral Tanaka later wrote.[143] His destroyers carrying waterlogged troops could not very well land those troops on Guadalcanal and expect them to be effective. The remaining troops were not enough to make a difference. He needed another way to get the troops to Guadalcanal. In the meantime, he had to withdraw, a decision affirmed by Combined Fleet and 8th Fleet.

In forcing the invasion convoy to turn back, this little airstrike by all eight SBD Dauntlesses of the tiny Cactus Air Force had transformed what the Americans called the Battle of the Eastern Solomons from a tactical draw into an Allied victory.

And in the process it taught the Japanese a lesson that was costly, albeit perhaps not nearly as costly as it should have been. A lesson that would guide Japanese strategy in the months ahead. As Admiral Yamamoto's chief of staff Admiral Ugaki put it: "It is apparent that landing on Guadalcanal by transport is hopeless unless the enemy planes are wiped out."[144]

CHAPTER 6

PRIDE GOETH...

Few civilizations are believed to have an equal, let alone better, understanding of war than the Romans. Not perfect, by any means – notable failures include the battles of Teutoburg Forest and Adrianople – but the Romans had war down to a science. Yet at a basic level, the Roman idea of how to handle a war was very simple: you find the enemy and then attack them.

The Carthaginian general Hannibal grasped this philosophy better than any of Rome's enemies, in part because, it is now believed, he had spies in Rome. And Hannibal figured out a way to turn it against the Romans: he would let the Romans find him at a place of his choosing and attack at a time of his choosing.

In 218 BC, Hannibal goaded the Romans into attacking him by charging across the Trebbia River in December when its swollen waters were barely above freezing and he slaughtered them.

The next year, Hannibal got the Romans to chase him into a narrow defile, with Lake Trasimenus on one side, and, on the other side, hills in which he had hidden his troops. And he slaughtered them again.

In response the Romans called for Quintus Fabius Maximus. Fabius had a new strategy. Instead of having his army attack Hannibal's, he would simply follow it, always camping in good defensive positions, but sending out patrols to pick off parties Hannibal had sent out to forage for supplies. One by one. Day after day. It was painful, arduous, and tedious, whittling down supplies and troops fighting under the Carthaginian banner. But it started to have an effect on Hannibal's army.

It also had an effect on Rome's politics. It wasn't sexy enough. It wasn't fast enough. They wanted Hannibal out now. So Fabius was thrown out. The result was Cannae, the worst defeat in Roman history until that time. And Fabius was then put back in. Fabius' strategy for dealing with Hannibal became the norm for Rome's legions. Those who departed from it paid dearly, with their troops' lives and sometimes their own. But the Fabian strategy, as it was called, would largely hold until Hannibal left Italy.

The Fabian strategy has become known by another name: war of attrition. Nibbling away at the enemy, day after day after grueling day.

War is often thought of as what we see in the movies. Giant battles with thousands of troops. Mass cavalry charges. Swarms of bombers. Fleets of thousands of ships. But not every day of a war is a Midway, a Normandy, a Gettysburg, a Jutland, an Eastern Solomons. Not even most days.

No, most days are snipers taking pot shots, a destroyer bombarding, a tussle between scout planes, a fight between patrols, a few planes on a bombing raid.

After Eastern Solomons, both the Allies and the Japanese realized Guadalcanal was not going to be easy or quick. So they girded themselves as best they could for a long campaign. There would be no Coral Seas or Midways or Eastern Solomons for a little while.

Now, the war became Fabian, not so much by choice as by necessity. Daily bombing raids that were too small to be decisive. Running reinforcements in by the handful. Bombardments by little destroyers. Patrols clashing in the jungle.

And floatplanes. Dropping flares and bombs at night.

It was in the days after Eastern Solomons that the campaign for Guadalcanal started settling into its attrition phase.

On August 26, Base Air Force got into its routine of attacking Henderson Field almost every day. This day it was 17 G4Ms escorted by nine Zeros. Warned by New Georgia coastwatcher Donald Kennedy at 11:24, Henderson Field got every flyable plane off the ground within 12 minutes.[1] A dozen Wildcats moved to high altitude to offer a suitable reception for the Bettys, who arrived at 12:03. The green Marine pilots who had never intercepted Japanese twin-engine bombers before marveled at the "beautiful target presented by the impeccable Japanese V formation three-fourths of a mile across."[2] The rookies' shooting, however, did not match the beauty of the target. Captain Smith later complained, "They wanted to shoot them all down. They did a lot of *general* shooting … and didn't get any bombers at all" (emphasis in original). Not quite. Base Air Force acknowledged two Bettys did not return, while two more "force-landed," which usually meant crash landed; three Zeros were write-offs as well, including one piloted by the Tainan Air Group's talented fighter leader Lieutenant (jg) Sasai Junichi.[3] All the remainder of the bombers were damaged to some degree. For this cost, the Japanese dropped some 50 bombs, which set off a fuel dump with 2,000 gallons of gasoline, which in turn detonated two 1,000lb bombs. They shot down one Wildcat with its pilot, 2nd Lieutenant Roy A. Corry.[4]

This became the standard practice for Base Air Force, whenever the weather would allow for passage down what Japanese aviators called the "Guadal Highway" (*Gadaru Gaito*). A typical air attack would consist of a mixture of 18 or 27 Mitsubishi G4M Type 1 bombers from all the air groups available at Rabaul, usually the Kisarazu and

Misawa air groups of the 6th Air Attack Force under Vice Admiral Yamagata Seigo. The 4th Air Group, so shredded in the initial air attacks against the Guadalcanal landings on August 7 and 8, was now restricted to reconnaissance. Starting to trickle in were some bombers from the famous Kanoya Air Group of the 21st Air Flotilla – now designated 1st Air Attack Force – the killers of the *Prince of Wales* and *Repulse*.

But the Kanoya would find that things had changed since those early days. For starters, now they needed fighter protection. Escort was usually provided by the Zeros of the famous Tainan Air Group from the 5th Air Attack Force. They would soon be augmented by fighters from the 6th Air Attack Force's 6th Air Group, who were also about to start trickling in. There would be 12 or 18 Zeros, usually deployed in two groups behind and to either side of the bomber formation. The bomber formation might be best described as a vee of vees of vees – a wide, flat "V" formed by nine-plane divisions, each in a "V" of its own formed by its three-plane sections, each of which also formed a "V." Typically, each bomber would be loaded with a 551lb bomb high-explosive bomb and six 132lb antipersonnel bombs, or ten 132lb antipersonnel bombs, which the Allies called "daisy cutters."[5]

In the Japanese Naval Air Force, this was fairly standard. Too standard, for a campaign that was becoming anything but. Indeed, standard practice for the Sea Eagles was to take off on or after sunrise and return no later than sunset to avoid the dangers of operating aircraft in the dark and around mountains. With a four-hour flight to Guadalcanal, that left a window of only, at its widest, perhaps 11:00 am and 3:00 pm for them to be over the target. The Americans figured out the window when the Japanese could arrive and dubbed it "Tojo Time."

That the Americans had figured out the scheduling was only part of the issue for the Japanese. There was also that *Ferdinand* network of coastwatchers in the Solomons. Jack Read and Paul Mason on Bougainville would see the Japanese strike just after takeoff and radio the first warnings. Donald Kennedy on New Georgia would see the strike approximately 45 minutes from Guadalcanal and radio a final warning. Between the obvious strike window and the warning from the coastwatchers, it was extremely difficult for the Japanese bombers to catch the American aircraft on the ground. The American bombers would have been sent east to ride out the attack, while the fighters would be positioning themselves to intercept. The Japanese were aware of the coastwatchers, but repeated searches and sweeps failed to make much more than a dent in *Ferdinand*, thanks in large part to the hostility of the native Melanesians that Japanese behavior had incurred.

And there were some handicaps that the Japanese Naval Air Force had inflicted on itself. For all the Japanese expertise in optics, especially long range and night vision, their bombsight did not live up to their reputation. Moreover, compared to their American adversaries, the Japanese had tiny bombs, their heaviest being 551lb; the heaviest American bomb was 2,000lb.

Similarly, the payload for the Mitsubishi G4M Type 1 land attack plane was 2,200lb. Part of the reason for this relatively small payload was that the G4M was designed to attack targets at sea, often with torpedoes. Strictly speaking, there was no American direct counterpart to the Betty. The closest was the Martin B-26 Marauder, which could attack targets at sea with a torpedo slung under its belly. But even the Marauder's early version could carry a payload of 3,000lb, the same as the B-25 Mitchell. Both were medium bombers like the Betty. The Japanese had no heavy bomber, no counterpart to the B-17 Flying Fortress or B-24 Liberator.

There was also the issue of pilot protection. The Japanese Naval Air Force had made a conscious decision to emphasize speed and maneuverability in its aircraft over an armored cockpit, shatterproof glass, or self-sealing fuel tanks, all of which added weight to the aircraft. It was an expression of confidence in the pilot, but it also meant that the pilot had better be perfect or he would soon be dead. And no pilot is perfect. Sakai Saburo's shock at the ability of the Grumman F4F Wildcat to take some ten minutes of punishment and keep flying is indicative of the difference. "A Zero can't take two seconds' fire from a Grumman," explained 1st Marine Air Wing assistant operations officer Major Joseph N. Renner, "and a Grumman can sometimes take as high as fifteen minutes fire from a Zero."[6] The Type 1 bomber was, if anything, even worse. Its nicknames included "Type 1 Lighter" and "Flying Cigar" for its propensity to catch fire very easily. The Cactus Air Force's John Smith developed tactics for a pilot to position himself for the easiest possible shot at the Betty's fuel tanks.

That was one reason the G4Ms needed fighter protection, but close escort by fighters was almost impossible thanks to another conscious decision – taking the radios out of all but a few of their Zeros. They found the radios too unreliable and too short-ranged to be effective, and it saved almost 40lb of weight. But it meant that fighter pilots could communicate with each other in flight only with hand signals or waggling wings. Not the speediest, most efficient, or most effective forms of communication in combat.

Finally, there was the target environment, which circles back to the issue of distance. The Lunga airfield was held by Americans and defended by Americans. An American aircraft damaged in combat was thus near a base to which it could return. An American aircraft shot down left the pilot both near a base and in an area with friendly native Melanesians. Damaged Japanese aircraft would have to make, as Sakai Saburo did, the long haul back up the Guadal Highway – 560 nautical miles to Rabaul and more than 400 to the emergency strip at Buka. The Shortland base complex, in which was located Buin, where Admiral Tsukahara had ordered construction of a new airstrip, was more than 300 miles away. The upshot was that an American pilot shot down stood a good chance of surviving, being recovered, and returning to duty. A Japanese pilot shot down was likely never to return to duty.

It added up to serious aerial losses for the Japanese. By August 26, Base Air Force was down to 29 serviceable bombers and 19 Zeros, with which they had to attack Guadalcanal and New Guinea. The 6th Air Attack Force was still arriving in a piecemeal fashion, so to tide them over Base Air Force needed a temporary attachment of 30 Zeros from the *Shokaku* and *Zuikaku*, all of which staged into Buka on August 28.[7] But these low numbers would not stay low. The Japanese planned a massive reinforcement effort so that by

September 20 Base Air Force would have 93 Zeros with long-range capability, 81 G4M bombers, six Type 99 dive bombers, four reconnaissance planes, and 14 flying boats.[8]

Also on August 28, Admiral Mikawa's 8th Fleet reconfigured its own contribution to Japanese air power, by putting all its seaplanes and their parent tenders into one organization that was given the title of "R-Area Air Force." This new organization under newly promoted Rear Admiral Jojima Takatsugu of the 11th Seaplane Tender Division would use its seaplane tenders – *Chitose*, *Kamikawa Maru*, *Sanyo Maru*, and *Sanuki Maru* – to operate floatplanes all over the R-Area.[9]

Once he figured out where exactly the "R-Area" was, Admiral Jojima assembled his forces in Shortland. His most powerful units would be the veterans *Kamikawa Maru* and *Chitose*. The *Kamikawa Maru* had about a dozen of those "float Zeros," the Nakajima A6M2-N Type 2. The *Chitose* had maybe 16 of those Type 0 observation seaplanes. These should not be confused with the Type 0 reconnaissance seaplane, of which the *Chitose* had seven.[10]

Admiral Jojima would anchor his *Chitose* in Shortland Harbor to serve as his headquarters while rotating his other tenders through Santa Ysabel's Rekata Bay, thus providing one meaning for "R-Area" and placing his forces only 135 miles north of Henderson Field. His seaplanes would dance in and out of the bay, as would his seaplane tenders, to avoid the inevitable Allied airstrikes.[11]

These started almost immediately, as B-17s were taking an interest in the area. On September 1, they had attacked the seaplane tender *Akitsushima* and the old destroyer *Akikaze* off Buka, doing "trifling" damage to the former.[12] The next day the *Sanyo Maru* packed much of its base personnel aboard *Patrol Boat 35* and departed Shortland, giving the staff all the luxury and comfort the old converted destroyer *Tsuta* could offer. Until 11:00 am or so, when a B-17 of the 11th Bombardment Group showed up, released a stick of bombs, and left the demoted destroyer dead in the water. At some point the patrol boat sank, taking her skipper, Reserve Lieutenant Kumai Zentaro, and 92 others with her, with 52 survivors.[13] But the Japanese just sent another patrol boat and opened the base on September 5. From the Rekata Bay area, the R-Area Air Force would be a persistent thorn in the Marines' side, especially with its rather rude habit of sending solitary floatplanes to loudly hang out over Lunga at night, dropping flares and the occasional bomb, and keeping the Marines awake. This annoyance would earn from the Marines the nickname "Louie the Louse."

The R-Area Air Force had solved issues of distance by moving closer. Base Air Force could not, at least not until the Buin airfield was complete. And that distance also posed issues of climate. The Solomons have volatile weather, and a storm brewing up over, say, New Georgia could prevent the Japanese from attacking Guadalcanal but allow American air operations to continue unimpeded. So could Rabaul's Tavurvur and Vulcan volcanoes, which nibbled away at aircraft and caused maintenance problems.

Weather was an issue on August 27 and 28, as airstrikes by Base Air Force were forced to return to base by bad weather. The weather did not keep a reinforcement, 14 new

P-400s, the remainder of the 67th Fighter Squadron, from reaching Henderson Field. But there was a little ground combat as General Vandegrift decided to try another sortie across the Matanikau with the 1st Battalion of the 5th Marine Regiment. The battalion was inexperienced, with a commander, Lieutenant Colonel William E. Maxwell, who tried to make up for the greenness with an insistence on strict adherence to orders and a ruthless response to perceived mistakes. Just as there had been with King Bode on the *Chicago*, the effect was hesitation and indecisiveness.

The sortie landed west of Kokumbona. But on top of the hesitation and indecisiveness came vague orders, problematic terrain, and a lack of intelligence on Captain Monzen and what was left of his construction laborers and Special Naval Landing Force troops. The result was paralysis, a stunted, indecisive advance, and ultimately the removal of Captain Maxwell.[14]

Not that the Japanese could take advantage. As he was returning to the Shortlands on August 26 after the Cactus Air Force successfully turned back his reinforcement convoy, Admiral Tanaka received an order from Admiral Tsukahara directing him to transport the remaining 300-odd troops to Guadalcanal in fast warships on the night of August 27. Tanaka wondered just how much thought had been put into this order, but orders were still orders. He dutifully directed the following:

> *Umikaze*, *Yamakaze*, and *Isokaze* will take the 390 troops now loaded in the transport, together with four rapid-fire guns and provisions for 1,300 troops and leave Shortland for Guadalcanal at 0500 hours under Commander Desron 24 [the 24th Destroyer Division]. At 2100 they will arrive at Cape Taivu to land troops and supplies. During the night they will return from Guadalcanal.[15]

It seemed simple enough. As soon as Admiral Tanaka arrived in Shortland, he discussed the situation with the army commander. They spent the entire sleepless night transferring troops, provisions, and munitions to three destroyers. Early next morning the three destroyers were headed to Guadalcanal, led by the commander of the 24th Destroyer Division, Captain Murakami Yonosuke.

After a few hours, Admiral Tanaka received a new order from Admiral Mikawa of the 8th Fleet, directing him to land the troops on Guadalcanal 24 hours later, on August 28. A flabbergasted Tanaka replied that the destroyers transporting the troops had already left. Mikawa came back with, "Recall destroyers at once. Am sending Desdiv 20 [20th Destroyer Division] to Shortland where it will be under Comdesron 2 [2nd Destroyer Flotilla]."

It was the third time Tanaka had received conflicting orders from his immediate superior and his immediate superior's superior. This was despite the fact that their headquarters were within walking distance of each other in Rabaul. He acidly commented:

> It was inconceivable that no liaison existed between the headquarters of Eleventh Air Fleet [Base Air Force] and Eighth Fleet, since both were located at Rabaul, and yet such seemed to

> be the case. I had again received contradictory and conflicting orders from the area commander and my immediate superior and was at a loss as to what to do. If such circumstances continue, I thought, how can we possibly win a battle? It occurred to me again that this operation gave no evidence of careful, deliberate study; everything seemed to be completely haphazard.[16]

But conflicting orders were still orders, and Admiral Tanaka had to have the destroyers he so recently sent away come back.

Tanaka was caught in the middle of a power struggle with General Kawaguchi Kiyotake of the Army's 35th Brigade. Kawaguchi had arrived at Truk on August 23 and was presented with orders from 17th Army that his troops were to head to Guadalcanal immediately on transports. To Kawaguchi, however, orders were more what you'd call guidelines than actual directives. Certainly he had no intention of stepping aboard slow, fat transports vulnerable to American air power from Guadalcanal. Nor would he go by fast, cramped destroyer. No, Kawaguchi preferred barges.

A typical barge, the Daihatsu Army Type A, was a 50-foot open creature with, when fully loaded, a top speed of 7 knots. It could carry some 70 men, 10 tons of cargo, or even one light tank. Kawaguchi's troops had advanced up to 500 miles by barge during their successful campaign in Borneo. How much of the success of this tactic was due to his opponents in Borneo, the colonial Dutch and later ABDACOM, having almost no air power, does not seem to have crossed the general's mind. He would land at Shortland, move to Gizo off New Georgia in the middle Solomons, and take barges from island to island every night down the rest of the Solomons to Guadalcanal.[17] It would be slow, but his troops would get there. Eventually.

The general left Truk on August 24, the day of the carrier battle of the Eastern Solomons. The following day, Admiral Tanaka's convoy was turned back by the Cactus Air Force with heavy losses. So the 17th Army sent General Kawaguchi new orders: some 600 of his men were to be rushed to Guadalcanal aboard four destroyers; the rest of the brigade would go to Rabaul with him, where they arrived four days later.[18]

Much of August 26 was spent transferring the 2nd Battalion of the 124th Infantry Regiment to the destroyers *Asagiri*, *Amagiri*, *Yugiri*, and *Shirakumo* – the four ships of the 20th Destroyer Division under Captain Yamada Yuji. This was why they were being added to Admiral Tanaka's command and his next high-speed destroyer convoy to land the night of August 28. Tanaka issued orders to this effect to Captain Murakami.

One slight catch: because of fuel issues, Captain Yamada's destroyers could not stop at Shortland. Instead they would hang east of the Solomons, operating independently of Captain Murakami's destroyers, and dash in on the night of August 28. "This further served to increase my pessimism about the success of the landing operation," Tanaka later wrote.[19]

There was one other slight catch: around 5:00 pm on August 28, a pair of radioless Dauntlesses piloted by 1st Lieutenant Danny Iverson and 2nd Lieutenant Hank Hise found the four destroyers loitering off Santa Ysabel, 60 miles north of Savo Island.[20] Iverson could not get into attack position, but Hise dove on one of the destroyers and missed. He raced back to Henderson Field and taxied right up to the Pagoda to report the contact. Not even a half-hour later, Lieutenant Colonel Mangrum led 11 Dauntlesses into the air looking for this new prey.

They found Captain Yamada's little flotilla at 6:05, just before sunset. The Navy Dauntlesses went after the *Shirakumo* and *Asagiri*. The *Enterprise*'s Lieutenant Caldwell planted a 1,000lb bomb on the quarterdeck of the *Shirakumo*, flooding an engine room and leaving her dead in the water.[21] Ensign Fink, rapidly acquiring a reputation of "never miss 'em," dropped his directly on the torpedo tubes of the *Asagiri*. The bomb's detonation set off the torpedoes, resulting in a massive, spectacular explosion that blew the *Asagiri* in two.[22] The Marine SBDs went after the other two destroyers. One sent a 1,000lb bomb into the *Yugiri*'s bridge, killing Captain Yamada and 31 others, and injuring 40.[23] A strafing run on the lone undamaged destroyer, *Amagiri*, resulted in the death of Marine Lieutenant Oliver Mitchell and his gunner Private P. O. Schackman by antiaircraft fire.

The *Amagiri* went on to have a busy evening. She first moved to pick up survivors from her sister *Asagiri*, rescuing 135 officers and crew and 83 soldiers, leaving 122 dead crew and troops. Then, accompanied by the battered *Yugiri*, the destroyer dragged the powerless carcass of the *Shirakumo*, who despite having no power suffered only two wounded, towards the Shortlands.[24]

Admiral Tanaka was dismayed, but not surprised. At 8:40 pm, Tanaka sent a signal to the effect of, "This [attack] made it more obvious than ever what sheer recklessness it was to attempt a landing operation against strong resistance without preliminary neutralization of enemy air power. If the present operation plan for Guadalcanal was not altered, we were certain to suffer further humiliating and fruitless casualties."[25]

Meanwhile, in an independent and unauthorized effort to avoid further humiliating and fruitless casualties, Captain Murakami, without orders, turned his three destroyers around at 7:25 pm and headed back toward Shortland. By the time Murakami informed Tanaka of his move around midnight, it was too late for the admiral to order him to turn back around.[26] Which was probably the point.

This left Combined Fleet and 8th Fleet's Admiral Mikawa none too happy. They chewed out Tanaka for Captain Murakami's turnabout. Tanaka publicly concurred with the decision of his subordinate, but, later calling the commodore's decision "inexcusable," he in turn privately chewed out Murakami.[27] Members of the 17th Army staff, not impressed with the chaos they were seeing from the Navy, considered scotching the reinforcement, but cooler heads prevailed, waiting until at least the next operation, scheduled for the very next day.[28]

August 29 saw the Japanese bring both air and sea power against the Marines on Guadalcanal. Very early that morning, three Mitsubishi G4Ms pulled off a hit and run. At dawn, Base Air Force sent 18 more G4Ms, escorted by 22 Zeros from the *Shokaku* and *Zuikaku* to pound the Lunga airfield.[29]

At the same time, the transport *William Ward Burroughs* and freighter *SS Kopara* anchored off Kukum, faithfully guarded by their five escorts: the old destroyer-minelayers

Tracy and *Gamble*, and grizzled veteran high-speed destroyer-transports *Colhoun*, *Gregory*, and *Little*. They had already had an eventful morning. At 8:05, the *Gamble*, commanded by Lieutenant Commander Stephen N. Tackney, spotted the conning tower of a submarine disappear beneath the waves some 60 miles southeast of Savo Island.

It did not take Lieutenant Commander Tackney long to get the scent and, starting at 8:44, the converted four-piper spent three hours tracking the submarine using, somewhat unusually, her magnetic anomaly detection system and blasting the submerged boat with depth charges.

After the last attack at 11:47, lookouts spotted a large air bubble break the surface of the water. The *Gamble* sailed through a large oil slick and her crew recovered fragments of deck planking. The Japanese submarine *RO-34*, hanging out to the west, heard several underwater explosions from the patrol area assigned to the submarine *I-123*, one of the earliest tormentors of the Marines on Guadalcanal. What she had heard was the *I-123*'s death at the hands of the *Gamble*.[30] And the day had only just started.

Safe for the moment in Lunga Roads after the failed ambush by *I-123*, the *William Ward Burrows* sent ashore the ground crews for Marine Fighting 223 and Marine Scout Bombing 232. But before she could offload supplies, including an SCR 270 air warning radar for Henderson Field, coastwatchers warned that the Japanese airstrike was on the way. The two transport ships were forced to head for the relative safety of Tulagi.

Once again, every flyable aircraft was scrambled from Henderson Field. By the time the Japanese arrived at 11:55 am, ten Wildcats under Captain Smith were ready to greet them. Attempting to intercept were 14 Airacobras, but their lack of an engine supercharger combined with a lack of an oxygen system meant they could not operate above 14,000 feet and were thus useless against both high-level bombers and Japanese Zeros. The Bettys came in at 17,000 feet and dropped their bombs. Henderson Field was cratered yet again. Smith's vengeful Wildcats mixed it up with the bombers and Zeros as they tried to make a getaway. One Wildcat was so shot up that it was cannibalized for parts. One Zero and one Betty were shot down, while a second G4M "crash-landed" at Buka. General MacArthur's 5th Air Force B-17s subsequently paid a visit to Buka, damaging four Zeros on the ground. The Cactus Air Force pilots landed at Henderson having to go through a slalom of bomb craters, marked for their safety and convenience.[31]

But the American side of the ledger for this day was not yet complete. The *William Ward Burrows*, in her effort to enter the harbor at Tulagi, ran aground and got stuck. Worse, the Japanese aviators had spotted her and reported "two transports, one cruiser, and two destroyers" off Lunga. Admiral Mikawa issued orders directly to Captain Murakami, leading the Japanese reinforcement run that night, to attack these American ships as soon as he had finished landing his troops.[32]

Landing at Taivu Point at 10:30 that night were 300 men of the second echelon of the Ichiki Detachment, ferried by Captain Murakami's 24th Destroyer Division, with 450 men of the 1st Battalion, 124th Infantry Regiment, landed by destroyers *Hatsuyuki*, *Shirayuki*, and *Fubuki* of the 11th Destroyer Division. Also around Taivu Point, the commodore could see, were 14 SBD Dauntless dive bombers, launched just after midnight to run cover for the helpless *William Ward Burrows* and her vital supplies. The Dauntlesses never saw Murakami's destroyer transports, but Murakami nevertheless bravely turned his tail and fled for Shortland.[33]

This second such act of bravery on the part of Captain Murakami in a little more than 24 hours – and a willful violation of direct orders at that – humiliated Admiral Tanaka, the commodore's immediate superior who had protected him 24 hours earlier, in front of the admiral's own superiors. Tanaka was "conscience stricken," and so livid he was left literally speechless. Murakami was immediately sacked.[34]

Realizing that their attacks on the Lunga airfield so far had not produced results commensurate with their losses, the next day Base Air Force switched things up and led with a sweep by 18 Zeros from the *Shokaku* and *Zuikaku*. Whatever surprise they had hoped to achieve by leading with fighters took a hit at 9:30 am when Bougainville coastwatcher Paul Mason warned of a large formation of single-engine aircraft; New Georgia coastwatcher Donald Kennedy reported their progress at 11:00 am.[35]

The warning got the Marines thinking of a dive-bombing attack. The Cactus Air Force had exactly 19 operational aircraft – eight Wildcats and 11 P-400s. Captain Brannon and the Army pilots were frustrated by the P-400s and wanted to do something – anything – to help the Marine pilots, and volunteered to join in. Captain Smith took the Wildcats and seven Airacobras to the air at 11:05, while the other four P-400s patrolled at about 1,000 feet over the still-helpless *William Ward Burrows* off Tulagi.

The P-400s' severe limitations because of their lack of oxygen and a supercharger cost them dearly. The Zeros ascended from a cloud and jumped Captain Brannon's Airacobras over Tulagi. The other seven P-400s, at 14,000 feet, dove to help them and were driven off. Captain Smith's Wildcats, seeing the Airacobras dive, dove to help them and caught the Zeros by surprise, shooting down eight in a few minutes. Two more Zeros crashed on the return flight to Buka. Four of the P-400s were shot down, however, with two of the pilots walking back to base. All eight of the Wildcats returned to Henderson Field, but three were so shot up they were written off and assigned to what was called the "Boneyard" to be cannibalized for spare parts.

It was a major victory for Captain Smith and the young Marine pilots of the Cactus Air Force, cutting to pieces the famous Sea Eagles of the vaunted *Kido Butai* that had smashed Pearl Harbor. They were rightfully proud of themselves. On the other hand, the Army pilots of the 67th Fighter Squadron – well-trained, experienced, and brave – were dejected. The squadron historian described their despair:

> We can't maneuver and dogfight with the Zero – what good are we? Our enlisted men are risking their lives every day trying to get the planes patched up – for what?… Hell, we can't fight. When the Japs come we're told to "go on reconnaissance." What good are we?[36]

Captain Brannon's pilots were all the more bitter because it wasn't supposed to be this way, or so they had been told. Originally the 67th Pursuit Squadron, the 67th Fighter

Squadron was to have been equipped with the standard Army Air Force fighter, the Curtiss P-40 Warhawk. The aircraft were shipped in crates disassembled, to be put together at their airfield in New Caledonia. When the mechanics opened the crates, they found two P-39 Airacobras and 45 P-400s, originally slated to go to the British in North Africa.[37] None of the pilots of the 67th had flown a P-400 and only two had flown a P-39. The mechanics also had little experience with the P-39/P-400, whose unusual features, including the placement of the engine behind the cockpit and a 20mm cannon in the nose, had the potential to complicate assembly. Naturally, the shipment included no assembly instructions, requiring the ground crews to experiment and guess which parts went where in sort of a blind puzzle.[38] To the men of the 67th, it was a broken promise and an example of how the Pacific got only the scraps left after the European Theater took all the good stuff. Yet the pilots and their ground crews had mastered this weird little plane, only to find it was worse than useless against the Zero.

The ineffectiveness of these "Klunkers," as the Army pilots derisively called the Airacobras, meant that Guadalcanal was currently defended by just five F4F Wildcats. These were still being refueled when, a little after 3:00 pm, 18 Bettys arrived over Guadalcanal escorted by 13 Zeros. The destroyer-transport *Colhoun*, in the Lunga roadstead, saw the bombers coming out of the sun at 15,000 feet, well above the altitude of her four 20mm antiaircraft guns, but the bombers still took the precaution of working their way in and out of the clouds. The *Colhoun* went to full speed since evasive maneuvers were now her only defense. And much of that was nullified when the Bettys dove to perform lower-level bombing runs.

The first dropped several sticks of bombs. Two were near misses but one exploded on the after searchlight platform. The blast wrecked a nearby lifeboat, dumping its oil, which promptly caught fire, and bent its davits to block the hatch to the engine room. The Type 1s made a second pass, with five out of a stick of six bombs splashing just 50 or 60 feet off the starboard side. This series of drenching detonations crumpled the foremast, blew two 20mm guns and one 4-inch gun clean off the ship, and propelled a lubrication pump from the after engine room through a bulkhead into the forward engine room. The *Colhoun* was already a flaming wreck when the Mitsubishis made a third pass, scoring two hits that killed everyone who had gathered in the after deck house, and the little destroyer-transport began to sink by the stern. Skipper Lieutenant Commander George B. Madden ordered abandon ship. Tank lighters from Guadalcanal quickly swarmed in and rescued as many of the crew as possible, including 18 wounded. But as the *Colhoun* sank she took 51 of her crew with her.[39]

The Japanese pilots managed to completely miss the *William Ward Burrows*, still aground off Tulagi. She had started unloading supplies into lighters in order to both get the supplies ashore and lighten the ship. The *Burrows* went full astern while the destroyer minelayer *Tracy* tugged at her via a towline, which promptly snapped. The air attacks halted salvage operations. And at 8:35 pm, 20 injured men from *Colhoun* were brought on board the *Burrows* for medical treatment. "There but for the grace of God go us," thought *Burrows* skipper Lieutenant Commander E. I. McQuiston. He later explained that had the *Burrows* not run aground, she would have been unloading supplies at Kukum with the *Colhoun* and would probably have been sunk with her. So the grounding was a blessing in disguise.[40]

A blessing not in disguise arrived at Henderson Field around 4:00 pm. Two B-17 pathfinders led Colonel William Wallace, the commander of the Marine Air Group 23, and the remainder of his command: 19 F4F Wildcats of Marine Fighting 224 under Major Robert E. Galer, and 12 SBD Dauntlesses of Marine Scout Bombing 231 under Major Leo R. Smith. The thin blue line of five Wildcats had just gotten some reinforcements, as did the Cactus Air Force's airstrike capability. The jubilation at their arrival was short, as the next day three of the new fighters disappeared on patrol.

Watching the reinforcements arrive was Admiral McCain, who was visiting General Vandegrift and inspecting the conditions at Henderson Field. When McCain returned to Espiritu Santo, he sent a dispatch to Admiral Nimitz and Admiral Ghormley estimating that Guadalcanal needed at least 40 high-altitude fighters for an adequate defense, clearly not the Airacobras. The beleaguered Army pilots had found a friend in McCain. "P-400s no good at altitude and disheartening to brave men who fly them," he said. "F4F-4 [Wildcat] more successful due in part to belly tanks on Zeros, in part to cool maneuvering and expert gunnery."[41]

Admiral McCain went on: "… 2 full squadrons of P-38s or F4Fs in addition to present strength should be put into Cactus at once, with replacements in training to the south." He wanted the two squadrons to replace the Airacobras. Immediately. "[T]he situation admits of no delay whatever." McCain closed his report with this declaration:

> With substantially the reinforcement requested, Cactus can be a sinkhole for enemy air power and can be consolidated, expanded, and exploited to [the] enemy's mortal hurt. The reverse is true if we lose Cactus. If the reinforcement requested is not made available, Cactus cannot be supplied and hence cannot be held.[42]

This statement got full support from Admiral Turner in a missive to Admiral Ghormley:

> Here in the Solomons we now have an unsinkable aircraft carrier which I believe may finally be multiplied into an invincible fleet adequate for a decisive move, but this will require patience, and the determined support by forces of a strength and character which you do not now have under your control… I believe that the immediate consolidation and extension of our Cactus position is now possible and advisable, and is a golden opportunity that ought not to be missed.[43]

Lacking all of the optimism of Turner's missive but none of its melodrama was the surprisingly prescient note of support from Admiral Ghormley:

> Cactus [is] not only a base of major value to the nation holding it but is [the] first foot of ground taken from an enemy who has had some cause to consider his armies invincible … It is my considered opinion that at this time the retention of Cactus is more vital to the prosecution of the war in the Pacific than any other commitment.[44]

For all his military faults, Robert Ghormley was a first-class diplomat, and perhaps it took a diplomat to understand, as Ghormley showed here, that Guadalcanal was now more than a military operation. It was emotional as well.

To be sure, Admiral Nimitz fully agreed with them. But the commander-in-chief of the Pacific Fleet had a lot of territory to defend and not nearly enough fighter aircraft with which to defend it. Hawaii and the West Coast were short 75 Wildcats and would get only 16 by mid-September.[45] And he had to supply Guadalcanal on top of that. The Army's generals Marshall and Arnold were still refusing to provide the P-38s to the Pacific.

From where would the aircraft come?

A position is only as good as its supply line. And the longer a supply line is, the more vulnerable it is, the less stable it is. The Japanese were finding this out the hard way with the distance to Guadalcanal from Shortland, much of which was vulnerable to the Cactus Air Force.

But the American supply line to Guadalcanal from Espiritu Santo was not much better. That area was within reach of the Betty bombers of Base Air Force in Rabaul. And though, for reasons known only to the US Navy, "The Slot" was not flooded with Allied submarines, the Japanese had vectored several submarines to cover the areas south and east of the Solomons. So Allied air coverage for this area was essential. But Henderson Field was not yet capable of providing it; that coverage had to come out of Espiritu Santo and carriers that the US Navy had covering that route.

Admiral Fletcher was present in the *Saratoga*; Admiral Noyes had come back with the *Wasp* the day after Eastern Solomons; and the *Enterprise* had been replaced by the *Hornet*, who came down from Pearl Harbor as the centerpiece of a task force commanded by Rear Admiral George Murray, former skipper of the *Enterprise*. Three aircraft carriers, playing a defensive role. Admiral Fletcher didn't like it. None of the carrier admirals liked it, to be sure. It limited the carriers' freedom of movement and made them easier for the enemy to find.

Admiral Fletcher's operational carriers spent the night of August 30–31 heading northwest toward San Cristobal, west of the Santa Cruz Islands. The night was largely uneventful, although not entirely so. At 2:10 am, in the deepest part of the night, the radar on the *Saratoga* and the *North Carolina* detected … something 9 miles to the west. And closing to about 11,000 yards. Admiral Fletcher sent the destroyer *Farragut* to investigate. The destroyer went out and found four ships headed due north. Fletcher ordered the *Farragut* to challenge the unidentified ships and the rest of his task force to make an emergency turn to starboard. The *Farragut* dutifully challenged the dark shapes, but got no response. The destroyer carefully crept closer to the mysterious ships. Maybe she could identify them.[46]

That the *Farragut* could not do, but she recognized the silhouettes of one of the ships. It was an aircraft carrier. The dumbfounded destroyer reported her finding.

"Are you sure you're not following this force?" the admiral asked.

"It is possible we are," answered the *Farragut*, mustering as much dignity as she could; the destroyer's highly trained professional sailors had indeed gotten their bearings mixed. They headed back to the task force.[47] The original radar contact, whatever it was, apparently vanished in the interim.

The next morning, at 7:41, destroyer *Macdonough*, on the *Saratoga*'s starboard bow, picked up something on sonar, only 400 yards dead ahead. The destroyer steamed onward to see if the contact would solidify.

It did – into a periscope that popped up out of the water only 10 yards off the *Macdonough*'s port bow. A scraping sound was heard coming from the bottom of the destroyer's hull. The sailors quickly dropped two depth charges – but forgot to arm them – as one torpedo malfunctioned and broke the surface of the water. The signalmen raised the warning flag for "submarine alert" while the voice radio broadcast the alarm, "Torpedo headed for carrier on course 50 degrees True!"[48]

The *Saratoga*'s Captain Ramsey ordered full speed and right full rudder to try to swing out of the way of the torpedoes he knew were coming. Indeed, could see were coming – all five of them.

But the *Saratoga*, physically bigger and not as nimble as the newer carriers, responded "sluggishly."[49] At 7:48, one torpedo grazed the carrier's starboard side bulge just aft of the island. Admiral Murray in the *Hornet* saw a geyser of water erupt higher than the *Saratoga*'s mast. Fighting 5's Lieutenant Howard W. Crews described the impact as "a dull thud and the ship heaved a couple of times like some old antiquated street car lurching along an equally old track." Others would say the big *Saratoga* "went into a fit and fairly lifted itself out of the water and then shook itself good," like a "house in a severe earthquake."[50]

On the towering flag bridge, Admiral Fletcher banged his head and blood poured over his face. He ordered a pharmacist's mate to bandage the wound, then went back to work. The admiral was one of 12 casualties on the *Saratoga*, none fatal, and several months later became the highest ranked naval officer to be awarded the Purple Heart, an honor for which he did not ask – Fletcher never even reported his injury, but was listed on the casualty list according to procedure – and did not want.[51]

The admiral was not nearly as injured as his flagship, whose wound was, however, serious only to the extent it disabled the carrier within range of the Japanese airbases at Rabaul. Mostly, the damage was annoying. The aftermost boiler room, one of 16 on the carrier, was flooded, while another suffered some flooding. Normally, on a steam turbine-powered ship, this sort of damage could be managed fairly easily, but the *Saratoga* had an innovative turboelectric propulsion system which was actually fairly resistant to damage. Yet this time, the torpedo had hit in exactly the wrong place for it, the shock overwhelming vibration dampeners and causing a short circuit that took the entire turboelectric drive offline.[52] Though she had made 16 knots with a 4-degree list to starboard, by 7:53, the *Saratoga* had drifted to a halt.[53]

Admiral Fletcher sent the *North Carolina* off to the *Hornet* while most of his destroyers circled the carrier. The destroyers *Macdonough* and *Phelps* maintained sonar contact with the *Saratoga*'s assailant, the Japanese submarine *I-26* under the command of Commander Yokota Minoru. Yokota had first picked up the *Saratoga* task force while running on the surface after midnight. It was *I-26* that had appeared on the radar before the *Farragut* went out to chase her tail, in the process losing the contact. As did the *I-26*, after she dove to make a submerged approach.

Three hours later, the *I-26* had found the *Saratoga* again, a visual sighting at 23,000 meters. But the carrier was heading away from the submarine, whose submerged speed was too slow to catch her until the *Saratoga* turned into the wind for flight operations. Commander Yokota found himself with a perfect shot at 1,000 meters, only to have his torpedomen botch preparing the torpedoes for launch.[54] But Yokota got a third bite at the apple and finally got one fish into the carrier.

After restoring power, which took less than five minutes, the *Saratoga* headed southeast, away from Rabaul, one propeller pushing her at 5 knots. The destroyers *Macdonough* and *Phelps* had depth charged the submarine twice with no effect except, it was alleged, sending shockwaves through the water that caused the carrier's list to increase to 6 degrees. The *Monssen* was left behind to keep the submarine occupied while the carrier cleared the area. The destroyer made several unsuccessful depth-charge attacks until the contact was lost at around noon. She claimed sinking the submarine, but the *I-26* made good her escape. Admiral Murray loaned the destroyer *Bagley* to Admiral Fletcher to take the *Monssen*'s place in the *Saratoga*'s screen.[55]

While this was going on, things were getting worse. The *North Carolina* reported a large group of unidentified aircraft on her radar, bearing 120 degrees True, distance 23 miles. The Japanese were hunting the crippled carrier. The *Bagley* stumbled across another submarine contact that she depth charged. As if matters were not complicated enough, the *Saratoga*, turning into the wind to send her aircraft off to Guadalcanal, Espiritu Santo, or any place that would take in homeless Wildcats, Dauntlesses, and Avengers, lost power again. When it rains, it pours, especially in the Solomons.

The destroyers circled the carrier while the cruiser *Minneapolis* rigged a tow line. By 12:36 pm, the carrier was again under way at 10 knots, using both her engines and the *Minneapolis*'s tow. Combined with a "brisk" wind, it generated enough of a headwind to launch 20 Dauntlesses and nine Avengers under Lieutenant Commander Kirn at 1:30 pm. Admiral Nimitz's report to Admiral King of the *Saratoga*'s misfortune described the launching of aircraft while under tow as a "unique performance."[56]

As soon as the *Saratoga* restored power, she made for home and a lengthy repair job that underwater holes in the hull normally require. This stretch of water, cursed by Japanese submarine sightings and now attacks, started earning its nickname: "Torpedo Junction."

With the *Saratoga*'s departure came the departure of Vice Admiral Frank Jack Fletcher. He had fought three major carrier battles in four months, in addition to commanding numerous carrier operations since the beginning of the Pacific War. The stress had certainly taken a toll on Fletcher, and he was due for a badly needed rest and break from the front. He would never return, at least in command of aircraft carriers. With Vice Admiral William F. Halsey, Jr, regarded as the US Navy's top carrier commander, still on medical leave that had kept him out of Midway, command of the South Pacific's carriers went to Rear Admiral Noyes. Eventually Fletcher was instead given command of the 13th Naval District, out of Seattle, Washington, and made Commander, Northwestern Sea Frontier. He would later be given the additional titles of Commander, North Pacific Ocean Area, one of the three Pacific Ocean areas under Admiral Nimitz.

Fletcher thus, as his biographer Stephen Regan aptly put it, "departed the bitter tempest quietly after a full year of sea duty surrounded by hard luck. He had been in more operations than any other admiral, yet in each case his successes were tempered with misfortune – often uncontrollable – and every victory was bittersweet."[57]

For all those operations, Fletcher is most remembered, fairly or otherwise, as the man who pulled out the carriers, abandoning the Marines, setting up the disaster at Savo Island, and imperiling the *Watchtower* landings, about which Fletcher seems to have given scant consideration despite the warnings from Admiral Turner and General Vandegrift.

Thus was answered Napoleon's question: "Is he lucky?"

One of Fletcher's final commands was to authorize 28 Wildcats from the *Saratoga* to fly off to Efate. This meant there were now 22 Dauntlesses, 15 Avengers, and the aforementioned 28 Wildcats at Espiritu Santo, just waiting for deployment.[61] Admiral Nimitz recommended they be transferred to Guadalcanal, a recommendation that was approved. Captain Ramsey sent a final message to his departing pilots:

> Your record of achievements is a matter of the greatest pride to us all and it is our fervent determination to rejoin you as expeditiously as humanly possible. In the meantime, carry on as you have in the past. No one could ask more.[62]

Nimitz didn't like it. Deploying carrier-trained pilots to a land base is an inefficient use of scarce carrier-trained pilots.[63]

But they were carrier pilots without a carrier. This deployment was one way of finding aircraft for Henderson Field. And, right now, the only way.

The "Victory Disease" with which the Imperial Japanese Navy was afflicted before Midway is as old as humanity. The ancient Greeks had a different term for it: hubris. In the English-speaking world it is more often expressed today with the old English saying "Pride goeth before a fall." After its successes in China, Malaya, the East Indies, the Philippines, and other places, the Imperial Japanese Army suffered from the same Victory Disease as the Navy. Unlike the Navy, however, the Army had not yet experienced such a disaster – like Midway – that it was compelled to self-inspect.

Perhaps the last person in the Imperial Navy to suffer from hubris was Admiral Mikawa, who had recognized the developing threat in the Solomons before anyone else. On August 31, Mikawa sent out a missive to the Combined Fleet warning that the piecemeal reinforcement of Guadalcanal would only lead to defeat, stating, "Every effort must be made to use large units all at once." Moreover:

> Enemy resistance and counter attacks in the Guadalcanal and Solomons area have been extremely stubborn and our operations of the first period were totally unable to cope with them. Unless operations are conducted in accordance with careful and detailed plans based on accurate information the probability of their success is slight.[64]

But old habits die hard, and Imperial General Headquarters was still feverish with Victory Disease, a fever that was not yet ready to break. Nevertheless, small changes were made. The same day they received Admiral Mikawa's message, they issued orders making the "immediate recapture of Guadalcanal" the top operational priority. All offensive operations in New Guinea were to be suspended until the island was recaptured.[65]

This could not have pleased General Hyakutake. He was still deep in his latest scheme to take Port Moresby. This time, it involved setting up a base at Milne Bay, Papua, from where they could sail around and take Port Moresby from the sea. After the usual bickering, he talked Admiral Mikawa into landing some Special Naval Landing Force troops there.

Around midnight on August 26, Admiral Maruyama had led his light cruisers *Tenryu* and *Tatsuta* and destroyers *Urakaze*, *Tanikaze*, and *Hamakaze*, and two subchasers in escorting two transports to land the naval infantry in "Rabi," what the Japanese called the entirety of Milne Bay. There the Japanese Special Naval Landing Force troops became bogged down in the face of much heavier than anticipated opposition and repeated air attacks. While General Hyakutake did not think barges were safe under these conditions for transporting his Army troops, he presumably thought they were perfectly fine for transporting naval infantry. A batch that was coming down by seven barges stopped for rest on Goodenough Island, where Royal Australian Air Force P-40s promptly destroyed the barges, stranding the troops.

Shortly thereafter, in the last hour of August 31, the Japanese General Kawaguchi Kiyotake stepped off not a barge, but the destroyer *Umikaze* and onto the soil of Guadalcanal at Taivu Point. With him in this eight-destroyer convoy – *Fubuki*, *Shirayuki*, *Kawakaze*, *Yudachi*, *Amagiri*, *Kagero*, *Suzukaze*, and the aforementioned *Umikaze* – were some 1,200 troops.[66]

It had been an adventurous journey for the general, at least in a political and bureaucratic sense. On August 30, while still at Shortland, he had continued to demand his barges and adamantly refused to move his 35th Brigade to Guadalcanal by destroyer despite what had happened to the barges on Goodenough Island. Admiral Tanaka continued trying to convince Kawaguchi that the barges were too slow and unseaworthy and moving by destroyer was the fastest and safest method available. But the persuasive power of his argument was reduced by the appearance in the Shortlands anchorage of the destroyers *Amagiri*, *Kagero*, and *Shirakumo*, the last at the end of a towline from the minelayer *Tsugaru*, who had taken over from the *Amagiri*.[67] Tanaka had scrounged up the destroyer *Yudachi* to replace the *Shirakumo* and try again to take Kawaguchi's troops to Guadalcanal, but Kawaguchi was insisting on his barges. Barges had made it in Borneo, the general believed, and if they could make it there, they could make it anywhere. Except, apparently, Goodenough Island.

Not since Hannibal coerced Carthage into giving him elephants had a general fought so hard for a means of transport so nonsensical, at least in the given circumstances. But Kawaguchi would not allow his troops to board any more destroyers unless he was ordered to do so by the Army. As such, Admiral Tanaka was forced to leave the general's troops behind and carry the rest of the Ichiki Detachment on the destroyer *Yudachi*, who brought them to Guadalcanal safely that night.[68]

The next day, 17th Army supported their general and gave him what he craved: permission to carry troops by barge. General Hyakutake had intended for General Kawaguchi to transport most of his supplies and artillery by the barges, with maybe one company of infantry with machine guns. But Kawaguchi was determined to make his dumb idea even dumber. The order said transport "as few men as possible" by barge, but it did not specify a number. It was the opening Kawaguchi needed to transport 1,000 men of the 124th Infantry Regiment under Colonel Oka Akinosuke, with some minimal artillery.[69] For its part, 8th Fleet did not support its hard-pressed admiral, Tanaka, and gave him a tongue lashing for not transporting Kawaguchi's troops to Guadalcanal. They followed it by sacking Tanaka and replacing his 2nd Destroyer Flotilla with Rear Admiral Hashimoto Shintaro's 3rd Destroyer Flotilla.

But with the general mollified, for now, Admiral Tanaka had one last assignment: to lead an eight-destroyer convoy to Guadalcanal to drop off General Kawaguchi and his men. Before boarding the destroyers, the general gave a speech to some officers:

> Gentlemen, I think our faith is our strength. Men who fight bravely, never doubting victory, will be the victors in the long run. Before we get to the battlefield we must sail three

> hundred miles and may very well encounter enemy attacks en route [...] But we have trained ourselves, haven't we? I swear to all of you we will smash the enemy. On to Guadalcanal!

"To Guadalcanal!" came the shout from the assembled men.[70] The troops were confident. Cocky. They promised to "wipe out every last Yankee."[71]

When they came ashore the night of August 31, they were greeted by the few remaining troops of the previous attempt to wipe out every last Yankee, the haggard, tattered remnants of the Ichiki Detachment. They led General Kawaguchi and his troops inland, covering their tracks as they went to avoid detection by American aircraft, to an abandoned native village at Tasimboko Point. There, Kawaguchi decided to sit tight. He would not start his attack until Colonel Oka and his troops had landed, whenever that would be.

However, the Ichiki's efforts at avoiding aerial detection were not entirely successful. Two P-400s showed up the next day. They did not see the Japanese, but they knew something was there and they started blindly strafing. Throughout the day, Airacobras, Wildcats, and Dauntlesses strafed and bombed the invisible troops. The Japanese lost 12 killed. A bomb blast damaged the general's hearing, causing him trouble speaking that he found "irritating."[72] Welcome to Guadalcanal, General Kawaguchi.

It was a welcome to which the Ichiki were accustomed. They were renamed the "Kuma" or "Bear" Battalion. But the new name did little to dispel the old dread that came with the air attacks.

A dread that normally lessens with night, though not this night. "Guard Company, rally!" came the shout through the dark of Tasimboko. Japanese troops hustled to defensive positions on the beach. General Kawaguchi went to his command post overlooking beach, where the sound of motors was now audible and getting louder – landing boats.

"Prepare to fire!" The infantry aimed their long, long rifles at the black shapes getting bigger and bigger.

"Fire!"

Multiple loud pops and cracks shook the night.

And a cry. In Japanese. "My arm! I've been hit!" "Cease firing!" shouted an officer. "They're friends." This opposed landing on a friendly shore cost the Japanese two dead and eight wounded.[73]

General Kawaguchi and his men were surprised by the reinforcements because it was a planned "sneak landing," to use Admiral Ugaki's description, by the destroyers *Urakaze*, *Uranami*, *Tanikaze*, and *Shikinami*.[74] Albeit not planned very well. The destroyers did not have enough landing boats, so they had to shuttle everyone to shore, which took longer. The surprise landing and the gunfire that resulted therefrom attracted attention. Flares appeared overhead and with them a trio of SBD Dauntlesses at about 1:30 am. The Japanese troops had to land amid strafing runs and falling bombs that caused slight damage to the *Shikinami*, killed five, and wounded six. The landing was aborted about halfway through. One Dauntless was damaged by gunfire and had to be written off.[75]

This was not going quite the way General Kawaguchi had drawn it up. He started to notice that he was not in Borneo anymore. He wondered if ordering Colonel Oka to get to Guadalcanal by the slowest means of transportation possible was perhaps not his best idea.[76]

Both to help cover the landing and on general principles, on September 2 Base Air Force sent 40 Mitsubishis – 18 G4Ms and 22 Zeros – to bomb Henderson Field. They arrived around 11:35 am to face a well-prepared Marine Fighting 224. Of the 22 Zeros, 13 were from *Kido Butai*, but they could not overcome cloud cover that prevented them from protecting their charges. Even so, one Japanese bomb torched an armed, fueled Dauntless near an ammunition dump. The burning SBD exploded, detonating its bomb in the process, and spewed flaming gasoline everywhere, including on a cache of 90mm ammunition. The shells began going off and caused several casualties among firefighters before the blaze could be brought under control. The vengeful Wildcats perforated three of the Bettys, while the Zeros were jumped by Marine Fighting 224 on the trip back and two were shot down. There were no American aerial losses.[77]

In addition to the intercepting Wildcats, as was now normal practice during Japanese air attacks, the Dauntlesses and Airacobras had taken off from Henderson Field. Usually, they would simply ride out the attack so they would not be destroyed on the ground. But now they had the idea that some *thing* was near Taivu Point and Tasimboko, so the Marine attack planes went there for plenty of bombing and strafing. In fact, the Dauntlesses and Airacobras spent much of the day there – 71 sorties, according to a Japanese war correspondent.[78] When they were done, the Tasimboko area was covered with craters, blackened stumps of trees, and burning palm fronds. One company commander described it:

> I received several near misses from these bombings and strafings. The enemy continued his bombing attacks almost all day long – four times in the morning and twice in the afternoon. Therefore, I stayed in the trench all day. I haven't any appetite. Although I think that these bombings are a test of intestinal fortitude, it is maddening to be the recipient of these daring and insulting attacks by American forces.[79]

Daring attacks were one thing, but, to the Imperial Army, insulting attacks were far worse. That night, General Kawaguchi received a way to return insults when the minelayer *Tsugaru*, destroyers *Kagero* and *Yugure*, and two patrol boats, escorted by the destroyers *Fubuki*, *Shirayuki*, and *Amagiri*, dropped off two field guns, two antitank guns, two antiaircraft guns, some 200 troops, and some supplies. One of the antiaircraft guns was damaged during unloading, however, and had to be sent back.[80] The gun was not the only thing damaged. As the ships hightailed it toward Shortland the next day, they were found by American scout planes. The *Tsugaru* suffered damage, 14 killed, and 30 wounded. The Americans were on to the reinforcement operations and had reset the schedule of their scout missions to catch these convoys, which the Marines on Guadalcanal had dubbed the "Cactus Express." However, because revealing the American code name for Guadalcanal – *Cactus* – was not permitted, a different name was substituted: "Tokyo Express."[81]

General Kawaguchi's troops were getting discouraged by the constant lashings by American aircraft, but he knew more troops were inbound. There was no reinforcement run scheduled for September 3, but a big one was to arrive September 4. So they continued to endure the attacks while Kawaguchi continued to wait for Oka.

Oka had been "overjoyed" when ordered to transport 1,000 men by 61 barges.[82] Like his superior General Kawaguchi, Oka considered his orders more what you'd call guidelines than actual directives. Kawaguchi had ordered Oka to use Gizo Island in the New Georgia group as the point of departure; Oka took his men by ship to the northwest coast of Santa Ysabel. Kawaguchi ordered Oka to proceed down the southern tier of the Solomons; Oka went down the northern tier. Kawaguchi ordered Oka to land at Taivu Point east of Lunga; Oka planned to land at Kamimbo Bay west of Lunga, which, to be sure, made more sense than Taivu Point. As Guadalcanal historian Richard Frank commented dryly, "In view of Kawaguchi's treatment of his orders, there is some poetic justice in Oka's response to Kawaguchi's directives."[83]

Colonel Oka's trip down was smooth enough, or at least as smooth as any trip by barge could be, and by September 3 he and his troops were at Finanana Point on the southeast end of Santa Ysabel. He sent notice to Colonel Kawaguchi that he was "approaching" Guadalcanal.[84]

All Oka and his men had to do was cross over to Guadalcanal. It was the longest part of the run – 57 miles – but they would do it at night. How hard could it be?

September was not just a new month on Guadalcanal, it was a new beginning. Certainly for General Kawaguchi and the Japanese, but also for the Americans.

On September 1, the *Betelgeuse* landed five officers and 387 men of the 6th Naval Construction Battalion. These men were generally much older than the Marine infantry, many older than draft age, which initially earned jeers from their Guadalcanal hosts. But these men were skilled tradesmen – carpenters, electricians, metalworkers, machinists, demolition experts, and the like – who had volunteered to put their skills to work in the war effort. The construction battalion was an American innovation, and the 6th was the first such unit to be deployed to a combat area. As the men worked to "... help make an airfield out of Henderson and ... clear a short grassy strip a mile to the east called Fighter 1," they earned a great deal of respect from the Marines.[85] And an affectionate nickname: "Seebees."

But the Seebees were not the only gifts from the holds of the *Betelgeuse*. Also delivered was one battery of 5-inch coastal defense guns – the same 5-inch gun that was on US Navy ships – of the 3rd Defense Battalion. No longer would the Marines have to endure shelling from the sea without answering. Now they could respond in kind.[86]

Additionally, some new troops were in the area. Not a lot, but some. One battalion of the 5th Marine Regiment had already rejoined its parent unit at Lunga. Lieutenant Colonel Merritt A. "Red Mike" Edson's 1st Raider Battalion completed its move to Guadalcanal from Tulagi on September 1, while the remnants of the 1st Parachute Battalion were to do so on September 3.[87] They would have to do until General Vandegrift could wrangle the 7th Marine Regiment from Samoa over Admiral Ghormley's wish to move it to Ndeni. Meanwhile, with several promotions taking effect, some people had new ranks. Major Richard Mangrum became lieutenant colonel while fellow Marine pilot Captain John Smith became a major. And it would be a new beginning for the *William Ward Burrows*.

The transport was still stuck on a reef off Tulagi. She had spent the past few days sweating out air attacks and surface strikes that somehow managed to miss her, and offloading as much of her equipment as she could, including a critical radar that was sent to Henderson Field. Some of the new, grandiosely designated "yacht patrol" boats – nicknamed "Yippies"– that were old fishing boats that the Navy had requisitioned, crews and all, came to help out, as did the destroyer minelayer *Gamble*. On September 2, two of the Yippies, *YP-3* and *YP-6*, worked on the *William Ward Burrows*' port quarter, while another, *YP-239*, worked on the starboard, and the *Gamble* joined in. Together with the *Burrows*' engines, they managed to finally yank the transport free.[88]

The *Burrows*' skipper, Lieutenant Commander McQuiston, had the ship anchor to make a damage assessment. Fortunately, the damage was very light and would not inhibit operations. So she headed to Kukum to continue offloading. Just in time for the *Gamble* to report a submarine contact. It was time to get moving, and the *William Ward Burrows* rang up some speed to get into the safety of Tulagi fast. Too fast, actually, to clear a reef. And the *Burrows* ran fast aground. Again.

The crews of the Yippies, mostly fishermen from San Diego, were suitably unimpressed with the Navy's seamanship.[89] But one, the *YP-239*, joined the *Gamble* and a small flotilla of landing boats in pulling the transport free – again – the following afternoon. Once again the damage was very light, and the *William Ward Burrows* proceeded to begin offloading the remainder of her cargo at Kukum and Tulagi.

The *William Ward Burrows* was not the only watercraft aground that day. So too were the barges of Colonel Oka, which were hidden at Finanana Point on Santa Ysabel but not hidden well enough to avoid detection by Marine scout planes after dawn on September 3. The scout planes were followed by 11 Dauntlesses, who strafed the grounded barges. That afternoon came seven Dauntlesses and two Wildcats to rake the boats with gunfire. Undaunted, Colonel Oka led his barges to San Jorge Island that night and carefully camouflaged them.

And, again, not well enough to avoid detection by the Americans. The morning of September 4 saw 13 Dauntlesses under Lieutenant Colonel Mangrum roar over the boats, machine guns blazing. Again and again and again. About a third of the boats were perforated. Colonel Oka and his fleet endured two smaller air attacks that afternoon.[90]

That night, a DC-3 (or, as the Navy designated it a Douglas R4D), transporting 57-year-old Marine Brigadier General Roy Geiger, commanding officer of the 1st Marine Air Wing, and two assistants, chief of staff Colonel Louis Woods and chief aide Lieutenant Colonel J. C. "Toby" Munn, landed at Henderson Field. A pilot to his bone marrow, Geiger was a flying veteran of World War I and the Marines' pre-eminent aviation specialist. Geiger was also a doer, not of paperwork, which he hated, but of supporting the ground troops, which he understood to be the *raison d'etre* of Marine aviation. And Geiger was prepared to implement that policy immediately. As soon as he set up shop in the Pagoda, he directed continued attacks against those barges that had appeared off Santa Ysabel.

The earlier attacks necessitated some quick patch jobs on the barges before their planned departure for Guadalcanal at 7:00 pm. They all were ready on time. The ocean, however, was not. Low tide kept them ashore until 9:30 or so.

Once the barges were finally under way they found the sea rough, not like the placid rivers of Borneo or the calmer coastal waters of Santa Ysabel. Water overtopped the gunwales and came in through the bullet holes. These barges were really not designed for, and not seaworthy in, such conditions. The water soaked the thoroughly annoyed troops and strained the engines. The boats unwillingly fanned out. And out. And out.

While Colonel Oka and his troops were taking the scenic route to Guadalcanal, the American destroyer transports *Little* and *Gregory* were taking the scenic route to nowhere. They had transported a detachment of Marine Raiders to Savo Island that day to investigate native reports of Japanese forces on the tiny island. But ten hours of scouring by Lieutenant Colonel Griffith and his men found nothing except for wreckage from the disastrous Battle of Savo Island.[91]

The Raiders arrived back at Kukum very late that afternoon. Lieutenant Colonel Edson sent him a message to keep the Raiders aboard the *Little* and *Gregory* that night, to save them the trouble of getting back on board the ships in the morning for an attack on Tasimboko. The message was never received, however, so the Raiders disembarked.[92] The missed message would be, in the words of one Marine historian, "a curiously fortuitous error."[93] Meanwhile the sun had gone down to give way to an unusually dark night.

Their job as chauffers for the 1st Marine Raider Battalion done, the *Little* and *Gregory* didn't want to go back to Tulagi because the abnormally low visibility could cause them to run aground like the *William Ward Burrows* had. So their group chief, Commander Hugh W. Hadley, decided to remain for a night on the Sound. There were no reports of enemy ships approaching, and even if there were, being sunk was preferable to running aground, or at least the US Navy bureaucracy thought so. The two destroyer-transports marked time between Guadalcanal and Savo Island at 10 knots, alternating between courses of 130 degrees and 310 degrees True.

The *Little*, leading the *Gregory*, had reached the eastern end of the patrol route and was turning right to 310 degrees a little before 1:00 am when they saw flashes and heard sharp reports to the east. "A good ways off," in the words of one of the boatswains.[94] It must be a Japanese submarine shelling Henderson Field, they guessed. The old destroyer-transports went to battle stations at 12:58 am.[95] Four minutes later, radar showed four contacts about 2 miles astern. Between them the two old ships had a total of four 4-inch guns. Whatever those four contacts were, they heavily outgunned the Americans. Hadley had the choice to either run or fight a hit-and-run-battle.

Time for pondering such existential questions ran out. Five flares appeared in the sky above them about a half-mile ahead and floated down.

From somewhere off the *Gregory*'s starboard quarter, a searchlight snapped open and pinned the *Little*. Shell splashes quickly followed. The *Gregory* opened up with every weapon she had that could be trained on their tormentors. But she, too was quickly pinned by a searchlight, this time from off her port quarter and the gunfire started coming her way as well.

Two quick hits on the port wing of the bridge killed most of the bridge crew, wounded her skipper, Lieutenant Commander Harry F. Bauer, cut off all communications, and disabled her fire-control system. A hit to her fireroom smashed a boiler, disabled her engines, and, appropriately, started a fire; another hit toppled her Number 2 stack. She was unable to fight, but could not get out of the fight. Three minutes after the first shots, Bauer was compelled to order the *Gregory* abandoned. The crewmen poured over the side, but two, Boatswain's Mate 2nd Class Clarence C. Justice and Coxswain Chester M. Ellis, helped the badly injured Bauer get away from the ship. When Bauer heard another man in the water crying for help, he ordered Justice and Ellis to help the drowning man. That was the last anyone saw of Bauer.[96]

The *Little* was also in dire straits. A quick hit to the stern disabled her steering engine and jammed her rudder. Another cracked the after fuel tanks, and the leaking fuel quickly caught fire. The after 4-inch mount was disabled and her main steam pipe was ruptured. In desperation, skipper Lieutenant Commander Gus Brynolf Lofberg, Jr, tried to beach the destroyer, but with the rudder jammed and the ship losing way because of the broken steam pipe, it was hopeless. He ordered her abandoned, but before everyone could get off another hit shattered the bridge, killing Lofberg and Commander Hadley.[97]

About a half-hour after the action began, their Japanese assailants approached – the *Yudachi*, *Hatsuyuki*, and *Murakumo* of the Japanese 11th Destroyer Division under Captain Sugino Shuichi. They had been part of the big destroyer convoy led by Admiral Hashimoto's flagship light cruiser *Sendai* and also included the destroyers *Kawakaze*, *Umikaze*, *Suzukaze*, *Shikinami*, *Uranami*, and *Ariake*. They had landed almost 1,000 soldiers of the renamed Kuma Battalion and the Aoba Detachment, formally the 4th Regiment of the 2nd Sendai Division. Captain Sugino had been ordered to shell the Lunga airfield on the way out, and was making a thoroughly miserable night for the Marines when he saw the flares that revealed the *Little* and *Gregory*. The flares surprised the Japanese as much as they did the Americans – they had been dropped by a US Navy PBY Catalina, trying to find the submarine that was suspected of shelling the airfield.

But the 11th recovered quickly, and with a total of 17 5-inch guns and 26 24-inch torpedo tubes among the *Yudachi*, *Hatsuyuki*, and *Murakumo*, they had the *Little* and *Gregory* outnumbered and badly outgunned. The *Yudachi*'s skipper was Commander Kikkawa Kiyoshi, a veteran of the Java Sea Campaign who had impressed even Admiral Ugaki with his command of the destroyer *Oshio*, especially in battle off Bali.[98] Even so, it had not been a contest.

And it was not a contest now, either. Passing between the two burning hulks, the three Japanese destroyers made a high-speed run to machine gun, blast, and depth charge the survivors in the water. The *Gregory* sank stern first at about 1:40 am; the *Little* sank on an even keel at 3:30 am.[99] After sunrise boats came out from Guadalcanal to pick up 12 officers and 226 men. Commander Hadley, Lieutenant Commander Lofberg, and 20 other men were killed on the *Little*, with 44 wounded. From the *Gregory*, in addition to Lieutenant Commander Bauer, whose gallantry earned him a posthumous Silver Star and a new destroyer named after him, ten men were killed and 26 wounded.[100]

The *Little* and *Gregory* and, for that matter, the *Colhoun*, had been unheralded ships, converted as they were from old four-piper destroyers that had proven overmatched in the Java Sea Campaign, but here, after their conversion, they had been incredibly useful.

And perhaps not appreciated nearly enough until half of these destroyer transports had been lost within a week. Admiral Nimitz would later say of this action, "Both of these small vessels fought as well as possible against the overwhelming odds ...with little means they performed duties vital to the success of the campaign." [101] Admiral Turner, in his own tribute, would describe the odds faced by the Little, Gregory, Colhoun, and other destroyer transports making the runs to Guadalcanal and Tulagi:

> The officers and men serving in these ships have shown great courage and have performed outstanding service. They entered this dangerous area time after time, well knowing that their ships stood little or no chance if they should be opposed by any surface or air force the enemy would send into those waters. On the occasion of their last trip they remained for six days, subjected to daily air attack and anticipating nightly surface attack.[102]

Perhaps Lieutenant Colonel Twining gave the most heartfelt eulogy: "Due to our close association with them before and during the war, we Marines felt keenly the loss of these brave little ships. To my mind, no group in the Pacific accomplished so much with so little."[103]

For his part, Commander Kikkawa had impressed not just Admiral Ugaki but his colleagues by landing troops, shelling the airfield, and sinking enemy ships in the space of a single night.

Yet when the night changed back to day, things changed. As the victorious *Yudachi*, *Hatsuyuki*, and *Murakumo* retired, they were found by two B-17s, who attacked but caused no damage. At around 4:30 am on September 5 light cruiser *Sendai* and destroyers *Kawakaze*, *Umikaze*, and *Suzukaze* paused their own withdrawal to guard Colonel Oka's landing barges for a bit.[104]

But Admiral Hashimoto's ships could not help bail out the leaking barges or herd the flotilla back together. Landfall on Guadalcanal was scheduled for 5:00 am, which came and went with the island not even in sight. The tallest peaks of Gadarukanaru started rising over the horizon at around 6:20 am. Colonel Oka's troops were heartened.

Only for about 20 minutes, however; then two "long-nosed planes" appeared. They were the last two operational P-400 Airacobras under Captain Dale Brannon. By this time, the *Sendai* and her destroyers had left to avoid the air attacks they knew were coming, but the barges could not.

The Americans found 15 barges some 500 yards off the coast of Guadalcanal, with Japanese troops wading ashore. This batch of infantry was led by Major Takamatsu Etsuo, commanding the 2nd Battalion of the 124th Infantry Regiment. Captain Brannon and his wingman roared in low and "cut a bloody X" in the midst of the landing troops with their .50cal machine guns and the espe ily brutal 20mm cannons. Joining in the vicious strafing were six Marine Fighting 224 Wildcats. Takamatsu had his troops fire back at their low-flying tormentors with small arms, which were effective enough to down one Grumman. But the Americans took their toll in Japanese lives, including that of Takamatsu himself.[105]

About two hours later, Captain Brannon and his wingman returned to shoot up the Japanese supplies aboard the grounded barges. The Wildcats had to stay behind to help defend Henderson Field from Base Air Force, who was attacking with 26 G4Ms and 20 Zeros. But the same weather that had roughed up the crossing for Colonel Oka's men had forced the bombers to jettison their loads and head back. All 18 operational Wildcats moved to intercept. One Betty was shot down and six others damaged, while one F4F and pilot were lost. Three others were damaged, including that of veteran Major Rivers Morrell, who was so badly wounded that he had to be airlifted out.[106]

Colonel Oka and his men were not in much better shape. Oka had finally made landfall with his badly leaking barge at about 11:20 am, some 7 miles southeast of Kamimbo. Initially he was able to round up only about 150 of his soaking-wet men. He later found out some 300 of them had landed at Kamimbo. The remainder of his 1,000 men were scattered from Santa Ysabel to Savo Island. His supplies were gone, which put them in not much better shape than their hosts on Guadalcanal, the redoubtable Captain Monzen and his Special Naval Landing Force troops.

Also stumbling ashore was Colonel Tsuji Masanobu, the army operations officer at Imperial General Headquarters who had invited himself onto this expedition to represent the army general staff. The highly intelligent Tsuji was a brilliant tactician who was known as the "god of operations," and had developed the plan for the conquest of Malaya and Singapore. In the words of Pacific War historian H. P. Willmott, "[T]here was no disputing [Tsuji's] industriousness, and equally there was no denying the fact that he achieved results."[107]

However, "Tsuji's unendearing traits combined extreme rudeness with irritability," Willmott says.[108] He possessed unmeasurable arrogance, an extreme racism, and misogyny to boot. After the surrender of Singapore, Tsuji helped plan the *Sook Ching* – the massacre of some 50,000 Malayan Chinese. He was then transferred to the Philippines. After the US surrender there, Tsuji tried to have all American prisoners killed. While he was not entirely successful in that effort, Tsuji had a hand in the brutal abuse and murder of prisoners in the Bataan Death March, as well as the execution of captured Philippine government officials.

But that was not all. Colonel Tsuji was a master of political intrigue, having taken part in many of the army machinations in the 1930s, which gained him the firm backing of General Tojo. He was a firm believer in *gekokujo*, the ritual insubordination that was a tradition in Japanese military circles. As a member of the often-rogue Kwantung Army in China, Tsuji was a supporter of war with the Soviet Union, and his insubordination helped spark the Nomonhan border incident. But once the Red Army had smashed the Japanese at Nomonhan, he became "the most determined single protagonist of war with the United States."[109] There is even evidence he plotted the murder of Prince Konoye, should the royal prime minister's last ditch negotiations with the US to avoid war have been successful. In the words of Willmott again, Tsuji "enjoyed an extremely unsavory reputation even in an Army hardly noted for its exacting standards of personal behavior."[110]

Tsuji's very presence showed the interest Imperial General Headquarters had in the Solomons situation. And Tsuji Masanobu fully intended to act.

The sinkings of the *Little* and *Gregory*, and the subsequent scattering of the Japanese barge convoy by the Cactus Air Force, were a microcosm of what the Guadalcanal campaign had become. It had developed, almost imperceptibly, but surely and well understood, into that most bizarre of tactical situations, perhaps unique in all of military history, in which the control of the waters around Guadalcanal changed every time the sun crossed the horizon.

When the sun came up every morning, the Stars and Stripes would be dominant. The only break would be the usual noontime Japanese air attack, which was only marginally effective. Except for that interlude, American aircraft would operate from Henderson Field, American reinforcement and supply convoys would come in, boats would shuttle between Lunga and Tulagi throughout the day. But everyone would clear Ironbottom Sound by sundown.

For when the sun went down every night, the Rising Sun would be dominant. All through the midnight hours, Japanese reinforcement and supply convoys came in, and Japanese surface ships and submarines would lob shells at Henderson Field. But everyone would clear Ironbottom Sound and be out of range of Henderson Field by sunrise.

"Like a broken record," Harold Buell of the *Enterprise*'s Dauntless squadron stationed at Henderson Field remembered, "the routine of noon bombings, morning and afternoon searches, night shellings, and harassment missions went on day after day with little variance."[111]

The key to the conundrum was Henderson Field. Whoever controlled Henderson Field controlled the air over Guadalcanal. The Combined Fleet had superiority over the Pacific Fleet. But as long as the Americans controlled Henderson Field, Japanese ships could not operate with any guarantee of safety during daylight hours. So when the night came, the Japanese could make their naval superiority felt.

As much as the South Pacific situation overall favored the Japanese, this curious strategic situation favored the Americans. The necessity of getting into and out of Guadalcanal waters by daylight meant the Japanese had to use only fast ships – usually destroyers – to run troops and supplies to Guadalcanal. But destroyers cannot carry significant amounts of troops and supplies, and almost nothing in the way of heavy weapons, meaning Japanese forces on Guadalcanal could never develop a critical mass of forces to overwhelm the Marine defenders of Henderson Field.

In short, the Japanese needed to capture Henderson Field to gain air superiority. But unless they gained air superiority they could not capture Henderson Field.

It was a dilemma without an obvious solution. So the Imperial Japanese Navy, the Imperial Japanese Army, and Imperial General Headquarters did what any self-respecting bureaucratic organization would do when faced with such a quandary – they kept doing what they were doing, hoping the next time would be successful. The only one who saw what was happening was Admiral Mikawa in Rabaul.

It was certainly not General Kawaguchi. He actively tried to tamp down expectations. "No matter what the War College says, it's extremely difficult to take an enemy position by night assault," he told a reporter. "If we succeed here on Guadalcanal, it will be a wonder in the military history of the world."[112]

Hyperbole aside, General Kawaguchi acted with much the same arrogance that Colonel Ichiki had. General Hyakutake had ordered Kawaguchi to "view the enemy strength, position, and terrain" to determine if it was "possible or not to achieve quick success."[113] No doubt with these orders in mind, General Kawaguchi had developed his plan of attack while he was at Shortland, having seen neither the enemy, nor the position, nor the terrain, with, apparently, only one hydrographic map of the northern coast of Guadalcanal to guide him.[114] He had fought in the jungles of Borneo and won, after all. And, in Kawaguchi's view, jungle is jungle.

On September 5, the 17th Army offered General Kawaguchi an additional infantry battalion that would arrive on or around September 11. But Kawaguchi had planned his attack for September 12, when there would be no moon. "It would not be advisable to postpone the day of attack to wait for reinforcements," he replied.[115] Kawaguchi did make several requests, including naval gunfire support, and air attacks on the airfield starting on September 9 and ending at sunset on September 12.

Some reinforcements were already in the pipeline, arriving the night of September 5. Five destroyers – *Yugure*, *Fubuki*, *Shirayuki*, *Amagiri*, and *Kagero* – landed 370 men and supplies at Taivu. The destroyers then proceeded to herd as many of Colonel Oka's survivors as they could to Kamimbo Bay. This latest reinforcement brought General

Kawaguchi up to about 6,200 men, more than enough to handle the Americans, he thought, believing the enemy numbered just 2,000.

The next day, however, brought heavy rain. The rain swelled the rivers and turned the few trails into ribbons of slippery, swallowing mud. Movement of the heavy guns slowed to a literal crawl. The troops were soaked, and, after barely a week, about half were already suffering from malaria and dysentery. Many were also enduring a fungal infection known as "crotch rot," a description of which is probably better left to the imagination.[116] Kawaguchi was forced to delay his attack one day to September 13.

The same rain that was taking a toll on General Kawaguchi and his troops also took a toll on the Marines. Eager to dish out some of what they had been taking from Base Air Force, 11 Cactus Air Force Dauntlesses took off to attack ships and shore installations at Gizo. The foul weather fouled the attack, which was almost completely ineffective. Worse, two Dauntlesses disappeared on the return leg.

But one pilot did return. Not one of the bomber pilots, but in fact one of the pilots of the three Wildcats that had disappeared a week earlier. In his tattered flight suit, 2nd Lieutenant Richard Amerine of Marine Fighting 224 had walked back 30 miles from Cape Esperance behind Japanese lines, having killed four Japanese and used his prewar entomology training to get his protein intake by eating nonpoisonous insects. His flight had turned foul because all their oxygen masks were badly leaking. At high altitude, Amerine had bailed before he lost consciousness due to hypoxia; presumably, the other pilots did not and their planes crashed.

There was some more good news. Despite the weather, the 6th Seebees completed a satellite airfield that was dubbed "Fighter 1" or, not quite as formally, the "Cow Pasture." It was not as advanced as Henderson Field proper – it was just dirt and had drainage issues – but it gave the Cactus Air Force some flexibility in dispersing its aircraft. And now it could launch fighters and bombers simultaneously.

And indeed at 4:00 pm Dauntlesses from the *Saratoga*'s Scouting 3 arrived from Espiritu Santo. So now based at Henderson were Dauntlesses from both the *Saratoga* and the *Enterprise*. Joining them the next day were four new Wildcats of Marine Fighting 223, led to Guadalcanal through more inclement weather by a friendly B-17 of the 11th Bombardment Group.

On September 7, General Kawaguchi moved his troops west from Tasimboko to Tetere. There he issued the plan of battle he had developed in Shortland to "route (sic) and annihilate the enemy in the vicinity of the Guadalcanal Island airfield."[117] It was, he believed, an improvement on Colonel Ichiki's simplistic approach. All Ichiki had done was land, march straight to the Marine positions, and launch a banzai charge. Bamboo spear tactics.

Kawaguchi would start with "tunneling through the jungle," as he called it, moving through the jungle screened from aerial eyes to a position just south of the airfield.[118] He believed the southern part of the American perimeter would be lightly defended, if at all. Colonel Oka's troops would position themselves to the west of the airfield. The Kuma

Battalion would position itself to the east. On the night of September 13, when all was set, then they would all launch a banzai charge.

But the general's mission took a greater level of urgency when at 11:00 pm he received a dispatch from the 17th Army, relaying a report from Tokyo that "a large enemy convoy with marines aboard arrived at the Fiji Islands on the 5th." The 17th Army asked General Kawaguchi how soon he could begin his attack. Kawaguchi answered September 12, maybe sooner if he made good progress through the jungle. Naturally, the 17th Army told Combined Fleet that the attack would begin September 11.[119]

General Kawaguchi and his troops set out before dawn the next day, September 8. As they did so, he saw American ships pass by, heading east. Where were they going? He got a hint later when he heard shooting and explosions. Were they attacking his supply base at Tasimboko? Maybe, but he was heading into the jungle now, leading a column almost 3 miles long, and could not turn around to take care of it.[120] The 300 troops he had left guarding it should be able to fend off the attack on their own.

Or so the general believed until a soldier ran from Tasimboko to make a panting report that the enemy had attacked the troops at the supply base and the defenders were outnumbered. He had run all this way to ask what they should do about it.

Kawaguchi was flabbergasted; this did not seem like a difficult question. "Confront the enemy," he ordered, probably with more than a hint of impatience.[121] Kawaguchi sent back one company of infantry and a machine-gun platoon to help.

Rabaul was alarmed by the news of the landing at Taivu. General Hyakutake did not need this. His Rabi attack had collapsed, and Admiral Matsuyama's light cruisers *Tenryu* and *Tatsuta* returned to Milne Bay on September 5 to rescue the naval infantry. Now he had this. Hyakutake ordered the New Guinea offensive suspended. General staff representatives on site thought General Kawaguchi should turn around to secure his rear, but Colonel Matsumoto successfully argued that the airfield was the real objective, whose capture or neutralization would make moot all other problems.[122]

In a near-panic, he informed Imperial General Headquarters that Kawaguchi's troops were now "sandwiched" between the American base at Lunga and American troops at Taivu.[123] In response, Tokyo alerted two battalions at Batavia in the East Indies to prepare to move quickly. The Army did not have nearly enough transport capacity, however, so the Navy sent the light cruisers *Isuzu* and *Kinu* to Tanjoeng Priok to escort a convoy carrying 780 troops of the 2nd Sendai Division and take them to the Solomons.[124] Additionally, Admiral Mikawa dispatched the light cruiser *Sendai* and managed to scrounge up eight destroyers – *Fubuki*, *Shirayuki*, *Yudachi*, *Kagero*, *Yugure*, *Uranami*, *Amagiri*, and *Shikinami* – all to go to Guadalcanal for a night bombardment in support of Kawaguchi.[125] More of the Aoba Detachment was embarked for transport to Guadalcanal. Base Air Force could not immediately help, as they had already launched their strike for the day directed at New Guinea, but they would rearm their G4Ms with torpedoes and attack later in the day.

All of which would have greatly amused the man responsible for the landing at Taivu: "Red Mike" Edson. Earlier, during the night of September 7, the 17th Army and the 8th Fleet sent the destroyers *Umikaze*, *Suzukaze*, and *Kawakaze* and the minelayer *Tsugaru* to drop off supplies and a battery of 75mm artillery from the Sendai Division.[126] This was apparently another "sneak landing," as no one had told General Kawaguchi or anyone in his command about it. However, this night there was no friendly fire incident and the reinforcement was completed successfully.

However, those American ships General Kawaguchi had glimpsed – the destroyer transports *Manley* and *McKean*, and the "yacht patrol" boats *YP-346* and *-298* – were carrying Lieutenant Colonel Edson's Raiders. General Vandegrift had been aware of a Japanese build up around him, but while his own intelligence told him the Japanese had landed just a few hundred troops, the native scouts were reporting the numbers were in the thousands. Edson had long argued for a hit-and-run raid befitting his Raiders; now one was a necessity to gain intelligence about the Japanese numbers. It would have been launched a few days earlier but for the sinking of the *Little* and *Gregory*. As it was, they were lucky the destroyers *Umikaze*, *Suzukaze*, and *Kawakaze* had missed them in the rain and thus had not repeated the *Little* and *Gregory* experience.

The loss of the *Little* and *Gregory* had not only delayed the raid, but forced the Marines to come in two waves, the Raiders first then the 1st Parachute Battalion. The Raiders stepped aboard the transports at Kukum, where Edson was handed another report stating the Japanese had as many as 3,000 troops. His Raiders could be outnumbered three-to-one. Edson shrugged it off and the flotilla got under way.[127]

Surprise was essential and the Americans did everything they could to avoid detection. But the Yippies just could not help themselves. The old fishing boats were noisy and not necessarily properly maintained, giving off red sparks from their stacks. Lieutenant Colonel Griffith commented, "[T]he Yippies announced their presence to all but the blind and deaf."[128]

Evidently, the Japanese were both. After some preliminary air attacks by two Wildcats and four Airacobras, the Raiders came ashore at Taivu Point at 5:20 or so and began moving inland just after dawn. They found the Japanese response puzzling. An antitank gun was on shore in perfect position – but it was unmanned. Many of the Japanese just stood around watching them. Maybe the Japanese had thought they were more unannounced reinforcements. Maybe the Japanese had seen something behind them – like the arriving cargo ships *Fuller* and *Bellatrix* pulling into Ironbottom Sound, escorted by destroyers *Hull*, *Hughes*, *Zane*, and *Hopkins*, and the destroyer-minesweeper *Southard*. This US convoy was only running supplies to Guadalcanal, but it gave the impression of a much larger landing instead of a mere raid.[129]

The Marines found two antitank guns, 37mm German models, abandoned. The Japanese appeared to have fled the beach area.[130] The Raiders moved on. Then they came under fire from an ancient "regimental" gun of 75mm caliber firing at point-blank range.[131] The Americans responded with some .30cal machine guns. The regimental guns were silenced and the Japanese fled again. The Raiders moved on again, following a trail of abandoned supplies. Resistance got tougher as the Marines approached Tasimboko, as the machine-gun company General Kawaguchi had sent back formed a fighting nucleus, but after a few strikes by Airacobras – the washout of a fighter was becoming an excellent ground support aircraft – the Japanese fled one last time and the Raiders entered Tasimboko.

And were stunned.

Tasimboko had become a Japanese base and supply depot. There were thousands of cans of food, mainly crab and sliced beef in soy sauce. Hundreds of bags of rice. Ammunition for machine guns, mortars, and artillery that totaled by one estimate some 500,000 rounds. Boxes stacked 10 feet high. A radio that the Raider communications officer said could reach Tokyo. Ten collapsible boats complete with motors. All told, two weeks of supplies for 6,000 troops.[132]

Not any more.

Lieutenant Colonel Edson wanted to take the captured supplies back, but there was simply no time and no room. The Raiders pocketed as many cans of sliced beef and crab as they could, while 50 Marines were ordered to bayonet the remainder of the thousands of cans. The hundreds of bags of rice were either dumped into Ironbottom Sound or spiced with urine or gasoline.[133] The big radio was completely destroyed. The captured artillery, including the two 37mm antitank guns and four 75mm guns, also of German manufacture, had their breech blocks removed and were redeployed to the bottom of Ironbottom Sound, where they were joined by shells with their fuses removed. The ammunition was destroyed except for 81mm mortar shells and ammunition for six captured machine guns, which were taken back with the Raiders.

Also going back with the Raiders were 21 cases of Japanese beer and 17 half-gallon jugs of *sake* as well as General Kawaguchi's white dress uniform. "The bastard must have been planning to shine in Sydney society," one Marine snorted.[134] Actually, Kawaguchi had been planning to wear it for the raising of the Rising Sun at Henderson Field. Instead, it was raised to the top of the masthead of the *Manley* as it headed back to Kukum.[135]

Meanwhile the Japanese engineers burrowed into increasingly dense jungle with machetes, swords, and bayonets. General Kawaguchi and his troops followed. For reasons known only to Kawaguchi, he had his troops split into four columns as they trekked through the dark jungle to their attack positions south and southeast of the airfield. Now the general learned that not all jungles are created equal, because Guadalcanal's jungle, in the words of historian Richard Frank, was like "compressing a spring – the longer you push, the harder it becomes."[136] Especially moving in the dark, as the Japanese were trying to do to avoid detection. The mud, the slime, the tangled undergrowth, the sharp, slashing vines, the hazardous roots, the steep hills, the treacherous ravines, the swollen creeks, the rotted trees, the rain, the sweat, the smell. Progress was slower than a crawl: at one point, the 1st Battalion of the 124th Infantry Regiment under Major Kokusho Yukichi was advancing one half-mile every two hours.[137] Kawaguchi and his men now truly understood that the jungles of Guadalcanal were a botanical hell.

General Kawaguchi was moving through this hell with only a hydrographic map of Guadalcanal's north coast and a compass that varied from 20 to 40 degrees off. "Thus we moved in a tremendous zigzag pattern and wasted a lot of time," Kawaguchi lamented.[138] His brigade headquarters column moved drunkenly, nearly ending up back on the coast. The other columns were not much better; on September 10, Kawaguchi's headquarters column, the Kuma Battalion, Major Kokusho's aforementioned 1st Battalion and the 2nd Battalion of the 4th Infantry Regiment under Major Tamura Masao all ran into each other. The Kuma made for Alligator Creek. The other three formed a column and continued on.[139] They occasionally heard dull booming sounds from the direction of the American positions, day and night. Encounters with Marine patrols were increasing. But there was some good news: a captured American aviator had revealed that, just as Kawaguchi had thought, the south side of the Lunga perimeter was weakly defended. Moreover, the Americans could not see Kawaguchi's troops under the jungle cover.[140]

Though they knew battle was coming, it was with some sense of relief that the hour of attack got close and the Kawaguchi Detachment neared the staging area, a hill some 3 miles south of the airfield.[141] The attack was to begin at 8:00 pm the following day, September 12, from three directions – Colonel Oka from the west, the Kuma Battalion from the east, and the main effort, General Kawaguchi's own, from the south. As the troops made their final preparations, he spoke to his company and platoon leaders. "You must put the enemy to rout and crush them by daybreak," the general said. "The time has come for you to give your lives for the Emperor."[142]

It was with such uplifting thoughts that, the next day, they heard more booming from the direction of the Marine positions. It was Base Air Force, attacking the Americans. North of the Solomons, the Combined Fleet was at sea, ready to prevent US Navy interference with General Kawaguchi's attack, and believing the airfield would soon be captured.

As the sun slid beneath the jungle to the west on September 12, General Kawaguchi's troops headed down the hill toward their attack positions. It was now that the general found out that there was a ridge between his troops and the airfield.[143] Located on the east bank of the Lunga River, this bare ridge had a weird shape, roughly north-south, or perpendicular to the airfield, with spurs jutting out from each side that gave it the appearance from overhead of a lizard or centipede.[144] It aimed like a dagger at his army. Curiously, Kawaguchi's hydrographic map of the north coast of Guadalcanal had not shown this ridge here. There was no time to go around it. He would simply have to attack over it.

The assault was to begin at 8:00 pm with three battalions swarming the tip of the ridge joined by a naval bombardment. The bombardment, from the indefatigable *Sendai* and destroyers *Shikinami*, *Fubuki*, and *Suzukaze*, came off without a hitch at 9:30, with General Kawaguchi's 3,000-odd troops still nowhere to be seen. Trying to hack their way through the jungle in the dark, the Japanese infantry had all gotten to their assembly areas late – in the case of the 3rd Battalion of the 124th Regiment under Lieutenant Colonel Watanabe

Kusukichi, two hours after the scheduled start of the attack. When Watanabe's and Major Kokusho's battalions attacked, they missed the ridge altogether and, while exchanging fire with Marines on top of the ridge, got bunched up in a swampy area between the ridge and the Lunga, where they became entangled with each other. Units got lost or intermingled. American artillery shells landing in their midst did not help things. By the time they got some sense of organization, it was too close to daylight to attack. Kawaguchi was furious. "Due to the devilish jungle, the brigade was scattered all over and was completely beyond control," he later wrote. "In my whole life I have never felt so helpless."[145] He had at least made contact with the American positions, however. Both Colonel Oka's troops and the Kuma Battalion had managed to miss them altogether in the dark.

Rabaul had heard very little radio chatter from the Americans and nothing from General Kawaguchi during the night. At 6:30 am Admiral Tsukahara had the Tainan Air Group send up two Nakajima J1N1 reconnaissance planes – known to the Allies as the "Irving" – under Lieutenant Hayashi Hideo, escorted by nine Zeros under Lieutenant Inano Kikuichi. One of the Irvings carried 17th Army staff officer Major Tanaka Koji, who was to determine if the airfield was now in Japanese hands and, if so, to land there to facilitate the staging in of the 6th Air Group. An air attack was also readied to strike suspected Marine positions at Taivu.

Approaching Guadalcanal, Lieutenant Hayashi saw Grumman Wildcat fighters aloft. Meanwhile, Lieutenant Inano saw several Wildcats gaining altitude and set up an ambush. So began a short aerial melee, which Hayashi missed while, first, Major Tanaka's plane, and then, ten minutes later, Hayashi's own plane each made a single pass over the airfield. Both reconnaissance planes radioed Rabaul, with Tanaka reporting he had seen 40 aircraft at the airfield and Hayashi reporting he had seen no aircraft at the airfield. These revealing reports cost the Tainan Air Group four Zeros and their pilots, including two more veterans.[146] Base Air Force made the safe, not to say obvious, conclusion that the Lunga airfield was still in enemy hands.

They had already reached the conclusion that Taivu was in enemy hands based on the September 8 landing, and that afternoon Vunakanau sent up 27 G4Ms from a mixed bag of air groups under Lieutenant Nakamura Tomoo of the Misawa Air Group to pound it, escorted by 12 Zeros. Expecting the Japanese to attack the airfield, 16 Grummans moved to meet them. As several Wildcats lashed at the Bettys and several more Wildcats were lashed by the Zeros, the Americans watched in bewilderment the bombers pass the airfield heading east. They saw the bombers dropping their bombs and assumed they were dumping their loads. Instead, the G4Ms were releasing their bombs over what they believed were enemy artillery positions on Taivu Point. For good measure, several of the Zeros went in and strafed the defending troops. None of the Japanese pilots noticed the white flag with the *hinomaru* the radioless troops at Taivu were desperately trying to display. No one had told Base Air Force that the Americans had left and the Japanese had reoccupied Taivu. One G4M was shot down, one more ditched. It was a high price to pay for bombing your own troops.

But it was not nearly the fiasco of the previous night, which was so bad that as noon arrived General Kawaguchi still did not even know where his own troops were, let alone the Marine positions. Nevertheless, Kawaguchi had to make preparations to attack and so issued his operational order with the attack scheduled to begin at 10:00 pm.[147] Kawaguchi spent much of the rest of the day trying to find and organize his scattered men into some form of coherent combat formation. Colonel Oka radioed asking for a delay in the attack so he could round some more of his own scattered troops, but Kawaguchi refused. The attack had been delayed long enough.

After dark arrived the Japanese started moving back to their attack positions. American artillery rounds landed in their midst to disrupt them. But last night would not be repeated.

"Banzai!"

"Totsugeki!"

General Kawaguchi's 3,000 men charged the ridge. And initially found nothing.

The Marine line on the ridge was much further back than General Kawaguchi had expected, forcing his troops to charge through open ground in the face of 105mm artillery and a brutal crossfire of .30cal machine guns backed by grenades.

Colonel Edson's earlier raid on Tasimboko had captured a treasure trove of Japanese documents. When he had returned on September 8, Edson went to report to the operations officer, Colonel Gerald Thomas. "This is no motley of Japs," Edson hissed, "but two or three thousand well-organized soldiers."[148] The captured documents were turned over to Captain Sherwood F. "Pappy" Moran, the 1st Marine Division's senior linguist, who spent much of the night translating them to the sounds of the cruiser *Sendai* and her destroyer attendants as they shelled Tulagi and sank the *YP-346*.

The next day Lieutenant Colonel Edson met with 1st Marine Division's operations staff. The various reports, captured documents, and aerial photographs were collated. Captain Moran said the captured documents confirmed there were several thousand Japanese on the island. Clemens' scouts reported a force of maybe 3,000 Japanese heading southwest from Tetere. This was corroboration – Edson, the documents, and the scouts. Colonel Thomas said it. "They're coming."[149]

But from where? Lieutenant Colonel Edson drew a forefinger, placed it on one of the aerial photographs of the Lunga area, and ran it along a ridge south of Henderson Field, with jungle on two sides, and the Lunga River on a third, while the fourth gently sloped down toward the runway. His analysis came in his normal soft, raspy voice. "This looks like a good approach."[150]

This brought up a longstanding disagreement between General Vandegrift and his staff. Though there were some 15,000 Marines on the island, there were not enough to maintain a continuous line around the perimeter. So the Marines created strong points guarding the beaches to the north and the coastal avenues to the east and west of the base. The staff thought the Marine defenses were facing the wrong way, that they should face the jungle to the south instead of the beach to the north. Vandegrift disagreed. He believed the Japanese would attack the same way they had earlier, along the coast. The jungle was virtually impenetrable and the Japanese would have to attack up that ridge.

So confident was Vandegrift that the Japanese would not attack on the ridge that, over the "profane" objectives of his staff, he was moving the division command post to the ridge. The old command post, which also served as his living quarters, was too close to the airfield and took more than a few stray bombs and loose shrapnel. Its nickname, "impact center," gave support to the general's argument, and he was tired of jumping in and out of bed every night. "I simply wanted a good night's sleep," Vandegrift later explained.[151]

Colonel Thomas and Lieutenant Colonel Edson strolled into the soon-to-be old command post. Unfolding a map, they announced to General Vandegrift that they knew where the Japanese would attack. "Where is that?" the general asked.[152]

Edson answered, "The ridge you insist on putting your new CP (command post) behind."[153]

General Vandegrift smiled gently. He had heard all their arguments on this issue before. He had rejected them before. And he rejected them now. The Japanese were going to attack along the coast, as they always did.

Colonel Thomas switched gears. The Raiders and Parachute battalions, having just completed the Tasimboko Raid after tough combat on Tulagi and Gavutu, needed a break. If this ridge was as safe as the general thought, perhaps it could serve as a "rest area" for these units. It could also discourage Japanese snipers and minor incursions. Vandegrift agreed.[154]

The morning of September 10, Lieutenant Colonel Edson announced to his Raiders and Parachutists, "Too much bombing and shelling here close to the beach. We're moving to a quiet spot." The troops were puzzled, since they found their present site in a coconut grove near Kukum quite quiet, but they started moseying the 1 mile south to the ridge.[155] The colonel smiled his famously humorless smile.

The Raiders' trek to the quiet spot was loudly interrupted by Base Air Force, who seemed to be stepping up its efforts of late. The previous day had seen 26 Bettys, escorted by the usual number of Zeros, go after shipping off Lunga, thinking it was the Tasimboko invasion force. It was an expensive mistake, for there was no invasion force, their bombs missed the shipping that was there, and they lost seven Bettys and three Zeros to the 16 Wildcats who scrambled to meet them. In turn, three Wildcats were shot down, with one pilot killed, one seriously wounded, and one, ace Captain Marion Carl, missing. A fourth Wildcat lost power on takeoff and spun into the ground, but the pilot was not seriously injured.[156] Today it was 27 Bettys and 15 Zeros who met five of the 11 Grummans who rose to meet them. Two of the bombers were shot down and a third forced to ditch, but for the loss of another Marine fighter ace, 2nd Lieutenant Zenneth Pond. This action left the Cactus Air Force with only 12 operational Marine Wildcats.[157]

Lieutenant Colonel Edson and his Raiders and Parachutists resumed their trudge to their rest area. Once they got there, Edson deployed them. Facing south, towards the jungle, he placed one company of the 1st Parachute on the left, with two more parachute companies lined up behind it and two companies of the 1st Raiders on the right, with three more raider companies lined up behind them. Across the ridge and in the jungle on the left and right, the latter was supported by the 1st Pioneer Battalion on the Lunga River. Edson had them dig foxholes, string barbed wire, and clear fields of fire of the annoying kunai grass.

Edson's men spent a quiet night on the ridge. The next morning they continued their preparations. There was no questioning why they needed to fortify a rest area and they continued their work even when they heard the siren.

The 1st Marine Division and the Cactus Air Force had a three-stage system of readiness: "Green," "Yellow," and "Red." "Green" meant remain calm, all is well. If a Japanese air attack was detected or suspected within an hour or so, "Yellow" alert would be declared, by which the four enlisted Marines who formed the "Pagoda Watch" raised a red flag, naturally, and cranked a siren. If everyone needed to take cover immediately, like for an imminent air attack or a bombardment, "Red" alert would be declared, in which the Pagoda Watch would raise a black flag, naturally, and sound the siren.[158] It worked for them. This time, the siren sounded and the black flag was up. Condition: Red.

It did not concern Edson or his men that much. The Japanese always bombed the airfield, now about a mile away. All 12 of the remaining Marine fighters that stood between Guadalcanal and the Japanese had scrambled. They had to engage 26 Bettys and 15 Zeros. But this time, something was different. The Japanese were not going after the airfield, they were going after the ridge.

Edson's ridge. Edson's rest area.

The Bettys dropped entire sticks of bombs, liberally mixed with the daisy cutters, on Edson's troops. Those who had taken their assignments to dig foxholes seriously and dove therein were left shaking but safe. Those who were caught in the open were killed or wounded.

The raid had cost the Japanese one Betty and one Zero, both shot down by Marine Fighting 224 skipper Major Galer, but the new Marine ace himself was forced to ditch his damaged fighter offshore and swim back. One Airacobra was destroyed on the ground, and Army Captain Brannon was so badly injured by a bomb he had to be flown out with two of his badly wounded pilots.[159] A total of 11 Americans were killed and 14 wounded.

Now the Cactus Air Force was down to 11 fighters against 51 the Japanese had at Rabaul.[160] And Lieutenant Colonel Edson's men now knew they'd been had. Far from being a rest area, this was going to be the target of a Japanese attack, an attack that was imminent.

"Some goddam rest area," a corporal grumbled. "Some goddam rest area!"[161]

While the Raiders were sorting themselves out, General Vandegrift had opened his new headquarters on the ridge. Lieutenant Colonel Twining called it "a beautiful spot for a dacha in the hills but hardly suitable for a command post."[162] It was here that the general took in two distinguished visitors: admirals Turner and McCain.

The general and the admirals had spent the air attack in the newly constructed dugout, but when the raid ended and they convened in the new command post, the mood was not nearly as pleasant. A visibly unsettled Admiral Turner silently handed a message to General Vandegrift. It was from Admiral Ghormley. As the Marine general perused the letter, the color drained from his face. He handed the letter to Colonel Thomas.

What is known is that the message contained Ghormley's assessment of the operational situation. Naval intelligence, likely including *Magic*, had determined a major Japanese offensive to retake Guadalcanal was imminent, as soon as ten days away. They were building up overwhelming naval, air, and ground forces at Rabaul and Truk for this effort. To stop this onslaught, Ghormley explained, he had not nearly enough resources. Not enough carriers. Not enough cruisers. Not enough destroyers. Not enough transports. Ghormley concluded he could no longer support the Marines on Guadalcanal. But, the admiral stated, he was not giving up. He was considering sending the 7th Marine Regiment to Guadalcanal to try to stop this offensive. Lieutenant Colonel Twining would later say there was a second, handwritten, personal note from the admiral to the general that essentially authorized him to surrender if it became necessary. If so, General Vandegrift and Colonel Thomas never acknowledged the letter, which has not been seen since.[163]

Admiral Turner then produced a bottle of Scotch and some glasses. "Vandegrift," he said, "I'm not inclined to take so pessimistic a view as Ghormley does." Turner was confident that he could successfully land the 7th Marine Regiment.

If General Vandegrift's mood was grim after reading the communication from Admiral Ghormley, it was certainly brightened late that afternoon. At 4:20 pm, 24 F4F Wildcats of Fighting 5 under Lieutenant Commander Leroy C. Simpler arrived, a contingent left behind by the *Saratoga*, to join the Cactus Air Force. Ghormley believed the carrier fighters were still under the command of Admiral Fletcher. Fletcher, still in nominal command at this point, had made Ghormley promise not to send them to Guadalcanal. Admiral Nimitz took a sword to his Gordian knot and transferred all the carrier aircraft "that could be spared" to Ghormley, who, for once, acted quickly and sent them up to Guadalcanal.[164]

The next day the new arrivals were forced to sink or swim. A false alarm at dawn was followed by coastwatcher warning, then radar confirmation, of the usual incoming strike by Base Air Force – 26 Bettys from the Kisarazu, Misawa, and Chitose air groups, escorted by 15 Zeros from the 2nd and 6th air groups. They were led by the Kisarazu's Lieutenant Nabeta Miyoshi, who had put a torpedo into the battleship *Prince of Wales* the previous December.[165] The Cactus Air Force scrambled 20 of the *Saratoga* fighters and a dozen of the Marines'.

The Wildcats got the warning slightly late and were not all at altitude when the Japanese arrived. But a wild air melee, joined by the radar-guided antiaircraft guns of the 3rd Defense Battalion, resulted nonetheless.[166] The Bettys' bombs demolished the main radio station and three Dauntlesses, and torched some gasoline. Base Air Force lost six G4Ms – their worst day since August 8 – and one Zero. No Wildcats were shot down, but two suffered heavy damage and one crashed during landing, killing the pilot.[167]

The Marines and Navy pilots on the ground watched in horror as the guns of Kawamura's Type 2 caught Lieutenant Johnson's SBD as it crossed in front of the floatplane on its landing vector. The Dauntless belched smoke and veered down to the left, crashing west of Henderson Field across the Lunga River where the 1st Amphibious Tractor Battalion was based and where the SBD's 500lb bomb exploded. There were no survivors.

There was little to be done. One vengeful Marine pilot climbed into a Wildcat to chase the float Zeros, but crashed on takeoff. The Rufes flew off without a scratch, arriving at Rekata at 6:10 pm.

The ambush was followed ten minutes later by a large formation of unidentified aircraft approaching at low altitude. There were still no fighters in the air, but the alerted men on the ground manned the heavy antiaircraft guns and trained them toward the approaching bogeys, while the Marines challenged them by radio.

At the last moment, they were identified. Lieutenant Commander Kirn was leading in 12 Dauntlesses of Scouting 3, while Lieutenant Larsen brought eight Avengers, all from the *Saratoga*.[176] No one had told Henderson Field to expect a reinforcement, but they were happy for any good surprise; any reinforcement was welcome, especially so soon after the ambush of Lieutenant Johnson. His was the second scout Dauntless lost on this day, the other disappearing at sea.

As the last light disappeared, the jungle to the south of the ridge "seemed to come alive."[177] At 6:30, apparently earlier than General Kawaguchi had planned, Major Kokusho, sword in hand, led his Japanese troops in bursting from the jungle...

"Banzai!"

"Totsugeki!"

... into the right side of the American line in the jungle west of the ridge. The Marines responded with grenades and machine-gun fire, but the Japanese forced them back. To prevent an encirclement, the Marines bent the line back, forming half of a horseshoe. Major Kokusho stopped to re-form his attack, only to see his men scattered by artillery. Once he was able to reorganize them and resume the march forward through the swamp between the ridge and the Lunga, he did not attack the Marines in their now unprotected right flank, but drove straight for the airfield. Until he and his men found a cache of rations. These soldiers, starving for almost a week, stopped to "gorge themselves" on Marine food.[178]

While this was going on, Louie the Louse made his first appearance of this night. He dropped a few bombs, and then, a little before 9:00 pm, a flare over the airfield. Everyone knew what that meant. The flare was a registration point for yet another naval bombardment, this time by seven destroyers *Yudachi, Uranami*, *Mirakumo*, *Kawakaze*, *Umikaze*, *Kagero*, and *Shirayuki*.[179] Most of their shells flew over the Marines and into the jungle beyond, where another attack was forming up.

A red rocket was shot up into the sky, and the rest of General Kawaguchi's 3,000 Japanese infantry charged forward against Lieutenant Colonel Edson's 800 Marines.

"Banzai!"

"Totsugeki!"

"Totsugeki" has a few too many syllables for a charge, and the Marines who heard it thought the Japanese were yelling "Gas attack!"[180] One company of Lieutenant Colonel Watanabe's battalion drove through the jungle, cutting off the Parachute company on the left. The Marines had to pull back, and now the left side of the line was bent backwards. The line was now a full horseshoe.

Major Tamura's battalion had the position of honor, if you could call it that: his men, with bayonets fixed, made a frontal charge up the ridge, through some 400 yards of open ground – the result of Lieutenant Colonel Edson's pullback – into the teeth of .30cal machine guns. Marine 105mm artillery rounds had pounded his staging area and perhaps compelled Tamura to attack earlier than he had planned.

Major Tamura's was only the first banzai charge of the night, but it set the pattern. The Japanese would thoughtfully shoot up a red flare, warning the Marines of an imminent banzai charge. Tamura's troops would charge. They would be cut down by machine-gun fire, grenades, and artillery. They would fall back and re-form. And it would start all over again.

The Japanese were suffering frightful casualties, but there were too many Japanese and not enough Marines. "There were so many of them that came over the ridge compared to what we had string out there," remembered one Marine. "You could shoot two and there would be six more."[181] Gradually, Lieutenant Colonel Edson's horseshoe was squeezed smaller and smaller.

Red Mike's presence was critical. One officer later commented, "[I]f there is such a thing as one man holding a battalion (plus the paratroopers) together, Edson did it that night. He stood just behind the front lines – stood, when most of us hugged the ground."[182] Standing just behind the line, he would challenge men who wavered, yelling, "the only difference between you and the Japs is they've got guts."[183] In this he was joined by Major Kenneth Bailey, who waved his pistol threatening to shoot anyone who left his post. Edson tried to round up every man he could find to augment his meager forces, bellowing, "Raiders, parachuters, engineers, artillerymen. I don't give a damn who you are. You're all Marines. Come up on this hill and fight!"[184] He would call down artillery barrages that were so close he and his own men were endangered. But there was no choice.

The Japanese had no counter to the Marine artillery, especially the 105mm howitzers. They tried mortar fire, but it was almost completely ineffective. Marines saw Major Tamura's men wrestle a 75mm "regimental" gun onto the ridge. The battle hung in the balance. This gun was critical, or would have been but for a faulty firing pin that rendered it useless.[185]

Nevertheless, the crush of Japanese numbers was having an effect. Edson had been pushed to his final defense position, the northernmost part of the ridge, within 1,000 yards of Henderson Field. His communication line to the division headquarters had been cut.

Fleet Admiral Ernest J. King, the driving force behind the Allied counteroffensive at Guadalcanal. (Naval History and Heritage Command)

Rear Admiral Richmond Kelly Turner, controversial architect of the invasion of Guadalcanal and Tulagi. (Naval History and Heritage Command)

Vice Admiral Frank J. Fletcher. His decision to withdraw the US carriers set in motion a chain of events that imperiled the Allied counteroffensive at Guadalcanal. (Naval History and Heritage Command)

Vice Admiral Robert F. Ghormley, commander of US Naval Forces in the South Pacific. His pessimistic take on the Guadalcanal offensive colored his tactical judgments. (Getty)

Japanese Vice Admiral Mikawa Gunichi, head of the 8th Fleet. He masterminded the attack at Savo Island, but failed to complete his mission to destroy the American transports. (Naval History and Heritage Command)

Admiral Kondo Nobutake commanded the Japanese battle fleet at Eastern Solomons and Santa Cruz. (Naval History and Heritage Command)

Rear Admiral Tanaka Raizo was the brilliant mastermind behind the "Tokyo Express," but his opinionated nature made him unpopular with colleagues and superiors. (Naval History and Heritage Command)

Japanese Vice Admiral Nagumo Chuichi, commander of the Carrier Striking Force *Kido Butai* at Pearl Harbor, Midway, Eastern Solomons, and Santa Cruz. (Naval History and Heritage Command)

The carrier *Enterprise* enters Pearl Harbor on May 26, 1942, shortly before the Battle of Midway. (Naval History and Heritage Command)

Scene on the flight deck of the carrier *Enterprise* on August 7, 1942, as she was supporting the first day of the Guadalcanal and Tulagi landings. (Naval History and Heritage Command)

The heavy cruiser USS *Quincy* in the glare of Japanese searchlights and sinking during the Battle of Savo Island, August 8, 1942. The flashes on the left are gunfire from the heavy cruiser USS *Vincennes*. Photograph probably taken from the Japanese heavy cruiser *Aoba*. (Naval History and Heritage Command)

The destroyer USS *Jarvis* sits off Guadalcanal damaged by Japanese air attack on August 8, 1942. Another victim of that attack, transport *George F. Elliott*, burns in the background. (Public Domain)

The view from the Japanese heavy cruiser *Chokai* during the Battle of Savo Island, August 9, 1942. The light is from parachute flares dropped by Japanese cruiser float planes. (Public Domain, Renga Kantui Fujo-su, KK Best Sellers)

HMAS *Canberra* after the Battle of Savo Island, August 9, 1942. She lists to starboard and is partially obscured by the destroyer *Blue*, tied up to port to the left of the image. On the right, approaching from astern, is the destroyer *Patterson*. (Naval History and Heritage Command)

USS *Enterprise* performing evasive maneuvers under heavy air attack on August 24, 1942. A fire is burning in the carrier's after 5-inch gun gallery, the result of a bomb hit. (Naval History and Heritage Command)

A Japanese Aichi D3A Type 99 "Val" carrier bomber, believed to be that of Petty Officer 2nd Class Iida Yoshihiro, disintegrates over the *Enterprise* after 20-mm gunfire set fire to its bomb, August 24, 1942. (Naval History and Heritage Command)

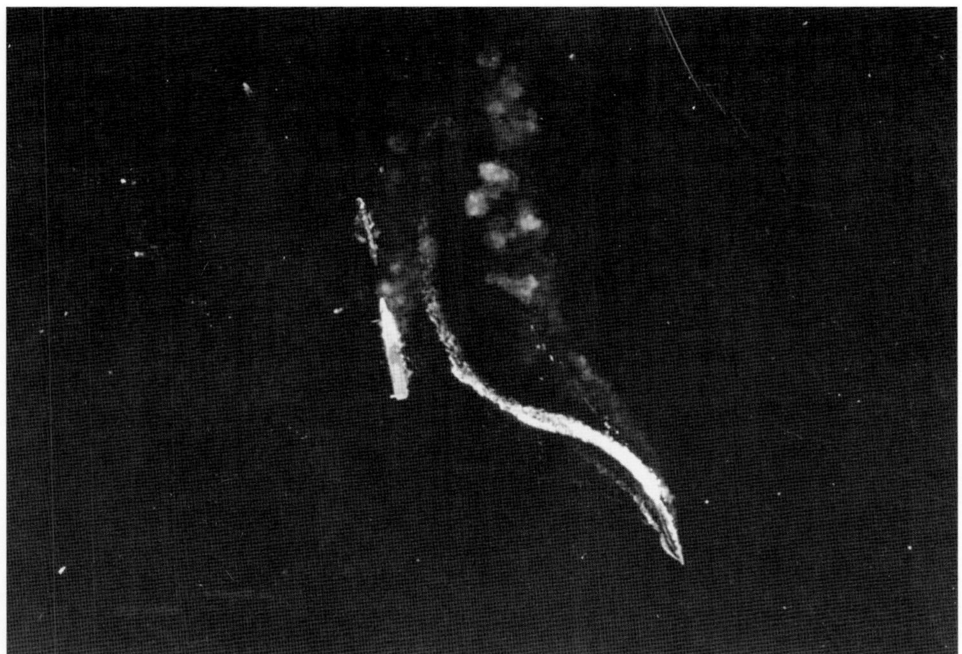

The disabled Japanese carrier *Ryujo* (center) under high-level attack by B-17s of the 11th Bombardment Group, August 24, 1942. The destroyer *Amatsukaze* (lower right) is getting under way, and the destroyer *Tokitsukaze* (top center) is backing away from the carrier's bow. (Naval History and Heritage Command)

Henderson Field, Guadalcanal, photographed from a plane from USS *Saratoga* (CV-3) in the latter part of August 1942, after US aircraft had begun to use the airfield. The view looks about northwest, with the Lunga River running across the upper portion of the image. Iron Bottom Sound is just out of view at the top. Several planes are parked to the left, and numerous bomb and shell craters are visible. (Naval History and Heritage Command)

The blazing carrier USS *Wasp* after she was struck by torpedoes from the Japanese submarine *I-19*, September 15, 1942. (Library of Congress)

US destroyer *O'Brien* (right) is hit by a torpedo from the Japanese submarine *I-19*. In the distance at left is the burning carrier *Wasp*, also torpedoed by *I-19*. (Naval History and Heritage Command)

Grumman F4F Wildcat fighters of Marine Fighting 121 at Henderson Field, Guadalcanal, 1942. In the background is a Lockheed P-38 Lightning. (US Navy National Naval Aviation Museum)

Grumman F4F Wildcat fighters parked at Henderson Field, Guadalcanal, 1942. (Naval History and Heritage Command)

Allied nemesis: the Japanese A6M2 Model 21 Type 0 Carrier Fighter, called "Zero" or "Zeke," prepares to launch from the carrier *Shokaku* on the morning of October 26, 1942, during the Battle of the Santa Cruz Islands. The drop tank is visible beneath the fuselage. (Naval History and Heritage Command)

The US Navy's primary carrier weapon, the Douglas SBD Dauntless dive bomber, flies over the carrier *Enterprise* (foreground) and Saratoga (background). The censor has scratched out the Enterprise's radar package atop her mast. (US Navy National Naval Aviation Museum)

The Japanese aircraft carrier *Zuikaku* (shown here) and sister *Shokaku* were Allied nemeses throughout the war. (Naval History and Heritage Command)

Heavy antiaircraft fire greeted the Japanese attackers off the Santa Cruz Islands on October 26, 1942. At left is the *Enterprise*, the main focus of the Japanese attacks. In the distance at right is the battleship *South Dakota*, firing her starboard 5-inch battery in an antiaircraft capacity. (Naval History and Heritage Command)

The carrier *Hornet* under attack off the Santa Cruz Islands on October 26. An antiaircraft shell has just exploded, spraying shrapnel off the carrier's starboard side. At center is a Nakajima B5N Type 97 "Kate" carrier attack plane, withdrawing after dropping its torpedo. Top center is a burning Aichi D3A Type 99 "Val" carrier bomber piloted by Warrant Officer Sato Shigeyuki, who was likely dead or wounded by this time. (Naval History and Heritage Command)

MAIN The "Val" piloted by Sato Shigeyuki slams into *Hornet*'s island superstructure and explodes, spewing burning fuel everywhere. Sato's bomb did not explode. (Naval History and Heritage Command)

INSET LEFT The heavy cruiser *Northampton* attempts to tow the disabled *Hornet*. (Naval History and Heritage Command)

Weird Japanese heavy cruiser/seaplane carrier thing *Chikuma* under an American dive-bombing attack during the Battle of the Santa Cruz Islands, October 26, 1942. A bomb has just hit the port side of the bridge, which is giving off the smoke at center. (Naval History and Heritage Command)

After a new wire had been run at around 2:30 am, Edson called Colonel Thomas. "My losses have been heavy. I need more men."[186]

General Vandegrift got on the line. "Can you hold?"

"We can hold," Edson replied, but he needed more ammunition and more men. Thomas started feeding in the companies of the reserve 2nd Battalion of the 5th Marines.[187] The Marines' ammunition was just about gone at around 3:00, forcing Major Bailey to crawl on his hands and knees under fire on the ridge to resupply the men.

The Japanese attacks were weakening. Once they had satiated their enormous hunger, Major Kokusho's battalion had charged the ridge, where the major was killed. Three Japanese companies had worked their way through to the edge of the field that contained the Fighter 1 airstrip. But they had no support and were quickly driven out. One Japanese officer actually broke through to Vandegrift's headquarters, startling the general with shouts of "Banzai!" and throwing his sword like a javelin to impale a gunnery sergeant. Division Sergeant Major Shepherd Banta, who was at that moment dressing down a clerk, turned and killed the Japanese officer with one shot from his pistol, then promptly returned to berating the clerk.[188]

Dawn brought an end to the main attacks, the back of the Japanese offensive broken. For all of General Kawaguchi's hopes for the flank attacks on the Marine perimeter to mislead the Americans, they accomplished nothing. Both Colonel Oka's and the Kuma Battalions' attacks were thrown back with heavy losses. Though there was sniper fire and isolated firefights, Edson's men still held the ridge, which would be renamed in his honor. And Henderson Field was safe. For now.

But the ridge was a gruesome sight. Total Japanese losses are difficult to determine, but by one estimate more than 800 Imperial Japanese Army officers and men were killed, with 505 wounded.

The Marines suffered 104 killed and 278 wounded.[189] It was a victory against the odds, a proud moment for the US Marine Corps, if not for the commander on Guadalcanal, General Vandegrift, who had committed one of his few misjudgments of the war.

But it continued the pattern of Japanese misjudgments, especially those by the Imperial Japanese Army. Arrogance, overconfidence, sloppiness.

"The Army," said one of Admiral Yamamoto's staff officers, "had been used to fighting the Chinese Army."[190]

The Marines on Guadalcanal needed reinforcement, because elsewhere in the South Pacific American forces were being nibbled at the edges, and not just by the Japanese.

With the Japanese operation at Milne Bay in full swing, General MacArthur had understandably asked for naval reinforcements. Admiral King agreed to have Admiral Nimitz order Admiral Ghormley to send back to the general the heavy cruiser HMAS

Australia and light cruisers HMAS *Hobart* and USS *Phoenix*, and six destroyers of Admiral Crutchley's reconstituted Task Force 44. Ghormley protested, but the ships were sent back in early September.

Less understandably, General MacArthur asked for one regiment of "experienced amphibious troops" complete with shipping with which to move them.[191] At the direction of the joint chiefs, Admiral Nimitz ordered Admiral Ghormley to prepare to turn over a regiment meeting these qualifications to MacArthur. An appalled Ghormley suspected MacArthur was trying to get the 7th Marine Regiment, which was en route from Samoa to the South Pacific Command area, where it was badly needed. Turner pointed out that the 7th Marines had been garrisoning Samoa for months and were thus not ready for immediate amphibious warfare. He took the chance to second General Vandegrift's repeated requests for one more regiment for Guadalcanal. Nimitz backed off, but he gave Ghormley no precise instructions as to what to do, so the South Pacific commander had to keep the forces available for transfer.[192]

With Admiral Noyes set to take over for Admiral Fletcher as carrier force commander, Admiral Ghormley met with Noyes in Nouméa on September 3. Ghormley was obsessed about the right flank of the South Pacific operating area – Espiritu Santo, Fiji, Samoa. Worried about submarines, he told Noyes that unless "promising targets" appeared, he wanted the carriers kept east of the Ndeni-Espiritu Santo line, roughly 166 degrees east. He later added he wanted the carriers kept south of the line of 12 degrees south.[193] This was well away from the Solomons, meaning no carrier support for the Marines on Guadalcanal.

Admiral Murray on the *Hornet* chafed under these restrictive orders that essentially amounted to abandoning the Marines. So, he made a sweep toward the southern Solomons, and by September 6 Murray had plunged 250 miles west of Admiral Ghormley's limit and within 75 miles of the Russell Islands south of Guadalcanal. Finding nothing, he turned the *Hornet* back toward Espiritu Santo.

Just before 1:00 pm, Ensign John Cresto, one of three Torpedo 3 Avengers on antisubmarine patrol, saw what he thought was a submarine conning tower between the plane guard destroyers and the battleship *North Carolina*. He dropped a 325lb depth charge. It wasn't a submarine, but torpedoes. The shockwave of his depth charge detonated two of the torpedoes, while the *Hornet* turned hard to port and the *North Carolina* hard to starboard to avoid a third.

Two hours later the destroyer *Russell* made a sound contact with the Japanese submarine *I-11*, skippered by Commander Shichiji Tsuneo, who had fired four quick torpedoes when he caught the *Hornet* passing by at a ludicrously close range of 765 yards. The submarine's sound gear picked up the detonations and Shichiji assumed they had sunk the carrier. Quite possibly, Ensign Cristo's quick thinking had saved the *Hornet*.

Only Commander Shichiji's quick thinking would save the *I-11*. The *Russell* hit the boat with six punishing depth charges that knocked out most of her batteries and started a leak near the stern. But Shichiji was able to nurse his boat back to Truk.[194]

Now Admiral Murray had to nurse his reputation. He had willfully violated Admiral Ghormley's order and, in essence, proven his point. He had to report the submarine contact, but in so doing Murray went on the offensive, calling Ghormley's operating order too restrictive and asking that the *Hornet* be permitted to operate within 300 miles of Guadalcanal and southeast of the island as necessary. Murray's case was not helped on September 7, when, at around 5:30 pm, a patrol of four Wildcats under the command of Lieutenant John F. "Jock" Sutherland strafed a submerging submarine near the task force. Ghormley was "astounded" that Murray had violated his order and "invited" Murray's attention to his order and suggested he move the *Hornet* east of the boundary.[195] It was the most backbone Ghormley would show during the entire campaign.

The *Hornet* crossed the sacred line of 166 degrees east near sundown on September 8 and sat down to refuel and wait for Admiral Noyes and the *Wasp*. While Admiral Murray had to deal with Ghormley, Noyes had to deal with the temperamental Admiral Turner as the *Wasp* escorted the transport *McCawley* northward. Turner flashed a draft operations plan for conveying the 7th Marines to Guadalcanal. His plan included two additional fighter and two additional scout bomber squadrons for Guadalcanal, and if Admiral McCain could not provide them, "presumably the carriers will help." Turner also wanted a constant antisubmarine patrol off Malaita-San Cristobal and carrier attacks on enemy forces threatening the reinforcement convoy. Noyes said it was impossible to provide the aircraft and he would not box his carriers in to provide the antisubmarine protection. In a blistering response to this refusal, Turner tore into the mild-mannered Noyes before taking his *McCawley* and her escorting New Zealand cruiser *Leander* off to Espiritu Santo, leaving a befuddled Noyes to take the *Wasp* up to join the *Hornet*.[196]

Noyes, now commanding both carriers, had far more dangerous issues with which to contend than Turner. Intelligence had estimated that the Combined Fleet was positioning Admiral Nagumo's carriers of *Kido Butai* and Admiral Kondo's Advance Force to resume the counteroffensive for Guadalcanal. As the sun rose on September 13, pilots of the *Hornet* ferried those 18 badly needed Wildcats to Guadalcanal. Then Noyes had the carriers race to the east toward Santa Cruz to keep that all-important flanking position and be prepared to strike.

Ghormley implemented Admiral Turner's plan for moving the 7th Marine Regiment to Guadalcanal, and at 5:15 on September 14, Turner took his normal flagship transport *McCawley* plus the transports *Crescent City*, *President Adams*, *President Hayes*, *President Jackson*, and *Alchiba*. The 7th Marines were finally going to join the fight. So important was this convoy that it would have its own screen: the new Task Force 64 under Rear Admiral Carleton Wright. Just created – "about a month late," grumbled Admiral King – Task Force 64 was to perform screening, escort, and attack functions, and it could always run errands.[197] It would consist of whatever cruisers and destroyers they could find lying around. For this mission, it consisted of the flagship heavy cruiser *Minneapolis*, light cruisers USS *Boise* and HMNZS *Leander*, and more than a dozen destroyers and minesweepers.

Admiral Turner had his ships head east to avoid Japanese aerial reconnaissance and get some semblance of protection from the *Wasp* and *Hornet*. The only problem was that Turner's course took him and the carriers into the same area where the *Saratoga* had been torpedoed a few weeks earlier. The Japanese had figured out some time ago that the sea routes from Espiritu Santo to Guadalcanal all passed through the same relatively small stretch of water, and had stationed a picket line of submarines along this route. The continued sightings of and attacks by Japanese submarines had already earned the stretch the moniker "Torpedo Junction." But there was little choice. If you wanted to supply Guadalcanal you had to go through Torpedo Junction.

Admiral Noyes had more on his mind than submarines, because he and the Combined Fleet were performing their own version of the *danse macabre* that would be repeated many times over the course of the campaign. The Americans would advance, the Japanese would pull back; then the Japanese would advance and the Americans would pull back. The distance between them remained much the same, and they couldn't quite come to grips with each other.

These few days were typical of the *danse macabre*. At around 11:00 am on September 13, a PBY out of Espiritu Santo reported two Japanese cruisers near Santa Cruz. Thinking it might be a major fleet element, Admiral Noyes raced toward it to launch an airstrike. But follow-ups found no cruisers. Meanwhile, at 11:10 am Special Duty Lieutenant (jg) Mizukura Kiyoshi, commanding one of the new Kawanishi H8K Type 2 "Emily" flying boats of the 14th Air Group, reported one of the American carriers. Now the Japanese raced toward the Americans, but the *Wasp* and *Hornet* pulled back out of strike range.[198]

The next day it was the reverse. Admiral Noyes was trying to keep the carriers positioned between Admiral Turner's convoy and the Japanese. At 10:45, a PBY commanded by Lieutenant Glen E. Hoffman reported four battleships and seven carriers 325 miles north-northwest of the *Wasp* and *Hornet* and closing. Did the Japanese even have seven aircraft carriers? No matter. Despite apparently being badly outnumbered, Admiral Noyes decided to launch an airstrike on this force to protect the transports. At 11:40, Hoffman issued an unsurprising correction to his earlier report, the contacts now being three battleships, four cruisers, four destroyers, and one transport. Hoffman had found Admiral Kondo's Advance Force, northwest of Santa Cruz, probing for the American carrier reported the previous day.[199]

Another report came in from a Catalina just before noon: a Japanese carrier, along with three cruisers and four destroyers. Lieutenant (jg) Baxter E. Moore, commanding this Catalina out of Espiritu Santo, had found Admiral Nagumo's *Kido Butai*. But he would not live to tell about it. Horrified listeners in the radio rooms of Admiral Noyes' ships heard Moore declare, "We're going down in flames." Neither he nor his crew were ever heard from again. Six Zeros from the *Shokaku* had found and destroyed the PBY.[200]

Noyes sent up an airstrike at 1:15 pm to deal with this obviously grave threat. Then, more than two hours later, the seaplane tender *Curtiss* relayed an update from Lieutenant Hoffman: now it was the Japanese who were heading away. Their own searches had found nothing and Admiral Kondo was heading north to refuel. The American airstrike returned having found nothing. The only attack that day was in the late afternoon by ten Flying Fortresses of the 11th Bombardment Group out of Espiritu Santo, who managed to nick the cruiser *Myoko* with a near miss.[201] Would the dance of death resume the next day?

The morning of September 15 found the two US carriers staying about 100 miles north of Admiral Turner's convoy. Knowing *Kido Butai* was on the prowl, Turner was edgy, waiting for developments to decide if he would continue toward Guadalcanal. An otherwise quiet morning ended when a Japanese Mavis flying boat, this one commanded by veteran Lieutenant Yoneyama Shigeru of the Toko Air Group, had spotted the reinforcement at about 11:05 am. Four *Wasp* Wildcats had been vectored to check it out, and one piloted by Lieutenant (jg) John McBrayer sent the Mavis down in flames. The Japanese were now onto them, Turner thought. The situation in his view was "not reassuring."[202]

Kido Butai and Pearl Harbor had not yet taught the US Navy the lesson of grouping its carriers for mutual protection and mass aircraft formations. According to American practice the two carriers were steaming in separate task forces, with Admiral Noyes' *Wasp* some 7 to 10 miles from Admiral Murray's *Hornet*. Both were heading southeast to conduct flight operations, which had just concluded. While they were still fueling and arming aircraft, at 2:42 pm they all began turning right to a base course of 280 degrees True – west-northwest – to resume the journey to Guadalcanal about 250 miles away.

Guarding the convoy was vital. But it was also a tedious job, a dangerous job, because they were steaming right through the dark heart of Torpedo Junction. Sonar contacts occurred at least every day. Making things worse, in the eyes of some sailors, was that the *Wasp* in particular seemed to be following predictable, straight-line courses.

"Every day at the same time we were at the same place going at the same speed on the same course," recalled *Wasp* radioman Lieutenant Leonard Gross. "We were making bets when something was going to happen."[203]

But hopefully not today. Today, it was a beautiful day. Bright, sunny. You could see for miles and miles. A little windy, though, with a 20-knot wind from the east-southeast. It made flight operations easier but also created whitecaps on the sea.

For the lookouts keeping watch over the sea, whitecaps were like static on a TV that obscured the true picture. It was easier to spot something on the water by its wake or the contrast between it and the blueness of the water. Whitecaps broke everything up, creating perpetual motion that made it difficult to see anything. Even seeing the white wakes of the escorting ships could be a chore, though it was much easier than seeing wakes where you didn't expect them.

On the bridge of the heavy cruiser *Pensacola*, Ben Blee, the officer of the deck, was not watching the whitecaps as his ship held station escorting the *Hornet*. He was watching the *Wasp* through his binoculars some 12,000 yards away. Something about the *Wasp* was bugging him. He saw smoke, quite a lot of it, rising from the carrier, from the side away from him, the starboard side. Blee also saw several aircraft floating past the *Wasp*'s stern into her wake. Must have been an aircraft accident, he thought, with those aircraft pushed over the side to eliminate fire hazards. Not a big deal; happens all the time. That the carrier had sent no message explaining it supported this view.

Still … that was an awful lot of smoke. As Blee continued to watch and wonder, the smoke kept coming, got worse, even. Explosions followed. The *Wasp* had never completed her turn and was still headed southeast. Yet she said nothing.[204]

Then the *Pensacola* picked up a frantic, frightening, but frustratingly fragmentary radio report, "… torpedo headed for formation, course zero-eight-zero!" What formation? Who sent this message?

Shortly thereafter came another message just as frantic, just as frightening, and just as fragmentary: "… torpedo just passed astern of me, headed for you!" It was followed by inaudible crosstalk on the radio.

The destroyer *Mustin*, in the *Hornet*'s screen, finally provided some clarity by hoisting the signal flag from her yardarm: "Torpedo." The task force had just settled on their new course of 280 degrees True when at 2:51 the *Hornet*'s loudspeakers blared with the boatswain's whistle, the bugle, and the call "General Quarters! All hands man your battle stations."[205] A few thought they felt a dull crash, like a torpedo hitting a distant target. Several men running to their posts recalled hearing an officer say, "The *Wasp* got three fish in her."[206]

The *Hornet* had to get aircraft in the air. Now. Since the *Wasp* was the duty carrier for the day and now looked like she could no longer handle it, the *Hornet* had to provide air cover for herself. She also had to clear space for the returning aircraft from the *Wasp* to land. On the bridge Captain Charles P. Mason rang up 30 knots and "Hard right rudder!" then "Now hard left rudder!," hoping the traditional method of zigzagging could throw off the enemy aim.[207] As heartless as it might sound, the *Hornet* had to protect herself, getting as far away as possible from the *Wasp* and whatever had brought her to grief. It was most probably a submarine, and a submarine could not move quickly while submerged. Seeing his charge's maneuvers, Captain George H. Fort of the *North Carolina* barked, "Right full rudder! Emergency flank speed!"[208]

In the *Hornet*'s air plot, Lieutenant Commander Francis Foley, the air operations officer, was looking out off the port beam toward the *Wasp* when he saw the destroyer *O'Brien*, 2,000 yards away, disappear in a giant geyser of water and smoke. Foley's assistant nonchalantly said "Scratch one Small Boy," and crossed out the destroyer's name on a blackboard of all the nearby screening vessels and their positions. Prematurely, as it turned out, since the *O'Brien* quickly reappeared, *sans* her bow. Foley was appalled. The little destroyer had taken a torpedo that would otherwise have hit the *Hornet*.

Before Foley had time to contemplate more than that, he felt a concussion from off the *Hornet*'s port quarter. The battleship *North Carolina* was still turning, just passing 295 degrees True, when a torpedo smacked her on the port side underneath the Number 1 turret, sending another plume of water, smoke, oil, and debris shooting up as high as her tower mast. As the water came crashing back down onto her deck, one crewman was washed over the side. The *North Carolina* took a 5-degree list, but shrugged off the hit, continuing to build up speed and keeping her station in the screen.

The messages started coming in to Admiral Murray on the flag bridge. The *O'Brien* signaled "Torpedo hit forward. CPO quarters destroyed … casualties. Can make 15 knots. Request permission to remain in company." Then came the battleship. "Large hole well below waterline. Five known dead. Damage under control. Can make 25 knots."[209]

Every man on the *Hornet* who could look astern did, watching in "dry-mouthed horror" as the *Wasp* drunkenly staggered in an apparent effort to get the wind to blow off the port quarter the huge pall of inky black smoke that was smothering her. At 3:09 they watched as "the most terrible flash they had ever seen" engulfed the *Wasp*'s island, blowing men into the air, into the sea, and sending another column of smoke billowing upward like a volcano. They saw what looked like flashes of gunfire coming from the doomed carrier; they were her aircraft and ammunition exploding. They saw sheets of flame around the *Wasp*'s waterline and in her wake – burning fuel on the water.

The men kept watching as some now homeless *Wasp* SBDs approached the *Hornet*. One dropped a message: "*Wasp* burning fiercely forward of island. Ten degree list to starboard (guess). 100 men or more aft on ft. deck. Destroyer close aboard. Eight *Wasp* planes due land 16:20. *Wasp* dead in water or just barely backing down. Ammunition on deck exploding."[210] What had caused all *this*? Multiple submarines, they were guessing. Had to be, one submarine couldn't do all *this*.

As the *Wasp* receded in the distance astern, in her mortal agony she presented a terrible and yet transfixing sight. The men of the *Hornet* were mesmerized, clustered in tight, small groups. Their jaws clenched. Watching their friend die. Just before the *Wasp* disappeared over the horizon, one officer handed his binoculars to a friend and muttered, "Take your last look at the *Wasp*."[211] Paying their respects. Vowing revenge. They would never forget the sunny, surreal afternoon of September 15, 1942.

What precisely happened to the *Wasp* has never been fully determined. The Japanese submarine *I-19* skippered by Lieutenant Commander Kinashi Takakazu had spent much of the morning tracking sound contacts. At 1:50 pm, he finally made visual contact, using his periscope, with the sources of the noise: one carrier, one heavy cruiser, and several destroyers, bearing 45 degrees True – northeast – distance 9 miles. Kinashi estimated the carrier was heading northwest. They were a long way away, but they were zigzagging, so maybe they would zig toward a good firing position for him.

They did better than that. At 2:20 pm, the force turned southeast to conduct flight operations. The carrier was headed almost straight for him. This was almost too good to be true. The *I-19* didn't need to move. Making no noise, the *I-19* would be almost impossible to detect before Kinashi could strike, unless the destroyers were running active sonar.

Kinashi estimated that the carrier was on course 130 degrees True – southeast – at 12 knots. He set for a gyro angle of 50 degrees starboard. And at 2:45, Kinashi launched a spread of what were much later determined to be six Type 95 oxygen-propelled torpedoes with a slightly diverging spread at the ludicrously close range of 985 yards.[212]

On the *Wasp*, Lieutenant Gross was making an entry in the carrier's war diary. To buy himself the time to do so, he played a classical concert over the ship's loudspeakers. Ensign John Jenks Mitchell had finished working in the *Wasp*'s starboard forward gun gallery in front of the island in brilliant sunshine paired with the somber tones of Franz Schubert's *Unfinished Symphony*. Mitchell was starting to head below when one of his gunners asked him, "Mr Mitchell, what's 'at funny-looking thing out there?" Mitchell turned to look. And saw it coming right at him.[213]

"I shouted an alarm in a voice that may be described as similar to a thrilled tenor," Mitchell later said.[214]

"TORPEDOES!!!"

Another call came at 2:45 from a lookout in the *Wasp*'s tripod mast.[215] Admiral Noyes' head swiveled to see, off the starboard bow, three torpedo wakes, barely a football field away. Still ascending; these had come from very close by. Next to the admiral, a mortified Ensign C. G. Durr pronounced in resignation, "These have got us."[216]

By the time gunnery officer Lieutenant Commander George Knuepfer, also standing watch in the tripod mast, saw the torpedoes, they were only 50 yards away. He shouted "Torpedoes! Hard left rudder!" Captain Forrest Sherman belayed that order, shouting for right full rudder.[217] The desperate hope was that the *Wasp* could still comb the wakes.

Answering in the negative were "two water spouts rearing high above the superstructure; smoke and flame bursting out amidships," in the words of *Wasp* fighter pilot Ensign Millard "Red" Thrash, who, high overhead flying air cover, watched in shock as the torpedoes struck.[218] The first torpedo stung the *Wasp* near the bow, cracking tanks holding volatile aviation fuel deep within the ship and flooding the forward powder magazines.

The concussion and explosion knocked out power in the forward part of the ship, whipsawed the tripod mast, left the *Unfinished Symphony* even more unfinished, and threw Ensign Mitchell 30 feet into the air, landing 60 feet away at the feet of Captain Sherman on the bridge's wing. Mitchell broke his leg, but, claimed his crewmates, he set a new world record for distance thrown by an explosion and surviving. "The record for a survivor in the last war," Mitchell recalled, "was believed to have been thirty feet high and a few feet away."[219]

The second torpedo pierced the hull aft of the first, just in front of the island, cracking open even more aviation gasoline tanks and flooding the forward bomb magazines. Some 20 seconds after the two torpedoes hit came a third explosion amidships, its source unclear. Some believe it was a third torpedo that had broached and struck the carrier at or above the waterline. Others believe that it was a detonation of gasoline vapors after only 20 seconds. In any event, the *Wasp* rocked and reeled, immediately developing a 15-degree list to starboard before coming back a bit to 11 degrees. The carrier also developed what is known as a bow trim, down 10 to 12 feet at the bow.[220]

Below decks were filled with the stench of aviation gasoline. The torpedoes had hit the aviation fuel stowage. Burning gasoline leaked from the ruptured tanks and pipes through the lower levels of the carrier and spilled into the ocean beyond, forming a sheet of fire around the carrier. Even worse, the aircraft fueling system had been active. Normally, when combat is expected, the system is drained and filled with carbon dioxide. But combat had not been expected, and the system was engaged to fuel some Wildcats on the flight deck.

There were also 16 aircraft – 12 Wildcats and four Dauntlesses – fully armed and fueled on the hangar deck forward of the Number 2 elevator waiting to be moved to the flight deck. Even with or aft of the elevator were ten Avengers armed but not fueled and six Dauntlesses armed and fueled. Suspended from the hangar overhead were four spare Wildcats, two forward and two aft.

Not anymore. The concussion from the torpedo hits jarred at least two fighters loose from their overhead brackets, sending them crashing to the deck or on top of people, with fatal results, or on top of other parked aircraft, smashing them to pieces and cracking open their own volatile fuel tanks. The remaining aircraft were bodily lifted by the shock to come crashing back to the deck, crushing their landing gear, rupturing their fuel tanks and releasing more volatile fuel, which promptly caught fire. In some areas, the fuel coming out of the outlets and leaks in the ruptured fuel lines was already burning, like flamethrowers.[221] According to Lieutenant Gross, "It was violent. The hangar deck was a wall of fire."[222]

In short, the *Wasp* was like the Japanese carriers at Midway: caught with her hangar deck full of armed and fueled aircraft. The damage control team in the forward part of the ship was not responding; they had been killed when the torpedo struck or shortly thereafter.[223] The forecastle was almost cut off by fire, trapping Lieutenant Gross and some 50 others and forcing them to abandon the ship. The central station for handling damage control lost power and had to be abandoned due to fumes and flooding.[224] Brave men rushed into the hangar deck to fight the rapidly spreading conflagration there, only to find their path blocked by a twisted, tangled mess of burning aircraft wreckage that could not be moved.

Worst of all, when they broke out the fire hoses, the water only dribbled out of the nozzles. They had no water pressure. The men stood around confused and dumbfounded. For all practical purposes, they had to fight the fires with no water.

All this despite the fact that her engines and machinery were still fully operational and, through some quick transferring of water and fuel loads, her starboard list had been reduced to 4 degrees and her reserve buoyancy meant there was no immediate danger of sinking. Even so, the situation was, as Admiral Turner might have said, "not reassuring."

For reasons that soon became apparent. Some three to five minutes after the initial hits, there was a fuel vapor explosion from deep within the ship, the area of the second and third decks between the island and the Number 2 elevator. The blast sent smoke and flames up the bomb elevator to the hangar deck and the flight deck, billowing around the island. A much bigger blast occurred in the same area at 3:05 pm that engulfed the island in flaming gases. Admiral Noyes was leaving the bridge and beginning to climb down a ladder when the explosion threw him forward onto the signal bridge, with his shirt, hair, and ears burned. The bridge area had to be abandoned. A quad 1.1-inch mount was blown off its base, with 20mm and 1.1-inch ammunition now cooking off.

A third detonation came at 3:10, this one coming amidships in the neighborhood of the Number 2 elevator. It sent up another column, with debris blown as much as 150 feet into the air. The elevator itself was physically lifted, to come crashing back down across its original opening, very much the worse for wear. The fire burned through the flight deck on its starboard edge forward of the island, as 5-inch ammunition in the starboard gun gallery above the first hit started cooking off. So did the 5-inch ammunition in the port-side gun gallery. The explosions and fire had destroyed the bulkhead between the hangar deck and the forward part of the ship, allowing the fire to cross the ship completely. The forward part of the carrier was an absolute inferno.

Captain Sherman described the *Wasp* as "pretty well shattered from number 2 elevator well down and forward at least to the splinter deck."[225] He turned the *Wasp* to try to get the wind to blow the smoke and flames away from the undamaged parts of the ship. She presented a gruesome sight. As seen by the distraught Ensign Thrash overhead, "Clouds of bright red fire erupted from both sides below the flight deck, billowing out 200 yards, leaving black smoke streamers and scattering little pools of fire on the water. Sprays of red, yellow, and green Very lights shot out like Roman candles."[226]

The *Wasp*'s escorts – cruisers *Salt Lake City* and *Helena*; and destroyers *Lansdowne*, *Duncan*, *Farenholt*, *Lardner*, and *Laffey* – tried to help. They came in and circled the carrier to prevent further attacks. Unfortunately, the destroyers could not use their fire hoses as all of the *Wasp*'s fires were internal, some deep within the carrier. The torpedo holes in the starboard side were leaking flaming gasoline on top of the water. Despite Captain Sherman's best efforts to escape the flaming fuel on the sea, the carrier just took it with her. Then there were the explosions, which threatened not just the *Wasp* but any ship alongside.

At 3:20 pm, Captain Sherman ordered the *Wasp* abandoned. The order shocked the men in the engine rooms, who had stayed at their posts and saw little evidence of the carrier's mortal injuries. But they shut down the engine rooms all the same and made their way topside for a second shock when they saw the virtual firestorm the *Wasp* had become. It took about 40 minutes to get the entire crew off the ship. As was tradition, Sherman himself was the last to leave the ship, immediately after Admiral Noyes.

It had taken barely a half-hour for a modern warship to be turned into a Pacific pyre. These afternoon events left everyone in both task forces stunned, though none even remotely as much as the men of the *Wasp*. Their home was now exploding "like a fourth of July bonfire: fuel, ordnance, planes, everything."[227] The fighters overhead, including that of Ensign Thrash, headed to the *Hornet* to protect her. They could not resist sneaking one last look at their home in its death throes. Not that they could see. As Thrash later explained, "My last view of the flat-top was blurred with tears."[228]

Many of the *Wasp*'s crew were in tears; others were simply dazed, unable to fathom what had happened so quickly to them. Unfortunately, tears and introspection were luxuries the Pacific Fleet could ill afford right now. The *Wasp* now put the other US ships in danger, as her gigantic smoke pall and illuminating fire threatened to act as a beacon for Japanese ships, aircraft, and submarines. The fires continued spreading aft, and at 5:47 there was a massive explosion from below the after flight deck, according to the destroyer *Lansdowne*. As the heavy cruiser *Salt Lake City* recorded it, "Tremendous explosions, huge column of white smoke (or steam) above carrier," resulting three minutes later in "much black smoke, list to starboard about 15–20 degrees, series of small explosions." The *Helena* also noted an extreme volume of smoke coming from the *Wasp*'s stern as a result of this explosion, and, along with the *Salt Lake City*, recorded two more detonations on the convulsing carrier at 5:57 and 5:58.[229]

Admiral Noyes, now aboard the destroyer *Duncan*, radioed, "*Lansdowne*, remain with the *Wasp*. Sink her with your torpedoes. Do not leave her until she has sunk."[230] The *Lansdowne* had picked up 41 officers and 406 men from the *Wasp*, including much of the carrier's engineering team. The assistant chief engineer confronted the *Lansdowne*'s skipper, Lieutenant Commander William R. Smedberg III, saying, "Sir, I secured the engineering plant of that ship and there's no fire aft or amidships of the ship. I think we can go back on board. I can get that ship under way and we can get that fire out."[231] Did he know something the other *Wasp* survivors did not?

Lieutenant Commander Smedberg gave this information to Admiral Noyes and requested permission to take the engineer and his men back to the carrier and to take the *Wasp* in tow. Evidently unimpressed, Admiral Noyes was adamant: "[S]ink her."[232] This was to be the first time the *Lansdowne* fired armed torpedoes. Smedberg called his torpedo officer to the bridge so they together could read the instructions for launching torpedoes.[233] It was apparently considered bad form to read the instructions for launching torpedoes until one had to actually launch them.

These torpedoes were supposed to be wonder weapons. The destroyers used the Mark 15, which in turn used the Mark 6 detonator. The Mark 6 included a contact exploder and a magnetic influence feature. This feature was intended to cause the torpedo to detonate when it entered a ship's magnetic field, which was, in theory, under it. The explosion was supposed to fracture the unarmored bottom of the ship, snapping the keel, and causing the ship to break in half. The magnetic influence feature was so secret that, of the men on board the *Lansdowne,* only Lieutenant Commander Smedberg and the torpedo officer knew about it.

Smedberg told his torpedo officer, "Set it for 15 feet under the keel." As *Wasp* survivors watched in dismay, at 7:08 pm, the *Lansdowne* fired a single torpedo at the carrier from a distance of 1,000 yards. As Smedberg described it, the torpedo, set for a depth of 30 feet, "made a perfect flight down to the middle of the carrier, and nothing happened."

This wonder weapon was certainly living up to the wonder part of the equation. "Set it at keel depth," Smedberg ordered. The *Lansdowne* crept closer to about 800 yards and fired. It "went right under the middle of the ship, and we never heard a sound. Nothing happened."

"Can you make that magnetic exploder inoperative?" a suitably impressed Lieutenant Commander Smedberg asked his torpedo officer. "Can you get rid of it? Obviously it isn't working." Deactivating the magnetic influence feature of the Mark 6 was a violation of current standing orders, but Smedberg was smart enough to know what was important and otherwise.

So was his torpedo officer, who with his men deactivated the magnetic influence feature. "We'll fire these set at ten feet," Smedberg said. The third torpedo detonated exactly where it was supposed to on the *Wasp*'s starboard side underneath the island near the original torpedo hits. Smedberg could at least stop wondering about the Mark 6 exploder. However, the torpedo hit had no obvious effect on the listing carrier.

It was already going down in the history books as a legendary performance for the Mark 15 torpedo and its Mark 6 exploder. The *Lansdowne* launched a fourth torpedo. It caused a large explosion on the starboard side. That was still not enough to sink the carrier, leaving the *Lansdowne* down to her last torpedo. Smedberg maneuvered the destroyer to the opposite side of the carrier and launched. Finally, at 8:15 pm the torpedo blew a hole into exactly what it was supposed to – the now- exposed unarmored bottom of the badly listing ship. Smedberg edged the destroyer away from the slowly sinking carrier, zigzagging to try to throw off the aim of the submarine that was out there gunning for him, he guessed – correctly; it was the *I-15*. But he kept the burning carrier in sight until, after almost two hours of work, the *Wasp* went bow first to her grave at 9:00 pm.

Much of this Japanese submarine attack of September 15, 1942 was blurred, due to several mysteries that were not solved for decades, if at all. One mystery concerns how many torpedoes hit the *Wasp* – two or three? Captain Sherman reported, "The third torpedo broached and then submerged but was close to the surface when it hit 50 to 75 feet forward of the bridge." The US Navy Bureau of Ships disagreed:

> About 20 seconds after the torpedoes struck, a third explosion – somewhat less severe – was felt. This was reported by the Commanding Officer to have been a torpedo, but it is believed to have been of internal origin inasmuch as the flight deck cover to bomb elevator A-423-ET was blown violently upward and flames appeared in the shaft.[234]

The question may seem largely academic – and largely unanswerable – except to the extent it relates to a second mystery: the number of submarines involved in the attack. When the *Wasp* was hit by two or three torpedoes, a fourth was seen to pass the carrier's bow. Shortly thereafter, the light cruiser *Helena*, off the carrier's port bow, sighted a torpedo passing astern, estimating its course at 60 degrees True – east-northeast. At 2:48, the destroyer *Landsdowne*, while turning to starboard, saw a torpedo pass under her, bow to stern, also heading 60 degrees True. She estimated it came from bearing 240 degrees True – southwest. The *Landsdowne* radioed a warning, which was the first one picked up by the *Pensacola*, but it was garbled enough that it lost the identification and misunderstood the course as 80 degrees True. Two minutes later the destroyer *Mustin*, far off the *Hornet*'s port bow, saw a wake off the port bow coming from an estimated 240 degrees True. The wake was seen passing 30 feet astern, indicating the torpedo had passed under her. She hoisted warning flags and radioed an alert, the second one picked up by the *Pensacola*. One minute after that, the *O'Brien* had to turn hard to starboard to avoid a torpedo that just missed astern; she was unable to avoid a second.[235]

Initially, it was believed that the *I-19* had hit the *Wasp* while the *I-15* had hit the *O'Brien* and *North Carolina*. This belief was based on a misidentification of the torpedo by the US Navy and the improbability – albeit not the impossibility – of a torpedo from the *I-19* missing the *Wasp* still having the range to reach the *Hornet* task force.

But after four decades and some painstaking research and tracking by the aforementioned Ben Blee of the *Pensacola*, it was determined that the *Landsdowne* and *Mustin* saw the same torpedo, one that ultimately hit the *North Carolina*. Tracked back to its source, this torpedo was originally intended for the *Wasp*, but missed either astern or under. The torpedo seen by the *Helena* was one that was either seen by or struck the *O'Brien*. Again, tracked back to its source, this torpedo was intended to hit the *Wasp*, but missed ahead.

All of these torpedoes came from the same source: Lieutenant Commander Kinashi Takakazu's *I-19*, even though Kinashi had no idea the *Hornet* task force was tucked in behind the *Wasp* group or that the vectors of his torpedoes would carry them there. His Type 95s had the range – barely – because when Kinashi launched his target was almost on top of him, less than 1,000 yards away. The torpedo that hit the *North Carolina* was at the very end of its run.[236]

The *I-19*'s attack was a confluence of skill, superior equipment, and incredible luck, resulting in perhaps the most devastating submarine attack ever launched against the US Navy. Even American observers, when the true origin of the attack was revealed, could only admit, "Well played." As Ben Blee himself said, "Lucky or not, this incredible accomplishment by the *I-19* ranks among the all-time record successes of submarine warfare in any navy. Captain Kinashi, I salute you!"[237]

The attack would have been still worth the salute, but not nearly as devastating if not for the third mystery: what caused the complete lack of water pressure in the *Wasp*'s firefighting and fire suppression systems that made fighting the carrier's fires impossible?

This was indeed a serious question for US Navy investigators, who summarized that the carrier had "an excellent fire main system, hangar sprinkling and water curtain systems." The Navy postulated, not unreasonably so, that the torpedo hits in the forward part of the *Wasp* ruptured the fire mains located there. That damage is what caused the lack of water pressure in the fire main system.[238] What Navy investigators found harder to understand was why the damaged part of the system was not isolated so that the amidships and aft sections of the water main system could continue functioning.[239] Without explicitly saying it, the Navy report implied the reason was human error.[240] One wonders, however, if the assistant engineer who approached Lieutenant Commander Smedberg on the *Lansdowne* and asked to reboard the *Wasp* to put out the fire had figured out the issues with isolating the damaged water mains.

Torpedoed along with the *Wasp* was the career of Rear Admiral Leigh Noyes. If Admiral King was respected but not liked, Noyes was the opposite – liked but not respected. Admiral King described Noyes as "mild and meticulous," but "Everyone knew he had trouble making decisions."[241] Lieutenant (jg) Thomas R. Weschler, a junior officer of the deck on the *Wasp*, found Noyes to be "tentative and unsure of himself."[242]

It was perhaps for that reason Admiral Noyes had leaned heavily on the *Wasp*'s Captain Sherman, who served as his de facto chief of staff. "I thought Admiral Leigh Noyes did not have the big picture," opined Lieutenant Weschler, "and that Captain Sherman was really the one who was carrying him."[243]

In more ways than one, it would seem. In the wake of the *Wasp* disaster, Admiral Ghormley wondered what exactly the *Wasp* was doing there guarding Admiral Turner's transports, since they could have been protected, he believed, by land-based air power alone. Ghormley went on to criticize Admiral Noyes for basically the same reason Lieutenant Gross did – crossing and recrossing the same course track multiple times. Noyes and Captain Sherman defended themselves vigorously, pointing out that the attack took place "150 miles from the nearest point of crossing an old track, and in an area which had not been entered or approached previously."[244]

But a further issue was in play, underlying why Torpedo Junction had in fact become Torpedo Junction. West of a certain line, command authority changed from Admiral Ghormley's South Pacific Command to General MacArthur's Southwest Pacific Command, the creation of which had created a firestorm of its own. Admiral Noyes interpreted his orders from admirals Nimitz and Ghormley to mean he could not cross that line; given his mild-mannered, non-confrontational personality, Noyes probably did not want to cross that line and possibly create a political incident. In fact, Admiral Nimitz intended no such restriction and had no problem whatsoever with Noyes intruding on MacArthur's zone.[245] This was another instance in which the lack of a unified command, due entirely to the political machinations of Douglas MacArthur and his allies, carried a material cost.

The loss of the *Wasp* stung a Pacific Fleet that had still yet to recover from the disabling of the *Enterprise* and *Saratoga*. Going down with the carrier were 46 aircraft – 24 Wildcats, 11 Dauntlesses, ten Avengers, and one Grumman J2F Duck amphibious biplane. The 25 *Wasp* aircraft in the air at the time of the attack – eight Wildcats and 17 Dauntlesses – landed on the *Hornet*.[246]

For the next month the *Hornet* would be the only operational US aircraft carrier in the Pacific.

And for now, Admiral Turner was very much alone. He had six slow, unarmed ships bearing badly needed troops and supplies for the Marines on Guadalcanal. His heaviest escorting ship was a single heavy cruiser. And he had just been stripped of his aerial protection. He and his ships were exceedingly vulnerable. Turner had them head back to the southeast.

But not for long. Kelly Turner was unquestionably courageous. He would make the tough decision; he would put himself in harm's way. At 3:00 pm on September 16, he turned the convoy toward Guadalcanal, risking a Japanese attack.[247] But Combined Fleet doctrine gave warships much higher priority for submarine attack than supply ships and the *Wasp* had just drawn the submarine attack. One can argue the *Wasp*'s sacrifice helped save the convoy.

Just before dawn on September 18, Admiral Turner and the convoy arrived safely in Lunga Roads. The 4,262 men of the 7th Marine Regiment and their supporting artillery from the 1st Battalion of the 11th Marines made an orderly entrance to Guadalcanal. They were joined by cargo ships *Macfarland*, *Tracy*, and *Bellatrix* bringing in emergency shipments of aviation fuel.[248]

It was a highly efficient unloading. The convoy put ashore 3,823 drums of fuel, 147 vehicles, 1,012 tons of rations, 82.5 percent of the organizational equipment, and nearly all of the ammunition, the first ammunition shipment to Guadalcanal since the invasion. Lieutenant Colonel Twining called it "undreamed-of wealth."[249]

For good measure, six Grumman Avengers formerly of the *Saratoga* came in to reinforce the Cactus Air Force. For entertainment, destroyers *Monssen* and *Macdonough* turned their 5-inch guns onto Japanese positions near Kokumbona, to the cheers of the Marines at Lunga. After perhaps the second-happiest day in the history of *Watchtower*, Turner's ships left in the early evening, taking with them 162 American wounded, eight Japanese prisoners, and the battered remnants of the 1st Parachute Battalion.[250]

Word of the 7th Marines' arrival on Guadalcanal quickly made its way to Rabaul. Base Air Force responded by launching an air attack, but bad weather turned the Mitsubishis back. The ubiquitous *Sendai* was sent down with destroyers *Shirayuki*, *Murakumo*, *Uranami*, and *Hamakaze*.[251] They arrived that night to find nothing, so perhaps out of boredom as much as anything else they exchanged fire with the Marine coast defense batteries at Lunga, with minimal damage to both sides.[252]

As they did so, destroyers *Arashi*, *Umikaze*, *Kawakaze*, and *Suzukaze* landed 170 men, four "regimental" guns, and supplies at Kamimbo. But now the Japanese faced a much different picture than just 24 hours earlier, with 19,200 Marines defending Henderson Field.

Never had the US Marines defending Guadalcanal been so strong.

And never had the US Navy defending Guadalcanal been so weak.

In Imperial Japanese Army dress uniform, Tsuji Masanobu stepped aboard the giant battleship *Yamato*, the flagship of the Imperial Japanese Navy's Combined Fleet.

He had been sent from Rabaul. On his shoulders rested the future of the Guadalcanal operation.

It had not been a good two weeks in Rabaul. The arrival of the rest of the 6th Air Attack Force – 26th Air Flotilla – ended Base Air Force's dark days at the end of

August when it was so low on fighters it had to borrow 30 of them from *Kido Butai*. All 15 of the remaining carrier fighters returned to their carriers on September 4.

This idea of two going out and only one coming back was becoming a pattern. General Hyakutake's Milne Bay operation had been a disaster, costing the Navy perfectly good if older naval infantry and leaving a detachment of the Special Naval Landing Force troops stranded on Goodenough Island. Admiral Mikawa sent out the destroyers *Isokaze* and *Yayoi* to retrieve them, but only the *Isokaze* came back, with the survivors of the *Yayoi*, who, just east of Normanby Island on September 11, had been disabled by a bomb hit from Boeing B-17s and Lockheed Hudsons and wracked with near misses that sent her to the depths.[253] Now came more bad news from Guadalcanal.

The defeat of General Kawaguchi's force brought a tectonic shift in Rabaul, which for once had nothing to do with its resident volcanoes, that resonated all the way to Tokyo. The first reaction was shock. The Americans had defeated the Imperial Japanese Army *again*? Can they do that? It was followed by another round of finger-pointing.

General Hyakutake decided to take command of the operation personally. He planned to bring artillery – field guns, 105mm howitzers, 150mm howitzers – and more troops, including the 2nd Sendai Division. This resulted in another series of arguments with the Navy.

The Navy insisted on transporting the Sendai division by its normal method of using destroyers. This was not acceptable to General Hyakutake because it meant transporting little in the way of supplies and almost no artillery, certainly not the big howitzers the Army wanted. Moreover, with not enough destroyers available, the troops would be transported in a piecemeal fashion. No, Hyakutake wanted transports. A large convoy, with a powerful escort of surface ships, to send in the Sendai Division and its artillery in one go. The Navy said it did not have the ships for that. "How can we shake a sleeve we don't have?" the Navy argued.[254]

Finally, General Hyakutake – vain and short-tempered as he was – bellowed, "If the Navy lacks the strength to escort the 2nd Division properly to Guadalcanal, we will go in transports without any escort. And 17th Army headquarters will lead the way!"[255]

However, Colonel Tsuji, who had been plucked from Guadalcanal after the Kawaguchi attack and taken back to Rabaul, was also quietly watching the conference. He now felt forced to intervene. Tsuji had a better understanding of the conditions there – the jungle, the lack of food, the American air power – than his superiors did.

Colonel Tsuji pulled General Hyakutake aside. Taking transports to Guadalcanal without protection against American air power was suicide, Tsuji knew. Let me fly up to Truk, Tsuji asked, so he could present Hyakutake's case to Admiral Yamamoto. The general agreed.

This he did on September 24. He was momentarily awestruck by the size of the *Yamato*. It was indeed the biggest, most powerful battleship in the world, as it was meant to be. But it never went out to fight. The flagship of the Combined Fleet had thus acquired the unflattering nickname "*Yamato* Hotel." Tsuji could see why.[256]

But his awe passed quickly. Not easily intimidated, certainly not by rank, Colonel Tsuji briefed chief of staff Admiral Ugaki and senior staff officer Captain Kuroshima Kameto as to his purpose, then the colonel was escorted to Yamamoto's cabin.[257]

The sight that greeted Colonel Tsuji, at least as he told it, did little to suggest a war going on. He found the admiral behind the attack on Pearl Harbor, commander of the Combined Fleet, sitting on the floor of his state room, writing *haiku*.

Colonel Tsuji went into his presentation, describing what he had seen, what the men had done, on Guadalcanal. Admiral Yamamoto listened quietly, occasionally nodding. "Our supply has been cut off for more than a month," Tsuji said. "Officers and men have to dig grass roots, scrape moss and pick buds from the trees, and drink sea water to survive."[258]

The next reinforcement must be transported at one time – troops and supplies – or else it would fail like the Ichiki and Kawaguchi attacks had failed. Colonel Tsuji finished his argument. "I beg you to provide it with a strong escort. If the Navy finds it impossible to do this, then Army Commander Hyakutake is determined to lead the convoy himself and is prepared to be wiped out in his attempt to retake the island."

Admiral Yamamoto responded, speaking slowly, as he often did in these situations. "If army men have been starving through lack of supplies, then the navy should be ashamed of itself." Tears rimmed his eyes. "Very well – I'll give you cover even if I have to bring the *Yamato* alongside Guadalcanal myself."

The war for Guadalcanal and the Solomons was about to get much, much bigger.

CHAPTER 7
"WHY NOT?"

On September 7, 1942, an older officer walked into the St Francis Hotel in San Francisco.[1]

What made it strange was his uniform. He was wearing an officer's cap with the crest of the US Navy, but it was like no Navy uniform the people around there had seen. It was like a khaki service dress uniform, except it was gray. Charcoal gray pants and jacket. Lighter gray shirt. Black tie. Gray shoulderboards with black stripes of rank. Charcoal gray hat.

It certainly matched the personality of the man who wore it: Admiral Ernest J. King, commander-in-chief of the US Fleet and chief of naval operations. He had personally designed this uniform which he was modeling this day, as he disliked the khaki service uniforms that had originally been issued, believing the color was more appropriate for land bases.

But the gray uniform was generally disliked in the Navy. And it was loathed by the man with whom Admiral King was meeting: Admiral Chester Nimitz, the blue-and-gold Navy service dress-wearing commander-in-chief of the Pacific Fleet.

Today was the start of one of their periodic conferences, this one of three days. The first day was filled with senior personnel matters. King had brought with him Admiral Halsey, finally cured of his lengthy bout of dermatitis and aching to return to the fight. Nimitz was happy to have Halsey take over his old command, the *Enterprise* task force, once again.

There was also a bit of musical chairs. Admiral King was eager to get rid of Rear Admiral John H. Towers, the chief of the Bureau of Aeronautics. Towers had accepted an offer from King to become the commander of the Air Force of the Pacific Fleet, which did not make Admiral Nimitz happy. The current commander, Rear Admiral Aubrey Fitch, was going to move to command the land-based air in the South Pacific, while the current commander there, Admiral McCain, who was close to King, would go to Washington to replace Towers. Everyone clearly still had a seat.

Admirals King and Nimitz, with their respective staffs, then went over the South Pacific situation. They took a close look at the disaster at Savo Island, especially the lack of intelligence, alertness, readiness, and flag officers, and the deployment. This led to other issues. "Calculated risks," or more accurately, lack of the same, a term Nimitz had used in his orders to Admiral Fletcher before Midway. "Inopportune fueling," another reference to Fletcher, for which he was now infamous. "Mixing forces." "Lack of coordination of operations." The new cruiser-destroyer attack and screening force designated Task Force 64 was created around this time – "about a month late," grumbled King.[2]

The common denominator was Vice Admiral Robert Ghormley, the commander of US forces in the South Pacific. Admiral King had soured on Ghormley after the South Pacific commander had joined with General MacArthur in that July memo predicting the Guadalcanal campaign would fail. And Ghormley had done nothing to improve that opinion. Now King asked Nimitz about Ghormley's state. How was he holding up physically and mentally? What was the state of his command and control of the South Pacific forces?

For his part, Admiral Nimitz was wondering about Admiral Ghormley himself. On September 7, the South Pacific commander had sent a missive to his superior Nimitz that read more like a session with a psychologist:

> I have to spill this to somebody so I am afraid you will have to be the goat, but I hope you will burn this after it is read.[3]

He didn't. Ghormley went on to complain that he wasn't getting the support he needed in the South Pacific, and wondered if Admiral King really understood what was happening. He went on to say that the carrier situation was "precarious" and then gave the following explanation of why he could not achieve anything:

> Some people are probably saying why don't I send surface forces to Guadalcanal in strength at night. The simple reason is, it is too dangerous to suffer possible loss under the present conditions where they have submarines, motor torpedo boats, surface forces and shore based aircraft to aid them in restricted waters.

To Nimitz this would simply have raised more questions. There were no reports of motor torpedo reports and Ghormley was seemingly not taking into account that there was US land-based air available for protection.

But perhaps the most disconcerting statement concerned Ghormley's view of his authority:

> A recent dispatch from Washington told me of several ships that had P-38s on board, but they have never given me authority to divert a ship. I do not want that authority, for in diverting a ship in order to get an airplane, I might divert the very ship that had the critical ammunition in order to tide over a tough situation in Australia.

Most commanders want more authority, stretching the bounds of their current authority in order to complete their objectives. Ghormley was doing the exact opposite, as if he didn't trust himself with it.

With this in mind, Admiral Nimitz told King he would check on how the South Pacific commander was doing.

Nimitz also spent time wrestling with Undersecretary of the Navy James Forrestal, who handled procurement, over the Pacific Fleet's constant shortage of oilers. Forrestal managed to wrangle the additional oilers Nimitz needed. The conference concluded shortly thereafter.

After giving his staff a free day in San Francisco, Nimitz, Admiral Halsey, and the staff flew back to Pearl Harbor. On September 12, Nimitz and Halsey went aboard the *Enterprise*, who had just arrived after Eastern Solomons to repair her battle damage. Nimitz was to award battle decorations.

Admiral Halsey had traditionally commanded the *Enterprise* task force. He had sailed the carrier into Pearl Harbor on December 8, 1941, when he and his crew saw the devastation first-hand. He had commanded it for the mission to take Jimmy Doolittle's B-25s to bomb Tokyo. The only reason Halsey had not commanded the *Enterprise* at Midway and after was because of the annoying dermatitis.

The men knew him well. Halsey's outgoing personality made him a natural leader. His aggression and contempt for the Japanese aggressors early in the war buoyed the spirits of his men. Widely regarded as the Pacific Fleet's top carrier commander and certainly its most popular, Halsey was a breed apart from Admiral Fletcher. Fletcher did everything by the book; Halsey didn't even have a library card.

With the men all lined up on deck, Admiral Nimitz stepped to the microphone. He waved for Admiral Halsey, who had been kept hidden, to step forward. "Boys, I've got a surprise for you. Bill Halsey's back!"

There was a moment of shocked silence as the words sank in. Then, wrote Foster Hailey of the *New York Times*, "officers and men alike forgot decorum and yelled and cheered and whistled until they were hoarse."[4]

Admiral Halsey's eyes welled.[5]

Tears were not restricted to Americans.

On the hill where he had led the Japanese attack on what would be called Edson's Ridge and what he called "Bald Mountain," the battered, bloodied General Kawaguchi, his uniform in shreds, looked toward the battlefield, bowed his head, and clasped his hands in a prayer for the fallen.[6] There were a lot of fallen on that ridge, the vast majority Japanese, and Kawaguchi knew it.

The reports he had received during the night battle had been horrific. "Battalion commander killed; battalion completely annihilated; whereabouts of the battalion commander not known."[7] A head count had revealed only some 800 effectives remaining, mostly from Colonel Watanabe's battalion.

General Kawaguchi went to find out why. "This powerful battalion," Kawaguchi remembered, "which I had counted on most, was thus completely mismanaged. When I heard of this, I could not help shedding tears of disappointment, anger, and regret."[8]

He sent for Colonel Watanabe to get an explanation. But Kawaguchi gave the colonel no chance. As Watanabe approached, Kawaguchi was enraged. "Coward," he shouted. "Commit *hara-kiri*!"[9]

But the general relented when he saw Watanabe's condition. The colonel could hardly stand, let alone walk. Watanabe explained the transit through the jungle had injured his feet and he could not lead his troops.[10] Before the battle Watanabe had taken his adjutant and two orderlies with him to go find General Kawaguchi. Unable to find the general, Watanabe headed back for his unit, except he got lost in the jungle. Then they were pinned down by American artillery, which Watanabe was unable to escape because his old war wound from Manchuria acted up so he could not move quickly.[11] He was unable to contact his unit to turn over command, so except for one company, his battalion basically just sat there during the battle and did nothing.

Kawaguchi still had to get his remaining men out of the combat zone. And it was most certainly still a combat zone. The last three flyable Airacobras of the 67th had strafed the Japanese troops. Heavy ground fire perforated two and forced them to return to the airfield, where a very busy September 14 for the Cactus Air Force, though still trying to clean up after the Battle of Edson's Ridge, was about to begin.

Two R4Ds had landed at Henderson Field, bringing in supplies and taking out wounded and captured equipment. One had already taken off when Donald Kennedy on New Georgia had sent warning of an approaching Japanese airstrike. Later, at 9:21, came another warning, this from Geoffrey Kuper on Santa Ysabel, of three aircraft going southeast. That was unusual.

The second R4D had hardly raised its landing gear when it found itself in the sights of a float Zero, one of three from the *Kamikawa Maru* operating out of Rekata Bay on Santa Ysabel that R-Area Air Force had sent on a mission to determine the status of the airfield. The Type 2 was forced to abort his attack by seven intervening *Saratoga* Wildcats, among the 30 Marine and Navy fighters sent up in response to these alerts. The float Zeros had no chance and all were shot down. One Wildcat was forced to land by a burnt-out engine.[12]

Next came yet another Japanese reconnaissance mission, this one from Base Air Force. Eleven Zeros from the 2nd Air Group under Lieutenant Kurakane Akira were launched to make a fighter sweep ahead of Lieutenant Hayashi in his Irving, again trying to determine the status of the airfield. One Zero was forced to ditch, another to abort, and two more had to make emergency landings at Buka, leaving seven to try to sweep two dozen defending Marine Wildcats from the sky. With odds like that, the Japanese were lucky to lose only one Zero, albeit that of another veteran fighter pilot, Petty Officer 1st Class Magara Koichi.[13]

Lieutenant Kurakane's Zeros were long gone before Lieutenant Hayashi arrived to check out the airfield. He looped around the island to approach from the south, but unlike the previous day, Hayashi did not escape notice. Bemused Navy and Marine fighter pilots, who had never seen the twin-engine Nakajima J1N before, thought it was a German Focke-Wulf. Hayashi's Nakajima ran into a swarm of Wildcats as it tried to observe the airfield. Four Grummans peppered the Irving with machine-gun fire, leaving it smoking as it entered a cloud and tried to speed away. Two more, 2nd lieutenants Kenneth D. Frazier and Willis S. Lees of Marine Fighting 223, chased the Irving for 50 miles at speeds in excess of 200 knots, shooting off pieces of the Nakajima until one of its engines just fell off. Then the Irving went down with no survivors.[14] This seems to have convinced Base Air Force that the airfield was indeed still in American hands.

It was around this time that a small motor launch huffed and puffed its way to the dock at Kukum. The boat was assigned to a Corporal Eroni, one of Martin Clemens' scouts, for the purpose of bringing downed aviators back to Henderson Field. In this case, he was bringing back ace Captain Marion Carl, who had disappeared five days earlier. Carl had actually bailed out of his shot-up Wildcat. Eroni had cared for him ever since.

The two borrowed a Jeep and drove to the Pagoda. General Geiger looked up, very pleasantly surprised. He had given Carl up for dead. Then the general gave a puckish smile.

Carl was in a friendly rivalry with Major Smith for top fighter ace. When Carl was shot down, he had 12 aerial victories to Smith's 11. But things had changed during Carl's five-day absence. Referring to Smith, who was in the room with them, General Geiger said, "Marion, I have bad news. Smitty has fourteen now; you still have only twelve.

"What are we going to do about that?" the general asked.

Captain Carl paused for a moment. Then he exploded "Goddammit, General, ground him for five days!"

Grounded fighters was what Admiral Jojima was hoping for. The disappearance of his morning reconnaissance flight had convinced Jojima that the airfield remained unfriendly. So he decided to get R-Area Air Force to launch further massed air attacks. This one, commanded by Lieutenant Horihashi Takeshi of the *Chitose*, would consist of 19 Mitsubishi F1M Type 0 observation seaplanes, called the "Pete" – eight from the *Chitose*, two from *Kamikawa Maru*, four from *Sanyo Maru*, and five from *Sanuki Maru* – each armed with two 132lb fragmentation bombs. These biplanes would have an escort of two float Zeros from the *Kamikawa Maru*. Since biplanes were not exactly cutting-edge aeronautical technology, this attack would take place at twilight, approaching from south of Guadalcanal, in the hope of catching the American fighters on the ground.

American radar spoiled Admiral Jojima's surprise, as it picked up the approaching Japanese at around 5:30 pm. Six Marine Fighting 224 and five *Saratoga* Wildcats were sent up. The two float Zeros were spotted first. One was shot down and the other driven off before the 19 Petes approached Henderson Field from the southeast, looking like some World War I reenactment. In the growing darkness, most of the Wildcats missed the biplanes, but not all. Two Petes were shot down, and a third, that of Lieutenant Horihashi, was so badly shot up that it capsized and burned as soon as it arrived back at Rekata. The bombing attack was almost entirely ineffective, destroying just one Airacobra that had already been written off. So ineffective, in fact, that Jojima largely gave up the idea of massed bombing attacks on the airfield in the future.[15]

While the air attacks continued, at 1:05 on October 14, General Kawaguchi led his forces away from the ridge. Still debating where exactly they should go, it was at 9:00 pm on October 15 that he finally ordered his troops to head west across the Matanikau and join Colonel Oka's troops. The Taivu Point position was east of the Lunga perimeter and required reinforcements to cross within sight of American troops. The Kokumbona area west of the Matanikau made more sense.

So General Kawaguchi and his troops set out for Kokumbona. They were crossing the upper reaches of the Lunga, on the lower ridges of Mount Austen, in the deepest jungle, with nearly every soldier involved in carrying wounded. And with no food – they had only taken a few days' rations from Tasimboko because they expected to quickly capture the airfield, after which they expected to dine on American food.

Arrogant. Overconfident. Sloppy.

By the time they arrived in Kokumbona at around 2:00 pm on September 19, General Kawaguchi's troops looked like ghouls – skeletal, barely moving, having shed their weapons out of physical weakness due to exhaustion, thirst, and hunger. The troops of Colonel Oka and Captain Monzen were not in much better shape, desperately low on food themselves. But not nearly as bad as the Kuma Battalion, who set out from Taivu Point trying to follow Kawaguchi to Kokumbona as well. They got lost in the jungle for three weeks, losing all their weapons and becoming near ghouls themselves. This in turn was a far better fate than that experienced by the laborers of the 11th and 13th construction units. These laborers, dragged from Korea and Okinawa to this dismal corner of the world to build the airfield now in American hands, were now summarily dismissed, marooned on Guadalcanal, and told to forage for themselves.[16] It was truly the "co-prosperity" in Japan's "Greater East Asia Co-prosperity Sphere."

Imperial General Headquarters didn't care about their conscripted laborers dying of starvation. But it did care about their own troops dying of starvation. So began a series of food runs of the Tokyo Express.

On the night of September 20, destroyers *Suzunami*, *Ushio*, *Yudachi*, and *Shikinami*, each towing a barge full of provisions and ammunition drawn from the seaplane carrier *Nisshin*, headed for the Japanese anchorage at Kamimbo. They were found in the dark by seven Navy Dauntlesses of Scouting 3 and three Marine Scout Bombing 231 Dauntlesses under the *Saratoga*'s Lieutenant Commander Kirn. Kirn himself slightly damaged the *Shikinami* with a near miss.[17] The next night it was the *Uranami*, *Shirayuki*, *Kagero*, and *Hamakaze* making the run. The Cactus Air Force found them again. Strafing caused the *Kagero* waterline damage that led to flooding near the bow. The destroyers were only able to offload two-thirds of their supplies before turning back to Shortland.[18] On September 24, a run that included *Suzukaze*, *Kawakaze*, *Urakaze*, and *Umikaze* carrying 280 men of the 4th Infantry Regiment had to be aborted when nine Dauntlesses and one

Avenger got near misses on the *Urakaze* and *Umikaze*.[19]

By this time, though, the new Japanese plan with the old name of Operation *Ka* was in motion.

Hanson Baldwin was the *New York Times*' military affairs correspondent. A 1924 graduate of the Naval Academy, he had served in the Navy before going into journalism. That background gave him access and insight that would be unheard of today.

On September 19, Baldwin accompanied Admiral Fitch on a visit to Guadalcanal. Fitch was familiarizing himself with his new command area. And Baldwin was doing what reporters do, gathering information and giving information.

Baldwin met General Vandegrift and gave him some rather disconcerting news. The reporter told the general that the American public were under the false impression that the Marines held most of Guadalcanal. The public was completely unaware of the conditions under which the troops were living and fighting. Washington was aware of those conditions, but "top officials" were deeply concerned about the situation and seemed ready to give up.[20] The attitude was even worse in Nouméa, where the harbor was packed with supply ships waiting to be unloaded because of the disorganization of Admiral Ghormley's headquarters, where defeatism had clearly taken hold.

Vandegrift bristled at the idea that his troops were on the verge of defeat. He pointed out that they had finally stopped the Japanese advance across the Pacific, during which the Japanese had suffered heavy naval and air losses, from which they might not quickly recover. In fact, the American offensive on Guadalcanal seemed to have taken them by surprise.[21]

Baldwin's question was blunt. "Are you going to hold this beachhead, General? Are you going to stay here?"

"Hell yes. Why not?"[22]

It would become General Vandegrift's most famous quote. Not as a battle cry – American troops were not going to storm enemy positions hollering "Why not?" But it was a message of optimism, of hope, in the face of a vicious enemy and weak-kneed or ambivalent superiors.

Those weak-kneed superiors were a major problem in this campaign, none bigger than Admiral Ghormley. Baldwin went to Pearl Harbor, where he told a similar story to Admiral Nimitz. The poor results of the South Pacific campaign so far had come from "overcaution and the defensive complex," an outgrowth of that defeatism.[23] Perhaps most surprisingly, Ghormley had never visited Guadalcanal. Despite being in Nouméa, "the Paris of the Pacific," he had never even left his flagship *Argonne*.

Baldwin later elaborated:

> [Ghormley] was almost despairing. He was heavily overworked and he said, "This is a shoestring operation, we haven't got enough of anything. We're just hanging on by our

AMERICAN AND JAPANESE BASES IN THE SOUTH PACIFIC, SEPTEMBER–OCTOBER 1942

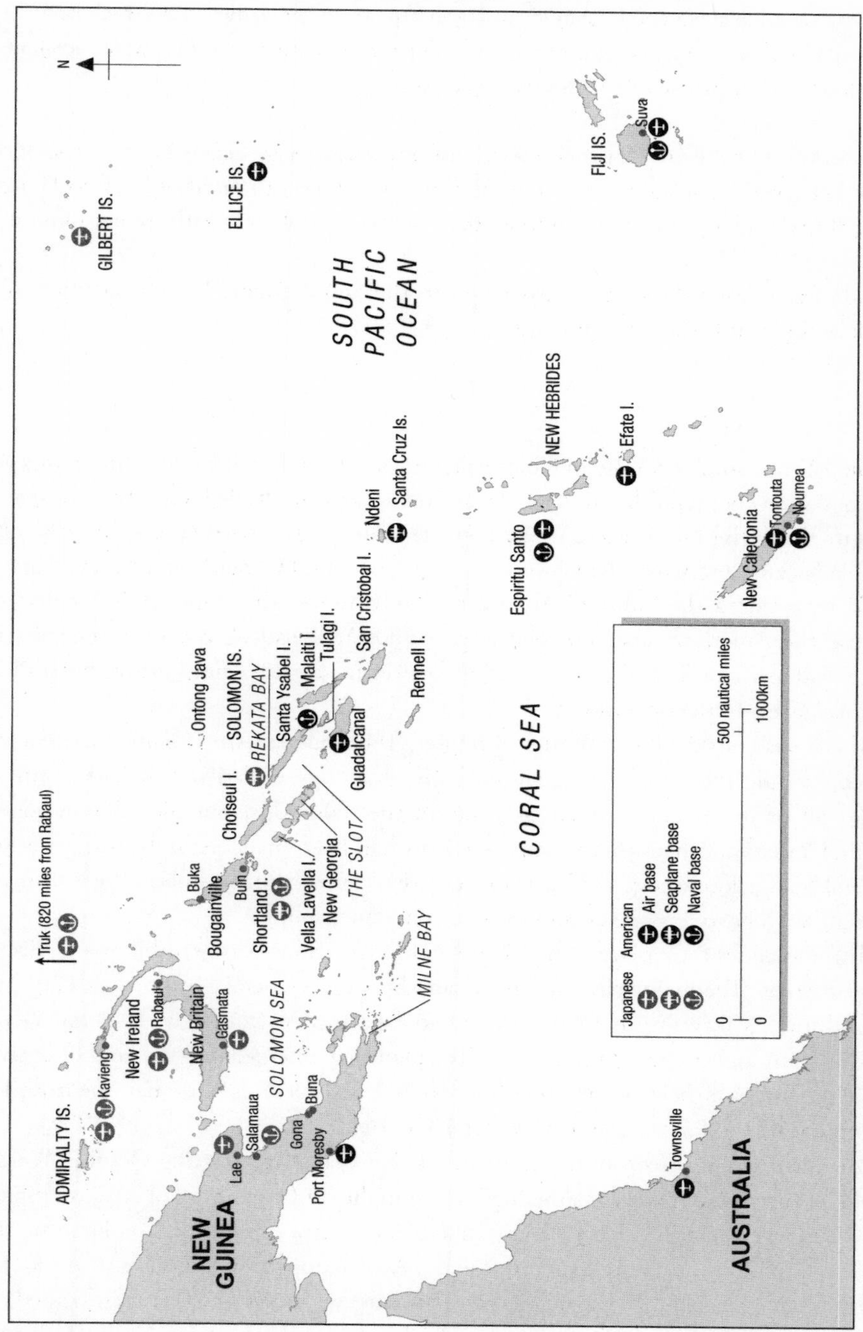

> teeth." He was very frank about this. Here was a time when you needed tough, hard, almost ruthless men. He was miscast, in my opinion. He should never have been in that job. He was a superb planner and he should have been kept as a planner, but I don't think he was a good operator… The staff didn't share these impressions entirely, but they were becoming infected. So the whole thing was very unpleasant.[24]

Baldwin was not the only journalist with this impression. Associated Press correspondent Clark Lee gave this insight: "It seemed to me some officers thought only of NOT losing more ships, and it was in that mood that we undertook our early operations in the Solomons."[25]

Admiral Nimitz decided he had to go to the South Pacific himself and personally check on his South Pacific commander.

Admiral Yamamoto's promise to Colonel Tsuji was the culmination of more than a week of negotiations between the Imperial Army and Navy at multiple levels. The negotiations came on the heels of some not-entirely-consistent analyses on what exactly was happening on Guadalcanal and why it had gone so wrong. The Naval General Staff believed that the island represented the "all-out" American counterattack; the Imperial Army disagreed because the Americans had not dedicated sufficient logistical assets for the offensive, which was perhaps a side benefit of the Americans' actually not dedicating sufficient logistical assets to the operation.[26]

There was considerable pointing of fingers. The Imperial Army blamed the Navy for not controlling the air over Guadalcanal. The Navy responded that it had committed almost all of its air and submarine assets to the Solomons, but did acknowledge, as Admiral Yamamoto had, that its supply efforts had been inadequate. In turn, the Army General Staff acknowledged at least privately that perhaps the "bamboo spear tactics" of charging with bayonets and swords needed some fine tuning.[27]

These analyses took place in the shadow of negotiations between the two services for the next steps. The major part was in Rabaul, between General Hyakutake's 17th Army and Admiral Mikawa's 8th Fleet, but essential parts were crafted at Imperial General Headquarters and on board the *Yamato*. The plan that emerged had the land offensive to retake the Lunga airfield starting on October 20. Back tracking from that, the troops and equipment had to be in place by October 13 or 14.

The plan would consist of five elements. 1. For two weeks starting October 1, troops would be run in to Guadalcanal by high-speed night runs consisting of any combination of 27 destroyers, a tactic the Japanese called "rat transportation." 2. At the same time, artillery, armor, more supplies, and other heavy equipment would be run in from Shortland by General Kawaguchi's beloved barges, which the Japanese called "ant transportation." 3. Runs on October 3 and 6 by the seaplane tender *Nisshin* to bring in heavy artillery. 4. Increased air attacks on the airfield, starting on September 26, the projected completion date for the new airfield at Buin. 5. A high-speed convoy that included five transports lent by Admiral Yamamoto to run reinforcements directly to Guadalcanal.[28]

It was a logical plan in general. It did represent a major change for the Combined Fleet inasmuch as the mission now was not the destruction of the Pacific Fleet but support for the Guadalcanal land offensive. It came with one catch, as plans always do: once the Combined Fleet was at sea, it could stay at sea no longer than two weeks. After that, it would have to refuel and resupply. Imperial Navy staffers tried to drill this important point into Colonel Tsuji and his Army colleagues; whether they understood it is anyone's guess.[29]

To carry out the plan, the 17th Army requested serious reinforcements. And it would get them, including the 2nd Sendai Division, the 38th Kanoya Division under Major General Ito Takeo – with a proud history of conquering Hong Kong, Sumatra, and Timor, and an equally sad history of war crimes – and the 8th Tank Regiment.

For now, though, it was all about that Base Air Force. On September 16, the 1st Air Attack Force – 21st Air Flotilla – began staging into Kavieng, north of Rabaul on New Ireland. First to arrive was commanding officer Rear Admiral Ichimaru Rinosuke, who had a reputation for being a "fire-eater," and much of the Kanoya Air Group.[30] Seven of the Kanoya's Zeros were sent to Rabaul to leaven the chewed-up Tainan Air Group. From the East Indies, the 3rd Air Attack Force – 23rd Air Flotilla – loaned elements of the 3rd Air Group, which the Japanese considered the equal of the Tainan Air Group in terms of air combat skills. They were brought to Kavieng by the new Japanese escort carrier *Taiyo*. The 23rd also loaned elements of the Takao Air Group with 20 G4Ms.

The 31st Air Group sent nine Type 99 carrier bombers, which were loaded alongside various other aircraft for delivery on board the *Taiyo*, which was due to deliver them to Truk. When she was 40 miles south of Truk, the escort carrier, under the escort of the destroyers *Akebono* and *Ushio*, was "smacked" in the stern by a Mark 14 torpedo, one of five fired by the US submarine *Trout*. With 13 dead, the *Taiyo* staggered into Truk later that day for emergency repairs. She was the first Japanese aircraft carrier hit by US submarine torpedoes.[31] She would not be the last.

The surviving aircrews of the badly mauled 4th and Yokohama air groups were finally sent back to Japan, and the survivors of the Chitose Air Group were sent back to the Marshall Islands, but for the exhausted survivors of the Tainan Air Group there would be no relief.[32] All told, these moves meant that, as of September 24, Base Air Force had 62 G4Ms, 77 Zeros, of which 48 were the long-range model, five Kawanishi Type 97 and one Type 2 flying boats, five Type 99 carrier bombers, five Mitsubishi C5M2 Type 98 land reconnaissance planes, known to the Allies as "Babs," and one Nakajima J1N1 reconnaissance plane. Admiral Tsukahara reorganized Base Air Force for improved efficiency, placing all the fighters under the 5th Air Attack Force and all the bombers under the 6th Air Attack Force. He also sent one Lieutenant Commander Mitsui Kenji, former air officer of the 4th Air Group, and ten communications personnel to monitor the weather and the Lunga airfield from the friendly confines of Mount Austen.[33]

Base Air Force now outnumbered the Cactus Air Force two-to-one in fighters and three-to-one in bombers. But, for now, bad weather kept it from exercising those numerical advantages.

The morning of September 19, transport *Shirogane Maru*, carrying elements of the 16th Construction Unit to Bougainville, took a torpedo in her engine room courtesy of the submarine *USS Amberjack* under Lieutenant Commander John A. Bole and went dead in the water. The destroyers *Amagiri* and *Hatsuyuki* went out to lug the disabled transport back to the Shortlands, where the *Shirogane Maru* was beached to keep her from sinking. Her cargo was unloaded but she was eventually declared a total loss.[34] Shortland was starting to get some heat, as a September 24 attack by 11th Bombardment Group B-17s staging through Henderson Field damaged seaplane tender *Sanuki Maru*, though she does not seem to have missed any combat time. One B-17 was shot down.[35]

The bad weather that had stymied Japanese efforts to bomb the Lunga airfield finally broke on September 27. At 10:30 am, the new, improved Base Air Force sent up nine G4Ms of the Kisarazu Air Group and nine from the Takao Air Group, making its first attack on Guadalcanal. They were escorted by 26 Zeros of the 3rd Air Group, with 12 from the 2nd Air Group serving as "air control."[36]

The incoming strike was picked up on radar early enough for nine Wildcats from Marine Fighting 223 and eight from Marine Fighting 224 to take off from Fighter 1, joined by 14 *Saratoga* Wildcats from Henderson Field itself. There was no semblance of squadron order, as everyone simply formed themselves up as best they could once in the air.

The Wildcats were helped immensely by the 12 "air control" Zeros completely missing them altogether. The Bettys from the Takao group saw a dozen approaching Wildcats, but could not warn the Zeros because the Zeros, of course, lacked radios.

The bombers managed to destroy one Dauntless on the ground while damaging three others along with five Avengers. Five Wildcats were perforated in the air battle and needed repairs. One Kisarazu Betty and one Takao Betty were shot down over Guadalcanal, while a second Takao Betty had to ditch at Rekata.[37] All of the rest had some form of damage. One Zero was shot down; one more had slight damage.

September 28 saw another massive raid by Base Air Force. Lieutenant Morita Rinji of the Misawa Air Group led 27 Mitsubishi G4Ms – nine each from the Misawa, Kanoya, and Takao air groups – escorted by 15 Zeros from the Tainan Air Group under Lieutenant Kawai. Today in the role of "air control" were 27 Zeros – 18 from the 6th and nine from the Kanoya air groups – under Lieutenant Kofukuda Mitsugi of the 6th. Though as "air control" Kofukuda was to sweep ahead of the main strike for Zeros, for reasons known only to him he took off 40 minutes after the main strike did. The attack thus got off to a bad start.

Things rapidly got worse. One of Lieutenant Kofukuda's Zeros had to abort. Then Lieutenant Kawai developed engine trouble and had to abort, initially taking eight other Zeros with him before he could turn over command of the close escort thanks – again – to the lack of radio. Two of the G4Ms had to abort as well.

With warning from Donald Kennedy and radar, 20 Marine Wildcats – ten each from Fighting 223 and 224 – and 15 *Saratoga* Wildcats took to the air. Going to 28,000 feet, Major John L. Smith looked at the approaching Japanese with some bemusement. Why were some two dozen Zeros too far behind the bombers to protect them? The Americans struck hard.

Lieutenant Morita's Betty was fatally hit by the *Saratoga*'s fighters; the other Bettys took Morita's spiraling out of formation as the signal for them to drop their bombs – on a jungle trail about 10 miles west of Henderson Field. Even so, G4M pilot Lieutenant Naka Seiji claimed to have destroyed seven aircraft on the ground.[38]

With the Zeros almost completely out of it, it was a slaughter. Major Galer later said, "you could look back up and there were wings, motors, and tail assemblies floating all around." Lieutenant Colonel Harold W. "Joe" Bauer, a visitor to Guadalcanal who had talked his way into this first combat of his career, wrote, "It was the greatest sight of my life to see Jap bombers fall out of the sky."[39]

Five Bettys were shot down, including Lieutenant Morita's command plane. One ditched at Rekata, one crash-landed at Buin, and one made it back but was a total loss. Eight Mitsubishi G4M Type 1 land attack planes were lost; all the rest suffered damage.[40] Forty-one were killed.

And with more performances like this, a new reality was slowly dawning on the American pilots. As usual, Admiral McCain was one of the first to pick up on it. Briefing staffers at Pearl Harbor, McCain described what was unthinkable just six months earlier. "The Japs are afraid of our F4F and will not attack it," he said. "It seems reasonable to suppose that we have now destroyed the cream of [the enemy's] naval air pilots." McCain emphasized that Guadalcanal could be held if fighter strength could be maintained at the present level. Unfortunately, he said, there were not yet enough fighters or pilots to do that.[41]

That afternoon saw celebration inside the Lunga perimeter, at least to the extent one could celebrate on Guadalcanal. And the news got even better with the arrival of reinforcements. Lieutenant Commander John Eldridge, skipper of the *Wasp*'s Scouting 71, led two more of his squadron mates, three Dauntlesses from Scouting 3, and four Avengers from Torpedo 8.[42] It was a good day at Lunga.

At Rabaul the atmosphere was markedly different. That night, a very ill Admiral Tsukahara convened a meeting of the staffs of the 5th and 6th Air Attack forces, with no shortage of yelling and finger-pointing. In two days, despite the assignment of what should have been an overwhelming escort of Zeros, Base Air Force had lost 11 bombers, almost 20 percent of its force. Why was this happening? What could be done to fix it?

The 11th Air Fleet historian put it in cold, laconic terms: "In today's attack our bombers suffered heavy damage; therefore it was decided that tomorrow's attack will be carried out by fighters."[43]

The battle of Edson's Ridge had bought the Marines some breathing room, nothing more. The Japanese would be back.

But the pause allowed the Americans to take stock of their situation and make some needed changes. The first change would be the aircrews.

By this time, most of the Marine pilots had been at Henderson Field for over a month. It was a unique situation for pilots inasmuch as they served as pilots but they basically lived as infantry. The aircrews were housed in tents in a coconut grove between Henderson Field and the beach. Not entirely unpleasant, in theory, though the aircrews called it "Mosquito Gulch." But a shortage of cots meant most of them slept on captured Japanese straw mats in the dirt that served as the floors of their tents. And when it rained, the dirt became a stinking black mud that could swallow cots or men whole.

That was when the pilots could sleep. Indeed, the single biggest problem was sleep. Every night the Japanese sent someone over – Louie the Louse or, lately, a twin-engine Betty that was dubbed "Washing Machine Charlie" – to loudly fly over the Lunga positions, light them with flares, and drop the occasional bomb, "just to keep the enemy forces there disturbed," as the Japanese would later explain.[44] It worked. When the siren wailed at night, the pilots had to hide in foxholes, just like the infantry.

They needed energy. They couldn't always get it. The food on Guadalcanal seemed suspiciously familiar – Spam, canned hash, sausage, Spam, captured Japanese rice, dehydrated potatoes, Spam, and whatever concoctions could be made thereof. With Spam. And coffee. Nothing hits the spot in 100-degree temperatures and 100-percent humidity like a cup of boiling hot coffee. But it was the only caffeinated beverage they had.

As delectable and varied as this menu seems, various emergencies and missions meant they could not always or even usually get three meals a day. During the day they had to fly fighter missions or bombing missions, often at high altitude, where the pure oxygen they had to breathe made them drowsy, and where the stomach gases from the food they ate expanded and caused agonizingly painful cramps.

This was on top of the normal stress of simply being a pilot. Being in your cockpit, all alone, with everyone you see in the air trying to kill you. And you have to decide which ones to kill. It may be a powerful experience, but it is also stressful, dehumanizing, and draining.

Draining was something Henderson Field badly needed. Taking off and landing are difficult under any circumstances, but the runway at Henderson added a level of adventure to which few pilots were accustomed. There were the standard bomb craters. There was also not enough Marston matting – perforated steel planks that could be hooked together to create a temporary runway – to cover the runway. So they had to deal with the dirt strip, which the official Marine Corps aviation history described in not-entirely complimentary terms:

> Henderson Field was a bowl of black dust which fouled airplane engines or it was a quagmire of black mud which made the take-off resemble nothing more than a fly trying to rise from a runway of molasses.[45]

The excitement did not end there, however. The Douglas SBD Dauntlesses were carrier planes, designed to land on aircraft carriers. They had hard-rubber wheels under their tails designed for landing on the tough wooden decks of aircraft carriers. But on the dirt runway of Henderson, these wheels "... chewed up the runway like a plowshare."[46] The engineers and Seebees had their hands full repairing the airstrip, combat or no combat. Repair teams and dump trucks full of dirt were kept at the ready for quick repairs.

All in all, the Cactus Air Force pilots had to endure circumstances that were "probably the worst any American airmen faced for a prolonged period during the war."[47] Unsurprisingly, the result was a number of pilots being declared unfit to fly by the medical staff of the 1st Marine Air Wing. Colonel Woods, the chief of staff, was indignant. "They've got to keep flying," he bellowed. "It's better to do that than get a Jap bayonet stuck in their ass!"[48] The simple fact was they didn't have enough pilots.

In general, the aviators of the Cactus Air Force were a hardy, cheeky bunch who took their lot with spunk and black humor that undoubtedly aided their survival. One of their favorite stories concerned a Marine Wildcat pilot who was cut off by Japanese Zeros. The defiant pilot radioed the rest of his flight, "Hey, fellows, come on over; I've got twelve of the bastards cornered."[49]

But the toll on the pilots was starting to show, with more operational accidents occurring. Very late in the afternoon of September 8, when a Japanese airstrike was expected, 16 Wildcats were scrambled to meet it. One crashed on takeoff. The others stayed aloft until after dark, when it became obvious there would be no attack. Then the fighters came in to land. Two ran into each other on the runway, wrecking both planes. A third got stuck in the mud and pitched over, becoming a total loss. Then a fourth crashed on landing. One pilot lamented, "At this rate we can whip ourselves without any help from the Japs."[50]

Other problems appeared as well. Dauntless pilots and radiomen on reconnaissance missions would make basic errors of identification and navigation. The Marine Dauntless pilots had not gotten a direct hit on a Japanese ship with a bomb since they hit the *Asagiri*. All aviators, but especially fighter pilots, would make mistakes in combat. And a very few didn't even want to fight any more. Calling such aviators "almost worthless," Major Galer explained it:

> A percentage of these pilots could be said to avoid combat, while the majority would accept but not look for combat… After a definite period a pilot who is undergoing daily alert periods and combat should be relieved before he is forced to request his relief from the Medical Department or before he is evacuated sick or wounded.[51]

Lieutenant Turner Caldwell of the *Enterprise* agreed. He used to believe pilot fatigue was a myth. "Now I know what [the medical staff] meant. There's a point where you just get to be no good; you're shot to the devil – and there's nothing you can do about it."[52]

But how long was that "definite period"? One experienced pilot thought it was six weeks; others thought it was a mere 30 days.[53] Either way, the only solution was to rotate the aircrews out. That process began on September 23, when five Dauntlesses of Marine Scout Bombing 141 arrived at Henderson Field. These were the first elements of Marine Air Group 14, who would little by little take over for Marine Air Group 23.[54]

Yet it was not just rotating the aircrews. Admiral Halsey had requested the "earliest practicable return" of the carrier pilots and aircrews. He hoped to use "the least tired" as cadre for replacement carrier air groups. Admiral Fitch replied that the carrier aviators would be returned when "transportation and the military situation permitted."[55] They permitted enough to give Halsey back the remaining pilots from the carrier *Enterprise* on September 27. But the Cactus Air Force would continue to rely on carrier pilots for some time to come.

This was because they would not be getting rid of the Japanese for some time to come. General Vandegrift had used the new troops to build up his defense, a series of strong points just inside the perimeter, with a reserve positioned to reinforce threatened sectors. But the general also had his eye on the Matanikau. Starting on September 24, Vandegrift had the 7th Marines lead a two-pronged strike, with one prong attacking across the Matanikau and the other taking boats to land in the Japanese rear.

The troops did not know what General Vandegrift hoped to accomplish by this mission, and neither did he, by his own admission.[56] Colonel Oka used a defense of interior lines to thwart a Marine assault bogged down by poor communications and coordination within the jungle. It took a blasting by the 5-inch guns of the destroyer *Monssen* to get some of the troops out. It was Vandegrift's second serious tactical misjudgment in two weeks. But this one was borne of frustration at being cooped up inside the Lunga perimeter, and a fear that the Japanese would build up across the Matanikau for a massive assault on Henderson Field.

Which was exactly what the Japanese were planning.

On the afternoon of September 28, a Consolidated PB2Y Coronado flying boat set down in Nouméa harbor. Out of it stepped Admiral Nimitz with his air officer and his Marine officer. They got into a launch that took him to Admiral Ghormley's flagship *Argonne*. They were on a fact-finding mission that promised to not be entirely pleasant.

The admiral had already gathered considerable important information. On the way down from Pearl Harbor he had stopped in Canton, where he crossed paths with Admiral McCain, on his way to Washington to work for Admiral King. Nimitz asked McCain for a short briefing on what to look for in the South Pacific.

"The first thing is to get as many reserve planes to [Espiritu Santo] as possible. Cactus cannot handle any more planes right now, but you have to be ready to feed them in all the time. Aviation gasoline supply at Cactus is the present most critical question."

This dovetailed into more issues of logistics. There was discussion of how admirals Noyes and Fletcher were doing. Then McCain added:

> I want to emphasize the aviation gas supply and relief for pilots at Cactus. We can fly VF [fighters] up but not back. It's a one-way wind. The Marine VF pilots are very tired. A relief for them is there now and the SBD pilots will be next. They have had no rest; they are just tired. They had to work during the day and could get no sleep at night.
>
> The Marines are not worried about holding what they have on Cactus but you have got to stop the Japs coming in.[57]

Nimitz would see just how right McCain was on this trip.

It started as soon as they landed in Nouméa, when Admiral Nimitz saw 80 cargo ships and freighters carrying badly needed supplies simply sat in the harbor, with the ships themselves badly needed elsewhere. They could not be sent to the front because they had not been combat loaded – the most important supplies stowed for first unloading, ammunition kept together, etc. –in the United States. They could not be unloaded in Nouméa because there were not enough docks, cranes, transport, or workers, which could usually handle only about 24 ships a month. They all had to be sent down to Wellington, New Zealand, to be unloaded and reloaded for combat in the midst of a longshoremen's strike.

The commander of the Pacific Fleet and his staff officers were directed to the wardroom. There was South Pacific Commander Admiral Ghormley, his chief of staff Admiral Callaghan, and Admiral Turner. Also there was General Arnold, head of the Army Air Force, who was on his own tour of the South Pacific; General MacArthur's chief of staff Major General Richard K. Sutherland; MacArthur's 5th Air Force Major General George Kenney; and Major General Millard Harmon, commander of Army Air in the South Pacific.

As he entered the wardroom, Admiral Nimitz noted with some unease the physical appearance of Admiral Ghormley, who to the Pacific Fleet commander looked exhausted, nervous, and overwhelmed. Nevertheless, Nimitz opened the conference around 4:15 pm:

> The purpose of my visit is to inform myself and members of my staff with conditions in the SoPac [South Pacific] area; and to inform myself on the problems of Admiral Ghormley and General MacArthur. We will begin the conference by having Ghormley or Harmon outline the situation…[58]

Admiral Ghormley started into his presentation:

> Our forces and position there are under constant pressure. Logistic supply is most difficult. We can send in only one ship at a time and from the eastward there is only one channel. Most of the Japs in the area are on Cactus […] The Japs are still getting in despite our air activity. Nobody knows exactly how many are on Cactus right now…

Well, at least Ghormley did not. Clearly it might have helped if he had actually visited the island. At one point Ghormley stated that Guadalcanal was down to 10,000 gallons of aviation fuel. Admiral Turner quickly corrected him: it was 5,000. His lack of knowledge about the situation on Guadalcanal left the other officers sharing uncomfortable looks.

"I liked Ghormley," General Kenney wrote, "but he looked tired and really was tired. I don't believe his health was any too good and I thought, while we were talking, that it wouldn't be long before he was relieved."[59]

Admiral Nimitz asked tough questions of his South Pacific commander. Nimitz was surprised to learn the battleship *Washington* was in Tongatabu, 1,800 miles from Guadalcanal. What exactly was the battleship accomplishing there? The *Washington* "was so far removed from the battle area that she might as well have been at Pearl or San Francisco, insofar as taking advantage of favorable opportunities is concerned."[60] Ghormley pled fuel shortages. How that justified keeping the battleship 1,800 miles away rather than somewhere closer like Nouméa he did not explain. Nimitz also thought Ghormley was keeping his cruiser task force too far from Guadalcanal "to do much about visiting enemy ships."[61]

Twice during the conference, staffers intruded to deliver urgent messages for Admiral Ghormley. Ghormley had been given two urgent messages from Guadalcanal. Both times he exclaimed, "My God! What are we going to do about this?"[62] It was as if he had no idea what to do, and didn't want to find out. It made a big impression on those present, especially Admiral Nimitz.

Admiral Ghormley and his staff appealed for more help from General MacArthur's forces, including, especially, mass raids by heavy bombers on Rabaul. General Kenney agreed to "try to burn the place down," but he also said that his units were stretched thin while "knocking off Jap convoys to Buna, maintaining air control over New Guinea, and helping out our ground forces."[63] Ghormley responded that he appreciated what MacArthur's forces were doing and wished them luck when they did attack Rabaul. Nimitz seethed at Ghormley's weak response.[64]

General Sutherland then presented General MacArthur's position, followed by Admiral Turner describing the South Pacific strategy. General Arnold was left to explain the global war, the grand strategy, and how, in the grand scheme of things, the South Pacific did not matter all that much. At least as he saw it.

General Arnold's tour of the South Pacific had allegedly been about fact finding, though the opinions he expressed made it sound as if it was more about confirmation bias. "It was obvious that the naval officers in this area were under a terrific strain," Arnold acknowledged later on. "It was also obvious that they had chips on their shoulders." He wrote, "It looked to me as if everybody on that South Pacific front had a bad case of jitters."[65]

General Arnold bristled at the Navy's requests for more aircraft from the Army. What had the Navy done with the aircraft the Army had already sent? Were they tied up in the shipping snarl at Nouméa? He wanted no more Army aircraft sent to the South Pacific until the Navy used what it already had.[66] That the Army aircraft available on Guadalcanal, the P-39 and P-400 Airacobras, were totally unsuitable for fighting Japanese Zeros did not matter to him.

The Navy's problem, General Arnold insisted, was not a lack of aircraft but a lack of airfields. It was a bizarre claim considering Espiritu Santo, Efate, and the rear airfields were nowhere near capacity. Indeed, no one had done more to block reinforcements to the Pacific than Arnold. And Arnold was not interested in learning anything that might change his mind.

As the 67th Fighter Squadron's Captain Dale Brannon was about to learn.[67] After the meeting with Nimitz, Brannon, the highest-ranking Army officer on Guadalcanal, was summoned to Espiritu Santo for a meeting with Arnold. For all of Arnold's study of the Pacific, he would not visit Guadalcanal. Instead Brannon was to brief him. Or so he thought.

When Brannon arrived, he sat at a table across from Arnold. Brannon was about to go into his prepared briefing when Arnold preempted him. "What the hell is going on with your people?" the head of the Army Air Force shouted.

Brannon was thrown for a loop. He started to go into his remarks about the P-400s, but Arnold cut him off. "They're doing a fine job in Australia!"

"They have P-39s in Australia, not P-400s, sir, and they have oxygen."

"That's not the case at all," Arnold snapped. The Airacobras were doing fine in New Guinea. They weren't on Guadalcanal. The Marines and Navy fliers got the news headlines for shooting down Japanese Zeros, but the Army pilots there ran from Japanese Zeros. Arnold didn't care about the Airacobras' effective ground-support role. Why weren't they shooting down Zeros over Guadalcanal? Arnold had the answer: it was the pilots.

General Arnold lunged across the table, pounding it with his fist. He snarled, "The problem is that you're a coward!" Arnold chose not to notice the bandage across Brannon's chin from injuries he suffered in the September 10 Japanese bombing attack. He went eye to eye with Brannon. "You have a whole squadron full of nothing but cowards!" Arnold stormed from the room, slamming the door behind him.

It was a sorry performance by Hap Arnold. Captain Brannon had been stunned into silence. As he headed back for Guadalcanal, he was shaking with rage.[68] Brannon had no idea that while this was going on, the 339th Fighter Squadron was created. It would eventually have the new P-38, and its head would be one of the original test pilots of the P-38 – Dale Brannon.

Meanwhile, on September 30, Nimitz got on a B-17 headed in the general direction of Guadalcanal – the pilot did not have a map of the Solomons. He got a first-hand experience of the difficulty of flight in the Solomon Islands when the pilot got lost in a storm. His air officer remembered they had a *National Geographic* map of the South Pacific on board, which helped them find Henderson Field.[69]

Despite the pouring rain, which secretly pleased Vandegrift since it showed the issues of the muddy runway, Admiral Nimitz inspected the flight operations, Edson's Ridge, and parts of the defense perimeter. That evening Nimitz dined with Vandegrift and the senior officers, then spoke with the general alone to get his real thoughts. Vandegrift and his troops were confident of holding Guadalcanal – both Nimitz and General Arnold had found that optimism increased the closer one got to the front – although he did have issues with the Japanese, obviously, but also with Admiral Turner. Turner fancied himself a genius in land warfare as well as naval warfare. Vandegrift disagreed. The general said what he needed most were more troops to hold the perimeter and more aircraft to beat back the constant Japanese air attacks.[70]

Later that night, over alcoholic beverages, the Pacific Fleet commander got into more theoretical issues. "You know, Vandegrift, when this war is over we are going to write a new set of Navy regulations," Nimitz said. "So just keep it in the back of your mind because I will want to know some of the things you think ought to be changed." It was a measure of how much Nimitz had been impressed by the Marine general.

He did not disappoint now. "I know one right now," Vandegrift said. "Leave out all reference that he who runs his ship aground will face a fate worse than death. Out here too many commanders have been far too leery about risking their ships."[71]

It was a standard prewar Navy philosophy that had been drummed into the heads of the skippers. Now it was getting people killed. It went a long way in explaining why, for instance, the lightly armed destroyer-transports *Little* and *Gregory* chose death at the hands of the Japanese rather than risk running aground off Tulagi in the dark and receive a fate worse than death from the Navy bureaucracy.

Nimitz smiled.

The next morning the admiral handed out merit citations, including one to a burly Marine sergeant who fainted out of sheer terror at being this close to a four-star admiral. As Vandegrift and Nimitz headed back to the Henderson Field runway in the rain – again – the admiral promised "support to the maximum of our resources."[72] The necessity of those resources was proven again when Nimitz's B-17 could not take off out of the mud and nearly spun off the runway into a deep ravine. After the rain stopped and the field dried a bit, Nimitz and his staff headed back to Espiritu Santo and then Nouméa, where he met Admiral Ghormley again on October 2.

This time, Nimitz directed the meeting. He wanted support for Guadalcanal, no doubt. The Army's Americal Division was being trained in New Caledonia. Against the wishes of its commander Major General Alexander M. Patch, Ghormley had refused to commit the division, believing it would be lost when Guadalcanal inevitably fell to the Japanese. Nimitz wanted it sent forward.

In fact, Admiral Nimitz gave very definite and very forceful instructions that left no doubt what he wanted from his South Pacific commander:

All-weather airfields, which meant a lot more Marston matting – a direct consequence of the difficult landing and takeoff Nimitz experienced at Henderson Field.
More storage for aviation gasoline.
Better housing for pilots, in particular Quonset huts instead of tents.
All-weather roads, which meant even more Marston matting.
Better communications.
Better cargo handling facilities.
Better repair facilities for aircraft. "Planes are too expensive and too hard to get to let only minor damage render them permanently unserviceable," Admiral Nimitz explained.
Better handling of mail, which could do wonders for morale.

Perhaps most importantly, he told Ghormley, "I want you to go up and see conditions for yourself. Callaghan can take care of things here while you are away."[73]

Admiral Nimitz also wanted ideas of future operations. Admiral Ghormley discussed the old holy grail of building an airbase at Ndeni, ignoring the mounting evidence that the Santa Cruz Islands were actually biological hazards that included their own particularly nasty strain of malaria that attacked the human brain. More disturbingly, the joint chiefs had ordered him to supply a plan and schedule for future operations last August. Ghormley had not done so, as he had not believed it to be worthwhile. This was a major failure on Ghormley's part. Nimitz left Nouméa the next day to make a few more inspections before returning to Pearl Harbor. His visit had not settled his concerns about Ghormley. If anything, what Nimitz had seen had intensified those concerns.

The Pacific Fleet commander hoped his instructions and admonitions to his South Pacific commander would be enough.

Admiral Tsukahara and Base Air Force had a problem.

When they sent bombers with fighters down to attack Guadalcanal, the Americans would simply ignore the fighters and go after the bombers. That struck the Japanese as rude. Their solution had been what they termed "air control"; a fighter sweep would lead the main bomber force, with a close fighter escort. However, the Americans, helped in part by radar and the coastwatchers, had still cut through the fighters and slashed away at the bombers.

Now Base Air Force tried a new tactic. Now the Japanese would lead with bombers, but just enough to get the Americans to scramble fighters. Then the bombers would turn back and let a swarm of Zeros pass by to deal with the Americans.

They first tried this tactic on September 29. Lieutenant Aioi Takahide led 27 Zeros from the 3rd Air Group and the Kanoya Air Group. They were joined at 10:00 am by nine Kanoya G4Ms from Kavieng.

At 8:45 Coastwatcher Jack Read on southern Bougainville reported fighters and bombers had passed overhead at 7:30 and were "now going yours." Due to the delay in reporting, fighters were almost immediately scrambled at Henderson Field. The Bettys turned around in the central Solomons, but no one seems to have seen them do so. When no attack materialized that morning, the fighters landed.

Only to be sent back up at 1:25 pm when radar detected a large flight of unidentified aircraft. Now it was 20 Marine Wildcats and 14 *Saratoga* Fighting 5 Wildcats. What resulted was an aerial battle that took bizarre turns because of heavy cloud cover. There were 27 attacking Japanese Zeros, but only 19 of them engaged the Americans. The 20 Marine Wildcats never fought at all; they never saw anyone to fight. It was the *Saratoga* Wildcats who held the line, losing one of their own, but ended up costing the Japanese four Zeros.[74]

It was another unhappy day for Base Air Force. Fighter pilot Petty Officer 3rd Class Abe Kenichi was taken aback by the skill and aggressiveness of the American pilots. He had been taught that the F4F Wildcat would break off an attack and dive away when the Zero fought back. But Abe didn't see that. He saw pilots who wanted combat with the Zeros, who did not fear the Zeros. Abe called it a "frightening surprise."[75] He might have also called it ominous.

There were no Japanese air attacks for the next few days, in part because of bad weather between Rabaul and Guadalcanal. But the bad weather helped cover the Tokyo Express. On October 1 it was the destroyers *Fubuki*, *Shirayuki*, *Hatsuyuki*, and *Murakumo* dropping off Major General Nasu Yumio and members of the 4th Infantry Regiment.[76] The Cactus Air Force tried to mount another night attack with five each of Dauntlesses and Avengers, but all they managed to accomplish was to give the *Hatsuyuki* steering issues, at the cost of losing all but one of the Avengers. As the Americans suffered their slings and arrows, so did the Japanese. Just before dawn on October 2, six B-17s of the 5th Air Force's 19th Bombardment Group bombed Rabaul and Simpson Harbor. One bomb plunged into the fantail of the light cruiser *Tenryu*, gnawing a 16-foot hole in her deck and damaging her superstructure, leaving 22 dead and 26 wounded. But the light cruiser received emergency repairs.[77]

For the period of early October, the Japanese strategy would be two intertwined tracks – bombing attacks by Base Air Force during the day and reinforcement of Guadalcanal by the Tokyo Express at night. Not every day, not every night. But enough to keep the Americans on edge while constantly nibbling away at their strength.

On October 2, Base Air Force again tried its bait-and-switch tactic by baiting the Cactus Air Force with bombers – this time nine Misawa G4Ms, who turned back – and the switch with 36 Zeros under the 6th Air Group's Lieutenant Kofukuda, though one 6th Zero had to abort and eight Tainan Zeros did a U-turn with the Type 1s. After picking up the strike on radar at 12:20 pm, the Cactus Air Force was ready, with 36 Wildcats – ten from Marine Fighting 223, 12 from Marine Fighting 224, and 14 from the *Saratoga*'s Fighting 5 – in the air. But the warning had actually come too late and the

Zeros had a significant altitude advantage over the Wildcats, an advantage they used skillfully. Now it was a disaster for the Cactus Air Force. Five Wildcats were shot down, though of these two pilots, Major John L. Smith and Major Bob Galer, returned. One more Wildcat apparently crashed from pilot hypoxia after oxygen failure. To top it off, two search Dauntlesses disappeared as well. And all they got was one Zero shot down.[78]

With the daily air attack over, it was now the turn of the nightly Tokyo Express run. Destroyers *Asagumo*, *Natsugumo*, *Minegumo*, *Murasame*, and *Harusame* ran in, dropped off troops and supplies, and ran out.

The first of the really big Tokyo Expresses came on October 3. For that, Base Air Force wanted a repeat of its ambush of the day before, with the same bait and switch. This time it was Lieutenant Ito leading 27 Zeros. But Ito wasn't from the Kanoya Air Group any more. On October 1, the famous Kanoya Air Group had been renamed the 751 Air Group and the Takao Air Group the 753 Air Group. After all, there's no better time to change the names of your air groups from something distinctive with which everyone was familiar to some semi-secret numeric code than in the middle of a critical phase of a critical air campaign.

So Lieutenant Ito of the 751 Air Group led 27 Zeros, who would play the switch when 15 unarmed G4Ms played the bait. Radar picked them up, Donald Kennedy warned, fighters scrambled. The Bettys turned back.

Once again, there was heavy cloud cover, which prevented Lieutenant Ito from seeing any defending fighters and vice versa, for the moment, at least. The Japanese fighters became separated in the clouds into three sections, none of whom could communicate with each other due to their lack of radios. One section of nine Zeros of the 3rd Air Group under Lieutenant (jg) Yamaguchi Sadao looped back looking for enemy fighters. And he found them – diving on him from behind.

The Americans had adjusted to the bait-and-switch technique by stacking the fighters vertically at multiple altitudes. Five Marine Wildcats under Captain Marion Carl had settled at about 30,000 feet when they saw Lieutenant Yamaguchi's section beneath them and dove like hawks on prey. Three Zeros were shot down, a fourth had to ditch, and a fifth, Yamaguchi's, crashed near the beach.[79]

The other two sections of Zeros never got into the fight, but Petty Officer 1st Class Imahashi Takeru from the 751 Group decided to lead his flight of three in strafing the airfield. The 3rd Defense Battalion had other ideas and trained all of its antiaircraft guns on the Zeros. Takahashi ended up embedding his Zero into the ground just west of the runway; the other two were heavily damaged but somehow managed to stagger back to base. The *Saratoga*'s fighter skipper Lieutenant Commander Simpler thought the attack was "without other objective than to measure the effectiveness of our antiaircraft fire."[80] It was the aerial version of the banzai charge.

Carl's fighters were the only ones able to engage the Zeros. Altogether six Zeros were shot down, two more crashed, and yet another two had to be written off for battle damage. Lieutenant Colonel Bauer, a guest in this flight of combat air patrol, shot down four by himself. For all that, the US lost one fighter, whose pilot parachuted to safety, and one that crash landed.[81]

It was an aerial victory that was cathartic for the Cactus Air Force after the previous day's disaster. But their main concern was the convoy they knew was coming that night. It would indeed be a giant Tokyo Express. Destroyers *Uranami*, *Makigumo*, and *Akigumo* were to drop off 320 men and 16 tons of supplies at Tassafaronga. Destroyers *Arashi*, *Kuroshio*, and *Hayashio* would do the same thing at Kamimbo.[82]

But the really significant reinforcement was the seaplane carrier *Nisshin*, with an escort of destroyers *Nowaki* and *Maikaze*, planning to stop at Tassafaronga as well. In her sizable hold she carried nine artillery pieces, including four 150mm guns, 330 troops, and General Maruyama Masao, commander of the 2nd Sendai Division. The *Nisshin* was so important to the Japanese that they had the air cover of six Zeros from the 2nd Air Group stay over her so long that they could not return to base and had to ditch.[83]

Eight Dauntlesses and three Avengers took off in the late afternoon and managed to miss the Japanese Zeros, but also managed to miss the *Nisshin* with their munitions. The *Nisshin* reached Tassafaronga and began offloading her troops and supplies. But she was surprised at 10:00 pm when a night attack by five Dauntlesses got a near-miss that started a leak in her engine room. The Americans were bombing a stopped ship, with the air full of flares, and still managed to get only a near-miss. Nevertheless, between the near-miss and increased American radio traffic, the Japanese decided to cut short her visit to Guadalcanal, and she left with 80 troops and two artillery pieces still on board. The big new destroyer *Akizuki*, with increased heavy antiaircraft armament, was dispatched from Shortland to meet the *Nisshin* to help cover her return.[84] The *Nisshin* would prove to be a thorn in the American side, delivering Japanese troops and supplies while eluding truly damaging strikes by US air power.

And this night, the *Nisshin* was truly damaging, for she had dropped off General Maruyama. Maruyama was the typical Imperial Japanese Army general – arrogant, overconfident, ruthless, with both the enemy and his own troops. In his Order of the Day for October 1, Maruyama said of Guadalcanal, "This is the decisive battle, a battle in which the rise or fall of the Japanese Empire will be decided. If we do not succeed in the occupation of these islands, no one should expect … to return alive."[85]

The next morning, the Cactus Air Force set out again to take out the *Nisshin*. Seven Dauntlesses and four Avengers took off after the seaplane carrier, but four of the SBDs under the *Saratoga*'s Lieutenant Commander Kirn had to dodge into a cloud to avoid Japanese floatplanes and never found the *Nisshin* again. The Avengers attacked without success. Again. To add injury to insult, during the fight a flight of B-17s from the 11th Bombardment Group came through on the way back home from an attack on Buka. One of the Type 0 reconnaissance seaplanes performed its own banzai charge by intentionally ramming one of the Flying Fortresses. The Japanese crew parachuted and was picked up by the *Akizuki*, but the B-17 crew was killed.[86]

Base Air Force did not attack Guadalcanal for the next two days because they were trying to cover a Japanese convoy to Buna on New Guinea. The Japanese had not given up on New Guinea, even as they tried to build up their forces on Guadalcanal, which continued the night of October 4, as destroyers *Shigure*, *Fubuki*, *Shirayuki*, *Murakumo*, and *Ayanami* dropped off 750 troops and supplies at Kamimbo.[87]

The Japanese reinforcements were getting too ridiculous even for Admiral Ghormley, though the risk-averse South Pacific commander was probably motivated more by his meetings with Admiral Nimitz. On October 1, Ghormley's operations officer asked the *Hornet*'s Admiral Murray, "How would you like to do an operation against Buin and Faisi?" It was music to Murray's ears. "That's exactly what we're here for; that's the only employment for carriers in this area; to go up and hit them and get out."[88]

A three-pronged strike was to take place October 5. One part involved the Cactus Air Force attacking the home of Louie the Louse, the Japanese seaplane base at Rekata Bay. A second part involved 11th Bombardment Group B-17s bombing the Buka airfield. Both strikes were intended to suppress Japanese air power for the main event – an attack by the air attack group of the carrier *Hornet* on the staging area for Japanese reinforcements, the harbors of Tonolei, on Bougainville, and Faisi, on the tiny island of the same name, one of the Shortland Islands and off the eastern tip of Shortland itself. The distance between the two harbors was some 25 miles. The waters between Bougainville, Shortland, and Fauro islands formed a large, vaguely triangular, sheltered anchorage. It was a "safe space" for ships, at least Japanese ones. The Japanese kept attacking the American staging area at Henderson Field; it was time to return the favor.

It was a good plan with one problem: weather. The day of the attack, October 5, the weather over the northern Solomons was stormy, with heavy rain and lightning. Only one of the B-17s found their target at Buka. Only eight Dauntlesses and three Avengers of the Cactus Air Force found Rekata Bay. Lieutenant Eldridge found his SBD the target of three Pete Type 0 observation seaplanes and was forced to ditch, but was rescued. The strike on Rekata accomplished very little.

The centerpiece of the operation, the *Hornet*'s airstrike, was scattered by the weather as well. Only two fighters and eight Dauntlesses found Tonolei, where they managed to shoot up some Toko Air Group seaplanes on the water, but little else. Only seven Avengers and five Wildcats found Faisi, where they ran into a little opposition from floatplanes but again accomplished very little.

But that afternoon scouting Dauntlesses from Henderson Field found the next Tokyo Express 170 miles west of Guadalcanal – destroyer *Asagumo* leading destroyers *Minegumo*, *Murasame*, *Natsugumo*, *Yudachi*, and *Harusame* in bringing 650 troops, two field guns, and ammunition to Guadalcanal.[89] An airstrike of nine Dauntlesses led by the *Saratoga*'s Lieutenant Commander Kirn was quickly launched. The Cactus Air Force pilots found the Japanese ships without air cover at 3:45 pm and went into their dive-bombing attacks. Once again, they could not land a clean hit. Two near-misses off both bows of the *Minegumo* caused flooding and reduced her best speed to 14 knots. The *Natsugumo* had to escort her back to Shortland.[90] The *Murasame* was also compelled to turn back after being damaged by near-misses. Two more strikes from Henderson Field could not find the three remaining destroyers, and managed to lose two Avengers in the dark as well.[91]

Nevertheless, the day was not a total washout from the standpoint of damage inflicted on the enemy or turning back part of a Tokyo Express. There was also a benefit of which the Americans were unaware. After she had launched her airstrikes, the *Hornet* had turned around to get as far away from Rabaul as possible. At 12:04 pm, her combat air patrol shot down one Betty from the Misawa Air Group on a reconnaissance mission. About 40 minutes later they shot down a second Betty, this one commanded by Petty Officer 2nd Class Yamada Shizuo.[92] Neither scout plane got off a contact report, but between the loss of two scout planes and the attack on the Shortlands anchorage, Base Air Force concluded there must be a carrier out there. Admiral Tsukahara decided not to attack Guadalcanal for the next few days while his scouts tried again to locate the American carrier so his G4Ms could take her out.

The Tokyo Express runs continued on October 6. Protected from air attack by rain, the *Uranami*, *Shikinami*, *Hayashio*, *Nowaki*, *Kuroshio*, and *Oyashio* managed to land four "regimental" guns, 450 Army troops, and 150 naval infantry of the 4th Maizuru Special Naval Landing Force at Tassafaronga.[93]

The next day the American nemesis *Nisshin* was sent out on another reinforcement run. But with an enemy carrier out there somewhere, the damage done by American flyers from Guadalcanal the previous day, and no air cover available for her, the *Nisshin* was called back. It was another fringe benefit of the otherwise ineffective attacks of October 5. But while the seaplane carrier was called back, the destroyers were not, and the *Shigure* led the *Ayanami*, *Fubuki*, and *Murakumo* on another successful run that night. The Americans simply could not stop these "rat transportation" runs.

However the Americans could and did stop the "ant" runs. For a while, anyway. The Japanese had been trying to run barges from Shortland to Rendova to carry heavy weapons and supplies, but the barges were not exactly seagoing creatures and even struggled in the littorals. Then the Americans attacked one of the intermediate bases for the barge runs. The ant transportation had to be suspended, which put more pressure on the Imperial Navy's supply convoys and especially the *Nisshin*.

The *Nisshin*'s delay was only a day, likely so they could get the new antiaircraft destroyer *Akizuki* to escort her. Now, with the *Harusame*, *Natsugumo*, *Asagumo*, and *Yudachi* as well as the *Akizuki* shepherding her, the *Nisshin* set out from Shortland on October 8 carrying six antiaircraft guns, two howitzers, and 180 troops. The destroyers carried an additional 560 troops. They successfully landed them that night. There was no trouble until the way back, although the *Nisshin* endured a bombing attack but took no damage.

The next Tokyo Express run was a milestone. The old light cruiser *Tatsuta* and destroyers *Shikinami*, *Hayashio*, *Nowaki*, *Kuroshio*, *Oyashio*, *Akigumo*, and *Uranami* were carrying 400 naval infantry of the 4th Maizuru Naval Landing Force, 700 Imperial Army troops – and General Hyakutake himself, finally making his appearance on the front lines.

Before he left Rabaul for Guadalcanal, General Hyakutake said, "The operation to surround and recapture Guadalcanal will truly decide the fate of the Pacific War."[94] That still did not make the operation important enough for Hyakutake to fully commit the fresh 38th Nagoya Division. He was saving as much of that division as he could for the new offensive in New Guinea.

General Hyakutake arrived to find that the Japanese had just been driven from the Matanikau River defense line by a spoiling attack engineered by General Vandegrift that virtually wiped out the 4th Regiment. Hyakutake also found out that many of the troops, especially those of the Kawaguchi Detachment, were starving. The 17th Army commander ordered new reinforcement convoys halted in favor of supply convoys. The supplies were so badly needed that Hyakutake wanted the convoys sent whether or not the Lunga airfield was suppressed.

But Admiral Yamamoto had no intention of allowing that to happen. The next run of the seaplane carrier *Nisshin* would include a strong escort of an entire division of heavy cruisers, and the admiral was working on an idea that had intrigued him for some time.

He had promised Colonel Tsuji that if necessary he would bring the *Yamato* to Guadalcanal and blast the airfield. Imperial General Headquarters had put a stop to that. Why send the biggest, most powerful battleship in the world to the front line when it can more usefully sit in the middle of Truk Harbor like a floating hotel with Yamamoto sitting on the floor of his stateroom writing *haiku*? No, the *Yamato* and her sister *Musashi* would not be going to Guadalcanal.

But the Japanese had other battleships.

CHAPTER 8
"I AM *AOBA*"

Normally, when one wants to protect something, one tries to surround it with something else. If surrounding the object to be protected is not possible, one tries to at least place something between the object and whatever could threaten it. But the Imperial Japanese Navy was not always normal.

The Imperial Navy had a peculiar habit of having the escorting warships hang out well behind the slow, unarmored, almost defenseless transports filled with troops. It made sense, in a way. If the enemy showed up blocking the transports, the enemy could cut these ships to pieces and kill the troops on board, but the warships would be all right.

It seemed to work at the Battle of the Java Sea, which was at its core an attempt by Allied ships to intercept a Japanese invasion convoy. The Japanese commander in charge of protecting the transports, Admiral Takagi Takeo, had decided having his cruisers some 200 miles behind the defenseless ships was good enough. And it was, until Allied ships showed up. Then, in a panic that his subordinates found amusing, Takagi had the cruisers race up to place themselves between the transports and the Allies. He arrived just in time, when the Allied ships were only some 20 miles from the convoy. In that respect, the battle was a near-run thing.

The Battle of the Java Sea was hardly the only time the Imperial Navy did not take protecting Army transports seriously. Just two nights later, off the Soenda Strait, the US cruiser *Houston* and Australian cruiser *Perth* managed to sneak into an anchorage filled with Japanese transports, getting between the transports and their guarding warships because those guarding warships were out to sea trying to intercept fleeing Allied ships. Arrogant. Overconfident. Sloppy.

Arrogant and overconfident might also be used to describe Vice Admiral Tsukahara, head of the Southeast Area and the 11th Air Fleet. He had demonstrated that he was something of a hothead too, figuratively speaking. Recently, however, Tsukahara had been a hothead literally, as he was suffering from dengue fever, malaria, and dysentery. Rabaul was not much better than Guadalcanal in terms of health effects.

So on October 8, Admiral Tsukahara relinquished command of the Southeast Area and the 11th Air Fleet to Vice Admiral Kusaka Jinichi, cousin to Admiral Nagumo's infamously cautious chief of staff Rear Admiral Kusaka Ryunosuke. Meanwhile the Buin airfield was completed – finally – at the southern end of Bougainville; the Americans would call it "Kahili." On October 10, the 6th Air Group completed staging into it. The 6th had the Mitsubishi A6M3 Model 32 Zero – the Allies would initially call it the "Hamp" – which had squared-off wings and, despite being newer than the A6M2 Model 21 "Zeke" Zero, had a far shorter range, which had restricted it to defending Rabaul. No longer. From Buin the Model 32s could both protect the Shortlands base complex and reach Guadalcanal. Now Base Air Force could attack Guadalcanal twice a day.[1]

Base Air Force could also cover the reinforcement convoys. Admiral Jojima's Reinforcement Group departed Shortland centered on seaplane carriers *Nisshin* and *Chitose*, carrying a total of four 150mm howitzers with towing vehicles, two field guns, one antiaircraft gun, and 280 troops of the Sendai Division, plus supplies. They were escorted by destroyers *Asagumo*, *Natsugumo*, *Yamagumo*, *Shirayuki*, *Murakumo*, and *Akizuki*, who were also carrying 289 naval infantry of the 4th Maizuru Special Naval Landing Force, 410 Army troops, a "regimental" gun, two battalion guns, two rapid-fire guns, and a mortar.[2] It was said that Jojima "could navigate a warship even on dry land."[3] It was a skill that might very well be needed before this campaign was over.

To cover Admiral Jojima, Base Air Force tried its new idea to wear down the Cactus Air Force. At 9:10 am, 18 Zeros of the Tainan Air Group under Lieutenant Commander Nakajima took off from Rabaul. Two soon aborted, but the remaining 16 were to perform a fighter sweep of the Lunga airfield. Following them by some 45 minutes was a second strike led by Misawa Air Group Lieutenant Commander Uchida Tomoyuki, with 45 Mitsubishi G4Ms – 18 from the 751 Air Group and nine each from the Kisarazu, Misawa, and 753 air groups – escorted by 29 Zeros – 12 from the 3rd Air Group, nine from the 751, and eight from the 2nd – under Lieutenant Ito. That is, 90 aircraft were headed for Guadalcanal. The idea was for the first strike to scare up American fighters, then the second strike would catch them on the ground refueling after the first strike.[4]

With no warning from coastwatchers, Lunga radar picked up the two formations inbound, 138 miles to the northwest. The Cactus Air Force sent up 15 Wildcats from Marine Fighting 121, 16 from Marine Fighting 223, and eight from the *Saratoga*, followed by 12 Airacobras. Heavy cloud cover created confusion in which the American fighters became scattered. Around 1:00 pm Lieutenant Commander Nakajima's 16 Zeros ended up wrestling with eight Fighting 121 F4Fs under Major Leonard Davis. Petty Officer 1st Class Nishzawa Hiroyoshi gouged the Grumman of 2nd Lieutenant Arthur Nehf, forcing him to ditch offshore. All 16 Zeros returned safely.

About 45 minutes later came the second strike, just slightly too early to catch the American fighters on the ground. Heavy clouds again confused the action. Unable to find the airfields, most of the G4Ms turned back, but the 18 Type 1s of the 751 Air Group under Lieutenant Commander Nishioka Kazuo ducked under the clouds to bomb the airfields. They hadn't found the airfields, either, and almost all the bombs landed several miles southeast of Fighter 1. Many of the Marine Wildcats had been low on fuel and about to land, but made one pass anyway, damaging four Bettys, with one later written off. Another, that of Petty Officer 1st Class Tashiro Eibu, was crippled then chased down and destroyed by Captain William C. Sharpsteen, flying a P-39 Airacobra of the 339th Fighter Squadron. In turn, Army 1st Lieutenant Howard Stern was killed when his Airacobra was shot down.[5]

In short, the new double strike tactic of Base Air Force had failed. But it might have succeeded if not for those meddling clouds. Admiral Kusaka was not willing to give up on this idea quite yet.

It was not the only experiment currently under way. Admiral Jojima's Reinforcement Group was assigned air cover in the form of flights of six Zeros each that rotated throughout the day. The last flight was ordered to stay on station until after sunset. Then, unable to make for Buin in the dark, the pilots were expected to ditch their Zeros in the Slot and be picked by destroyers. The Japanese got it half right; the pilots, all from the 6th Air Group, ditched their Zeros as ordered, but five of the pilots were never seen again.[6] It was a small but telling unforced error, further eroding the rapidly dwindling number of Sea Eagles.

Also speeding toward Guadalcanal to assist the Reinforcement Group was the so-called Bombardment Group, consisting of the truncated 6th Cruiser Division and two destroyers, whose job was to bombard Guadalcanal. This little force was sailing under the command of Rear Admiral Goto Aritomo. Goto had spent almost his entire career at sea, with little in the way of staff or shore postings. That seagoing experience had made him an accomplished, respected expert in torpedo tactics, which in turn helped earn him command of the 6th Cruiser Division. Then again, the lack of staff or shore postings may have denied Goto the political connections needed to get something better than the 6th, which was not necessarily a first-line command, consisting of four older, under-gunned heavy cruisers of the almost-identical *Aoba* and *Kako* classes. But Goto had made the most of it and the 6th had performed extremely well in the ambush off Savo Island.

Extremely well, at least until the admiral started the victory celebration a wee bit early and discontinued his ships' antisubmarine protocols as they approached port. Now, the 6th had only three cruisers of the almost-identical *Aoba* and *Kako* classes, and the *Kako* was not one of them, having paid the ultimate price for not maintaining vigilance.

Perhaps that incident gave Admiral Goto his first misgivings about the entire Guadalcanal operation. He had shared his reservations with Admiral Tanaka that perhaps their bosses were not taking this campaign seriously enough. There his reservations remained. Goto was a colorful old sea dog and far from stupid. He knew further criticism could be career-ending.

But his reservations were in the wind on this October 11. The Americans had never contested by sea a transport mission at night; there was no consideration that they would do so this night. And Admiral Goto's ships were ready; he had had them practicing shore bombardment since September. By 6:12 pm, his force was in the "center route" to Guadalcanal – one of the Japanese names for The Slot – some 120 miles northwest of Guadalcanal on a course of 110 degrees True – east-southeast – and a speed of 22 knots, soon increased to 30 knots.[7] They were dealing with intermittent squalls that the admiral found most annoying, though in theory they helped cover his approach. Goto had his ships in a T-shaped formation, the heavy cruisers *Aoba*, *Furutaka*, and *Kinugasa* in a central column, destroyer *Fubuki* 3,300 yards to port of *Aoba*, and destroyer *Hatsuyuki* 3,300 yards to starboard.

At 10:20 pm, the *Nisshin* signaled the Reinforcement Group had reached the landing zone on Guadalcanal, where no enemy ships were present; 20 minutes later, Admiral Goto received a message that the weather over Guadalcanal was "fair."[8] After another half-hour, Goto's aide Captain Kijima Kikunori noted continuous spurts of heat lightning to starboard, but they carried no thunder, though there were more squalls.

A little before 11:30, the navigator reported Savo Island was 20 miles ahead and would be visible in half an hour. The heat lightning and showers had dissipated. The *Aoba*'s skipper Captain Hisamune Sojiro turned to Admiral Goto and said, "Admiral, lookouts report flickering lights dead ahead."

The admiral wasn't worried. "It could be the reinforcement group," Goto responded. "Answer them. Find out that they want."[9] The *Aoba* flashed a recognition signal, following the common practice of first identifying herself: "I am *Aoba*." There was no answer. They tried again. "I am *Aoba*." Again no answer.

The lack of a response was reported to Admiral Goto. Though some on the cruiser's bridge were suspicious, to the admiral it was a curiosity, nothing more.[10] Goto told Captain Hisamune to hold course. "Steady on course 125 degrees."[11]

The *Aoba* came out of another rain squall at 11:40 pm. About to enter more restricted waters, at night, with a darkened target, Admiral Goto ordered speed cut to 26 knots. A lookout reported three ships dead ahead at a distance of 11,000 yards – about 5 miles.[12] They had to be the Reinforcement Group unloading troops and equipment on Guadalcanal, just as they were supposed to.

Just as she was supposed to, the flagship used her Aldis lamp to identify herself to the friendly ships by flashing the recognition signal: "I am *Aoba*."

The range to the ships ahead closed to 7,000 yards. With no response to the recognition signal. Stunned lookouts yelled that those ships were actually enemy. Enemy? Couldn't be, Admiral Goto thought. No enemy ships were reported in this area. The flagship's Aldis lamp flashed again, "I am *Aoba*."[13]

Admiral Goto leaned on the polished wood railing atop the starboard bridge bulkhead. Watching the heat lightning that had returned, just off the port bow. Strange. It was silent, like heat lightning often is, but this wasn't the white flashes in the clouds you'd normally expect. Instead, it was orange flashes close to the water…[14]

Those weren't lightning flashes. Those were gunflashes. The Reinforcement Group must have mistaken his ships for the enemy. Admiral Goto was being targeted by his own forces.

"Put your rudder over – reverse course!" Admiral Goto shouted to Captain Hisamune. The order went out in plain language over the voice radio to the other ships.[15] The gunfire was coming from almost dead ahead, but slightly to port. Best to turn away from it. Battle stations were not ordered. The gunfire was obviously a horrible mistake. Goto was not going to compound it by shooting at his own ships. Instead, the Japanese flagship tried to stop the gunfire by identifying herself. Exasperated signalmen flashed the Aldis lamp again: "I am *Aoba*."

The flagship heeled over as she turned to starboard, presenting her broadside to the guns now targeting her. A storm of shells battered the *Aoba*. At least one cut into cruiser's flag bridge. It did not explode, but its momentum created enough shrapnel to cut down most of the bridge crew. Admiral Goto was knocked to the deck, badly wounded.

Captain Kijima carried his admiral below decks for treatment and comfort. But Admiral Goto's wounds were mortal.

As Goto Aritomo slowly slipped away, Captain Kijima tried to console him as best he could. He told Goto that he could die with an easy mind because they had sunk two American heavy cruisers.[16]

The admiral was not assuaged. Painfully, Goto Aritomo growled at the men who had ended his life – "Bakayaro!," which might be most politely translated as "Stupid bastards!"[17]

Captain Kijima went back to the shattered bridge. He had lied to his admiral. The same salvo that had wounded his admiral had slashed communications, knocked out the fire director, and disabled the forward main battery before it could fire a shot. But Goto Aritomo would not, could not, accept Kijima's explanation. Kijima knew, and the other skippers in the task force knew, what the admiral refused to see.

The ships shooting at them were not from the Reinforcement Group, not even Japanese. They were from the US Navy.

Much like Admiral Goto, Rear Admiral Norman Scott believed he was shooting at his own ships. He was frantic. He had destroyers out there, he knew not where. And he had not even ordered his ships to open fire.

Norman Scott was a survivor of the Battle of Savo Island, if a distant survivor. He had been in Savo Sound that horrid August night, on board his then-flagship light antiaircraft cruiser *San Juan*, commanding a group that also included the Australian light cruiser *Hobart* and American destroyers *Monssen* and *Buchanan*. Scott had not been involved in the combat, though.

But he had studied all the information that could be gleaned from the Battle of Savo Island. Admiral Scott was determined that such a disaster would not happen again, not on his watch. And Scott now had a chance to put his studies into practice. On September 20, Admiral Ghormley had given command of the "Screening and Attack Force" to Scott, taking over for Admiral Wright.

Norman Scott was ready for battle. Scott had been "one of the best-liked men in the class" of 1911 at the Naval Academy.[18] He had done a tour of duty in the office of the Chief of Naval Operations, but made everyone's life miserable because he wanted to be at sea. He got his wish.

As commander of this still-new task force, Admiral Scott had established a reputation as "kind of like a junior Halsey."[19] The popular Scott was ready for battle. Were his men? "We would talk about it constantly," said Chick Morris of the light cruiser *Helena*. "The talk was always of the impending clash with the enemy's warships. Were we good enough? None of us knew. We had never been through the real thing."[20] Scott aimed to make them good enough.

In theory, Admiral Scott's force was to have six cruisers and nine destroyers. In practice, it never had this many ships and was filled with whatever cruisers and destroyers could be spared or were no longer needed to escort the *Enterprise*, *Saratoga*, and *Wasp*. These few ships were pulled this way and that, hither and yon in various duties, but whenever they had a free moment, during those last few weeks of September and the first week of October, Scott made sure they got in a lot of gunnery practice and a lot of practice in what Marine gunner Private Clifford Spencer on the heavy cruiser *San Francisco* called "Night Fighting Course 101."

"For the next two weeks we held daily gunnery practice and high speed night tactical maneuvers, every night, all night," recalled Spencer. "We were at general quarters every night and had mock battles with opposing ships, all moving at flank speed. Some fun!"

But Spencer was not complaining. "The object of the practice was to have everyone sharpen their night vision and spot the enemy before he saw you. With training, helmsmen were able to maintain ship intervals with more expertise and direct more energy to finding the enemy ships, allowing you to get off those very important first salvos."[21]

There is no substitute for combat experience, but relentless training can help one survive that first combat experience, replacing fear with procedure, instinct, muscle memory. "Admiral Scott had to instill behavior into his ships and crews that the Japanese had perfected over many years. The Admiral had days or at best a few weeks. We bitched and probably whined a lot, but by God, we learned!"[22]

This was how Admiral Scott earned the respect and the love of the men under his command. It was exhausting, it was dangerous – during one exercise on September 30 the *San Francisco* collided with the minelayer *Breese*, which in a time not much earlier would have cost a skipper his command – but his men knew Scott was preparing them for survival. "In Texas the battle cry had been 'Remember the Alamo!' Here the rally cry was 'Remember Savo Island!'" remembered Spencer.

In the interim, Admiral Ghormley had put his plans to seize an airfield site on Ndeni on hold – again – so he could send infantry reinforcements directly to Guadalcanal. These infantry were not Marines, but US Army. In the early months of 1942, Admiral King had compelled a generally unwilling US Army to send troops to New Caledonia because it was specifically listed in the Arcadia declaration as part of the "main air routes which must be secured" by securing "essential air bases." The Army found some loose units here and there totaling some 17,000 troops and sent them to Nouméa in a secret convoy that arrived in March, where General Patch set up headquarters for the defense of New Caledonia. Those loose units were arranged into a full Army division. One without the standard numerical designation, for now anyway. Private 1st Class David Fonseca of the 26th Signal Company suggested a contraction of "America" and "Caledonia." Thus, the Americal Division was born, the only US Army division formed outside United States territory.

Now one of those previously loose units, the 164th Infantry Regiment, was to be deployed to Guadalcanal as the vanguard of the Americal Division. The regiment, along with 210 men of the 1st Marine Air Wing and supplies for the 1st Marine Division, was loaded onto the transport *Zeilin* and Admiral Turner's flagship transport *McCawley* on October 8. The next day they sailed from Nouméa, with a close escort of destroyers *Gwin*, *Nicholas*, and *Sterett*, and three mine layers. Providing air cover was the only operational American carrier left in the Pacific, the *Hornet*, while protecting the right flank was a task force centered on the only operational American battleship left in the Pacific, the *Washington*.

It fell to Admiral Scott's ships to cover the left flank of the transports. On October 7, Scott left Espiritu Santo with only the heavy cruisers *San Francisco*, his flagship, and *Salt Lake City*, light cruiser *Boise*, and destroyers *Farenholt*, *Buchanan*, and *Laffey*. His orders were to go to a spot near Rennell Island and wait. When air reconnaissance showed Japanese ships moving toward Guadalcanal, Scott would take his ships to the Savo Island area to intercept them. Scott's specific mission was to "search for and destroy enemy ships and landing craft." That was fine with the aggressive, confident Scott. It was not fine with Admiral Ghormley, who understandably regarded Scott's force as too small for this mission, so the light cruiser *Helena* and the destroyers *Duncan* and *McCalla* were found near Espiritu Santo and ordered to join Scott's force.

Ever conscious of the lessons of Savo Island, Admiral Scott held one last night battle practice on October 8. The next day Scott issued his preliminary battle plan. It incorporated as many of the lessons of Savo Island as he could.

A huge issue at Savo had been the mistaken belief they were under fire from friendly ships, so Admiral Scott placed a premium on identification. Both for that reason and because many of the ships had not worked together before, Scott decided to keep a simple column formation. The cruisers would be in the center with the destroyers in front and back. It was hoped this formation would improve communications and identification. The destroyers were to illuminate targets as soon as possible after radar contacts, to launch torpedoes at large ships, and fire their guns at enemy destroyers. The destroyers in the lead were reminded to be alert for turn signals by voice radio or blinker, and to watch for turns if the voice radio failed.

As for the cruisers, the heavy cruisers were to use continuous fire against small ships at short range, rather than full gun salvos with long intervals; this was standard operating procedure for the US Navy, but it essentially constantly advertised the ship's position with the continuous gun flashes. The cruisers *Salt Lake City* and the *Helena* were, with the destroyers, to keep watch on the disengaged side. The cruisers were to open fire without orders from Admiral Scott.

Again with the identification issue, ships compelled to fall out of formation were to do so on the disengaged side, and head to Tulagi if unable to make 15 knots. A ship becoming separated from the formation was not to rejoin until after requesting permission, giving bearing of approach in voice code.

The admiral also borrowed liberally from the Japanese side. If the Japanese resorted to illuminating with searchlights, the Americans were to "counterilluminate", a military word if there ever was one. Admiral Scott figured that if the Japanese could use floatplanes, so could the Americans. Each cruiser was to launch two floatplanes to scout the shore for enemy landings and the sound for enemy ships. The aircraft were to maintain contact with the enemy until the approach of the Task Force, then to drop bombs and floatlights to indicate the enemy's position. Planes were to report any information regarding the enemy, even if there wasn't any. Flares were not to be used unless expressly ordered by the admiral. Upon the completion of their mission, or in the event that tactical scouting was impossible, the planes were to land at Tulagi.

Admiral Scott had tried to think of everything. It was as complete a plan as was possible, and was certainly reasonable under the circumstances. But it wasn't perfect.

One problem was radar, that new device whose potential most in the US Navy did not understand, including, despite his best efforts, Admiral Scott. That was especially true of the new SG search radar, the type of radar with the overhead display that most resembles radar as it is known today. All of the cruisers carried radar, but only light cruisers *Boise* and *Helena* carried the new SG search radar. Yet Scott, as admirals traditionally did, chose as his flagship what he believed was his strongest ship, the heavy cruiser *San Francisco*. However, both the *San Francisco* and the *Salt Lake City*, the latter with her ten 8-inch guns arguably more powerful than the former with nine, each carried the SC radar, whose display looked more like an EKG and required interpretation through a top-secret decoder ring or something. Worse, radio intelligence had determined that the Japanese could detect SC radar transmissions because of its wide metric band. Scott ordered the SC radars switched off during transit, restricting use to the centimetric SG radar and the even narrower-band fire control radars. The admiral was going to have to get his contact information from the *Boise* and *Helena*, instead of seeing it himself.

And then there were the torpedoes. For some time, US Navy submarines had strongly suspected there were serious mechanical problems with their torpedo, the Mark 14. The Bureau of Ordnance denied any problems. Then Admiral King got involved. Shortly thereafter in late August, a notice had been issued that tests had proven the torpedoes were running some 10 feet deeper than set.[23] Because the Navy had been too cash-strapped to test the torpedoes with actual warheads and instead used dummy warheads, which were lighter than real warheads, the torpedoes' depth setting had been calibrated incorrectly. Once the depth issue was identified, the problem was relatively easy to fix.[24]

But the problems did not end there. The Mark 14 would be detonated by the Mark 6 exploder, which included a contact exploder and a magnetic influence feature. This feature was intended to cause the torpedo to detonate when it entered a ship's magnetic field, which, in theory, was when the torpedo was under the ship. In theory. However, the size of the magnetic field varied depending on where one was on the earth, so the magnetic field of a ship off, say, Newport, Rhode Island, home of the US Navy's Newport Torpedo Station, was of a different size and shape than the magnetic field of a ship off, for instance, Guadalcanal.

Since the beginning of the war, the submariners had reported a never-ending stream of premature explosions and non-explosions from its torpedoes. They were suspicious something was wrong with the Mark 6, especially that magnetic influence exploder, but the Navy Bureau of Ordnance and the Newport Torpedo Station refused to even consider the matter and blamed the malfunctions on user error.

The Navy's destroyers usually did not launch their torpedoes under the slow and carefully documented conditions that submarines did, so they could not know for sure. But they had escaped success with their torpedo, the Mark 15, which also used the Mark 6. As it was, a month earlier the skipper of the destroyer *Lansdowne*, Lieutenant Commander Smedberg, had to deactivate the magnetic influence feature in order to get his Mark 15 torpedoes to actually sink the blazing carrier *Wasp*. The Mark 6 was supposed to be a wonder weapon; so far its users were only left wondering.

Meanwhile Admiral Scott was wondering when the enemy would show up. On the afternoons of October 9 and 10, Scott's force positioned itself near Rennell Island to be able to make the 20–25-knot dash to arrive off Savo Island by 11:00 pm. But there were no sightings and each night Scott went back south again. He flew off four of his cruiser floatplanes to Tulagi where they would spend the evening and return the next afternoon.

This was about the time – 1:45 pm – that an 11th Bombardment Group B-17 reported two cruisers and six destroyers some 210 miles from Guadalcanal heading down The Slot at 25 knots on a course 120 degrees True – southeast.[25] Admiral Scott plotted their course and speed; they would arrive off Guadalcanal at about 11:00 pm. At 4:07 pm, Scott got his ships moving toward Savo Island. The cruisers were in a column, the flagship *San Francisco* in front, followed by the *Boise*, *Salt Lake City*, and *Helena*. In front of the column was a 2,500-yard semicircle of destroyers, with the *McCalla* and *Buchanan* to port, the *Farenholt* dead ahead, and the *Duncan* and *Laffey* to starboard.[26]

The impending action gave Admiral Scott an aerial tangle. He had ordered his cruisers to send off all but one of their floatplanes to Tulagi, which they started to do around 4:00 pm. However, this was when the floatplanes they had sent the day before started returning, pursuant to their previous orders. Scott wanted to send them back, but they were suffering from contaminated gasoline and had to be taken aboard. While being hoisted aboard, the *San Francisco*'s floatplane bounced off the hull and was damaged.

Scott ordered the *Buchanan* to recover the crew and sink the plane, which delayed the destroyer rejoining the formation until 10:00 pm and possibly complicated the night battle plan.[27] The US Navy just could not get the hang of floatplanes.

Another report of the enemy had come in at 6:10 pm, this from Cactus Air Force SBDs. Again it was two enemy cruisers and six destroyers, speed 20 knots, again on course 120 degrees True, now some 110 miles from Guadalcanal. Were these the same ships reported earlier? It seemed so. Were these the only ships coming? No other sightings had been reported. Admiral Scott ordered his ships to battle stations, mainly as a precaution.[28] He didn't expect combat for another five hours or so and that combat was to be with an invasion convoy with unarmed and lightly armed transports.

For that reason, four hours later, Admiral Scott started putting his ships in a combat state of mind. The floatplanes were to be launched at 10:00 pm, and at the appointed hour the *Salt Lake City*, *Boise*, and *San Francisco* catapulted theirs into the air. The *Helena* did not receive Scott's order to launch the floatplane. Her skipper Captain Gilbert Hoover was unwilling to leave the fire hazard aboard in a night combat action and so dumped it over the side.[29]

Meanwhile, just after the *Salt Lake City*'s floatplane was blasted into the air, improperly stowed flares kept on board ignited. The plane immediately crashed, leaving a "ring of fire" that burned for two minutes about 600 yards off the starboard side of the column.[30] The hideous nature of the fire convinced the American witnesses that no one could have survived, but both crewmembers did.[31]

Not to be outdone, 90 minutes later the floatplane from the *Boise* developed engine trouble and had to plop down near Tulagi, where, without power, she had to bob in the water waiting for rescue.[32] The US Navy still could not get the hang of floatplanes.

The Americans were very fortunate that Admiral Jojima's ships, hidden by a jut of land, missed the fire. And even more fortunate that Admiral Goto, who did see the fire, concluded it was some sort of message from Jojima's ships. And still more fortunate in the judgment of Commander Yokota Minoru, whose submarine *I-26*, rapidly becoming an American nemesis, had spotted a "cruiser" at 10:26 pm southwest of Guadalcanal. An Allied ship approaching Guadalcanal at night was very unusual, so Yokota decided he would report the contact – after attacking it. He had his boat dive and approached the cruiser column, but struggled to get into attack position.[33] Admiral Scott's American surprise was still safe. For now.

Around 10:30, when the force was 23 miles southeast of Savo Island, the force changed course to 75 degrees True – east-northeast – heading directly toward Savo. A few minutes later Admiral Scott ordered the five destroyers to go to battle formation, join the cruiser column, which Captain Robert G. Tobin, head of Destroyer Squadron 12, acknowledged. His command ship *Farenholt* moved in front, followed by *Duncan* and *Laffey*, while the *Buchanan* moved behind the *Helena* and the *McCalla* moved behind the *Buchanan*, forming a column 3 miles long.[34]

At 10:50 Lieutenant John A. Thomas in the *San Francisco*'s floatplane reported, "One large, two small vessels, one six miles from Savo off northern beach Guadalcanal. Will investigate closer."[35] The report was not "well understood" aboard the *San Francisco*'s flag bridge.[36] "*One six?" What does that mean? Sixteen? Or one ship 6 miles from Savo Island? What does "large" mean? A battleship? Are these ships moving?*

Right on schedule, at 11:00 pm, Commodore Tobin's destroyer *Farenholt*, in the lead, sighted Savo Island dead ahead.[37] Admiral Scott changed course to 50 degrees True to assume a blocking position west of Savo, with a clean horizon for radar searches to avoid the land interference that had complicated things at the Savo Island disaster in August. The column of American ships kept steaming along, trying to keep the gap between Savo Island and Guadalcanal plugged. At 11:30, Lieutenant Thomas, in the *San Francisco*'s floatplane, reported, "one large ship, two small ships, 16 miles east of Savo, one mile offshore."[38] A slightly more coherent report.

As the ships assumed battle formation, the tension aboard the ships ratcheted up, especially for the vast majority of the men, for whom this was going to be their first combat. On the destroyer *Duncan*, Boatswain's Mate 3rd Class Roy Boehm, manning the Number 2 5-inch mount, was watching for targets. Another gunner was nervously pacing through the mount's entrance hatch.

"See anything yet?" the gunner muttered.

"Yes," Boehm responded.

There was a moment of apprehensive silence from the gunner. Then he asked the obvious, "What do you see?"

"The dark."

"Boehm, I don't want any of your bullshit tonight," grumbled the gunner.[39]

On the *Boise*, radar technician Vincent Langelo said several prayers, including the Lord's Prayer and a reasonable facsimile of the 23rd Psalm. He observed, "All over the ship, the men braced themselves for action. They were like tigers, crouched backward, ready to leap at their prey."[40]

As the *Boise* and the rest of the column scooched more and more to the northeast, it opened up a gap between it and Guadalcanal that would only get wider and wider. Admiral Scott had to turn around and head back to the southwest to keep the blocking position and keep that gap plugged. All his ships had to do was turn around. In all of the training through which Scott had put his ships, they had never practiced this maneuver, not at night, but how hard could it be?

So at 11:32 pm, when four miles off Savo Island, Admiral Scott radioed, "Signal. Execute to follow. Column left to course two three zero."[41] He was telling his ships to prepare for a course change.

In naval parlance, when an admiral commanding a fleet orders a "turn," it means all the ships so ordered are to change to the same course at the same time. It can be called a "simultaneous turn," but there are other versions of this term used for clarity. If a group of ships is steaming line ahead – that is, in a column – a simultaneous turn will put the ships in a line abreast formation – that is, a line – so it can be called a "line turn," while an "echelon turn" staggers the turn so the ships steam in the same direction but with each ship at an angle from the other ships in the formation.

But if a group of ships are in a column and are expected to turn and "follow the leader," the turn is called a "column movement," though perhaps "column turn" might be better for clarity. The column of ships becomes like a train or a centipede. The lead ship goes to a spot on the water and turns and moves on. The next ship follows the first ship to the same spot, turns in the same direction, and moves on following the first, and so forth.

The order to actually turn – the column movement – came by voice radio: "Execute column left to course 230."[42]

In the *Farenholt* in front, Commodore Tobin had the destroyer turn to port to assume course 230 degrees True – southwest. The *Farenholt* was followed by the *Duncan* and the *Laffey*.

Commodore Tobin looked at the cruisers who were behind him in the column. Or were supposed to be. Because the *San Francisco*, Admiral Scott's flagship, had turned at the same time the *Farenholt* did. The flagship had not followed the destroyers ahead of her but had cut inside them. And the other cruisers were following the *San Francisco*. Tobin's three destroyers were cut out of the formation. A bemused Tobin wondered if he had misinterpreted the order. Were the lead destroyers, the cruisers, and the trailing destroyers supposed to execute column turns by group? So that the trailing destroyers would be ahead? Were his ships supposed to be cut out? He later reported:

> At 2332 force reverse course left to 230 degrees true, cruisers executing column movement immediately. FARENHOLT turned to left followed by DUNCAN and LAFFEY. I gave orders to the Captain of the FARENHOLT to slow as necessary to remain astern of the cruisers until it could be ascertained whether DDs [destroyers] which had been in the rear were following cruisers in formation, or had turned to take new van positions.[43]

It was not his fault, nor was it Admiral Scott's fault. Not anyone's fault, really. The *San Francisco* had only one voice radio for the Talk Between Ships frequencies. That radio was on the flag bridge, not the navigation bridge, where the cruiser's skipper Captain Charles H. McMorris was. Despite being Scott's flag captain, McMorris had not received Scott's full order.[44]

As soon as Commodore Tobin saw that the trailing destroyers *Buchanan* and *McCalla* were following the cruisers, he had his three destroyers race up the starboard side of the cruiser column intending to take the lead once again. The force was thrown into confusion. Just as the Japanese showed up.

In reality they had shown up a little earlier. At 11:25 the SG radar on the *Helena* picked up unidentified contacts on a bearing of 315 degrees True at the extreme range of 28,000 yards. The contact was updated and plotted every 15 seconds.[45] For whatever reason, news of the contact never reached Admiral Scott.

A minute later, the *Salt Lake City*'s SC radar, operating against orders, picked up unidentified ships on bearing 273 degrees True 16,000 yards away. They were heading on a course of 120 degrees True at a speed of about 20 knots. The radar operators on the *Salt Lake City* guessed that the 20-knot speed was probably too slow for aircraft.[46] For whatever reason, news of this contact never reached Admiral Scott, either.

At 11:38 pm, it was the SG radar on the *Boise* that picked up unidentified ships bearing 295 degrees True, range of about 14,000 yards.[47] Again, a report of this contact never reached Admiral Scott.

It was not until 11:41, 16 minutes after her radar initially detected enemy ships, that the *Helena* reported to Admiral Scott a "surface radar contact, bearing 298."[48] The range would have been helpful. So would course and speed. The *San Francisco* trained out her fire control radar toward this target, and the *Helena*'s report was repeated to the other ships.[49]

Another two minutes and it was the *Boise* that was reporting in, this time, "five bogeys bearing 065."[50] Admiral Scott was perplexed. *Bogeys?* That was a term for unidentified aircraft. Were there enemy aircraft around here? In fact, radar was so new that its terminology had not yet been standardized, so the *Boise* was simply reusing familiar terms.

And that bearing of 65 degrees? What was that? True or relative? Normally the bearing is given in term of degrees "True" – that is, with reference to 0 degrees as true north. The *Boise* had said "relative," but the word was garbled over the radio. A relative bearing – relative as to the one reporting the contact – is meaningless unless one knows the position and course of the one reporting the contact. The true bearing for the *Boise*'s contact was 295 degrees.

This worried Admiral Scott. Were his wayward destroyers the reported radar contacts? He could not open fire if he did not know where his ships were. Commodore Tobin was even more worried. His three destroyers were now at about the midpoint of the cruiser column and directly in the line of fire from the cruisers to these reported radar contacts.

With growing alarm, at 11:44 Scott radioed Tobin. "Are you taking station ahead?" At that time, Tobin was wondering if he should have his ships slow down and simply follow the cruisers and trailing destroyers in column. Tobin inferred that the admiral's question meant he wanted Tobin's destroyers back at the front of the column. After a few seconds of consideration, Tobin responded, "Affirmative; coming up on your starboard flank."[51] Certainly, the *Farenholt* was. Tobin assumed he was being followed by the *Duncan* and *Laffey*.

But the *Duncan* was having some wacky ideas of her own. Her gunnery radar had picked up the contacts. When the *Farenholt* slowed down to determine if the rear destroyers were staying in the rear, the *Duncan* had to slow down to avoid hitting her. *Duncan* skipper Lieutenant Commander Edmund B. Taylor did not know why the *Farenholt* had slowed down. Perhaps it was to charge at the Japanese ships that had showed up on the *Duncan*'s fire control radar. It must be, because those ships were poised to ambush the Americans as they turned. Not good. So Taylor decided to have the *Duncan* charge. The little destroyer dashed at 30 knots toward the big Japanese ships to close the range to launch torpedoes.

Without telling Commodore Tobin or, for that matter, Admiral Scott. As Taylor looked astern, he saw to his horror that no one, not even the *Farenholt*, was following him. His little ship was charging all by herself. But it was too late to turn back now.

It was around this time that the flagship *San Francisco*, whose fire control radar had been trained in the direction of the contacts, finally detected the incoming ships as well, at the perilously close range of 5,000 yards. Marine Clenroe Davis heard one of the radar operators report by phone to the bridge that unidentified ships had appeared on his display. The man fell silent as he listened to the response of the apparently incredulous officer on the bridge. Then the radar operator politely replied, "Well, sir, these islands are traveling at about 30 knots."[52]

Admiral Scott knew the Japanese were here. Much, much closer than he would have liked. But he wasn't quite sure where they were because he wasn't sure where his own destroyers were. Somewhere to starboard and behind him, was all he knew. Scott's entire force, entire plan, had been thrown into confusion because his ships could not execute a simple column turn, a maneuver that had slipped through the cracks of the admiral's preparation. After all that determination to not have another Savo Island, all that study, all that training, all that practice, all that effort to keep his ships together, Scott was just like the cruiser captains at Savo Island – afraid to open fire out of fear of hitting his own ships.

Admiral Scott was, but his skippers were not. The *Boise* and *Helena* had been tracking the Japanese for some 20 minutes. They knew the targets were Japanese. They had good firing solutions. Moreover, as Captain Ernest G. Small of the *Salt Lake City* later said, "It was one of those things that naval officers wait twenty years to see. We crossed their T."[53]

The cruiser skippers knew that the US column was perpendicular to and now less than 3 miles in front of the Japanese column. That is, the American ships were a horizontal capping the Japanese vertical, forming a "T," a classic maneuver in which the ships in the cross could fire all of their guns but the ships in the vertical could respond with only their forward guns. And the admiral didn't seem to realize it.

The cross would not last long. They had to take advantage of it. Now.

Not surprisingly, the *Boise* and *Helena* were getting impatient. A lookout on the *Helena* reported, "Ships visible to the naked eye." This announcement prompted a disgusted ensign to grumble to the navigator, "What are we going to do? Board them?"[54]

It was rather odd, the impatience to open fire, because Admiral Scott's original orders for how to handle this engagement had said the cruisers were to open fire without his permission. But it seems none of the skippers were comfortable in doing so.[55] The *Helena*'s skipper Captain Hoover decided to press the issue, which brought to the forefront what was in retrospect a bizarre quirk of the General Signals Procedure book.

Over the voice radio, specifically the Talk Between Ships circuit, Hoover sent to Admiral Scott a two-word message: "Interrogatory Roger." According to the signals procedure, this was to be interpreted as a request for permission to commence action, in this instance, "Request permission to open fire."[56] If the response was "Roger," then that permission had been granted.

What Admiral Scott's people on the *San Francisco* heard in these same words, though, also according to signals procedure, was "Did you receive my last message?" This was the *Helena*'s report of a radar contact. In that instance, a response of "Roger" means "I have received your message." The flagship responded by voice radio, "Roger."[57]

It's not clear if the *Helena* actually received this response. In the light cruiser's radio room, Lieutenant C. G. Morris interpreted the response from Admiral Scott to be "Wait."[58] Which does not fit the context for "Roger."

But with time to spring their surprise slipping away, Captain Hoover quickly tried again. "Interrogatory Roger." This time, the *San Francisco*'s reply was heard loud and clear, "Roger."[59]

Lieutenant W. D. Fisher, the *Helena*'s signal officer, shouted to Captain Hoover, "Permission granted!"

Finally. The *Helena*'s skipper snarled, "Open fire!"[60]

And at 11:46 pm, five minutes after Commander Yokota's *I-26*, unable to get into attack position, sent a too-late-to-be-of-use warning of the cruisers' presence, the 15 6-inch guns of the *Helena*, which had been loaded for a half-hour, bloomed and boomed in the night. Within a minute, the *Salt Lake City* chipped in with ten 8-inch shells. At about the same time, the *Boise* sent another 15 6-inch shells. Not wanting to be left out, the *San Francisco* joined in as well.

The *Duncan*'s Roy Boehm remembered the shock of it:

> The night erupted … American warships opened up with everything in a gigantic continuous explosion of bright flashes and flaming meteors. It was like being in the heart of a violent electrical storm. Star clusters bursting high aloft bathed the desperately maneuvering mixture of friendly and enemy ships with eerie shadows and reflections. Streaks of flames belched from every big gun.[61]

Like Boehm, Admiral Scott was shocked. He had given no specific order to open fire. Were his cruisers firing on his destroyers? It sure seemed that way. Lieutenant Morris called it "one of the most dramatic misinterpretations of signals in naval history."[62]

The largest and closest of the Japanese ships, *Aoba*, was snowed under by an avalanche of gunfire from the *Boise*, *Salt Lake City*, *Farenholt*, and *Laffey*. It was probably one of the *Boise*'s shells that wrecked the *Aoba*'s bridge and fatally injured Admiral Goto. With their fearless and perhaps clueless leader incapacitated, the Bombardment Group followed Goto's last order – to turn around – and then sluggishly milled around in confusion, with the only objective being to get out.

The *Helena*'s main battery aimed at two different but unspecified targets. One was apparently the *Hatsuyuki*, on the port wing of the Japanese formation. The other target seems to have been the *Duncan*, who had gotten way too close to the Japanese, passing the *Aoba* in the opposite direction. The *Laffey*, seeing the *Helena* open fire, decided to drop back and try to fall in behind the trailing destroyer *McCalla*. Her skipper, Lieutenant

Commander William E. Hank, understandably wanted no part of being caught in the crossfire between the Japanese and his own ships.[63]

"Cease firing, our ships!" shouted Admiral Scott into the voice radio. He was very concerned that his cruisers, who had been firing for only some 90 seconds, were firing on the lost destroyers of Destroyer Squadron 12. But no one stopped firing. Scott repeated his order. Then the *Salt Lake City* ceased fire. Scott physically went up to the *San Francisco*'s navigation bridge to personally order Captain McMorris to stop shooting. The *Boise* and *Helena*? Well, they never stopped firing, so they evidently did not get the order. Evidently.

Admiral Scott got on the voice radio to Commodore Tobin. "How are you?" the admiral asked. "[Destroyer Squadron 12] is okay," Tobin answered. To be more precise, Tobin and his ship *Farenholt* were okay. He had no idea where the *Duncan* and *Laffey* had gone or what had happened to them, though he didn't tell his admiral that.

"Were we shooting at [you]?" Scott asked. A befuddled Tobin replied, "I do not know who you were firing at."[64] Completely frustrated, the admiral ordered, "All Squadron 12 turn on recognition signals." Four of the five destroyers lit up their recognition lights, white and colored lights arranged in a sequence that changes by day, mounted on the side of the bridge. Ominously, the lone destroyer that did not was the *Duncan*. Of the four that did, only two, the *Buchanan* and *McCalla*, were where they were supposed to be.

With that settled, at least as much as it was going to be, at 11:51 Admiral Scott barked into the voice radio, "Commence firing, commence firing!"[65] The confusion caused by the botched column turn and the *Duncan*'s charge had given the Japanese four minutes to gather themselves and try to escape.

One of those ships showed a very big return on the radars of the *San Francisco* and *Salt Lake City*. Both cruisers snapped on their searchlights and pinned their target, which showed a white band on one of her smoke stacks. The US Navy never used such recognition symbols. The ship was obviously Japanese. Admiral Scott was shocked to see a Japanese ship so close, only some 1,400 yards away. But at least now he was certain the targets were not American ships. At least not this target.

This was the destroyer *Fubuki*, who had been holding position on the starboard beam of Admiral Goto's flagship *Aoba*. The destroyer had given an outsized radar return because she had been in the process of reversing course to starboard, thus presenting her port broadside and largest possible profile to the radar.

The American 8-inch cruisers let the *Fubuki* have it, joined by many of Admiral Scott's other ships. The Japanese destroyer had Allied blood on her hands; it had been she who first spotted and reported the aforementioned *Perth* and *Houston* off northwest Java as they tried to escape the Japanese in the East Indies, helping to sink both. Now the bill was due. *Fubuki* captain Lieutenant Commander Yamashita Shizuo seems to have still been in shock, or else shared Admiral Goto's belief that he was the victim of friendly fire, for the destroyer never fired a shot or even trained out any of her tubes carrying the deadly Type 93 torpedoes as she tried to scurry away. Japanese records claim the *Fubuki* received four hits; the Americans believe the actual figure was much higher. Whatever it was – and four 8-inch shell hits would be a serious issue for any destroyer – the *Fubuki* did not last long. The avalanche of American arms caused an explosion aboard the revolutionary destroyer that sent her to the depths at 11:53, barely six minutes after the shooting began, taking with her Yamashita and about half her crew.[66]

Near the *Fubuki* was the *Farenholt*, still trying to get back to the front of the American column and almost there, being even with the *San Francisco* to port. Also to port was whoever smacked the *Farenholt* with at least two hits, both on the port side, one jamming the torpedo mount, the other at the water line, destroying the plotting room and disrupting all power, lighting, and communications in the forward part of the ship. The *Farenholt* developed a "heavy" list to port, and Commodore Tobin looked to exit this particular stage.[67]

Like the *Fubuki*, the *Aoba* was still completing her turn to starboard. She had several fires burning and her foremast had been toppled, but she gamely fired back with her aft 8-inch turret, the only one still operational. On the navigation bridge, Captain Hisamune tried to steer an erratic course to throw off the vicious gunfire, but it was not enough to keep the aft turret from being destroyed by an explosion and and fire after only seven shots.[68] Only Hisamune's order for the cruiser to make smoke brought her some relief and a chance to escape.

Behind the *Aoba* in the Japanese cruiser column was the *Furutaka* under Captain Araki Tsutau. Araki saw what was happening to the *Aoba* ahead of him and determined the situation was "not good."[69] With the American column having crossed their "T" from left to right, Araki guessed that a left turn would enable him to more quickly return fire with his entire battery and take his ship out of the main line of fire. The *Furutaka* started turning left. Then he saw the *Aoba* in deep trouble, so he turned right to try to take some of the heat off of his flagship. And he did, for a price.

After she fired one salvo from her secondary battery at 11:48 the *Furutaka* started taking the avalanche of gunfire, especially from the *Salt Lake City*. It was apparently a salvo from the *Salt Lake City* that, a minute later, smashed the *Furutaka*'s aft 8-inch turret. At 11:51, as the old Japanese cruiser was in the midst of her turn and parallel to the American column, a shell exploded on the port torpedo tubes, igniting several of the Type 93 torpedoes there and starting a large fire that now served as a nice point of aim in the darkness.[70]

As the *Furutaka* turned to starboard, she was being stalked by destroyer *Duncan*, the "one ship Navy," as C. W. Kilpatrick cheekily named her.[71] Lieutenant Commander Taylor ordered hard to starboard to try to get out of the American line of fire. But then he saw the *Furutaka* and swung left again to try for a good firing solution. The destroyer's 5-inch guns got in some good licks on the cruiser's superstructure and launched one torpedo. But, as Roy Boehm described it:

> In the middle of the storm, *Duncan* found herself occupying a precarious no-man's-land between the guns of the enemy and the guns of her own ships... Alone and trapped

> between enemy and friendly guns, *Duncan* became a lightning rod attracting fire from both sides.[72]

Especially from the *Furutaka*, the *Hatsuyuki*, and, Boehm believed, the *Boise*. The *Duncan* was walloped between the Number 2 5-inch mount and the bridge, starting a serious fire. Another shell collapsed the smoke stack. Several American shells, believed to be 6-inch, perforated her hull and superstructure. After launching one more torpedo the *Duncan* swung away to port, her rudder jammed, burning like a comet.[73]

So, for that matter, was the *Furutaka*. At 11:54, her forward starboard engine room was hit and flooded by an actual American Mark 15 torpedo, probably from the *Duncan*, though it could have been from a spread of five from the *Buchanan*.[74] A minute later a shell went into her aft port engine room. At the same time, her main battery got a short near-miss on the *Salt Lake City* at 11:55 that sprayed the American cruiser with shrapnel and also sent a shell into the *Boise* that torched skipper Captain Edward J. Moran's quarters. Captain Araki's ship got off maybe 30 8-inch shells, but she had to deal with not just the damage, flooding, and loss of speed, but also the humiliation of being the first confirmed hit during the Guadalcanal campaign by an American surface-launched torpedo on an enemy ship.[75]

Behind the *Furutaka* was the *Kinugasa*. Her skipper, Captain Sawa Masao, was known for being aggressive, but even he wanted no part of what he was seeing up ahead. The wily skipper, like the *Furutaka*'s Captain Araki, saw that the American column was heading left to right in front of him, so that if he turned left he would escape their fire and attention more easily. Unlike Captain Araki, Sawa decided it was more important to save his own skin than that of his admiral. So, "[l]ess gallantly but more sensibly," in the words of Guadalcanal historian Richard Frank, Sawa swung the *Kinugasa* hard to port.[76] It saved his ship. For now.

At around this time it occurred to Admiral Scott that he should probably report that he was in combat with the Japanese. At 11:54 he sent a three-word message to Admiral Ghormley and General Vandegrift: "Engaging heavy cruisers." A very informative message that C. W. Kilpatrick described as "designed to keep both recipients awake the rest of the night."[77]

At midnight, Scott sent a very different voice message to his force: "All ships cease firing." Evidently he feared that his formation was coming apart, as often happens in night engagements, and he wanted to straighten it up. To that end, one minute later, the admiral ordered, "Flash recognition lights and form column. [Destroyer Squadron 12] acknowledge."[78] This last message apparently generated no response, for Scott had to repeat it four more times, calling various ships out by name to acknowledge receipt. Those that did, did so with the word, "Roger." The significance of this word would be re-examined after this night. Two did not; the *Boise*, which never even obeyed the first order to stop firing, and the *Duncan*, whose radio suite had been destroyed.

In the absence of the leading destroyers, Admiral Scott's flagship *San Francisco* was now leading the American column, which had by now crossed the Japanese front and was steaming away from it. By this time the Japanese ships had turned around and were heading west-northwest toward Shortland, trying to build up speed. Without formal orders, Scott turned the *San Francisco* to course 290 degrees True – west-northwest – to lead the cruiser column in continuing the fight with the retreating Bombardment Force on a roughly parallel course. As he did so, the burning *Farenholt*, now listing 9 degrees, cut in front of the flagship heading south-southwest and continued away from the battle.

Four fires were visible to the Americans. One was the *Farenholt*; three were unidentified. Of those, one was the *Duncan*, all by herself; one was the *Aoba*, who some mistook for being sunk since she had completely covered herself with a smokescreen so soon after being hit hard; and one, the biggest, was the *Furutaka*, now crawling along at 5 knots. For the Japanese it was now every ship for herself. They were all fleeing, thinking only of escape.

Except for one: *Kinugasa*.

Alone among the Japanese skippers, Captain Sawa had recovered from the shock of the American attack. Some 4 miles north of the *San Francisco*, the *Kinugasa* was screened from the pursuing squadron by the burning *Aoba* and *Furutaka*, and the aggressive Sawa was determined to strike back. And unlike the other Japanese skippers this night, Sawa had remembered the Japanese credo: *When in doubt, launch torpedoes.*

The *Salt Lake City* had developed a horribly inaccurate firing solution on the *Kinugasa* and spewed eight ten-gun salvos which she thought straddled but actually all missed. Speeding for Shortland at 30 knots, Captain Sawa struck back with a salvo that landed just astern of the *San Francisco*, who had resumed firing at the *Aoba.*

By a hard right rudder at 12:06, the *Boise* had narrowly dodged two Long Lance torpedoes the *Kinugasa* had spit out. SG radar found a contact off the starboard beam. Captain Moran ordered the searchlight snapped open, trying to pin the contact. All it did was serve as a nice point of aim for the *Kinugasa*. With her forward turrets masked by her superstructure, the old Japanese cruiser let loose with her aft turret.

With only one dual turret, at long range, with no radar, the *Kinugasa* was "shooting beautifully with twin eight-inch mounts," according to the *Boise*'s Captain Moran. "She straddled us repeatedly along the forward half of the forecastle, and made two known hits."[79] More hits than that, according to the *Boise*'s damage report. One shell, possibly from the secondary battery, hit just below the left gun of Turret 1. At the same time, one 8-inch salvo sent one Type 91 armor-piercing shell into the barbette of Turret 2, and another plunging into the water to pierce the *Boise*'s hull below the waterline and bounce into the magazine for Turret 2, where it exploded. The hit started a fire that quickly spread to the magazines for Turret 1 and forced the abandonment of all three forward turrets and started flooding. Yet another 8-inch hit, also below the waterline, worsened the flooding. It was indeed a "beautiful" job of shooting by Captain Sawa's crew, who had managed to get the Type 91 shell, designed to dive into the water and hit the target below the waterline, to do exactly that.[80] With her forward turrets ablaze, the *Boise* sheared out of line to port.

An explosion in a magazine is normally a bad thing. If the entire magazine detonates, the ship could be completely destroyed, as the Americans and the Japanese had seen and would see during this campaign. But the *Boise*'s did not. The crewmen in the magazine, almost all

The Battle of Cape Esperance

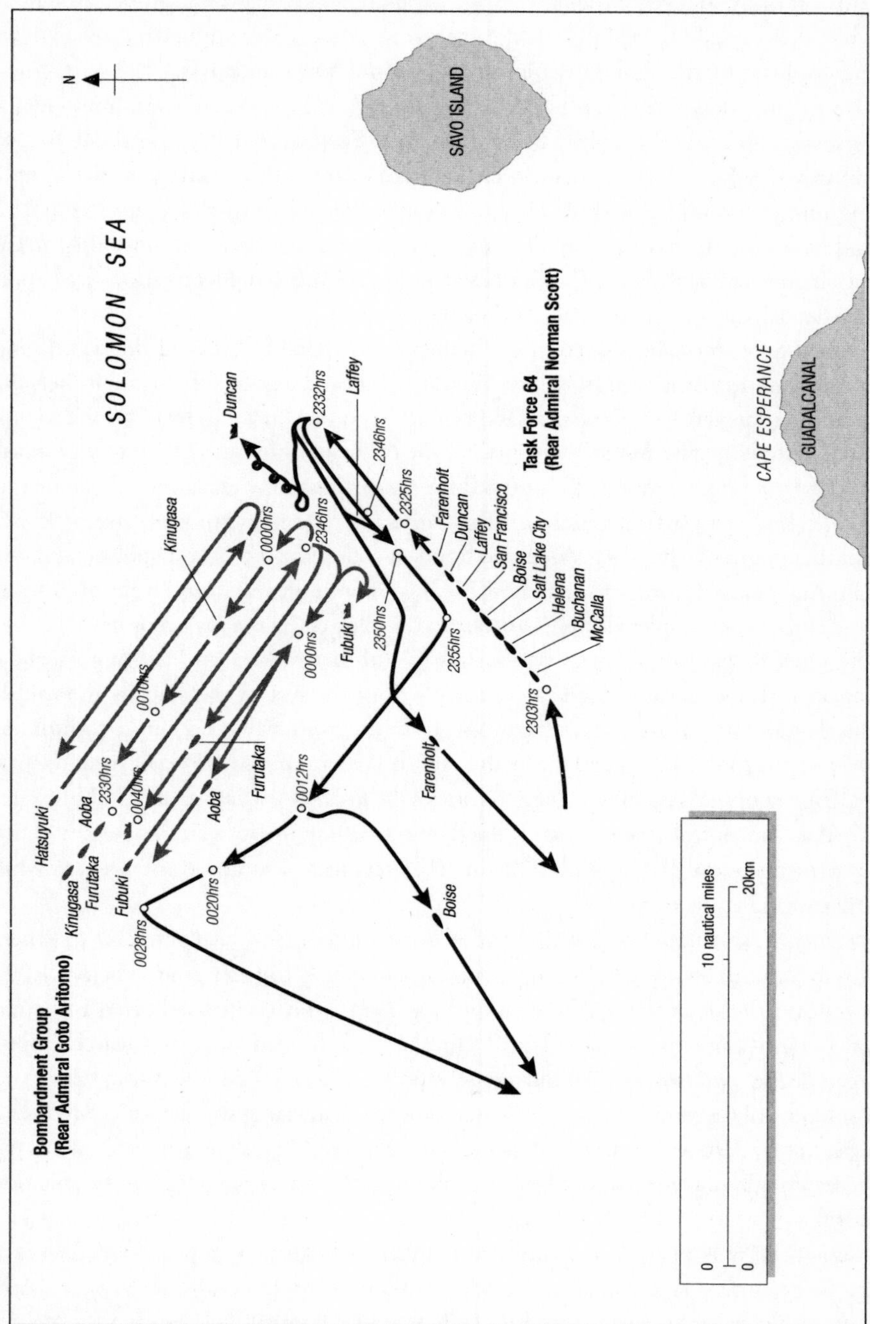

of whom were killed, had practiced safety first and sealed the powder within tanks, which did not cook off easily, and very little powder was exposed. Moreover, the flooding caused by the same hits that caused the explosion had the perverse effect of drowning the most dangerous of the fires. Even so, the light cruiser lost 107 dead and 35 wounded.

Covering the *Boise*'s exit stage port was the *Salt Lake City*. Captain Sawa calmly switched targets to the old cruiser, now backlit by the blazing *Boise*, and at 12:14 am sent an 8-inch shell burrowing through the American cruiser's armor beneath the bridge at the waterline, causing minor flooding. A second hit two minutes later ruptured the steam line from the forward boiler room, starting a fire that forced the room's abandonment until the fire could burn itself out five hours later.[81] The *Salt Lake City* lost some speed. Her own gunfire responses were ineffective due to her comically bad firing solutions.

Admiral Scott thought discretion the better part of valor and backed off. The *Kinugasa* sped away from the Americans to safety. The *Aoba*, hit by about 40 6-inch and 8-inch shells, staggered away as well. The *Furutaka* had been hit by some 90 rounds from 5-inch to 8-inch gun and, incredibly, one American torpedo. One of the last hits, at 12:05 am, had smashed the forward port engine room and ruptured the steam line to the aft starboard engine room, the only engine room still operational.[82] The cruiser lost power and thus the means to escape or fight the progressive flooding. After two hours of futile efforts to restore power, at 2:08 am Captain Araki gave the order to abandon ship. Just 20 minutes later, and eight minutes after the evacuation was completed, the *Furutaka* was swallowed by the sea, stern first.

The *Duncan* was in not much better straits. With her rudder jammed to port, she was circling at 15 knots because the bridge, cut off from the rest of the ship by the midships inferno that also pretty much cut off the bow from the stern, could no longer communicate with the engine room. Taylor and the bridge crew had to jump into the water from the bridge wings. The rest of the crew tried in vain to control the fire that the Office of Naval Intelligence described as "uncontrollable," but with the flames reaching the forward magazines, the ship was ordered abandoned at around 2:00 am. The crew had to jump off the *Duncan* while it was still moving at 15 knots.[83]

Meanwhile, with combat ended, Admiral Scott tried to herd his command together for the trip to Espiritu Santo. But he had a few wayward sheep to lasso. A little before 1:00 am Scott ordered the destroyer *McCalla* to find the *Boise*, who was last reported to be about 12 miles south-southwest of Savo Island. The *McCalla* headed there and searched for the damaged cruiser with no success, but she sighted a burning unidentified ship very close to Savo and possibly aground. Several explosions aboard the blazing ship kept the *McCalla* at a distance, but by 2:20 am the fires had died down a bit; the *McCalla* approached and snapped on her searchlight to reveal the ship's hull number: "485" – the destroyer *Duncan*, abandoned and adrift.

The *McCalla*'s skipper, Lieutenant Commander William G. Cooper, decided to leave a salvage party under Lieutenant Commander Floyd B. T. Myhre with the *Duncan*. Myhre's team gradually brought the uncontrollable fires under control and decided the destroyer could be salvaged. After making yet another futile search for the *Boise*, the *McCalla* set out to recover the *Duncan*'s crew, aided by aircraft and boats from Guadalcanal, starting at about 6:30 am. By noon, 195 of the *Duncan*'s crew were rescued, most by the *McCalla*. Then the destroyer tried to tow the *Duncan* by the stern, the only way she could be towed, but a bulkhead collapse spelled the end and the *Duncan* sank a little after noon.[84]

By then, Admiral Scott and his ships were heading southeast toward Espiritu Santo. Scott had thoughtfully requested air cover for the trip back, and received it. Less thoughtfully, he had not told the *McCalla* that the *Boise* had rejoined the task force during the night. But they were in a celebratory mood. They had won the battle, based on their overoptimistic projections of Japanese losses. It was the first US victory over the Japanese in a surface engagement – at night, to boot – since the Battle of Balikpapan that past January, which had largely been against defenseless Japanese transports.

And it was a victory. A tactical one, at least. There was just one problem. The Japanese had still managed to land all their reinforcements on Guadalcanal – the Sendai Division, the artillery, the supplies, everything. Admiral Scott had not known there were two Japanese forces in the vicinity, could not tell that the *San Francisco*'s floatplane was watching not the approaching Japanese cruisers, but the reinforcement convoy, in which the seaplane carriers *Nisshin* and *Chitose* were mistaken for cruisers.

Admiral Jojima had completed his job and led his ships back up The Slot. But he dropped off a few. The destroyers *Asagumo* and *Natsugumo* were ordered to meet the *Kinugasa*, who had held up in order to cover the Reinforcement Group's withdrawal. And the Japanese still had to rescue survivors of the *Furutaka*, with whom the *Hatsuyuki* was already packed. The *Shirayuki* and *Murakumo* were ordered to recover the remaining survivors. It was the logical thing to do. It was the humane thing to do. And it was a bad idea.

At 5:15 am, Lieutenant Colonel Albert D. Cooley, head of newly arrived Marine Air Group 14, personally led 16 Dauntlesses (11 Marine, five *Wasp* Scouting 71) with an escort of 16 Marine Fighting 121 Wildcats under Major Davis and eight Airacobras up from Guadalcanal to look for any leftovers from the action of the previous night. His strike found the *Shirayuki* and *Murakumo* north of the Russell Islands. The 11 Marine SBDs dove on the two destroyers with only a near-miss on the *Murakumo* to show for it.[85] The five *Wasp* Scouting 71 SBDs under Lieutenant Commander John Eldridge searched a bit further before finding the *Hatsuyuki* near Santa Ysabel. They did not get a hit, either, but the day was still young.[86]

Next up at 8:00 am were seven Dauntlesses of the *Saratoga*'s Scouting 3 and Marine Bombing 141 led by the *Saratoga*'s Lieutenant Commander Kirn and six Avengers of the *Saratoga*'s Torpedo 8 under Lieutenant Larsen, escorted by Major John Dobbins and 14 Marine Wildcats from Marine Fighting 121 and 224. They followed the trail of oil left by the *Murakumo* after the first attack to the two destroyers, now near New Georgia. The fighters strafed the two destroyers to suppress antiaircraft fire while the bombers maneuvered into attack position. Once again, the dive bombers got no hits, though they did get three near-misses on the *Murakumo*, now packed with survivors of the *Furutaka*. But Swede Larsen split his flight of Avengers in half to execute a perfect anvil attack on the hard-pressed

Murakumo, scoring a torpedo hit on the destroyer's port side. Her engineering plant wrecked, the destroyer staggered to a halt in a cloud of steam, settling in the water.

Now the Japanese had to rescue survivors of the *Furutaka* and the *Murakumo*. Destroyers *Asagumo* and *Natsugumo* bailed on the *Kinugasa* to help their beleaguered tin can mates. They, along with the *Shirakumo*, were circling the *Murakumo* southeast of New Georgia when the Cactus Air Force next paid its respects at 3:45 pm. Lieutenant Commander Eldridge led 11 Dauntlesses – all armed with 1,000lb bombs – from the *Saratoga*'s Scouting 3, the *Wasp*'s Scouting 71, and Marine Scout Bombing 141, joined by Swede Larsen's Avenger, four Army Airacobras, and five Wildcats from the *Saratoga*'s Fighting 5.

While the fighters again strafed the destroyers' decks to suppress antiaircraft fire, the Dauntlesses did their work. Two near-misses rocked the *Natsugumo* and wrenched open her hull plating, then Lieutenant Commander Eldridge planted his bomb just aft of amidships on the destroyer, causing a devastating explosion that left the *Natsugumo* slowly rolling over.[87]

Now the Japanese had to rescue survivors from the *Furutaka*, the *Murakumo*, and the *Natsugumo*. The *Asagumo* came over and took off the *Natsugumo*'s crew, except for her skipper, Commander Tsukamoto Shutaro, and 15 others, who were killed. The *Natsugumo* completed her rollover and sank at 4:27, 39 minutes after she was hit.[88]

The *Murakumo*, with 22 dead, was still not going anywhere. The *Shirayuki* took off her remaining crew, including her skipper, Lieutenant Commander Higashi Hideo, and scuttled her with a Type 93 torpedo.[89] Having learned their lesson – for now – the remaining destroyers sped off for the Shortlands.

And the score card for this Battle of Cape Esperance was finalized. The Americans had lost one destroyer and 163 men; the Japanese had lost one heavy cruiser, three destroyers, and some 565 men. Admiral Tanaka later called it "a crushing defeat for the Japanese Navy."[90] In terms of ego, it was. They took a lot of pride in their night-fighting ability. They could not believe the US Navy had bested them.

> Throughout the night battle off Savo Island, Providence abandoned us and our losses mounted. Especially since the enemy used radar which enabled them to fire effectively from the first round without the use of searchlights, the future looked black for our surface forces, whose forte was night warfare.[91]

It was such an embarrassment that someone had to pay. Admiral Goto's chief of staff, Captain Kijima, was sacked. Captain Araki of the *Furutaka* was defiant, tossing blame back at Base Air Force's faulty reconnaissance and 8th Fleet's inability to understand the situation, which, while a cliché, comes down to one thing: if it expected Admiral Goto's force to enter combat, why did it send the Reinforcement Group ahead of it? It was a stupid decision that was the basis for all the Japanese mistakes at Cape Esperance. Arrogant. Overconfident. Sloppy. This time, it cost them.

But the mission had been a success. And for that, General Vandegrift and his men would pay dearly. Sooner than anyone expected.

CHAPTER 9
ALL HELL'S EVE

October 13, 1942 carried the promise of a new day for the 1st Marine Division. The Americal Division's 164th Regiment, with some 2,200 men, was set to land. Its arrival would bring the number of American troops on Guadalcanal up to some 23,000. The Cactus Air Force had 90 operational aircraft: 39 Dauntlesses, 41 Wildcats, four P-400s, and six P-39s. Things were looking up.

Where there was yet another Japanese air attack. Indeed, it was another one of those double air attacks Admiral Kusaka was trying out. Leading off were 27 G4Ms (nine each from the Kisarazu, Misawa, and 753 air groups) led by the 753's Lieutenant Makino Shigeji, escorted by 18 Zeros (nine each from the 3rd and 751 air groups) under Lieutenant Aioi. Following two hours later were 15 G4Ms from the 751 under Lieutenant Commander Nishioka with 18 Zeros of the Tainan Air Group under Lieutenant Kawai.[1]

With warning from coastwatcher Donald Kennedy and radar, the Cactus Air Force managed to scramble 42 Wildcats and 13 Airacobras. All but four of them, however, missed the Japanese arrival at 12:02 pm. With no opposition, the 24 Bettys (three had aborted) missed Admiral Turner's transports off Lunga and lazily bombed both Henderson Field and Fighter 1. They managed to destroy one B-17, slightly damage 12 other planes, and, ominously, set alight 5,000 gallons of aviation fuel. The Japanese thought they had destroyed some 20 aircraft on the ground and were pleased with their efforts. Only four Marine 121 Wildcats managed to catch the Japanese some 30 minutes after the bombing, while 2nd Lieutenant Joseph L. Narr shot up one Zero so badly it had to fatally ditch off Rekata. In return, Narr was forced to ditch, but was recovered.[2]

The second strike was picked up on radar at 1:35 pm. A dozen Marine Wildcats were ready to intercept, but they themselves were bounced by the Tainan Zeros. The Bettys claimed to have destroyed 30 aircraft on the ground, which overstated the actual damage by 30. Five of the Tainan Zeros tangled with Captain Joe Foss' Wildcats, shooting up Foss, who managed to get back to Henderson. So in truth no losses for either side.

Admiral Kusaka was pleased with the results as they were inaccurately presented to him.[3] He would keep up the two-strike tactic.

Later that afternoon eight B-17s of the 11th Bombardment Group, led personally by Colonel Saunders, landed at Henderson, hoping to get a bed for the night after a difficult mission attacking Buka just north of Bougainville.[4]

It was at 6:18 pm that things got a little strange. An artillery shell exploded inside the Marine perimeter just west of the Henderson Field runway. That was new. Where did that come from?

General Vandegrift had been worried about Japanese artillery shelling the airfield, which was why he kept trying to push the Marine perimeter west of the Matanikau. Unfortunately, the 1st Marine Division had no sound-and-flash unit to locate howitzers, so they were blind. He watched his cook, Butch Morgan, put on his old World War I helmet and head for the shelter. The general asked him, "Where are you going?"

"Bombs."

"No, those aren't bombs. They're either howitzers or guns."

Morgan paused to think about it. Then he concluded, "Hell, nothing but artillery – I'm going back to work."[5]

The shell detonations, all 150mm, continued for some 45 minutes. One landed close to the Fighting 5 ready tent, where General Geiger had been talking with the *Saratoga* fighter skipper Lieutenant Commander Simpler. Simpler and others went scurrying for cover. But Geiger just stood there, his fingers plugging his ears. Simpler said, "General, you know you should seek shelter as fast as possible in such a danger."

The air general replied, "Yes, I know, but I am not going to let a goddamn Jap cause me to get my last clean uniform dirty."[6] But Geiger would, and quickly did, move many of the Cactus Air Force fighters further southeast to Fighter 1.

Another 150mm shell splashed about 25 yards from Admiral Turner's flagship *McCawley*. A little too close for comfort. Escorting destroyers *Gwin*, *Nicholas*, and *Sterett* were dispatched to bombard the Point Cruz area west of the Matanikau, from where the shells were coming. As far as anyone could tell, anyway. The shells were in fact courtesy of the 1st Battery, 4th Heavy Field Artillery Regiment, 150mm howitzers.

All in all, it was not the reception for which the 164th Infantry Regiment, now temporarily camped on the beach, had hoped. But it could have been worse. And it soon was.

In the midnight air of October 13, photographer Lieutenant Soule of the Marine intelligence unit, lay in his bunk. Trying to sleep and failing.

Soule heard *put-putting*. An underpowered aircraft overhead. Not Washing Machine Charlie, because it was single-engine. Must be Louie the Louse. It sounded like a popcorn machine, according to Captain Foss.[7]

Flares were being dropped for artillery. Like most of the Marines, Soule's reserve of energy was low. Always tired, and unable to get any sleep because of that plane. "Damn that plane, keeping us awake."[8]

But there was something different about these flares. They were much more colorful. Red over the western edge of the runway. White in the center over the Pagoda. Green over the east.[9] Like Christmas in October. And well-spaced, like they were bracketing the Marine positions.

Meanwhile, Corporal Frank Blakely, at the 1st Marines message center near the beach, thought he heard "a sound like from the channel like a cork being pulled from a champagne bottle, a gentle *pop*."[10]

A gentle pop. The seconds passed. And then the world exploded.

"Outside, a thousand rockets burst in the sky," recalled Soule. "The blast blew me from my bunk."[11]

At the Pagoda, the siren started its eerie wail in the dark, announcing Condition Red, as shown by the black flag in the night. Some Marines, used to this routine, tried to sleep through it. General Vandegrift didn't have that option. He, Colonel Thomas, and a few staffers went into the bomb-proof trench cut out of a coral ridge. Another bombardment, nothing they hadn't been through before, they assumed.

But inside the bunker, Colonel Thomas listened. He knew it almost immediately. This wasn't the normal bombardment. "My God, those aren't 5-inchers they're throwing at us!"[12]

The talented writer Corporal Gallant was with one of the gun crews on the beach when "[W]ithout warning of any kind, the sound of a heavy freight train filled the air, the earth shook, there was a series of great explosions and the ground shook again."[13]

"What the hell? What was that?" exclaimed one of the gunners.

"Where'd it come from? I didn't see any flash!" said another.

"I didn't hear anything before, either," Gallant responded. He looked out toward the water.

"You see anything out there?" the corporal was asked. From the beach, Gallant kept peering out into the darkness.

And was stunned by a giant red-yellow explosion, like a ship had blown up, but billowing out.

"Look! You see that?" Corporal Gallant yelled. "It's a ship … they're coming from a ship!"

"We ain't never had no ship shoot like that!" another member of the gun crew managed to force out of a throat tightened with terror. "Great God."

There was another giant flash, another cloud billowing toward them, in the dark out to sea.

"That ain't no cruiser!" another crewman panted.

"It's one of their damn battleships… That's what it is," shouted the gunner. "No doubt about it, by God… A damn battleship… The bastards are trying to kill us with a stinking battleship!"[14]

The nerve. Was there no limit to the depths to which the Japanese would sink? Not even just one battleship. Two battleships: the *Kongo* and her sister ship *Haruna* of the

Combined Fleet's 3rd Battleship Division, under the command of Rear Admiral Kurita Takeo. Admiral Yamamoto was keeping his promise to bring the battleships alongside Guadalcanal if necessary, even if it wasn't exactly the *Yamato*, with these two *Kongo*-class battleships. Converted from battlecruisers, the *Kongo*s were lightly armored for battleships but were fast, rated for 30 knots. Kurita had protested at the thought of sending his battleships into the restricted waters of Ironbottom Sound. Yamamoto said the battleships were going, and either Kurita could command them or Yamamoto would command them himself.

After such an offer he obviously could not refuse, Admiral Kurita headed south with a screen formed by the ubiquitous Rear Admiral Tanaka and his 2nd Destroyer Flotilla, with the light cruiser *Isuzu* and destroyers *Oyashio*, *Kuroshio*, *Hayashio*, *Umikaze*, *Kawakaze*, *Suzukaze*, *Takanami*, *Makanami*, and *Naganami*. The battleships' magazines carried the new Type 3 shell. This shell had a casing that would burst and spread 470 individual incendiary submunitions over a wide area. It was originally designed for an antiaircraft role, but the Japanese decided it could work well for bombardment of aircraft on the ground, fuel and ammunition dumps, and other flammable land targets.

Unnoticed by Allied scout planes, Admiral Kurita's force had come down from the north to pass the south side of Savo Island at 1:31 am, when they slowed to 18 knots and turned to course 77 degrees True – east-northeast. With a gunnery officer from the *Yamato*, Lieutenant Funashi Masatomi (whose presence attested the importance Admiral Yamamoto attached to this operation) on Mount Austen spotting for the battleships, along with four seaplanes for illumination, the flagship *Kongo* opened fire at 1:33 am at a range of 29,500 yards, followed at 1:35 by the *Haruna*.[15]

The immediate result within the American perimeter was pandemonium. About 150 men crammed into the Pagoda tunnel and the underground operations room. If they could make it that far. According to Lieutenant Colonel Twining, "[T]he earth seemed to turn into the consistency of Jell-O, making it difficult to move or even remain upright."[16]

For coastwatcher Martin Clemens:

> The ground shook with the most awful of convulsions, and there was dust and smoke everywhere. Our tent was in confusion, as a jagged piece of red-hot steel snapped off the tent pole above our heads[…] The top of the tent collapsed over us, together with a few tons of earth that had been blown out of the immense shell craters.[17]

To Captain Joe Foss, "It seemed as if all the props had been kicked from under the sky and we were crushed underneath."[18]

On board the ships of Admiral Kurita's flotilla, there was excitement and celebration, according to Admiral Tanaka:

> The ensuing scene baffled description as the fires and explosions from the 36-cm. shell hits on the airfield set off enemy planes, fuel dumps, and ammunition storage places. The scene

> was topped off by flare bombs from our observation planes flying over the field, the whole spectacle making the Ryogoku fireworks display seem like mere child's play. The night's pitch dark was transformed by fire into the brightness of day. Spontaneous cries and shouts of excitement ran throughout our ships.[19]

On the American side, the psychological toll was crushing. Private Leckie:

> [T]he Americans were passing through an agony not to be repeated in World War II. It was a terror of the soul. It was as though the roar of colliding planets was exploding in their ears. Self-control was shattered, strong faces went flabby with fear, men sobbed aloud or whimpered, others put their pistols to their heads. It was not possible to pray.[20]

The *Kongo*'s skipper, Captain Koyanagi Tomiji, was being very careful, spacing his salvos a minute apart so gunnery officer Lieutenant Commander Ukita Nobue could make sure the guns were on target.[21] They could not afford to waste the very limited supply ofType 3 shells. The *Haruna*, for her part, was using Type 1 armor-piercing shells, a weird choice against a land target. It seems the Japanese wanted to churn the ground to make repairs to the runways more difficult.

The Marines could only respond with their 5-inch coastal defense guns, which lacked the range to reach the battleships. Admiral Tanaka's *Isuzu* and his destroyers shelled the Marine positions themselves to suppress the guns, and shone their searchlights to blind the Marine gunners. Welcome to Guadalcanal, 164th Infantry.

At 2:13 am, the shelling stopped. Captain Joe Foss joined other Marines, soldiers, and pilots, poked their heads out, and crawled out, to see the aftermath.[22] Fire, fire everywhere. Lieutenant Colonel Walter L. J. Bayler, the Cactus Air Force communications officer, saw a "ghastly blaze of light."[23]

The Japanese saw a "lake of fire."[24] The scene was worthy of Milton. Except it was not Satan and his rebellious angels chained to it, but helpless American troops. Navy Lieutenant Frederick Mears joined about 70 men in a single truck hoping to go to the beach and get out of the main impact area. "Men were yelling, even crying and trying to hide behind one another or force their way to the bottom of the truck."[25]

Sitting on a bench in the Pagoda Hill dugout, the leadership of the 1st Marine Division relaxed a little. Colonel Thomas spoke up. "I don't know how you feel, but I think I prefer a good bombing or artillery shelling."

Standing near the doorway, General Vandegrift nodded. "I think I do…"

His thought was cut off by a massive explosion that knocked over everyone on the bench like bowling pins.[26] Joe Foss, the image of Marine toughness, dove back into his foxhole, landing on top of his superior Major Leonard Davis with such force that Foss "almost killed" the major.[27]

It had only been the eye of the hurricane. The *Kongo* and *Haruna* had reached the eastern terminus of their run and had ceased fire while turning around. Now heading back to the west along the coast, the battleships had resumed shelling, with the *Kongo* now using the Type 1 armor-piercing shells and the *Haruna* using Type 0 high explosive. With the fire obscuring landmarks ashore, Lieutenant Commander Ukita had to use a mechanical "shelling disc" to ensure adequate coverage of the salvos.[28]

The Marines had never been through anything like this. Not with artillery this big. Not in the war, not in the long history of the Marines.

"At the height of the bombardment the express train roar of the bursting salvos was so loud that it overloaded the capacity of the human ear," remembered Captain Foss. "Those two hours were simply indescribable. Nothing like them can be imagined."[29]

Writing later, General Vandegrift agreed. "Unless the reader has experienced naval or artillery shelling or aerial bombing he cannot easily grasp a sensation compounded of frustration, helplessness, fear and, in case of close hits, shock."[30]

There had always been a surreal quality to Guadalcanal, the Marines and Army troops knew, the paradise that wasn't. But never more so than on this night. The rumbling thunder that came from no storm. The quaking that came from no shifting tectonic plate. The wail of the siren that warned of no tornado. The bright blasts of the guns of battleships barely visible in the dark. A lake of fire in a land so drenched by rain it never really dries.

Some of the toughest men in the world were helpless to defend themselves, to stop this blasting, hiding in foxholes and trenches, scratching, clawing, pressing ever deeper into the ground to dodge the fire and shrapnel flying a few feet off the ground, that one millimeter possibly being the difference between life and death.

And, in a twisted version of the Pied Pieper – rats. Tens of thousands of rats poured forth from the jungle, from food stores, apoplectic at the commotion and carnage that had gripped the land and shaken it, not understanding what was happening, only that they needed to get away, they knew not how, squeaking, screaming, scratching, clawing, frantic.[31]

The surrealism extended to the victims as well. Captain Foss and Major Davis sorted themselves out to more comfortable positions. Foss started absentmindedly beating a tune on Davis' helmet. As the blasts continued, Davis exploded as well. "For God's sake, stop that! It makes me nervous!"[32]

Meanwhile, an ammunition dump was exploding and a gasoline dump was blazing fiercely near the foxhole 2nd Lieutenant Danny Doyle, a newly arrived pilot for Marine Fighting 121, shared with three other men. Doyle leaned over to one of the others and asked, "Say, do you think it would reveal our position if I lit a cigarette?"[33]

But in the midst of this enemy naval bombardment, some Marines wondered, *Where on earth is the US Navy?* "It was the hopelessness, the feeling that nobody gave a curse whether we lived or died," said Lieutenant Commander John E. Lawrence, Cactus Air Force air information officer.[34]

Well, the US Navy was there. Just not in the form of warships or even submarines. Deployed to Tulagi on October 12 was one section of Motor Torpedo Boat Squadron 3 under Lieutenant Commander Allen Montgomery. Better known as PT boats, these were basically oversized wooden motor boats with torpedo tubes and machine guns. With the devastating power of the battleships apparent, Montgomery led his four PT boats out to attack anything that moved.

But they promptly got separated. Since they rode low in the water, they didn't have much in the way of vision. *PT-38*, commanded by Lieutenant (jg) Robert L. Searles, saw a "light cruiser" – the only one present that night was the *Isuzu* – and fired four torpedoes, three of which malfunctioned. The target fired back, apparently with machine guns, as *PT-38* passed within 100 yards of the stern. *PT-60*, with Lieutenant Commander Montgomery aboard but commanded by Lieutenant (jg) John M. Searles, Robert's brother, mistook gunflashes for hits on a destroyer. *PT-60* had a few uncomfortable moments as she was chased off by the destroyer *Naganami*, at which point she ran aground.[35] The PT boat attack was mostly ineffective.

Admiral Kurita saw the gunflashes from the destroyers brushing off the PTs and concluded the destroyers were duking it out with a submarine. Kurita wanted none of that. Since the shelling was almost complete anyway, the admiral decided to end it five minutes early. The *Kongo*'s gunnery officer Lieutenant Commander Ukita later insisted that Kurita was more concerned about running aground than he was about the PTs.[36] But Kurita was already known for being a bit jittery, a reputation that would only increase.

In that sense, the PTs did drive the battleships away. At 2:56 am, after firing 973 shells, the *Kongo* and *Haruna*, their towering pagoda masts resembling aloof totems in the dark, and their companions glided out of Ironbottom Sound. They were replaced by two Washing Machine Charlies. Two Mitsubishi G4Ms harassed the beleaguered Americans by circling the Lunga perimeter loudly and dropping the occasional bomb, relieved by two more G4Ms who kept it up until dawn. At which point the 150mm guns took over. The guns were now dubbed "Millimeter Mike," or, more popularly for those averse to the metric system, "Pistol Pete."[37]

To the Americans on Guadalcanal, this night became "The Bombardment," or "All Hell's Eve." Or quite simply, "The Night of the Battleships."

When dawn finally came the Americans came out of their dugouts, foxholes, and trenches, to a shocking, demoralizing scene of abject devastation. The optimism of just 24 hours before was gone.

Palm trees were leveled, palm fronds littered the ground, along with shrapnel, splinters, baseplates, incendiary tubes. Tents were perforated, if they stood at all. Half the Pagoda was rubble. The radio station was knocked out. Henderson Field had 13 craters, 13 holes in the Marston matting. Burning, wrecked aircraft littered the edges of the runways. Of the 39 SBD Dauntless dive bombers present the day before, only seven were operational, which was seven more than there were operational Avengers. Two of the 11th Bombardment Group's B-17s were destroyed, with a third damaged.

At Fighter 1, General Geiger's move of the fighters now seemed prescient. The runway was far less damaged than that at Henderson. Only six Airacobras remained, but 18 of 30

Marine Wildcats were operational.[38] Most fortunately for the Americans on Guadalcanal and most amazing considering the severity of the bombardment, only 41 were killed.

Most unfortunately for the Americans on Guadalcanal, almost the entire supply of aviation fuel was torched. All over the base gasoline was burning.

At 5:00 am, Admiral Yamamoto issued an order stating American air power on Guadalcanal was "suppressed" and thus the 2nd and 3rd Fleets – Admiral Kondo's battleships and *Kido Butai* – were to head south and destroy the US fleet, especially the carrier *Hornet*.[39] So it was quite an unpleasant surprise to Lieutenant Commander Mitsui and his comrades on Mount Austen when at 5:40 am two SBD Dauntlesses took off from Henderson Field for the dawn search and two Marine Wildcats took off for the dawn patrol.

These operations revealed the "High Speed Convoy." Six transports – *Sado*, *Sakito*, *Sasako*, *Azumasan*, *Kyushu*, and *Nankai*, all *Maru*s – were carrying some 4,500 troops: the Imperial Army's 16th Regiment, two battalions of the 230th Infantry Regiment, and 824 men of the 4th Maizuru Special Naval Landing Force; a battery each of 100mm guns and 150mm howitzers; the 38th Field Antiaircraft Battalion; the 45th Field Antiaircraft Battalion; one company of the 47th Field Antiaircraft Battalion; the 1st Company of the 38th Engineer Regiment; the 1st Independent Tank Company; and one section of the 38th Division Signal Company, plus ammunition and provisions. They were escorted by Rear Admiral Takama Tamotsu's 4th Destroyer Flotilla with the new antiaircraft destroyer *Akizuki* serving as his flagship and destroyers *Yudachi*, *Harusame*, *Samidare*, *Murasame*, *Shigure*, *Shiratsuyu*, and *Ariake*. And they were only 140 miles away.

Inside the Lunga perimeter, sleep-deprived Marine engineers and mechanics and Seebees got to work. The surviving B-17s took off using the only 2,000 feet of available runway at Henderson. The damaged Pagoda, long believed to be a convenient point of aim for bombs and shells, was bulldozed. It took three hours to get the radio repaired enough and moved into the Pagoda Hill tunnel for General Vandegrift to get off an urgent message to Ghormley: "Urgently necessary that this force receive maximum support of air and surface units."[40] He added, "absolutely essential aviation gas be flown here continuously."[41] The Cactus Air Force pilots called it a "virtual SOS."[42]

However, US Navy surface units were in no position to help. Admiral Scott's task force was resupplying and could not get to Lunga before dawn on October 15. The lone operational US carrier in the Pacific, the *Hornet*, was refueling. Another one of those "inopportune fueling" situations. And in any event she could not take on *Kido Butai* by herself. Admiral Nimitz's assessment was "our position is not favorable to prevent a major enemy landing."[43]

But even if Admiral Ghormley was not in a position or of the disposition to help, a few people were in a position to do so. Admiral Aubrey Fitch, who had replaced Admiral McCain as head of land-based air forces in the South Pacific, was prepared to assist. Fitch had commanded the *Lexington* carrier task force at Coral Sea; in fact, during that battle, Admiral Fletcher had deferred air operations to Fitch. The loss of the *Lexington* did not diminish Fitch's reputation much, if at all. Highly respected and a good mix of aggression and caution, Fitch recognized the danger of the situation. He did not have a lot to offer from Espiritu Santo, but what he did have he sent – 17 SBD Dauntlesses (six of which were from the *Enterprise*) and 20 Wildcats of Marine Fighting 212 under Lieutenant Colonel Bauer.

Four of the P-400 Airacobras managed to take off to try to pin down Pistol Pete, who was still shelling the western end of the Henderson Field runway. But they could not find him and they soon had much bigger concerns.

Coastwatcher Donald Kennedy on New Georgia warned of an incoming strike. Fighters were scrambled, but when nothing showed up on radar, the fighters came back down to refuel, only for the strike to show up on radar a little before noon. The bombardment apparently left the radar out of adjustment. As a result, its warning and the subsequent scramble was a little too late.

If the Lunga airfield still had functional aircraft to take off from a functional runway, Admiral Kusaka hoped to fix that with another double strike. First up at 8:10 am were 27 G4Ms – nine each from the Kisarazu, Misawa, and 753 air groups – under Lieutenant Nabeta, though one Kisarazu bomber had to abort. Their escort was 18 Zeros – nine from the 751 Air Group, six from the Tainan, and three from the 3rd – under Lieutenant Ito. Henderson Field scrambled 25 Wildcats, but it was too late for them to gain altitude for effective defense. Nabeta's bombers roared in from the southwest – they may have looped around after passing New Georgia, in order to throw off the timing of the launch of defensive fighters – and dropped their payloads on the already cratered main runway, where they counted 50 aircraft. What they saw were wrecks, damaged aircraft pushed to the side of the runway and used for cannibalizing spare parts, in the Boneyard. Almost all the effective American aircraft had been moved to Fighter 1, which the Japanese missed completely. There were no losses on either side.[44]

An hour later came Base Air Force's second strike. Lieutenant Doki Asamu led 12 Mitsubishi G4Ms of the 751 Air Group with an escort of 15 Zeros – nine from the 2nd Air Group and six from the 3rd – under Lieutenant Kurakane. This time, they found very angry, vengeful Wildcats ready and waiting for them overhead – nine Marine Fighting 224 Grummans under Major Galer. In the four minutes from 1:02 to 1:06 pm, Galer's Marine pilots slashed through Doki's Bettys, quickly shooting down two and crippling a third that later exploded in midair. One Wildcat, that of 2nd Lieutenant Koller C. Brandon, was lost.[45]

The remaining Bettys split up to bomb both Henderson Field and Fighter 1 – ineffectually – only to run into more Wildcats from the *Saratoga*. One was shot up so badly it had to crash-land at Buin; another ditched at Rekata. All this time, Lieutenant Ito's Zeros were overhead, apparently checking out the scenery. They certainly were not protecting their bombers, but then again they didn't lose any Zeros, either. Total losses for Base Air Force were five G4Ms, with several more heavily damaged. According to the Japanese, "the bombing raid was not very successful."[46]

While this was going on, Lieutenant Colonel Munn, one of General Vandegrift's staff officers, drove to the 67th Fighter Squadron's area, where he found three Army pilots and a mechanic. Munn briefed them:

> I want you to pass the word along that the situation is desperate. We don't know whether we'll be able to hold the field or not. There's a Japanese task force of destroyers, cruisers, and troop transports headed this way. We have enough gas left for one mission against them. Load your airplanes with bombs and go out with the dive bombers and hit them. After the gas is gone we'll have to let the ground troops take over. Then your officers and men will attach themselves to some infantry outfit. Good luck and goodbye.[47]

Lieutenant Colonel Munn's words were punctuated by exploding Japanese artillery shells nearby that twice forced the men to take cover. Already, the *Saratoga* pilots led by Swede Larsen, with no serviceable Avengers, had taken up arms to fight alongside the infantry.[48] The bombardment had flipped the field from only 24 hours before.

While all this was going on, the Seebees were still trying to repair Henderson Field and ground crews were trying to cobble together some flyable aircraft from all the pieces of aircraft lying around. Working feverishly all day, throughout the Japanese air attacks, the fires, and Pistol Pete, the mechanics managed to slap together enough aircraft for a few airstrikes at the approaching reinforcement group.

First was a group of four Dauntlesses, seven Airacobras, and 17 Wildcats, who arrived over the convoy at 3:45. They accomplished nothing except losing one Wildcat. By draining the gas from the two damaged B-17s, the Cactus Air Force sent up a second airstrike of the same seven Airacobras and nine *Saratoga* Dauntlesses under Lieutenant Commander Kirn, escorted by eight Wildcats. They found the convoy at 6:05 pm east of Santa Ysabel, with the transports in two columns. Heavy antiaircraft fire and six Zeros from the 6th Air Group out of Buin harassed the attackers into scoring only a near-miss on the destroyer *Samidare* and brought down the Airacobra of 1st Lieutenant Edgar E. Barr, who was recovered. The six Zeros were not, having ditched at Rekata.[49]

Even though eight Dauntlesses of the *Enterprise*'s Fighting 6 arrived just before dark, the night promised to be another difficult one for the Americans on Guadalcanal. That night light cruisers *Yura* and *Sendai*, the seaplane carrier *Nisshin* – again – and destroyers *Asagumo*, *Akatsuki*, and *Ikazuchi* landed 1,129 troops, four field guns, four rapid-fire guns, ammunitions and provisions on Cape Esperance. With them was destroyer *Shirayuki*, who delivered a midget submarine base for Kamimbo. Guarding them was Admiral Mikawa with his flagship heavy cruiser *Chokai*, heavy cruiser *Kinugasa*, and destroyers *Amagiri* and *Mochizuki*. When that was done and while the destroyers stood guard, the cruisers spent a half-hour lobbing 752 8-inch shells into the Lunga perimeter. It was unpleasant, but nothing like the night before. The Marines shrugged it off.

What they could not shrug off was the view that greeted them the next morning. "Brazen and bold," in full view of the Marines inside the Lunga perimeter, the six transports of the High-Speed Convoy were anchored and offloading troops, guns, and supplies.[50] That was just … insulting. Admiral Takama assumed that the bombardments by the battleships and cruisers and army artillery would keep the flyers at the Lunga airfield grounded. But just in case, Takama had six Type 0 observation seaplanes from the R-Area Air Force, 12 Zeros from Base Air Force, and 11 Zeros from the carrier *Junyo* to protect them.

General Geiger's men were now scrounging parts to make aircraft flyable and scrounging aviation gasoline to fuel them. As they pieced individual aircraft together, they sent them up in individual attacks, accomplishing little except to put the men in danger. *Saratoga* fighter pilots Lieutenant Carl W. ("Pat") Rooney and Lieutenant (jg) E. T. ("Smokey") Stover made repeated strafing runs "below masthead height" on the transports, until Stover ran into a Type 0 observation seaplane, piloted by Petty Officer 1st Class Sakuma Kiichi of the *Sanuki Maru*, diving at him.[51] Stover made a head-on run and opened fire, but missed. So did Sakuma. It turned into an aerial game of chicken, though Sakuma's apparent belief that it was a good idea to play such a game in a fabric-covered biplane with a heavily armored monoplane fighter doesn't speak well of Japanese training practices. Neither pilot turned. Stover's Wildcat drove through the Pete float biplane, slashing off a wing and a wing strut. Sakuma spun into the ground. Stover managed to regain control of his fighter and land, where his right wing sagged with a foot-long gash, in which was caught "a yard square strip of black fabric containing part of a blood-red Rising Sun, edged with a gray circle."[52] Stover kept it, as well he should. The ground crews also found four 25mm shell holes in Stover's Wildcat.

In the interim, just as the Cactus Air Force was approaching its last drop of aviation gas, one of General Geiger's staff officers remembered that Colonel Woods, who had moved to Espiritu Santo, had managed to assemble hidden emergency stashes of gas. Geiger bellowed, "By God, find some!"[53]

And they did. Stashed away in swamps and thickets were a total of 465 barrels, enough for two days of operations.[54] Admiral Fitch had arranged for an airlift of R4Ds and C-47s to run a dozen drums apiece to Henderson Field, braving the fire of Pistol Pete to land. Fitch had also arranged for the old four-piper *McFarland*, now a seaplane tender, to bring in 40,000 gallons along with a dozen torpedoes. Yippies were running another 200 drums from Tulagi.

General Geiger stopped the pinprick attacks and at 10:15 sent up five Marine Fighting 121 Wildcats under Major Davis escorting a dozen Dauntlesses, two P-39 Airacobras with 500lb bombs, four P-400 Airacobras with 100lb bombs – and a PBY-5A Catalina flying boat with a Mark 13 torpedo slung under each wing. This was Geiger's personal Catalina, flown by Geiger's personal pilot, Major Jack R. Cram. Cram had talked a reluctant Geiger into allowing him to take the Catalina to mount a torpedo attack on the Japanese transports. Catalinas were ponderous aircraft used for scouting, no one had ever used a Catalina for a daylight torpedo attack, and Cram had never dropped a torpedo before. Other than that, Cram's plan was airtight.

After saying goodbye to the other pilots, Major Cram went up in the PBY. Aerial opposition was provided by six Tainan and three 3rd Air Group Zeros under Lieutenant (jg) Ono Takeyoshi. But the fighters focused on the Dauntlesses dropping their bombs, shooting down three, while Cram slipped in and dropped his torpedoes. Cram believed he got a hit – because of course he was going to get a hit the first time he ever dropped a torpedo. The Dauntless crews believed they had gotten a hit. Certainly, between them, the *Sasago Maru* was hit, starting a large fire. She had to be beached to prevent her sinking, a total loss, but her troops, tanks, and guns were landed successfully. The Airacobras did not get a hit, but one of the newly arrived 339th Fighter Squadron flown by Captain William Sharpsteen torched one Zero, apparently that of Seaman 1st Class Iwase Jisuke.[55]

As Major Cram came in for a landing, he was chased by two Zeros from the Tainan Air Group, flown by Petty Officer 2nd Class Sakurai Chuji and Seaman 1st Class Sugawara Yozo. They both perforated the PBY, but missed Lieutenant Roger A. Haberman's damaged Wildcat from Marine Fighting 121, which was trying to land. Wheels down and coming in to land, Haberman sent a burst of .50cal that detonated Sakurai's fighter. Sugawara made a lame strafing run and headed out. Grateful for the assistance, Cram landed safely, as did Haberman.[56]

At 11:45, transport *Nankai Maru*, having completed her offloading, headed out, escorted by destroyer *Ariake*. She got out just in time, because five minutes later a flight of nine B-17 Flying Fortresses under Major Ernest R. Maniere of the 11th Bombardment Group arrived. The B-17s had flown over Henderson Field, where men ran out from cover to the runway to cheer on the Flying Fortresses.[57] Zeros moved in to engage the B-17s, but did not stop them from landing at least one bomb on the *Azumasan Maru*, igniting a fatal fire that forced her to be beached to prevent her sinking. Nor did they stop the B-17s from all returning safely to Espiritu Santo. Her troops, tanks, and guns were landed successfully, but the tank fuel and ammunition she carried were lost.[58]

Base Air Force had yet to make its daily air attack, and Admiral Kusaka was certainly not going to miss a chance like this. Lieutenant Makino Shigeji of the 753 Air Group led 23 G4Ms – nine from the Misawa Air Group, eight Kisarazu, and six 753 – in an attack on Lunga at 12:45 that resulted in "some damage to planes and runways," according to the Marines.[59] With the Cactus Air Force busy elsewhere, the Japanese had almost no aerial opposition.

So their escort of eight Zeros – five from the 751 Air Group and three from the 3rd – under Lieutenant (jg) Baba Masayoshi of the 751 Air Group – dropped back to join nine Zeros from the 2nd Air Group under Lieutenant (jg) Futagami Tokitane to cover the unloading transports. But Japanese fighter protection was strangely ineffective this day, largely because of the lack of radios in the Zeros that would allow ground observers to vector them to intercept incoming attackers. That was how, at 1:15 pm, yet another strike of SBD Dauntless dive bombers broke through to wreak more havoc. One well-placed bomb killed everyone on the bridge of the *Kyushu Maru* and started a major fire. Not knowing there was no one at the helm, the engineering crew kept the engines running at full speed, and the *Kyushu Maru* drove herself high onto the beach at Bunina Point near Kokumbona. Her troops, tanks, and guns were landed successfully, but the tank fuel and ammunition she carried were lost when the ship burned herself out, becoming yet another total loss.[60]

Admiral Takama was not pleased with this situation. Far from being knocked out, the Americans were relentlessly attacking his transports and drawing blood. Their bombs had cost him three ships. Their strafing runs had wrought chaos, scattering landing parties and destroying barges and supplies. Takama pulled his ships out and had them mass north of Savo Island where they could maneuver to avoid the air attacks. And they did so when another attack of four Dauntlesses of Bombing 6 arrived at 5:40. The attack failed, but Takama's hopes to resume the unloading after dark were dashed when the Army representative waived him off with the message, "Moon bright, do not come."[61] So Takama headed back to Shortlands. All 4,500 troops had been landed, but maybe only two-thirds of the supplies, at a cost of three transports, six Zeros, and one Type 0 observation seaplane so spectacularly brought down. Air operations had cost the Americans three Wildcats, three Dauntlesses, and one Airacobra.[62] The Cactus Air Force still lived, but it was on the ropes.

Help was on the way, though. The *McFarland* was en route with those 40,000 gallons of aviation fuel and 12 torpedoes. And even before the latest crisis a supply convoy had been sent from Espiritu Santo. The convoy consisted of cargo ships *Alchiba* and *Bellatrix* towing some gasoline barges, with motor torpedo boat tender *Jamestown* and fleet tug *Vireo*, escorted by destroyers *Meredith* and *Nicholas*. The gasoline was urgently needed on Guadalcanal, but Pacific Fleet intelligence and *Magic* was, ominously, unable to pinpoint the carriers of *Kido Butai*. For that reason, at 6:08 am Admiral Ghormley had everyone turn back. But the *Vireo*, with a top speed of 14 knots, was struggling to keep up. So she was detached with the *Meredith* as an escort while the rest raced on ahead towards Espiritu Santo.[63]

At 10:50 am, a Type 0 reconnaissance seaplane from the *Chitose* found the *Meredith* and *Vireo* and attacked unsuccessfully.[64] Then came a report that two Japanese ships were nearby. The report was inaccurate, but together these incidents spooked the *Meredith* skipper Lieutenant Commander Harry Hubbard enough to order the *Vireo* abandoned. After the entire crew had been taken aboard the *Meredith*, the destroyer positioned herself to scuttle the tug, which was when, at 12:25, the expected air attack arrived. It consisted of eight Zeros, 21 Aichi Type 99 carrier bombers, and nine Nakajima Type 97 carrier attack planes. They were all from the *Zuikaku*, who with her sister ship *Shokaku* was cruising east of the Stewart Islands, in futile attempts to find the *Hornet*.[65] The *Meredith*, having just recovered the *Vireo*'s crew and preparing to scuttle her, must have been moving slowly, if at all, because it took only ten minutes for the Sea Eagles to plaster the destroyer with several bomb hits and even got three torpedoes into her. Fearing their boat would be sunk, the crew of the *Vireo* had left for the safety of the *Meredith*, so, naturally, it was the *Meredith* that was sunk, while the Japanese completely ignored the *Vireo* and her tow.[66]

Apparently angry at their losses of one Val and two Kates to the destroyer's antiaircraft fire, the Japanese proceeded to strafe the survivors in the water.

A patrolling PBY found the *Vireo* and the tug abandoned and adrift the next day. It was two days later when the destroyers *Grayson* and *Gwin* were able to fish 88 survivors out of the Coral Sea; 237 men were lost.[67] The *Vireo* and her tow were not. But before she could become the *Mary Celeste* of the Pacific, on October 21 the *Grayson* ran into her – literally. The resulting damage apparently light, the *Grayson* dropped off a salvage crew who successfully brought the *Vireo* and her tow back to Espiritu Santo.[68]

The sacrifice of the *Meredith* and *Vireo* did bring one critical benefit: the *Zuikaku*'s airstrike was so focused on them it missed the *Alchiba*, *Bellatrix*, *Jamestown*, and *Nicholas* heading back to Espiritu Santo. A later airstrike of five Vals managed to get only a few near-misses on the *Bellatrix*.[69]

But other help was also on the way: an angry *Hornet* task force under a vindictive Admiral Murray eager to punish the punishers of Guadalcanal. Having finally finished her inopportune refueling, the carrier was heading back. As she did so, her radar picked up a Mavis flying boat commanded by Warrant Officer Yaguchi Toshihito of the Toko Air Group 30 miles away on its return leg to Shortland. Veteran lieutenants (jg) George Formanek and Rickard Hughes were vectored out, and Formanek detonated the flying boat in midair. If Yaguchi even saw the *Hornet*, he never sent out a contact report.[70] Barely taking notice, the carrier kept on course to cover Henderson Field and stop the nighttime bombardments. Admiral Ghormley had also directed the *Washington* task force under Rear Admiral Willis Augustus Lee and Admiral Scott's task force to hook up and position themselves west of Guadalcanal to intercept these nighttime convoys and bombardments. But no one could get there before that night.

That night it was the turn of the victor of the Battle of the Java Sea, Vice Admiral Takagi Takeo, to blast the Lunga airfield, with the flagship of the 5th Cruiser Division, heavy cruiser *Myoko*, and the *Maya*, sister to the luxurious *Chokai*, and an escort of light cruiser *Isuzu* and destroyers of Admiral Tanaka's 2nd Destroyer Flotilla. The *Maya* tossed up 450 more of those Type 3 incendiaries and Type 91 armor-piercing shells, while the flagship *Myoko* chipped in with 462 8-inch shells. Two of the escorting destroyers added 253 rounds of 5-inch ammunition.[71]

For the Marines, this was getting ridiculous. At dawn on October 16, the Cactus Air Force had only nine Wildcats, 11 Dauntlesses, and seven Airacobras operational. "I don't think we have a goddamn Navy," snarled General Geiger to the *Saratoga*'s Lieutenant Commander Simpler. Geiger spoke for a great many within the Lunga perimeter. But Simpler was going to defend his service. "We have one, general, and I think I can find it." Simpler went out in the last flyable *Saratoga* Wildcat and found the *Hornet*, who nevertheless would not let him land. Simpler headed back and found the *Hornet*'s aircraft joining Marine and Army pilots in some of their seven attacks on the Japanese landing zones and supply drops near Kokumbona.[72] The Cactus Air Force needed the help, because the strain was showing. On one mission involving four P-400 Airacobras, one had a bomb, but only one .30cal machine gun functioning; the second had a bomb but no functioning guns, the third and fourth had most of their guns functional, but no bombs. The 67th Fighter Squadron's history does not describe it in glowing terms. "The day … was a weary succession of taking off, bombing and strafing, landing to refuel and rearm, and taking off again."[73]

The helping hand of the *Hornet* was not only at Guadalcanal, but at Rekata Bay, where they pounded the annoying R-Area Air Force's staging area. They claimed to have destroyed everything of military value, including eight Rufes, five biplanes, three twin-float seaplanes, and all shore installations. Multiple airstrikes found no ships off Guadalcanal, though. "It is regretted that more suitable targets were not available," commented Commander Walter F. Rodee of the *Hornet*.[74]

Even more regrettably, the Japanese found the *Hornet*. Lieutenant Hinata Yoshihiko of the Toko Air Group radioed that he had found the carrier 60 miles southeast of Guadalcanal on a course of 300 degrees True – northwest. In return, Hinata's Type 97 flying boat was discovered by Lieutenant (jg) Frank Christofferson of Bombing 8, flying an SBD on inner air patrol looking for submarines. Christofferson made five attacks that emptied his guns, only to take a 20mm hit from Hinata's tail gun. Christofferson was forced to ditch near the destroyer *Morris*, who picked up him and his gunner unharmed.

Hornet fighter pilots Lieutenant Tom Johnson and Ensign Phil Souza went hunting for the crafty Kawanishi, but struggled finding it in the clouds. Then Souza saw "the biggest airplane I had ever seen," Hinata's very large Type 97 flying boat, which responded to attack with "tracers the size of red ping pong balls." Hinata was able to evade Johnson and Souza by ducking into a cloud, but when he came out he found Souza with Lieutenant (jg) Robert H. Jennings waiting for him. They caught the giant flying boat in a vicious crossfire. The Mavis exploded, as Mavises so often did, its "[e]ngines with the propellers still spinning" fell away, and the burning aircraft disintegrated some 18 miles from the *Hornet*.

Yet Lieutenant Hitaka had done his job. By now, Admiral Nagumo's *Kido Butai* was heading north to refuel, but there was still Admiral Kusaka's Base Air Force. In response to his contact report, multiple airstrikes were launched, including one of nine Type 99 carrier bombers under Reserve Lieutenant Kitamura Norimasa of the 31st Air Group, escorted by 12 Zeros of the 6th Air Group under Lieutenant (jg) Kawamata Katsutoshi that took off at 3:00 pm from Buin hunting for the *Hornet*. Right on cue, at 4:05 pm, coastwatcher Donald Kennedy warned of hearing a "fair number" of aircraft passing over New Georgia heading southeast.[75] Also right on cue, at 5:00 pm 11 Wildcats of Marine Fighting 121 under 1st Lieutenant Edwin C. Fry scrambled.

The Japanese pilots prowled the Coral Sea south of Guadalcanal but did not find a carrier. Lieutenant Kitamura decided to head back after a detour over Lunga. There, at 5:30, Kitamura found the *McFarland*. At 1:20 pm, the old destroyer had anchored about 300 yards off Lunga and began unloading oil drums and torpedoes. She also began pumping aviation fuel into oil drums on a barge tethered to her starboard side.

For the trip out, she began taking on board the ground crews from Marine Air Group 23 and the last of the pilots from the *Saratoga*'s Fighting 5. The *McFarland* had offloaded about half her cargo, largely because, aside from one false alarm, she had no interference, since Base Air Force was too busy looking for the *Hornet* to bother them. Until now.

On the advice of his old friend Lieutenant Commander Simpler, the *McFarland*'s skipper, Lieutenant Commander John C. Alderman, cut loose the barge and got under way. The Vals, each armed with two 132lb bombs, all dove on the old destroyer as Lieutenant Fry's fighters apparently missed them completely. The first bomb hit the *McFarland* amidships on the port side, but the rest of the bombs missed astern. Except for the last bomb.

This landed on the *McFarland*'s stern, where it detonated the depth charges, blowing off the stern and sending white-hot fragments into the desperately needed 20,000 gallons of aviation fuel on the barge, which went up in flames. The *McFarland* lashed out with her 20mm antiaircraft guns, which sent the Val of Reserve Ensign Kawaga Atushi up in flames and down into the water. The remaining Vals strafed Kukum before heading home.

The Japanese may have evaded Lieutenant Fry's defending Wildcats, but they could not evade Lieutenant Colonel "Joe" Bauer, who had just arrived from Espiritu Santo with 19 Marine Fighting 212 Wildcats, seven Dauntlesses, and four R4Ds bringing in aviation fuel and taking out wounded and crews set to be pulled out, including the *Saratoga*'s Fighting 5. With his fuel tanks almost dry, Bauer was waiting until his charges had landed when he saw the blazing *McFarland* and a line of Vals heading away at an altitude of about 200 feet. Flying on empty did not bother Bauer. In full view of those at Lunga, he roared after the Vals at full speed and started gobbling them up like Pac-Man, shooting down Warrant Officer Iwami Kenzo, Petty Officer 3rd Class Tokuoka Masahiro, and Petty Officer 3rd Class Ozeki Mitsuo, one by one by one. Bauer later grumbled that if he had the gas he would have shot down all eight of them.

The determination of Joe Bauer helped turn this small mission into a costly one for Base Air Force. Lieutenant Kitamura's Vals landed at Buin at 8:30 pm. Having already lost four Type 99s, a fifth broke up on the runway. Lieutenant Kawamata's escorting Zeros got tangled up with four B-17s who had guided Bauer's flight in to Guadalcanal and accomplished nothing. Steering by engine, Lieutenant Commander Alderman guided the *McFarland* toward Tulagi, but she lost power and had to be towed in by *YP-239* around midnight. From her crew and passengers there were nine killed, 28 wounded, and 18 missing.

It was a gruesome end to the day, but October 16 ended far better than the previous three nights had. Before the attack, the *McFarland* had landed 20,000 gallons of precious aviation fuel. Moreover, once Joe Bauer landed, he gave a rousing speech that provided a desperately needed morale boost. Despite the body blows of the past three days, thanks to the toughness of the pilots, the ground crews, the mechanics, and the Seebees, the Cactus Air Force was still alive.

Bloodied, to be sure, but unbroken.

Yet the Japanese smelled that blood in the water. And now on land. They were coming.

The bombardment by the *Kongo* and *Haruna* may have caused ground tremors on Guadalcanal, but it sent aftershocks all the way to Washington.

On October 16, a reporter asked Secretary of the Navy Frank Knox, "Do you think we can hold Guadalcanal?" Knox answered:

> I certainly hope so and expect so… I will not make any predictions, but every man will give a good account of himself. What I am trying to say is that there is a good stiff fight going on. Everybody hopes we can hold on.[76]

It was not an answer that could or would buoy the spirits. Already the Marines were tired of "weak-kneed reports by some official about our precarious situation."[77] Knox was a politician, but he had been an Army officer. He should have known better. But at least he was no longer an officer leading men into battle, nor had he been for decades. Others did not have that excuse.

By General Vandegrift's estimate, the Japanese now had some 15,000 troops on Guadalcanal. Enough to make a land attack on the Lunga perimeter. That same day, he sent a message to admirals Nimitz, Ghormley, and Turner:

> Our force exceeds that number but more than half of it is in no condition to undertake a protracted land campaign due to incessant hostile operations… The situation demands two urgent and immediate steps: A. Take and maintain control of sea areas adjacent to CACTUS to prevent further enemy landings and enemy bombardment such as this force has taken for the last three nights; B. reinforcement of ground forces by at least one division in order that extensive operations may be initiated to destroy hostile force now on CACTUS.[78]

Admiral Ghormley quickly responded with a message to admirals Nimitz and King – and all the ships under his command:

> Urgently need this area one additional army infantry division. Present forces … insufficient to garrison present bases and therefore obviously inadequate [to] support offensive operations. Have neither on hand nor in sight sufficient forces to render CACTUS secure against present infiltration tactics.[79]

In other words, even in this crisis Admiral Ghormley was still unwilling to take forces from the rear bases in order to support the Marines on Guadalcanal. It went back to his original belief that the Guadalcanal offensive would fail and those rear bases would then need to be defended.

What was it Admiral King had said about "Mak[ing] the best of what you have?"

And if Admiral Ghormley was not willing to use all the forces already under his command, how would Admiral King convince generals Marshall and Arnold, always stingy with reinforcements for the Pacific, to give him more?

But that was not all. Despite the emergency on Guadalcanal, Admiral Ghormley yanked the *Hornet* away from her supporting position and sent her to the southeast, out of range of the Japanese, where she would hopefully meet the *Enterprise* soon. After receiving reports from Canberra that a Japanese carrier force was west of the Santa Cruz Islands, at 4:00 pm on October 16, Admiral Ghormley sent another dispatch to admirals Nimitz and King:

> This appears to be all out enemy effort against CACTUS, possibly other positions also. My forces totally inadequate [to] meet situation. Urgently request all available reinforcements possible.[80]

For Admiral Nimitz, it was the last straw.

CHAPTER 10
THE LION COMES

An army of sheep led by a lion is more to be feared than an army of lions led by a sheep.

This quote or some variant thereof is usually attributed to Alexander the Great. It is a sound piece of wisdom. And when a Consolidated PB2Y Coronado flying boat set down in Nouméa at 2:00 pm on October 18, there was little doubt that the VIP aboard was a lion.

Vice Admiral William F. Halsey had arrived. Halsey was in Nouméa to take over the *Enterprise* task force. But the *Enterprise* was not yet ready for him, so he was touring his area of operations, familiarizing himself with it, visiting the bases he would use, and talking to the people with whom he would be dealing.

As the propellers stopped spinning, a boat carrying Admiral Ghormley's flag lieutenant came alongside to carry Admiral Halsey to the flagship *Argonne* to speak with his new superior. Halsey stepped aboard. The lieutenant saluted him and gave him an envelope. Inside that envelope was another envelope, marked "SECRET." Halsey opened the envelope:

> CINCPAC: You will take command of the South Pacific area and South Pacific forces immediately.

Admiral Halsey had to read it twice. "Jesus Christ and General Jackson! This is the hottest potato they ever handed me!"[1]

The new commander of the South Pacific forces was still digesting his new assignment when he stepped aboard the *Argonne* to meet with the old commander of the South Pacific forces, Vice Admiral Robert Ghormley, who had been informed of his removal the previous day. Ghormley greeted Admiral Halsey warmly – the two had been friends since their Naval Academy days – but the meeting felt awkward.

"This is a tough job they've given you, Bill," Admiral Ghormley said.

"I damn well know it!" Halsey replied. They both went to Ghormley's cabin, where Halsey was briefed on the situation in and around Guadalcanal.[2]

Questions about Ghormley's fitness for command had been building since planning began for the Guadalcanal campaign. He did not attend planning meetings in Koro, sending a representative instead, which displayed a curious lack of interest in an operation he had been ordered to "command in person in the operating area" by Admiral King.[3] Admiral Nimitz's late September visit was in part to check on Ghormley. Nimitz returned to Pearl Harbor hoping for the best, but he was deeply concerned about Ghormley's mindset. He later told his wife, "Ghormley was too immersed in detail and not sufficiently bold and aggressive at the right times."[4]

To use an analogy to today's world where sports coaches are known for "playing to win" versus "playing not to lose," Admiral Ghormley played as if he had already lost. During his September 28 meeting with Admiral Nimitz, Ghormley had reacted to two urgent messages from Guadalcanal with the exclamation, "My God! What are we going to do about *this*?"[5] Nimitz was quite unsettled by the defeatism contained in that statement. Ghormley was not resourceful; quite the opposite, he was loath to use the resources he had because they would be needed when the Guadalcanal offensive failed.

Moreover, Ghormley had isolated himself. Local French officials had denied him the use of a headquarters ashore, so he confined himself to the *Argonne*, where, in the sweltering cabins with no air conditioning, he worked very hard. But cabin fever seems to have set in and affected both his judgment and his mood. The isolation had practical drawbacks as well. Ghormley would write:

> I did not know, from actual contact, the ability of the officers, nor the material condition of the ships nor their readiness for battle, nor did I know their degree of training for warfare such as was soon to develop in this area. Improvement was acquired while carrying out combat missions.[6]

Sun Tzu wrote, "It is said that if you know your enemies and know yourself, you will not be imperiled in a hundred battles." And here Ghormley was admitting he did not know himself. Knowing was his job. Indeed, he still had not visited Guadalcanal.

The final straw seems to have been his panicked October 15 message calling his forces "totally inadequate" to meet a Japanese carrier attack that never materialized.[7] That same night, Admiral Nimitz met with his staff members who had accompanied him on his South Pacific tour. Some of them noticed his normally warm blue eyes were an icy gray.

Admiral Nimitz opened the meeting with a short lecture. Apparently referring to Ghormley's message, he stated, "I don't want to hear, or see, such pessimism. Remember, the enemy is hurting too."[8] It was apparent, the admiral said, that the Japanese were about to launch a major offensive. He wanted his staff's impressions of the situation, specifically concerning Admiral Ghormley. Ghormley, said Nimitz, was an intelligent and dedicated officer. But, he asked, was Ghormley tough enough to handle the situation? Could he inspire the men under his command?

After some discussion, the staff officers unanimously answered both questions with a resounding "no." Admiral Nimitz finished the discussion with, "All right, I'm going to poll you." He pointed to each man in turn and asked, "Is it time for me to relieve Ghormley?" Each man responded to the question with the same one-word answer: "Yes."[9]

They started talking about potential replacements. Admiral Turner was the natural choice; he was a brilliant strategic thinker who had headed the Navy's War Plans office before the war. Turner was also familiar with the area and its challenges. However, he was also arrogant and irascible, qualities that had alienated the Marines and especially General Vandegrift.[10]

Admiral Halsey's name came up. He was recently off the injured list and ready for action. Halsey was a pilot, known as a fighter, and very popular throughout the Navy, especially with enlisted men.[11] Like Turner, though, Halsey was combative and short-tempered, and they wondered if his combat leadership skills would translate into an effective theater commander. Halsey had once been given an assignment to command the Norfolk Navy Yard. He told the Navy's personnel chief, who at that time was Nimitz, that he didn't feel suited to administering an industrial establishment, which was exactly what the South Pacific command was.[12]

Admiral Nimitz adjourned the meeting and went back to his quarters to ponder the issues. Late that night he was called to the phone. A small group of staff officers wished to speak with the admiral to express their opinion. Nimitz agreed to give them five minutes, and the officers, none of whom had any knowledge of the earlier meeting, were invited in. In his pajamas, Nimitz listened as they got straight to the point. Admiral Ghormley should be replaced, they said. With Admiral Halsey. Nimitz thanked them for their concern and said he would consider their opinion.[13]

After a sleepless night, the next morning Admiral Nimitz sent a message to Admiral King: "In view Ghormley's [latest dispatch] and other indications including some noted during my visit I have under consideration his relief by Halsey at earliest practicable time. Request your comment."

King's response was prompt, succinct, and brutal: "Affirmative."[14]

The news of Admiral Halsey's appointment spread like the proverbial wildfire across the South Pacific. The effect was electric, with cheers and celebration among the officers and sailors of the fleet. "We were absolutely elated when we heard the news," said assistant gunnery officer Ed Hooper of the battleship *Washington*. "It was a shot of adrenalin for the whole command; things had been getting pretty wishy-washy down there."[15] The *Atlanta*'s Robert Graff took a slightly different angle:

> During wartime it's important how the leadership, starting with the Chief of Naval Operations, gets a message across to everybody in every ship, submarine, airplane, and shore station. You need to hear it said that that this is an extraordinary moment in your life and in the life of the country, and that you're not going to let it down. Until that day, we had received no such message.[16]

If the effect on the fleet was electric, the effect on Guadalcanal was nuclear. Lieutenant Commander Roger Kent, an air information officer there, described the atmosphere upon hearing the news: "One minute we were too limp with malaria to crawl out of our foxholes; the next we were running around whooping like kids."[17] Two Marines embarked on a scientific discussion of the true value of "The Old Man," as they knew Admiral Halsey. One claimed Halsey was worth two battleships and two carriers; the other insisted Halsey was worth two battleships and three carriers. This largely theoretical disagreement was settled only with increasing volume and, ultimately, some physical debate.

Admiral Halsey went straight to work. By word-of-mouth and even by posted signs he made everyone aware of his wartime credo: "Kill Japs! Kill Japs! Kill more Japs!" He almost immediately ended the quixotic quest to build an airbase at Ndeni, thereby releasing the forces involved to Guadalcanal. He told Pearl Harbor he would need his best staffers sent down to serve at his headquarters; Admiral Ghormley's old staffers had absorbed his defeatism, which Halsey did not want on his staff.

Halsey officially moved the fleet base from distant Auckland to more convenient Nouméa. He demanded 1 million square feet of covered storage space for supplies. Just in case the Free French were as obdurate as they had been with Admiral Ghormley, he sent his intelligence officer to meet with the Free French governor about getting a headquarters set up ashore. When the governor demurred and kept demurring for a month, Halsey himself came ashore with a contingent of Marines and seized the local headquarters of the High Commissioner for Free France in the Pacific for his own, as well as the former residence of the Japanese consul.[18] At his new headquarters Halsey installed a plaque that said it all about his management philosophy:

Complete with black tie
You do look terrific
But take it off here
This is still South Pacific.[19]

Halsey was informal. His men would no longer wear ties in the steamy Solomons. His people would wear informal khakis. He worked hard to eliminate distinctions, and thus rivalries, between the services. People would not be of the Navy or the Army any more, just warriors of the South Pacific Fighting Forces. He would pull in Army technicians to service the fleet and bases, and he wanted their cooperation publicized. "I would like to see it widely advertised that the army is helping us here. I have never seen anything like the spirit here in this neck of woods. It is a real United States service."[20]

Since the centerpiece of the South Pacific was Guadalcanal, Admiral Halsey wanted to know everything about the island and its environs. Unfortunately:

> I began my new job under the crippling handicap of never having seen Guadalcanal, the keystone of the area I was defending. My information about it was not even second-hand,

> since Bob Ghormley and his Chief of Staff, Rear Admiral Daniel J. Callaghan, had never had an opportunity to see it either.[21]

Halsey did the next best thing: he asked the men in command in and around Guadalcanal to fly to Nouméa and brief him.

So, on the night of October 20, Admiral Halsey met with General Vandegrift, Army General Alexander M. Patch, Major General Millard F. Harmon, the senior army officer in the South Pacific, Lieutenant General Thomas Holcomb, the Commandant of the Marine Corps, who was in Nouméa on an inspection tour, Major General C. Barney Vogel, who had just arrived as commander of the I Marine Amphibious Corps, Admiral Turner and Ghormley's other subordinate commanders, and Halsey's staff, such as it was.

Generals Vandegrift and Harmon told their stories to Admiral Halsey. Vandegrift said his troops were "practically worn out," with not nearly enough sleep or food but more than enough combat for the past two months.[22] He said his troops needed material support and eventual relief, emphasizing that General Patch's Americal Division be sent in as well as the remainder of the 2nd Marine Division.[23] It was necessarily a very, very long briefing. When they finished, Halsey cut to the chase. "Are we going to evacuate or hold?'

Vandegrift replied, "I can hold, but I've got to get more active support than I've been getting."

It was an answer that irked Admiral Turner. He protested that their already small logistical capacity was getting smaller every day. On Guadalcanal there was no base; Ironbottom Sound had no space to maneuver. There were not enough warships to protect the supply convoys, who had to run the gauntlet of Japanese submarines to get to Guadalcanal.

General Vandegrift looked at Halsey. The new South Pacific commander understood that what Admiral Turner said was completely true. And also completely irrelevant.

Halsey was decisive. He nodded. "All right. Go on back. I'll promise you everything I've got."[24]

Getting Vandegrift everything Halsey got came with its own dangers, about one of which Halsey was about to learn. Recall destroyer *O'Brien* was torpedoed with the *North Carolina* in the same attack that sank the *Wasp* on September 15 in Torpedo Junction. Despite the fact that a single torpedo hit is usually enough to sink a destroyer, the damage to the *O'Brien* seemed to create more of a shark mouth on her bow than a serious danger. Skipper Commander Thomas Burrowes had her stop in Espiritu Santo and Nouméa for emergency repairs to make the trip back to San Francisco. She left Nouméa on October 10 with the destroyer *Lang* and the fleet oiler *Cimarron*, reaching Suva on October 13, where they repaired patches that had started leaking in the forward engine room. That was a bad sign.[25]

The signs did not improve after they left on the afternoon of October 16. The leaks returned, slowly but surely getting worse. By the morning of October 18, cracks had formed in the forward engine room patch, the shell, and, most worrisome, the keel. Commander Burrowes headed the *O'Brien* to the nearest port, Pago Pago, jettisoning as much topside weight as he could. The ship's creaking and groaning gave way to "the noise of a pistol shot" as a shell plate cracked open at 3:37 the next morning. Forget the nearest port; the *O'Brien* headed for the nearest land, only 40 miles away.

It might as well have been 4,000 miles. At around 6:00 am on October 19, the bottom fell out. Literally. The *O'Brien*'s keel snapped and the destroyer's bottom cracked wide open. The *O'Brien* was now held together only by her shell and her main deck, and within 30 minutes the main deck started splitting. The bow and stern sections started grinding and working separately. What had happened was the explosion of the torpedo had caused a "severe flexural vibration of the ship girder" – the keel – weakening both it and its connecting support members. The emergency repairs had not been enough to shore up the structural damage.[26] As a result, the *O'Brien* had progressively cracked up and was now disintegrating. The end was coming fast; the crew was completely evacuated by 7:01 am, all picked up by the *Lang* and the *Cimarron*. Only 45 minutes later, the *O'Brien* broke almost completely in half and folded like a jackknife. The stern sank at 7:57 am, the bow quickly following.

But Admiral Halsey's introduction to Torpedo Junction was not yet complete. While he was meeting everyone on October 20, Rear Admiral Willis Augustus Lee was having his task force centered on the new battleship *Washington* support a supply run to Guadalcanal. With the battleship was the heavy cruiser *San Francisco*, once again the flagship of Rear Admiral Scott, and *Chester*, now the flagship of Rear Admiral Wright, light cruiser *Helena*, light antiaircraft cruiser *Atlanta*, and destroyers *Aaron Ward*, *Walke*, *Behnam*, *Laffey*, *Buchanan*, *Lansdowne*, *McCalla*, *Fletcher*, and *Lardner*.

At 7:30 that night, Admiral Scott led the *San Francisco*, *Helena*, *Chester*, *Laffey*, *McCalla*, *Walke*, and *Buchanan* to split off and head for Espiritu Santo to refuel. Scott had the cruisers form a column, zigzagging at 19 knots as an antisubmarine measure.

That failed. At 9:20 pm, off San Cristobal, the *Chester*, last in the cruiser column, took one torpedo in the forward engine room. A second crossed in front of the bow. Both were courtesy of the Japanese submarine *I-176* and its skipper Lieutenant Commander Tanabe Yahachi, who as skipper of the *I-168* had finished off the *Yorktown* after Midway. Not quite as devastating this time, but bad enough. The *Chester* lost power and drifted to a stop with a 500-square-foot gash. The cruiser's forward engine room and Number 3 fireroom were flooded, and two of her engines were disabled. Both of her SOC floatplanes had to be jettisoned. The *Laffey* and *McCalla* were detailed to assist the *Chester*, while the remainder of Admiral Scott's ships, now joined by the *Fletcher*, continued on. Power was restored in short order and she was able to limp at 8 knots to Espiritu Santo. The *Chester* would be out of action for almost a year. Tanabe and the *I-176* escaped. Again.[27]

Nevertheless, the most serious issue in the South Pacific command continued to be air power. As of October 18, the 1st Marine Air Wing had only 74 aircraft available – 32

Wildcats, 27 Dauntlesses, a measly four Avengers, and 11 Airacobras. By comparison, Base Air Force had 55 Zeros, 49 Bettys, 13 Vals, one land reconnaissance plane, and five flying boats. To support Guadalcanal, all the nearby bases had been stripped to the point where they barely had enough to defend themselves. Espiritu Santo, for example, had only 16 fighters left to protect it.[28]

The only replacements en route to Guadalcanal were eight Dauntlesses and two Avengers being shipped on the carrier *Enterprise*, but no one knew when they would arrive. General Geiger reported a "critical shortage of fighters" to Fleet Air West Coast at San Diego, who were loading the escort carrier *Altamaha* for shipment to the South Pacific. When she left port, she would be carrying, among other things, 50 Wildcats. But she would not leave until November 3, and would take three weeks to get there.[29] So, in terms of air power, Admiral Halsey would be on his own until mid-November.

Admiral Nimitz had found his lion. But could this lion become the king of the Solomons jungle?

While Allied command in the South Pacific was changing and reorganizing itself, a single-file column of some 5,500 troops of the 2nd Sendai Division, led by Lieutenant General Maruyama Masao, was worming its way through the jungle closer to the weak link in the Marine lines defending Henderson Field.

General Hyakutake's plan to finally take Henderson Field was overly complicated, as Japanese plans tended to be. This time it was the result of compromise. Colonel Matsumoto Hiroshi, the operations officer for the Sendai Division, wanted to attack near the coast. The politically powerful Lieutenant Colonel Tsuji Masanobu of the 17th Army, who also represented Imperial General Headquarters, wanted to attack from heights several miles inland to the south of Henderson Field. Hyakutake figured: why not attack both?

And so began this latest Imperial Japanese Army attack on the Henderson Field perimeter. The Sendai Division's 4th Infantry Regiment – the Aoba Detachment – supported by tanks and artillery, would attack Marine positions along the Matanikau River near the coast to the west, complete with a flanking move. Somehow, this effort by a unit that was already pretty badly chewed up by early October actions, also along the Matanikau River, was supposed to be both a diversion from the real attack and a real attack. Meanwhile, two more regiments of the Sendai, the 16th and 29th, plus the 230th Regiment of the 38th Nagoya Division, would have worked their way around the Henderson Field perimeter to perform the real attack – a two-pronged assault – from the south, where the Marines would least expect it, having covered that sector with only two battalions of the 7th Marine Regiment. Imperial General Headquarters set the night of October 21 for the attack.

This plan required close coordination between units, which could be problematic on an island that's mainly primordial jungle. General Hyakutake had anticipated this issue and sent engineers to cut a path through the jungle for General Maruyama's troops before they stepped off on October 16. It became known as the Maruyama Road, no more than 2 feet wide.[30]

The troops hacked their way through dense foliage, crossing hills, ridges, streams, and rivers, often in monsoon-like rains that turned the Maruyama Road into a quagmire, making every step a major physical effort and always in stifling humidity. Not surprisingly, the march took longer than anticipated. And it went downhill from there.

On October 20, General Maruyama radioed 17th Army headquarters that the attack would have to be delayed by one day, to October 22. In notifying his troops, General Hyakutake announced, "The time of the decisive battle between Japan and the United States has come."[31] When October 22 came, however, Maruyama radioed again, delaying the "time of the decisive battle between Japan and the United States" to October 23.

North of the Solomons, the ships of the Imperial Japanese Navy waited impatiently. Collectively called the "Support Force" under Admiral Kondo, although Admiral Yamamoto himself exercised direct control from the *Yamato* sitting comfortably in Truk, they were arrayed in three major groups forming a triangle. To the west was the so-called "Advance Force," with the carriers *Junyo* and *Hiyo* under Rear Admiral Kakuta Kakuji; the 3rd Battleship Division with *Kongo* and *Haruna* under Vice Admiral Kurita Takeo; heavy cruisers *Myoko* and *Maya* under Vice Admiral Tagaki; two more heavy cruisers, flagship *Atago* and her sister-life partner *Takao* under the direct command of Kondo; and Admiral Tanaka's 2nd Destroyer Flotilla with flagship light cruiser *Isuzu* and 12 destroyers.

About 100 miles east of the Advance Force was the "Main Body," consisting of the reconstituted Japanese Carrier Striking Force *Kido Butai*, with Admiral Nagumo leading fleet carriers *Shokaku* and *Zuikaku*, now with new light carrier *Zuiho* and a minimal escort of heavy cruiser *Kumano* and eight destroyers.

The carriers' escort was so small because most of it was about 100 miles to the south. Using an organizational breakdown similar to that used at Eastern Solomons, this group under Rear Admiral Abe Hiroaki was – again – the so-called "Vanguard Force." It featured the 11th Battleship Division with the *Hiei* and *Kirishima* under Abe's direct command; one member of the 7th Cruiser Division, *Suzuya*, under Rear Admiral Nishimura Shoji; the traditional escorts of *Kido Butai* of the 8th Cruiser Division, the heavy cruiser/seaplane carriers *Tone* and *Chikuma* under Rear Admiral Hara Chuichi; and the 10th Destroyer Flotilla under Rear Admiral Kimura Susumu with flagship light cruiser *Nagara* and seven destroyers.

These were a lot of ships to keep at sea at the same time. The 17th Army had been told its naval support could remain at sea for only two weeks or so because of fuel issues; whether the 17th actually appreciated it is unclear. Much of the Navy's impatience was rooted in these concerns, which indeed started to manifest themselves. Oilers had to be sent back to Truk to siphon fuel from the *Yamato* and *Mutsu* to keep the fleet operating. Admiral Kondo's ships had already been forced to withdraw once to refuel. But just before they did, Kondo had Admiral Kakuta's *Junyo* and *Hiyo* perform the first carrier raid on Guadalcanal since August.

It did not go well. Expecting to find anchored transports, the attacking aircraft – 18 Zeros and 17 Kates armed with bombs – instead found destroyers *Aaron Ward* and *Lardner* shelling Japanese supply dumps near Kokumbona at around 7:00 am. Nine Kates from the *Hiyo* bombed what they identified as a *Honolulu*-class cruiser; which destroyer it actually was is unclear. They all missed. One Kate was shot down and a second was damaged and had to land at Buin. Then eight Kates from the *Junyo* tried to attack, but were ambushed by eight Fighting 121 Wildcats under Major Davis, part of 25 Wildcats launched before dawn in response to a warning from *Magic* of the planned attack. Only three of the Kates managed to drop their payloads, and all missed; six Kates were shot down and the remaining two, badly damaged, had to crash-land at Buin. The vengeful escorting Zeros shot down two Wildcats, losing one of their own.[32]

That was it for Admiral Kondo, and his ships moved off to refuel again. Vice Admiral Kusaka's Base Air Force stepped up operations in advance of the big offensive that was due to start … whenever. On October 18, coastwatcher Jack Read, operating near Buka, reported a dozen fighters headed southeast. It was actually nine Zeros under Lieutenant (jg) Baba Masayoshi of the Kanoya Air Group. The report reached Henderson Field at 10:30 am.[33] A half-hour later, Colonel Joe Bauer called in his pilots for a briefing. But it was more than a briefing. It was a motivational speech – one that would turn tried and true conventional wisdom on its head:

> Be an aggressor. You're out there to shoot down enemy planes. Have complete faith in your armor and confidence in your ability to shoot down the enemy when you have him in your sights… When you see Zeros, dogfight 'em![34]

Up until this point, the conventional wisdom, learned from painful, bitter experience, was "Never, *ever* dogfight a Zero," because a Zero could and did outperform American fighters such as the F4F Wildcat or the P-40 Warhawk. The Americans were forced to use the tactic of "Boom and Zoom" – take one pass at a Zero and speed away, then try again. But not anymore. Now, for the most part, they were no longer facing the Japanese pilots who attacked Pearl Harbor, sank the *Prince of Wales* and *Repulse,* and rampaged through the Indian Ocean. The skill level of Japanese pilots had decreased markedly. Admiral Halsey was bringing a new aggressiveness, and now Colonel Bauer was too.

Thirty-two Marine Wildcats took to the air. While flying to meet the enemy, they overheard a report from coastwatcher Donald Kennedy on New Georgia of more aircraft heading southeast: "sounds like a fair number."[35] It was the second part of the Base Air Force attack, 15 Bettys led by Lieutenant Nabeta escorted by seven Zeros. A full day of air battles using Joe Bauer's new philosophy cost the Japanese four Zeros and three Bettys at a cost of two Wildcats shot down, with both pilots rescued, and a third lost due to accident, the pilot killed. Lieutenant Nabeta claimed he had set Henderson Field afire; his bombers had actually missed it entirely, hitting the pioneer battalion bivouac area instead, killing seven and wounding 18.[36]

The next day, October 19, was not nearly as successful for the Cactus Air Force. The first attempted intercept of a Japanese fighter sweep failed, with one Wildcat performing a mysterious and fatal swan dive from 18,000 feet into Ironbottom Sound. The second – 16 F4Fs – was ambushed by nine Zeros of the 6th Air Group under Lieutenant Miyano Zenjiro. The Wildcats dove away from the Zeros, but lost two of their number, though both pilots were recovered. No Zeros were shot down. Upon the pilots' return, a furious Colonel Bauer tore into them, demanding, "Why didn't you stay and fight?" and threatening to ship them all out.

As General Maruyama took longer and longer to hack his way through the jungle, the costs of waiting multiplied. On October 21, the *Hiyo*, converted to a carrier from an ocean liner hull, suffered a fire in her starboard generator room. The fire was put out within 90 minutes, but the damage to her engineering spaces limited her speed to 16 knots, too low to keep up with the fleet or even to operate aircraft in the absence of a headwind. Admiral Kakuta transferred his flag to the *Junyo.* Using only her port engines, the *Hiyo*, escorted by destroyers *Isonami* and *Inazuma*, headed back to Truk for emergency repairs. Of her air group, three Zeros, one Val, and five Kates were transferred to the *Junyo* to bring her air group up to full strength, while 17 Zeros and 17 Vals were sent to Rabaul, eventually staging into Buin, to operate with Base Air Force.[37]

A final worrying factor for the Combined Fleet amidst the waiting for the army to attack was the American aircraft carriers. For some time, the Japanese carriers north of the Solomons had been doing that *danse macabre* with the carrier *Hornet*, the only operational US carrier in the Pacific, south of the Solomons. Much to the angst of Admiral Nagumo and the Japanese, US Navy Catalina flying boats out of Espiritu Santo were very good when it came to finding the Japanese carriers. So, when the Japanese headed south to try to attack the *Hornet*, the *Hornet* would move south. When the Japanese gave up and headed back north again, the *Hornet* would head back north, too.

It only got worse when their own scouts lost track of the *Hornet*, starting on October 16. Radio intelligence detected messages to her, so they knew she was there. But the Japanese could not find her visually, though they did find the battleship *Washington* and some cruisers in the vicinity of Rennell Island. Why could they find the battleship and not the carrier? Was the battleship to lure them into a trap? That's what the Japanese would do – use a few of their extremely limited supply of ships as bait. Yamamoto warned his ships at sea to maintain search patrols to the east.[38]

Moreover, on October 15, Japanese radio intelligence determined that a major US task force had just left Pearl Harbor headed for the South Pacific. They figured correctly this was the *Enterprise* task force.[39] The clock was ticking.

But the 17th Army could not get its act together. October 23 saw the date of the attack pushed back yet again to October 24. During that time, the perfidious Lieutenant Colonel

Tsuji connived to get the veteran General Kawaguchi, the most experienced senior officer on Guadalcanal, leading the right flank of the attack, removed; Kawaguchi was a "loser" and not nearly enough of a war criminal for Tsuji. He was replaced with Colonel Shoji Toshinaro, who let it be known he did not want the job on the eve of battle.[40]

But though the attack had been postponed – again – no one had bothered to tell the units conducting the sort-of-diversionary attack along the coast of the latest delay. They attacked on schedule at around 6:00 pm on October 23 and were easily repulsed. The 1st Marine Division lost 25 killed and 14 wounded. The Japanese lost some 600 troops and gained no ground whatsoever.

The constant delays got under the skin of Admiral Yamamoto and, especially, Admiral Nagumo. In the late afternoon of October 24, the commander of the much-reduced *Kido Butai* sat in his cabin pondering the meaning of two reports he had received. One was an October 20 news story from United Press, declaring "a major sea and air battle is expected in the near future in the Solomon Islands area."[41] The other was a breakdown of the American ships spotted by his scouts since his carriers had arrived. The enemy carriers had been missing for a week.[42]

As Admiral Nagumo considered this information, or lack thereof, Commander Takada Toshitane of his staff came in and warned, "Sir, radiomen report they are suddenly getting great numbers of undecipherable messages, evidently from nearby enemy submarines and aircraft."[43]

"Very well," replied the admiral wearily, who figured the Americans had located his carriers again. "Call Chief of Staff Kusaka quickly." Kusaka quickly confirmed that his ships were still in the process of refueling.

"Any reports on enemy carriers?"

"No, sir."

The catastrophe at Midway had noticeably aged Admiral Nagumo. His hair had grayed; his face was worn and wrinkled. It had affected him in other ways as well. "At Midway," he thought aloud, "the enemy struck us at a time of his choosing. Now, too, there is no doubt that the enemy pinpoints our position as if on a chessboard, but we are running blind…"

"Excuse me, sir." The voice was Commander Takada's. "May I suggest sending a message to *Yamato* asking for instructions?"

After a few moments of silence, it was Admiral Kusaka who spoke up. "All right, Takada, take this message: 'From Kusaka, 1st Air Fleet Chief of Staff, to Vice Admiral Ugaki, Combined Fleet Chief of Staff: May I suggest halting our southward advance until we receive definite word that the Army has captured Guadalcanal airfields? There seems to be a possibility of our being trapped if we continue going like this.'" Nagumo nodded silently and the message was sent.

It was after midnight when they received the response: "From Ugaki to Kusaka: Your Striking Force will proceed quickly to the enemy direction. The operation orders stand, without change."

The response was coldly military, but its firmness only hinted at the rage at Admiral Nagumo in Combined Fleet headquarters on the *Yamato*. This was part of a long-simmering feud between Nagumo and Admiral Yamamoto as to the degree of risk with which *Kido Butai* should operate. For weeks Yamamoto had indirectly pressed Nagumo to take the carriers south and attack, but did not make it a direct order. Each time, Admiral Kusaka convinced Nagumo that to do so would lead to another Midway. Avoiding another Midway was foremost in Nagumo's mind. And perhaps not just for tactical reasons; Admiral Yamamoto continued to hold Nagumo responsible for the Midway disaster.[44]

When the message was passed to Admiral Yamamoto, he flat-out refused to consider it. Admiral Ugaki was angry himself, calling the proposal "outrageous," "arbitrary," and "irresponsible and presumptuous" because it would leave the southeast, the most likely avenue for enemy attack, uncovered, and would leave Admiral Kondo's battleships with only the *Junyo* for air cover.[45]

The anger on the *Yamato* was matched by the disappointment and resignation on the *Shokaku*. Admiral Nagumo snorted in disgust and ordered, "All right, start fueling the carriers."

The anger on the *Yamato* and the apprehension on the *Shokaku* both contrasted with the eagerness and borderline arrogance on the *Junyo*, where Admiral Kakuta Kakuji was considering the same information Admiral Nagumo had, and was reaching some very different conclusions. He turned to his air officer, Lieutenant Commander Okumiya Masatake. "Well, what do you say, Masatake?"

Lieutenant Commander Okumiya said impassively, "Sir, October 27 is America's Navy Day."

Admiral Kakuta leapt from his chair with a laugh. "Very good, very good. Let's hustle and prepare a nice Navy Day gift for those cocky Yanks!"[46]

It was – finally – the night of October 24 that the great pincer attack on the south side of the Henderson Field Marine perimeter took place. Except that Colonel Shoji's pincer got lost in the rain and the jungle and missed the battle entirely. That can happen when you change commanders on the eve of battle.

Nevertheless, after midnight, a phone call came in to General Maruyama's headquarters. It was Colonel Matsumoto, his operations officer, acting as a liaison with Colonel Shoji's troops.

"The right flank attacked the airfield!" Colonel Matsumoto shouted. "The night attack is a success!"

"Banzai!" replied General Maruyama.[47]

And so, 50 minutes after midnight on October 25, 17th Army sent the victory message: "2300 Banzai! – A little before 2300 (11:00 pm) the right wing captured the airfield."[48] Finally! The long national nightmare was over!

With Henderson Field now out of the way, Admiral Yamamoto ordered Admiral Kondo to take the various elements of his fleet and head south to meet the Americans. Already the area around Guadalcanal was crawling with Japanese naval units, mostly from Admiral Mikawa's 8th Fleet. On the way was Rear Admiral Takama Tamotsu's so-called "No. 2 Attack Unit," consisting of light cruiser *Yura* and destroyers *Akizuki*, *Harusame*, *Murasame*, *Samidare*, and *Yudachi*. Their role had been to bombard Henderson Field while still in enemy hands and then drop troops near Koli Point to cut off the Americans' escape route.

Early that morning, an Imperial Army Air Force Mitsubishi Ki-46 twin-engine "Type 100 command reconnaissance plane" – called "Dinah" by the Allies – from the 76th Independent Air Squadron appeared over Henderson Field. Told that Henderson Field was in Japanese hands, the mission of squadron commander Captain Kirita Hideo and his crew was to report on the progress of General Maruyama's attack. Lazily, the Mitsubishi buzzed low over Henderson Field, looking for the Rising Sun flag and friendly troops. It received an unfriendly burst from an antiaircraft gun that sent the Dinah plummeting into the ground next to the runway.[49] Clearly, Henderson Field was not yet entirely friendly.

In fact, several hours after Colonel Matsumoto called to report "The night attack is a success!" he called again: "I was mistaken about the success of the right flank. They crossed a large open field and thought it was the airfield. It was a mistake."[50]

What exactly prompted Colonel Matsumoto to give the impression Colonel Shoji's right wing had captured Henderson Field remains a mystery. It may have been a lie. It may have been a product of war fever or malarial fever, more likely the latter.[51] But the 17th Army compounded the error by evidently trying to cover it up. They first announced at 2:00 am there was continued fighting near the airfield, then only at 6:23 am finally admitted that Henderson Field was still in American hands.[52]

At 7:00 am, the search Dauntlesses out of Henderson found three Japanese destroyers – *Akatsuki*, *Ikazuchi*, and *Shiratsuyu*, forming the "No. 1 Attack Unit" – just 35 miles northwest of Cape Esperance and closing in. Fast.[53] Later, at 8:30 that morning, the "No. 2 Attack Unit" was spotted some 100 miles from Cape Esperance.

But Henderson was not in a position to do anything about it just yet. The rain had turned the runways into quagmires. Coastwatchers had warned of an incoming flight of Zeros. From Rabaul, Base Air Force was sending 28 fighters, divided into four hourly flights. Each was to circle the field for two hours, then land if they could see the airfield was in Japanese hands. En route were nine Zeros of the 3rd Air Group under Lieutenant (jg) Yamaguchi Sadao, back in action after being shot down on October 3, and subsequently rescued by Imperial Army Troops.

Colonel Bauer selected Captain Joe Foss to lead a flight of six Fighting 121 Wildcats out of the muck that was Fighter 1 at the moment. At about 9:45, the Marine Grummans took off without flaps to avoid the worst of the mud. They had gotten to only about 1,500 feet before six Zeros pounced. Foss and his pilots held the Japanese off until about

6,000 feet, where most of the fighting took place. Two Zeros were shot down at a cost of one Wildcat, whose pilot, 2nd Lieutenant Oscar M. Bate, bailed out and walked back to Henderson Field. The remaining seven Zeros ended up sparring with a second flight of seven Marine Fighting 121 F4Fs under Major Davis, with no loss to either side.[54]

Meanwhile, the Japanese destroyers *Akatsuki*, *Ikazuchi*, and *Shiratsuyu* of the 6th Destroyer Division under Commander Yamada Yusuke had arrived off Lunga and were making merry mischief. The first ships to fall foul of the intruders were the *Trever* and *Zane*, two old former four-piper destroyers repurposed as minesweepers, at least one of which was misidentified by the Japanese as a light cruiser.[55] They had transported PT boats, ammunition, and aviation gasoline to Tulagi and were transporting a Marine surveying team when, at around 10:00 am, they were warned about three Japanese "cruisers" charging in to Ironbottom Sound. Commander Dwight Agnew, skipper of the *Trever* and commanding the group of minesweepers, had no choice but to run for Sealark Channel.

The chase began. Commander Agnew rang for as much speed as he could get – 29 knots, causing a boiler casing on the *Trever* to burn completely through. Even with *Trever* melting a boiler, Commander Yamada's ships still had at least a 6-knot advantage in speed. They started shelling the two old minesweepers, with the shell splashes "feet, not yards" away from the *Zane*.[56] Commander Agnew ordered evasive maneuvers and had his guns respond, more for morale purposes since they could not reach the destroyers. Because Sealark Channel was too close to the intruders, Agnew steered just north of Sealark toward the reef-studded Naggela Channel, hoping the destroyers would run aground or at least have their progress impeded. But the Japanese gained on the old minesweepers, and their guns started scoring. The *Zane* took a hit amidships that knocked out a gun and killed three. The old four-pipers were overmatched. They needed help to escape.

And they got it, in the form of four Marine Fighting 212 Wildcats commanded by 1st Lieutenant Tex Stout. Their strafing distracted the three Japanese vessels enough for the minesweepers to escape. Commander Yamada's destroyers looped around and headed west along the coast of Lunga, where they found the tug *Seminole* and the patrol boat *YP-284* unloading cargo.

The Yippie's skipper Lieutenant Carl Rasmussen saw the three destroyers and radioed Tulagi, asking if they were friendly. With a reply in the negative he ordered full speed back to Tulagi, but at 10:50 the boat was cut to pieces by Japanese gunfire. She quickly sank with the loss of three Marine passengers. The *Seminole* didn't even try to fight back, but instead moved to beach herself to preserve what she could of her cargo of pack howitzers and gasoline. It was no use, as the 5-inch shells set fire to the gasoline and forced the crew to abandon ship, after which the tug sank at 11:20. One life was lost.[57]

Commander Yamada was not done yet. The "No. 1 Attack Unit" arrived off Lunga and started to bombard American positions with 5-inch shells. This time, however, the 6th Destroyer Division had picked on someone who could fight back – the Marine 3rd Defense Battalion, with those 5-inch coastal defense guns. At 10:53, the Marines scored one hit on the *Akatsuki*, setting fire to the magazine for the Number 3 mount, killing four and severely injuring one. Yamada's destroyers retreated behind a smoke screen.[58]

The strafing by Lieutenant Stout's Wildcats had helped drive the destroyers away and now, low on ammunition, the Wildcats tried to land. But eight Zeros of Lieutenant (jg) Futagami Tokitane got there first. As the first section of three started strafing the airfield, Marine 1st Lieutenant Jack Conger swung behind them. He set one afire and pumped his remaining ammunition into a second, which ground observers confirmed crashed. Conger was ready to face the third, which was apparently Futagami himself, when he realized he was out of ammunition. At the last second, he decided to try to slice the Zero's tail off with his propeller, which he later admitted was "a crazy thing to do," but give him credit for resourcefulness and determination. His propeller cut the Mitsubishi's fuselage in half, but sent his Grumman into a dive, forcing Conger to bail out. His parachute had barely opened before he splashed; his last target was never seen again.

Having downed three Zeros, Lieutenant Conger was very nearly killed by a flaming fourth, which plunged into the water only 100 feet away. Its pilot, Petty Officer 2nd Class Ishikawa Shiro, plopped in the water only 20 yards away, shot down by 1st Lieutenant Lawrence Faulkner. A PT boat came out from Lunga to pick up Conger, who suggested they pick up Ishikawa and take him prisoner. Ishikawa had other ideas. He thrust his pistol in Conger's face and pulled the trigger; the waterlogged gun only clicked. Ishikawa then pointed the gun at his own head and pulled the trigger; the pistol clicked again. Conger bashed Ishikawa over the head with a jerry can, a sailor took his gun, and the dazed Japanese pilot was hauled aboard.[59]

The tag team air battles continued. At 11:30 Captain Joe Foss led four other Wildcats up. At 12:45, he spotted below him six Zeros of the famous Tainan Air Group led by Warrant Officer Yamashita Shohei, "sailing along with splendid calm and indifference" over Lunga.[60] Foss dove in to close on one Zero, riddling it with his guns and causing it to explode, but barely missing its flaming engine flying out of the wreckage. Another Zero, apparently that of Yamashita, overshot Foss, and he turned to tail it and give it some "liberal treatment." The four surviving Zeros broke off around 1:05 pm and headed back, but Yamashita's fighter was so shot up he had to ditch on the way back to Rabaul.

While Captain Foss was holding off Zeros, five Dauntlesses of Scouting 71 under the direction of Lieutenant Commander Eldridge managed to take off to do something about some of the Japanese ships that were hanging around Lunga. At 1:05 pm, Eldridge and his crews found the cruiser *Yura* and the destroyers of the No. 2 Attack Unit in the northern entrance to Indispensable Strait some 30 miles northeast of Florida Island.[61]

Lieutenant Commander Eldridge himself led off, dropping a 1,000lb bomb from 3,000 feet that exploded in the *Yura*'s engine room. One of his pilots got a near-miss on the cruiser as well. The *Yura* coasted to a stop, settling by the stern. The large destroyer *Akizuki* took a hit from a small bomb amidships and two near-misses that ruptured hull plating and flooded her after engine room. The starboard propeller stopped and her speed was cut to 23 knots.[62] Admiral Takama informed Admiral Mikawa of the attack. Mikawa, in his own words, "decided to assemble his forces in the rear area until the recapture of the Guadalcanal airfield was definitely reported."[63] In other words, Takama was to return to Shortland.

If he could. The Americans were not through with him. Next came three P-39 Airacobras of the 67th at 2:35. They scored no hits, nor did three SBDs under the command of Lieutenant Ray Davis of Bombing 6. By this time, the *Yura*'s damage control had managed to restore some power, but they could not control the flooding. Skipper Captain Sato Shiro asked Admiral Takama for permission to beach the light cruiser on Fara Island, which Takama granted.[64]

But the Americans would make even that short trip difficult. At 4:30 pm, Lieutenant Commander Eldridge led three Dauntlesses of Scouting 71, four Airacobras of the 67th Squadron, and three Marine Wildcats in another strike on Admiral Takama's beleaguered group. The *Yura* took at least one bomb hit that set her afire and the *Akizuki* took one near-miss. Thirty minutes later came six B-17s of the 11th Bombardment Group from Espiritu Santo under Major Edmundson. From 13,500 feet, they piled on, dropping 46 500lb bombs (two more failed to drop), claiming three to six hits on the biggest target, the *Yura*.[65]

Night was almost here, but it could not come soon enough to save the *Yura*. Admiral Takama ordered the cruiser scuttled. Takama moved his flag from the damaged *Akizuki* to the *Murasame*, and both ships took off the *Yura*'s crew. At 6:30, *Harusame* and *Yudachi* fired torpedoes at the abandoned cruiser. Not even this was simple. The *Yura* broke in two, the bow sinking, but the stern remaining afloat until the *Yudachi* dispatched it with gunfire around 7:00 pm off Cape Astrolabe, Santa Ysabel.[66] The *Akizuki* suffered heavy damage to her boiler room, 11 dead and 22 injured, but she made it back to Japan.[67]

It was a significant success for the Americans on a day in which the 1st Marine Air Wing was under siege. Five Zeros of the Tainan Air Group appeared over Lunga around 2:00 pm, at about the same time as a raid of 16 Betty bombers from Rabaul escorted by 12 Zeros from the *Hiyo* operating out of Buin appeared. They were met by 11 Wildcats under Major Davis, resulting in a wild melee that resulted in the loss of two Bettys, one Tainan Zero, and one *Hiyo* Zero. Then a little before 4:00 pm came 12 Val dive bombers and 12 Zeros from the carrier *Junyo* under Lieutenant Shiga Yoshio. With no aerial opposition, the *Junyo* strike bombed and strafed Henderson Field at will, then returned to their carrier with no losses. But they also inflicted no losses on the Americans; all they did was hit the Boneyard of wrecked aircraft south of the runway.[68]

The siege, at least the aerial portion of it, was over for the moment. The Japanese had launched 82 aircraft in six waves against Henderson Field. Of those 82, 11 Zeros, two Bettys, and one Army reconnaissance plane were lost, along with their crews; two more damaged Zeros were written off. For all this effort, the Japanese had shot down exactly two Wildcats, of which both pilots survived. Another four were shot up and six were damaged by operational accidents or the quagmire of an airstrip. That left exactly eight fighters immediately flyable.

But after this "Dugout Sunday," as it became known because the day-long series of air attacks had kept the men in their dugout shelters, Henderson Field was still in American hands. The 1st Marine Air Wing was in desperate shape, but the Marines and soldiers had done their part, holding back the Japanese attack by land, by air, and even a little by sea.

The question remained: could the US Navy do its part?

CHAPTER 11
NOT QUITE MIDWAY

The Imperial Navy's fears about the cost of the repeated delays in the 17th Army's attack on Henderson Field were being realized.

At 12:45 pm on October 24, mere hours before the Sendai Division was to attack, the USS *Enterprise* group met the *Hornet* group northeast of the New Hebrides, forming Task Force 61 under Rear Admiral Kinkaid.[1] Task Force 61 had two component parts. One was Task Force 16 under Kinkaid's personal direction, featuring the *Enterprise* screened by the new battleship *South Dakota*, heavy cruiser *Portland*, light antiaircraft cruiser *San Juan*, and seven destroyers. Task Force 17, still under Rear Admiral Murray, had the *Hornet* screened by the heavy cruisers *Northampton* and *Pensacola*, light antiaircraft cruisers *San Diego* and *Juneau*, and six destroyers. In Admiral Halsey's words, "Until the *Enterprise* arrived, our plight had been almost hopeless. Now we had a fighting chance."[2]

The reason? Admiral Halsey believed "Carrier power varies as the square – two carriers are four times as powerful as one."[3] Halsey's mathematic proof of this formula was somewhat lacking. So, too, was his intelligence information. Pearl Harbor thought Halsey's ships would only face the *Shokaku* and *Zuikaku*, two fleet carriers. In fact, they were also facing one light carrier, the *Zuiho*, as well as the *Junyo*, the latter larger than a light carrier if not quite a fleet carrier, which could be counted as three or even four aircraft carriers, with the power, under Halsey's formula, of nine or even 16 carriers. The numbers perhaps expose the bizarre nature of Halsey's formula.

Nevertheless, as Halsey told Admiral Nimitz a few weeks later, "I had to begin throwing punches almost immediately. As a consequence quick decisions had to be made."[4]

And Admiral Halsey made them, sending out orders to Admiral Kinkaid: "[M]ake a sweep around north Santa Cruz Islands thence southwesterly east of San Cristobal to area in Coral Sea in position to intercept enemy forces approaching [Guadalcanal-Tulagi]."[5] It was a bold, aggressive move, unlike anything seen from Admiral Ghormley, going outside the air cover, such as it was, of Espiritu Santo, into waters visited by no American carrier in two months. The idea was to place the *Enterprise* and *Hornet* outside the range of Japanese air power on Rabaul, but able to strike from the east at the flank of, and hopefully ambush, the Japanese carriers.[6]

In short, it was to be another Midway. These were the same maneuvers that enabled the badly outnumbered US Navy to win at Midway.

But past performance is no guarantee of future results.

It was almost dawn on October 25 when Admiral Nagumo was awakened by an aide. He gave the admiral a report from one of *Kido Butai*'s protecting fighters: "I have shot down an enemy plane, apparently a scout."

That news got the little admiral bolt upright. "Cut refueling! Turn the carriers around and head due north!" In fact they actually headed north-northeast at 20 knots, sending out numerous scout planes.[7] Admiral Nagumo was assuming the scout had made a full contact report. The turn was intended to throw off subsequent American searches and attacks.

While *Kido Butai* was headed north, Admiral Kondo had received a report from Base Air Force that one of its scout planes had sighted two battleships, four heavy cruisers, one light cruiser, and 12 destroyers 30 miles east of Rennell Island.[8] Overstated in strength, this was Admiral Lee's Task Force 64, built around the battleship *Washington*. Frustrated by their inability to locate the American carriers, Kondo ordered Nagumo to attack this group; maybe the battleship would point the way to the missing carriers. But Nagumo refused, reasoning that the 340-mile distance from his carriers to the battleship was too long for his aircraft.[9]

Admiral Nagumo's about-face and the subsequent inability to strike at the battleship seems to have been the final straw for Admiral Yamamoto. That afternoon, Nagumo received a message from Yamamoto. Among the highlights from the deliberately insulting dispatch was Yamamoto "urging" Nagumo to attack "with vigor."[10]

Now it was Admiral Nagumo's turn to be angry. He summoned Kusaka and showed him the message, saying he could not ignore it. Nagumo asked for the support of his longtime chief of staff.

"I admit I've objected to your suggestions, but you are the commander and must make the final decisions," said Admiral Kusaka. "It's your battle. If you really want to head south, I'll go along with your verdict." After this empty show of support, Kusaka went on to remind the admiral that they had not yet located the enemy fleet, while they would likely be found by B-17s from Espiritu Santo. Kusaka concluded with pure sophistry. "But now that your mind is made up, I want you to know that we shall not be destroyed without first destroying the enemy."[11]

With that reassurance in hand, Admiral Nagumo had his fleet refuel and, at about 9:00 pm, turned to head south at 20 knots.[12]

Admiral Halsey was indeed hitting the ground running, but in the process he may have run over a few of his subordinates, in particular Admiral Kinkaid.

One of Admiral Halsey's administrative priorities was to assemble as many of his old staff as he could. These were people who knew his ways, knew how to handle him, and shared his aggressive philosophy. The defeatism of Admiral Ghormley would be eradicated.

Among these staffers was Commander Leonard J. "Ham" Dow. Dow had been Admiral Halsey's communications officer, but he was currently on the *Enterprise*, on which he had served as fighter director officer since before the war. Halsey later told Admiral Nimitz that he debated for a long time whether he should order Dow to join him and leave the *Enterprise* looking for a new fighter director officer – on the eve of battle, no less. He believed with fleet communications so poor he needed someone he could trust. In addition, Commander John H. Griffin, aboard the *Enterprise* as a member of Admiral Kinkaid's staff, could immediately replace him. Griffin had been the head of the Fighter Director School on Oahu, had been trained by the Royal Air Force, and had a deep understanding of the theory of fighter direction. That Griffin had never directed fighters in a carrier battle apparently did not bother Halsey.[13]

In fairness, communications were indeed a major issue for Admiral Halsey, though not necessarily related to the staff. Halsey's plan for another Midway by having the carriers "[M]ake a sweep around north Santa Cruz Islands" had, as he explained to Admiral Nimitz about a week later, one caveat: the carriers were to sweep past Santa Cruz only "if no enemy comes down." In other words, if no large enemy force appeared north of the Solomons. Somehow, that particular aspect of the plan did not make it into Halsey's orders to Admiral Kinkaid.[14] It's always the little things.

As ordered, Admiral Kinkaid spent most of October 25 headed northwest at 22 knots. The *Enterprise* kept a combat air patrol operating while the *Hornet* kept a strike spotted on deck to be launched as soon as the enemy carriers were located. To locate said carriers, Admiral Fitch sent out from Espiritu Santo ten Catalinas and six B-17s. The seaplane tender *Ballard* braved the malaria and moved to Vanikoro, at the south end of the Santa Cruz Islands, to maintain the PBYs.

The reports came in fast and furious. At 9:48 am after a mauling by a few Zeros from the *Junyo*, Lieutenant Mario Sesso's B-17 reported contact with Admiral Kondo's Advance Force. Admiral Fitch sent a dozen B-17s after this force. Ten minutes later, a Catalina commanded by Lieutenant (jg) Warren B. Matthew, after a mauling by two Petes from the *Kirishima* that produced 76 holes, reported finding Admiral Abe's Vanguard Force.

It was at 10:00 am that the first truly interesting report came in, from a Catalina commanded by Lieutenant (jg) Robert G. Lampshire. He initially reported "unidentified task forces," which he later specified were carriers launching fighters. At 11:03 he added two more carriers to his report. Course 145 degrees – southeast – speed 25 knots. That is, bearing 287 degrees True – northwest – and 355 miles from Admiral Kinkaid; also, 250 miles northeast of Henderson Field and able to support an attack thereon.[15]

These were interesting times indeed. Monitoring all the sighting reports from Nouméa, Admiral Halsey reached his own conclusions. He dispatched an order to Admiral Kinkaid and Admiral Lee, one that would encapsulate the new attitude emanating out of Nouméa and electrify the men fighting in the South Pacific. The order read simply, "Strike, Repeat, Strike. ComSoPac sends action CTF61 and 64."[16]

Unfortunately, at that moment Admiral Kinkaid had his hands full. While flying combat air patrol, Wildcat pilot Lieutenant (jg) William K. Blair suffered a mechanical breakdown that greatly reduced his engine power and made it almost impossible to fly straight and level with his gear down. He was allowed to attempt a forced landing on the *Enterprise*, but in trying to execute the hazardous landing he did not lower his tailhook, nor did the landing signal officer notice it. As a result, Blair's Wildcat ripped through the crash barrier, bounced and plowed into parked SBDs forward, knocking one overboard and wrecking three more in addition to Blair's fighter. Five aircraft were totaled. Fortunately, although four were injured, no one was killed. But since he had destroyed five US planes at once, Blair's ruthless squadron mates called him a "Japanese ace."[17]

Because the American and Japanese carriers were on almost a head-on course and thus rapidly closing the range, Admiral Kinkaid calculated that an afternoon airstrike on the Japanese carriers might be feasible. He sped up to 27 knots. But he faced a problem whose scope had been underrated – the wind was coming from the southeast, as it almost alwys did in theis region. From behind him. To conduct flight operations he had to turn almost completely around, which meant to launch an attack his carriers had to steam into well within the maximum range of their aircraft. The Japanese, with the wind coming straight at them, had no such issue and could launch as they steamed along. This was a serious disadvantage for the Americans.

Rather curiously, instead of using the aircraft already spotted and ready for launch on the deck of the *Hornet*, Admiral Kinkaid had the *Enterprise*'s Air Group 10 prepare for the afternoon attack. His logic appears to have been twofold. First, the *Enterprise*'s Wildcats had wing fuel tanks, which gave them slightly longer range than those of the *Hornet*, who only had belly tanks.[18] Second, Kinkaid seems to have studied the battles of the Coral Sea, Midway, and Eastern Solomons, and concluded that the US airstrikes needed a second wave, like the Japanese managed to do. His plan therefore was to prepare the *Enterprise* strike while closing the range. Then, once Air Group 10 had found the Japanese, the follow-up strike from the *Hornet* could be immediately launched.[19]

More properly, the *Hornet* strike would be the follow-up to the follow-up, because the *Enterprise* strike would be preceded by six pairs of Dauntlesses also launched by the *Enterprise*. Launched at 1:36, 12 members of Scouting 10 under Lieutenant Commander James R. "Bucky" Lee would search the sector of 280 degrees True – slightly northwest – to 10 degrees True – slightly northeast – to a range of 200 miles. The *Enterprise* would then launch a strike of 16 Wildcats, 12 Dauntlesses, and seven Avengers to go out 150 miles to attack whatever the scouts found.[20]

But the strike group was star-crossed. Timing and fuel seemed to be major issues for the pilots. Lieutenant (jg) Stanley "Swede" Vejtasa of Fighting 10, a former SBD pilot, was furious. By his calculations, they were still 250 miles from the Japanese carriers. It was an "impossible mission" for the green pilots of Air Group 10 because their aircraft simply did not carry the fuel for it. Vejtasa slammed down his chart board and loudly opined that Admiral Kinkaid was a "stupid ass." He stormed to the flag bridge looking for blood, later saying, "I didn't give a damn if they court-martialed me."[21]

This supposedly lowly lieutenant proceeded to loudly lecture the admiral's staff that this lengthy mission would end with the green pilots making their first night landings on the *Enterprise*. After saying his piece, he returned to find Lieutenant Commander James Thomas, head of Bombing 10, waiting for him. "Don't be so hasty," Thomas said. "We'll do an out and in."[22] That, indeed, was Admiral Kinkaid's plan: the strike group was to travel out 150 miles on the median line of the search – 325 degrees True, or northwest – then, if no Japanese ships were found, to return.

But the launch itself, taking place at 2:08 pm, was completely botched. Of the planned 16 Wildcats, only 11, under the command of Fighting 10 executive officer Lieutenant Commander William "Killer" Kane, took off. Of those 11, three missed the rendezvous with the other fighters and had to return to the *Enterprise*. Of the planned 12 Dauntlesses, only five took off, under Lieutenant Commander Thomas. Of the seven Avengers, six under Lieutenant Albert P. "Scoofer" Coffin took off, though one suffered a bent wingtip during its takeoff run when the prop wash of the plane ahead of it drove its wing into the deck.[23] Also taking off was Air Group 10 head Commander Richard K. Gaines, flying in the back of the formation in a command TBF to evaluate the attack and the damage caused, but with no command responsibilities on this mission.

Commander Gaines may have wished he had command, however, because things did not get much better. Lieutenant Commander Thomas, assuming the Japanese carriers had continued steaming toward the *Enterprise*, led the attack group on a course of 287 degrees True, much closer to the southern end of the scouts' search arc than the median. That may not have been an issue if the Japanese had indeed kept closing the range.[24]

At around 2:30, Army 1st Lieutenant John H. Buie led a flight of six B-17s over Admiral Abe's Vanguard Force, where they made an unsuccessful bombing attack on the battleship *Kirishima*. At 3:10, Buie reported that he had seen the Japanese headed back to the north. If the Vanguard Force was headed back north, then the carriers were, too. They were not closing the range, but opening it. Thomas would never find them in his modified search and, in fact, the carriers were now out of range. Admiral Kinkaid, not wanting to break radio silence, did not immediately recall the strike, figuring that with only a 150-mile leg, they would be back at their scheduled time, 5:35 pm, just about sundown.[25]

However, after takeoff, Lieutenant Commander Thomas received garbled orders by radio that suggested to him he needed to take the strike out not 150 miles but 200 miles instead.[26] Given that 200 miles was the range for the scouting Dauntlesses launched earlier, it's easy to imagine that somehow their range was mixed in with Thomas' orders.

What followed, however, was not. After having found no Japanese and perhaps thinking he had taken his strike too far to the south, Lieutenant Commander Thomas on his own initiative decided to take the strike out an additional 80 miles to the north. For those not mathematically inclined, the airstrike had traveled 280 miles, or almost twice what Admiral Kinkaid had intended. Kinkaid would later call Thomas' decisions here "excess zeal."[27]

All that remained was to see how much of a price the excess zeal would exact. The return trip for the strike group was complicated by dwindling fuel, receding light, and an *Enterprise* that had to steam away from them to recover the scout Dauntlesses, which she did between 5:12 and 6:02 pm, pulling the carrier an additional 20 miles away.[28] The evening turned "pitch black," with low clouds, haze, and no visible horizon. "It was one of the scariest days of my life," Wildcat pilot Ensign Edward "Whitey" Feightner later said. "I flew ten minutes with my fuel gauges reading zero."[29]

The pilots kept formation by following the "reddened exhaust stacks" of the other aircraft. Flying at an altitude of 17,000 feet to keep a lock on the *Enterprise*'s homing signal, the Wildcat pilots ran low on oxygen and had difficulty transferring fuel from the wing tanks due to poor suction. The poor suction seems to have caused the F4F of Lieutenant Don Miller to lose power some 40 miles short of the carrier. He waved goodbye and was seen to bail out, but that was the last anyone saw of him.[30] A lack of oxygen was plaguing the Dauntless piloted by Ensign Jefferson H. "Tiny" Carroum; the oxygen system had sprung a leak, and flying at high altitude had caused him a splitting headache and drowsiness, symptoms of hypoxia.[31]

Sure enough, when the group reached the point where they thought the *Enterprise* should be, almost all of them found empty sea. All but Lieutenant Vejtasa. As the SBDs jettisoned their payloads in an attempt to squeeze more out of their remaining fuel, the resulting explosions revealed to him an oil slick. Remembering that the *Enterprise* had been trailing oil, he followed the narrowing oil slick in the dark and led the remaining aircraft back to the carrier a little after 6:30 pm.[32]

But, just as Lieutenant Vejtasa had warned, landing after dark was a completely new experience for most of the pilots. The result was mild chaos. Vejtasa landed "almost simultaneously," with the F4F immediately behind him flown by Ensign Feightner, making his first night landing. Ensign Carroum, his judgment apparently clouded by hypoxia, disregarded a waveoff signal from the landing signal officer and came in anyway, bouncing off the *Enterprise*'s island and plowing into a Dauntless that had landed ahead of it, trashing both, and delaying landing operations until they could be cleared. Two SBDs and three TBFs were forced to ditch because their fuel ran out in the landing circle. Destroyers fished out all of the aircrews except for Seaman 1st Class Arthur Browning of Torpedo 10.[33]

The airstrike had been a self-inflicted disaster. It had resulted in the loss of two lives, one Wildcat, four Dauntlesses, and three Avengers, while inflicting no damage whatsoever on the enemy. The pilots and Admiral Kinkaid's staff started pointing fingers at each other over who was responsible for the debacle. Lieutenant Vejtasa, much to his surprise, was never disciplined for his outburst at Admiral Kinkaid's staff, probably because he had been proven right. Nor was Ensign Carroum punished, likely a recognition that hypoxia had impaired his judgment.[34]

It was a bad day all around. Losing 12 aircraft is not a good way to start a battle that everyone knew was close. The *Hornet*'s Captain Charles Mason felt "like the night before the Big Game."[35] Commander John Crommelin, the *Enterprise*'s air officer, gathered his pilots in the wardroom for what was described as "an excellent, earnest flight talk never forgotten by those present."[36] In his Alabama accent, "Uncle John," as he was known, declared:

> This may be the beginning of a great battle. You men do not need to be babied and I don't intend to hold your hands. We know that the Jap task force we are looking for will have a three-to-one superiority over us. Four of our PBY patrols sighted the Jap task force [...]
>
> You men will have the privilege tomorrow of proving the worth of your training, your schooling, our way of life against the Japs.
>
> The offensive strength we have in the Pacific is at the moment in the hands of you men in this room and of those on the *Hornet*.
>
> On you rests the safety of our Marines at Guadalcanal who have fought magnificently. Last night they were bombarded again, and the Japs made an assault on our position, but they held, proving their worth. Wherever we have met the Jap at sea with our carriers, despite overwhelming odds, we have stopped them.
>
> The Japs are determined to drive us out of the South Pacific. If they get through to Guadalcanal with their carriers tomorrow, the Japs will take it. If Guadalcanal falls, our lifeline to Australia will be menaced. To stop them, you must knock out their carrier force. [...]
>
> There is no room for waste and no excuse for misses. If you're going to miss with your bomb, you might as well stay home and let a *good* pilot take your place. [...]
>
> We are on the right side of this war. God is with us. Let's knock those Jap bastards off the face of the earth.[37]

He closed his speech with the promise, "If you get back to the ship and into the groove, we'll get you aboard."[38] Every aviator on the *Enterprise* knew the record of John Crommelin. No one wanted to disappoint him. As they slept that night, the crews heard his words ringing in their ears "... over and over and over and over again."[39]

While Commander Crommelin was giving his rousing speech, Admiral Yamamoto was sending a message that, in its memo form, was not quite as rousing:

> (1). Army units plan to storm Guadalcanal airfield this evening at 2100; accordingly there is great likelihood that the enemy fleet will appear northeast of the Solomons.

(2). The Combined Fleet will seek to destroy the enemy fleet on October 26.
(3). All forces will take appropriate action to (2) above.
(4). [Guadalcanal] Support Force will operate as designated by Commander-in-Chief.[40]

It was left to Admiral Kondo to put the message in a more motivational form, which he sent out at 10:40 pm to the men under his command: "Commander-in-Chief, Combined Fleet, orders that since there is a great possibility that we will engage in a decisive action, aircraft of all units continue searching and tracking operations regardless of weather and enemy planes, in an attempt to discover the size and nature of the enemy forces."[41]

Aircraft were already doing just that, just not Japanese ones. Admiral Fitch had sent out a Catalina night tracker and five armed Catalinas to search out to 500 miles. The hope was that they could find the Japanese carriers in time for Admiral Kinkaid to launch the strike group still spotted on the deck of the *Hornet*. When it became clear the Japanese carriers would not be in range that night, the *Hornet* was allowed to stand down, but her aircraft were kept armed, fueled, and spotted on deck for immediate launch. In this position, Admiral Murray suggested to Admiral Kinkaid that the *Enterprise* continue providing air cover the next morning so the *Hornet*'s pilots could get some sleep and still be positioned to launch immediately. Kinkaid agreed.[42]

In the meantime, those PBYs were making nuisances of themselves. October 26 was but a minute old when the radar of a Catalina piloted by Lieutenant (jg) George Clute detected "the enemy" some 300 miles northwest of Task Force 61. Guided by radar, he honed in on what he believed was a cruiser and launched two torpedoes before exiting. The cruiser turned out to be the Japanese destroyer *Isokaze* of Admiral Abe's Vanguard Force. The torpedoes were easily avoided.[43] It was Clute, apparently, who made a very helpful, laconic contact report revealing he had met "the enemy" but leaving out such details as its course, speed, and composition.[44]

"Air raid! Air raid!"

The alarm had gone up on the Japanese carrier *Shokaku* a little before 3:00 am.[45] Commander Takada ran to the bridge just in time to see in the moonlight some 5,000 meters astern four giant columns of water rise where the *Zuikaku* was supposed to be. Many a breath was held until the pillars fell away, revealing the carrier to be undamaged.

The bombs from the Catalina piloted by Lieutenant Glen Hoffman had fallen 300 meters to starboard. Then a flare burst, a brilliant tactic by Hoffman that blinded the Japanese antiaircraft gunners long enough for him to escape. As he did so, at 3:10 he radioed a contact report to his seaplane tender *Curtiss* at Espiritu Santo the position of "One large carrier, six other vessels on a southerly course speed 10."[46]

Commander Takada stumbled down the ladder to his admiral's cabin, where Admiral Nagumo was conferring with his chief of staff Admiral Kusaka. Takada reported the attempted bombing of the *Zuikaku*. Neither Nagumo nor Kusaka rose from their chairs. They just looked at each other and said in unison, "Let's turn around."[47]

In rapid succession came orders flashed from the flagship: "All ships turn 18 degrees to starboard." After the turn had started, "Speed of advance 24 knots." Then, once the turn was completed, "All ships of this force steady on course 0 degrees [True]."[48]

Admiral Nagumo went on to order the ammunition and fuel removed from the aircraft on the hangar decks. They had been the death knell for his carriers at Midway. They would not be again.

As the night went on the Japanese naval commanders were informed that the army's attack on Henderson Field had failed yet again. That defeat did nothing, however, to turn attention away from an engagement that now seemed imminent. At around 4:00 am, the flight crews on the carriers began preparing their aircraft using red-shaded flashlights for illumination in the dark. Admiral Nagumo, incongruously wearing snow-white gloves – always a necessity in the South Pacific – watched nervously from the *Shokaku*'s bridge. At approximately 4:15 am Admiral Abe's Vanguard Force launched seven scout planes from the *Tone* and *Chikuma*, then headed north to maintain station with the carriers.[49] The scout planes were to search to the south, beyond Guadalcanal.

A half-hour later – an hour before sunrise – came *Kido Butai*'s own search planes: four Kates from the *Shokaku*, four from the *Zuikaku*, and five from the *Zuiho*, searching out to 300 miles in an arc from 50 to 230 degrees True – generally northeast to southeast.[50] The crews then prepared 22 fighters for combat air patrol and 64 aircraft for the first airstrike – the *Shokaku* with four escort Zeros and 20 Type 97 Kates armed with torpedoes; the *Zuikaku* with eight Zeros, 22 Type 99 Vals, and one unarmed Kate to maintain contact; and the *Zuiho* with nine Zeros and one unarmed Kate as strike evaluator. The strike would be commanded by the *Shokaku*'s veteran Lieutenant Commander Murata Shigeharu.[51] Then the Japanese simply hunkered down to wait.

They didn't have to wait for long. At 6:58 am, the radios on the carrier *Shokaku* crackled to life. "Large enemy unit sighted. One carrier, five other vessels."[52] The report came from *Shokaku* Warrant Officer Ukita Tadaaki, flying a scout on the 110-degree bearing – slightly southeast – from *Kido Butai*, though Ukita used the wrong call sign, which confused matters and was bad form.[53] After snooping around for a bit, Ukita amplified his report: *Saratoga*-class carrier escorted by 15 other vessels, bearing 125 degrees, distance 210 miles.

The skippers of *Kido Butai* who read the sighting report groaned. They had expected the Americans to be ahead of them or even slightly to the right. Instead, the Americans were to the southeast.[54] They had been about to ambush the Japanese. Admiral Yamamoto had been right.

Now, after weeks of not knowing where the US carriers were, they finally had them. They had a 64-plane airstrike ready to go. It could be in the air within 30 minutes.

On the bridge of his flagship *Shokaku*, Admiral Nagumo smiled.

It was 5:12 am when the *Enterprise* picked up a rebroadcast from the seaplane tender *Curtiss* sitting in Espiritu Santo: "One large carrier, six other vessels on a southerly course speed 10." The message, including their position, had come in at 3:15 am.

Admiral Kinkaid was livid. This report was two hours old. He had already launched his scouts – eight pairs of SBDs, each lugging a 500lb bomb, covering 235 to 000 degrees True – southwest to north – out to 200 miles. If Kinkaid had had this report, he would not have launched so many scouts, instead saving his Dauntlesses for an airstrike that he could have launched immediately.

Kinkaid himself may not have had the report, but several ships in his task force did, having picked up the original broadcast. They did not relay it to the *Enterprise* because they assumed she had picked it up as well. Admiral Halsey later called it a "serious communication delinquency," a major understatement from a man not generally known for such.[55] Even with this information two hours old, Kinkaid's staff and pilots tried to get him to launch that *Hornet* airstrike that had been spotted the previous day. Kinkaid demurred. They had lost 12 aircraft and two aviators that same previous day on a search-and-destroy mission. He would not risk them on such a mission again.[56]

Instead the search Dauntlesses joined ten Catalinas and six B-17s that had taken off at 3:30 am for a dawn search.[57] There were so many Japanese "forces" in the area that one couldn't help but stumble over one or more fairly quickly. Scouts Lieutenant Vivien W. Welch and Lieutenant (jg) Bruce A. McGraw were flying almost due west when, about 85 miles out, they found a Kate flying on an opposite course about 3 miles to starboard. Obviously, it was a scout; the Number 2 scout plane from the *Shokaku*, to be precise.[58] They ignored the enemy aircraft and continued on their way. And Vice Versa. At 6:17, the US Navy pilots found two battleships, one heavy cruiser, and seven destroyers, heading to the north at a speed of 20 knots. It was Admiral Abe's "Vanguard Force." No carrier, though, so they continued on their way again.

But after finding no carriers, Welch and McGraw headed back. They crossed Abe's force again, which, due to the sighting of enemy scouts, had changed course to 300 degrees and raised his speed to 30 knots. Angry at the continued harassment, the *Tone* and a few destroyers opened up on the two Dauntlesses without effect. As they continued on their way back, they passed by the same Kate, again headed in the opposite direction. Once again, neither side attacked the other. Their job was to scout, not to shoot. And, as it turned out, the Kate had not spotted their carrier either. Welch, McGraw, and their crews returned around 9:31 am.[59]

Admiral Abe had good reason to run away. Flying the adjacent search sector north of Welch and McGraw, the SBDs of ensigns Howard R. Burnett and Kenneth B. Miller also stumbled across the Vanguard Force. Burnett sent a contact report, then both dove on the *Tone*. Again, the *Tone* fired back; this time the concussion of exploding antiaircraft shells "caused [Burnett's Dauntless] to spin approximately 4,000 feet before it could be brought under control and the dive reentered."[60] Burnett regained control in time to drop his bomb with Miller, though they both missed the *Tone*. They then returned to the *Enterprise*.[61]

But those were just appetizers. Lieutenant Commander Bucky Lee, commander of Scouting 10, was the senior search pilot that morning, and had naturally assigned the juiciest search sector to himself. Lieutenant Strong had pulled Lee aside and told him, "I think you'll find the yellow-bellies are in your sector. When you discover them, give us the word, loud and clear."[62]

Strong was right. At 6:45 am, Lee and Lieutenant (jg) William E. Johnson stumbled across an aircraft carrier. At 6:50, circling 15 miles out, Lee, as Strong had requested, reported one carrier heading 330 degrees at a speed of 15 knots. In short order, he and his cohort found two more. But not only did they see the carriers, the carriers saw them, too. The force changed course and made smoke screens.[63] The *Shokaku* immediately launched nine Zeros, followed by the *Zuikaku* with eight. These joined three fighters from the *Zuiho* already in the air.[64] Lee kept radioing in his find, but could not get an acknowledgment. Then the Zeros caught up with the two SBDs, which separated, trying to elude their pursuers. Two Zeros hung onto Lee and chased him for 40 miles before giving up. Johnson had ducked into a cloud, then managed to drive off one fighter, which was immediately replaced by five more. Johnson successfully evaded them, and both returned to the *Enterprise* independently.

The warning as to their presence and the fierce resistance it brought frustrated Lieutenant Commander Lee's plan to unite the search Dauntlesses in a dive-bombing attack on the Japanese carriers, but his repeated if unacknowledged sighting reports did result in more SBDs over *Kido Butai*, just as Lieutenant Strong had intended. Lieutenants (jg) Leslie J. Ward and Martin D. "Red" Carmody moved east of the carriers trying to get into attack position, but were themselves subject to a whipping counterattack by the same Zeros harassing Johnson. They were forced to turn back.

Next to join the fray were Lieutenant Strong himself and Ensign Charles B. Irvine. They had picked up Lieutenant Welch's report and moved to intercept Admiral Abe's battleships until they picked up Lieutenant Commander Lee's report; then, as Strong had intended, they moved to intercept Admiral Nagumo's carriers. Strong was still smarting after a verbal thrashing he had received two months earlier after merely reporting on and shadowing the Japanese carrier *Ryujo* and not dropping his bomb on her. He would not make that mistake again.

While the covering Zeros were harassing lieutenants Ward and Carmody, Lieutenant Strong and Ensign Irvine found "two very large carriers separated by about 15 miles, launching aircraft."[65] Irvine followed Strong closely as they crept from cloud to cloud, stalking the nearest carrier. Positioning himself with the sun behind him and almost no wind effect, Strong reached his pushover point and took the plunge from 13,000 feet, followed quickly by Irvine. They both aimed for the forward part of the flight deck decorated with a large Rising Sun as a means of identification, which was, to the Americans, a conveniently placed target.

"Hell divers," the Japanese called these Douglas SBD Dauntless dive bombers, the same ones who had screamed from the sky to bring death and destruction at Midway. Then it had been too late when the lookouts had spotted the Dauntlesses. Zeros had gone into maximum climb; gunners had frantically trained their antiaircraft batteries upward but it had been to no avail. And here screamed the hell divers again.

The panicked, pathetic defense at Midway looked masterful compared with today. Stunned, stupefied at the hell diving from the clouds, yet again, the Japanese gunners got off a burst or two of wild antiaircraft fire, more for the principle of the thing than anything else, while the fighters were nowhere to be found. "It was just a dive bomber's paradise, something that you dream about, hope to see maybe once in your life," Lieutenant Strong later said.[66] The howling, picture-perfect plunge from 13,000 feet ended below 1,500, where Strong released his bomb, quickly followed by Ensign Irvine.

It was Lieutenant Strong's gunner, Aviation Radioman 1st Class Clarence Garlow, who rendered the verdict: "Your bomb was a hit, Mr Strong," Garlow said. "Mr Irvine got one, too."[67]

To show their appreciation of the success of Strong and Irvine, as the Dauntlesses pulled out of their dives amidst heavy but inaccurate antiaircraft fire, the Japanese, in the words of Strong, "had a reception committee waiting for us of 12 Zeros at the bottom of the hill."[68] The 12 gradually dwindled to three angry Zeros from the *Zuikaku* led by Lieutenant (jg) Yoshimura Hiroshi, who chased the pair for 50 miles as Strong and Irvine practiced a version of the scissoring maneuver introduced by Lieutenant Commander John S. "Jimmy" Thach, formerly of the *Yorktown*, by which two aircraft would weave back and forth, one trying to lure a chasing attacker into the sights of the other. Effective with forward-firing fighters, it worked even better with Dauntlesses that could fire to the rear as well.

Lieutenant Strong's bomber was perforated in the rear, but a Zero flown by Seaman 1st Class Nakagami Koichi misjudged and pulled up to make another pass too soon. "Right then, I laced into a burst of fire," said Garlow, the SBD's rear guns lashing into the belly of Nakagami's fuselage. "The gasoline started shooting out and he hit the water hard and burst into flames."[69] After some 45 minutes of this chase, Strong and Irvine lost the two remaining Zeros in a squall. Having cheated death once, as they headed home they sought to cheat it again. Irvine called back to his gunner, Aviation Radioman 3rd Class Elgie Williams, who himself had perforated a Zero, and asked, "I feel like a smoke; what about you?"[70]

Lieutenant Strong thought his target was the fleet carrier *Shokaku*. It was actually neither the *Shokaku* nor her sister *Zuikaku*, but the light carrier *Zuiho*, sister to the *Shoho* that had been sunk some five months earlier, the news of which was shared with the memorable phrase "Scratch one flattop!"

And with this attack on the *Zuiho* the US Navy could scratch one more flattop, at least temporarily. One of the bombs had blown a 15-meter hole in the flight deck far aft, destroying three Zeros parked there, wrecking her arresting gear, and starting a small but obnoxious fire.[71] Overall damage was light and the *Zuiho*'s survival was never in doubt, but the bomb had struck a tender spot on the light carrier. Her wrecked arresting gear could not be repaired at sea, and without it she could not recover aircraft. This "remarkably effective" attack had left the carrier useless for the current operation.[72] An extremely annoyed Admiral Nagumo ordered the *Zuiho* to leave her fighters behind while she broke off for Truk.[73]

The sneak attack further agitated Admiral Nagumo and his chief of staff Admiral Kusaka. After the first strike had launched, Nagumo watched impatiently as Kusaka kept pushing everyone on the *Shokaku* to work faster.[74] The *Zuiho*'s plight conjured up images of Midway, with fully armed and fueled aircraft in the hangars that the helldivers had turned into weapons against the Japanese carriers. Fueling operations for the second wave on the *Shokaku* and *Zuikaku* immediately stopped and, in an almost panicked reaction, the fueling carts were pushed overboard.[75]

Then the crews had to go faster and faster, under the whipping tongue of Admiral Kusaka, to get the second strike ready. Lieutenant Shingo Hideki, the fighter squadron commander, would lead eight Zeros in escorting 20 Val dive bombers under Lieutenant Commander Seki Mamoru. Deciding not to wait for the *Zuikaku* to finish arming 14 Kate torpedo bombers, Nagumo launched the *Shokaku*'s part of the airstrike starting at 8:10.[76]

Now, with two airstrikes away, there was very little left to defend *Kido Butai* from air attack. But Admiral Kusaka did not care. Described by one author as "cautious and outspoken by nature," Kusaka was normally very outspoken about the need for caution.[77] Not now. While *Kido Butai* had turned sneak attacks into a science – as with Pearl Harbor and Darwin – they did not much appreciate the same skill in their opponents. The sneak attack that had cost them the *Zuiho* brought up bad memories of Midway that left Kusaka seething.

"Bring spears, enemy," Kusaka hissed. "Anything!"[78]

Lieutenant Commander Lee's was the first fresh information on the Japanese carriers this morning, and Admiral Kinkaid was determined to act on it.

The admiral's staff plotted the location as bearing 300 degrees True, distance 185 to 200 miles, a distance that would increase because the Japanese carriers were now heading north. At 7:08 am, the Americans changed course to 330 degrees True and upped speed to 27 knots to close the range on the Japanese. A little after this, the heavy cruiser *Northampton* used flags to signal to Admiral Murray that she had an unidentified radar contact 28 miles to the southwest, odd since neither the *Hornet* nor the *Enterprise* had the contact on their radar. The blip circled all the way to the southeast and closed to 20 miles. At 7:37, the battleship *South Dakota* radioed that she had detected Japanese radio chatter. Somehow, this information never made it to Admiral Kinkaid.[79]

On orders flashed from Admiral Kinkaid, Admiral Murray had the *Hornet* turn into the wind, which involved basically reversing course, and from 7:32 to 7:43 am launched the original moonlight strike she still had spotted on her flight deck: 15 SBDs of Bombing 8 and Scouting 8 under Lieutenant Commander William J. "Gus" Widhelm; six TBFs of

Torpedo 6 under Lieutenant Edwin B. "Iceberg" Parker; and eight F4Fs, each with a belly tank, of Fighting 72 under Lieutenant Commander Henry Sanchez. Captain Mason returned the carrier to the 330-degree course and prepped the second wave for launch.

At around the same time, the *Enterprise* turned into the wind to launch her second air cover of the day of 11 Wildcats. She also slapped together some aircraft for an airstrike of her own. "Preparations, such as they were, strongly suggest a last minute improvisation as much to clear the flight deck of plans as to hit the enemy," opined the respected Pacific War historian John Lundstrom of this strike.[80] It comprised three SBDs of Bombing 10 flown by pilots of Scouting 10 under Lieutenant (jg) George Glen Estes, eight TBFs of Torpedo 10 under Lieutenant Commander Jack Collett, and eight F4Fs of Fighting 10 under the irrepressible Lieutenant Commander Jimmy Flatley, flying with a broken foot. *Enterprise* air group leader Commander Gaines once more joined the strike in a command TBF as strike evaluator.

Admiral Kinkaid had given the strike verbal orders to rendezvous with the *Hornet* strike if feasible, but as the pilots took off from the *Enterprise* they saw a placard that read "Proceed without *Hornet*." Nothing like a little contradiction in orders to start the day. The *Hornet*'s strike passed the *Enterprise*'s as the latter's was forming up. The savvy veteran Lieutenant Commander Flatley had a bad feeling about not joining with the *Hornet*'s group.[81]

At least the first *Hornet* group. There was also the second *Hornet* group, which the carrier had quickly armed, spotted, and launched, completing all by 8:10 in an admirably efficient performance. This second wave had nine SBDs under Lieutenant John J. Lynch, nine TBFs under Torpedo 6 executive officer Lieutenant Ward F. Powell, curiously armed with bombs instead of torpedoes, and eight F4Fs, but one of the fighters had to immediately return when the oil pressure went out. The *Hornet* Air Group skipper Commander Rodee joined this group as strike evaluator in a command Avenger known as the "Sea-Hag."[82]

Three groups of attack aircraft from the *Hornet* and *Enterprise* had launched. Three airstrikes, in theory. Each acting independently, making no effort to coordinate with the others. The eminent Guadalcanal historian Eric Hammel pointed out, "[T]here was no US doctrine allowing the subordination of one air-group commander to another, nor the meshing of squadrons of one air group with like squadrons of another." Not yet, anyway. Hammel went on to comment:

> [T]he US strike groups went off as a stream of separate mixed units, each one composed of whatever aircraft happened to be available at the time of the launch. Indeed, each of the three strike groups lacked internal cohesion; each was itself strung out over distances of several miles.[83]

In fairness, the *Hornet*'s first group had been planned and spotted since the previous day, but one could argue the *Enterprise* strike fit this description. In fact, most of the US airstrikes after Coral Sea would fit at least one element of this description. It had carried a price at Midway. Would it now?

Lieutenant Commander Widhelm's group from the *Hornet* was in the lead, but had fractured; the bombers and four fighters were at 12,000 feet while the Avengers and four fighters hugged the sea under 1,000 feet, each group losing sight of the other. Behind them and to starboard was the *Enterprise* strike, four fighters from Fighting 10 on either bow above the Avengers.

They were about 60 miles from the *Hornet* when Ensign Phil Souza, flying a Wildcat in the back of the formation, saw something curious a few miles away to starboard. Aircraft – a lot of them. Flying in the opposite direction. Towards the *Hornet*. They were not friendly.

"Hey, Johnny!" Souza called to his section leader, Lieutenant Thomas C. Johnson. Souza also alerted Lieutenant Commander Sanchez. Sanchez, in turn, radioed the *Hornet*, "24 dive bombers, Red Base. Approach. Stand by for bombing attack." Lieutenant Commander Widhelm also radioed a warning. Ominously, neither received an acknowledgment.[84]

What Ensign Souza had seen was Lieutenant Commander Murata's 20 Kates and four Zeros from the *Shokaku* and nine Zeros from the *Zuiho*. Though most of the Dauntlesses missed seeing the Japanese, Lieutenant Commander Widhelm, Ensign Souza, and others eyeballed the passing enemy strike, keeping their guard up and their tail guns trained on the Sea Eagles. Murata and some of his pilots returned the favor.

Like the Old West, it was rival gangs passing each other, staring each other down, waiting for one wrong move, one glance, one turn, one shot, to begin a free-for-all. But they were professionals. They had their orders. They were to attack the enemy carriers. Everything else was "only chicken feed," to use Lieutenant Commander Widhelm's term.[85] They now knew that neither side had really gotten the jump on the other, although the Japanese had launched about a half-hour earlier and had a significant edge in numbers and striking power. All they could do was wonder if, once the mission was complete, they would have a ship to which to return.

To help make sure he did, Lieutenant Commander Murata radioed the *Shokaku* that 15 enemy bombers were coming.[86] Above Murata, the flight from the *Zuikaku* missed Lieutenant Commander Widhelm's flight entirely. For that matter, Murata's flight missed the Avengers from the *Hornet* passing below them.

But the Japanese strike still had two approaching American air formations inbound, over each of which they had the advantage in numbers. Next in line were the Avengers and the few escorting Wildcats the *Enterprise* had quickly slapped together. Having just formed up and still gaining altitude, almost all of their radios were still turned off.

While radio silence had been ordered, airstrikes usually did not keep it. The silence was disconcerting to Lieutenant Commander Collett, leading the *Enterprise*'s torpedo bombers. He asked his Aviation Radioman 1st Class Tom Nelson if the radio was broken. Nelson checked. Someone had changed the channel away from that used by the torpedo bombers. Typical. Someone always changes the channel and never tells anyone. Nelson turned it back…

"Bogeys!" The yelp had come from the newly adjusted radio. For all the good it would do. The Avenger started to shiver, its right wing dipping. Nelson looked to starboard to see Lieutenant Commander Collett's wingman Ensign Robert E. Oscar with a look of "sheer horror" on his face.[87] Smoke began to fill the compartment, "flames gushing from the engine to the cockpit."[88] Nelson called to Collett, but there was no response; Collett had already bailed. Nelson tried to help the turret gunner Aviation Metalsmith 1st Class Stephen Nadison, Jr. get out, but Nadison had not put on his parachute harness. There was no time; the Avenger was corkscrewing into the water. Nadison signaled to Nelson to go. Nelson parachuted to the water; neither Nadison nor Collett was ever seen again.[89] They never saw what had hit them.

It had been Lieutenant Hidaka Saneyasu, leading the nine Zeros from the *Zuiho* who had been escorting Lieutenant Commander Murata's strike. He had watched Lieutenant Commander Widhelm's *Hornet* strike pass without orders from Murata to attack. That just would not do. Presumably Hidaka decided it better to apologize later than ask permission now. He would only perform a hit-and-run on them, then he could return to guarding the Type 97s. What could go wrong?

From higher altitude, Lieutenant Hidaka split off from Lieutenant Commander Murata and had his Zeros form a line and loop a 180-degree descending turn behind Torpedo 10. Attacking from out of the sun, Hidaka's fighters dove on the unsuspecting Avengers. With their Wildcat escort on either side in front of them, Torpedo 10 was literally blindsided.

No American saw Hidaka himself target the lead Avenger of Lieutenant Commander Collett, and set fire to the engine. The next one to go was the Avenger of Ensign John M. Reed. Turret gunner Aviation Radioman 3rd Class Murray Glasser saw pieces of plane fly past him, and then sensed fire licking him. Reed shouted over the intercom, "Bail out! Bail Out!" Glasser was the only one to escape before the TBF exploded in midair. Behind Reed, Aviation Radioman 3rd Class Charles E. Shinneman, the tunnel (ventral) gunner on Lieutenant Macdonald Thompson's TBF, saw Reed's "engine coming by our wingtip, the prop still spinning."[90]

Shinneman then saw holes "like live coals in a piece of paper" appear inboard on the port wing of Lieutenant (jg) Richard K. Batten's Avenger. The damage caused a fire in the wing's hydraulics, which caused the port aileron to stand straight up. Batten's tunnel gunner Aviation Metalsmith Rexford B. Holmgrin called out "Mr Batten, our wing is on fire!" Batten dropped out of formation and announced on the radio he was going to ditch because the TBF was burning. However, the fire burned out, the aileron fell off, and the tough Grumman kept on flying. Unable to jettison the torpedo because of the loss of hydraulics, Batten turned around, hoping to make it back to the *Enterprise*.[91]

The Avengers of Torpedo 10 were in trouble. But the Grumman TBF Avenger was a relatively new aircraft. Its first combat had only been at Midway back in June, a last minute addition to the atoll's defenses. Today would be its second major action operating from carriers, the first being Eastern Solomons. The Japanese in general had little experience against the Avenger. Like most American aircraft, it was a tough bird. It was also blessed with ample rear-facing weaponry – the .50cal dorsal turret gun and the .30cal ventral tunnel gun – as Lieutenant Hidaka's pilots were about to discover.

The first to learn this was Petty Officer 3rd Class Takagi Shizuta, one of Lieutenant Hidaka's wingmates. As Takagi dove from the starboard quarter, the turret gunners got the range with their .50cals. At a range of 100 yards, Takagi's Zero burst into flames and started losing altitude as he continued firing into the wing of Lieutenant Marvin D. Norton. Finally, the Mitsubishi "pulled up about 50 or 75 feet above the flight and exploded in a fireball."[92] It was a spectacular way to go.

And it may well have been what attracted the attention of the Wildcat mother ducks that a snake had snuck up behind them and was gobbling their ducklings one by one. On the left, the veteran Lieutenant John "Jack" Leppla led three green fighter pilots. He ordered them to drop wingtanks to increase their maneuverability. Preparing to get into the fight, Ensign Willis B. "Chip" Reding dropped his wingtank; his engine promptly lost all fuel suction, sputtered, and died. Not the way he wanted to start this aerial battle.

As Ensign Reding's Wildcat plunged toward the ocean below, Ensign Raleigh "Dusty" Rhodes, his own drop tank not releasing and ultimately set afire due to Japanese bullets, followed Reding down to see what he could do, which was not much. In the meantime the Zeros shot off most of his instrument panel, his canopy, even his goggles – all without even scratching him. The electric gunsight hung by its wiring, which was just as good because his guns were now useless. But the plane kept flying. Reding was finally able to get his engine restarted, just in time to be narrowly missed, as Rhodes had been, by the falling wingtank of Ensign Albert E. Mead, Lieutenant Leppla's wingman. So far, it was not a good day for wingtanks.

The issues with the wingtanks cost Leppla, who also had a malfunctioning gun, and his pilots any chance of a coherent response. Worse, they had still not reached altitude, so the tried-and-true tactic of diving to gain speed to pull away from the Zeros could not be used.[93] They were on their heels.

On the starboard bow of the beleaguered Avengers, Lieutenant Commander Flatley was maneuvering to stay in position when he saw the carnage behind him. Flatley ordered his Wildcats to drop their own wingtanks and then charged in. Only one Zero was within reach, that of Petty Officer 3rd Class Matsumoto Zenpei. The entire flight of four Wildcats combined to bring him down.

But that was all they could do. Lieutenant Thompson was now the Avenger last in formation. He called out to ventral gunner Shinneman, "Zero coming up underneath us!" The Zero, flown by either Lieutenant (jg) Utsumi Shuichi or Petty Officer 1st Class Kawasaki Masao, charged up and fired, missing astern. As the fighter pulled away, Shinneman "put about a half canister of .30s into his cockpit. He drifted off on a wing below us and out of sight."[94]

Lieutenant Thompson led the remaining Avengers in forming up with the Dauntlesses. It reminded Lieutenant Commander Flatley that he was on an escort mission. He was deeply frustrated that he and his men "had not been sufficiently alert."[95] But he had to protect the strike aircraft. And so Flatley made the agonizing decision to leave Lieutenant Leppla and his struggling Wildcats, cut off far behind Flatley, to their fate.

It was not long in coming. Lieutenant Hidaka and his wingman Petty Officer 1st Class Mitsumoto Jiro had Lieutenant Leppla and Ensign Mead by the throat. The beleaguered Americans practiced a version of the weaving tactic pioneered by Lieutenant Commander Thach, but one in which Mead did all the maneuvering. Leppla "seemed to fly straight ahead and I don't believe fired a shot," said Mead. "I shot for both of us and believe I got three." He got one, either Utsumi or Kawasaki, who had joined the fight unseen and was shot down unseen.[96]

But the odds were too great. Ensign Mead heard "popcorn popping" as Japanese bullets hit the back of his armored cockpit. His instruments were shattered and his ankle was injured. Then a head-on attack from either Hidaka or Mitsumoto finished off his fighter, forcing Mead to nurse it into the water.

Some distance away, Ensign Rhodes was trying to nurse his shattered F4F back to the *Enterprise* "to show the guys."[97] Rhodes managed to reunite with Ensign Reding, and they, too, performed Lieutenant Commander Thach's scissoring that baffled their Japanese pursuers. Rhodes glimpsed what he believed to be Lieutenant Leppla's Grumman. It was in deep distress, with a Zero coming from the front and a Zero on its tail. Later Rhodes glimpsed a parachute; he hoped it was Leppla.[98]

Rhodes's engine burned out and froze at 2,500 feet. As he tried to ditch the Wildcat, Japanese bullets severed his rudder cables. That was it. Rhodes remembered his old flight instructor had emphasized "never attempt to bail out under 500 feet."[99] But his flight instructor was not here to scold him. Rhodes popped open his canopy and deployed his parachute, which pulled him up out of the cockpit and set him hard but safely into the water.[100]

Ensign Reding tried to keep watch over Rhodes, but the three Zeros on his tail had other ideas. Reding pushed his engine to full power and hit the deck. With his electrical system down, he could not fight back, but Rhodes noticed that one of the three Zeros chasing Reding was smoking.[101] Though Rhodes had glimpsed a parachute he thought was Lieutenant Leppla, the inertness of Leppla's Wildcat made Ensign Mead suspect he was dead or unconscious in the cockpit.[102] Like an aerial El Cid, Leppla's Wildcat just kept flying, quivering slightly. It was never seen again.

The *Enterprise* strike had been roughly halved – three Dauntlesses, four Avengers, and four Wildcats. Three Wildcats and two Avengers shot down, one Wildcat and two Avengers damaged enough to turn back; five men dead, four in the water. Lieutenant Commander Flatley's fighters were now severely restricted in their options because Lieutenant Hidaka had forced them to drop their wingtanks early.

As for Lieutenant Hidaka, he had indeed made one pass at the *Enterprise* strike, just as he had planned. It had cost him almost half his command, much of his fuel, and almost all of his ammunition. He decided he could not catch up to Lieutenant Commander Murata and ordered the five remaining Zeros to head back to *Kido Butai*, where they told tales of fighting six Grummans and eight Dauntlesses, shooting down all of them, of course.[103] Forcing Murata to go without fighter escort was, in the view of Hidaka and his pilots, a small price to pay for such a victory.

After all, Murata, the best torpedo attack pilot in the world, had never really needed fighter escorts before. What are the odds he would need them now?

Suspicions were building on the *Enterprise* that something was seriously wrong.

The first hint came at 8:11 am, when Admiral Kinkaid signaled to the task force that he believed their position was known to the Japanese. On what he based this belief is unclear, though by this time the reports from the *Northampton* and *South Dakota* may have indirectly made their way to him. A little later, at 8:30, they picked up a garbled message from Lieutenant Commander Sanchez: "Stand by for bombing attack." The CXAM radar on neither the *Enterprise* nor the *Hornet*, whose had been salvaged from the battleship *California*, had detected incoming aircraft. Rather prudently, Admiral Kinkaid ordered, "Launch all planes immediately. Jap planes coming in."[104]

In compliance with the admiral's order to literally clear the decks, the *Enterprise* launched one fully armed and fueled Avenger, that of Lieutenant (jg) George Welles. He was supposed to simply ride out the attack and return, but no one told him that. So, acceding to the democracy that is inherent in a military torpedo plane, Welles had his crew, Aviation Metalsmith 2nd Class Earl B. Bjerke and Aviation Radioman 3rd Class Lee F. Hollingsworth, vote on what they should do. "We all voted to go kill something," Hollingsworth later explained. Then they set off to take on the entire Imperial Japanese Navy all by themselves.[105]

The task force started picking up snippets of radio chatter from Air Group 10. What was happening was unclear, except they were in some sort of battle, well before one was anticipated. Admiral Murray deduced from these and transmissions from *Hornet* strike aircraft that the Japanese were approaching from 275 degrees, and informed Admiral Kinkaid of such at 8:43. Kinkaid guessed that the *Enterprise* was in the path of this strike and, one minute later, told Murray that the *Enterprise* would handle fighter direction for this incoming attack.[106]

Fighter direction was a sore point for the *Hornet*. The *Hornet* had an efficient fighter direction system under the experienced fighter director officer Lieutenant Allan Foster Fleming. Fleming had proven himself very good at fighter direction and the *Hornet*'s Fighting 72 had complete confidence in him. They were aware that the fighter director officer on the *Enterprise*, Commander Griffin, was new at the job and had not been in combat. There was a lot of bitterness among the *Hornet*'s pilots that the inexperienced Griffin was directing air defense over Fleming. That bitterness would only increase.

Commander Griffin was operating under multiple handicaps, some self-imposed. No one had told him that Admiral Kinkaid believed the Japanese had found his task force. Griffin kept the fighters providing air cover, now numbered at 37 – 22 from Fighting 10 over the *Enterprise*, and 15 from Fighting 72 over the *Hornet*.[107] Not wanting to expend their fuel and oxygen until necessary, Griffin kept them at 10,000 feet. It was among the complexities of being a fighter director: one had to think in terms of fuel and oxygen and ammunition and altitude and time. It was much easier and faster to lose altitude than to gain it, so it was best for interceptors to be positioned at higher altitude, but gaining altitude used precious fuel and staying at high altitude used precious oxygen.

The CXAM radar on the *Enterprise* as well as the *Hornet* continued to show no unidentified contacts. Commander Griffin decided he had time to vector the fighters into the proper position. Listening in on the radio traffic, Griffin heard someone refer to dive bombers "off to port." Thinking this message came from a nearby aircraft, Griffin warned the fighters aloft about it. However, it came from one of the besieged Air Group 10 pilots and Griffin could only give a relative bearing, because that was all he had. Giving a relative bearing was a major annoyance of fighter pilots, because the relative bearing was usually from the carrier and half the time the pilots could not see the carrier. All the report did was confuse and infuriate the pilots. Griffin's inexperience was beginning to show.

Despite the growing sense that an air attack was imminent, the CXAM radar on the *Enterprise* and the *Hornet* continued to show nothing. At 8:41 am, however, the CXAM radar on the heavy cruiser *Northampton*, flagship of Rear Admiral Howard Good, commander of the *Hornet*'s screen, had picked up unidentified aircraft bearing 295 degrees True (northwest), distance 70 miles. No one on the carriers thought to ask for a third opinion, while Admiral Good simply assumed the carriers had already detected the bogeys. He informed them by flag hoist. By this time, the *Hornet*'s screen was arranged with the heavy cruisers *Pensacola* and *Northampton* on the carrier's port and starboard quarters respectively and the light antiaircraft cruisers *San Diego* and *Juneau* on the port and starboard bows respectively, with destroyers *Morris*, *Mustin*, and *Hughes* in front, while the *Barton*, *Russell*, and *Anderson* were astern.[108]

It was not Commander Griffin on the *Enterprise* but Lieutenant Fleming on the *Hornet* who was the first carrier fighter director to pick up the incoming strike. Griffin was still confused as to the situation. So, at 8:55, Fleming ordered two *Hornet* fighter divisions – four Wildcats under Lieutenant Edward W. "Red" Hessel and four under Lieutenant Robert Rynd – to head west and check out "a fairly large bogey" 35 miles away, providing a "perfect vector."[109] Ten miles away from the *Hornet*, the CXAM radar on the *Enterprise* finally detected unidentified aircraft, bearing 255 degrees True, distance 45 miles. By now, Griffin was also dealing with a rain squall that had protectively hidden the *Enterprise* but did nothing to help his understanding of the rapidly developing situation. He vectored two *Enterprise* fighter divisions toward the bogeys, but tethered them 15 miles from the *Enterprise*. He explained, "Large group now 20 miles from base."[110]

Lieutenant Hessel knew 10,000 feet was not enough altitude and immediately had his group start climbing. His wingman, Lieutenant (jg) Thomas J. Gallagher, "who could see like an eagle," was the first to spot the tiny specks ahead that soon became a "compact, formidable looking column" of 55 fighters, dive bombers, and torpedo bombers at 17,000 feet. Gallagher immediately reported in. Once Lieutenant Fleming got the specifics, like a well-oiled machine, he vectored in the two remaining divisions of *Hornet* defenders, comprising seven fighters. However, they had been hamstrung by Commander Griffin's orders to stay at 10,000 feet. In turn, Griffin himself sent in lieutenants Swede Vejtasa's and Frederic Lewis "Fritz" Faulkner's divisions of *Enterprise* Wildcats, frantically extolling them, "Climb, climb!"[111]

But they could never make it in time.

Japanese eyes had, to the Americans, a nasty habit of outperforming American radar in surface engagements. Now they applied that habit to carrier engagements as well. It was 8:53 am, two minutes before the American carriers' CXAM radars detected the Japanese, when the *Hornet*, with two cruisers and four destroyers, was sighted by a member of Lieutenant Commander Murata's strike from the *Shokaku*.[112] The *Enterprise*, hidden by the squall, was not spotted.

Leading 20 torpedo-armed Type 97s on this strike, but thanks to Lieutenant Hidaka's improvisation protected by only four Zeros, Lieutenant Commander Murata had his radioman Petty Officer 1st Class Mizuki Tokunobu transmit, "Assume attack formation." Mizuki was used to air attacks; it was he, as radioman for Commander Fuchida Mitsuo, who had transmitted the phrase "*Tora tora tora*" at Pearl Harbor.[113]

Lieutenant Commander Murata had been at Pearl Harbor as well, leading the first torpedo attack on the battleships at Pearl Harbor and himself launching the first aerial torpedo of the war. The *Junyo*'s Okumiya Masatake considered Murata "one of the world's foremost authorities" on torpedo attack.[114] Murata had torpedo attacks down to a science. Like a professor studying a math problem, he had coolly chosen to use "Attack Method B," a version of the famous anvil attack.[115]

But Murata had to wait a few minutes. The *Zuikaku*'s group above him finally got the target in sight at 8:58. Then Murata had Mizuki transmit "All forces attack."[116] He led his Type 97s in a high-speed dive to avoid the eight enemy fighters that had suddenly appeared ahead of him. Then he split off to the south with 11 of the Type 97s and all four remaining Zeros. Nine Type 97s under Lieutenant Washimi Goro headed north.

The eight *Hornet* Wildcats did not follow. Thanks to the foresight of Lieutenant Hessel, they were in position to face the 21 dive bombers from the *Zuikaku* under Lieutenant Takahashi Sadamu, which were in a column of three seven-plane divisions. Above and behind the Vals were eight *Zuikaku* fighters under Lieutenant Shirane Ayao.

With no threatening Zeros for the moment, Lieutenant Hessel aimed at what he believed was the strike leader, which was indeed Lieutenant Takahashi. Hessel made three passes. "Frantic maneuvers saved [Takahashi] from being shot down, but his plane was so seriously damaged that the rudder jammed and the bomber flew in wide circles."[117] Since he was the leader, much of his strike group started following him in these circles.[118] Takahashi's wingman, Petty Officer 2nd Class Nishimori Toshio, was damaged and driven out of formation by the aforementioned Lieutenant Gallagher, who shortly thereafter took on a few too many Vals, was shot up, and had to ditch.[119]

Two more of Hessel's Wildcats passed through the first two divisions and started shooting up the third group, with Lieutenant Claude R. Phillips damaging the Val commanded by Petty Officer 2nd Class Tsuchiya Yoshiaki. Lieutenant Shirane's Zeros now came in and shot up the Wildcat flown by Phillips, forcing him to return – or try to – and then shot down another Wildcat flown by Lieutenant (jg) John R. Franklin, who was killed.[120]

Lieutenant Rynd's division had worked its way behind the Japanese third division of Vals and started slashing away, only to be surprised by the *Zuikaku* Zeros. Rynd's wingman, Ensign George Wrenn, tried to engage one of the Zeros by following his leader into a steep climb, only to lose airspeed, requiring him to dive to stay aloft. Wrenn regained speed, but a nearby Zero forced him to keep diving. Rynd was also chased off. Lieutentant (jg) Kenneth C. Kiekhofer and Lieutenant (jg) Paul Landry never even got to the dive bombers. Kiekhofer shot up a Zero but saw Landry diving out of control toward the sea, victim of a second Zero that proceeded to chase Kiekhofer into a cloud.[121]

Nevertheless, the eight *Hornet* Wildcats, given how badly they were outnumbered, had done a decent job. The attack by the *Zuikaku* dive bombers had fallen apart. Only the second section got through in any semblance of a formation. Apparently three Vals, all from the third section, were shot down; another three suffered heavy damage. Lieutenant Takahashi flew his crippled Type 99 in wide circles for six hours, never diving on the *Hornet* and ultimately having to ditch.[122] For this, Fighting 72 lost three Wildcats, with two pilots killed and a third in the water.

The second section, under Lieutenant Tsuda Toshio, plowed ahead, only to be met by the remaining seven Wildcats of the *Hornet* group, who promptly flew over them without doing anything. Three under Lieutenant Alberto C. Emerson never saw or got word of the Vals, but four under Lieutenant Louis K. "Ken" Bliss turned around. They caught up with the only damaged Val commanded by Tsuchiya at the back of Tsuda's section. Tsuchiya had his pilot, Petty Officer 3rd Class Kato Motomu, lead the Americans on a chase that took them down and away from the other Vals. Bliss and his wingman Lieutenant (jg) Robert E. Holland managed to cause Tsuchiya's bomber to gush black smoke, but it kept diving toward the *Hornet*.[123]

As did the rest of Lieutenant Tsuda's Vals. At 9:05, the *Hornet*'s lookouts saw seven bombers in a column. The carrier was busy changing course to 40 degrees True – northeast – to close with the *Enterprise*. The carrier was as ready as she could be.

Antiaircraft guns manned, aircraft fueling system drained of fuel and filled with inert carbon dioxide, damage control teams positioned, flammables stowed, men not needed told to take cover. Sailors came to the flag bridge to close the windows with steel shutters, but Admiral Murray had other ideas. "Leave them open," he said. "I want to see the show too."[124] Indeed, it was far easier to take than blindly feeling the shocks and wondering what they were.

Captain Mason ordered his gunnery officer, "Commence firing at any target in sight." To his chief engineer, "Make full speed and maintain it until further orders."[125] She got up to 28 knots. Lieutenant Commander Oscar Dodson, the communications officer for the *Hornet* and Admiral Murray, raced up to the signal bridge near the mainmast, guessing he would be needed to calm the 18 young, inexperienced signalmen there facing their first combat. When Dodson got there, he found that, if anything, they were too calm – many were not even wearing their helmets or protective jackets. Dodson fixed that in short order.

"Stand by to repel attack," boomed the loudspeakers on the *Hornet*.[126] At 9:09 the *Hornet*'s 5-inch battery opened fire on Lieutenant Tsuda's dive bombers at a range of 10,500 yards. One minute later, Tsuda's Type 99s reached their pushover points and began diving from astern, emerging from a cloud base at 5,000 feet. The last bombers dove at increasingly shallow angles as the carrier moved away from them.[127] As the Japanese closed in, the long-range 5-inch guns were joined by medium-range quadruple 1.1-inch mounts and, lastly, the short-range 20mm guns.

Lieutenant Tsuda's bomb created a huge water plume off the *Hornet*'s bow. His wingman, Petty Officer 2nd Class Miyakashi Katsuhi, planted a bomb on the flight deck near the centerline, from where it penetrated three decks to detonate in the crew's mess room.[128] Behind him came Petty Officer 2nd Class Kitamura Ichiro, who plunged downward and into the water with his bomb still attached only 30 feet off the starboard bow, a victim of antiaircraft fire.

The parade of death continued with three more Vals. One was strafing with its twin 7.7-mm machine guns. Manning one of the 1.1-inch guns, Private 1st Class Vic Kelber was about to shout a badly needed profanity at the Val when someone yelled, "Kelber, you're bleeding." Kelber raised his hand to his cheek and felt that it was wet. One of the 7.7mm rounds had entered his mouth and exited through his cheek. Kelber spit out a mouthful of blood and teeth and looked through the gunsight to track another Val.[129]

Leading the last three was Lieutenant (jg) Shimada Yozo. His Type 99, piloted by Petty Officer 1st Class Taka Asatero, sent a bomb into the flight deck near the stern just 20 feet from the starboard side, detonating just below the flight deck and killing 30 in the starboard after gun gallery. Private Kelber was thrown from his seat and wrapped around his gun "like a wet rag."[130] Shimada had Taka head away, but American 20mm guns lashed at the Type 99, forcing Shimada to bail out. Taka was never found.[131] Following them were petty officers 3rd Class Hirayama Akitatsu and Yano Shoichi, both of whom circled around to complete their dives from ahead, one of whom got a third bomb hit on the *Hornet*. It pierced the flight deck not far from the second hit, sliced downward three decks, and detonated in the chief petty officers' mess.[132]

Last, but not least, was the smoking Type 99 of Tsuchiya piloted by Kato. Kato started his dive on the *Hornet* from astern. His bomb came out, either jettisoned or dropped. It plopped into the carrier's wake, quickly followed by Tsuchiya's bomber.[133]

There was no time for a breather, barely enough for even a paragraph break. Lieutenant Commander Murata's torpedo bombers were now coming in. His escorting fighters, now reduced to four thanks to Lieutenant Hidaka, tried to clear a path for him. In so doing they roared into Lieutenant Bliss' division of Wildcats. Bliss' first inkling that he was under attack was a 7.7mm round that appeared in his instrument panel. The Zero then passed him and slowed up, apparently to look at his handiwork. Bliss fired a quick burst, after which his ammunition ran out. The Zero burst into flames. Bliss was ultimately forced to ditch his Grumman and marvel at the damage done to his plane, mostly without his knowledge. Both his assailant and his victim was veteran pilot Warrant Officer Hanzawa Yukuo.[134]

A costly loss, but it was enough to get Lieutenant Commander Murata through yet another attack. It was frustrating for the *Hornet*'s gunners. Marine gunner Martin J. Melvin, Jr., called the attacks "pitiless … amalgamated hell. It seemed to me those Japs would never stop coming in."[135] The *Hornet*'s turn to the northeast to close with the *Enterprise* had thrown off Murata's calculations. Now he was coming from astern, which was the worst angle at which to execute a torpedo attack.

But Lieutenant Commander Murata was the best in the world. He had proved it at Pearl Harbor. Murata's section came roaring in between the *Northampton* and *Anderson*, where it started becoming a chess match between him, trying to stay ahead of the starboard beam, and the *Hornet*'s Captain Mason, trying to keep the carrier's stern facing them.

The first flight was Murata himself, Warrant Officer Matsushima Tadashi, and Petty Officer 1st Class Kawamura Zensaku. When about 1,500 yards off the starboard quarter, the first Type 97, apparently that of Matsushima, launched his torpedo but then burst into flames from antiaircraft fire, spinning into the water off the carrier's starboard side. The others came within 1,000 yards before releasing their torpedoes and then turning right off the starboard beam to parallel the *Hornet*'s course and pull away to escape. One of these Kates, apparently that of Murata, was hit in the port fuel tank, which started to smoke and then caught fire. Like a "flaming meteor," it veered to port and crashed in spectacular fashion off the *Hornet*'s starboard side. Kawamura escaped.[136]

Still hoping for his ship to escape, Captain Mason had kept the *Hornet* presenting as small a target as possible. Seeing the torpedoes approach, Mason ordered "Right full rudder," hoping to swing out of the way. From the carrier's bridge, Mason watched the torpedoes pass under the overhang of the flight deck and disappear from view.

After what seemed like a few minutes, Lieutenant Commander Harry Holmshaw, the command duty officer, said from behind Mason, "I guess they missed us, sir."

"Well," Mason said, "it seems as though there's been enough time."[137]

Right on cue, the *Hornet* suffered an underwater explosion in her forward engine room at 9:14. The ship was lifted up and heeled over to port.[138] Working in the island, Lieutenant Stephen Jurika "felt as though the ship was a rat being shaken by a bull terrier. My teeth rattled." The shock violently threw him against a bulkhead, making him think he had serious injuries. In the forward engine room, "all hell broke loose," as the torpedo blew a 4-foot hole in the starboard bulkhead and "an avalanche of oil and sea water" gushed in.[139] Lights went out all over the ship as the *Hornet* immediately lost power. Her engines stopped and she developed a 10.5-degree starboard list. Twenty seconds later the second torpedo struck aft near the antiaircraft magazines.[140] Badly hurt, the *Hornet* started losing headway.

And the late Lieutenant Commander Murata's attack had just begun. Captain Mason had reduced his target as much as possible, but Murata in his last ever attack had still managed a bullseye. His remaining pilots tried to match it. The second three Kates roared in behind the *Anderson* toward the *Hornet*'s stern, as Murata had. One Type 97, that of Petty Officer 1st Class Okizaki Yukio, was set afire by 20mm gunfire, forcing him to jettison his torpedo. It didn't help, and his carrier attack plane crashed off the *Northampton*'s port bow. The other two torpedo bombers dropped their torpedoes too early, missed to starboard, and crossed behind the carrier's stern to fly along the port side and escape.[141]

The third section was a carbon copy of the second. One Type 97, that of Petty Officer 2nd Class Kodama Kiyomi, was forced to jettison his torpedo after antiaircraft fire left his plane trailing smoke. The other two dropped their torpedoes too early – again – and missed to starboard – again. They then banked to port and escaped. Kodama's Kate passed in front of the *Pensacola*, caught fire, and crashed.[142]

The pilots of the two remaining Type 97s decided the *Hornet* was too difficult a target and instead split up to go after the heavy cruiser *Pensacola* from off either bow in a small anvil attack. Warrant Officer Nakai Taneichi ended up dropping his torpedo off the port beam. Petty Officer 2nd Class Kobayashi Yoshihiko circled to the right to come from starboard. The *Pensacola*'s skipper, Captain Frank L. Lowe, turned the cruiser toward the incoming Kobayashi. Antiaircraft fire torched the plane, but Kobayashi turned the Kate into a kamikaze and tried to crash into the *Pensacola*. He missed the bow by a few feet before splashing about 100 feet to port. Nakai saw the big plume of water and concluded his torpedo had hit.[143]

In the interim, the first division of the *Zuikaku*'s dive bombers had sorted itself out somewhat, without their leader Lieutenant Takahashi, who was still circling uncontrollably and had inadvertently led them to the north. Lieutenant (jg) Yoneda Nobuo, Takahashi's second in command, organized the six remaining Type 99s and continued heading north to approach the *Hornet* from port. In so doing, he smashed into four *Enterprise* Wildcats under Lieutenant Swede Vejtasa.

Lieutenant Vejtasa's division of Wildcats, along with that of Lieutenant Faulkner, had been sent earlier by Commander Griffin to help the *Hornet*, but they remained hamstrung by Griffin's earlier order to stay at 10,000 feet that now left them looking up at the Vals.

However, by this time, Griffin had completely lost control of the fighters. In a brutal assessment of his performance, the respected naval historian Vincent P. O'Hara would say that Griffin "completely failed to deliver effective information to the fighters."[144] For the leaders of Fighting 10 realized long before Griffin that the *Hornet* was in big trouble and needed help fast. Of the 22 *Enterprise* Wildcats aloft, at least 21 were now racing to defend their sister in deep distress.

Before Vejtasa's Wildcats could engage the reorganized Vals, the last Type 99 in the formation, the Val of Petty Officer 2nd Class Nishimori Toshio that had been damaged earlier, just started its dive without waiting for the others. Vejtasa himself sent the Type 99 into a flaming, fatal dive. But the remaining Wildcats could not stop the Vals, nor could four Wildcats under Lieutenant Faulkner, nor could two orphaned fighters from the *Enterprise*.

Lieutenant Yoneda's five bombers reached their pushover points and began their dives. And into a hailstorm of antiaircraft fire from, especially, the light antiaircraft cruisers *San Diego* and *Juneau* and the destroyers *Morris* and *Barton*. Four gamely held their dives and dropped their bombs. No hits, and they pulled up to head for home.

The fifth dive was made by Warrant Officer Sato Shigeyuki, flying fourth in the formation. Apparently damaged by antiaircraft fire, Sato's Type 99 was spitting fire underneath when it appeared over the *Hornet*'s starboard quarter. Sato himself may have been dead, dying, or unconscious, because the aircraft never wavered from its dive. And it never dropped its bomb. "For a thousand feet I never took my eye off him, and he never wavered an inch from a straight line to the signal bridge," said war correspondent Charles McMurtry.[145] Despite – perhaps because of – the torrent of shrapnel flying towards it, it just kept coming.

And slammed into the *Hornet*'s island.

Sato's starboard wing hit the port edge of the *Hornet*'s stack, ripping away the signal halyards and the starboard wing with them. Then the fuselage bounced off the island and embedded itself into the flight deck about 15 feet away, where the burning wreck exploded, spewing flaming gasoline on the signal bridge, the island, the flight deck, and into the ready room for Scouting 8 one deck below. All, ironically, without its 250kg bomb exploding. It ended up "rolling around outside the ready room."[146]

Lieutenant Commander Dodson, on the signal bridge to "settle" the young signalmen there, was protected from the spewing fuel by a leg of the mainmast, but his charges were not. They were incinerated by burning aviation gasoline. Dodson tried to beat out the flames with his gloves, only to have to ditch the gloves when they themselves caught fire. He could just stand in horror and watch his men thrash in agony, hearing their howls of unimaginable pain, until, one by one, the writhing and screaming stopped. One uninjured signalman, frantic with sorrow as he watched his twin brother burn to death in a pool of flaming gasoline, rushed into his brother's arms to die together "locked in a final embrace."[147]

Still to be heard from was Lieutenant Washimi with nine torpedo-armed Type 97s from the *Shokaku* that were to be the second part of the late Lieutenant Commander Murata's anvil attack, which was torn asunder by Captain Mason's changes in course.

Washimi had no fighter escort, thanks to Lieutenant Hidaka's abandoning his charges to gain glory for his emperor. He faced being torn asunder by fighter opposition. *Enterprise* Wildcats Ensign Donald Gordon and Ensign Gerald V. "Jerry" Davis flew over the Kates and then around to target the lead Type 97, which turned out to be Washimi's. A burst from Gordon drove Washimi into the sights of Davis, who riddled the Kate and left it smoking, forcing Washimi to turn away. They let him go to focus on the Kates still making their runs.

With Lieutenant Washimi out of the picture for the moment, command of the Type 97s fell to Petty Officer 2nd Class Akiyama Hiroshi. However, he had just picked up Lieutenant Macgregor Kilpatrick on his tail. Kilpatrick started "pecking away" at Akiyama's plane, killing his tail gunner. In desperation, Akiyama dove to an altitude of 10 feet, but Ensigns Davis and Gordon joined Kilpatrick. Ultimately it was Gordon who set Akiyama's plane afire. It was never seen again.[148]

Hornet Ensign George Wrenn had been forced to dive away from the Vals, but found himself in prime position to intercept the Kates of Lieutenant Washimi's section. Wrenn targeted the Type 97 of Petty Officer 2nd Class Suzuki Katsu, first killing Suzuki's tail gunner, then riddling the unprotected tail until the Kate started smoking, forcing Suzuki to abort. Next to Suzuki was Petty Officer 1st Class Sano Gonari. Wrenn quickly set Sano's Type 97 afire. Sano tried to kamikaze into the *Juneau*, but he had no chance against the antiaircraft cruiser's portside guns and was downed just short of the ship.

Wrenn, Davis, and Gordon were compelled to break off pursuit by the heavy antiaircraft fire that started slashing away at the Kates as the passed over the destroyer *Morris*, who apparently knocked down the Type 97 of Petty Officer 1st Class Mitsumori Yoshio. The remaining four Type 97s stayed on their runs, but had to engage in creative maneuvering to evade the heavy antiaircraft fire, especially from, naturally, the *San Diego* and *Juneau*. The disruption caused by the Wildcats and the antiaircraft fire ruined the torpedo attack, and no torpedoes hit the rapidly slowing *Hornet*, though three barely missed the *Northampton*.[149] The four Kates escaped.

By now, Lieutenant Ishimaru Yutaka, who had led the third division of dive bombers from the *Zuikaku*, had assembled the four remaining Type 99s and circled south of the *Hornet*. They were starting to move in on the now-disabled carrier when they stumbled across another three Wildcats from the *Enterprise*, these under Lieutenant Albert D. "Dave" Pollock. Ishimaru had begun his dive, but Pollock followed the second and sent him into a flaming spin. He and his wingmates were forced to break off by antiaircraft fire. Ishimaru and his wingmates completed their dives and dropped their bombs on the rapidly slowing carrier, but all missed.[150]

The Type 99s sped away at low altitude under heavy antiaircraft fire, but ran afoul of yet another group of Wildcats from the *Enterprise*. The indefatigable Lieutenant Vejtasa ended a long dive by torching one Kate; Lieutenant Stanley E. Ruehlow torched one more, the identities of the fallen Japanese unclear. Only Lieutenant Ishimaru, his Val lacerated, was able to escape. Barely.[151]

There were two more attackers who would not escape, but had no intention of doing so. One was a burning Val that appeared off the *Hornet*'s port quarter. The identities of its crew are a mystery, but it may have been the Val that had been hit by Lieutenant Pollock. The carrier's antiaircraft screen opened up on the bomber and riddled it further, but it kept coming in a "shallow dive."[152] It dropped its bomb, which missed about 50 yards ahead of the still-slowing carrier.

The plane itself missed the carrier as well, but had enough altitude for another pass. With the antiaircraft guns continually lashing away, the Type 99 pulled out of its shallow dive over the starboard bow, then, in "a lazy glide," turned around over the *Northampton* back towards the *Hornet*. The dive bomber crossed in front of the carrier's bow to her port side, then veered into the hull, crashing into the port gallery walkway just forward of the 5-inch antiaircraft battery. The burning fuselage penetrated the hull as far as the Number 1 elevator pit, spewing burning metal on the hangar deck and leaving yet another serious fire in its wake.[153]

Captain Mason had now noticed the *Hornet* was slowing down, which with her engines out was not surprising. Mason asked the helmsman, "Does she respond to helm?"

"No, sir," came the answer. "The rudder is jammed hard right."[154] That wasn't good. Even if the carrier could move, it would be only in circles.

There was one final proto-kamikaze, this one a battered Kate, apparently the one piloted by Lieutenant Washimi. He had jettisoned his torpedo to keep his perforated plane in the air for his plan to plow into the port side of the *Hornet*. But the Type 97 could not stay in the air and instead plopped into the water off the port bow.[155]

With Lieutenant Washimi's charge aborted, the air attack that would seemingly never end finally ended, leaving behind it half of America's carrier power in the Pacific completely unable to launch and recover aircraft, with a 10.5-degree list to starboard; and with major fires burning out of control on the signal bridge, flight deck, ready rooms, Number 1 elevator pit, and hangar deck – and no electrical power with which to fight them, no power to move the ship.

Admiral Murray looked down from his useless flag bridge on his useless flagship and saw barely recognizable creatures coming out of the smoking wreck of the signal bridge. In the lead was a chief signalman, fumbling for a way through the smoke for four other sailors who were themselves carrying two more sailors. All were barely clothed, wearing only charred scraps of their uniforms. All the human skin visible looked red, seen only through an oily black film.

"Where are you taking these men?" Admiral Murray asked the chief.

Even in what was clearly an emergency, the chief came to attention for this most senior of officers. "To the dressing station, sir."

But the route to the dressing station was blocked; only a ladder was available to get through the sealed bulkheads and hatches. "Bring them in here, man," the admiral responded, referring to his flag bridge.

The two men were carried in and laid down gently on the deck. The chief, fighting back tears, knelt beside them. Two signalmen with the least burns ran off to get medical help.

Admiral Murray went over to the chief and said, "Go below to the dressing station." It was an order.

"Sir, must I? I'd rather…"

"Yes, you must."

Very reluctantly, the chief left. Having spared the chief from what was now inevitable, the admiral himself now knelt beside the two badly burned men on the deck of his flag bridge. One, just 17 years old, looked up at him.

"Sir, am I being brave enough?"

Choking back tears of his own, the task force commander could only nod. A moment later, his voice cracking, Admiral Murray was able to say, "Yes, son. Just take it easy." It was all he, or anyone, could do for the boy at this point. The young sailor died on the deck of the flag bridge.[156]

Outside, back on the shattered signal bridge itself, the radio squawked a question from one of the escorting ships: "Is [the *Hornet*] hurt?" Commander Dodson responded, "Affirmative."

With that question settled, a bleeding signalman on the signal bridge raised his flags and started waving them in the semaphore code, signaling to the nearest ship, "We are ready to receive messages."[157]

CHAPTER 12

AND THEN THERE WAS ONE

The attack was over, but the battle was not. The Japanese were winging their way to the northwest, or trying to, but they continued to stumble across stray, avenging Wildcats. And a Dauntless.

Lieutenant (jg) Howard Burnett, assigned to Scouting 10 but with the attitude of a fighter pilot, had almost completed his return leg when he blundered into the air battle over the *Hornet*. His SBD was shot up, losing an engine cylinder and his hydraulics, and his fuel line punctured so gasoline pooled in the cockpit at his feet. Ignoring his flammability, Burnett found a Type 97, flown by Petty Officer 2nd Class Miya Hatsuhiko of the *Shokaku*, flying just 50 feet over the water, and made a firing pass that forced it to ditch. As Miya and his crew escaped the Kate and inflated their rubber life raft, Burnett turned around and, with his gunner Aviation Radioman 3rd Class Robert Wynn, proceeded to strafe them, making certain the raft was permanently deflated. None of Miya's crew returned.[1]

Lieutenant Shirane's remaining Zeros continued to spar with vindictive Wildcats here and there. The *Hornet*'s Lieutenant Emerson and his wingmen had overshot the fight over the carrier, but came across a flight of Zeros ahead and below. Swooping in like vultures, they shot down before the Zeros knew what hit them and scattered, beginning a series of dogfights. The *Enterprise*'s Lieutenant (jg) James D. Billo and Ensign James E. Caldwell saw Emerson's Wildcat under attack by "what looked like seven or eight Zeros," so they swooped in and Billo torched one, only to be chased away by another.[2]

Then Lieutenant Billo heard what was apparently Ensign Caldwell on the radio, announcing "Going in to the water." Another pilot wished him "Good luck." Caldwell replied, "I hope they pick me up." Billo may have seen Caldwell drifting down in a parachute, but that was the last anyone saw of him.

Also disappearing in these last moments of combat was *Enterprise* Ensign Lyman "Squeak" Fulton. Fulton and wingman Ensign Steve Kona had been rushing back to the *Enterprise* to battle a reported torpedo attack – a false alarm, for now – when Fulton all of a sudden turned back toward the *Hornet* without explanation. He vanished into a cloud and was never seen again. It is assumed he was shot down.[3]

And so the Japanese all headed home. Their mission had been a success. It had taken approximately ten minutes. For this complex but swift effort, the Japanese left the *Hornet* completely disabled and believed they had shot down 20 of 30 Wildcats they had faced. In actuality, they had shot down six, with two pilots eventually rescued.[4]

Nevertheless, the Japanese losses were brutal. Of the 53 aircraft from *Kido Butai* that had attacked the *Hornet* task force, only 15 – seven fighters, four dive bombers, and four torpedo bombers – returned. Of the losses, 24 were combat losses in the combat area, while 14 more crashed or had to ditch on the way back. Among the losses were respected veteran Zero pilots warrant officers Osanai Suekichi and Hanzawa Yukuo, and, of course, Lieutenant Commander Murata Shigeharu.

The loss of Lieutenant Commander Murata, perhaps the finest torpedo attack pilot in the world, and his vast knowledge of aerial torpedo attack theory was huge for the Japanese Naval Air Force. Commander Genda Minoru, who helped plan the Pearl Harbor attack, would later say of him, "Murata knew no fear, he was calm and cold as a rock in zero weather, was never nervous, and under the worst of circumstances always smiling."[5] Eminent historian John Lundstrom called Murata "happy-go-lucky" and "one of the outstanding naval aviators of the war."[6]

Most of those 15 Japanese aircraft were so scattered that they headed back in ones and twos. The exception was the torpedo squadron from the *Shokaku*. At a prearranged rendezvous point north of the *Hornet*, Lieutenant (jg) Suzuki Takeo gathered together the five remaining Type 97s from Lieutenant Commander Murata's division of the torpedo attack and headed north. The remaining five from Lieutenant Washimi's attack gathered southwest of the *Hornet* and headed home.

On their way, one of them saw a second American aircraft carrier northeast of the one they had just left burning. At 9:20, they reported its location to Admiral Nagumo: 20 degrees True, 15 miles from the first, course 0 degrees True, speed 24 knots.[7]

The carrier was the *Enterprise*, the last operational US Navy carrier in the Pacific.

For Admiral Nagumo and the men of *Kido Butai*, the morning had not been entirely pleasant. Nagumo himself had been on edge, of course, with memories, lessons of Midway on his mind, as they would be for anyone in his position. It was for this reason that the *Shokaku*, *Zuikaku*, and *Zuiho* had gotten their air cover and first strike launched as quickly as possible. The *Shokaku* had gotten her second strike launched almost as quickly, although the *Zuikaku* not so much.

But the lessons of Midway were manifesting themselves in other ways as well. Just before launching the first strike, Admiral Nagumo, not quite trusting his scouting reports, had the *Shokaku* launch something called a "Yokosuka D4Y1-C Type 2 carrier reconnaissance plane," called "Judy" by the Allies. It was a sleek, beautiful dive bomber whose kinks were still being worked out, but whose high speed in theory made it good for reconnaissance work. In theory.

So far, the Judy's main claim to fame was its work at Midway, where Admiral Nagumo had launched one to firm up the sighting of the US carrier. And the Judy dutifully had flown all the way out to the reported position of the US carrier and had found all three. She dutifully radioed her findings back to *Kido Butai*. However, her radio was not working so she had to fly all the way back to report her findings, by which time three-fourths of *Kido Butai* was in flames.

So Admiral Nagumo tried his luck with the Type 2 again. The Judy dutifully flew all the way out to the reported position of the US carrier and found it. She dutifully radioed her findings back to *Kido Butai*. However, her radio was not working. Again. So she had to fly all the way back to report her findings. Again. At least this time she found only one-third of *Kido Butai* in flames, which was an improvement.[8] It might help explain why the Japanese took the radios out of the Zeros.

Another lesson of Midway was the necessity of early warning of enemy aircraft. Lookouts, battleships making smoke screens, and the like had not been sufficient at Midway. By the time the lookouts had shouted "hell divers," the Dauntlesses were already in their dives.

With that in mind, the *Shokaku* had received that Type 21 air search radar. And it had already worked, though its good performance at Eastern Solomons had been wasted by poor communications. Today, it had not prevented a mob of scouting SBDs from materializing over *Kido Butai* and knocking out the *Zuiho*. But at 8:40 am, the radar atop the *Shokaku*'s island had detected unidentified aircraft bearing 135 degrees True – southeast – distance 145 kilometers (78.2 miles). It was commendable work by the inexperienced Japanese radar technicians, far better than their American counterparts at Savo Island. Or, for that matter, today.[9]

In response, Admiral Nagumo quickly tossed up all the fighters he could, which was 23 – nine from the *Shokaku* and seven each from the *Zuikaku* and *Zuiho*. Then Nagumo decided to proceed to the north to put as much distance between his carriers and the large mass of unidentified aircraft. However, the *Zuikaku* could not, because she still had to launch her second wave against the US carrier, which required her to turn into the southeast wind. She was detached with two destroyers for escort.[10]

It was not until 9:00 am that the *Zuikaku* was able to send up four Zeros led by Warrant Officer Katsuma Shigemi and 16 Type 97s led by Lieutenant Imajuku Shigeichiro. As sluggish as the aircraft handling was on the carrier, the launch did not go smoothly, as two PBY Catalinas poked their noses in the midst of the strike as it was forming up. One PBY under Lieutenant (jg) Enos J. Jones came in from the southeast and saw "a large cargo vessel" escorted by two destroyers, a description that likely would have offended *Zuikaku*'s skipper, Captain Nomoto Tameteru. As it was, three Type 97s with minimal antiair armament managed to chase the flying boat away.[11]

A second PBY, this one under Lieutenant (jg) George F. Poulos, came in from the southwest, found a Japanese carrier, and backed out to report it in. Or tried to. His radio operator had to resend it again and again. Headed back north to firm it up, the PBY was jumped by Katsuma's Zeros, which, after making several firing passes, thought they had shot him down. Poulos and his crew disagreed. But neither Poulos' nor Jones' reports got to Admiral Kinkaid until that afternoon.[12]

Admiral Nagumo was not the only one having trouble with US reconnaissance planes. So was Admiral Abe's Vanguard Force to the south. Three Zeros from the *Zuiho* under Warrant Officer Okamoto Shigeru were vectored out to assist him.[13]

By now, the first strike had reached its target. Admiral Nagumo and his staff had copied Lieutenant Commander Murata's message to his strike planes to "Assume attack formation" and "All forces attack." They continued to listen in on whatever chatter they could pick up, including the chatter on the American frequencies, which they had intercepted. Finally, at 9:15, an unidentified Japanese radioman sent the message " … one *Saratoga*-class carrier is on fire."[14] On the bridge of the flagship *Shokaku*, the message caused jubilation.

That was cut short after only a few minutes.

Ensign Phil Souza had been the first to spot those Japanese planes passing in the other direction about a half-hour earlier. It was not a good feeling. But even worse was the feeling he had right now – that those Japanese planes were targeting him.

About 20 minutes after passing the Japanese, Lieutenant Commander Widhelm and his *Hornet* pilots sighted ship wakes ahead. Any excitement that these might be the Japanese carriers rapidly turned to disappointment when the wakes were revealed to belong to the *Tone* and *Chikuma* of the 8th Cruiser Division, escorted by destroyers *Tanikaze* and *Urakaze*. They had gotten themselves separated from Admiral Abe's Vanguard Force as it had headed due east trying to close on the American carriers. Widhelm wanted carriers. They moved on.

But the frustration was growing. At 8:50, Lieutenant Commander Widhelm radioed his fighter escort Lieutenant Commander Sanchez, "Gus to Mike: Do you see carriers?" The radios in Widhelm's group squawked back, "Mike to Gus: No carriers in sight out here. Let's return." Widhelm and his pilots seethed at the response. When they returned, he would have to have a word about this with Sanchez, with whom he did not get along. They continued their search.

After another 20 miles, Lieutenant Commander Widhelm came across more ships – the rest of Admiral Abe's Vanguard Force, with the flagship battleship *Hiei* and sister

Kirishima, heavy cruiser *Suzuya*, and the 10th Destroyer Flotilla with flagship light cruiser *Nagara* and destroyers *Makigumo*, *Akigumo*, *Yugumo*, and *Isokaze*. The two battleships would be of major interest, so Widhelm reported them in, while *Isokaze* alerted Abe to the potential air attack.

Already aware of the potential air attack were the three Zeros from the *Zuiho*. Completely unaware of the Zeros were the eight Wildcats escorting the *Hornet* Dauntlesses. Four were escorting the Avengers at low altitude, and four, Lieutenant Commander Sanchez's flight that included Ensign Souza, were with the Dauntlesses at high altitude. By the time Souza had that sinking feeling that he was in someone's gunsights, it was too late; Warrant Officer Okamoto's *Zuiho* fighters were already above and behind them.

Ensign Souza expressed a professional appreciation at how the Japanese pilots had gotten them in their sights. He also appreciated the artistry of the Japanese Zeros, noting the aircraft were "beautiful and shiny" as they tried to kill him.[15] Then he released his droptank. Naturally, it failed to drop. Now Souza had to deal with the Zeros in a hamstrung Wildcat. Okamoto's Zeros made one pass through Souza's group, riddling Souza's right wing with 20mm cannon fire, sending Souza's flight leader Lieutenant Johnson spinning to a watery grave, and wounding both the Wildcat and the person of Lieutenant (jg) William V. Roberts, Jr. In return, Souza's guns caused the Zero of Petty Officer 1st Class Seki Kazuo to explode.

With one pass, it was over. Seeing a badly wounded Roberts flying a riddled Wildcat leaking gasoline, and with his own fighter barely flyable, Souza told Roberts, "Let's get out of here," and headed back to the task force. Division leader Lieutenant Commander Sanchez seems to have taken a snap shot at a Zero but otherwise missed the whole encounter and was left behind, wondering where his fighters and Dauntlesses had gone.

Warrant Officer Okamoto was not done, however. He and his lone remaining wingman spotted Lieutenant John C. "Jack" Bower with four Wildcats escorting Avengers and similarly oblivious to Okamoto's presence. Okamoto made a pass at Bower's group, shooting down Bower himself before the Americans regrouped and took out Okamoto. Then the American and Japanese fighters headed back to their respective carriers.

The six Avengers under Lieutenant Parker continued onward, blissfully ignorant of the ambush and disappearance of their fighters as well as the disappearance of their accompanying dive bombers. Lieutenant Commander Widhelm had spotted the ambush and turned right – almost due north – to avoid it. Five minutes into this course to the north he saw yet more ship wakes. "Contact bearing about 345," he announced, and set out to investigate. The contacts resolved themselves into one large aircraft carrier and another, smaller one that was spewing black smoke.

Lieutenant Commander Widhelm radioed, "I have one in sight and am going after them." The Dauntlesses of Scouting 8 and Bombing 8 were deployed in diamond-shaped sections of four in a column stepped down to the rear, like the underside of a staircase made of Dauntlesses. It was an unusual formation, a departure from the traditional "V"-shaped sections of three all combining to make up a big, flat "V". In this formation the SBDs could much more easily combine and focus their defensive firepower.

They would need to, as they had lost their fighter cover. And the combat air patrol of *Kido Butai* was in position and ready. A burst of heavy gunfire directed the Zeros to the attackers. The first to take on Widhelm's dive bombers were four Zeros from the *Shokaku* led by Petty Officer 1st Class Omori Shigataka, a veteran survivor of the *Akagi* at Midway. His group determinedly slashed at the formation, especially Widhelm in the lead. Omori himself came straight on at the *Hornet* pilot. Widhelm filled the Zero's engine with .50cal rounds, causing it to explode. In a last-gasp move, Omori tried to ram Widhelm's Dauntless, but Widhelm deftly avoided it and the Zero disintegrated. Omori's wingmates thought he had succeeded, however, taking out the enemy leader at the cost of his own life. As a result, Omori received a posthumous double promotion to special duty ensign.[16]

But the lost Omori was replaced by five more Zeros from the *Zuikaku*. The Dauntlesses kept barreling through, but their formation began to loosen. One unidentified Zero from the *Zuikaku* waited outside the US formation, "stalking us," until he saw the American flight leader was distracted. Then he raced overhead and riddled Lieutenant Commander Widhelm's Dauntless, puncturing the engine and causing an oil leak. Widhelm tried to hold formation, to coax just a little more mileage out of the Dauntless, but his engine overheated and ultimately seized up at around 9:25.[17]

As a result, Lieutenant Commander Widhelm could not go through with his dive-bombing attack and had to relinquish the lead in the formation, ultimately to Lieutenant James E. "Moe" Vose of Bombing 8. But he wasn't happy about it. And he let it be known. Giving an original meaning to the term "talk radio," Widhelm went into a lengthy soliloquy worthy of Shakespeare on what he thought of being abandoned by Lieutenant Commander Sanchez and the other fighters. The *Hornet* pilots who heard Widhelm's dissertation "admired the range of his vocabulary." Even Ensign Phil Souza of Sanchez' section found the monologue "very hilarious."[18] Widhelm had to ditch the SBD in the midst of *Kido Butai*.

But the Americans, too, were scoring to a degree. *Zuikaku* Petty Officer 1st Class Kamei Tomio dove in on the Dauntless formation, fired his guns, then pulled up for another pass. Kamei pulled up, but the wings of his Zero did not. One wing flew off, then part of the other, and the fuselage plunged into the water below.[19]

The Zeros kept hacking away at the block of Dauntlesses, little by little pulling the formation apart, forcing it into lower and lower altitudes to disrupt the attack. Another SBD was shot down, two more were forced by damage to turn back, but Lieutenant Vose was "as cool as could be," said Lieutenant (jg) Ralph V. Hovind. "He looked just like a deacon driving a buckboard to church."[20] The Americans finally overtook the fleeing *Shokaku*. At 9:27, the five Dauntlesses of Scouting 8 reached the pushover point and began their dives, followed quickly by Lieutenant Vose and the Dauntlesses of Bombing 8.

It was not an easy dive. They had lost altitude trying to evade the Zeros, but they made their shallower plunges. "The skies were filled with white and yellow smoke," from the bursts of antiaircraft fire at the howling dive bombers.[21] The falling bombs looked like "silver streaks, which appeared like thunderbolts" as they went down on the carrier.[22] At the last second, the *Shokaku*'s skipper, Captain Masafumi Arima, wheeled her around. The first four bombs fell into the sea.

But then the bombs started hitting. The first or second hit came from Lieutenant Vose leading Bombing 8. On the *Amatsukaze*, Commander Hara watched helplessly as "the whole deck bulged quietly and burst. Flames shot from the cleavages."[23]

Behind Vose, Lieutenant Fred L. Bates was stunned to find a charred piece of the *Shokaku*'s wooden flight deck plop into his lap, a souvenir of Vose's hit, before Bates dropped his own bomb.[24] As he pulled out down low and looked back, he saw the carrier's after elevator blown into the air. It was his bomb, apparently, that struck near the aft elevators on the port side, destroying two 127mm antiaircraft guns and killing almost everyone nearby.[25] One bomb, evidently dropped by Lieutenant Hovind from a damaged Dauntless, barely missed the carrier's island, landing just aft. The *Shokaku*'s flight deck amidships was pummeled. The 1,000lb bombs left it an inferno, so shattered it "looked like an earthquake fault zone."[26] The center elevator was trashed. Beneath the flight deck, the nearly empty hangar deck was devastated.

The last man in the Bombing 8 formation was Lieutenant (jg) Stanley R. Holm. He was unable to get the *Shokaku* lined up and instead went after the nearby antiaircraft destroyer *Teruzuki*. He got a near-miss; then, while pulling out of the dive, he emptied his .50cal on the heavy cruiser *Kumano*.[27]

The Dauntlesses roared low away from *Kido Butai*, chased by some angry Zeros. One "real hot shot" Japanese pilot raked three Dauntlesses in a row with gunfire, but his ammunition ran out before he could finish any of the tough birds off. He pulled up to one of those he had hit, Lieutenant (jg) Roy Gee, saluted him, and flew away. Lieutenant Hovind had something similar happen to him. Lieutenant Vose gathered nine SBDs for the trip home, while the other four headed back on their own.[28]

Lieutenant Vose would claim the SBDs got four hits on the *Shokaku*; watching the attack from a life raft, Lieutenant Commander Widhelm counted six.[29] Watching somewhat more comfortably than Widhelm from the *Amatsukaze*, Commander Hara groaned in despair.[30] The Americans had done it again. Just like Midway. Despite all the preparation, all the precautions, the new radar, launching all the aircraft and properly positioning fighters, still the Americans had succeeded.

Well, not quite. Word was passed to the bridge of the *Shokaku*: "We can go 32 knots, sir!"[31] The fires were serious, communications were out, and flight operations were impossible. But the engines were intact and there was no damage below the waterline. The fueling system had been emptied. There were only two aircraft, both Type 97s, on the carrier. One near the island was destroyed; the second near the stern somehow survived. So, unlike Midway, the hangar deck was not packed with fueled and armed aircraft, bombs in themselves. The fires were bad, but survivable.

The *Zuikaku* came out of her fortuitous squall to find out she now had to take in all the aircraft still aloft from herself, *Shokaku*, and *Zuiho*. The vaunted *Kido Butai* was now down to one operational aircraft carrier.

But the Japanese still had one other carrier out there.

Fragmenting. Carrier aviation theory, such as it was at this point in time, advocated massed airstrikes as the best way to attack the enemy. But the strength of even a massed airstrike can dissipate if it fragments, losing aircraft here and there to navigation erors, mechanical problems, mistiming, and whatnot. And the Americans had not even launched a massed airtrike. The American airstrikes had been sent up in driblets, stayed aloft in driblets, and, as the lone attack by the *Hornet* Dauntlesses showed, broke up into even smaller driblets. This fragmenting did not help the efficacy or the survivability of the airstrikes.

The small strike from the *Enterprise* had been reduced in numbers and range by Lieutenant Hidaka's attack. Four Wildcats, five Avengers, and three Dauntlesses. At 8:55, Lieutenant Commander Flatley suggested they link up with the *Hornet*'s second strike, whom he could see behind him, for mutual protection and support. No luck.

Both Flatley and Lieutenant Thompson, leading the Avengers, had picked up Widhelm's report of an enemy carrier, but did not know he had turned north and thus could not place it. They had passed Admiral Hara's 8th Cruiser Division when Thompson saw something to the west: Admiral Abe's Vanguard Force. The Wildcats and Avengers turned toward it. The three SBDs under Lieutenant Estes missed the turn and flew into a cloud.

So the Wildcats and Avengers checked out the Vanguard Force: two battleships, a heavy cruiser – but no carriers. Flatley would not agree to continue the search further; the loss of the wingtanks severely limited the range of his fighters. At 9:30, Thompson turned back to try to pick off the cruiser, the *Suzuya*, on the western edge of the Vanguard Force. The four Avengers moved in to aim at the port side and at 9:37 released their torpedoes. Only two successfully dropped. The *Suzuya* turned away to starboard and combed the wakes. A second attack by one Avenger off the starboard bow was easily evaded as well. The fourth torpedo would not release and had to be jettisoned. After that not-entirely-successful effort, they all headed home.

The second strike from the *Hornet* never made it out even this far. Lieutenant Lynch, leading the Dauntlesses, had overheard Lieutenant Commander Widhelm's question to Lieutenant Commander Sanchez, and the response that question received: "No carriers in sight out here." Lynch figured that if a strike that had launched 20 minutes before them had not found them, the carriers must be out of range. He had not picked up Widhelm's later contact reports, so there was no way he could have known that enemy carriers were close by. No way he could have known that the answer Widhelm had received had in fact not come from Sanchez, but from the Japanese, who had intercepted the American fighter direction and search and attack frequencies.[32]

Lieutenant Lynch told Commander Rodee that, unless otherwise ordered, he would go back and attack these Japanese ships they had passed earlier. Rodee made no reply as he never received Lynch's message.[33] So Lynch took his nine SBDs, with three fighters for escort as well as Rodee and his escorts, and headed back. The nine TBFs under Lieutenant Powell, armed with bombs and two fighters flown by Lieutenant Jock Sutherland and Lieutenant (jg) Henry "Hank" Carey, did not turn back and stayed on course.

At 9:26, the SBDs made bombing attacks on the *Chikuma*. Within a minute, one 1,000lb bomb smashed the port side of the bridge, disabling the main battery directors and killing much of the bridge crew. Though skipper Captain Komura Keizo's head was roaring because his eardrums had burst, he had the presence of mind to order an evasive course change. Five minutes later, a bomb from Scouting 8 crashed into the starboard side of the superstructure. Komura shouted, "Jettison torpedoes!"[34]

Those Americans left without taking any losses, only to be replaced by more. Lieutenant Estes and his three Dauntlesses, who made three runs on what they thought was the battleship *Kongo* but was, of course, the *Chikuma*. Of their three dives with 1,000lb bombs, one resulted in a near-miss, and one either hit or was an extremely close miss to starboard, because it left a "big hole" in the starboard side that flooded a boiler room and cost her speed. As he and his flight exited the area, Lieutenant Estes spotted a lone Wildcat "flying all over the sky."[35] It was Lieutenant Commander Sanchez, who was oblivious to both the controversy the Japanese had started in his name as well as his location. Estes pointed the way back, and was surprised when Sanchez nonchalantly lit a cigarette and sped on ahead.

By this time, the *Chikuma* had 190 killed, including her executive officer, and 154 wounded, including Captain Komura.[36] Two more torpedo groups that should have been converging on *Kido Butai* were now converging on her. One group was Lieutenant Parker's six *Hornet* Avengers.

Parker's crew had completely missed the aerial battle that had cost them their fighter escort, had missed the absence of that fighter escort, and had missed the Dauntlesses turning to the north to avoid the aerial battle the Avengers had missed. They had also missed Lieutenant Commander Widhelm's reports of the position of the Japanese carriers, due in part, no doubt, to the unreliability of American radios. When he reached the end of his outbound leg, Parker searched 50 more miles to the north and west. But he was still too far south, and now too far west; to top it off, he was running out of fuel. He had seen nothing resembling an aircraft carrier, so Parker decided to go back and attack the force of battleships they had passed.[37] But Parker missed them, too, so he aimed for Admiral Hara's cruisers.

Lieutenant Parker had selected Admiral Hara's flagship *Tone* as his target and at 9:51 began running a classic anvil attack from both bows. However, Parker's torpedo would not drop and two more ran erratically. Another proud moment for US torpedoes. Parker thought they had hit with the three that dropped, but the *Tone* avoided them all.[38]

By sheer coincidence, Lieutenant Parker's Avengers from the *Hornet* had arrived over Admiral Hara's ships at the same time as Lieutenant Powell's nine Avengers and their two Wildcat escorts from the *Hornet*. Despite not finding the Japanese carriers, the Japanese carriers had found them, as two Zeros from the *Zuikaku* jumped them when they reached the end of their search leg. Lieutenant Sutherland set up a Zero, flown by Seaman 1st Class Takayama Takashi, on an almost perfect full deflection shot from an incredible 400 yards. Sutherland kept pouring lead into the Zero until it exploded only 100 yards ahead, forcing Sutherland to dodge the flaming debris.[39]

With that excitement over, Parker's group was ready for more. From astern they came up on the *Chikuma*, where by now Captain Komura had to be wondering what his cruiser had done to earn such unwanted attention. The result was one hit from a 500lb bomb through an aft torpedo mount, which would have detonated the torpedoes there and probably destroyed the ship if Komura had not dumped them earlier. The lessons of Midway had been learnt, where a similar jettisoning of torpedoes once she was vulnerable had saved the cruiser *Mogami*.[40]

Nevertheless, in the face of these carrier air attacks, the entire Vanguard Force turned around to open the range to the American flattops. The American air attacks on the *Suzuya* and *Tone* and especially the heavy damage to the *Chikuma* left Admiral Abe concerned about more air attacks. Many of his men wondered if Abe was really concerned or just timid. Either way, it would very shortly have an effect.

The American aircraft, unhurt, turned to head back. As they did so, they saw a large pillar of smoke to the north. Only about 50 miles or so. That was the carrier they had been seeking. But they had never found it. Or were they just impatient? It was too late in any case; their munitions had been expended, and not on the most valuable target available. Frustrated, they pressed onward for home.

Or what was left of it.

Returning from their morning search and their harassment by Zeros, Scouting 10's Lieutenants Ward and Carmody were nearing the end of their mission and the end of their fuel. They were coming up on where the *Enterprise* was supposed to be, only to find empty sea.

The homing beacon from the *Enterprise* was working, though, and they followed it. As the two Dauntlesses moved along, warily eying the fuel gauges, they saw a tower of smoke on the horizon. It was the *Hornet*. She couldn't take them on board.

Times were getting desperate for lieutenants Carmody and Ward. "We agreed to ditch together at the same time," Carmody later said. "Then all of a sudden the *Enterprise* came out from under a squall." And just in time, too – they ran out of fuel while landing on the carrier. "Both Les and I had to be pushed out of the arresting gear," said Carmody.[41]

When the *Enterprise* came out of that squall, the men topside were shocked and horrified with the grim view that greeted them. There was their sister *Hornet*, dead in the water, a big cloud of smoke where her flight deck was supposed to be, surrounded by three destroyers trying to treat her obviously grievous injuries.

With the *Hornet*'s communications down, at 9:41 Admiral Kinkaid radioed Admiral Good, commanding the *Hornet*'s screen from the *Northampton*, to ask if the *Enterprise* should recover the *Hornet* "chickens" – aircraft – still in the air. The answer was a discouraging but not surprising "Affirmative." Kinkaid, in turn, radioed Admiral Halsey with two words: "*Hornet* hurt."[42]

The reply from the commander of American forces in the South Pacific suggests he was a little slow on the uptake: "Operate from and in positions from which you can strike quickly and effectively. We must use everything we have to the limit."[43]

Everything they had was rapidly dwindling to nothing. The fires on the *Hornet*, now "a dim, infernal, sweltering place where grimy figures bent over the wounded and beat at burning gasoline with bare hands," were taking up a good part of her screen.[44] Commander Marcel A. E. Gouin, the *Hornet*'s air officer, coordinated damage control efforts with the destroyers who came alongside to help fight the fires. First was the *Morris*, who moved to the starboard side and passed three hoses to the carrier. One was used to extinguish the fire on the signal bridge; the other two were hauled across the flight deck to battle one of the fires on the forecastle. It came at a cost, as ocean swells drove the short little destroyer into the *Hornet*'s side and smashed her superstructure and antennae.[45]

Next the *Russell* moved off the port bow to deal with the fire in the elevator pit and other fires in the forecastle. The swells kept driving her into the carrier's side, knocking off her starboard anchor and bashing in a good part of her bridge and superstructure. On one occasion, a depth charge was jolted into the water. Fortunately, it had been set on "safe" and did not explode.

Creeping in through the smoke caused by the *Hornet*'s fires, the *Mustin* came in off the starboard quarter, but swells kept bashing her into the carrier's side, too, so she switched to the port quarter so her hoses could be used to fight the fires in the chiefs' quarters and storerooms, which seemed to be the most persistent fires. By these and many superhuman efforts, including a 200-man bucket brigade, by 10:00 am the fires were under control.[46]

The next objective was to get the powerless *Hornet* moving. Admiral Good's flagship, heavy cruiser *Northampton*, would tow the carrier. There were only two complications. The first was that the carrier's rudder was jammed to starboard, which could force the cruiser to tow her in a circle. The second was that towing a ship left both very vulnerable. Good needed air cover. Over the disabled carrier right now was Lieutenant Emerson with three *Hornet* Wildcats and Lieutenant Billo from the *Enterprise*. But their fuel was running low and they couldn't stay aloft much longer. He needed help from the *Enterprise*.

The *Enterprise* had her own problems. She was now solely responsible for combat air patrol, antisubmarine patrol, search, and airstrikes. That was a lot of balls to juggle in the air. To complicate matters further, the aircraft from both the *Enterprise* and the *Hornet* were on their return flight, desperately low on fuel. The *Enterprise* had to land these aircraft while sending up more for an unescorted SBD strike on the Japanese. In short, the *Enterprise* had only 11 Wildcats available for defense.[47]

And she would need them very, very soon. Around 9:30 am, Admiral Good reported that the excellent CXAM radar operators on the *Northampton* had detected a large force of incoming aircraft, bearing 315 degrees True – northeast – distance 76 miles. Seven minutes later the *Northampton* had the contacts at 290 degrees and 35 miles. Then the battleship *South Dakota* picked them up at 9:45, 325 degrees and 55 miles. Finally, at 9:53, the *Enterprise* herself, 340 degrees and 45 miles.[48]

However, the *Enterprise* was still having issues trying to recover her aircraft, put up a strike, and put up and keep up air cover. A traffic jam was building both on and over the flight deck. Commander Griffin was trying to keep the air cover by landing a few Wildcats, refueling and reloading them right on the flight deck, then spotting and launching them immediately, like a pit stop in auto racing.

One of those chickens running out of fuel was the battered Avenger of Ensign Dick Batten. He had put out the fire in the cockpit, but he still could not dump his torpedo. At 9:59, Batten tried to land on the *Enterprise*, but the carrier waved him off; the flight deck was still crowded with fighters that had just landed; in any case, landing a damaged TBF still carrying its torpedo was not necessarily the smart thing to do in this situation. Unable to land, Batten ditched his Avenger two minutes later off the carrier's port quarter and some 1,500 yards ahead of the destroyer *Porter*. He and his crew got out of their sinking plane and set up their life raft. Despite the imminent air attack, the *Porter* was ordered to pick them up; she was the closest ship, and her dual-purpose twin 5-inch mounts were useless in an antiaircraft role because the guns could not elevate enough.

Skipper Lieutenant Commander Dave Roberts ordered the *Porter* to come to a complete stop so her bow waves would not swamp Ensign Batten and his crew. The wreck of the Avenger was on the port side, but Batten's raft would go to the starboard side, which was leeward and thus easier to take them aboard.[49]

Like most of the topside crew, Seaman 2nd Class Ross Pollock was watching the recovery of Ensign Batten and his crew from his position as loader of one of the port side 1.1-inch mounts, when he was distracted by some movement to port. Pollock turned his head and saw a fighter diving and strafing. Was it strafing the *Porter*? No, it was friendly. It was strafing something in the water off the port side. What was it?

Seaman Pollock watched as the fighter dove while firing its guns, pulled up, and then dove again. The *Porter*'s antiaircraft guns opened on the fighter, flown by the unrelated *Enterprise* pilot Lieutenant Dave Pollock. Not wanting to be shot down by a friendly ship, Pollock quickly veered away out of the range of the destroyer's guns. Ross Pollock was perplexed. What was it?[50]

He figured it out. Just in time to hear Seaman 1st Class Don Beane, a lookout on the port wing of the bridge, shout at the top of his lungs, "Fish!" Lieutenant Commander Roberts and his executive officer turned and looked at Beane.[51] Another lookout shouted, "Torpedo wake on the port bow!"[52] Lieutenant (jg) Bill Wood, the officer of the deck, ran from the port wing of the bridge into the pilot house to ring emergency flank speed to the engine room, where Machinist's Mate 1st Class Al Anundsen threw the throttle forward. The propellers started to churn the water.[53]

Then Anundsen heard a loud, sharp *Crack!* Like two stones being smacked together. The *Porter* immediately lost all power and seemed to settle in the water.[54] Ross Pollack felt the ship rise as he was thrown against his gunshield, trying to avoid the hot fragments flying through the air.

The torpedo struck the transverse bulkhead between both boiler rooms, flooding both. The damage was limited – but it was limited to the one area that produced the *Porter*'s power. She could not move or fight. She would have to be towed in an active battle area infested with Japanese submarines.

The *Enterprise* and her escorts had moved on ahead except for the destroyer *Shaw*, that Pearl Harbor veteran who had survived a spectacular bomb hit in drydock that blew off her bow. She was looking for the submarine that was believed to have launched the torpedo that pierced the *Porter*. The disabled destroyer's crew was ordered to assemble on deck, where they could hear the creaking and groaning below as bulkheads collapsed from the inrushing water. One particularly violent shock literally rattled men near the stern, who promptly jumped into the water, just in time for the *Shaw* to attack the suspected submarine with a string of eight depth charges whose explosions promptly blew the men back onto the *Porter*.[55]

Without power, the *Porter* could not move and it was too dangerous to tow her, so at 10:55 the *Shaw* was ordered to come alongside and take off the crew, which was accomplished quickly with no panic. Once Commander Roberts and Lieutenant Wood had made one last sweep of the ship for anyone left behind, they and division commander Captain Charles Cecil became the last ones to step off the *Porter*.[56]

The sad duty of putting the *Porter* under fell to the *Shaw*. The Pearl Harbor veteran circled around and at 12:08 pm fired two Mark 15 torpedoes at point-blank range.[57] Both hit the *Porter*; but, of course, being American torpedoes, neither detonated. So the *Shaw* pumped 50 5-inch rounds into the derelict's hull, sending her rolling to starboard and sinking stern first. Nine sailors had been killed; one sailor and one officer had just vanished, their bodies never recovered. Nine sailors were badly burned by the escape of superheated steam from the wrecked boiler rooms; four later died.[58]

Precisely who torpedoed the *Porter* – aside from the *Shaw* – remains disputed. Many American sources credit the Japanese submarine *I-21*. While the I-boat's skipper Commander Matsumura Kanji and crew would probably love to take the credit for the kill, Japanese sources insist that the *I-21* and, for that matter, all their submarines involved in the operation were scouting south of Guadalcanal.

No, the *Porter*'s executioner was not a submarine, but something much more bizarre – the TBF Avenger of Ensign Dick Batten. When he ditched his Grumman, the impact released the torpedo that was jammed underneath. The Mark 13 torpedo, naturally, then went on a circular run.[59] It was yet another proud moment for American torpedoes.

It was a distraction the *Enterprise* task force did not need. The Japanese attack was just about on top of them. This was the second strike launched by the *Shokaku*, 19 Type 99s under Lieutenant Commander Seki escorted by five Zeros under Lieutenant Shingo. Seki was not going after the *Hornet*. The 9:20 sighting report from the *Shokaku*'s returning strike just confirmed the building suspicions, thanks to the Japanese interception of the American fighter director frequencies, that there was a second American carrier out there.

At 9:27, Admiral Nagumo signaled, "There appear to be two carriers, one as yet unknown, estimated south of *Saratoga*'s [actually *Hornet*'s] position, 8 degrees 35 minutes south, 166 degrees 45 minutes east." Lieutenant (jg) Sakumuki Tsugimi, flying the Type 97 from the *Zuikaku* with a mission of making and keeping contact, amplified Nagumo's message at 9:37 with the report, "Another large enemy force, one carrier, one light cruiser, six destroyers, speed 20 knots, position 8 degrees 37 minutes south, 166 degrees 37 minutes east[.]"[60] Seki knew he was looking for a second carrier. So did the *Enterprise*, which carried a radio intelligence unit under Major Bankson T. Holcomb.

The *Enterprise* radar was tracking Seki's strike coming from the north and circling to the east.[61] But, once again, Commander Griffin was struggling to effectively position the patrolling fighters, largely because the carrier's CXAM radar was performing poorly. It had been the last of the search radars to detect the incoming strike. By that time, Lieutenant Commander Seki already had the carrier in sight.

Moreover, Seki's aircraft were now so close that the radar could not determine their altitude. Griffin had a total of eight Wildcats at high altitude over the *Enterprise* and 13 circling at low altitude, one of which was damaged and trying to return. Of the eight Wildcats at high altitude, Griffin kept sending the four F4Fs under Lieutenant Commander Kane running to and fro trying to find the incoming attackers, simply to determine their altitude. They had determined that the attack was developing to the north and northeast and ultimately vectored Kane and all the *Enterprise* Wildcats there, which was the right place. But Griffin had initially guessed the incoming aircraft were torpedo planes and thus their altitude was "probably low."[62] It wasn't, and Griffin never ordered them to gain altitude. It's much easier to move from high altitude to low altitude than vice versa. Griffin had positioned them too low. Again. Guadalcanal historian Eric Hammel gave the effects of the fighter direction this brutal assessment: "For all practical purposes, the fighter response was nil."[63]

Unlike Commander Griffin, Admiral Kinkaid was better able to position his assets to meet the incoming strike. Kinkaid had the *Enterprise* change course to 235 degrees to position the strike astern. The course change put the battleship *South Dakota* and her powerful antiaircraft battery in the path of the incoming Japanese, 2,500 yards aft of the carrier. The destroyer *Conyngham* filled the hole left by the *Porter* and *Shaw* by dropping back from her position in front to the starboard quarter. Veteran heavy cruiser *Portland* was positioned off the port bow and the light antiaircraft cruiser *San Juan* off the starboard bow. The other destroyers were positioned in a 1,500-yard-radius circle around the *Enterprise*.[64]

Lieutenant Commander Seki could see the *South Dakota* and beyond her the *Enterprise*. Seki could also see 20 planes on the *Enterprise*'s flight deck. In juggling all those chickens, the carrier had let one hit the deck like a sack of wet cement. She had been trying to get her quick strike of ten SBDs launched, but only one of them was spotted for launch on deck. Others were fully fueled and armed and thus ready for launch, except they were parked forward. Still other Dauntlesses were on the hangar deck still being fueled and armed. In short, the *Enterprise* was much like the carriers of *Kido Butai* at Midway – she had fueled and armed aircraft on her flight or hangar decks. The danger was grave.

At 11:08, Lieutenant Commander Seki ordered, "All forces attack."[65] There were no fighters to oppose him because they were all too low. Seki organized his dive bombers into a line of three divisions. Naturally, the third one of seven bombers, escorted by the five Zeros, went first. The first section went second; the second section went third.

Because of scattered cloud cover at 6,000 feet, the *Enterprise* did not see the Type 99s until 10:15, after Lieutenant Commander Seki had started his dive. With her fighters poorly positioned and the bombers diving, the carrier was in deep trouble. But the *Enterprise* had an advantage the *Hornet* did not: 16 40mm Bofors antiaircraft guns in four quadruple mounts. While she was under repair at Pearl Harbor, the "Bofors," as it was called, replaced all but one of the hated 1.1-inch quadruple mounts, because, though they had a slower rate of fire, they were more reliable, had greater range, and greater striking power. The Bofors was one of the most effective antiaircraft guns in the world.

On top of that, the *Enterprise* had received fire-direction radar for her eight 5-inch guns and an increase in the number of 20mm Oerlikons, which were also effective antiaircraft guns. The *Enterprise*'s antiaircraft battery was much stronger than the *Hornet*'s. The carrier opened up, as did the battleship *South Dakota* astern – her fire was so voluminous she was described as a "volcano" and a "ring of fire" – by the destroyer *Maury* off the starboard bow.[66]

The screaming dives of the fixed-landing gear Type 99s was mixed with antiaircraft bursts as the bombers entered a typhoon of hot steel. In the *Enterprise*'s sky control, Lieutenant Commander Elias B. "Benny" Mott II, the assistant gunnery officer, would later say, "As each plane came down, a veritable cone of tracer shells enveloped it. You could see it being hit and bounced by exploding shells."[67] Gunnery officer Lieutenant Commander Orlin Livdahl was with Mott in sky forward, the position from which the antiaircraft guns were directed. He was sure that "the amount of gunfire put out by the fleet far surpassed the prodigious volume at Eastern Solomons[.]"[68]

One of the first to learn the effects of the new antiaircraft package was Lieutenant Commander Seki himself. Diving from off the starboard bow, "Lieutenant Commander Seki's plane seems to have taken several direct hits soon after he gave the order to attack… [T]he bomber enter[ed] the dive and suddenly beg[an] to roll over on its back. Flames shot out of the bomber and, still inverted, it continued diving toward the enemy ship."[69] Seki's plane disintegrated. Its bomb splashed just off amidships as new skipper Captain

Osborne B. Hardison threw the *Enterprise* into a hard port turn. Hardison, an experienced pilot who understood the physics of dropping bombs, spent this battle holding his helmet in his left hand so he could look straight up at the diving bombers.[70]

In the face of this "unprecedented barrage," none of the remaining six Type 99s scored any bomb hits either, which Lieutenant Commander Mott attributed to the "volume and accuracy of the [antiaircraft] fire, which ruined their aim if it did not kill them outright."[71] Having killed outright the first Val of Lieutenant Commander Seki, it also killed outright the third, fifth, and seventh Vals – those of Petty Officer 2nd Class Itaya Yoshimi, Petty Officer 1st Class Someno Fumio, and Seaman 1st Class Hiroso Goichi. Lieutenant Shingo's Zeros tried to draw antiaircraft fire off the Vals as they tried to escape the US formation.[72]

The second group to attack was the first division, commanded by Lieutenant Arima Keiichi with his seven Type 99s attacking from astern. He was going against a cunning captain in Hardison, who had taken over from Captain Davis on October 21. The *Enterprise* was sailing away from the Japanese, forcing them into shallower and shallower dives, with a corresponding reduction in accuracy. For his part, Arima noticed no defending fighters, but the antiaircraft fire was "much more severe" than the Eastern Solomons action.[73]

As Arima punched through a cloud at 8,000 feet, Lieutenant Commander Mott shouted at his gunners through a bullhorn, "Four o'clock – four o'clock – get him!"[74] They didn't. Arima's bomb, dropped by pilot Petty Officer 1st Class Furata Kiyoto, pierced the flight deck 20 feet from the forward edge, passed through the forecastle deck, and exploded in midair just off the port bow.[75] It bounced Bucky Lee's Bombing 10 Dauntless off the bow, carrying to his death gunner Aviation Machinist's Mate 1st Class Sam Davis Presley, who had jumped into the rear seat to fire the twin .30cals at the Vals as they pulled out of their dives, set fire to a Scouting 10 Dauntless, which was pushed off the deck, and blew 1.1-inch battery officer Lieutenant (jg) Marshall Field IV (of the Chicago newspaper and department store Marshall Fields family) out of the 1.1-inch gun director on the forecastle and onto the flight deck, where he lay unconscious with wounds in his neck, arm, and leg.[76] They were merely flesh wounds. Like Field, the *Enterprise* had gotten off lucky.

But not with the next bomb. About a minute later, a second bomb hit the flight deck almost on the center line 10 feet aft of the forward elevator, piercing the deck to strike a girder and break in two, causing two distinct explosions.[77] One part blasted through the hangar deck, setting three SBDs trussed to the overhead afire. They were lowered and dumped over the side, along with three other Dauntlesses. The other exploded on the third deck, devastating officers' quarters, wiping out a repair party almost totally, and starting a fire in the pit to elevator Number 1 that disabled the elevator.[78]

The bombing was nerve-wracking for the pilots stuck on board with no way to fight back. Radioman Slim Colley was sweating out the attack playing the card game ace deucy with a pilot. "You had to do something," he said. "Everyone was almost a basket case at the end of the attack." "It was really something for a greenhorn to feel those bombs when they hit near the ship," said Lieutenant Carmody. "The whole ship would just shake." Even coffee was affected. In the Bombing 10 ready room, 'We had a huge 50-cup coffee urn sitting on a table, which tipped over," remembered Lieutenant (jg) Robert D. Gibson. "We were all swimming around on the deck in hot coffee."[79]

Lieutenant Yamada Shohei's second division was attacking third. It was the only one harassed by Wildcats before its dive, and then by only two – one flown by Ensign Feightner, the other by Ensign Maurice N. "Wick" Wickendoll. Feightner sent one plummeting to the water in flames. Wickendoll, hamstrung by having only one working gun, was largely ineffective. Two more, those of Lieutenant Blair and Ensign Gordon, harassed the Type 99s during their dives, destroying two more Vals, although how much was due to them and how much to the heavy antiaircraft fire is unclear.[80]

It was a bomb from this second division – that was attacking third – that at 10:20 got a serious near-miss on the *Enterprise*, about 10 feet from the starboard quarter. It opened a seam in the side plating 3 inches wide for a length of 50 feet. As the ship shuddered from top to bottom, the main turbine bearing was damaged; three fuel tanks, one of them full, ruptured; and the mast was rotated half an inch, knocking out of alignment a suite of antennae mounted there. One SBD was bounced off the deck into the sea, and another was bounced into the starboard 20mm gallery. It was dangerously perched there until Captain Hardison did a hard turn to port, which threw the Dauntless over the side.[81]

The Val that got the damaging near-miss was pursued by an avenging Lieutenant (jg) Richard Z. Hughes of the *Hornet*'s Fighting 72, who sent the Japanese into a fiery death. It was one of the few highlights of another pitiful performance by Commander Griffin's fighter direction team. A dozen Wildcats wanted to join the fight, but were once again out of position, which left the fighter pilots livid.

Another Val, pulling out of its dive, passed over the destroyer *Cushing*. The destroyer's 20mm forward battery trained on the dive bomber, and promptly jammed. In response to this outrageous misfortune, a signalman on the *Cushing*'s bridge pulled out his .45cal pistol and fired all seven shots at the bomber. The Val's rear gunner thumbed his nose at the signalman and joined his retiring mates.[82]

At 10:30 one of the *Shokaku* pilots reported that a carrier burned and listed to starboard; he got it half right in the case of the *Enterprise*. The cocky Lieutenant Arima reported his mission completed and sneered, "Good health to two enemy carriers."[83]

Arima had some right to be pleased, but an awful lot of his comrades had given their lives for their emperor, which did not help the effectiveness of the Japanese Naval Air Force. When the remaining Type 99s joined up for the trip home – under the watchful eye of a PBY commanded by Lieutenant (jg) Norman S. Haber, who had fought off five of Lieutenant Shingo's Zeros to report it – there were only nine of them. Of the 19 Type 99s, ten had been shot down – three by Wildcats and seven by the new and improved antiaircraft defenses. Among the dead were *Shokaku* air group leader Lieutenant Commander Seki and Lieutenant Yamada, a Pearl Harbor veteran, who was killed at some point during his attack. The Sea Eagles were rapidly running out of veterans. For this cost, they had damaged the *Enterprise* and killed 44 of her crew, but she was not crippled and was still operational.

However, her ability to juggle her chickens in the air was hampered by the jammed Number 1 elevator. Many of the Wildcats trying to protect her were now low on fuel and ammunition, but the *Enterprise* was having problems bringing anybody in. Just how badly was revealed at 10:20 when the *South Dakota*'s secondary battery and destroyers *Conyngham* and *Smith* opened fire on a submarine surfacing 4,000 yards from the *Smith*. Why an enemy submarine would surface in broad daylight in the midst of an enemy formation that included destroyers and battleships was a question apparently asked by no one, except by the destroyer *Preston*, who realized the submarine was actually the ditched TBF Avenger flown by Lieutenant Norton. The Avenger was sunk by the gunfire; the *Preston* had to dodge the *South Dakota*'s 5-inch shells as she moved to pick up Norton and his crew.[84]

At 10:30 am, Admiral Kinkaid received a message from Admiral Good on the *Northampton*. It was good news, sort of: "[*Hornet*] stopped burning. Request fighter coverage."[85] But there was no way. The *Enterprise* had barely enough fighters to defend herself, let alone the *Hornet*. And she would have to defend herself very soon; at 10:35 the *Enterprise* radar had a contact at bearing 330 degrees that, five minutes later, resolved itself into another large group of unidentified aircraft.

Having apparently learned from his previous mistakes, Commander Griffin had told 11 Wildcats on station to climb. Then he seems to have forgotten about seven of them. He vectored two fighters under Lieutenant Commander Kane and two more under Lieutenant Pollock to check out the contact, but said nothing to Lieutenant Vejtasa leading four Wildcats or the three under Lieutenant Faulkner. Undeterred, Vejtasa went out there anyway, while Faulkner went to the west, in the process going through a cloud and losing contact with wingman Ensign Gordon F. Barnes, who crashed off the *South Dakota*'s starboard quarter. The destroyer *Maury* moved in to pick him up.

The large bogey was the *Zuikaku*'s second strike: 16 Type 97s with torpedoes, one Type 97 as observer, all under Lieutenant Imajuku, with an escort of four Zeros under Warrant Officer Shigemi Katsuma. Imajuku planned yet another anvil attack for the *Enterprise*, and he kept eight carrier attack planes in a first division under himself to attack from the starboard bow, while eight more under Lieutenant Yusuhara Masayuki would attack from the starboard bow. Before entering a squall that had formed between the *Enterprise* and the Japanese carriers, the Japanese formation split.

And ran into a buzzsaw of Wildcats. The third time was the charm for Commander Griffin.

The first to engage were two of Lieutenant Vejtasa's four Wildcats who had independently decided to intercept the attackers. Vejtasa led Lieutenant Leroy E. "Tex" Harris in slashing at Lieutenant Yusuhara's division. Vejtasa and Harris shot up two before combining to set fire to the Type 97 of Petty Officer 1st Class Toshida Ken'ichiro, which went down shortly thereafter.

Hoping to lose his tormentors, Lieutenant Yusuhara led the Type 97s straight into the squall with Vejtasa and other Wildcats hot on their tails. Lieutenant Pollock perforated the Nakajima of Petty Officer 3rd Class Kikuchi Yasuo, while Vejtasa hacked away at three more, but all kept going.

Lieutenant Imajuku led his eight carrier attack planes in at wave-top level, flying under the storm and straight into the arms of Wildcats who were low on fuel and ammunition waiting to land on the *Enterprise*. The *Hornet*'s Ensign Wrenn took off after Imajuku, who was caught in a crossfire between Wrenn, the 20mm guns of the *Maury*, and the port 5-inch battery of the *Enterprise*. Imajuku's Kate lost its port wing and cartwheeled into the water. Ensign James H. Dowden of Fighting 10 knocked out another. That was the good news, but in turning to deal with the attacking Kates, the *Maury* had to stop its recovery of Ensign Barnes and was never able to relocate him.

The remaining six Type 97s bored in against heavy antiaircraft fire. Petty Officer 1st Class Kawada Tadayoshi dropped his torpedo from the *Enterprise*'s starboard beam and roared down the starboard side. The carrier's starboard gunners all targeted the Kate, but all missed. It was said that the Kate's gunner extended his arm and raised his middle finger as a gesture of his respect for the US Navy.[86] He might have changed his mind had he known his torpedo had also missed.

Petty Officer 1st Class Kawabata Oyoshi did not like the setup and flew past the carrier looking for another opportunity. Three Type 97s under Lieutenant (jg) Ito Tetsu were happy with the setup and combined for a well-executed torpedo attack off the *Enterprise*'s starboard bow, releasing three torpedoes abreast. Captain Hardison was able to turn the carrier to starboard and comb the torpedoes. The Kates got off scot free. For now.

The three torpedoes bubbled onward, toward the heavy cruiser *Portland*. Her engineers had been trying to correct, of all things, a sudden steering breakdown at 10:53 that caused her to swing out of control to port, when they saw the torpedoes with no way to avoid them. They felt three "separate, sharp and severe jolts" at 10:55. The torpedoes had all thunked against the cruiser's side, but coming as their runs ended and they lost momentum, apparently not hard enough to detonate the warheads.[87]

Two more Type 97s, those of Special Duty Ensign Suzuki Nakakura and Petty Officer 1st Class Yukawa Nagao, could not get into a good attack position for the *Enterprise*, so they turned to port to attack the battleship *South Dakota* from astern. Yukawa dropped his torpedo and turned away. Suzuki was not so lucky. Antiaircraft guns having torched his Type 97, Suzuki tried dropping his torpedo like a bomb on the battleship's fantail. The torpedo sailed completely over the stern to plop into the water 20 yards off the port quarter. Then Suzuki himself flew over the stern and splashed 200 yards beyond. Yukawa saw Suzuki's splashes and concluded he had gotten a hit.[88]

Trying to execute the anvil with Lieutenant Imajuku's group, the one damaged and five healthy Nakajimas of Lieutenant Yusuhara's division burst out of the cloud aimed at the *Enterprise*. The *Enterprise*'s Lieutenant Vejtasa hung onto them like a leech and thoroughly disrupted the timing of the attack, but he ran out of bullets as he was shooting up the Kate of Seaman 1st Class Takei Kiyomi. Vejtasa "gave serious consideration to cutting off his tail with my prop as we had discussed in our training," but was forced to pull up by American flak.[89] With his Type 97 burning and unable to reach the carrier, Takei turned toward the destroyer *Smith* off the *Enterprise*'s port quarter to make a proto-kamikaze run. At 10:48, he drove his Type 97 into the destroyer's 5-inch Mount 2, the torpedo breaking free and landing on deck, the fuselage continuing onward onto Mount 1, where it exploded and blew itself over the side. Burning gasoline was spewed everywhere and detonated the warhead for the torpedo. With its bow an inferno, the *Smith* sheered out to starboard.[90]

This caused a problem for the *Enterprise*. Captain Hardison had just avoided the three torpedoes launched by Lieutenant Ito's Kates when the *Smith* appeared ready to plow into the carrier's stern. The skipper turned hard to port to swing the stern out of the way. Still lurking to starboard like a maritime vulture, Petty Officer Kawabata saw this as his chance to launch his torpedo. He came in and launched his torpedo from dead ahead of the carrier, an aerial version of what submariners called the "down the throat" shot. It could be a difficult shot to avoid. Especially when the torpedo is first seen when it's only 800 yards away.

But Captain Hardison swung to starboard to swing the stern out of the way – again – and the torpedo passed only 100 yards away from the starboard side. For good measure, the aforementioned now-recovered Marshall Field used his 1.1-inch mount in the forecastle to knock Kawabata's Kate out of the sky and force it to ditch only a few hundred yards away. As the crew crawled out of the sinking Type 97, Lieutenant Commander Mott used the bullhorn to call attention to the survivors. He wanted prisoners. The gunners did not and, to Mott's horror, blasted what was left of the Kate and its crew.

The remaining five Type 97s of Lieutenant Yusuhara's attack bored in through very heavy flak. Having had to deal with Imajuku, the *Smith*, and Kawabata, Captain Hardison kept the *Enterprise* in her dance, maintaining a stern facing to the nettlesome Nakajimas. Four dropped their torpedoes, only one of which even came close and was easily avoided. But the fifth, piloted by Seaman 1st Class Oma Rinzo and commanded by Petty Officer 1st Class Yamauchi Kazuo, for reasons known only to Oma, just flew up to the *Enterprise*'s stern. Two landing signal officers, lieutenants James G. Daniels and Robin Lindsey, manned rear .30cals in Dauntlesses aft on the carrier's flight deck and apparently wounded or killed Oma, causing his Kate to spin out and crash near the cruiser *Portland*. Daniels, Air Group 10 landing signal officer, said shooting down the Kate was "the most fun I've had."[91]

The remaining Nakajimas headed out at wave-top height toward the *Zuikaku* and safety, but not before two of Lieutenant Ito's planes had blundered into ensigns Feightner and Gordon and the ubiquitous Lieutenant Swede Vejtasa. Feightner targeted the nearer Kate and Vejtasa joined him by emptying his guns. Trailing fire, the Kate staggered onward for 5 miles before crashing. It was Vejtasa's fifth Kate and seventh kill overall for this flight.[92]

Ensign Gordon wanted to knock down the other Kate, which would be a neat trick since he was out of bullets. He decided to come in head-on. The Japanese pilot had been glancing back when he looked ahead again and was shocked to see an American fighter coming straight at him on a collision course. He dipped his left wing to roll out of the way, but at an approximate altitude of 10 feet, the wing dipped into the water, causing the Type 97 to cartwheel into the sea and explode. It was, indeed, a neat trick.[93]

The Japanese had attacked the *Enterprise* with 16 Type 97s. They came out with eight.

The destroyer *Smith* was left to manage the conflagration on her bow as best she could. The intense heat forced her skipper, Lieutenant Commander Hunter Wood, to clear the bridge at 10:49. After a fashion, they were able to re-establish control from the secondary conn. Wood was able to phone directions to helmsman Chief Quartermaster Frank Riduka, who steered the *Smith* through the formation into the wake of the speeding *South Dakota*. The spray put out most of the fires on the bow and enabled the *Smith*'s crew to get control of the situation. The attack cost the destroyer 57 officers and men, but she and her crew did get some important prizes out of it: nine Navy Crosses, 13 Silver Stars, two Bronze Stars, and, from the remnants of Yamauchi's Type 97, a document that contained the newest aircraft codes for the Imperial Japanese Navy.[94]

Like the *Smith*, the *Enterprise* went back to licking her wounds, while also trying to manage the chickens still flying. They all hoped for a breather to rest, refuel, and rearm.

They got a half-hour.

There was still one Japanese aircraft carrier out there. Not part of *Kido Butai*, indeed never part of the Japanese Naval Air Force's "A-Team," it was the weird *Junyo*. Her cruise liner roots meant her engines could not produce the speed of the carriers of *Kido Butai*. She was so slow that she struggled to launch heavy torpedo-armed Type 97 carrier attack planes in the absence of a strong headwind, so slow that Commander Hara called her "the most sluggish carrier in service."[95]

With her sister *Hiyo* currently out of action, the *Junyo* alone formed the 2nd Carrier Division, under Rear Admiral Kakuta Kakuji. The beefy Kakuta was highly aggressive. His answer to every tactical problem was to attack. Okumiya Masatake would later say Kakuta "would not hesitate to sail his ship directly into the enemy fleet and ram the largest enemy carrier he could find."[96] It tended to simplify things a great deal.

That morning, when Admiral Kakuta learned the enemy was 330 miles away, he stamped his feet like an angry six-year-old in a toy store. He ordered full speed to the southeast. To the shock of her escorting destroyers, the *Junyo* "sprang" away from her escorting destroyers. It took them an hour to catch up.[97]

At 9:05, the *Junyo,* calculating range to the Americans to be about 280 miles, launched 17 Type 99s under Lieutenant Yamaguchi Masao, escorted by 12 Zeros under Pearl Harbor veteran Lieutenant Shiga Yoshio, to attack the US Navy carriers.[98] Now the *Junyo* could prepare a second strike of seven Type 97s armed with torpedoes. Admiral Kakuta was happy.

The beleaguered carrier USS *Enterprise* was not. She had 18 Wildcats in orbit – 13 from the *Enterprise*, five from the *Hornet*, and almost all low on fuel and ammunition. She was struggling to land them because her Number 1 elevator – the most forward of the carrier's three aircraft elevators to the hangar deck – was damaged, fortunately in the up position, and no one wanted to risk using it. Then the Number 2 elevator – amidships – got stuck. In the down position.

As if things were not complicated enough, at 10:58, after the *Zuikaku*'s torpedo attack, the drive motor for the big CXAM radar stopped rotating. Now the *Enterprise* was blind to incoming attackers.

Lieutenant Dwight M. B. "Brad" Williams, the radar officer – the first in the US Navy to be so designated – figured the bedspring antenna, jarred by that bomb from the *Shokaku* and shaken by strafing, had been knocked out of alignment, causing the drive motor to go out. Williams grabbed his toolbox and climbed the mast to the highest and most exposed point on the *Enterprise* to fix the radar. Lieutenant Williams held on to the *Enterprise*'s radar antenna with one hand while trying to fix it with the other. It quickly became evident that this was a two-handed job, so he lashed himself to the big bedspring antenna and worked on the drive motor.

Without radar, all Commander Griffin could tell the fighters was "Remain close to base; no definite bogeys now," which was technically true, for the *Enterprise*.[99]

But it was not for the *South Dakota*, whose radar at 11:01 picked up unidentified aircraft 45 miles to the northwest, about which Griffin was never told. Nor for the *Portland*, who at 11:10 advised unidentified aircraft to the west; however, Admiral Kinkaid said they were friendly. The issue with the Number 2 elevator was fixed, and at 11:15, the *Enterprise* started taking aircraft on board again. There were some 36 aircraft in the carrier's landing circle.[100] Three *Hornet* Wildcats, including that of Lieutenant Commander Sanchez, touched down, followed by four more from both carriers.

The next was the *Hornet*'s Ensign Souza, all alone. He had escorted the damaged Wildcat of wounded Lieutenant Roberts all the way back to the *Hornet*. But it was for naught. The *Hornet* was in no shape to be taking anyone aboard. To make matters worse, the light antiaircraft cruiser *Juneau* opened fire on them, soon followed by other jittery ships. An exasperated Souza shouted into the radio, "Christ sake stop shooting at me! I haven't a hell of a lot of gas!"[101]

His friend Lieutenant Roberts had none. Despite his serious wounds, Roberts tried gliding all the way back to the *Enterprise* task force, but went down just short of the formation. Roberts got out of his sinking fighter and deployed his dye marker, but while Ensign Souza tried to get the attention of screening destroyers, the badly wounded Roberts disappeared.

Ensign Souza could not get the destroyers' attention because, at that moment, they were dealing with the second strike from the *Zuikaku*. Souza even helplessly watched the destroyer *Smith* get hit. Now he was finally set to land his shot-up Wildcat on the

Enterprise. He touched down and the arresting gear yanked his fighter to a stop. Then the aircraft handlers all bolted for cover.

Working fast and under the most difficult conditions imaginable, Lieutenant Williams fixed the drive motor for the radar. In the radar room, desperate to get the CXAM back in operation, someone ordered the radar turned on, and the big bedspring antenna started rotating, with Williams still lashed to it. But it did reveal the unidentified aircraft just 20 miles away. Unlike Admiral Kinkaid, Commander Griffin had a bad feeling about this. "They may not all be friendly," he announced.[102]

It was an understatement, which Griffin corrected with, "All planes in the air prepare to repel attack." At 11:19 the *South Dakota* opened fire with her antiaircraft battery, but it turned out to be some fighters from the *Hornet*, who were none too pleased about that. Then someone got a visual on the unknown intruders. "Bandits reported above clouds. All planes in air standby to repel attack approaching from north. Above clouds! Above clouds!"[103]

Lieutenant Shiga had the "bastards," as the *South Dakota* called them in her report, charge downward out of the aforementioned clouds, with only half his command. Shiga had told his inexperienced pilots, "Don't separate. That's an order." But separate they did.[104]

Shiga had lost sight of Lieutenant Yamaguchi when Yamaguchi had led the nine Type 99s of his division into a cloud. As soon as Shiga saw a carrier "with a bone in its teeth" through a break in the clouds, he signaled for the Zeros to drop their tanks – which actually dropped – and Lieutenant Miura Naohiko led the remaining eight Type 99s down on to the *Enterprise* at 11:21.[105]

By now, for the besieged *Enterprise,* the Japanese air attacks had crossed from dangerous and deadly to obnoxious. The combat air patrol pilots had exhausted their ammunition, their fuel, and their patience. The antiaircraft gunners were just sick and tired of these insufferable attacks. And as the gunners were trying to repel the repellant, as the ship was heeling over in evasive turns, Lieutenant Williams was still lashed to the radar going round and round. His angry shouts and curses got no attention over the noise of the guns, and Williams rotated with his radar a dozen times before someone noticed and stopped the CXAM long enough for him to climb off.[106]

Diving from the stern at a shallow angle, the Japanese faced no fighter opposition but were heading into the teeth of the 40mm Bofors and 20mm Oerlikons. Lieutenant Miura's Val was set afire and crashed. His wingman, Petty Officer 1st Class Yabuki Katsuyoshi, had the tail blown off his Val. His other wingman, Petty Officer 2nd Class Kataoka Yoshiharu, dropped his bomb, and then followed it straight into the water in the wake of the *Enterprise*. The *Enterprise*'s evasive maneuvers had caused Ensign Souza's Wildcat, its landing gear collapsed, to slide on its belly toward the starboard 5-inch gun gallery. The handlers on deck had to push it overboard. To Souza this was a small tragedy; he had left his sunglasses on its gunsight.[107]

The next section was led by Warrant Officer Honmura Masataka. He managed to drop a bomb that glanced off the port bow near the waterline and detonated less than 10 feet from the hull. The concussion dented and ruptured hull plating. None of the other dropped bombs came close to hitting, but Lieutenant Williams, still trying to climb down from the radar, was stunned to look up and see a ball falling toward him from above. As it got closer and closer, the ball resolved itself into the shape of a bomb that just missed him, but fell off to starboard and exploded, destroying his hearing for weeks afterward.[108]

Lieutenant Yamaguchi's Aichis managed to lose track of each other in the clouds. They never managed to find the *Enterprise*, but they did find some other American ships.

Yamaguchi and three friends dove on the battleship *South Dakota*, who had just been admonished by Admiral Kinkaid over the voice radio for firing at friendly aircraft who were now intermixed with enemy aircraft. The order inhibited the use of the highly effective flak guns. The *South Dakota*'s skipper, Captain Thomas Gatch, had been watching the air attacks from a catwalk in front of the armored conning tower. Advised to move inside, Gatch refused, saying he wouldn't "duck for any damned bomber."[109]

Such thinking worked for the first three bombs, which straddled the battleship's bow, but the fourth struck squarely on the top of 16-inch Turret 1. The turret was so heavily armored that the crew inside didn't even know they had been hit.[110] But Captain Gatch immediately did. Shrapnel severed his juggler vein; if it hadn't been for the immediate availability of a corpsman who stopped the bleeding, he would have died. After the bleeding was stopped Captain Gatch went back on duty with his arm and neck immobilized, his arm positioned over his head due to the nature of the wound.[111] The battleship temporarily lost steering control and veered toward the *Enterprise*.

The remaining five Type 99s dove down on the light antiaircraft cruiser *San Juan*. This was normally a very stupid thing to do, but because Admiral Kinkaid had discouraged the use of antiaircraft fire, her barrels were mostly silent. She immediately took three near-misses. A fourth glanced off the starboard side and detonated in the water, damaging her hull. Then one bomb passed completely though her stern to detonate underneath her keel. The entire ship was lifted out of the water and twisted sideways. The shock activated the smoke generator, causing the *San Juan* to belch so much smoke that everyone around her was convinced she was burning, a belief buttressed by the fact that she was steaming in circles.[112]

Two large ships steaming out of control at the same time was a bit nerve-wracking for those around them, especially the destroyers. The *Maury*'s skipper G. L. Sims observed, "During [this] attack adjacent ships seemed to change identity with marked rapidity."[113] But the *South Dakota* quickly regained steering control, while the *San Juan* had merely suffered a tripped circuit breaker that froze the rudder and was cleared up in a matter of minutes.

Lieutenant Yamaguchi's Aichis broke for home, but got themselves ensnared in the jammed landing circle for the *Enterprise*. Here were the Wildcats returning from the *Hornet*'s second strike and they still had their ammunition. Four Vals, including Yamaguchi's, were shot down, two by the *Hornet*'s Lieutenant Sutherland. One Val from Lieutenant Miura's group was downed by the *Hornet*'s Lieutenant (jg) Henry A. "Al" Fairbanks.[114]

Lieutenant Commander Flatley's four *Enterprise* Wildcats were returning from escorting their tiny strike. When Flatley saw Zeros prowling around, he decided to try those scissoring tactics from Lieutenant Commander Thach. His guinea pig would turn out to be the veteran Lieutenant Shiga, who had managed to separate himself from all the other Japanese and decided it was a good idea to attack four Grumman fighters by himself.

This one-on-four fast break turned out better than most one-on-four fast breaks, but nevertheless not how Lieutenant Shiga had intended. He made three or four passes, but every time he got a Wildcat in his sights, he found himself in the sights of another. Ultimately, he gave up and flew away. It occurred to the highly intelligent Shiga that this new tactic was why so many Zeros had been shot down of late.[115] He would later say, "That teamwork was very good." The performance was summed up as "No runs, no hits, and no errors."[116]

Lieutenant Commander Flatley would give the maneuver the name by which it has become famous: "The Thach Weave." He accurately described it as "undoubtedly the greatest contribution to air combat tactics that has been made to date."[117]

While Lieutenant Shiga was trying his one-on-four, two of his Zeros tried a two-on-one. The one was the PBY Catalina of redoubtable Lieutenant Haber. The two fighters seemed to think all they needed to do was show up and the PBY would be shot down. Haber, having already fought off five Zeros, had other ideas. The Japanese pilots later claimed to have shot down Haber's "Consolidated," but Haber set his PBY down safely in Espiritu Santo four hours later with no rudder or elevator control and with 144 bullet holes – 78 between the rear blisters and the tail.[118]

The returning Dauntlesses from the *Hornet* also threw themselves into service to defend their home away from home. Three Scouting 8 SBDs led by Lieutenant Edgar E. Stebbins caught sight of three of Lieutenant Yamaguchi's Vals speeding away low over the water and turned to give chase. Stebbins was slowly catching up to the trailing Val, which moved lower and lower to stay out of Stebbins' gunsights. As Stebbins was about to shoot, to his shock, the Val's wing caught the water, causing the plane to cartwheel to a spectacular end, without firing a shot.[119] It was a neat trick for the second time today.

Not as neat was the trick pulled by the three returning Dauntlesses under the *Enterprise*'s Lieutenant Estes. The SBDs' gunners were shooting away merrily at a Zero, only to discover that it was actually the SBD of the *Hornet*'s Lieutenant Holm. Estes later apologized to Holm. Privately, however, Estes was livid at his gunners. For not only had they failed to identify their target as an American plane before shooting at it; they hadn't even hit it.[120]

But the costs were rapidly adding up. During these aerial battles, two Wildcats, flown by Fighting 10's Ensign Davis and Fighting 8's Lieutenant (jg) Morrill I. Cook, and one Avenger, piloted by Torpedo 6's Lieutenant (jg) Rufus C. Clark, disappeared. The *Enterprise* simply had to bring these aircraft down.

The carrier resumed flight operations, but she was in desperate shape. Her forward elevator was out, which slowed striking aircraft below. As of 11:40 am, in the air were no fewer than 73 aircraft: 28 Wildcats (nine *Hornet*, 19 *Enterprise*); 24 Dauntlesses (21 *Hornet*; three *Enterprise*), none of which had folding wings; and 21 Avengers (15 *Hornet*, six *Enterprise*). All were critically low on fuel.

The *Enterprise* had to recover as many planes as possible. Commander Crommelin had promised, "If you get back to the ship and into the groove, we'll get you aboard." The "groove" was, basically, the final approach for landing on the carrier. Moreover, "the fate of US carrier air operations in the Pacific for the next several months literally hung upon Landing Signal Officer Lieutenant Jim Daniels' decision-making powers."[121]

Daniels got to work. The first to land were the Wildcats, who were the worst off in terms of fuel. Not all of them made it. Lieutenant Billo was waved off twice. Running out of fuel, he ditched and was picked up by the destroyer *Preston*. The *Preston* heroically fished 11 aviators out of the drink without being torpedoed. Not yet, anyway.

Lieutenant Daniels managed to land more than 60 aircraft, some badly damaged. Exhausted from flapping his arms and feeling the strain, Daniels turned over this particular orchestra to senior landing signal officer Lieutenant Robin Lindsey, who would bring in the last 30.

The flight deck kept getting more and more full, the mass of stopped aircraft moving further and further aft, leaving fewer and fewer arrester wires for the landing planes to catch. When aircraft packed the flight deck so far that the only remaining available arrester wires were the Number 1 and 2 wires – those farthest aft – the bridge ordered the landings halted. But Commander Crommelin kept the *Enterprise* turned into the wind. She would keep landing aircraft as long as there was any room at all.

Lieutenant Lindsey proved himself a true virtuoso. As Lieutenant Daniels would elaborate: "He played those pilots like a master, slowing them down, easing the tension by signaling Roger – 'Everything OK' – then bringing them in slowly and carefully – no waveoffs allowed – until he got everyone aboard."[122]

And he did. In 43 minutes Crommelin, Daniels, and Lindsey landed 47 planes – 23 Wildcats and 24 Dauntlesses – without an accident. The last was that of the indefatigable Swede Vejtasa.[123] In so doing, they saved American naval air power in the South Pacific. Five Wildcats had to ditch, but no Dauntlesses did.

Her flight deck bursting, the *Enterprise* cut off landings to strike aircraft below before recovering the remaining 21 Avengers still in the air. Some were actually vectored to check out a suspicious contact. That turned out to be the PBY Catalina of the redoubtable Lieutenant Haber and his crew, on their merry way back to Espiritu Santo, where they could report a successful scouting mission, a repulse of seven Zeros who thought them shot down – twice – and 144 bullet holes. Tough guys, these Catalina crews.

The Avengers were running out of time while the *Enterprise* sorted the Wildcats from the Dauntlesses so the latter could be struck below while the former were rearmed and refueled. The *Hornet*'s Commander Rodee, in his command Avenger, had extra fuel, so he headed down to Espiritu Santo. The *Enterprise* was finally able to launch a force of 25 protective fighters at 12:51, the first aircraft she had been able to launch in more than four hours.[124] The deck was quickly cleared and at 1:18 they were able to take ten Avengers aboard. Eight were forced to ditch, their crews all rescued.

She would later launch 13 SBDs to head to Espiritu Santo in order to relieve overcrowding on the carrier. While spotting this group, the Avenger of Lieutenant Welles returned, his planned one-plane attack on the Combined Fleet aborted by three Japanese Zeros who forced him to jettison his torpedo. He could not land, but was able to ditch; he and his crew were rescued by the destroyer *Maury*.

Admiral Kinkaid knew they were lucky. The *Enterprise* was still – barely – operational. He believed, correctly, there were still one or two undamaged Japanese carriers out there. Kinkaid had to make a very difficult and painful decision, but he did so "without hesitation." He had to get the *Enterprise* out of danger. He signaled Admiral Halsey and Admiral Murray: "I am proceeding southeastward toward [Efate]. When ready proceed in the same direction." At 11:55 Kinkaid signaled Admiral Good, "If Murray safe direct him to take charge salvaging operations. Have been under continuous air attack. Otherwise you take charge."[125]

As damage reports continued coming in, at 3:40 Kinkaid was forced to report to Admiral Halsey that the damage to the *Enterprise* was far worse previously thought. Halsey understood the danger and ordered all forces to "retire to southward."[126]

Heading on a course of 123 degrees True, speed 27 knots, the *Enterprise*, now carrying 84 aircraft, was already doing so.

But could the *Hornet*?

By this time, despite the damage to the *Shokaku* and the *Zuiho*, the reportedly heavy damage done to the American carriers was leaving the Japanese feeling good about themselves. On the bridge of the *Junyo*, Admiral Kakuta listened to the reports coming in with satisfaction. He turned to his air officers and said, "Our men have become quite proficient. The ship functions as a team. Perhaps we shall compensate for Midway."[127]

The *Junyo* and two destroyers were on their way to join the *Zuikaku*. Admiral Kondo had been informed of the *Shokaku*'s situation and at 10:18 had ordered *Junyo* to essentially take her place. Kondo had also been informed of the heavy damage to American ships. Sensing total victory within his grasp, Kondo had the Advance Force and Admiral Abe's Vanguard Force dash toward the Americans.

But there was some inkling that this particular silver cloud had a dark lining. Lieutenant Commander Okumiya watched the *Junyo*'s strike return:

> Lookouts sighted the planes straggling in toward the carrier; only six Zeros flew formation. The remainder flew in from all directions. We searched the sky with apprehension. There were only a few planes in the air in comparison to the number launched several hours before. We could see only five or six dive bombers. The planes lurched and staggered onto

> the deck, every single fighter and bomber bullet-holed. Some planes were literally flying sieves. As the pilots climbed wearily from their cramped cockpits they told of unbelievable opposition, of skies choked with antiaircraft shellbursts and tracers.[128]

The senior surviving bomber pilot from the attack was a junior-grade lieutenant, Kato Shunko. In reporting the results of the attack to *Junyo* skipper Captain Okada Tametsugu, Kato "was so shaken that at times he could not speak coherently. Young and lacking experience in circumstances where his friends died all around him, he had suffered a nasty shock."[129]

It was a story repeated on the *Zuikaku* and other ships as well. Three carrier attack plane squadron leaders, including the irreplaceable Lieutenant Commander Murata, had been lost. Two of three carrier bomber squadron leaders, including Lieutenant Commander Seki, were gone, as were most of the section leaders – 148 aviators in all. The young and inexperienced pilots who did return were so shell-shocked that they could not even give a coherent report. Consequently, Admiral Nagumo believed there were three US carriers – one crippled and two undamaged.

Nagumo radioed at 11:32, "Cancel assumption that there is an enemy carrier south of the first carrier."[130] He wanted Kakuta to ignore the damaged carrier and go after the other two, one being east of the damaged carrier, the other being northeast. In fact, there was only one carrier – undamaged, as far as Nagumo was concerned – the *Enterprise*, who was now indeed south of the "first carrier," the *Hornet*, and going further south. If the reader is getting confused here, imagine how the Japanese felt.

Not that it mattered much to Admiral Kakuta. He had only the vaguest idea of where these alleged two undamaged carriers were. But he was going to attack them. Kakuta launched his second strike at 1:06. Lieutenant Irikiin Yoshiaki would lead seven Type 97s escorted by eight Zeros – five from the *Junyo*, two from the *Zuikaku*, and one from the *Zuiho* – under the *Zuikaku*'s Lieutenant Shirane.[131]

At around the same time, the Americans' nemesis *Zuikaku* launched her third airstrike of the day, under Lieutenant (jg) Tanaka Ichiro of the *Zuiho*. The *Zuikaku* had managed to scrape together seven Type 97s – five from the *Zuiho* and two from the *Zuikaku*, six armed with bombs – under Tanaka's direct command, and two Type 99 bombers – one *Shokaku* and one *Zuikaku* – under the *Zuikaku*'s Petty Officer 1st Class Hori Kenzo. They were escorted by five Zeros – three from the *Zuikaku* and two from the *Shokaku* – under Lieutenant (jg) Kobayashi Hohei.[132]

The Japanese were not done yet. The *Zuikaku* went back to recovering as many aircraft as she could. They were desperately needed. That both strikes were led by very junior officers showed the wide swath of devastation that had been scythed through the aviators' senior ranks. Even now, a badly wounded Lieutenant Ishimaru, his observer already dead, was staggering back toward the *Zuikaku*. But he never made it; his beaten-up Type 99 was forced to ditch near the destroyer *Amatsukaze*. Commander Hara's crew brought Ishimaru aboard, but as they were treating his injuries Ishimaru muttered, "Mother!" and died. Ishimaru was one of 16 pilots picked up by the *Amatsukaze*, three of whom died.[133]

"Air Staff, go to the hangar deck and see how many of our remaining planes can be sent out immediately for further attacks," *Junyo*'s Captain Okada ordered. "Prepare nine fighters and six dive bombers for attack. Planes will take off immediately after servicing."[134]

It had been barely a half-hour since the badly shaken Lieutenant Kato had returned. Lieutenant Commander Okumiya sympathized with the young pilot, who, he would later write, "had literally gone through hell."[135] But the sympathy was little comfort to Kato when Okumiya told him he was to attack again. The lieutenant burst from his seat. "Again? Am I to fly again today?"

"Ton-chan!" The voice coming from across the room was Lieutenant Shiga's, using Kato's nickname. "This is war! There can be no rest in our fight against the enemy ... we cannot afford to give them a chance when their ships are crippled. Otherwise we will face those same ships again. We have no choice... We go!"

Lieutenant Kato stood up and said quietly, "I will go."[136] Shiga was not minimizing Kato's reluctance, for he had his own concerns. This next strike would have them return after dark. An operations officer asked if Shiga could do that.

"It's not a question of returning," replied Shiga. "It has to be done. If possible, send out a homing signal. If you don't send it out, I'll come back anyway. Then watch out!" It was a joke, mostly.[137]

Admiral Kakuta watched the preparations for this next attack in total silence. Lieutenant Commander Okumiya later wrote:

> The *Junyo* was a good ship. [Kakuta] ordered full steam ahead in the direction of the enemy. That was his only message to his men. So long as the ship continued on this course, every airplane capable of being launched from the deck would be launched to attack enemy forces... [Kakuta] was a hard but a courageous taskmaster.[138]

And on that comforting note, Admiral Kakuta courageously sent the aviators in six Zeros and four Type 99 dive bombers up at 3:35.[139] It was a "ludicrous situation," Okumiya thought, that these few planes were now more powerful than all the rest of the surface ships in the Advance Force.[140] Even so, the six Zeros and four dive bombers were nothing short of pitiful.

Unless they were unopposed.

The continuous air attacks on the *Enterprise* had been a godsend of sorts for the *Hornet*. Their fury at the performance of Commander Griffin as fighter director officer exceeded even that of the *Enterprise* pilots, but they had more pressing matters requiring their attention.

As their strike aircraft had returned, most of the pilots could see that the *Hornet* was in no shape to recover them and proceeded on their own to the *Enterprise*. Nevertheless, Admiral Good in the *Northampton* felt it necessary to signal "Go to Big E" – twice – to one group of three Wildcats, seven Dauntlesses, and six Avengers.[141] Unfortunately, the light antiaircraft cruiser *Juneau* was on the same bearing as the aircraft receiving the signal. When the message was repeated, the cruiser's skipper, Captain Lyman K. Swanson, thought it was meant for him, so he hauled out of formation and made full speed for the *Enterprise*. Admiral Murray realized that a mistake had been made, but before anyone could correct it he told Captain Mason, "Let her go. 'Big E' needs her more than we do."[142] So did Dauntless pilot Evan Fisher and radioman George Ferguson of Bombing 8, who had to ditch their damaged Douglas and were picked up by the cruiser.[143]

With the fires put out, the engineering team started trying to find a way to get some power back on the carrier. Water in the fuel lines had caused the fires in the boilers to go out. They had found an uncontaminated tank and were trying to get one of the boilers lit. Once that was done, they would get the steam to power the after engine room.

But she had no power yet and Japanese surface forces were too close for comfort. They had to get the *Hornet* moving. The cruiser *Northampton* was moving into positon for a tow. The crew of the *Hornet* put the end of a 1,200-foot, 1.25-inch-thick cable over the side. The *Northampton* moved in to pick it up, but when she had trouble getting into position, a rather brave sailor dove over the bow 60 feet into the water, took the end, and swam with it to the cruiser. By 11:05, the *Northampton* had it fastened and the men of the *Hornet* were winching it back to fasten to the port anchor.

But about five minutes later all the work came to a screeching halt. A Japanese plane had come out of the clouds. It looked like a Val. A snooper.

"Here comes the Lone Ranger," snorted someone among the antiaircraft guns. Gallows humor is almost always welcome in war.

The destroyers attending the *Hornet* cast off and pulled away. The gunners opened up on the bomber, who made a rather odd approach to the *Hornet*. The Americans watched his bomb fall.

"Yes, and here comes Silver, high-ho!"[144]

The bomb splashed to starboard of the *Hornet* and aft of the *Morris*. Close but not dangerously close – and not particularly explosive. Then, somehow evading the guns of every ship in the task force shooting at him, the plane roared out to altitude to continue watching.

As it turned out, the plane was not a Val at all, as the witnesses had assumed, but a Kate, a Type 97 flown by the *Zuiho*'s Warrant Officer Tanaka Shigenobu, who had decided to try to disrupt the salvage efforts. However, he did not have a bomb or a torpedo. He came in low like a glide bombing run and dropped a smoke marker.[145] Well played.

At least it was, until Tanaka stumbled across the SBD Dauntless of Lieutenant (jg) Forrester C. Auman of the *Hornet*. Auman came at Tanaka directly and riddled the Kate, then for good measure pulled up alongside so his tail gunner Aviation Radioman 3rd

Class Samuel P. McLean could pound Tanaka with his twin .30cal machine guns. Tanaka was never seen again.[146]

No harm, but some foul, since the towing operation was delayed by about 30 minutes. The *Northampton* moved back into position, a sailor dove overboard again, and the cable was secured at 11:34 am. At 12:23, the cruiser got under way, slowly, carefully trying to build up momentum to pull the *Hornet* forward.

This was not the easiest thing, with the carrier's rudder jammed 30 degrees to starboard. Imagine towing a car with its wheels turned left. The *Hornet* kept yawing to the right behind the *Northampton*. Still, the cruiser's skipper, Captain Willard A. Kitts, kept making adjustments to compensate for the yawing. Slowly, he built up the speed. One knot … two … three … four …

TWANG!

It sounded like gun shots. The carrier veered to starboard. The line went slack. The pelican hook holding it to the *Northampton* had snapped.[147]

Back to square one.

But the *Hornet* had a towing cable of her own, 10 tons, 1,200 feet, and 2 inches thick. It was the pride of Chief Boatswain Percy Bond. They just had to get it out of the pit for the Number 2 elevator. Hundreds of men went to work hauling it out.

Meanwhile, Admiral Murray had come to the reluctant conclusion that he could no longer command the force from the *Hornet*. He took the *Russell*'s whaleboat to the *Pensacola*, where the sailors who greeted him thought he looked "tired and despondent."[148]Admiral Good also transferred his flag to the *Pensacola*, since he could not command the screening ships from the *Northampton* as she was trying to tow the *Hornet*.

As they prepared to tow her again, the *Hornet* began transferring all her wounded and excess personnel to the destroyers circling the carrier "like Indians around a wagon train," especially the *Russell*, who took another backhanded blow from the swaying carrier.[149] By 2:40 pm, some 800 men had been transferred to the *Russell* and *Hughes*.

While this was going on, the *Northampton* was able to begin towing again at 1:30 pm. Slowly, carefully, Captain Kitts again built up speed. One knot, two … three … all the way to six knots, heading east to avoid Torpedo Junction.

Meanwhile efforts continued to get the *Hornet* moving on her own. Chief Engineer Pat Creehan and his men had managed to get one boiler lit and were building up pressure to get power to the after engine room. Commander Henry Moran, the *Hornet*'s damage control officer, crawled on the bottom of the *Hornet's* hull, including 70 feet though a flooded tunnel, to the stern to straighten the rudder. In so doing he had made his assessment of the carrier's structural wounds. They were bad, but she was salvageable. Things were looking up.

And in looking up, they saw the 12 aircraft from the *Junyo* under Lieutenant Irikiin. The *Northampton*'s CXAM radar had detected Irikiin hanging out to the northwest, where he seemed to "mill around for some time" hoping to find the two mythical undamaged American carriers. Unable to find them, Irikiin decided to go for the sure kill with the disabled *Hornet*. [150]

The number of attack planes was pitiful, but with no aerial opposition it would not matter. Admiral Murray asked Admiral Kinkaid for fighter support, but he knew there was no way Kinkaid could grant it. The men of the *Hornet* did not, though. On top of having the poor fighter direction of the *Enterprise* to blame for putting them in this mess, now they had the *Enterprise* to blame for abandoning them.

At 3:13, Lieutenant Irikiin started moving in. The *Northampton* cut the tow line and moved to join the other escorts in a protective circle around the carrier. Every antiaircraft gun that was able, and even a few of the main batteries, opened fire on the nettlesome Nakajimas. But the fire was not nearly as powerful as the Nakajimas had faced that morning, because of the mistake that sent the light antiaircraft cruiser *Juneau* away.

The Type 97s roared in from the *Hornet*'s starboard side. "With our air cover gone, the Japs pretty much had their own way," remembered Gunner's Mate Alvin Grahn.[151] Lieutenant Irikiin flew over the *Russell* and dropped his Type 91 torpedo. His six torpedo-armed mates dropped theirs as well against a carrier that was dead in the water. Four missed. A fifth hit and did not explode. But the sixth, dropped by Irikiin himself, with "a sickly green flash" buried itself in the *Hornet*'s side just aft of Lieutenant Commander Murata's earlier hit.[152]

In exactly the wrong place for the *Hornet*. Now, not only was the forward engine room flooded, but the after engine room as well. There was no way to restore power to get the carrier moving again on her own. The list increased back to 14 degrees.

Angry, heartbroken, the antiaircraft gunners lashed at the assassins of the *Hornet*, in the process hitting the talented Lieutenant Fleming, who had half his face blown off by antiaircraft shrapnel as he watched the proceedings. Executioner Lieutenant Irikiin pulled up after making his drop, then banked right, all the way into the water ahead of the *Northampton*. Antiaircraft fire had finally gotten him. Too late.

Flak also caught the Kate of Warrant Officer Yokoyama Takeo, who crashed off the *Hornet*'s port side. On the return leg two Zeros, under Petty Officer 1st Class Suzuki Kiyonobu and Seaman 2nd Class Nakamoto Kiyoshi, got separated from the returning strike and were never seen again. Three more Zeros later ditched. It was a very expensive attack.

But a successful one. It was now impossible for the *Hornet* to move under her own power, and she could not be towed because her towing cable had been ruined when the *Northampton* had been forced to cut it. There were no other towing cables available. And even if there was, she could never be towed fast enough to escape the Japanese surface forces known to be advancing on her position. The only choice was to scuttle her. Captain Mason gave the order to prepare to abandon ship.

This order became critical at 3:43 when the list increased to 20 degrees after a near-miss from the bombs of Petty Officer 1st Class Hori's two Type 99 dive bombers of the *Zuikaku*'s strike. About ten minutes later, Lieutenant Tanaka came in with six Type 97s armed with bombs, who planted all of one bomb on the *Hornet*'s flight deck near the stern, which did not do much except hasten the evacuation of the carrier. The wounded came off first, including Al Fleming, who would survive. Captain Mason was the last person to depart the *Hornet* at 4:27, after the ship had been evacuated "in a quiet and orderly manner[.]"[153]

Not that quiet. During the abandonment, Lieutenant Commander Dodson overhead one sailor ask another if he would reenlist. The answer became famous: "Goddammit yes! On the new *Hornet*!"[154]

Some 20 minutes later, Lieutenant Shiga's pitiful strike arrived. Lieutenant Kato's Type 99s put one more bomb on the flight deck, starting a fire that quickly burned itself out. They all returned safely to the *Junyo*, who avoided the wrath of Shiga by activating her beacon.[155]

Even so, Mason was not giving up totally on his ship. Once he got aboard the destroyer *Mustin*, he began discussing plans to put a salvage crew aboard the *Hornet* the next morning. She was not, in fact, sinking. That was a problem – the Japanese were coming and might be able to salvage her. Mason had to be given the bad news that at 6:40 pm Admiral Murray had ordered Commander Arnold E. True, who commanded the carrier's screening destroyers, to finish off the *Hornet*. A grim and emotional but relatively simple duty. In theory.

At 7:03 pm, after a very deliberate setup, the *Mustin* fired eight Mark 15 Model 1 torpedoes, each with the Mark 6 Model 1 exploder, at the *Hornet*'s port side, one at a time with a range of 2,000 to 3,000 yards.[156] The depth was set at 26 feet for the first three torpedoes, at 10 feet for the next four, and at 15 for the last torpedo. The speed was set at intermediate for the first five shots and low for the last three. Commander True and his crew, as well as Captain Mason and survivors of the *Hornet*, watched the torpedo wakes, "running hot, straight, and normal," disappear in the encroaching dark. They prepared themselves for the coming explosions.

But not for what happened next. The second Mark 15 torpedo reappeared, leaping into the air like a dolphin about 300 yards off the *Mustin*'s starboard quarter, at which point it exploded, showering the ship with fragments. The third Mark 15 also reappeared – astern of the carrier, running on a course about right angles to the angle at which it was fired. The fourth apparently exploded, though no one could tell where. What happened to the first and eighth torpedoes is anybody's guess. The fifth, sixth and seventh torpedoes did actually hit the *Hornet* and exploded like they were supposed to – but the badly listing carrier still did not sink and showed no signs she would do so any time soon.

After these "most discouraging results" according to Commander True, the *Mustin* was now out of torpedoes.[157] She had one job, which she could not do, in part because of torpedoes that did not work but also in part because she had, for some unknown reason, aimed at the undamaged port side, hitting which would have served to counter the starboard list.[158] By this time, Japanese floatplanes from Admiral Abe's force – one each from the *Nagara*, *Isuzu*, and *Maya* – were overhead, just outside antiaircraft range, watching the proceedings with, no doubt, some combination of amusement and bemusement.[159] Informed of the situation, at 7:40 Admiral Murray ordered the destroyer *Anderson* to finally end the *Hornet*'s agony.

The *Anderson* came over and launched eight Mark 15 torpedoes at a range of less than 2,000 yards. Soon after launch, one of the torpedoes turned about 3 degrees to the right and disappeared. A second torpedo detonated prematurely. Six of the torpedoes hit the carrier and exploded, but the effect was described as "negligible."[160] Now the *Anderson* was out of torpedoes. She had one job, which she could not do, because again the torpedoes did not work and again had been aimed at the undamaged port side.

As historian Samuel Eliot Morison put it, the "[r]esults were not complimentary to American torpedo performance[.]"[161] As Eric Hammel put it more succinctly, "[T]he results were humiliating[.]"[162] Indeed, this episode of the attempted scuttling of the *Hornet*, more than any other, was the pinnacle in the legend of the Mark 15 torpedo and its Mark 6 exploder.

But the *Mustin* and *Anderson* had no time to consider the dark humor of their situation. They were out of torpedoes. The other remaining American ships had fled the area. They and they alone had the job of denying the Japanese the use of the *Hornet*. They were keenly aware of those floatplanes overhead and what those floatplanes meant. They could not have known, however, that the situation was even more serious than they had realized. From Truk, Admiral Ugaki had ordered Admiral Kondo to attempt to capture and tow away the *Hornet*. The order was decrypted and read with extreme consternation at Pearl Harbor.[163]

The *Anderson* tried gunfire, firing 130 5-inch shells into the *Hornet*, trying to detonate the magazines or the fuel tanks. No luck, although the darkened hulk brightened with several fires. Also brightening was the sky – the Japanese floatplanes had started dropping flares to illuminate the area for incoming warships. At 9:15, a single surface contact appeared on the *Mustin*'s radar. It was not friendly. The Americans' time was running out, but the *Hornet* would not sink.[164]

Probably on the verge of panic, starting at 9:30, both the *Mustin* and the *Anderson* pumped more 5-inch shells into the *Hornet*'s hull. More fires bloomed on the empty carrier.[165] More contacts bloomed on the *Mustin*'s radar. They were out of time. If they stayed any longer, they risked facing about half of the Imperial Japanese Navy. Without torpedoes.

At 9:46, the *Mustin* and *Anderson*, after firing another 150 5-inch rounds each, with Japanese floatplanes watching them, sped off "leaving the hulk burning fiercely from end to end."[166]

Hot on their heels were the destroyers *Akigumo* and *Makigumo*, who arrived on the scene just 20 minutes later. They found a blazing wreck with a number "8" on her hull, which, the Japanese learned, identified her as the *Hornet*. Aided by the floatplanes, their unit, the 10th Destroyer Flotilla, pressed on, trying to catch the fleeing *Mustin* and *Anderson*. They gave up around midnight.[167]

Admiral Abe arrived with his battleships at around 11:20 pm and found the *Hornet* burning with induced explosions and a 45-degree list to starboard. Abe signaled Admiral Kondo about the state of the *Hornet*, while his staff put their heads together trying to figure out how they were going to tow the blazing carrier. Before they could do so, Kondo acknowledged Abe's message and, considering her "hopeless," ordered him to sink the carrier.[168]

By now, the fires on the *Hornet* were so intense that her hull was incandescent in places. The *Akigumo* and *Makigumo* positioned themselves and each launched two Type 93 torpedoes at the wreck. No premature detonations, no erratic runs, no disappearing without a trace with these Long Lances. All four hit the carrier and exploded, and at 1:35 am on October 27, the *Hornet* disappeared in a hissing shroud of steam as she slid beneath the waves, taking with her 118 of America's finest.[169] And with that, what would become known to history in the West as the Battle of the Santa Cruz Islands was over.

Just over the horizon, on the bridge of the *Junyo,* Admiral Kakuta and Lieutenant Commander Okumiya could see the glow from the fires on the *Hornet*.[170] They could see the glow dim as the carrier sank. The Imperial Japanese Navy had won a great victory. On Navy Day, no less. Kakuta could celebrate.

In the bowels of the *Junyo*, Lieutenant Shiga and his pilots could celebrate the victory, too. Amidst all the empty chairs at the dinner tables where their fellow aviators had sat only 24 hours before. Amidst all the plates of food sitting uneaten. Amidst the silence.

Shiga Yoshio did not feel like celebrating.[171]

Neither the US Navy nor any navy is "one big happy fleet." There are rivalries between ships, even within ships. Even during war. But when survivors of a naval disaster come aboard, those rivalries are put aside. The survivors become part of the family.

The *Enterprise* now had at least 20 new family members who had been fighter pilots on the *Hornet*. They came on board with nothing more than the clothes on their backs. The carrier opened to them, finding them quarters and personal items. In the fighter ready room, the newcomers sat in upholstered seats while the devoutly religious Jimmy Flatley performed his own welcoming ritual by anointing them with holy water. Jock Sutherland protested that he was not Roman Catholic. Flatley smiled and said, "It won't do you any harm."[172]

The *Enterprise* fighter pilots and their new brethren from the *Hornet* undoubtedly compared notes as to their experiences that day. How Swede Vejtasa had shot down five Kates in one mission, shot down seven overall this day; Flatley wrote in Vejtasa's flight logbook, "Greatest single combat flight record in the history of air warfare."[173] How George Wrenn had himself shot down five. And how air defenses were handled that day, especially the deployment of the fighters.

Lieutenant Commander Flatley was deeply concerned about the morale of his pilots. Those who had taken part in the defense of the *Enterprise* and *Hornet* considered the battle "an unmitigated disaster."[174] The pilots had been ready. When they intercepted Japanese, they had disrupted or destroyed them. They had done their job. But they had seen far too many Japanese just fly over their heads.

THE BATTLE OF SANTA CRUZ, 12:00–24:00HRS

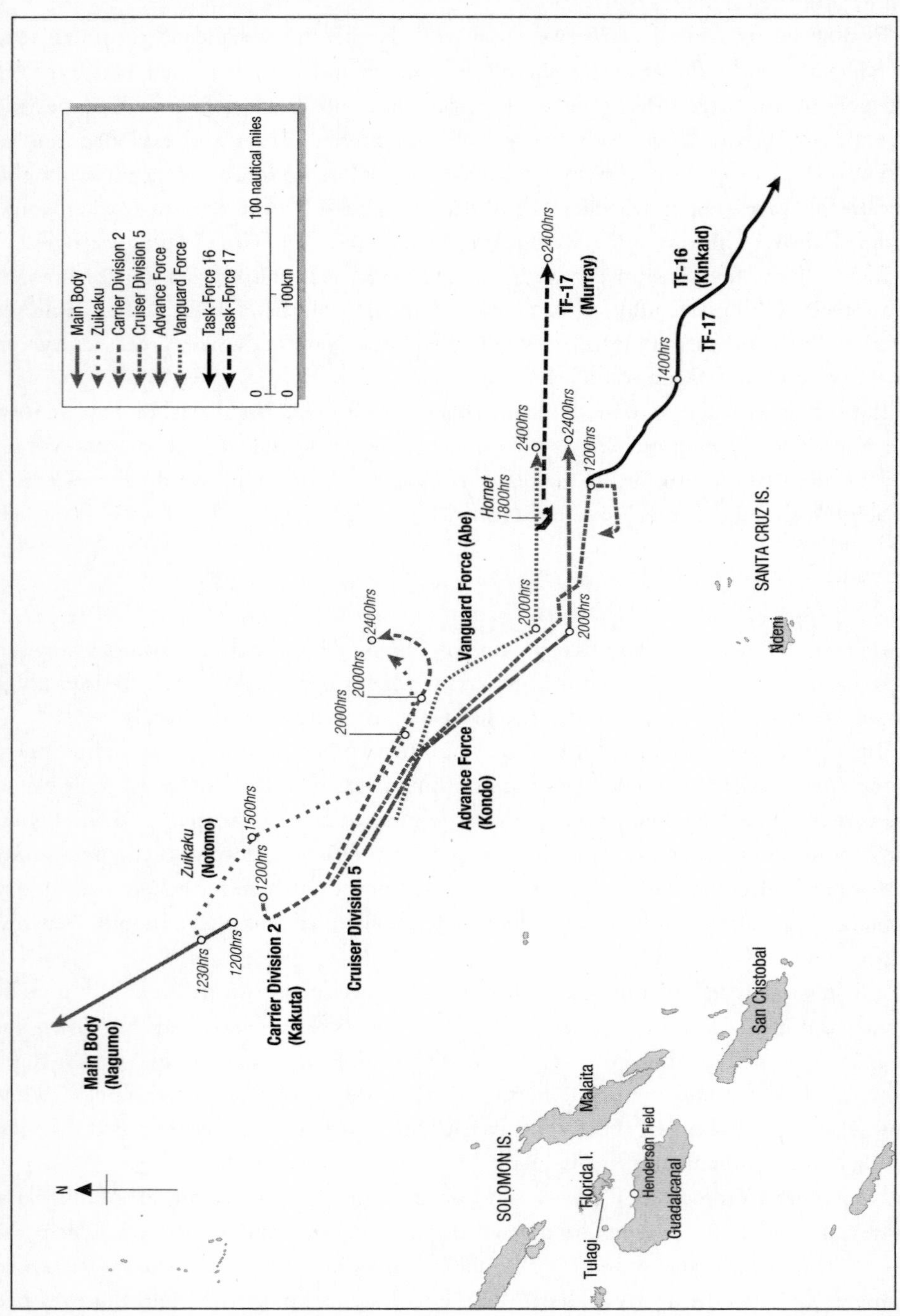

To Flatley they vented their anger at the fighter direction of the *Enterprise* in the form of one Commander Griffin. "Inadequate," Flatley would call it. Sanchez called it "ineffective." Even Captain Hardison would later call it a "disappointment."[175]

Late that night, Lieutenant Commander Flatley and Commander Crommelin hunted down Ensign George Givens, a junior fighter director officer, and ordered him to bring the radio logs and the fighter direction battle plot to the wardroom. Givens dutifully brought the ordered items to the wardroom, where they were spread out on a table. Givens didn't expect the Spanish Inquisition.

But Jimmy Flatley and John Crommelin were ready. Their chief weapon was surprise. And fear. With ruthless efficiency, Flatley and Crommelin pointed to specific instances in the records in front of them, bombarding Givens with questions like "Why this?" and "Why that?" Givens did his best to explain the various contacts and the fighter director officer's responses. The one who could really answer those questions was Commander Griffin, who, to his credit, was conducting his own examination of the fighter direction and his own performance.[176]

As unhealthy as it sounds, the anger of the pilots, of men like Jimmy Flatley, their cheekiness, their rage at being denied the chance to strike the enemy with full force, was badly needed right now. The *Enterprise* was now the only operational American aircraft carrier in the Pacific. And barely operational at that.

A sign appeared in her hangar, a message of defiance: "*Enterprise* versus Japan."[177]

EPILOGUE:

FAR FROM SATISFACTORY, FAR FROM HOPELESS

Nights in the Solomons were always strange territory. Almost unimaginably dark. Dank. Hot. Full of frightening, sinister noises. As if the world had returned to the old days, when stories abounded of the unspeakable horrors that happened in the night once one ventured outside safe, walled towns.

Even so, the night had always been Japanese territory. It certainly was not American territory. The Americans still endured unspeakable horrors in the night. Retreating from Santa Cruz through Torpedo Junction, Admiral Kinkaid's already-battered *Enterprise* task force suffered yet another injury. A little after 4:00 am, the destroyer *Conygham* reported a possible submarine contact, which was actually the Japanese submarine *I-15*.[1] The *Enterprise* made an emergency turn to port without signaling. The remaining ships in the task force turned to conform to the carrier's evasive maneuvers, except for the battleship *South Dakota* and the destroyer *Preston*. While in her turn, the destroyer *Mahan* found the battleship looming in front of her. The *Mahan*'s bow sliced into the *South Dakota*'s starboard quarter, leaving an anchor in the battlewagon's wardroom as a souvenir of the occasion. The *Mahan*'s bow was crumpled and bent to port, the rudder was jammed 30 degrees to port, and a fire was blazing in the forward hold. The fire put out and the rudder cleared, both ships headed to Nouméa. The *South Dakota*'s damage was almost enough to send her back to the US, but the repair ship *Vestal* was able to patch her up.[2]

Japanese submarines always infested Torpedo Junction, now more than usual in an effort to catch fleeing US ships. Admiral Lee's Task Force 64, with the battleship *Washington*, light antiaircraft cruiser *Atlanta*, and destroyers *Lardner*, *Lansdowne*, *McCalla*, and *Buchanan*, was no stranger to submarine attacks, having lost the *Chester* to torpedo damage a week earlier. At around 3:30 am, incoming torpedoes from the *I-24* were sighted, but they missed so badly that the *Washington* barely noticed them. Later, at 5:42 am, there was an explosion off the battleship's port quarter. It was yet another torpedo, one that had broached and detonated in the *Washington*'s sizable wake. A second torpedo crossed ahead of the battleship's bow from port to starboard. Both came with the compliments of the *I-21*, whose skipper, Commander Matsumura Kanji, heard the explosion and took it as a hit on the battleship.[3] The *Washington* continued her charmed existence.

Which was an anomaly for the Americans right now, especially at night. Both the Imperial Army and the Imperial Navy had geared their tactics toward taking advantage of the night, though as of late, the Army's tactics had proven deficient in the face of modernity. The Navy, despite Cape Esperance, still took pride in its night-fighting capability, still could go into a night battle and expect victory.

Admiral Kondo had the night-battle theory in mind immediately after the Battle of the Santa Cruz Islands as he tried to gather his forces for a continued pursuit of the Americans. But the night was becoming less and less friendly. Out of the dark in the wee hours of October 27 came three PBY Catalina flying boats to harass *Zuikaku* and *Junyo*. One PBY, piloted by Lieutenant Melvin K. Atwell, got a near-miss off the starboard beam of the antiaircraft destroyer *Teruzuki*, killing seven and wounding more than 40.[4] Lieutenant (jg) Donald L. Jackson piloted a second that nearly mugged the *Junyo* with a torpedo, but the carrier was able to avoid it.

Still, it was enough to spook the admiral into hustling his remaining carriers *Zuikaku* and *Junyo* out of the area. Many of the surface units milled around north of the Santa Cruz Islands, picking up four downed American aviators – ensigns Dusty Rhodes and Al Mead, Aviation Machinist Mate 3rd Class Murray Glasser, and Aviation Radioman 1st Class Tom Nelson – and three of their own. But they could do little in the way of operations because their fuel situation was getting dire; for instance, the fuel bunkers of Admiral Abe's destroyers were down to 30 percent.[5] When searches on October 27 revealed no American carrier forces nearby, Admiral Yamamoto ordered all ships to withdraw.

In response to this "Battle of the South Pacific," as the Japanese would call the Battle of the Santa Cruz Islands, Emperor Hirohito issued an imperial rescript:

> The Combined Fleet is at present striking heavy blows at the enemy Fleet in the South Pacific Ocean. We are deeply gratified. I charge each of you to exert yourselves to the utmost in all things toward this critical turning point in the war.[6]

It's hard to argue that Santa Cruz was anything less than a Japanese tactical victory. The Japanese had literally chased the Americans from the field, or, more properly, the sea. In so doing, the Japanese had sunk one aircraft carrier. The Americans had sunk one destroyer. That's an uneven exchange even before considering that the destroyer the Americans had sunk was one of their own. The Japanese suffered severe damage to the

Shokaku and serious damage to the *Zuiho* and *Chikuma*, which would keep them out for extended periods of time. The Americans had suffered heavy damage to the *San Juan* and *Smith*, relatively light damage to the *South Dakota*, and heavy damage to the *Enterprise*, the last remaining (mostly) operational American carrier in the Pacific. By any measure, it was a Japanese tactical victory.

Whether it was a strategic victory for Japan is not nearly as clear. It can be (and has been) argued that because the Japanese now possessed the only fully operational carrier force in the Pacific, the battle was a Japanese strategic victory.[7] And, indeed, in theory, in the *Zuikaku* and the *Junyo*, the Imperial Japanese Navy did possess the only fully operational carrier force in the Pacific. In theory.

But just because a carrier force is "operational" does not mean it is effective. The effectiveness of a carrier force depends on its aircraft and especially its aviators. Toward the end of the Santa Cruz action, the *Junyo* sent six Type 97 torpedo planes against the *Hornet*. Of the six torpedoes they dropped, two hit, and only one exploded. Then came two Type 99s from the *Zuikaku*, six *Zuikaku* Type 97s armed with bombs, and, lastly, four Type 99s from the *Junyo*. Together, they got a total of two hits and one near-miss, all against a carrier that was disabled and stationary, with no air cover and reduced antiaircraft protection.

Such a performance does not speak well of their effectiveness.

It was the result of Japanese carrier aircraft losses in the Santa Cruz action that might be best described as devastating to Japanese naval aviation. In the face of a poorly coordinated American air defense, the Sea Eagles had been sitting ducks. On the morning of October 26, the four Japanese carriers had 203 carrier aircraft available – 82 fighters, 63 bombers, 57 attack planes, and one reconnaissance plane. By the evening of October 26, they were down to 104 – 55 fighters, 22 bombers, and 27 attack planes. One day of action had cost them almost half their carrier planes – 67 shot down and 28 more ditched, usually the result of battle damage.[8] That same day cost the Japanese Naval Air Force 145 aviators – 20 percent of the fighter pilots committed to Santa Cruz, 39 percent of the torpedo plane aviators, and 49 percent of the dive bomber aviators.[9]

The Japanese had not lost just quantity, but quality as well: three carrier attack plane squadron leaders, including Lieutenant Commander Murata, two of three carrier bomber squadron leaders, including Lieutenant Commander Seki, and 18 section leaders.[10] The consequence of these losses could be seen in the sloppy and undisciplined, albeit still fatal, late attacks on the *Hornet*. By comparison, while the Americans had lost 80 aircraft, they lost only 26 aviators, of which 22 were killed. The casualties included four section leaders and one squadron commander, Lieutenant Commander Collett of the *Enterprise*.[11]

It was a problem that had now caught up to the Imperial Japanese Navy and especially *Kido Butai*. Of the 765 elite carrier aviators from *Kido Butai* who had attacked Pearl Harbor, 409 were now dead. At the beginning of the war, the Japanese Naval Air Force had 3,500 Sea Eagles. They had anticipated needing as many as 15,000 new pilots for the war, but they only trained "several hundred" per year.[12]

Because the damaged *Shokaku* could train no one, the *Zuikaku* was sent back to Japan to train a new air group for *Kido Butai*. Only one Japanese carrier was left on station, the *Junyo*, with 27 Zeros (many from the *Zuiho*), 12 Type 99 carrier bombers, and nine Type 97 carrier attack planes.[13] Admiral Nagumo would later call Santa Cruz "a tactical win but a shattering strategic loss for Japan."[14]

Admiral Yamamoto did not seem to mind too much, because he believed he had sunk four American aircraft carriers at Santa Cruz, leaving them with none remaining in the South Pacific. And he was close to the truth, at least in the latter. But he was not going to risk his relatively few remaining attack planes against the battle-hardened US Marine and Navy fliers on Guadalcanal. He would let Admiral Kusaka's Base Air Force take care of them.

However, the Americans did have one carrier left in the South Pacific – the *Enterprise*, though badly damaged and hampered in air operations. While still en route to the relative safety of New Caledonia, Admiral Halsey called the senior officers of all branches in Nouméa and told them to pool their mechanics for the repairs to the *Enterprise* and other ships and aircraft.[15]

But not having seen the *Enterprise* yet, Admiral Halsey was assuming the worst about the carrier's condition. He went so far as to ask Admiral Nimitz to get one or more British aircraft carriers sent to the South Pacific. Nimitz forwarded the request to Admiral King.[16] In turn, Nimitz ordered Halsey to prepare a coordinated defense plan for the rear bases. They were bracing for the worst.

And the worst looked more and more likely. The *Enterprise* limped into Nouméa, where she was swarmed by men from the repair ship *Vulcan*. They estimated it would take three weeks to repair the carrier.[17] That wasn't good.

But unlike his predecessor, Admiral Halsey was defiant in the face of adversity. In an October 31 letter to Admiral Nimitz, Halsey vowed to "patch up what we have and go with them." He went on to say, "I will not send any ship back to Pearl Harbor unless it is absolutely necessary. This may mean operating the *Enterprise* with a slightly reduced complement of planes and under difficulties, but under the present circumstances, a half a loaf is better than none."[18]

That half a loaf got slightly bigger with the October 28 recovery of Lieutenant Commander Widhelm and his radioman George Stokely by a PBY. They joined the rest of the remaining carrier aviators from the *Enteprise* and *Hornet* at the Tontouta airbase some 40 miles northwest of Nouméa. What to do with these highly skilled and battle-hardened aviators would be a question for Admiral Halsey as he pondered his next move.

The Japanese still had a numerical advantage in every major warship category in the Pacific – more aircraft carriers, more battleships, more cruisers, more destroyers. A numerical advantage in aircraft as well. And they had more of those major warships and aircraft close to the South Pacific theater than the Allies did. They remained poised to move on Guadalcanal, with a crushing bombardment of the airfield by battleships, followed by Imperial Army troops landing to overwhelm the Marine defenders. But their most powerful striking arm, the Sea Eagles, was shattered.

The Americans could oppose this collection of forces with one beaten-up aircraft carrier, albeit one who now had the best carrier air group in the Pacific. Two new battleships, one of which was damaged. And they had an unsinkable airfield on Guadalcanal that had resisted all Japanese attempts to capture or reduce it. Both the carrier and the airfield were home to experienced, battle-hardened aviators; the airfield could house more. On the battered but tough aviator shoulders rested the fate of Guadalcanal.

That was a very long list of advantages for the Japanese, a very short one for the Americans. But as Admiral Nimitz explained, "While our situation in the Southern Solomons is far from satisfactory, it is far from hopeless."[19]

In Admiral Halsey, the Americans, for the first time in the campaign, had an aggressive commander who was determined to exploit those few advantages to the fullest. How well he did so would determine if the Americans could withstand the next Japanese attack to retake Guadalcanal.

For the next attack would be their strongest yet. It had to be. After all the lives, ships, and aircraft lost since August; after two carrier battles at Eastern Solomons and Santa Cruz; after two major surface battles at Savo Island and Cape Esperance; and quite a few smaller ones, for all practical purposes, nothing had changed. The Americans still controlled Henderson Field but the Japanese were still in position to capture it. The Americans still controlled the skies over Guadalcanal but the Japanese could still challenge it. The American Stars and Stripes still flew over the waters around Guadalcanal during the day, but the Japanese Rising Sun still flew over those same waters at night.

The pressures were building on both sides, and something had to change. And change it would.

But could Halsey change enough to save Guadalcanal?

NOTES

Prologue

1. Traditionally, Japanese names feature the surname preceding the given name, which is how they will be presented here.
2. "Combined Fleet" (*Rengo Kantai*) was the term used for all of the main combat components of the "Imperial Japanese Navy" (*Dai Nippon Teikoku Kaigun*). The defense districts of the Japanese home islands and the naval craft deployed to fight in China, for instance, were not part of the Combined Fleet.
3. The emperor's given name of Hirohito is used here because of its familiarity to readers, but it should be noted that in Japan its use is considered improper. In Japan, he is properly called by his posthumous name, Showa, the name of the era of his rule.
4. David Bergamini, *Japan's Imperial Conspiracy* (London: William Morrow, 1971), 44. Iris Chang, *The Rape of Nanking: The Forgotten Holocaust of World War II* (New York: Penguin, 1998), 4, says the number of women who were raped was as high as 80,000.
5. Estimates of the number of dead vary between 100,000 and 300,000. Because so many were burned, buried in mass graves or dumped into the Yangtze by the Japanese, the actual number will never be known.
6. Japanese aircraft had a dual naming system that Allied observers found confusing. One name for an aircraft was the manufacturer's alphanumeric project code; the other was the official military designation, which consisted of a reference to the year the aircraft entered service according to the Japanese calendar plus a description of the aircraft. To use the Zero as an example, "Mitsubishi A6M Type 0 Carrier Fighter," "Mitsubishi A6M" was the manufacturer's project code, Type 0 is a reference to the Imperial year 2600, or 1940 in the Gregorian calendar, and "Carrier Fighter" describes the aircraft's function. Because of this unwieldy name combination, the Allies eventually chose a naming system of their own for Japanese aircraft – fighters were given male names (i.e. "Zeke," "Oscar") while bombers were given female names (i.e. "Betty," "Kate").
7. H. P. Willmott, *Empires in the Balance: Japanese and Allied Pacific Strategies to April 1942* (Annapolis: Naval Institute Press, 1982), 55.
8. Willmott, *Empires in the Balance*, 63, 61–62.
9. S. C. M. Paine, *The Wars for Asia 1911–1949* (Cambridge: Cambridge University Press, 2012), 176.
10. Bergamini, *Japan's Imperial Conspiracy*, 739. Bergamini also quotes Yamamoto as gloomily saying, "I expect to die on the deck of my flagship, the battleship *Nagato*. In those evil days you will see Tokyo burnt to the ground at least three times. The result will be prolonged suffering for the people" (739).
11. See Jeffrey R. Cox, *Rising Sun, Falling Skies: The Disastrous Java Sea Campaign of World War II* (Oxford: Osprey, 2014) for a more detailed explanation.
12. Richard B. Frank, *Guadalcanal: The Definitive Account of the Landmark Battle* (New York: Penguin, 1992), 22.
13. John Prados, *Combined Fleet Decoded: The Secret History of American Intelligence and the Japanese Navy in World War II* (Annapolis: Naval Institute Press, 1995), 279.
14. Frank, *Guadalcanal*, 24.
15. John Prados, *Islands of Destiny: The Solomons Campaign and the Eclipse of the Rising Sun* (New York: NAL Caliber, 2012), 13.
16. Stanley Coleman Jersey, *Hell's Islands: The Untold Story of Guadalcanal* (College Station, TX: Texas A&M University Press, 2008), 997, 1025.
17. Eric Hammel, *Carrier Clash: The Invasion of Guadalcanal and the Battle of the Eastern Solomons August 1942* (Pacifica, CA: Pacifica Military History, 1997), 1970; William Bruce Johnson, *The Pacific Campaign in World War II: From Pearl Harbor to Guadalcanal* (London; New York: Routledge, 2006), 173.
18. John B. Lundstrom, *First Team and the Guadalcanal Campaign: Naval Fighter Combat from August to November 1942* (Annapolis: Naval Institute Press, 1994), 1459–76.
19. Jersey, *Hell's Islands*, 1078.

20 Lundstrom, *First Team*, 1473.
21 Toshikazu Ohmae, "The Battle of Savo Island," in *The Japanese Navy in World War II in the Words of Former Japanese Naval Officers* (2nd edn), ed. David C. Evans (Annapolis: Naval Institute Press, 1986), 222.
22 Richard W. Bates, *The Battle of Savo Island, August 9, 1942. Strategical and Tactical Analysis* (Newport, RI: Naval War College, 1950), 8.
23 Lundstrom, *First Team*, 1459, 1476.
24 John Toland, *The Rising Sun: The Decline and Fall of the Japanese Empire 1936–1945* (New York: Random House, 1970), 7771. Japanese radio intelligence gathering was centered on a secret unit located in the Tokyo suburb of Owada officially titled the "Central Radio Intelligence Group" (Prados, *Combined Fleet Decoded*, 592). Nevertheless, histories tend to give it the international media conglomerate-sounding name of "Owada Communications Group." See e.g., Prados, *Islands of Destiny*, 41.
25 Jersey, *Hell's Islands*, 1096, 1120.
26 Frank, *Guadalcanal*, 59.
27 Jersey, *Hell's Islands*, 1123, 1104–13.
28 Ibid., 1619.
29 Lundstrom, *First Team*, 1476.
30 Ibid., 1493.
31 Jersey, *Hell's Islands*, 1619. In order to be approachable for readers not versed in military history, all times are in 12-hour format. Additionally, the use of military and maritime terminology, designations, and acronyms that might be unfamiliar or confusing to non-military readers, will be kept to a minimum.

Chapter 1

1 Samuel Eliot Morison, *The Two-Ocean War: A Short History of the United States Navy in the Second World War* (Boston, Toronto: London: Little, Brown, and Company, 1963), 35.
2 See Cox, *Rising Sun, Falling Skies* for a more detailed explanation.
3 William Tuohy, *America's Fighting Admirals: Winning the War at Sea in World War II* (St. Paul, MN: Zenith Press, 2007), 733.
4 Frank, *Guadalcanal*, 4.
5 Morison, *Two-Ocean War*, 35.
6 Brig Gen Samuel B. Griffith, USMC (ret.), *The Battle for Guadalcanal* (Toronto; New York; London; Sydney: Bantam, 1980), 5.
7 Tuohy, *America's Fighting Admirals*, 741.
8 Morison, *Two-Ocean War*, 138–9.
9 James D. Hornfischer, *Neptune's Inferno: The US Navy at Guadalcanal* (New York: Bantam, 2011), 333.
10 Frank, *Guadalcanal*, 6.
11 "Foreign Relations of the United States, The Conferences at Washington, 1941–1942, and Casablanca, 1943 Document 114," Office of the Historian, United States Department of State, https://history.state.gov/historicaldocuments/frus1941–43/d114.
12 Frank, *Guadalcanal*, 7–8; Vice Admiral George Carroll Dyer, USN (Ret.), *The Amphibians Came to Conquer: The Story of Admiral Richmond Kelly Turner* (Washington, DC: US Government Printing Office, 1971), 234, 239–40
13 "Foreign Relations of the United States, The Conferences at Washington, 1941–1942, and Casablanca, 1943 Document 114."
14 Dyer, *Amphibians*, 238.
15 Ibid., 244–5.
16 Maurice Matloff and Edward M. Snell, *United States Army in World War II: The War Department, Volume III:* "Strategic Planning for Coalition Warfare 1941–1942" (Washington: Office of the Chief of Military History, Department of the Army, 1953), 147.
17 Frank, *Guadalcanal*, 11.
18 Dyer, *Amphibians*, 241, 242.
19 Matloff and Snell, "Strategic Planning," 154–5.
20 Dyer, *Amphibians*, 243.
21 Griffith, *Battle for Guadalcanal*, 9–10.
22 Dyer, *Amphibians*, 243.

23 Thomas B. Buell, *Master of Seapower: A Biography of Fleet Admiral Ernest J. King* (Annapolis: Naval Institute Press, 1980), 3944.
24 Matloff and Snell, "Strategic Planning," 157.
25 Buell, *Master of Seapower*, 4438.
26 William Manchester, *American Caesar: Douglas MacArthur 1880–1964* (New York: Back Bay Books, 1978), 5591.
27 Williamson Murray and Allan R. Millett, *A War to Be Won: Fighting the Second World War* (Cambridge, MA; London: Belknap Press of Harvard University Press, 2000), 2606.
28 Manchester, *American Caesar*, 5591; Buell, *Master of Seapower*, 3949.
29 Walter R. Borneman, *The Admirals: Nimitz, Halsey, Leahy, and King – The Five-Star Admirals Who Won the War at Sea* (New York; Boston; London: Little, Brown, and Company, 2012), 280.
30 Admiral Nimitz's first suggestion to head the South Pacific Command was Vice Admiral William S. Pye, whose main claim to fame was, in a meeting on December 6, 1941, loudly declaring, "The Japanese will not go to war with the United States. We are too big, too powerful, and too strong." Gordon Prange, *At Dawn We Slept; The Untold Story of Pearl Harbor* (New York: Penguin, 1981), 470.
31 Frank, *Guadalcanal*, 15.
32 Griffith, *Battle for Guadalcanal*, 11.
33 General Alexander A. Vandegrift, USMC, and Robert B. Asprey, *Once a Marine: The Memoirs of General A. A. Vandegrift, USMC* (New York: W. W. Norton & Co., 1964), 104; Buell, *Master of Seapower*, 4106; Griffith, *Guadalcanal*, 11.
34 Hornfischer, *Neptune's Inferno*, 582.
35 Richard F. Newcomb, *The Battle of Savo Island: The Harrowing Account of the Disastrous Night Battle Off Guadalcanal that Nearly Destroyed the Pacific Fleet in August 1942* (New York: Owl Books, 2002), 52.
36 Dyer, *Amphibians*, 252–3.
37 Tuohy, *America's Fighting Admirals*, 1156–64.
38 Prados, *Islands of Destiny*, 36.
39 John B. Lundstrom, *Black Shoe Carrier Admiral: Frank Jack Fletcher at Coral Sea, Midway, and Guadalcanal* (Annapolis: Naval Institute Press, 2006), 311.
40 Tuohy, *America's Fighting Admirals*, 1156.
41 Lieutenant General Merrill B. Twining, USMC (Ret.), *No Bended Knee: The Battle for Guadalcanal* (New York: Presidio, 1996), 86, 54.
42 As Robert Leckie (*Challenge for the Pacific – Guadalcanal: The Turning Point of the War* (New York: Bantam, 1965), 632 note) states, in traditional practice, "The word 'Marines' is interchangeable with 'regiment' … thus, to say First Marines is to mean First Marine Regiment[.]" (See also Frank (*Guadalcanal*, 46, n. 5.) While acknowledging that this is the preferred and long-standing habit in the military and among military historians, it may become confusing for the non-military reader. For that reason, the custom will generally not be used here.
43 Frank, *Guadalcanal*, 46–7, 17.
44 In the designation "JN-25," "JN" means "Japanese Navy" and "25" references this being the 25th such code identified.
45 Toland, *Rising Sun*, 7676; Frank, *Guadalcanal*, 32; Lundstrom, *Black Shoe*, 308.
46 Toland, *Rising Sun*, 7676; Frank, *Guadalcanal*, 32.
47 Frank, *Guadalcanal*, 32–3.
48 Murray and Millett, *War*, 2800; Lundstrom, *Black Shoe*, 309–10.
49 Matloff and Snell, "Strategic Planning," 261; Frank, *Guadalcanal*, 33.
50 Buell, *Master of Seapower*, 4466.
51 Toland, *Rising Sun*, 7676; Frank, *Guadalcanal*, 33; Hornfischer, *Neptune's Inferno*, 497; Borneman, *Admirals*, 284.
52 Matloff and Snell, "Strategic Planning," 262.
53 Toland, *Rising Sun*, 7676–97; Frank, *Guadalcanal*, 33–4
54 Toland, *Rising Sun*, 7704; Manchester, *American Caesar*, 5622; Murray and Millett, *War*, 2851.
55 Lundstrom, *Black Shoe*, 313.
56 Frank, *Guadalcanal*, 34, 35.
57 Dyer, *Amphibians*, 272; Lundstrom, *Black Shoe*, 312.
58 Prados, *Combined Fleet Decoded*, 235–6.

59 Prados, *Combined Fleet Decoded*, 358; Frank, *Guadalcanal*, 29.
60 Prados, *Combined Fleet Decoded*, 358.
61 Dyer, *Amphibians*, 274. For clarification, Dyer says the version of events proffered by Samuel Eliot Morison, *History of United States Naval Operations in World War II, Vol V: The Struggle for Guadalcanal August 1942–February 1943* (Edison, NJ: Castle, 1949), 12–14, in which an Allied reconnaissance plane spotted the airfield on July 4, was actually the work of *Magic*.
62 Tuohy, *America's Fighting Admirals*, 1150; Frank, *Guadalcanal*, 36.
63 Lundstrom, *Black Shoe*, 321.
64 Hornfischer, *Neptune's Inferno*, 588.
65 Frank, *Guadalcanal*, 37.
66 Lieutenant Colonel Frank O. Hough, USMC; Major Verle E. Ludwig, USMC; Henry I. Shaw, Jr., *History of U.S. Marine Corps Operations in World War II, Volume I: Pearl Harbor to Guadalcanal* (Washington, DC: Historical Branch, G-3 Division, Headquarters, U.S. Marine Corps; 1958), 248–9.
67 Details of the meeting come from Vandegrift and Asprey, *Once A Marine*, 110–1.
68 Ibid., 111.
69 Prados, *Combined Fleet Decoded*, 358.
70 Dyer, *Amphibians*, 285–6.
71 Dyer, *Amphibians*, 383.
72 Frank, *Guadalcanal*, 38.
73 Lundstrom, *Black Shoe*, 321.
74 Hornfischer, *Neptune's Inferno*, 513.
75 Newcomb, *Battle*, 53.
76 Dyer, *Amphibians*, 286.
77 Lundstrom, *First Team*, 1237–94.
78 Hough, Ludwig, and Shaw, *Pearl Harbor*, 48.
79 In 1942, a publication called *Joint Action of the Army and the Navy* (Short Title: FTP-155), prepared by a Joint Board of Army and Navy officers, specifically governed all Joint Overseas Expeditions (Chapter VI). Although *Watchtower* was not joint inasmuch as it was entirely a Navy operation, FTP-155 Chapter VI was used as kind of a how-to manual for overseas expeditions. Section VI, Paragraph 84 covered "Naval organization for landing."
80 Lundstrom, *First Team*, 723.
81 Ibid., 854–71. Because the numeric designations for the squadrons did not always match up with their carriers at this point in the war and could thus be confusing for the uninitiated, squadrons and pilots will normally be referenced here by the name of their carrier.
82 See e.g. Leonard Ware, *United States Navy Combat Narrative: The Landing in the Solomons 7–8 August 1942* (Washington, DC: Publications Branch, Office of Naval Intelligence, United States Navy, 1943), 7.
83 Hough, Ludwig, and Shaw, *Pearl Harbor*, 47.
84 Newcomb, *Battle of Savo Island*, 58.
85 Lundstrom, *Black Shoe*, 326.
86 Ibid., 353.
87 Dyer, *Amphibians*, 283–4.
88 Twining, *No Bended Knee*, 57.
89 Johnson, *Pacific Campaign*, 143.
90 T. Grady Gallant, *On Valor's Side: A Marine's Own Story of Parris Island and Guadalcanal* (New York: Doubleday, 1963), 3144–60, 3076–93.
91 Leckie, *Challenge*, 1114.
92 Hough, Ludwig, and Shaw, *Pearl Harbor*, 49–50.
93 Johnson, *Pacific Campaign*, 53.
94 Twining, *No Bended Knee*, 59.
95 Ibid., 57.
96 Dyer, *Amphibians*, 283–4.
97 Bruce Loxton and Chris Coulthard-Clark, *The Shame of Savo: Anatomy of a Naval Disaster* (Annapolis: Naval Institute Press, 1997), 62; Hornfischer, *Neptune's Inferno*, 1887.
98 Dyer, *Amphibians*, 284.
99 Twining, *No Bended Knee*, 59, 61.

100 Hough, Ludwig, and Shaw, *Pearl* Harbor, 250.
101 Richard W. Bates, *The Battle of Savo Island, August 9, 1942. Strategical and Tactical Analysis* (Newport, RI: Naval War College, 1950), 22-A Table 2, 23.
102 Ware, *Landing*, 16; Bates, *Battle of Savo Island*, 22-A Table 2, p. 23.
103 These are not the famous Curtiss Helldivers. The famous Curtiss Helldiver was the Curtiss SB2C Helldiver that became the main US carrier dive bomber late in the Pacific War after it had replaced the Douglas SBD Dauntless. This is the other Curtiss Helldiver. The SBC was also a dive bomber, but it, the last biplane purchased for the US Navy, was long obsolete.
104 Bates, *Battle of Savo Island*, 22-A Table 2.
105 Ware, *Landing*, 13–14.
106 Prados, *Combined Fleet Decoded*, 359.
107 The story of Lieutenant Colonel Twining's photographic mission comes from Twining, *No Bended Knee*, 41–7.
108 Dyer, *Amphibians*, 302.
109 Lundstrom, *Black Shoe*, 326–7.
110 Prados, *Islands of Destiny*, 51.
111 Vandegrift and Asprey, *Once A Marine*, 120.
112 Ibid., 120.
113 Dyer, *Amphibians*, 301.
114 Vandegrift and Asprey, *Once A Marine*, 120.
115 Dyer, *Amphibians*, 302.
116 Vandegrift and Asprey, *Once A Marine*, 120.
117 Toland, *Rising Sun*, 7793.
118 Vandegrift and Asprey, *Once A Marine*, 120.
119 Hornfischer, *Neptune's Inferno*, 782.
120 For a discussion as to the circumstances under which Admiral Turner's remark came to light, see Lundstrom, *Black Shoe*, 336, 580 n. 25.
121 Dyer, *Amphibians*, 300.
122 Leckie, *Challenge*, 1170, 6078.
123 Dyer, *Amphibians*, 302.
124 Ibid., 301–2.
125 Bates, *Battle of Savo Island*, 2.
126 Twining, *No Bended Knee*, 56–7.
127 Vandegrift and Asprey, *Once A Marine*, 122.
128 Twining, *No Bended Knee*, 52.
129 Dyer, *Amphibians*, 311.
130 Frank, *Guadalcanal*, 57.
131 Vandegrift and Asprey, *Once A Marine*, 122.
132 Dyer, *Amphibians*, 294.
133 Twining, *No Bended Knee*, 54.
134 Dyer, *Amphibians*, 297.
135 Ibid., 317–18.
136 Lundstrom, *Black Shoe*, 350–1; Prados, *Islands of Destiny*, 56.
137 Hough, Ludwig, and Shaw, *Pearl Harbor*, 248; Twining, *No Bended Knee*, 55.

Chapter 2

1 Johnson, *Pacific Campaign*, 167.
2 Frank, *Guadalcanal*, 57–8.
3 Prados, *Islands of Destiny*, 888–92.
4 Dyer, *Amphibians*, 328.
5 Ibid., 328.
6 Morison, *Two-Ocean War*, 166–7.
7 Twining, *No Bended Knee*, 62.
8 Richard Tregaskis, *Guadalcanal Diary* (New York: Random House, 1943), 32.
9 Ware, *Landing*, 30–2.

10 Twining, *No Bended Knee*, 62.
11 Lundstrom, *First Team*, 1401–17.
12 Ibid., 1416–31.
13 Lundstrom, *Black Shoe*, 353, 355–6.
14 Ware, *Landing*, 41.
15 Twining, *No Bended Knee*, 64.
16 Lundstrom, *First Team*, 1641; Lundstrom, *Black Shoe*, 355.
17 Lundstrom, *Black Shoe*, 357.
18 Saburo Sakai, Martin Caidin, and Fred Saito, *Samurai* (New York: J. Boylston & Company, 2001), 2525.
19 Sakai, Caidin, and Saito, *Samurai*, 2545.
20 Ibid., 2545.
21 Lundstrom, *First Team*, 1736–53.
22 Sakai, Caidin, and Saito, *Samurai*, 2568.
23 Ibid., 2583.
24 Ibid., 2583.
25 Ibid., 2584.
26 Ibid., 2584.
27 Ibid., 2599.
28 Lundstrom, *First Team*, 1895.
29 Sakai, Caidin, and Saito, *Samurai*, 2629.
30 Lundstrom, *First Team*, 1911–29.
31 Lundstrom, *Black Shoe*, 357.
32 Lundstrom, *First Team*, 2126.
33 Ware, *Landing*, 55; Lundstrom, *First Team*, 2153.
34 Lundstrom, *First Team*, 2215; Lundstrom, *Black Shoe*, 359.
35 Morison, *Struggle for Guadalcanal*, 24; Bates, *Battle of Savo Island*, 53; Frank, *Guadalcanal*, 90.
36 Gallant, *On Valor's Side*, 3765.
37 Ibid., 3765–83.
38 Tregaskis, *Guadalcanal Diary*, 42.
39 Lundstrom, *Black Shoe*, 360.
40 Bates, *Battle of Savo Island*, 54, 70–1.
41 Bates, *Battle of Savo Island*, 83–4; Newcomb, *Battle of Savo Island*, 73.
42 Lundstrom, *Black Shoe*, 372.
43 Lundstrom, *Black Shoe*, 372.
44 Dyer, *Amphibians*, 387.
45 Ibid., 387.
46 Flight decks normally have designated spots for aircraft depending on whether the carrier is in a launching or recovering phase. For that reason, positioning aircraft on the flight deck is known as "spotting." If, for instance, four fighters are to be launched, they would first be "spotted" – in this case, positioned to launch – and then launched.
47 Dyer, *Amphibians*, 387.
48 Lundstrom, *First Team*, 2366.
49 Ibid., 2343–58, 14590 n. 2.
50 The story of the fighter direction comes from Lundstrom, *Black Shoe*, 364–5.
51 Ibid., 364.
52 Ibid., 364.
53 Ware, *Landing*, 77.
54 Lundstrom, *First Team*, 2429.
55 Newcomb, *Battle of Savo Island*, 71; Osamu Tagaya and Mark Styling, *Mitsubishi Type 1 Rikko 'Betty' Units of World War 2* (Oxford: Osprey, 2001), 998.
56 Ware, *Landing*, 78.
57 Robert Sinclair Parkin, *Blood on the Sea: American Destroyers Lost in World War II* (Cambridge, MA: Da Capo Press, 1995), 72.
58 Lundstrom, *First Team*, 2477.
59 Lundstrom, *Black Shoe*, 365–6.

60 Bates, *Battle of Savo Island*, 85.
61 Lundstrom, *Black Shoe*, 367.
62 Tregaskis, *Guadalcanal Diary*, 53.
63 Lundstrom, *Black Shoe*, 568; Bates, *Battle of Savo Island*, 85.
64 Loxton and Coulthard-Clark, *Shame*, 117.
65 Newcomb, *Battle of Savo Island*, 88.
66 Galfrey George Ormond Gatacre, *A Naval Career: Report of Proceedings, 1921–1964* (Manly, New South Wales, Australia: Nautical Press, 1982), 169–70.
67 Hornfischer, *Neptune's Inferno*, 1213.
68 Newcomb, *Battle of Savo Island*, 89.
69 John J. Domagalski, *Lost at Guadalcanal: The Final Battles of the* Astoria *and* Chicago *as Described by Survivors and In Official Reports* (Jefferson, NC; London: MacFarland, 2010), 428; Hornfischer, *Neptune's Inferno*, 1151.
70 Hornfischer, *Neptune's Inferno*, 1151.
71 Domagalski, *Lost*, 1263.
72 Twining, *No Bended Knee*, 78.
73 Ibid., 78.

Chapter 3

1 The Imperial Japanese Navy used the term *sentai* to refer to a division of cruisers or battleships, with each *sentai* organized according to type of warship but the unit designations themselves making no such distinction. Thus, the numerical designation references not the number of cruiser or battleship divisions, but the number of *sentai*. Not surprisingly, the use of *sentai* often results in confusion, so the traditional English-language practice of referencing the "cruiser division" or "battleship division" will be used here.
2 Loxton and Coulthard-Clark, *Shame*, 125.
3 Ohmae, "Battle of Savo Island," 220.
4 Ibid., 219.
5 Bruce Gamble, *Fortress Rabaul: The Battle for the Southwest Pacific, January 1942–April 1943* (Minneapolis, MN: Zenith Press, 2013), 4.
6 Simpson Harbor was named after – and by – Royal Navy Captain Cortland Simpson, whose main claim to fame was sailing into Simpson Harbor.
7 Masatake Okumiya, Jiro Horikoshi, and Martin Caidin, *Zero!* (Pickle Partners Publishing, 2014), 130; Lundstrom, *First Team*, 1553.
8 Gamble, *Fortress Rabaul*, 4. At one point in the 1980s, Rabaul recorded 14,000 measurable earthquakes in one month.
9 Prados, *Islands of Destiny*, 25. Rabaul was eventually destroyed in 1994 by another combined eruption of Tavurvur and Vulcan.
10 Sakai, Caidin, and Saito, *Samurai!*, 1245. Lakunai was the worst airfield Sakai had seen until he was shipped to Lae a few days later, at which point Lae immediately became "the worst airfield [Sakai] had ever seen, not excluding Rabaul or even the advanced fields in China" (ibid., 1284). Prados, *Islands of Destiny*, 25.
11 Prados, *Islands of Destiny*, 15.
12 Ohmae, "Battle of Savo Island," 222–3.
13 Bates, *Battle of Savo Island*, 7. Aside from this task force leaving a base thousands of miles closer to the 8th Fleet operating area a day earlier than they had reported, the Naval War College calls this intelligence report "reasonably accurate."
14 Bates, *Battle of Savo Island*, 8; Loxton and Coulthard-Clark, *Shame*, 123.
15 Eric Hammel, *Guadalcanal: Starvation Island* (Pacifica, CA: Pacifica Military History, 1987), 1474.
16 Gamble, *Fortress Rabaul*, 216; Bates, *Battle of Savo Island*, 45.
17 Newcomb, *Battle of Savo Island*, 21.
18 Bates, *Battle of Savo Island*, 43.
19 Newcomb, *Battle of Savo Island*, 21. Time is from Bates, *Battle of Savo Island*, 43.
20 Gamble, *Fortress Rabaul*, 216.
21 Newcomb, *Battle of Savo Island*, 22. Time is from Bates, *Battle of Savo Island*, 44.
22 Bates, *Battle of Savo Island*, 44.

23 There are inconsistent accounts as to who was the officer commanding in attendance at this meeting, Admiral Yamada or Admial Mikawa: see the accounts of Sakai, Caidin, and Saito (*Samurai!*, 2507), Newcomb (*Battle of Savo Island*, 22–23), Gamble (*Fortress Rabaul*, 216) and Hammel (*Carrier Clash*, 1070). The account given here is from Newcomb and Sakai, with allowance that Newcomb apparently understandably interpreted Sakai's "admiral" as a reference to Mikawa.

24 Hammel, *Starvation*, 1474. Time is from Bates, *Battle of Savo Island*, 44, which has a slightly different wording for the message and adds the clarification "This report certainly indicated that Tulagi was in danger of falling."

25 As the Japanese prepared to occupy the Buka airfield, on January 2, 1942, the Australians demolished and blocked the runways to prevent aircraft from taking off or landing. The next day, the Australians were ordered to prepare the runways for aircraft fleeing from Rabaul to land. "Buka Airfield Bougainville Province Papua New Guinea (PNG)," *Pacific Wrecks*, www.pacificwrecks.com.

26 Okumiya, Horikoshi, and Caidin, *Zero!*, 2748.

27 Gamble, *Fortress Rabaul*, 218.

28 Bates, *Battle of Savo Island*, 51. The submarines were *RO-33*, *I-121*, *I-122*, and *I-123*.

29 Leckie, *Challenge*, 718; Twining, *No Bended Knee*, 73.

31 Gamble, *Fortress Rabaul*, 220–21. Lieutenant General George Kenney, head of Allied Air Forces and the 5th Air Force under MacArthur, would later write that 150 aircraft were parked "wingtip to wingtip on both sides of the runway at Vunakanau." At the time of the attack there were no actual aircraft at Vunakanau.

32 Ohmae, "Battle of Savo Island," 226.

33 Bates, *Battle of Savo Island*, 46.

34 Loxton and Coulthard-Clark, *Shame*, 125; Ohmae, "Battle of Savo Island," 227.

35 Toland, *Rising Sun*, 7875.

36 Sakai, Caidin, and Saito, *Samurai!*, 2681–2864. After collapsing before his superiors, Sakai Saburo was treated to emergency surgery on his fractured skull – without anesthesia. On August 12 Sakai was flown back to Japan for treatment on his injured right eye. He was never able to regain full sight in that eye and was consequently grounded until the last days of the war.

37 Bates, *Battle of Savo Island*, 49.

38 Ohmae, "Battle of Savo Island," 228.

39 Bates, *Battle of Savo Island*, 50.

40 Ohmae, "Battle of Savo Island," 227.

41 Bates, *Battle of Savo Island*, 50, 68. Ohmae ("Battle of Savo Island," 227–8) says that they detected a submarine to the south and changed course to the east to avoid it, and were able to do so. It is impossible to reconcile Ohmae's statement with the details of *S-38*'s encounter with the Japanese ships in Bates, which indicates the Japanese ships did not actually avoid the *S-38*, but instead ran over it, though they did avoid attack. At some point after the encounter with *S-38*, the Japanese force did change course from 140 degrees True to 80 degrees True, that is, from southeast to slightly north of east.

42 Newcomb, *Battle of Savo Island*, 33.

43 Loxton and Coulthard-Clark, *Shame*, 129–30; Bates, *Battle of Savo Island*, 100. A bitter Admiral Gatacre later commented on the accuracy of the Hudson's report: "At least the aircrew could count up to eight!" (Gatacre, *Naval Career*, 173).

44 Bates, *Battle of Savo Island*, 73.

45 *Aoba* Tabular Record of Movement (TROM), Imperial Japanese Navy Page, www.combinedfleet.com; Bates, *Battle of Savo Island*, 74.

46 Ohmae, "Battle of Savo Island," 228.

47 Ibid., 230.

48 Ibid., 230, 228.

49 This is an amalgamation of Bates, *Battle of Savo Island*, 75, 77, and Loxton and Coulthard-Clark, *Shame*, 131–2, 288 n. 30, 31. Bates says, "At 1915 Commander Cruiser Force (Admiral Mikawa) shot off signal flares to guide the AOBA plane back to the cruisers, but the plane failed to return, having been shot down over Tulagi." What is presented here follows Bates to the extent that Mikawa did shoot up signal flares to guide the floatplane back, but agrees with Loxton that the floatplane was not shot down and did return to base. The alleged loss of the *Aoba*'s floatplane over Tulagi is commonly reported, usually ascribed to a fighter from the *Wasp*, but there does not seem to be support for it. The story may be a garbled recollection of Lieutenant Commander Snowden's downing of what he thought was a float Zero and was actually an Aichi E13A1 floatplane from the *Kako*.

50 Ohmae, "Battle of Savo Island," 230.
51 Bates, *Battle of Savo Island*, 76.
52 Ohmae, "Battle of Savo Island," 230.
53 Bates, *Battle of Savo Island*, 75.
54 Ibid., 77.
55 Bates, *Battle of Savo Island*, 77; Ohmae, "Battle of Savo Island," 230–1.
57 Ohmae, "Battle of Savo Island," 231.
58 Ibid., 231. Since Captain Ohmae drafted the message, His words are used here instead of the more commonly used translation from Bates, *Battle of Savo Island*, 77: "Let us attack with certain victory in the traditional night attack of the Imperial Navy! May each one calmly do his utmost!"
59 Bates, *Battle of Savo Island*, 77.
60 In its analysis of the Battle of Savo Island, the Naval War College is brutal in its assessment of the Japanese air attacks: "The operations of the FIFTH Air Attack Force (25th Air Flotilla) on August 8th contributed little of direct value to the Japanese overall effort against the Allied forces at Tulagi and Guadalcanal, except to delay unloading operations of the transports" (Bates, *Battle of Savo Island*, 81).
61 Bates, *Battle of Savo Island*, 219–20.
62 H. P. Willmott, *The Battle of Leyte Gulf: The Last Fleet Action* (Bloomington, IN; Indianapolis: Indiana University Press, 2005), 779.
63 Loxton and Coulthard-Clark, *Shame*, 132–33; Newcomb, *Battle of Savo Island*, 41–2.
64 Bates, *Battle of Savo Island*, 78.
65 Bates (*Battle of Savo Island*, 106) says, "[W]hen one considers the pilot's problem of operating over hostile surface forces, in low visibility and on a moonless night, his performance must be rated unusually creditable and reflected merit on the Japanese ship-based pilots." However creditable their performance, this particular Japanese pilot and air crew apparently never returned to their mother ship.
66 Loxton and Coulthard-Clark, *Shame*, 167.
67 Bates, *Battle of Savo Island*, 78.
68 Ohmae, "Battle of Savo Island," 232.
69 Bates, *Battle of Savo Island*, 107; Ohmae, "Battle of Savo Island," 232. The Naval War College (Bates) is used here except for his timing of sighting the ship, which appears to be ten minutes later than the Japanese time as related by Captain Ohmae.
70 Ohmae, "Battle of Savo Island," 232.
71 Bates, *Battle of Savo Island*, 107.
72 Ohmae, "Battle of Savo Island," 232–3. Bates (*Battle of Savo Island*, 110) insists that the *Blue* was headed southwest, or away from the *Chokai* when the latter sighted the former. The Naval War College's belief must be balanced against the Japanese records, Captain Ohmae's specific recollection, and the post-war analysis by Morison. Loxton and Coulthard-Clark (*Shame*, 171–3) go into a discussion of the dispute here and point out that the actions of the Japanese force, specifically: 1. Admiral Mikawa's initial course change in response to the *Blue* sighting; and 2. The *Tenryu* turning toward the *Blue* are indicative of the *Blue* approaching the Japanese, not moving away from them. This writer disagrees with the former but agrees with the latter, and finds the Naval War College's case here unpersuasive.
73 Newcomb, *Battle of Savo Island*, 43.
74 Ohmae, "Battle of Savo Island," 233.
75 Bates (*Battle of Savo Island*, 108) insists that the ship sighted at this time was not the *Ralph Talbot*, but "evidently was a two-masted schooner" that had been observed by a scout plane from the *Enterprise* on August 7 northwest of the Russell Islands. Loxton and Coulthard-Clark (*Shame*, 173–4) go into a discussion of the evidence in this factual dispute. Loxton's conclusion is that the Naval War College's finding that no Japanese ship saw the *Ralph Talbot* at this time is "not justified." This writer finds Loxton's analysis persuasive and has used it as a basis for the narrative here. It should be pointed out that the idea of this mysterious ship the skilled Japanese identified as a "destroyer" – and was roughly where a destroyer who arguably did not fulfill her picket duty should have been – was instead a schooner is a little too convenient.
76 Bates, *Battle of Savo Island*, 108.
77 Loxton and Coulthard-Clark, *Shame*, 171.
78 Bates, *Battle of Savo Island*, 110–1.
79 Morison, *Struggle*, 36.
80 Hammel, *Starvation*, 1848–65.

81 Loxton and Coulthard-Clark, *Shame*, 175.
82 Gatacre, *Reports*, 174.
83 Loxton and Coulthard-Clark, *Shame*, 171.
84 Jack D. Coombe, *Derailing the Tokyo Express: The Naval Battles for the Solomon Islands that Sealed Japan's Fate* (Harrisburg, PA: Stackpole, 1991), 23.
85 The sighting reports of Admiral Mikawa's ships by the Australian Hudsons have been controversial. The delay in their relay to Admiral Turner was blamed by Morison (*Struggle*, 25) on the Hudson's crew for failing to report the sighting until after they leisurely completed their search, had landed, and even had tea. This version of events was later repeated by numerous historians. Savo Island historian Bruce Loxton spent years researching the claim, as a result of which he would call it "almost completely unjustified," and "untrue" (Loxton and Coulthard-Clark, *Shame*, 144–5). After decades of lobbying by the Hudson's radio operator Eric Geddes, in 2014 the US Navy's Naval History and Heritage Command stated, "RADM Morison's criticism, in particular, was unwarranted." "Eric Geddes: Sole survivor of WWII RAAF aircrew wins fight to erase historic slur over Savo Island bloodbath" - ABC News (Australian Broadcasting Corporation) Adam Harvey October 28, 2014 09:18:21 Pacific War of WW2 The Battle of Savo Island - August 9, 1942 (http://www.ww2pacific.com/hudsonrep.html#10).
86 Toland, *Rising Sun*, 7960.
87 Ibid., 7960.
88 Ibid., 7960.
89 Ibid., 7960.
90 Ibid., 7960.
91 Gatacre, *Reports*, 171.
92 Bates, *Battle of Savo Island*, 3, 108–9.
93 Loxton and Coulthard-Clark, *Shame*, 180.
94 Bates, *Battle of Savo Island*, 109.
95 Ibid., 114.
96 Ohmae, "Battle of Savo Island," 235.
97 Ibid., 235.
98 Loxton and Coulthard-Clark, *Shame*, 176–7.
99 Ohmae, "Battle of Savo Island," 235.
100 Bates, *Battle of Savo Island*, 115.
101 Loxton and Coulthard-Clark, *Shame*, 180.
102 Coombe, *Derailing*, 23.
103 Loxton and Coulthard-Clark, *Shame*, 111.
104 Loxton and Coulthard-Clark, *Shame*, 180; Bates, *Battle of Savo Island*, 127.
105 Coombe, *Derailing*, 24.
106 Apparently enraged by the inability to launch torpedoes at this time, Commander Walker sacked his torpedo officer shortly after the battle.
107 Bates, *Battle of Savo Island*, 137.
108 Domagalski, *Lost*, 1421.
109 Loxton and Coulthard-Clark, *Shame*, 180; Mackenzie J Gregory, "H.M.A.S. Canberra and the Battle of Savo Island," *Ahoy – Mac's Web Log – Naval, Maritime, Australian History and more*, http://ahoy.tk-jk.net.
110 Loxton and Coulthard-Clark, *Shame*, 180–1.
111 U.S.S. BAGLEY (386) "Night Engagement August 9, 1942 – Tulagi Guadalcanal Area August 13, 1942" ("*Bagley* Report"), 1.
112 Loxton and Coulthard-Clark, *Shame*, 192.
113 Ibid., 198.
114 Ibid.,198. Some of the rumors were that Chambers had to pull a gun on Sinclair to get him to relinquish command.
115 Bates, *Battle of Savo Island*, 134–5.
116 *Bagley* Report, 1.
117 Bates, *Battle of Savo Island*, 118–19.
118 Ibid., 120; Loxton and Coulthard-Clark, *Shame*, 183.
119 Bates, *Battle of Savo Island*, 128, says, "It is unfortunate that (Captain Getting) did not advise his immediate superior in command of the *Chicago* Group of his contacts with the enemy. Whatever may have been the

reason for this failure, it in no way relieved him of the responsibility for alerting the command to the presence of the enemy." As to how Getting was supposed to alert the *Chicago* when the *Canberra*'s radio had been smashed and the cruiser was without power, the Naval War College was rather vague.

120 Domagalski, *Lost*, 1510.
121 Ibid., 1421.
122 Bates, *Battle of Savo Island*, 130.
123 Morison, Two-Ocean War, 172.
124 Domagalski, *Lost*, 1421.
125 Ibid., 1435, 1508.
126 Ibid., 1488.
127 Bates, *Battle of Savo Island*, 132.
128 Ibid., 132.
129 Domagalski, *Lost*, 1488.
130 Bates, *Battle of Savo Island*, 132–3.
131 Ibid., 133.
132 Ibid., 133.
133 Vincent P. O'Hara, *The US Navy Against the Axis: Surface Combat 1941–1945* (Annapolis: Naval Institute Press, 2007), 1852; Bates, *Battle of Savo Island*, 138.
134 Bates, *Battle of Savo Island*, 166–7.
135 Ibid., 256.
136 Ibid., 298.
137 Newcomb, *Battle of Savo Island*, 169.
138 Bates, *Battle of Savo Island*, 162.
139 Interrogation Nav No.83, USSBS No.407, 13–14 November 1945: Interrogation of Rear Admiral Akira Siji, Captain Kenkichi Kato, and Captain Nobuye Ukita.
140 Ibid
141 Domagalski, *Lost*, 1582.
142 Ibid., 1550.
143 Ibid., 1563.
144 Newcomb, *Battle of Savo Island*, 128.
145 Domagalski, *Lost*, 1563.
146 Ibid., 1613.
147 Bates, *Battle of Savo Island*, 153.
148 Domagalski, *Lost*, 1633; Newcomb, *Battle of Savo Island*, 128.
149 Unless otherwise noted, the events on the *Astoria*'s bridge are from Domagalski, *Lost*, 1676–93.
150 Winston B. Lewis and Henry A. Mustin, *United States Navy Combat Narrative: The Battles of Savo Island, 9 August 1942 and the Eastern Solomons, 23–25 August 1942* (Washington, DC: Publications Branch, Office of Naval Intelligence, United States Navy, 1943), 21.
151 Bates, *Battle of Savo Island*, 194.
152 Ibid., 143; Newcomb, *Battle of Savo Island*, 134.
153 Bates, *Battle of Savo Island*, 178.
154 Ibid., 179.
155 Ibid.,182.
156 Ibid., 182–3.
157 Newcomb, *Battle of Savo Island*, 132.
158 Bates, *Battle of Savo Island*, 183–4.
159 Gatacre, *Reports*, 176; Bates, *Battle of Savo Island*, 140; Newcomb, *Battle of Savo Island*, 124.
160 Newcomb, *Battle of Savo Island*, 124.
161 Bates, *Battle of Savo Island*, 142–3.
162 Ibid., 144.
163 Ibid., 144. Dennis Warner, Peggy Warner, and Sadao Seno, *Disaster in the Pacific: New Light on the Battle of Savo Island* (Annapolis: Naval Institute Press, 1992), 147; Bates, *Battle of Savo Island*, 169.
164 Loxton and Coulthard-Clark, *Shame*, 225.
165 Warner, Warner, and Seno, *Disaster*, 148.
166 Ibid., 147.

167 Bates, *Battle of Savo Island*, 175.
168 Ibid., 176–7.
169 Bates, *Battle of Savo Island*, 177; *War Damage Report No. 29 USS Astoria (CA34), USS Quincy (CA39), USS Vincennes (CA44) Loss in Action Battle of Savo Island August 9, 1942*, Preliminary Design Branch Bureau of Ships Navy Department, 21 June, 1943, 13.
170 Bates, *Battle of Savo Island*, 231, 233, 249.
171 Ibid., 233, 234.
172 Ibid., 289–90.
173 Ibid., 238.
174 Ibid., 236.
175 Ohmae, "Battle of Savo Island," 236–7.
176 Bates, *Battle of Savo Island*, 238–9.
177 Ibid., 239.
178 Ohmae, "Battle of Savo Island," 236.
179 Bates, *Battle of Savo Island*, 239.
180 Newcomb, *Battle of Savo Island*, 133–4.
181 Bates, *Battle of Savo Island*, 240; Newcomb, *Battle of Savo Island*, 134.
182 Bates, *Battle of Savo Island*, 241; Newcomb, *Battle of Savo Island*, 134.
183 Bates, *Battle of Savo Island*, 242, 290–1.
184 Ibid., 245–6.
185 Ibid., 248.
186 Ibid., 248.
187 Ibid., 247.
188 Ohmae, "Battle of Savo Island," 236.
189 Ibid., 236.
190 Ibid., 237–8.
191 Gatacre, *Reports*, 176–7.
192 Ohmae, "Battle of Savo Island," 244.
193 Toland, *Rising Sun*, 8070.
194 Ibid., 8070.
195 Ohmae, "Battle of Savo Island," 239.
196 Frank, *Guadalcanal*, 116.
197 Bates, *Battle of Savo Island*, 228.
198 Ibid., 257–8.
199 Ibid., 228.
200 Ibid., 309.
201 Ohmae, "Battle of Savo Island," 239.
202 Gatacre, *Reports*, 171.
203 Domagalski, *Lost*, 2741.
204 Bates, *Battle of Savo Island*, 280; Loxton and Coulthard-Clark, *Shame*, 215.
205 Bates, *Battle of Savo Island*, 281.
206 Ibid., 281.
207 Loxton and Coulthard-Clark, *Shame*, 215.
208 Domagalski, *Lost*, 2741; Loxton and Coulthard-Clark, *Shame*, 215.
209 Bates, *Battle of Savo Island*, 280–1.
210 Loxton and Coulthard-Clark, *Shame*, 215.
211 Ibid., 171.
212 Bates, *Battle of Savo Island*, 287.
213 Ibid., 284.
214 Lundstrom, *Black Shoe*, 57.
215 Frank, *Guadalcanal*, 119.
216 Bates, *Battle of Savo Island*, 288.
217 Morison, *Struggle*, 54.
218 Bates, *Battle of Savo Island*, 284.
219 Newcomb, *Battle of Savo Island*, 191.

220 Loxton and Coulthard-Clark, *Shame*, 242–3.
221 Bates, *Battle of Savo Island*, 282.
222 Loxton and Coulthard-Clark, *Shame*, 243.
223 Newcomb, *Battle of Savo Island*, 169.
224 Loxton and Coulthard-Clark, *Shame*, 243.
225 Ibid., 243–4.
226 Ibid., 244.
227 Ibid., 245–6.
228 Newcomb, *Battle of Savo Island*, 188–9.
229 Domagalski, *Lost*, 2616.
230 Breakdown of Allied deaths by ship: *Quincy*-389, *Vincennes*-342, *Astoria*-235, *Canberra*-85, *Ralph Talbot*-14, *Patterson*-10, and *Chicago*-2. Breakdown of Japanese deaths by ship: *Chokai*-34, *Tenryu*-23, and *Kinugasa*-1. Frank, *Guadalcanal*, 117, 121.
231 Domagalski, *Lost*, 1510.
232 Hornfischer, *Neptune's Inferno*, 89.
233 Commander James C. Shaw, USN, "Jarvis: Destroyer That Vanished," *Proceedings Magazine*, February 1950, Vol. 76/2/564, 126.
234 Bates, *Battle of Savo Island*, 274–5.
235 Shaw, "Jarvis: Destroyer That Vanished," 126.
236 Ibid., 126.
237 Bates, *Battle of Savo Island*, 278.
238 Shaw, "Jarvis: Destroyer That Vanished," 127.
239 Bates, *Battle of Savo Island*, 337.
240 Domagalski, *Lost*, 2693.
241 *Meiyo Maru* and *Tsugaru* TROMs.
242 Eric Lacroix and Linton Wells II, *Japanese Cruisers of the Pacific War* (Annapolis: Naval Institute Press, 1997), 307.
243 Time is from Lacroix and Wells, *Cruisers*, 307, adjusted for local time. The *Kako* TROM has the torpedoes striking two minutes earlier.
244 *Kako* TROM.
245 Theodore Roscoe, *United States Submarine Operations in World War II* (Annapolis: Naval Institute Press, 1949), 153. Newcomb, *Battle of Savo Island*, 209, says of the torpedo hits on the *Kako*: "[F]or once American torpedoes detonated." This was only because these torpedoes were older Mark 10s, not the new Mark 14s, which had a habit of detonating everywhere except against an enemy ship.
246 Roscoe, *Submarine Operations*, 153.
247 Coombe, *Derailing*, 29.

Chapter 4

1 Vandegrift and Asprey, *Once A Marine*, 132–3.
2 Twining, *No Bended Knee*, 85.
3 William Manchester, *Goodbye, Darkness: A Memoir of the Pacific War* (New York: Back Bay Books, 1979), 2372.
4 Johnson, *Pacific Campaign*, 200.
5 Morison, *Struggle*, 4.
6 Ibid., 4.
7 William J. Owens, *Green Hell: The Battle for Guadalcanal* (Central Point, OR: Hellgate Press, 1999), 15.
8 Johnson, *Pacific Campaign*, 201.
9 Ibid., 204.
10 Ibid., 204; Foss, *Flying Marine*, 670–88.
11 Ibid., 201.
12 Manchester, *Goodbye, Darkness*, 2372–88.
13 Leckie, *Challenge*, 2278.
14 Johnson, *Pacific Campaign*, 203.
15 Manchester, *Goodbye, Darkness*, 2629.

16 Ibid., 2372.
17 Twining, *No Bended Knee*, 88.
18 Jersey, *Hell's Islands*, 2635.
19 Major John L. Zimmerman, USMCR, *The Guadalcanal Campaign: Marines in World War II Historical Monograph* (Washington, DC: Historical Section, Division of Public Information, Headquarters, US Marine Corps, 1949), 63–4.
20 Vandegrift and Asprey, *Once A Marine*, 133–4; Lundstrom, *First Team*, 2783.
21 Twining, *No Bended Knee*, 93.
22 Prados, *Islands of Destiny*, 66.
23 Warner, Warner, and Seno, *Disaster*, 79.
24 Frank, *Guadalcanal*, 142.
25 Ibid., 141–2.
26 Ibid., 171–2.
27 Ibid., 143–4.
28 Lundstrom, *First Team*, 2908.
29 Raizo Tanaka, "The Struggle for Guadalcanal," *The Japanese Navy in World War II in the Words of Former Japanese Naval Officers* (2nd ed.), ed. David C. Evans (Annapolis: Naval Institute Press, 1986), 160–1.
30 Leckie, *Challenge*, 2225.
31 Also called the Battle of Khalkyn Gol ("Khalka River").
32 Richard Fuller, *Shokan: Hirohito's Samurai* (London: Arms and Armour Press, 1992), 107.
33 Griffith, *Guadalcanal*, 98.
34 William H. Bartsch, *Victory Fever: Japan's First Land Defeat of WWII* (College Station, TX: Texas A&M University Press, 2014), 76.
35 Frank, *Guadalcanal*, 146.
36 Ibid., 147.
37 Tanaka, "Struggle for Guadalcanal," 161.
38 Ibid., 164.
39 Bartsch, *Victory Fever*, 82.
40 Tanaka, "Struggle for Guadalcanal," 163–4.
41 Toland, *Rising Sun*, 8099.
42 Hammel, *Carrier Clash*, 2502.
43 Leckie, *Challenge*, 2185. A slightly different translation appears in Toland, *Rising Sun*, 8119.
44 Toland, *Rising Sun*, 8119.
45 Lewis and Mustin, *Combat Narrative*, 44.
46 Frank, *Guadalcanal*, 122.
47 Loxton and Coulthard-Clark, *Shame*, 256–9; Gregory, "H.M.A.S. Canberra and the Battle of Savo Island."
48 Frank, *Guadalcanal*, 123; see also Dyer, *Amphibians*, 360–1.
49 Johnson, *Pacific Campaign*, 187.
50 Frank, *Guadalcanal*, 134.
51 Lundstrom, *First Team*, 2783.
52 Ibid., 2769–83.
53 Ibid., 2783–2801.
54 Prados, *Islands of Destiny*, 69–70.
55 Ibid., 70; Frank, *Guadalcanal*, 161.
56 Lundstrom, *First Team*, 2831.
57 Morison, *Struggle*, 67.
58 Lundstrom, *First Team*, 2964.
59 Ibid., 2981–98.
60 Wings at War, Vol. 3, 12.
61 Hough, Ludwig, and Shaw, *Pearl Harbor*, 275.
62 Owens, *Green Hell*, 16.
63 *I-123* TROM.
64 *I-122* TROM.
65 Prados, *Islands of Destiny*, 67.
66 Frank, *Guadalcanal*, 129.

67 Owens, *Green Hell*, 63.
68 Dick Camp, "Star-Crossed Translator," *Leatherneck, Military.com*; www.military.com; Hammel, *Starvation*, 2318.
69 Frank, *Guadalcanal*, 130.
70 Camp, "Star-Crossed Translator."
71 Jersey, *Hell's Islands*, 2768.
72 Prados, *Islands of Destiny*, 89.
73 Leckie, *Challenge*, 2080.
74 Griffith, *Guadalcanal*, 88.
75 Leckie, *Challenge*, 2097.
76 Martin Clemens, *Alone on Guadalcanal: A Coastwatcher's Story* (Annapolis: Naval Institute Press, 1998), 198.
77 Jersey, *Hell's Islands*, 2768.
78 Hough, Ludwig, and Shaw, *Pearl Harbor*, 276; Frank, *Guadalcanal*, 131.
79 Leckie, *Challenge*, 2156.
80 Frank, *Guadalcanal*, 131.
81 Jersey, *Hell's Islands*, 2795.
82 Leckie, *Challenge*, 2173.
83 Jersey, *Hell's Islands*, 2804–13.
84 Matome Ugaki, Donald M. Goldstein (ed.), and Katherine V. Dillon (ed.), *Fading Victory: The Diary of Admiral Matome Ugaki* (Pittsburgh: University of Pittsburgh Press, 1991), 185; Hammel, *Carrier Clash*, 2188; Morison, *Struggle*, 70; Tanaka, "Struggle for Guadalcanal," 162 (where Admiral Tanaka mistakenly has the *Yamakaze* instead of the *Arashi*); Leckie, *Challenge*, 2173; *Hagikaze* TROM.
85 Jersey, *Hell's Islands*, 2851.
86 Hammel, *Starvation*, 2726.
87 Bartsch, *Victory Fever*, 95.
88 Zimmerman, *Guadalcanal Campaign*, 62.
89 Clemens, *Alone*, 208.
90 Leckie, *Challenge*, 2288.
91 Hornfischer, *Neptune's Inferno*, 2103.
92 Clemens, *Alone*, 208.
93 Hammel, *Carrier Clash*, 2455; Vandegrift and Asprey, *Once A Marine*, 139; Hornfischer, *Neptune's Inferno*, 2103.
94 Hornfischer, *Neptune's Inferno*, 2103.
95 Clemens, *Alone*, 208.
96 Leckie, *Challenge*, 2300. The name "Ishimoto" on Guadalcanal and Tulagi has been associated with a shadowy Japanese intelligence operative. Postwar research initially associated "Ishimoto" with one Ishimoto Terushige, who worked as an interpreter for the Japanese. Research by historian Stan Jersey has conclusively proven that Ishimoto Terushige had no hand in any war crimes and was not even in the area during the brutal interrogation of Sergeant Major Jacob Vouza. The name "Ishimoto" is used here because the Imperial Japanese Army officer in question has not been identified and the name "Ishimoto" has been recognized and used as identification, as Jersey suggests, for all Japanese interpreters and intelligence officers. Stan Jersey, "The Mysterious Mr. Moto on Guadalcanal," *Pacific Wrecks* http://www.pacificwrecks.com/people/veterans/ishimoto/index.html.
97 Bartsch, *Victory Fever*, 82; Toland, *Rising Sun*, 8118.
98 Toland, *Rising Sun*, 8135.
99 Jersey, *Hell's Islands*, 2831–40.
100 Leckie, *Challenge*, 2189.
101 Unless otherwise noted, the story of Sergeant Major Vouza's confinement comes from Clemens, *Alone*, 209.
102 Hammel, *Starvation*, 2760.
103 Leckie, *Challenge*, 2357.
104 Bartsch, *Victory Fever*, 140, 142.
105 Leckie, *Challenge*, 2391.
106 Clemens, *Alone*, 209–10.
107 Lundstrom, *First Team*, 3109; Zimmerman, *Historical Monograph*, 69–70.
108 Vandegrift and Asprey, *Once A Marine*, 142.

109 Ibid., 142.
110 Ibid., 143–4.
111 Leckie, *Challenge*, 2417.
112 Bartsch, *Victory Fever*, 217, 218, 284.
113 This is largely based on the account of Leading Private Morihiro Masao, who witnessed the suicide of several officers, one of whom he presumed to be Colonel Ichiki. Bartsch, *Victory Fever*, 218, 284; Fuller, *Shokan*, 107.
114 Tanaka, "Struggle for Guadalcanal," 164.
115 Leckie, *Challenge*, 2485–501.

Chapter 5

1 Lundstrom, *First Team*, 3045.
2 Ibid., 3011–28.
3 Ibid., 3028, 3045; Tanaka, "Struggle for Guadalcanal," 164.
4 Frank, *Guadalcanal*, 163–4.
5 Lundstrom, *First Team*, 3011–28.
6 Hammel, *Carrier Clash*, 2757; Lundstrom, *First Team*, 3070.
7 Lundstrom, *First Team*, 3079.
8 Ibid., 3084.
9 Ibid., 3050.
10 Ibid., 3097.
11 Craven, *Army Air Forces in World War II*, Vol. IV, p. 18.
12 O'Hara, *US Navy*, 83.
13 Theodore Roscoe, *United States Destroyer Operations in World War II* (Annapolis: Naval Institute Press, 1953), 175.
14 O'Hara, *US Navy*, 83.
15 Parkin, *Blood*, 80.
16 Morison, *Struggle*, 81.
17 Prados, *Islands of Destiny*, 67.
18 O'Hara, *US Navy*, 83.
19 Roscoe, *Destroyer Operations*, 175.
20 Parkin, *Blood*, 81.
21 Lundstrom, *First Team*, 3118–34.
22 Ibid., 3112–29; O'Hara, *US Navy*, 83–4.
23 Lundstrom, *First Team*, 3177.
24 Tanaka, "Struggle for Guadalcanal," 165–6.
25 Lewis and Mustin, *Combat Narrative*, 52; *I-19* TROM.
26 Lundstrom, *First Team*, 3194–213.
27 Prados, *Islands of Destiny*, 70.
28 Ibid., 70.
29 Lundstrom, *First Team*, 3227.
30 Ibid., 3318–34; Lewis and Mustin, *Combat Narrative*, 54.
31 Lundstrom, *First Team*, 3334.
32 Ibid., 3345.
33 Ibid., 3345–63.
34 Ibid., 3382.
35 Ibid., 3391–3408; Lundstrom, *Black Shoe*, 440.
36 Lundstrom, *First Team*, 3416.
37 Ibid., 3444.
38 Ibid., 3488–503.
39 Ibid., 3455.
40 Ibid., 3557.
41 Ibid., 3550.
42 Tameichi Hara, Fred Saito, and Roger Pineau, *Japanese Destroyer Captain: Pearl Harbor, Guadalcanal, Midway – The Great Naval Battles as Seen Through Japanese Eyes* (Annapolis: Naval Institute Press, 1967), 98.

43 Hammel, *Carrier Clash*, 3510.
44 Hara Chuichi is also known as Hara Tadaichi.
45 Hara, Saito, and Pineau, *Destroyer Captain*, 98.
46 Lundstrom, *First Team*, 3160.
47 Lundstrom, *Black Shoe*, 434.
48 See, e.g., Hara, Saito, and Pineau, *Destroyer Captain*, 97–8; Morison, *Struggle*, 82.
49 Ugaki, Goldstein, and Dillon, *Fading Victory*, 191.
50 According to naval historian Mark E. Stille (*The Imperial Japanese Navy in the Pacific War* (Oxford: Osprey, 2014), 844), "The [*Ryujo*'s] small flight deck, small elevators, and unfavorable elevator placement made aircraft operations difficult and greatly reduced the ship's effectiveness."
51 See e.g. Tanaka, "Struggle for Guadalcanal," 166 (Admiral Tanaka said, "the *Tone* and *Ryujo* [...] with two destroyers were serving as indirect escort to my reinforcement group"); Lundstrom, *Black Shoe*, 432, 434. Paul S. Dull (*A Battle History of the Imperial Japanese Navy (1941–1945)*, (Annapolis: Naval Institute Press, 1978, 198) went so far as to say there was "no known evidence" the *Ryujo* was intended as a decoy.
52 Lundstrom, *First Team*, 2933.
53 Tanaka, "Struggle for Guadalcanal," 166.
54 Hara, Saito, and Pineau, *Destroyer Captain*, 97.
55 Lundstrom, *First Team*, 3575.
56 Hara, Saito, and Pineau, *Destroyer Captain*, 99; Lundstrom, *First Team*, 3575.
57 Hara, Saito, and Pineau, *Destroyer Captain*, 99.
58 Lundstrom, *First Team*, 3575; Hara, Saito, and Pineau, *Destroyer Captain*, 99.
59 Hara, Saito, and Pineau, *Destroyer Captain*, 99.
60 Ibid., 99.
61 Ibid., 98; Lundstrom, *First Team*, 3602.
62 Lundstrom, *First Team*, 3614; Lewis and Mustin, *Combat Narrative*, 56.
63 Hara, Saito, and Pineau, *Destroyer Captain*, 99–100.
64 Ibid., 100; Lundstrom, *First Team*, 3632.
65 Lundstrom, *First Team*, 3480; Lewis and Mustin, *Combat Narrative*, 56.
66 Lundstrom, *First Team*, 3464–87.
67 Lewis and Mustin, *Combat Narrative*, 56; Frank, *Guadalcanal*, 178.
68 Hara, Saito, and Pineau, *Destroyer Captain*, 100.
69 *Ryujo* TROM; *Ryujo* Data Page – *Nihon Kaigun*; Lundstrom, *First Team*, 3647.
70 Lewis and Mustin, *Combat Narrative*, 57.
71 *Ryujo* TROM; *Ryujo* Data Page – *Nihon Kaigun*; Lundstrom, *First Team*, 3647.
72 Lewis and Mustin, *Combat Narrative*, 57.
73 Hara, Saito, and Pineau, *Destroyer Captain*, 100–101; Tanaka, "Struggle for Guadalcanal," 166.
74 Hara, Saito, and Pineau, *Destroyer Captain*, 101.
75 Lundstrom, *First Team*, 3661, 3653.
76 Ibid., 3653–72.
77 Hara, Saito, and Pineau, *Destroyer Captain*, 101–2; Tanaka, "Struggle for Guadalcanal," 166.
78 Hammel, *Carrier Clash*, 4137.
79 Hara, Saito, and Pineau, *Destroyer Captain*, 101.
80 Ibid., 101.
81 Ibid., 101.
82 *Ryujo* TROM.
83 Hara, Saito, and Pineau, *Destroyer Captain*, 101.
84 Ibid., 101–2.
85 Lundstrom, *First Team*, 3454.
86 Dull, *Battle History*, 200.
87 Hara, Saito, and Pineau, *Destroyer Captain*, 101.
88 Ibid., 104.
89 Ibid., 98.
90 Lundstrom, *First Team*, 3687.
91 The Type 0 Reconnaissance Seaplane should not be confused with the Type 0 Observation Seaplane.

92 Ibid., 3687.
93 Ibid., 3704.
94 Ibid., 3724.
95 Ibid., 3732.
96 Ibid., 3769–77.
97 Ibid., 3731.
98 Lundstrom, *Black Shoe*, 446.
99 Lundstrom, *First Team*, 3792; Lundstrom, *Black Shoe*, 446.
100 Lundstrom, *First Team*, 3798.
101 Lundstrom, *Black Shoe*, 446.
102 Lundstrom, *First Team*, 3798.
103 Ibid., 3815.
104 Ibid., 3832.
105 Ibid., 3865–907.
106 Ibid., 3831.
107 Ibid., 3927.
108 Ibid., 3927–50.
109 Frank, *Guadalcanal*, 182.
110 Lundstrom, *First Team*, 3968.
111 Ibid., 3970.
112 Warships Associated With World War II in the Pacific – USS NORTH CAROLINA https://www.nps.gov/parkhistory/online_books/butowsky1/northcarolina.htm.
113 Lundstrom, *First Team*, 3948–62.
114 Ibid., 3978–88.
115 Lewis and Mustin, *Combat Narrative*, 65.
116 Lundstrom, *First Team*, 3978.
117 Warships Associated With World War II in the Pacific – USS NORTH CAROLINA.
118 Lundstrom, *First Team*, 4018.
119 Ibid., 4005.
120 Ibid., 4025.
121 Ibid., 4035.
122 Frank, *Guadalcanal*, 182.
123 Lundstrom, *First Team*, 4068.
124 William Thomas Generous, Jr, *Sweet Pea at War: A History of USS* Portland (Lexington, KY: University Press of Kentucky, 2003), 63.
125 Generous, *Sweet Pea*, 63–4.
126 Frank, *Guadalcanal*, 182.
127 Lundstrom, *First Team*, 3732.
128 Ibid., 4397–420.
129 Ibid., 4420.
130 Morison, *Struggle*, 100.
131 Lundstrom, *First Team*, 4461–79.
132 Ibid., 4479–90; *Chitose* TROM; Frank, *Guadalcanal*, 187–8.
133 Frank, *Guadalcanal*, 188.
134 Tanaka, "Struggle for Guadalcanal," 167.
135 Lundstrom, *First Team*, 4603.
136 Ibid., 4603–20.
137 Tanaka, "Struggle for Guadalcanal," 167.
138 Lundstrom, *First Team*, 4620; Tanaka, "Struggle for Guadalcanal," 169; *Jintsu* TROM.
139 *Jintsu* TROM; Lundstrom, *First Team*, 4620, which calls the near-miss "damaging"; *Kinryu Maru* TROM; Curiously, the *Boston Maru* TROM does not mention it.
140 Martin Caidin, *The B-17: The Flying Forts* (New York: iBooks, 2001), 3619.
141 On January 4, 1942, the Japanese heavy cruiser *Myoko*, anchored in the Gulf of Davao, Philippines, was hit by a bomb from a B-17.

142 Interrogation Nav. No. 8, USSBS No. 46, Interrogation of Commander H. Sekino and Commander Masatake Okumiya, 17 October 1945, 31. Toland, *Rising Sun*, 8221; Leckie, *Challenge*, both of whom identify his given name as "Kiyono." Martin Caidin (*The B-17*, 3619) says, "[Hatano's] superiors were little pleased with him …" It is probably revealing that Admiral Tanaka ("Struggle for Guadalcanal," 169) points out that the *Mutsuki* "with no headway" took direct hits.
143 Tanaka, "Struggle for Guadalcanal," 169.
144 Ugaki, Goldstein, and Dillon, *Fading Victory*, 193.

Chapter 6

1 Thomas G. Miller, *The Cactus Air Force* (New York: Bantam, 1981), 62.
2 Miller, *Cactus*, 62.
3 Frank, *Guadalcanal*, 194–5; Lundstrom, *First Team*, 5355.
4 Frank, *Guadalcanal*, 194–5; Miller, *Cactus*, 62.
5 Lundstrom, *First Team*, 5347.
6 Robert Sherrod, *History of Marine Corps Aviation in World War II* (Washington, DC: Combat Forces Press, 1952), 83.
7 Lundstrom, *First Team*, 5336.
8 Frank, *Guadalcanal*, 197.
9 Lundstrom, *First Team*, 5373–94. Jojima Takatsugu is sometimes rendered as Joshima Takaji, or some combination thereof.
10 Lundstrom, *First Team*, 5373–94.
11 Ibid., 5394.
12 *Akitsushima* TROM.
13 *PB-35* TROM.
14 Frank, *Guadalcanal*, 195–7.
15 Admiral Tanaka's experience with this reinforcement comes from Tanaka, "Struggle for Guadalcanal," 169–71.
16 Ibid., 170.
17 Hough, *Pearl Harbor*, 301, who says Kawaguchi was "a barge man."
18 Frank, *Guadalcanal*, 199.
19 Tanaka, "Struggle for Guadalcanal," 171.
20 Why two SBD Dauntlesses were ordered to fly scouting missions without radios has never been explained.
21 *Shirakumo* TROM; Miller, *Cactus*, 63.
22 *Asagiri* TROM; Frank, *Guadalcanal*, 199–200; Miller, *Cactus*, 63.
23 *Yugiri* TROM. Admiral Tanaka (Tanaka, "Struggle for Guadalcanal," 171) identifies the commander of the 20th Destroyer Division as Captain Arita Yuzo and states he was killed in the American bombing attack that sank the *Asagiri* and damaged the *Yugiri* and *Shirakumo*. Most histories have understandably followed Tanaka's lead (see e.g. Frank, *Guadalcanal*, 200). Miller (*Cactus*, 63) even says Arita was killed on the *Asagiri*. However, the TROM for the *Asagiri* makes no mention of the destroyer division commander being on board at the time of her loss. Furthermore, the TROM for the destroyer *Yugiri* states that a bomb hit to the bridge left "32 dead, including Comdesdiv 20 (Captain Yamada Yuji [46]), and 40 injured[.]" Finally, the TROM for the Japanese escort carrier *Kaiyo* states that on August 1, 1944, Captain Arita Yuzo assumed command.
24 *Asagiri* TROM; Frank, *Guadalcanal*, 200; *Shirakumo* TROM.
25 Frank, *Guadalcanal*, 200; Tanaka, "Struggle for Guadalcanal," 172.
26 Frank, *Guadalcanal*, 200; Tanaka, "Struggle for Guadalcanal," 172.
27 Tanaka, "Struggle for Guadalcanal," 172. "Commodore" is a title used for a captain who commands more than one ship.
28 Frank, *Guadalcanal*, 200.
29 Miller, *Cactus*, 64; Frank, *Guadalcanal*, 200; Hammel, *Starvation*, 3268–86.
30 Unless noted otherwise, the sinking of the submarine *I-123* comes from the *I-123* TROM.
31 Frank, *Guadalcanal*, 200; Hammel, *Starvation*, 3266.
32 Tanaka, "Struggle for Guadalcanal," 173–4.
33 Miller (*Cactus*, 660) says Captain Murakami fled "incontinently" back to Shortland.
34 Tanaka, "Struggle for Guadalcanal," 174.
35 Hammel, *Starvation*, 3281.

36 Sherrod, *History*, 82.
37 Because the P-39 Airacobra and the P-400 were mostly the same plane, the name "Airacobra" will be used for both for ease of reference.
38 Hammel, *Starvation*, 3195–211.
39 Frank, *Guadalcanal*, 202; Curt Clark, *Four Stack APDs: The Famed Green Dragons* (Paducah, KY: Turner Publishing Company, 2003), 59; Miller, *Cactus*, 68.
40 *William Ward Burrows*, Dictionary of American Naval Fighting Ships.
41 Lundstrom, *First Team*, 4968.
42 Frank, *Guadalcanal*, 214.
43 Morison, *Struggle*, 114–5.
44 Frank, *Guadalcanal*, 214.
45 Lundstrom, *First Team*, 4979–97.
46 *I-26* TROM; Lundstrom, *Black Shoe*, 471; Morison, *Struggle*, 110–11.
47 Lundstrom, *Black Shoe*, 471.
48 Ibid., 471.
49 Lundstrom, *First Team*, 4917.
50 Lundstrom, *Black Shoe*, 471.
51 Ibid., 471–2.
52 Joseph Czarnecki, "Turboelectric Drive in American Capital Ships," *NavWeaps*, http://www.navweaps.com/index_tech/tech-038.htm.
53 Lundstrom, *Black Shoe*, 472.
54 *I-26* TROM.
55 Lundstrom, *Black Shoe*, 472–3.
56 Lundstrom, *First Team*, 4928.
57 Stephen D. Regan, *In Bitter Tempest: The Biography of Admiral Frank Jack Fletcher* (Ames, IA: Iowa State University Press, 1994), 223.
58 Dyer, *Amphibians*, 391. It should be pointed out that Admiral Fletcher makes no mention here of fuel running low in his carrier task forces as influencing his decision. Fletcher would later dispute the belief that dwindling fuel played a role, citing the message from Admiral Ghormley informing Admiral Nimitz of the withdrawal as the source of that belief. Fletcher said his actual intent was to set up a fueling rendezvous only if Ghormley approved the withdrawal.
59 Dyer, *Amphibians*, 391.
60 Frank, *Guadalcanal*, 94.
61 Lundstrom, *First Team*, 4956.
62 Miller, *Cactus*, 70.
63 Lundstrom, *First Team*, 4979.
64 Griffith, *Guadalcanal*, 117.
65 Ibid., 117.
66 Zimmerman, *Historical Monograph*, 76–7; Frank, *Guadalcanal*, 205.
67 *Tsugaru* TROM.
68 Tanaka, "Struggle for Guadalcanal," 174–5.
69 Michael S. Smith, *Bloody Ridge: The Battle That Saved Guadalcanal* (Novato, CA: Presidio, 2000), 1627. Colonel Oka's given name has been variously rendered as Akinosuku, Akinosuke, and Akinosuka.
70 Toland, *Rising Sun*, 8241. While in Shortland, General Kawaguchi caught a lieutenant loitering on deck with a cigarette. While the young officer mumbled an excuse for his inaction, Kawaguchi pushed him overboard. "There are some lazy ones," the general explained.
71 Toland, *Rising Sun*, 8253.
72 Smith, *Bloody Ridge*, 1786.
73 Hammel, *Starvation*, 3386.
74 Ugaki, Goldstein, and Dillon, *Fading Victory*, 203; Smith, *Bloody Ridge*, 1785.
75 Toland, *Rising Sun*, 8310; Smith, *Bloody Ridge*, 1793; Frank, *Guadalcanal*, 205.
76 Hammel, *Starvation*, 3405.
77 Frank, *Guadalcanal*, 205; Hough, *Pearl Harbor*, 295–7.
78 Toland, *Rising Sun*, 8302.
79 Smith, *Bloody Ridge*, 1810.

80 What is presented here is an amalgamation and interpretation of Frank (*Guadalcanal*, 205–6), Smith (*Bloody Ridge*, 1810) and the TROMs for the *Tsugaru*, *Kagero*, *Yugure*, *Amagiri*, *Fubuki*, and *Shirayuki*.
81 Miller, *Cactus*, 78.
82 Hammel, *Starvation*, 3367–84.
83 Frank, *Guadalcanal*, 212.
84 Ibid., 212; Smith, *Bloody Ridge*, 1760; Toland, *Rising Sun*, 8319.
85 Twining, *No Bended Knee*, 115; Hough, *Pearl Harbor*, 295.
86 Zimmerman, *Historical Monograph*, 79–80.
87 Smith, *Bloody Ridge*, 1716.
88 The account of the freeing of the *William Ward Burrows* from her first grounding, her subsequent second grounding, and her freedom from her second grounding come from DANFS – *William Ward Burrows*.
89 Twining, *No Bended Knee*, 113.
90 Frank, *Guadalcanal*, 212.
91 Griffith, *Guadalcanal*, 126.
92 Hammel, *Starvation*, 3404.
93 Zimmerman, *Historical Monograph*, 80.
94 Morison, *Struggle*, 119.
95 Hammel, *Starvation*, 3424.
96 Morison, *Struggle*, 120.
97 Ibid., 120.
98 Ugaki, Goldstein, and Dillon, *Fading Victory*, 205.
99 O'Hara, *US Navy*, 1974.
100 Frank, *Guadalcanal*, 212.
101 Clark, *Green Dragons*, 60.
102 Frank, *Guadalcanal*, 212.
103 Twining, *No Bended Knee*, 116.
104 Smith, *Bloody Ridge*, 1755; TROMs for *Kawakaze*, *Umikaze*, and *Suzukaze*.
105 Frank, *Guadalcanal*, 213.
106 Ibid., 213.
107 Willmott, *Empires*, 242.
108 Ibid., 242.
109 Stuart D. Goldman, *Nomonhan, 1939: The Red Army's Victory that Shaped World War II* (Annapolis: Naval Institute Press, 2012), 173. The quote is from General Tanaka Ryukichi, who was chief of the Military Service Bureau in the Army Ministry in 1941.
110 Willmott, *Empires*, 242.
111 Prados, *Islands of Destiny*, 87.
112 Toland, *Rising Sun*, 8353.
113 Leckie, *Challenge*, 3043.
114 Ibid., 3043; Smith, *Bloody Ridge*, 2134.
115 Smith, *Bloody Ridge*, 1830.
116 Inui Genjirou, "My Guadalcanal" (http://www.nettally.com/jrube/Genjirou/genjirou.htm).
117 Smith, *Bloody Ridge*, 1843.
118 Leckie, *Challenge*, 3043.
119 Smith, *Bloody Ridge*, 1898.
120 Griffith, Guadalcanal, 130.
121 Ibid., 129–30. Twining (*No Bended Knee*, 117) opined, "[This] incident was illustrative of the frequent lack of initiative by Japanese troop leaders at every level."
122 Smith, *Bloody Ridge*, 2119.
123 Griffith, *Guadalcanal*, 130.
124 Smith, *Bloody Ridge*, 2119; *Isuzu* and *Kinu* TROMs.
125 Frank, *Guadalcanal*, 222; *Fubuki*, *Shirayuki*, *Yudachi*, *Kagero*, *Yugure*, *Uranami*, *Amagiri*, and *Shikinami* TROMs.
126 Smith, *Bloody Ridge*, 1951.
127 Ibid., 1929–51.
128 Griffith, *Guadalcanal*, 129.

129 The timing of the supply convoy's arrival was purely coincidental. Lieutenant Colonel Edson and his men did not know about the convoy, and when it approached, they feared it was Japanese. One captain remembered, "We considered ourselves doomed." George W. Smith, *The Do-Or-Die Men: The 1st Marine Raider Battalion at Guadalcanal* (New York: Pocket Books, 2003), 211.
130 These guns are commonly misidentified as 47mm Japanese antitank guns. 2nd Lieutenant Inui identifies the caliber as 37mm. These were German-manufactured PaK 35/36 37mm antitank guns, captured from the Chinese Nationalists (Smith, *Bloody Ridge*, 4038 n. 4). For a long time the Germans had supplied weapons and even advisors to Chiang Kai-shek's army.
131 This was the Type 41 75mm Mountain Gun, a license-built copy of the German Krupp M.08 Mountain Gun. The gun was accepted for production in 1908. Once the gun was superseded by the Type 94 75mm Mountain Gun in 1934, the Japanese designated the Type 41 a "regimental" gun and four were assigned to each infantry regiment.
132 Smith, *Bloody Ridge*, 2076; G. Smith, *Do-Or-Die Men*, 211.
133 Twining, *No Bended Knee*, 117; G. Smith, *Do-Or-Die Men*, 211.
134 Toland, *Rising Sun*, 8320–35.
135 Leckie, *Challenge*, 3078.
136 Frank, *Guadalcanal*, 224.
137 Smith, *Bloody Ridge*, 2151.
138 Ibid., 2151.
139 Frank, *Guadalcanal*, 224.
140 Ibid., 229.
141 Toland, *Rising Sun*, 8384.
142 Ibid., 8384–400.
143 Ibid., 8417.
144 Smith, *Bloody Ridge*, 2094.
145 Frank, *Guadalcanal*, 222.
146 Lundstrom, *First Team*, 5756, 5799–5816.
147 Smith, *Bloody Ridge*, 2548.
148 Griffith, *Guadalcanal*, 131; Smith, *Bloody Ridge*, 2087.
149 Griffith, *Guadalcanal*, 131–2.
150 Ibid., 132.
151 Vandegrift and Asprey, *Once A Marine*, 151.
152 Leckie, *Challenge*, 3106.
153 Vandegrift and Asprey, *Once A Marine*, 151.
154 Twining, *No Bended Knee*, 116.
155 Smith, *Bloody Ridge*, 2214.
156 Miller, *Cactus*, 86–7; Eric Hammel, *Air War Pacific Chronology: America's Air War Against Japan in East Asia and the Pacific 1941–1945* (Pacifica, CA: Pacifica Military History, 1998), 2701.
157 Miller, *Cactus*, 87; Hammel, *Air War*, 2701; Frank, *Guadalcanal*, 226.
158 Lundstrom, *First Team*, 5226–42.
159 Miller, *Cactus*, 87–8; Hammel, *Air War*, 2719; Frank, *Guadalcanal*, 226.
160 Lundstrom, *First Team*, 5307.
161 Griffith, *Guadalcanal*, 135.
162 Twining, *No Bended Knee*, 119.
163 Twining, *No Bended Knee*, 121; Frank, *Guadalcanal*, 228 n. 1.
164 Griffith, *Guadalcanal*, 133–4.
165 Lundstrom, *First Team*, 5412.
166 Ibid., 5431.
167 Frank, *Guadalcanal*, 228; Lundstrom, *First Team*, 5581–618.
168 Smith, *Bloody Ridge*, 2370. The deaths of the three pilots are normally attributed to the *Sendai*. Smith's research indicates the *Sendai* had stopped firing before the pilots were killed.
169 Frank, *Guadalcanal*, 233.
170 Lundstrom, *First Team*, 5782–99.
171 Smith, *Bloody Ridge*, 2479.
172 Twining, *No Bended Knee*, 124; Smith, *Bloody Ridge*, 2538.

173 Lundstrom, *First Team*, 5921.
174 Smith, *Bloody Ridge*, 2538.
175 The account of the attack by the two Rufes comes from Lundstrom, *First Team*, 5945–59.
176 Ibid., 5959.
177 Smith, *Bloody Ridge*, 2583.
178 Ibid., 2650.
179 *Yudachi, Uranami, Mirakumo, Kawakaze, Umikaze, Kagero*, and *Shirayuki* TROMs.
180 Frank, *Guadalcanal*, 237.
181 Smith, *Bloody Ridge*, 2667–84.
182 Ibid., 2752.
183 G. Smith, *Do-Or-Die Men*, 268.
184 Twining, *No Bended Knee*, 124.
185 Smith, *Bloody Ridge*, 2722.
186 Ibid., 2756.
187 The conversation between Lieutenant Colonel Edson and headquarters is an amalgamation of M. Smith, *Bloody Ridge*, 2756; G. Smith, *Do-Or-Die Men*, 273; and Griffith, *Guadalcanal*, 133–4.
188 Griffith, *Guadalcanal*, 144.
189 Smith, *Bloody Ridge*, 2946–62; Griffith, *Guadalcanal*, 145–6.
190 Interrogation Nav. No. 13, USSBS No. 96, Interrogation of Captain Yasuji Watanabe, 15 October 1945.
191 Griffith, *Guadalcanal*, 132.
192 Griffith, *Guadalcanal*, 132–3; Frank, *Guadalcanal*, 216.
193 Lundstrom, *First Team*, 5044.
194 *I-11* TROM.
195 Lundstrom, *First Team*, 5066.
196 Ibid., 5090.
197 Frank, *Guadalcanal*, 216–7.
198 Lundstrom, *First Team*, 6150.
199 Ibid., 6167.
200 Ibid., 6167–86.
201 Ibid., 6186–203.
202 Lundstrom, *First Team*, 6207–26; Frank, *Guadalcanal*, 247.
203 Keith Rogers, "WWII memories remain vivid for Navy veteran, 91," *Las Vegas Review-Journal*, December 7, 2012, http://www.reviewjournal.com/news/military/wwii-memories-remain-vivid-navy-veteran-91.
204 Capt Ben W. Blee, USN, "Whodunnit?" *Proceedings*, United States Naval Institute, 108, 7/953 (July 1982), 42–3.
205 Alexander T. Griffin, *A Ship to Remember: The Saga of the* Hornet (New York: Howell, Soskin, 1943), 189–90.
206 Lisle A. Rose, *The Ship That Held the Line: The USS* Hornet *and the First Year of the Pacific War* (Annapolis: Naval Institute Press, 1995), 188; Griffin, *Ship to Remember*, 190.
207 Griffin, *Ship to Remember*, 191.
208 Blee, "Whodunnit?" 43.
209 Rose, *Ship That Held the Line*, 188.
210 Griffin, *Ship to Remember*, 193–4.
211 Ibid., 194.
212 The *I-19*'s approach and launch on the *Wasp* come from the *I-19* TROM.
213 Rogers, "WWII memories"; Rose, *Ship That Held the Line*, 187.
214 Rose, *Ship That Held the Line*, 187.
215 Eric Hammel, *The Death of the USS* Wasp *September 15, 1942* (Pacifica, CA: Pacifica Military History, 2016), 96.
216 Frank, *Guadalcanal*, 248; Eric Hammel, *Carrier Strike: The Battle of the Santa Cruz Islands October 1942* (Pacifica, CA: Pacifica Military History, 1999), 732.
217 Frank, *Guadalcanal*, 248; Hammel, *Carrier Strike*, 732.
218 Lundstrom, *First Team*, 6250.
219 Rose, *Ship That Held the Line*, 187.
220 *War Damage Report No. 39 USS Wasp (CV7) Loss in Action South Pacific September 15, 1942*, Preliminary Design Branch Bureau of Ships Navy Department, 15 January, 1944 ("*Wasp* Report"), 3.

221 Hammel, *Death of the Wasp*, 132, 164.
222 Rogers, "WWII memories."
223 *Wasp* Report, 10.
224 Hammel, *Carrier Strike*, 812–30.
225 *After Action Report U.S.S. WASP* ("Sherman Report").
226 Lundstrom, *First Team*, 6283–95.
227 Rose, *Ship That Held the Line*, 188–9.
228 Lundstrom, *First Team*, 6343.
229 Sherman Report, *Wasp* Report, 8.
230 Vice Admiral William R. Smedberg, III, USN (Ret.), "As I Recall...Sink the Wasp!" *Proceedings*, United States Naval Institute, 108, 7/953 (July 1982), 48.
231 Smedberg, "As I Recall …" 48–9.
232 Ibid., 49
233 Except where indicated otherwise, the account of the scuttling of the *Wasp* comes from Smedberg, "As I Recall …" 49, and Hammel, *Carrier Strike*, 990.
234 *Wasp* Report, 5.
235 Blee, "Whodunnit?" 46.
236 Ibid., 47.
237 Ibid., 47.
238 The quotation is from *Wasp* Report, 10. *Wasp* Report, 6–7, explains the fire main system's arrangement. *Wasp* Report, 2, explains the lack of pressure.
239 *Wasp* Report, 9: "It is noted, however, that the reference does not contain any mention of attempts to cut out the damaged portion of the fire main forward of the engine room or the portion of the gasoline mains aft of frame 63."
240 The Navy did give an out for the crew of the forward engine room, where the valves for isolating the damaged pipes forward were located, in *Wasp* Report, 10.
241 Lundstrom, *Black Shoe*, 223–4.
242 Ibid., 332.
243 Ibid., 332.
244 Ibid., 481–2.
245 Rose, *Ship That Held the Line*, 184–5.
246 Lundstrom, *First Team*, 6327.
247 Griffith, *Guadalcanal*, 155.
248 Miller, *Cactus*, 122–3.
249 Twining, *No Bended Knee*, 129.
250 Hough, *Pearl Harbor*, 311.
251 Frank, *Guadalcanal*, 251–2; *Shirayuki*, *Murakumo*, *Uranami*, and *Hamakaze* TROMs.
252 Frank, *Guadalcanal*, 251–2.
253 *Yayoi* TROM; Robert J. Cressman, *The Official Chronology of the U.S. Navy in World War II* (Washington, DC: Contemporary History Branch, Naval Historical Center, 1999).
254 Toland, *Rising Sun*, 8577.
255 Ibid., 8569.
256 Except where otherwise noted, the account of Colonel Tsuji's meeting with Admiral Yamamoto comes from Hiroyuki Agawa, *The Reluctant Admiral: Yamamoto and the Imperial Navy* (Tokyo; New York: Kodansha, 1979), 328, although Agawa is careful to note "whether this story is true or not is uncertain."
257 Captain Kuroshima was actually the planning genius behind the Pearl Harbor attack and the Centrifugal Offensive. He was considered a brilliant eccentric. When an idea came to him Kuroshima would lock himself in his cabin, darken the portholes, and work naked at his desk day and night while chain-smoking cigarettes and burning incense. Agawa, *Reluctant Admiral*, 222.
258 Toland, *Rising Sun*, 8583.

Chapter 7:

1 Except where otherwise noted, the account of the September 7–9, 1942, San Francisco conference comes from E. B. Potter, *Nimitz* (Annapolis: Naval Institute Press, 1976), 186–8.

2 Frank, *Guadalcanal*, 216–7.
3 Hornfischer, *Neptune's Inferno*, 2471–87.
4 John Wukovits, *Admiral "Bull" Halsey: The Life and Wars of the Navy's Most Controversial Commander* (New York: St Martin's Press, 2010), 88.
5 Fleet Admiral William F. Halsey, USN, *Admiral Halsey's Story* (--: Pickle Partners Publishing, 2013), 2346. Halsey misidentifies the *Enterprise* as the *Saratoga*.
6 Smith, *Bloody Ridge*, 2794; Toland, *Rising Sun*, 8520.
7 Smith, *Bloody Ridge*, 2794.
8 Ibid., 2945.
9 Griffith, *Guadalcanal*, 147.
10 Leckie, *Challenge*, 3444.
11 Frank, *Guadalcanal*, 241.
12 Lundstrom, *First Team*, 6000–33.
13 Ibid., 6051.
14 Ibid,. 6051–68.
15 Ibid., 6073–142.
16 Frank, *Guadalcanal*, 261.
17 Ibid., 266; Cressman, *Official Chronology*; *Shikinami* TROM.
18 Frank, *Guadalcanal*, 266; *Kagero* TROM.
19 Frank, *Guadalcanal*, 267; *Suzukaze*, *Kawakaze*, *Urakaze*, and *Umikaze* TROMs.
20 Frank, *Guadalcanal*, 266.
21 Leckie, *Challenge*, 3604.
22 Hanson W. Baldwin, "US Hold in Solomons Bolstered," *New York Times*, 11/3/1942, 4.
23 Wukovits, *Admiral "Bull" Halsey*, 33.
24 Hornfischer, *Neptune's Inferno*, 3811.
25 Wukovits, *Admiral "Bull" Halsey*, 33.
26 Frank, *Guadalcanal*, 252–6.
27 Ibid., 244, 252–6.
28 Ibid., 267–8.
29 Ibid., 268–9.
30 Lundstrom, *First Team*, 6652–68.
31 Ibid., 6660–78; *Taiyo* TROM.
32 Lundstrom, *First Team*, 6678.
33 Ibid., 6678.
34 *Shirogane Maru* TROM.
35 Hammel, *Air War*, 2878.
36 Lundstrom, *First Team*, 6726.
37 Ibid., 6874.
38 Ibid., 7055.
39 Ibid., 7011.
40 Ibid., 7171.
41 Ibid., 7183.
42 Miller, *Cactus*, 103–4.
43 Ibid., 105.
44 Ibid., 73.
45 Sherrod, *History*, 82.
46 Ibid., 83.
47 Frank, *Guadalcanal*, 209.
48 Miller, *Cactus*, 85.
49 Vandegrift and Asprey, *Once A Marine*, 163.
50 Ibid., 84.
51 Ibid., 85–6.
52 Tregaskis, *Diary*, 221.
53 Frank, *Guadalcanal*, 210; Miller, *Cactus*, 74.
54 Hammel, *Air War*, 2862.

55 Lundstrom, *First Team*, 6632.
56 Frank, *Guadalcanal*, 274.
57 Edwin P. Hoyt, *How They Won the War in the Pacific: Nimitz and His Admirals* (Guilford, CT: Lyons Press, 2012), 2428–44.
58 Except where noted otherwise, the account of the September 28 conference comes from Hoyt, *How They Won*, 2476–604.
59 Prados, *Islands of Destiny*, 102–3.
60 Hornfischer, *Neptune's Inferno*, 2897–912.
61 Ibid., 2912.
62 Hammel, *Carrier Strike*, 1713.
63 Gamble, *Fortress Rabaul*, 242.
64 Prados, *Islands of Destiny*, 103.
65 Hornfischer, *Neptune's Inferno*, 2917, 2934.
66 Ibid., 2934.
67 The account of the meeting between General Arnold and Captain Brannon comes from Donald A. Davis, *Lightning Strike: The Secret Mission to Kill Admiral Yamamoto and Avenge Pearl Harbor* (New York: St Martin's Press, 2005), 157–8.
68 Dale Brannon would not reveal what General Arnold had called his men for another 60 years. Davis, *Lightning Strike*, 158.
69 Potter, *Nimitz*, 192.
70 Ibid., 192.
71 Ibid., 193–3.
72 Potter, *Nimitz*, 193.
73 Unless specified otherwise, details of the October 2 meeting come from Hoyt, *How They Won*, 2492–2591.
74 Lundstrom, *First Team*, 7211–321.
75 Ibid., 7315.
76 Frank, *Guadalcanal*, 278.
77 *Tenryu* TROM.
78 Lundstrom, *First Team*, 7376, 7361, 7486.
79 Lundstrom, *First Team*, 7563–83; Frank, *Guadalcanal*, 279.
80 Lundstrom, *First Team*, 7619–38.
81 Ibid., 7653.
82 Frank, *Guadalcanal*, 279.
83 Lundstrom, *First Team*, 7665.
84 *Nisshin* TROM; Frank, *Guadalcanal*, 280.
85 Prados, *Islands of Destiny*, 106.
86 Frank, *Guadalcanal*, 280; *Akizuki* TROM.
87 Frank, *Guadalcanal*, 280.
88 Lundstrom, *First Team*, 7683.
89 *Asagumo*, *Minegumo*, *Murasame*, *Natsugumo*, *Yudachi*, and *Harusame* TROMs.
90 *Minegumo* TROM; Frank, *Guadalcanal*, 281; Hammel, *Air War*, 3030.
91 Frank, *Guadalcanal*, 281; Hammel, *Air War*, 3030.
92 Lundstrom, *First Team*, 7820–39.
93 Frank, *Guadalcanal*, 281; *Uranami*, *Shikinami*, *Hayashio*, *Nowaki*, *Kuroshio*, and *Oyashio* TROMs.
94 Hammel, *Carrier Strike*, 1260.

Chapter 8:

1 Lundstrom, *First Team*, 8118.
2 *Chitose* TROM; Frank, *Guadalcanal*, 294; Morison, *Struggle*, 151.
3 Prange, *At Dawn We Slept*, 265.
4 Lundstrom, *First Team*, 8138–48.
5 Ibid., 8163.
6 Frank, *Guadalcanal*, 296; Lundstrom, *First Team*, 8181.
7 C. W. Kilpatrick, *The Night Naval Battles in the Solomons* (Pompano Beach, FL: Exposition-Banner, 1987), 42.

8 O'Hara, *US Navy*, 2061; Frank, *Guadalcanal*, 299; Kilpatrick, *Night Naval Battles*, 44–5.
9 Coombe, *Derailing*, 83.
10 Morison, *Struggle*, 153.
11 Coombe, *Derailing*, 83.
12 Coombe, *Derailing*; Frank, *Guadalcanal*, 301.
13 Frank, *Guadalcanal*, 301–2.
14 Coombe, *Derailing*, 86–7.
15 Kilpatrick, *Night Naval Battles*, 51.
16 Interrogation Nav. No. 106, USSBS No. 464,, Interrogation of: Captain Kikunori Kijima and Admiral Keizo Komura, 27 November 1945.
17 Hara, Saito, and Pineau, *Destroyer Captain*, 126–7.
18 Hornfischer, *Neptune's Inferno*, 2607.
19 Ibid., 2607–23.
20 Ibid., 2639.
21 Ibid., 2639.
22 Ibid., 2698.
23 Anthony Newpower, *Iron Men and Tin Fish: The Race to Build a Better Torpedo During World War II* (Annapolis: Naval Institute Press, 2006), 106–7.
24 Newpower, *Iron Men*, 110.
25 Charles Cook, *The Battle of Cape Esperance: Encounter at Guadalcanal* (Annapolis: Naval Institute Press, 1992), 18.
26 Henry V. Poor, Henry A. Mustin, and Colin G. Jameson, *United States Navy Combat Narrative: The Battles of Cape Esperance, 11 October 1942 and Santa Cruz Islands, 26 October 1942* (Washington, DC: Publications Branch, Office of Naval Intelligence, United States Navy, 1943), 5–6; Frank, *Guadalcanal*, 296.
27 Poor, Mustin, and Jameson, *Combat Narrative*, 6.
28 Ibid., 7.
29 Kilpatrick, *Naval Night Battles*, 44.
30 Frank, *Guadalcanal*, 298; Kilpatrick, *Naval Night Battles*, 44.
31 Frank, *Guadalcanal*, 298.
32 Kilpatrick, *Naval Night Battles*, 47.
33 *I-26* TROM.
34 Kilpatrick, *Naval Night Battles*, 44.
35 There are multiple versions of this message, all with slight variations. This version comes from Cook, *Cape Esperance*, 38.
36 Poor, Mustin, and Jameson, *Combat Narrative*, 8.
37 Kilpatrick, *Naval Night Battles*, 45.
38 Ibid., 47.
39 Roy Boehm, "The Roy Boehm account of the sinking of USS Duncan DD 485," *USS Duncan Reunion Association*, www.ussduncan.org (excerpted from Roy Boehm and Charles W. Sasser, *First SEAL* (New York: Atria, 1997)).
40 Vincent A. Langelo, *With All Our Might: The WWII History of the* USS Boise *(CL-47)* (Austin, TX: Eakin Press, 2000), 96.
41 Kilpatrick, *Naval Night Battles*, 47–8. The Office of Naval Intelligence Narrative (Poor, Mustin, and Jameson, *Combat Narrative*, 9) omits the word "column" from the text of the message, but later says, "The four cruisers executed column left about, the *San Francisco* leading, followed by the *Boise*, *Salt Lake City*, and *Helena*," thus confirming it was a column turn that was ordered, not a simple turn.
42 Kilpatrick, *Naval Night Battles*, 47–8.
43 Commander Destroyer Squadron TWELVE, "Report of Action off Savo Island, Solomons, Night of 11–12 October, 1942," dated October 23, 1942 ("*Farenholt* Report").
44 Morison (*Struggle*, 154–5), says Admiral Scott intended for the lead destroyers to have their own column turn while the cruiser column followed by the rear destroyers executed one column turn. The lead destroyers were then to speed up to take their lead positions in the column again. "There was nothing unusual in ordering this somewhat complicated procedure ..." Morison insists, but does not give a justification for it. He adds that Commodore Tobin held the lead destroyers up to make sure the maneuver went smoothly. Tobin, in his report, does not give the text of Scott's order nor does he say what he thought his ships were supposed to do,

but says he held up his destroyers until it could be "ascertained" what the trailing destroyers were doing. From this it may be inferred that Tobin did not know what the trailing destroyers were supposed to do.

45 Kilpatrick, *Naval Night Battles*, 47.
46 Frank, *Guadalcanal*, 299–300; Kilpatrick, *Naval Night Battles*, 47.
47 Poor, Mustin, and Jameson, *Combat Narrative*, 10.
48 Kilpatrick, *Naval Night Battles*, 49.
49 Poor, Mustin, and Jameson, *Combat Narrative*, 11.
50 Kilpatrick, *Naval Night Battles*, 49.
51 *Farenholt* Report.
52 Kilpatrick, *Naval Night Battles*, 49; Hornfischer, *Neptune's Inferno*, 3185.
53 Roscoe, *Destroyer Operations*, 181.
54 Frank, *Guadalcanal*, 301.
55 The sources are in agreement that Admiral Scott's original orders instructed the cruisers to open fire without specific orders from him. Scott himself admitted as much. Why no one did so has never been explained.
56 Lieutenant C. G. Morris, USNR, *The Fightin'est Ship: The Story of the Cruiser* Helena (Rockville, MD: Wildside Press, 2005), 42.
57 Kilpatrick, *Naval Night Battles*, 49–50.
58 Morris, *Fightin'est Ship*, 42.
59 Kilpatrick, *Naval Night Battles*, 50.
60 Morris, *Fightin'est Ship*, 43.
61 Boehm, "ÚSS Duncan."
62 Morris, *Fightin'est Ship*, 43.
63 Cook, *Cape Esperance*, 65–6.
64 Kilpatrick, *Naval Night Battles*, 54.
65 Ibid., 55.
66 Ibid., 55–6; O'Hara, *US Navy*, 2119.
67 *Farenholt* Report.
68 Lacroix and Wells, *Japanese Cruisers*, 309–10.
69 O'Hara, *US Navy*, 2119.
70 Lacroix and Wells, *Japanese Cruisers*, 308.
71 Kilpatrick, *Naval Night Battles*, 57.
72 Boehm, "USS Duncan."
73 Boehm, "USS Duncan"; O'Hara, *US Navy*, 2089–2108; Frank, *Guadalcanal*, 304.
74 Lacroix and Wells, *Japanese Cruisers*, 308–9; *Furutaka* TROM.
75 Newpower, *Iron Men*, 124.
76 Frank, *Guadalcanal*, 303.
77 Kilpatrick, *Naval Night Battles*, 58.
78 Ibid., 60.
79 Hornfischer, *Neptune's Inferno*, 3433.
80 Lacroix and Wells, *Japanese Cruisers*, 110. In War damage Report No. 24, *USS Boise (CL47) Gunfire Damage Savo Island 11-12 October 1942*, Preliminary Design Branch Bureau of Ships Navy Department, 25 January 1943 ("*Boise* Report"), 9–10, the US Navy Bureau of Ships marveled at the unique performance of the Type 91. By the end of the Guadalcanal campaign, American shells had also demonstrated an ability to plunge into the water to pierce the enemy hull below the waterline.
81 Kilpatrick, *Naval Night Battles*, 63; O'Hara, *US Navy*, 2147.
82 Lacroix and Wells, *Japanese Cruisers*, 308–9.
83 Unless noted otherwise, the story of the abandonment and attempted salvage of the *Duncan* is from Poor, Mustin, and Jameson, *Combat Narrative*, 20–3.
84 Frank, *Guadalcanal*, 308.
85 Miller, *Cactus*, 118.
86 Lundstrom, *First Team*, 8196; Miller, *Cactus*, 118.
87 Miller, *Cactus*, 119.
88 *Natsugumo* TROM.
89 *Murakumo* TROM.
90 Tanaka, "Struggle for Guadalcanal," 181.
91 Griffith, *Guadalcanal*, 179.

Chapter 9:

1 Lundstrom, *First Team*, 8263–80.
2 Ibid., 8280–96.
3 Ibid., 8290–309.
4 Ibid., 8343.
5 Vandegrift and Asprey, *Once A Marine*, 174.
6 Lundstrom, *First Team*, 8316.
7 Hammel, *Starvation*, 5203; Frank, *Guadalcanal*, 316.
8 Hornfischer, *Neptune's Inferno*, 3642.
9 Sherrod, *History*, 99; Miller, *Cactus*, 121.
10 Hammel, *Starvation*, 5203.
11 Hornfischer, *Neptune's Inferno*, 3642.
12 Vandegrift and Asprey, *Once A Marine*, 174.
13 Gallant, *On Valor's Side*, 5656.
14 Corporal Gallant's experience on the beach comes from Gallant, *On Valor's Side*, 5657–75.
15 Prados, *Islands of Destiny*, 116; Frank, *Guadalcanal*, 317.
16 Twining, *No Bended Knee*, 151.
17 Clemens, *Alone*, 256.
18 Colonel Joe Foss, USMC (ret.), *Joe Foss: Flying Marine* (--: Pickle Partners Publishing, 2013), 459.
19 Tanaka, "Struggle for Gudadalcanal," 181–2.
20 Leckie, *Challenge*, 4384.
21 Prados, *Islands of Destiny*, 117.
22 Foss, *Flying Marine*, 466.
23 Lundstrom, *First Team*, 8345.
24 Toland, *Rising Sun*, 8767.
25 Frank, *Guadalcanal*, 317.
26 Vandegrift and Asprey, *Once A Marine*, 176.
27 Foss, *Flying Marine*, 466.
28 Frank, *Guadalcanal*, 317–8.
29 Foss, *Flying Marine*, 466.
30 Vandegrift and Asprey, *Once A Marine*, 175.
31 Hammel, *Starvation*, 5233.
32 Foss, *Flying Marine*, 466.
33 Miller, *Cactus*, 122; Hammel, *Starvation*, 5253.
34 Hornfischer, *Neptune's Inferno*, 3691.
35 Frank, *Guadalcanal*, 318; Cressman, *The Official Chronology of the US Navy in World War II*.
36 Interrogation Nav No. 83, USSBS No.407, 13–14 November 1945. Interrogation of: Rear Admiral Akira Siji, Captain Kenkichi Kato, and Captain Nobuye Ukita.
37 Lundstrom, *First Team*, 8345; Frank, *Guadalcanal*, 318–9.
38 Lundstrom, *First Team*, 8370.
39 Frank, *Guadalcanal*, 319; Lundstrom, *First Team*, 8370.
40 Vandegrift and Asprey, *Once A Marine*, 177.
41 Frank, *Guadalcanal*, 320.
42 Lundstrom, *First Team*, 8375–91. Only one of the coastwatcher station's three masts was still standing. The teleradio aerial had caught in a palm tree. When the crew radioed out to make a test of signal strength and readability, the answer came back at once: "Seems much improved. Have you been making adjustments?" (Hornfischer, *Neptune's Inferno*, 3674).
43 Frank, *Guadalcanal*, 320.
44 Lundstrom, *First Team*, 8391–408.
45 Ibid., 8410–30.
46 Miller, *Cactus*, 124–5.
47 Ibid., 125.
48 Lundstrom, *First Team*, 8430.
49 Ibid., 8431–47.
50 Ibid., 8464.

51 Ibid., 8480.
52 Ibid., 8496.
53 Hoyt, *How They Won*, 163.
54 Frank, *Guadalcanal*, 322.
55 Lundstrom, *First Team*, 8515.
56 Ibid., 8515–33.
57 Ibid., 8524.
58 Ibid., 8533; *Azumasan Maru* TROM.
59 Lundstrom, *First Team*, 8541.
60Prados, *Islands of Destiny*, 121; Lundstrom, *First Team*, 8560; *Kyushu Maru* TROM.
61 Frank, *Guadalcanal*, 324.
62 Lundstrom, *First Team*, 8566.
63 Hammel, Air War, 3164–80.
64 Lundstrom, *First Team*, 8587; Miller, *Cactus*, 134.
65 Morison, *Struggle*, 179; Frank, *Guadalcanal*, 325.
66 Frank, *Guadalcanal*, 324–5.
67 Ibid., 324–5. The experience of the survivors of the *Meredith* and the *Vireo* was a horror. Two days of thirst and blazing sun, some floating in the water to become magnets for sharks. At one point, a shark leapt onto a life raft and bit off a chunk of a dying man's thigh.
68 Cressman, *The Official Chronology of the US Navy in World War II.*
69 Frank, *Guadalcanal*, 325.
70 Lundstrom, *First Team*, 8583.
71 *Maya* TROM, Frank, *Guadalcanal*, 326.
72 Hammel, *Air War*, 3197.
73 Miller, *Cactus*, 136.
74 Lundstrom, *First Team*, 8736.
75 Except where otherwise noted, the story of the *McFarland* and Lieutenant Colonel Bauer comes from Lundstrom, *First Team*, 8735–93.
76 Frank, *Guadalcanal*, 333.
77 Ibid., 333.
78 Toland, *Rising Sun*, 8796.
79 Hornfischer, *Neptune's Inferno*, 3825.
80 Lundstrom, *First Team*, 8794.

Chapter 10:

1 Halsey, *Admiral Halsey's Story*, 2362.
2 Ibid., 2402.
3 Frank, *Guadalcanal*, 55.
4 Potter, *Nimitz*, 197.
5 Hammel, *Carrier Strike*, 1713.
6 Hornfischer, *Neptune's Inferno*, 2625.
7 Lundstrom, *First Team*, 8793.
8 Potter, *Nimitz*, 196.
9 Ibid., 196.
10 Frank, *Guadalcanal*, 333–4; Hammel, *Carrier Strike*, 1845.
11 Halsey qualified as a pilot in 1934 at the age of 51 in order to get command of the carrier *Saratoga*. His flight instructor (later admiral) Bromfield Nichol would later describe Halsey's piloting skills: "The worse the weather, the better he flew" (Hoyt, *How They Won*, 2688).
12 Hornfischer, *Neptune's Inferno*, 3972.
13 Potter, *Nimitz*, 196–7.
14 Ibid., 197.
15 Hornfischer, *Neptune's Inferno*, 3930.
16 Ibid., 3930.
17 Halsey, *Admiral Halsey's Story*, 2498.
18 Ibid., 2498; Hornfischer, *Neptune's Inferno*, 3981.

19 Hornfischer, *Neptune's Inferno*, 3948–64.
20 Ibid., 3964.
21 Halsey, *Admiral Halsey's Story*, 2502.
22 Toland, *Rising Sun*, 8834.
23 Hammel, *Carrier Strike*, 1899.
24 Halsey, *Admiral Halsey's Story*, 2502–20.
25 Except where otherwise noted, the account of the sinking of the *O'Brien* comes from *War Damage Report No. 28 USS O'Brien (DD-415), Torpedo Damage and Loss, 15 Sept–19 Oct, 1942* ("*O'Brien* Report").
26 Of the emergency repairs to the *O'Brien*, the Bureau of Ships concluded that, among other things, "Not enough material was installed adequately to replace what had been damaged." (*O'Brien* Report, 11).
27 *I-176* TROM; *Chester* entry in Dictionary of American Naval Fighting Ships; *Washington* and *Buchanan* war diaries.
28 Lundstrom, *First Team*, 9008, 9055, 9002.
29 Ibid., 9033.
30 Frank, *Guadalcanal*, 341.
31 Ibid., 342.
32 Lundstrom, *First Team*, 8845–69.
33 Ibid., 9056.
34 Barrett Tillman, *US Marine Corps Fighter Squadrons of World War II* (Oxford: Osprey, 2014), 650; Lundstrom, *First Team*, 9063.
35 Lundstrom, *First Team*, 9077.
36 Ibid., 9095.
37 Ibid., 9342; *Hiyo* TROM.
38 Lundstrom, *First Team*, 9360.
39 Frank, *Guadalcanal*, 370.
40 Ibid., 347. For more detailed explanations of the replacement of General Kawaguchi, see Toland, *Rising Sun*, 8866–83, and Frank, *Guadalcanal*, 346–7.
41 Okumiya, Horikoshi, and Caidin, *Zero!*, 3941.
42 Except where otherwise noted, the account of the proceedings involving Admiral Nagumo on the *Shokaku* are from Hara, Saito, and Pineau, *Destroyer Captain*, 115–6.
43 Ibid., 115.
44 Toland, *Rising Sun*, 8947; Edwin P. Hoyt, *Guadalcanal: The Desperate Struggle That Turned the Tide of War* (New York: Jove, 1983), 182.
45 Hoyt, *Guadalcanal*, 182; Frank, *Guadalcanal*, 372; Lundstrom, *First Team*, 9370.
46 Hara, Saito, and Pineau, *Destroyer Captain*, 116.
47 Toland, *Rising Sun*, 8910.
48 Hornfischer, *Neptune's Inferno*, 4104.
49 Lundstrom, *First Team*, 9384.
50 Toland, *Rising Sun*, 8902–19.
51 Frank, *Guadalcanal*, 354.
52 Toland, *Rising Sun*, 8935; Morison, *Struggle*, 201–2.
53 Hammel, *Carrier Strike*, 1990; Lundstrom, *First Team*, 9378–95; *Akatsuki* TROM.
54 Lundstrom, *First Team*, 9401.
55 Frank, *Guadalcanal*, 358.
56 Morison, *Struggle*, 194–5.
57 Ibid., 196.
58 *Akatsuki* TROM; Frank, *Guadalcanal*, 359.
59 Lundstrom, *First Team*, 9405–18; Frank, *Guadalcanal*, 259.
60 Lundstrom, *First Team*, 9435.
61 Hammel, *Carrier Strike*, 2091.
62 Ibid., 2089; *Yura* TROM; *Akizuki* TROM.
63 Hammel, *Carrier Strike*, 2129.
64 Ibid., 2107.
65 Ibid., 2107–27; *Akizuki* TROM; *Yura* TROM.
66 Ibid., 2127; *Yura* TROM.
67 Hammel, *Carrier Strike*, 2120; *Akizuki* TROM.
68 Lundstrom, *First Team*, 9466.

Chapter 11:

1 Halsey, *Admiral Halsey's Story*, 2577.
2 Ibid., 2578.
3 Ibid., 2577.
4 Lundstrom, *First Team*, 9234.
5 Frank, *Guadalcanal*, 371.
6 Halsey, *Admiral Halsey's Story*, 2577.
7 Hara, Saito, and Pineau, *Destroyer Captain*, 117.
8 Hammel, *Carrier Strike*, 3115; Lundstrom, *First Team*, 9558.
9 Lundstrom, *First Team*, 9569.
10 Toland, *Rising Sun*, 8947.
11 Ibid., 8948–64.
12 Hara, Saito, and Pineau, *Destroyer Captain*, 117.
13 Lundstrom, *First Team*, 9295–309.
14 Ibid., 9250.
15 Ibid., 9519, 9540.
16 Ibid., 9552. There are two commonly held myths regarding this order. The first is that it read "Attack, Repeat, Attack," which comes from Admiral Halsey himself (*Admiral Halsey's Story*, 2593) paraphrasing the order. The second is the timing of the order, which, again thanks in part to Admiral Halsey (*Admiral Halsey's Story*, 2593), is commonly believed to have been the early morning hours of October 26. The order actually went out early afternoon on October 25.
17 Ibid., 9540; Stephen L. Moore, *The Battle for Hell's Island: How a Small Band of Carrier Dive Bombers Helped Save Guadalcanal* (New York: New American Library, 2015), 304.
18 Lundstrom, *First Team*, 9557.
19 Hammel, *Carrier Strike*, 3112.
20 Lundstrom, *First Team*, 9575, 9557.
21 Moore, *Hell's Island*, 305.
22 Ibid., 305–6.
23 Lundstrom, *First Team*, 9576.
24 Ibid., 9598.
25 Ibid., 9598.
26 Moore, *Hell's Island*, 306.
27 Poor, Mustin, and Jameson, *Combat Narrative*, 34.
28 Lundstrom, *First Team*, 9615.
29 Moore, *Hell's Island*, 308.
30 Lundstrom, *First Team*, 9615.
31 Moore, *Hell's Island*, 307.
32 Lundstrom, *First Team*, 9632; Moore, *Hell's Island*, 308.
33 Lundstrom, *First Team*, 9632–49.
34 Moore, *Hell's Island*, 305–6, 309.
35 Rose, *Ship That Held the Line*, 223.
36 Lundstrom, *First Team*, 9679.
37 Hammel, *Carrier Strike*, 3252–72; Commander Edward P. Stafford, USN, *The Big "E"* (New York: Ballantine, 1962), 163–4; Barrett Tillman, *Enterprise: America's Fightingest Ship and the Men Who Helped Win World War II* (New York: Simon & Schuster, 2012), 115–6.
38 Lundstrom, *First Team*, 9679.
39 Stafford, *The Big "E"*, 164.
40 Hammel, *Carrier Strike*, 3272.
41 Ibid., 3293.
42 Lundstrom, *First Team*, 9661–79, 9682.
43 Hammel, *Carrier Strike*, 3311.
44 Frank, *Guadalcanal*, 379; Poor, Mustin, and Jameson, *Combat Narrative*, 36; Lundstrom, *First Team*, 9723.
45 Hara, Saito, and Pineau, *Destroyer Captain*, 118; Morison, *Struggle*, 203.
46 Lundstrom, *First Team*, 9715.
47 Hara, Saito, and Pineau, *Destroyer Captain*, 117.

48 Ibid., 118.
49 Ibid., 118.
50 Lundstrom, *First Team*, 9723, 9731.
51 Ibid., 9843–62.
52 Hammel, *Carrier Strike*, 3524.
53 Lundstrom, *First Team*, 9835.
54 Hara, Saito, and Pineau, *Destroyer Captain*, 118.
55 Lundstrom, *First Team*, 9835.
56 Ibid., 9750.
57 Ibid., 9661–79.
58 Ibid., 9757.
59 Poor, Mustin, and Jameson, *Combat Narrative*, 41.
60 Ibid., 43.
61 Lundstrom, *First Team*, 9775.
62 Hammel, *Carrier Strike*, 3566.
63 Poor, Mustin, and Jameson, *Combat Narrative*, 42.
64 Lundstrom, *First Team*, 9775.
65 Moore, *Hell's Island*, 318.
66 Ibid., 318.
67 Hammel, *Carrier Strike*, 3584–605.
68 Moore, *Hell's Island*, 319.
69 Ibid., 320.
70 Ibid., 320.
71 Lundstrom, *First Team*, 9872.
72 *Shokaku* TROM.
73 Hara, Saito, and Pineau, *Destroyer Captain*, 118.
74 Toland, *Rising Sun*, 8989.
75 Lundstrom, *First Team*, 9883.
76 Ibid., 9881.
77 Mark E. Stille and Gerard Howard, *Santa Cruz 1942: Carrier Duel in the South Pacific* (Oxford: Osprey, 2012), 291.
78 Toland, *Rising Sun*, 8989.
79 Lundstrom, *First Team*, 9794.
80 Ibid., 9820.
81 Ibid., 9812–29.
82 Ibid., 9794.
83 Hammel, *Carrier Strike*, 3675.
84 Lundstrom, *First Team*, 9905–23; Hammel, *Carrier Strike*, 3695.
85 Rose, *Ship That Held the Line*, 227.
86 Hammel, *Carrier Strike*, 3695; Lundstrom, *First Team*, 9923.
87 Lundstrom, *First Team*, 9945.
88 Frank, *Guadalcanal*, 384.
89 Hammel, *Carrier Strike*, 3752.
90 Lundstrom, *First Team*, 9967.
91 Ibid., 9967–82.
92 Ibid., 9950.
93 Stafford, *The Big "E"*, 171.
94 Lundstrom, *First Team*, 10009.
95 Frank, *Guadalcanal*, 384.
96 Lundstrom, *First Team*, 10015–27.
97 Stafford, *The Big "E"*, 171.
98 Ibid., 171–2.
99 Lundstrom, *First Team*, 10043.
100 Stafford, *The Big "E"*, 172.
101 Ibid., 172–3.

102 Lundstrom, *First Team*, 10025.
103 Ibid., 10059.
104 Lundstrom, *First Team*, 9905–23, 10399; Hammel, *Carrier Strike*, 4353.
105 Lundstrom, *First Team*, 10399.
106 Ibid., 10417.
107 Ibid., 10403.
108 Poor, Mustin, and Jameson, *Combat Narrative*, 56.
109 Rose, *Ship That Held the Line*, 232.
110 Lundstrom, *First Team*, 10454.
111 Ibid., 10454.
112 Ibid., 10439.
113 Ibid., 10439.
114 Okumiya, Horikoshi, and Caidin, *Zero!*, 4064.
115 Lundstrom, *First Team*, 10469.
116 Ibid., 10469.
117 Okumiya, Horikoshi, and Caidin, *Zero!*, 4084.
118 Lundstrom, *First Team*, 10507.
119 Ibid., 10527.
120 Ibid., 10487.
121 Ibid., 10507.
122 Okumiya, Horikoshi, and Caidin, *Zero!*, 4084.
123 Lundstrom, *First Team*, 10545.
124 Hammel, *Carrier Strike*, 4607.
125 Ibid., 4607.
126 Ibid., 4682.
127 Lundstrom, *First Team*, 10563.
128 War Damage Report No. 30 USS Hornet (CV7) Loss in Action Santa Cruz 26 October 1942 ("*Hornet* Report"), 3; Lundstrom, *First Team*, 10563.
129 Hammel, *Carrier Strike*, 4722.
130 Ibid., 4722.
131 *Hornet* Report, 3; Lundstrom, *First Team*, 10580.
132 *Hornet* Report, 5; Lundstrom, *First Team*, 10580–97.
133 Lundstrom, *First Team*, 10597.
134 Ibid., 10608.
135 Rose, *Ship That Held the Line*, 235.
136 Lundstrom, *First Team*, 10616–36; 10662. The identification of the first two Kates destroyed as those of Warrant Officer Matsushima and Lieutenant Commander Murata, in that order, is a deduction based on Lundstrom's description of the damage to each Kate and a photograph showing a Kate, identified as that of Murata, streaming smoke. This much better fits the description of the damage to the second Kate. The reader should be cautioned, however, that Lundstrom, perhaps the most respected Pacific air war historian, does not himself reach this conclusion, but leaves it open-ended, saying that Murata was one of these two Kates.
137 Hammel, *Carrier Strike*, 5002.
138 Ibid., 5013.
139 Rose, *Ship That Held the Line*, 245.
140 *Hornet* Report, 5; Lundstrom, *First Team*, 10580–97.
141 Lundstrom, *First Team*, 10652.
142 Ibid., 10664.
143 Ibid., 10664.
144 Vincent P. O'Hara, "The Battle of Santa Cruz Prelude Campaign and Battle 11th October to 26th October 1942," *The Thunder of the Guns: Battles of the Pacific War*, http://www.microworks.net/pacific/battles/santa_cruz.htm
145 Rose, *Ship That Held the Line*, 236.
146 Lundstrom, *First Team*, 10718.
147 Hammel, *Carrier Strike*, 4888.
148 Lundstrom, *First Team*, 10750–66.

149 Ibid., 10762–98.
150 Ibid., 10798
151 Ibid., 10827–46.
152 Ibid., 10816.
153 *Hornet* Report, 7; Lundstrom, *First Team*, 10816.
154 Hammel, *Carrier Strike*, 5051.
155 *Hornet* Report, 2; Lundstrom, *First Team*, 10816.
156 Hammel, *Carrier Strike*, 5053–73.
157 Ibid., 5051.

Chapter 12:

1 Lundstrom, *First Team*, 10798–816; Moore, *Hell's Island*, 330–1.
2 Lundstrom, *First Team*, 10866.
3 Ibid., 10866.
4 Ibid., 10885–910.
5 Prange, *At Dawn We Slept*, 197.
6 Lundstrom, *First Team*, 10644.
7 Ibid., 10839.
8 Hara, Saito, and Pineau, *Destroyer Captain*, 120. While not specifically mentioning a D4Y, Type 2, or Judy, Hara first describes how a "scout bomber came in, wagging its wings for identification, to make a neat landing on the *Shokaku*'s deck." (120). Very shortly thereafter, *Amatsukaze* stopped to pick up the crew of a crippled bomber that had to ditch near the *Shokaku*'s stern (120). The version presented here interprets "scout bomber" to mean the D4Y Type 2 Judy.
9 Lundstrom, *First Team*, 10068–86; Frank (*Guadalcanal*, 387) called it "the best radar performance on either side all day[.]"
10 Lundstrom, *First Team*, 10086; *Zuikaku* TROM.
11 Lundstrom, *First Team*, 10094; Hammel, *Carrier Strike*, 3905–24.
12 Lundstrom, *First Team*, 10094; Hammel, *Carrier Strike*, 3905–24.
13 Lundstrom, *First Team*, 10682.
14 Okumiya, Horikoshi, and Caidin, *Zero!*, 4034; Lundstrom, *First Team*, 10682.
15 Lundstrom, *First Team*, 10127.
16 Ikuhiko Hata, Yasuho Izawa, and Christopher Shores, *Japanese Naval Air Force Fighter Units and Their Aces* (London: Grub Street, 2011), 6788–93.
17 Lundstrom, *First Team*, 10230.
18 Ibid., 10230.
19 Ibid., 10218.
20 Moore, *Hell's Island*, 325.
21 Hara, Saito, and Pineau, *Destroyer Captain*, 120.
22 Ibid., 120.
23 Ibid., 120.
24 Lundstrom, *First Team*, 10245.
25 Ibid., 10245; *Shokaku* TROM; Hammel, *Carrier Strike*, 4098–116.
26 *Shokaku* TROM.
27 Hammel, *Carrier Strike*, 4133.
28 Lundstrom, *First Team*, 10252–67.
29 Frank, *Guadalcanal*, 387; Hammel, *Carrier Strike*, 4116.
30 Hara, Saito, and Pineau, *Destroyer Captain*, 120.
31 Toland, *Rising Sun*, 9023.
32 Lundstrom, *First Team*, 10099–117.
33 Hammel, *Carrier Strike*, 4193.
34 Toland, *Rising Sun*, 9050; *Chikuma* TROM.
35 Lundstrom, *First Team*, 10327.
36 *Chikuma* TROM.
37 Lundstrom, *First Team*, 10267.

38 Hammel, *Carrier Strike*, 4266.
39 Lundstrom, *First Team*, 10338.
40 *Chikuma* TROM.
41 Moore, *Hell's Island*, 332; Hammel, *Carrier Strike*, 5314.
42 Lundstrom, *First Team*, 10928–45.
43 Ibid., 10945.
44 Griffin, *Ship to Remember*, 258.
45 Hammel, *Carrier Strike*, 5093–115.
46 Ibid., 5093–115; Poor, Mustin, and Jameson, *Combat Narrative*, 59.
47 Lundstrom, *First Team*, 10935.
48 Ibid., 10968.
49 Hammel, *Carrier Strike*, 5406.
50 Ibid., 5412.
51 Ibid., 5425.
52 Frank, *Guadalcanal*, 411.
53 Hammel, *Carrier Strike*, 5424–43; Stafford, *The Big "E"*, 177.
54 Hammel, *Carrier Strike*, 5443.
55 Ibid., 5477.
56 Ibid., 5496.
57 Lundstrom, *First Team*, 11018.
58 Hammel, *Carrier Strike*, 5498, 5443, 5517.
59 Ibid., 5518.
60 Lundstrom, *First Team*, 10968.
61 Ibid., 10986.
62 Ibid., 11031.
63 Hammel, *Carrier Strike*, 5663.
64 Lundstrom, *First Team*, 11013–31.
65 Ibid., 10986.
66 Ibid., 11153.
67 Ibid., 11057.
68 Hammel, *Carrier Strike*, 5700.
69 Okumiya, Horikoshi, and Caidin, *Zero!*, 4060.
70 Lundstrom, *First Team*, 11071; Stafford, *The Big "E"*, 178.
71 Lundstrom, *First Team*, 11065.
72 Ibid., 11071; Hammel, *Carrier Strike*, 5700.
73 Lundstrom, *First Team*, 11074.
74 Ibid., 11082.
75 Poor, Mustin, and Jameson, *Combat Narrative*, 64; Lundstrom, *First Team*, 11082.
76 Lundstrom, *First Team*, 11082; Hammel, *Carrier Strike*, 5707–27, despite misidentification as Marshall Field, Jr.
77 Hammel, *Carrier Strike*, 5739.
78 Poor, Mustin, and Jameson, *Combat Narrative*, 64; Lundstrom, *First Team*, 11098; Hammel, *Carrier Strike*, 5739–75.
79 Moore, p. 336.
80 Lundstrom, *First Team*, 11099.
81 Poor, Mustin, and Jameson, *Combat Narrative*, 64; Lundstrom, *First Team*, 11135.
82 Hammel, *Carrier Strike*, 5808.
83 Lundstrom, *First Team*, 11117.
84 Poor, Mustin, and Jameson, *Combat Narrative*, 64; Lundstrom, *First Team*, 11148.
85 Lundstrom, *First Team*, 11374.
86 Hammel, *Carrier Strike*, 5497.
87 Frank, *Guadalcanal*, 391.
88 Lundstrom, *First Team*, 11307.
89 Moore, *Hell's Island*, 338.
90 Frank, *Guadalcanal*, 390–1.

91 Lundstrom, *First Team*, 11340.
92 Ibid., 11359.
93 Ibid., 11359–77; Hammel, *Carrier Strike*, 6032.
94 Hammel, *Carrier Strike*, 6160.
95 Hara, Saito, and Pineau, *Destroyer Captain*, 118–9.
96 Okumiya, Horikoshi, and Caidin, *Zero!*, 4156.
97 Hara, Saito, and Pineau, *Destroyer Captain*, 118–9.
98 Toland, *Rising Sun*, 9042.
99 Lundstrom, *First Team*, 11488.
100 Ibid., 11499.
101 Ibid., 11420.
102 Ibid., 11516.
103 Ibid., 11516.
104 Morison, *Struggle*, 218; Toland, *Rising Sun*, 9042.
105 Toland, *Rising Sun*, 9026.
106 Stafford, *The Big "E"*, 189–90.
107 Lundstrom, *First Team*, 11542, 11555.
108 Stafford, *The Big "E"*, 190.
109 David Byron Kimball, *Henry Stewart: An American Life* (unpublished, 2006), 21.
110 Hammel, *Carrier Strike*, 6367.
111 Kimball, *Henry Stewart*, 21.
112 Hammel, *Carrier Strike*, 6387.
113 Frank, *Guadalcanal*, 393.
114 Lundstrom, *First Team*, 11600, 11637, 11625.
115 Toland, *Rising Sun*, 9042.
116 Lundstrom, *First Team*, 11675.
117 Ibid., 11675–87.
118 Lundstrom, *First Team*, 11688; Louis B. Dorny, *US Navy PBY Catalina Units of the Pacific War* (Oxford: Osprey, 2013), 1117–22.
119 Lundstrom, *First Team*, 11656.
120 Ibid., 11656.
121 Hammel, *Carrier Strike*, 6504.
122 Lundstrom, *First Team*, 11798.
123 Hammel, *Carrier Strike*, 6590.
124Lundstrom, *First Team*, 11848.
125 Ibid., 11747.
126 Ibid., 11870.
127 Okumiya, Horikoshi, and Caidin, *Zero!*, 4097.
128 Ibid., 4117.
129 Ibid., 4137.
130 Lundstrom, *First Team*, 11717.
131 Ibid., 11887–906.
132 Ibid., 11906.
133 Hara, Saito, and Pineau, *Destroyer Captain*, 122.
134 Okumiya, Horikoshi, and Caidin, *Zero!*, 4117.
135 Ibid., 4137.
136 Ibid., 4156.
137 Toland, *Rising Sun*, 9061.
138 Okumiya, Horikoshi, and Caidin, *Zero!*, 4156.
139 Lundstrom, *First Team*, 11937.
140 Okumiya, Horikoshi, and Caidin, *Zero!*, 4176.
141 Lundstrom, *First Team*, 11429–49; Hornfischer, *Neptune's Inferno*, 4356.
142Rose, *Ship That Held the Line*, 250.
143 Lundstrom, *First Team*, 11449.
144 Rose, *Ship That Held the Line*, 255.
145 Lundstrom, *First Team*, 11147.

146 Ibid., 11464.
147 *Hornet* Report, 11.
148 Hammel, *Carrier Strike*, 6781.
149 Rose, *Ship That Held the Line*, 258.
150 Lundstrom, *First Team*, 11931-50.
151 Hornfischer, *Neptune's Inferno*, 4373.
152 Morison, *Struggle*, 220; Hammel, *Carrier Strike*, 6889.
153 Rose, *Ship That Held the Line*, 264.
154 Morison, *Struggle*, 221.
155 Toland, *Rising Sun*, 9079.
156 *Hornet* Report, 3.
157 Poor, Mustin, and Jameson, *Combat Narrative*, 72.
158 *Hornet* Report, 3.
159 Frank, *Guadalcanal*, 398.
160 Poor, Mustin, and Jameson, *Combat Narrative*, 73.
161 Morison, *Struggle*, 221–2.
162 Hammel, *Carrier Strike*, 7124.
163 Frank, *Guadalcanal*, 398.
164 Poor, Mustin, and Jameson, *Combat Narrative*, 73; Morison, *Struggle*, 222; Frank, *Guadalcanal*, 398–9.
165 Poor, Mustin, and Jameson, *Combat Narrative*, 74.
166 Ibid., 74.
167 Hammel, *Carrier Strike*, 7147; Frank, *Guadalcanal*, 399.
168 Hammel, *Carrier Strike*, 7147; Ugaki, Goldstein, and Dillon, *Fading Victory*, 251.
169 Frank, *Guadalcanal*, 399; Hammel, *Carrier Strike*, 7147.
170 Okumiya, Horikoshi, and Caidin, *Zero!*, 4233.
171 Toland, *Rising Sun*, 9077.
172 Lundstrom, *First Team*, 11877.
173 Moore, *Hell's Island*, 338.
174 Lundstrom, *First Team*, 11889.
175 Ibid., 12445.
176 Ibid., 11877–94, 12245.
177 Joel Shepherd, "... And then there was one patched-up carrier," *USS ENTERPRISE CV-6, The Most Decorated Ship of the Second World War*, http://www.cv6.org

Epilogue:

1 *I-15* TROM.
2 *South Dakota* DANFS; *Mahan* War Diary.
3 *I-21* TROM; *Washington* War Diary.
4 Morison, *Struggle*, 223; Frank, *Guadalcanal*, 399; *Teruzuki* TROM; Lundstrom, *First Team*, 12011.
5 Prados, *Islands of Destiny*, 157.
6 Morison, *Struggle*, 224.
7 See, e.g., John Prados, "Solving the Mysteries of Santa Cruz," *Naval History Magazine*, October 2011 Volume 25, Number 5.
8 Lundstrom, *First Team*, 12134. "Aviators" includes both pilots and observers.
9 Lundstrom, *First Team*, 12134. "Aviators" includes both pilots and observers.
10 Frank, *Guadalcanal*, 400–1; Lundstrom, *First Team*, 12134.
11 Lundstrom, *First Team*, 12219.
12 Thomas Alexander Hughes, *Admiral Bill Halsey: A Naval Life* (Cambridge, MA: Harvard University Press, 2016), 3431; Murray and Millett, *A War to be Won*, 591
13 Lundstrom, *First Team*, 12150.
14 Hughes, *Admiral Bill Halsey*, 3431–47.
15 Halsey, *Admiral Halsey's Story*, 2610–29.
16 Prados, *Islands of Destiny*, 149–50.
17 Stafford, *The Big "E"*, 198–9.
18 Hughes, *Admiral Bill Halsey*, 3447.
19 Wukovits, *Admiral "Bull" Halsey*, 103.

BIBLIOGRAPHY

Official publications

After Action Report U.S.S. WASP 24 September, 1942 ("Sherman Report")

Bates, Richard W., *The Battle of Savo Island, August 9, 1942. Strategical and Tactical Analysis* (Newport, RI: Naval War College, 1950)

Commander Destroyer Squadron TWELVE, "Report of Action off Savo Island, Solomons, Night of 11–12 October, 1942," dated October 23, 1942 ("*Farenholt* Report")

Cressman, Robert J., *The Official Chronology of the U.S. Navy in World War II* (Washington, DC: Contemporary History Branch, Naval Historical Center, 1999)

"Foreign Relations of the United States, The Conferences at Washington, 1941–1942, and Casablanca, 1943 Document 114," Office of the Historian, United States Department of State

Hough, Lieutenant Colonel Frank O., USMCR; Major Verle E. Ludwig, USMC; Henry I. Shaw, Jr., *History of U.S. Marine Corps Operations in World War II, Volume I: Pearl Harbor to Guadalcanal* (Washington, DC: Historical Branch, G-3 Division, Headquarters, U.S. Marine Corps, 1958)

Interrogation Nav. No. 13, USSBS No. 96, Interrogation of Captain Yasuji Watanabe, 15 October 1945.

Interrogation Nav. No. 106, USSBS No. 464, Interrogation of Captain Kikunori Kijima and Admiral Keizo Komura, 27 November 1945.

Interrogation Nav. No. 8, USSBS No. 46, Interrogation of Commander H. Sekino and Commander Masatake Okumiya, 17 October 1945.

Lewis, Winston B., and Henry A. Mustin, *United States Navy Combat Narrative: The Battles of Savo Island, 9 August 1942 and the Eastern Solomons, 23–25 August 1942* (Washington, DC: Publications Branch, Office of Naval Intelligence, United States Navy, 1943)

War Damage Report No. 24, USS Boise (CL47) Gunfire Damage Savo Island 11–12 October 1942, , Preliminary Design Branch Bureau of Ships Navy Department, 25 January 1943 ("*Boise* Report")

War Damage Report No. 29 USS Astoria (CA34), USS Quincy (CA39), USS Vincennes (CA44) Loss in Action Battle of Savo Island August 9, 1942, Preliminary Design Branch Bureau of Ships Navy Department, 21 June 1943

War Damage Report No. 30 USS Hornet (CV8) Loss in Action Santa Cruz 26 October 1942 ("Hornet Report"), Preliminary Design Branch Bureau of Ships Navy Department, 8 July, 1943

War Damage Report No. 28 USS O'Brien (DD-415), Torpedo Damage and Loss, 15 Sept-19 Oct, 1942, Preliminary Design Branch Bureau of Ships Navy Department, 24 June, 1943

War Damage Report No. 39 USS Wasp (CV7) Loss in Action South Pacific September 15, 1942, Preliminary Design Branch Bureau of Ships Navy Department, 15 January 1944

Ware, Leonard, *United States Navy Combat Narrative: The Landing in the Solomons 7–8 August 1942* (Washington, DC: Publications Branch, Office of Naval Intelligence, United States Navy, 1943)

Zimmerman, Major John L., USMCR, *The Guadalcanal Campaign: Marines in World War II Historical Monograph* (Washington, DC: Historical Section, Division of Public Information, Headquarters, US Marine Corps, 1949)

USS Bagley (386) "Night Engagement August 9, 1942 - Tulagi Guadalcanal Area August 13, 1942" ("*Bagley* Report").

Wings At War Commemorative Edition Pacific Counterblow (The 11th Bombardment Group and The 67th Fighter Squadron in the Battle For Guadalcanal) Paperback – 1992 by Intelligence Office of Assistant Chief of Air Staff (Author). Wings at war series, no. 1-6 : an interim report.

Books and articles

Agawa, Hiroyuki, *The Reluctant Admiral: Yamamoto and the Imperial Navy* (Tokyo; New York: Kodansha, 1979)

Baldwin, Hanson W., "US Hold in Solomons Bolstered," *New York Times*, 11/3/1942

Bartsch, William H., *Victory Fever: Japan's First Land Defeat of WWII* (College Station, TX: Texas A&M University Press, 2014)

Bates, Richard W., *The Battle of Savo Island, August 9, 1942. Strategical and Tactical Analysis* (Newport, RI: Naval War College, 1950)

Bergamini, David, *Japan's Imperial Conspiracy* (London: William Morrow, 1971)

Bergerud, Eric M., *Fire in the Sky: The Air War in the South Pacific* (Boulder, CO: Westview Press, 2000)

Blair, Jr., Clay, *Silent Victory: The US Submarine War Against Japan* (Annapolis: Naval Institute Press, 1975)

Blee, Capt Ben W., USN, "Whodunnit?" *Proceedings*, United States Naval Institute, 108, 7/953 (July 1982), 42–7.

Boehm, Roy, and Charles W. Sasser, *First SEAL* (New York: Atria, 1997)

Borneman, Walter R., *The Admirals: Nimitz, Halsey, Leahy, and King – The Five-Star Admirals Who Won the War at Sea* (New York; Boston; London: Little, Brown, and Company, 2012)

Buell, Thomas B., *Master of Seapower: A Biography of Fleet Admiral Ernest J. King* (Annapolis: Naval Institute Press, 1980)

Caidin, Martin, *The B-17: The Flying Forts* (New York: iBooks, 2001)

Chang, Iris, *The Rape of Nanking: The Forgotten Holocaust of World War II* (New York: Penguin, 1998)

Clark, Curt, *Four Stack APDs: The Famed Green Dragons* (Paducah, KY: Turner Publishing Company, 2003)

Clemens, Martin, *Alone on Guadalcanal: A Coastwatcher's Story* (Annapolis: Naval Institute Press, 1998)

Cook, Charles, *The Battle of Cape Esperance: Encounter at Guadalcanal* (Annapolis: Naval Institute Press, 1992)

Coombe, Jack D., *Derailing the Tokyo Express: The Naval Battles for the Solomon Islands that Sealed Japan's Fate* (Harrisburg, PA: Stackpole, 1991)

Cox, Jeffrey R., *Rising Sun, Falling Skies: The Disastrous Java Sea Campaign of World War II* (Oxford: Osprey, 2014)

Craven, W. F., and Cate, J. L. (eds), *Army Air Forces in World War II*, Vol. IV: *The Pacific: Guadalcanal to Saipan August 1942 to July 1944* (Washington, DC: Office of Air Force History, 1983)

Davis, Donald A., *Lightning Strike: The Secret Mission to Kill Admiral Yamamoto and Avenge Pearl Harbor* (New York: St Martin's Press, 2005)

Domagalski, John J., *Lost at Guadalcanal: The Final Battles of the* Astoria *and* Chicago *as Described by Survivors and in Official Reports* (Jefferson, NC; London: MacFarland, 2010)

Dorny, Louis B., *US Navy PBY Catalina Units of the Pacific War* (Oxford: Osprey, 2013)

Dull, Paul S., *A Battle History of the Imperial Japanese Navy (1941–1945)* (Annapolis: Naval Institute Press, 1978)

Dyer, Vice Admiral George Carroll, USN (Ret.), *The Amphibians Came to Conquer: The Story of Admiral Richmond Kelly Turner* (Washington, DC: U.S. Government Printing Office, 1971)

Foss, Colonel Joe, USMC (ret.), *Joe Foss: Flying Marine* (Pickle Partners Publishing, 2013)

Frank, Richard B., *Guadalcanal: The Definitive Account of the Landmark Battle* (New York: Penguin, 1992)

Fuller, Richard, *Shokan: Hirohito's Samurai* (London: Arms and Armour Press, 1992)

Gallant, T. Grady, *On Valor's Side: A Marine's Own Story of Parris Island and Guadalcanal* (New York: Doubleday, 1963)

Gamble, Bruce, *Fortress Rabaul: The Battle for the Southwest Pacific, January 1942–April 1943* (Grand Rapids, MI: Zenith Press, 2013)

Gatacre, Galfrey George Ormond, *A Naval Career: Report of Proceedings, 1921–1964* (Manly, New South Wales, Australia: Nautical Press, 1982)

Generous, Jr., William Thomas, *Sweet Pea at War: A History of USS* Portland (Lexington, KY: University Press of Kentucky, 2003)

Goldman, Stuart D., *Nomonhan, 1939: The Red Army's Victory that Shaped World War II* (Annapolis: Naval Institute Press, 2012)

Goldstein, Donald M., and Dillon, Katherine V., (eds), *The Pacific War Papers: Japanese Documents of World War II* (Dulles, VA: Potomac, 2004)

Griffin, Alexander T., *A Ship to Remember: The Saga of the* Hornet (New York: Howell, Soskin, 1943)

Griffith, Brig Gen Samuel B., USMC (ret.), *The Battle for Guadalcanal* (New York; Bantam, 1980)

Halsey, Fleet Admiral William F., USN, *Admiral Halsey's Story* (Pickle Partners Publishing, 2013)

Hammel, Eric, *Air War Pacific Chronology: America's Air War Against Japan in East Asia and the Pacific 1941–1945* (Pacifica, CA: Pacifica Military History, 1998)

Hammel, Eric, *Carrier Clash: The Invasion of Guadalcanal and the Battle of the Eastern Solomons August 1942* (Pacifica, CA: Pacifica Military History, 1997)

Hammel, Eric, *Carrier Strike: The Battle of the Santa Cruz Islands October 1942* (Pacifica, CA: Pacifica Military History, 1999)

Hammel, Eric, *The Death of the USS* Wasp *September 15, 1942* (Pacifica, CA: Pacifica Military History, 2016)

Hammel, Eric, *Guadalcanal: Decision at Sea: The Naval Battle of Guadalcanal November 13–15, 1942* (Pacifica, CA: Pacifica Military History, 1988)

Hammel, Eric, *Guadalcanal: Starvation Island* (Pacifica, CA: Pacifica Military History, 1987)

Hara, Tameichi, Fred Saito, and Roger Pineau, *Japanese Destroyer Captain: Pearl Harbor, Guadalcanal, Midway – The Great Naval Battles as Seen Through Japanese Eyes* (Annapolis: Naval Institute Press, 1967)

Hata, Ikuhiko, Yasuho Izawa, and Christopher Shores, *Japanese Naval Air Force Fighter Units and Their Aces* (London: Grub Street, 2011)

Hornfischer, James D., *Neptune's Inferno: The US Navy at Guadalcanal* (New York: Bantam, 2011)

Hoyt, Edwin P., *Guadalcanal: The Desperate Struggle That Turned the Tide of War* (New York: Jove, 1983)

Hoyt, Edwin P., *How They Won the War in the Pacific: Nimitz and His Admirals* (Guilford, CT: Lyons Press, 2012)

Hughes, Thomas Alexander, *Admiral Bill Halsey: A Naval Life* (Cambridge, MA: Harvard University Press, 2016)

Jersey, Stanley Coleman, *Hell's Islands: The Untold Story of Guadalcanal* (College Station, TX: Texas A&M University Press, 2008)

Johnson, William Bruce, *The Pacific Campaign in World War II: From Pearl Harbor to Guadalcanal* (London; New York: Routledge, 2006)

Kilpatrick, C. W., *The Night Naval Battles in the Solomons* (Pompano Beach, FL: Exposition-Banner, 1987)

Kimball, David Byron, *Henry Stewart: An American Life* (unpublished, 2006)

Lacroix, Eric, and Linton Wells II, *Japanese Cruisers of the Pacific War* (Annapolis: Naval Institute Press, 1997)

Langelo, Vincent A., *With All Our Might: The WWII History of the* USS Boise *(CL-47)* (Austin, TX: Eakin Press, 2000)

Leckie, Robert, *Challenge for the Pacific – Guadalcanal: The Turning Point of the War* (New York: Bantam, 1965)

Lockwood, Charles A., *Sink 'em All; Submarine Warfare in the Pacific* (New York: E. P. Dutton & Co., 1951)

Loxton, Bruce, and Chris Coulthard-Clark, *The Shame of Savo: Anatomy of a Naval Disaster* (Annapolis: Naval Institute Press, 1997)

Lundstrom, John B., *Black Shoe Carrier Admiral: Frank Jack Fletcher at Coral Sea, Midway, and Guadalcanal* (Annapolis: Naval Institute Press, 2006)

Lundstrom, John B., *First Team and the Guadalcanal Campaign: Naval Fighter Combat from August to November 1942* (Annapolis: Naval Institute Press, 1994)

Manchester, William, *American Caesar: Douglas MacArthur 1880–1964* (New York: Back Bay Books, 1978)

Manchester, William, *Goodbye, Darkness: A Memoir of the Pacific War* (New York: Back Bay Books, 1979)

Matloff, Maurice, and Edward M. Snell, *United States Army in World War II: The War Department, Volume III:* "Strategic Planning for Coalition Warfare 1941–1942" (Washington: Office of the Chief of Military History, Department of the Army, 1953)

Miller, Thomas G., *The Cactus Air Force* (New York: Bantam, 1981)

Moore, Stephen L., *The Battle for Hell's Island: How a Small Band of Carrier Dive Bombers Helped Save Guadalcanal* (New York: New American Library, 2015)

Morison, Samuel Eliot, *History of United States Naval Operations in World War II, Vol V: The Struggle for Guadalcanal August 1942–February 1943* (Edison, NJ: Castle, 1949)

Morison, Samuel Eliot, *The Two-Ocean War: A Short History of the United States Navy in the Second World War* (Boston, Toronto; London: Little, Brown, and Company, 1963)

Morris, Lieutenant C. G., USNR, *The Fightin'est Ship: The Story of the Cruiser* Helena (Rockville, MD: Wildside Press, 2005)

Murray, Williamson, and Allan R. Millett, *A War to Be Won: Fighting the Second World War* (Cambridge, MA; London: Belknap Press of Harvard University Press, 2000)

Newcomb, Richard F., *The Battle of Savo Island: The Harrowing Account of the Disastrous Night Battle Off Guadalcanal that Nearly Destroyed the Pacific Fleet in August 1942* (New York: Owl Books, 2002)

Newpower, Anthony, *Iron Men and Tin Fish: The Race to Build a Better Torpedo During World War II* (Annapolis: Naval Institute Press, 2006)

O'Hara, Vincent P., "The Battle of Santa Cruz Prelude Campaign and Battle 11th October to 26th October 1942," *The Thunder of the Guns: Battles of the Pacific War*, http://www.microworks.net/pacific/battles/santa_cruz.htm

O'Hara, Vincent P., *The US Navy Against the Axis: Surface Combat 1941–1945* (Annapolis: Naval Institute Press, 2007)

Ohmae, Toshikazu, "The Battle of Savo Island," in *The Japanese Navy in World War II in the Words of Former Japanese Naval Officers* (2nd ed.), ed. David C. Evans (Annapolis: Naval Institute Press, 1986), 212–44.

Okumiya, Masatake, Jiro Horikoshi, and Martin Caidin, *Zero!* (Pickle Partners Publishing, 2014)

Owens, William J., *Green Hell: The Battle for Guadalcanal* (Central Point, OR: Hellgate Press, 1999)

Paine, S. C. M., *The Wars for Asia 1911–1949* (Cambridge: Cambridge University Press, 2012)

Parkin, Robert Sinclair, *Blood on the Sea: American Destroyers Lost in World War II* (Cambridge, MA: Da Capo Press, 1995)

Peattie, Mark, *Sunburst: The Rise of Japanese Naval Air Power, 1909–1941* (Annapolis: Naval Institute Press, 2013)

Poor, Henry V., Henry A. Mustin, and Colin G. Jameson, *United States Navy Combat Narrative: The Battles of Cape Esperance, 11 October 1942 and Santa Cruz Islands, 26 October 1942* (Washington, DC: Publications Branch, Office of Naval Intelligence, United States Navy, 1943)

Potter, E. B., *Nimitz* (Annapolis: Naval Institute Press, 1976)

Prados, John, *Combined Fleet Decoded: The Secret History of American Intelligence and the Japanese Navy in World War II* (Annapolis: Naval Institute Press, 1995)

Prados, John, *Islands of Destiny: The Solomons Campaign and the Eclipse of the Rising Sun* (New York: NAL Caliber, 2012)

Prados, John, "Solving the Mysteries of Santa Cruz," *Naval History Magazine*, October 2011 Volume 25, Number 5

Prange, Gordon, *At Dawn We Slept: The Untold Story of Pearl Harbor* (New York: Penguin, 1981)

Regan, Stephen D., *In Bitter Tempest: The Biography of Admiral Frank Jack Fletcher* (Ames, IA: Iowa State University Press, 1994)

Roscoe, Theodore, *United States Destroyer Operations in World War II* (Annapolis: Naval Institute Press, 1953)

Roscoe, Theodore, *United States Submarine Operations in World War II* (Annapolis: Naval Institute Press, 1949)

Rose, Lisle A., *The Ship That Held the Line: The USS* Hornet *and the First Year of the Pacific War* (Annapolis: Naval Institute Press, 1995)

Sakai Saburo, Martin Caidin, and Fred Saito, *Samurai* (New York: J. Boylston & Company, 2001)

Sakaida, Henry, *Imperial Japanese Navy Aces 1937–45* (Oxford: Osprey, 1998)

Samuels, Alfred, *The USS* Ralph Talbot *and her Gallant Men* (Charlottesville, VA: Publishers Syndication International, 1991)

Shaw, Commander James C., USN, "Jarvis: Destroyer That Vanished," *Proceedings Magazine*, February 1950, Vol. 76/2/564, 118–27.

Shepherd, Joel, "… And then there was one patched-up carrier," *USS ENTERPRISE CV-6, The Most Decorated Ship Of The Second World War*, http://www.cv6.org

Sherrod, Robert, *History of Marine Corps Aviation in World War II* (Washington, DC: Combat Forces Press, 1952)

Smedberg, III, Vice Admiral William R., USN (Ret.), "As I Recall … Sink the Wasp!" *Proceedings*, United States Naval Institute, 108, 7/953 (July 1982), 47–9.

Smith, George W., *The Do-or-Die Men: The 1st Marine Raider Battalion at Guadalcanal* (New York: Pocket Books, 2003)

Smith, Michael S., *Bloody Ridge: The Battle That Saved Guadalcanal* (Novato, CA: Presidio, 2000)

Stafford, Commander Edward P., USN, *The Big "E"* (New York: Ballantine, 1962)

Stille, Mark E., *The Imperial Japanese Navy in the Pacific War* (Oxford: Osprey, 2014)

Stille, Mark E., *The Naval Battles for Guadalcanal 1942: Clash for Supremacy in the Pacific* (Oxford: Osprey, 2013)

Stille, Mark E., and Gerard Howard, *Santa Cruz 1942: Carrier Duel in the South Pacific* (Oxford: Osprey, 2012)

Stille, Mark E., and Wright, Paul, *US Heavy Cruisers 1941–45: Pre-war Classes* (Oxford: Osprey, 2014)

Stille, Mark E., and Wright, Paul, *US Navy Light Cruisers 1941–45* (Oxford: Osprey, 2016)

Tagaya, Osamu, *Imperial Japanese Naval Aviator 1937–45* (Oxford: Osprey, 1988)

Tagaya, Osamu and Mark Styling, *Mitsubishi Type 1 Rikko 'Betty' Units of World War 2* (Oxford: Osprey, 2001)

Tanaka, Raizo, "The Struggle for Guadalcanal," in *The Japanese Navy in World War II in the Words of Former Japanese Naval Officers* (2nd ed.), ed. David C. Evans (Annapolis: Naval Institute Press, 1986), 156–211

Tillman, Barrett, *Enterprise: America's Fightingest Ship and the Men Who Helped Win World War II* (New York: Simon & Schuster, 2012)

Tillman, Barrett, *US Marine Corps Fighter Squadrons of World War II* (Oxford, Osprey, 2014)

Toland, John, *The Rising Sun: The Decline and Fall of the Japanese Empire 1936–1945* (New York: Random House, 1970)

Tregaskis, Richard, *Guadalcanal Diary* (New York: Random House, 1943)

Tuohy, William, *America's Fighting Admirals: Winning the War at Sea in World War II* (St. Paul, MN: Zenith Press, 2007)

Twining, Lieutenant General Merrill B., USMC (Ret.), *No Bended Knee: The Battle for Guadalcanal* (New York: Presidio, 1996)

Ugaki, Matome, Donald M. Goldstein (ed.), and Katherine V. Dillon (ed.), *Fading Victory: The Diary of Admiral Matome Ugaki* (Pittsburgh: University of Pittsburgh Press, 1991)

Vandegrift, General Alexander A., USMC, and Robert B. Asprey, *Once A Marine: The Memoirs of General A.A. Vandegrift, USMC* (New York: W. W. Norton & Co., 1964)

Warner, Denis, Peggy Warner, and Sadao Seno, *Disaster in the Pacific: New Light on the Battle of Savo Island* (Annapolis: Naval Institute Press, 1992)

Willmott, H. P., *The Battle of Leyte Gulf: The Last Fleet Action* (Bloomington, IN; Indianapolis: Indiana University Press, 2005)

Willmott, H. P., *Empires in the Balance: Japanese and Allied Pacific Strategies to April 1942* (Annapolis: Naval Institute Press, 1982)

Winton, John, *Ultra in the Pacific: How Breaking Japanese Codes & Ciphers Affected Naval Operations Against Japan* (London: Leo Cooper, 1993)

Wukovits, John, *Admiral "Bull" Halsey: The Life and Wars of the Navy's Most Controversial Commander* (New York: St Martin's Press, 2010)

Wukovits, John, *Tin Can Titans: The Heroic Men and Ships of World War II's Most Decorated Navy Destroyer Squadron* (Boston: Da Capo Press, 2017)

Online sources

Camp, Dick, "Star-Crossed Translator," Leatherneck, Military.com (www.military.com/content//MoreContent1?file=Leatherneck_Translator_080404), retrieved February 14, 2017.

Czarnecki, Joseph, "Turboelectric Drive in American Capital Ships," *NavWeaps* (http://www.navweaps.com/index_tech/tech-038.htm), retrieved March 3, 2017.

Geddes, Eric, "Sole survivor of WWII RAAF aircrew wins fight to erase historic slur over Savo Island bloodbath" – ABC News (Australian Broadcasting Corporation) by Adam Harvey October 28, 2014, *Pacific War of WW2* The Battle of Savo Island – August 9, 1942 (http://www.ww2pacific.com/hudsonrep.html#10), retrieved February 21, 2017.

"My Guadalcanal," Inui Genjirou (http://www.nettally.com/jrube/Genjirou/genjirou.htm).

Gregory, Mackenzie J., "H.M.A.S. Canberra and the Battle of Savo Island" Ahoy – Mac's Web Log – Naval, Maritime, Australian History and more (http://ahoy.tk-jk.net/Savo/Savo11HepburnsConclusions.html); accessed January 19, 2016.

"WWII memories remain vivid for Navy veteran, 91," Keith Rogers, *Las Vegas Review-Journal*, December 7, 2012 (http://www.reviewjournal.com/news/military/wwii-memories-remain-vivid-navy-veteran-91).

Warships Associated with World War II in the Pacific – USS NORTH CAROLINA (https://www.nps.gov/parkhistory/online_books/butowsky1/northcarolina.htm), retrieved February 27, 2017.

William Ward Burrows, Dictionary of American Naval Fighting Ships.

Chester Dictionary of American Fighting Ships (DANFS), US Naval History and Heritage Command, https://www.history.navy.mil/research/histories/ship-histories/danfs.html; *Washington* and *Buchanan* war diaries.

Tabular Records of Movement ("TROMs") for Japanese ships mentioned in the text come from *The Imperial Japanese Navy Page*, www.combinedfleet.com, edited by Jonathan Parshall, Tony Tully, Bob Hackett, Allyn D. Nevitt, Sander Kingsepp, Peter Cundall, and Gilbert Casse.

INDEX

References to maps are in **bold**.